D0021914

THE
UNMADE
BED

ALSO BY LAURA CHESTER:

Nightlatch (1974)
Primagravida (1975)
Watermark (1978)
Chunk Off & Float (1978)
Proud & Ashamed (1978)
My Pleasure (1980)
Lupus Novice (1987)
Free Rein (1988)
In the Zone (1988)
The Stone Baby (1989)
Bitches Ride Alone (1991)

Riding Tides: 20th Century American Women Poets (1973)
Deep Down: New Sensual Writing by Women (1988)
Cradle & All: Women Writers on Pregnancy and Birth (1989)
The Unmade Bed: Sensual Writing on Married Love (1992)

THE UNMADE BED

Sensual Writing on Married Love

Edited by

LAURA CHESTER

HarperCollins*Publishers*

With special thanks to Pancho and Stella Elliston.

Copyright acknowledgments will be found at the end of this book.

THE UNMADE BED. Copyright © 1992 by Laura Chester. All rights reserved. Printed in the United States of America. No part of this book may be used or reproduced in any manner whatsoever without written permission except in the case of brief quotations embodied in critical articles and reviews. For information address HarperCollins Publishers, Inc., 10 East 53rd Street, New York, NY 10022.

Designed by Alma Orenstein

Library of Congress Cataloging-in-Publication Data

The Unmade bed : sensual writing on married love / edited by Laura Chester.—
1st ed.
    p. cm.
  ISBN 0-06-016609-6 (cloth)
  1. Erotic literature, American. 2. Marriage—Literary collections.
3. American literature—20th century. 4. Love stories, American.
5. Love poetry, American. I. Chester, Laura.
PS509.E7U56 1992
810.8′03538—dc20   91-50461

For Mason Rose

two by two in the ark of
the ache of it

—DENISE LEVERTOV

Contents

PART II   THE HOT BED

PART III   THE MARRIAGE BED

Part IV   THE BOVARY BED

Part V   THE BROKEN BED

Part VI   THE FOREVER BED

Foreword

The image of the well-loved, unmade bed satisfies the soul somehow. The senses respond to this picture of pleasure, with its mess of pillows and feather comforters. A sumptuous disarray of sheets reminds us that the best of all conjugal comforts is rarely nice and neat. So this anthology of contemporary American writing is a literary loosening of the linens, replacing enmity with intimacy, drudgery with enjoyment.

I realize that there are many committed relationships that are not legally bound. Nonetheless, I wanted to explore what was particular to the marriage bed, from the early thrills of "The Newlywed Bed" to the more mature response of husband and wife as they continue to please each other. The themes of long-lasting love and sensuality intertwine throughout this book with many complications, for modern marriage is never static or easy.

Indeed it can almost be frightening when a marriage partner gets up and goes to sleep elsewhere. The bedroom turns from haven to horror, and one can't help but remember Big Mama in *Cat on a Hot Tin Roof*, pointing at the bed and yelling, "When a marriage goes on the rocks, the rocks are *there*, right there!"

Soon enough the question is always asked—how to keep that marriage simmering. I have included a section of particularly erotic writing, "The Hot Bed," where married passion is explored. A loosened familiarity and strengthened trust can give a couple access to a special sensual freedom, a place where fantasy and experiment often play their part.

But the heat of attraction can also turn to disillusionment. We can no longer remain naive about marriage. It is simply not all going to be white roses and doves fluttering about the couple on the cake. On the other hand, commitment is no longer the dirty word it used to be, and monogamy is clearly back in favor.

It also seems to me that the best marriages occur when a couple shares a sense of humor. The poets and prose writers included here bring a mature and yet often humorous perspective found lacking in more sentimental publications that focus on the lifting of the veil.

In this day devoid of ceremony, the wedding itself is one of the few events where we are encouraged to let ritual nourish us, but this anthology focuses more on what follows. What happens when a couple faces the decision—to have or not to have children. "The Marriage Bed" is the smallest of stage sets, where so much of life is enacted, but it can become an even bigger arena when a couple becomes a family.

Up to this point there has been a certain amount of sensual availability, and when husband and wife begin to focus on procreation a new dimension of stress can arise. With an infant in the foreground, it can be more difficult for a married couple to retain their initial ardor. A new kind of love fills the bed, and the bond is both tested and inevitably deepened.

Many American writers reflect the idealistic cultural belief that we should be able to find it all in one person. Either this can lead to a perennial rediscovery, where what we have sown resumes growing, or it can lead to serial monogamy, where the same mistakes are too often played out again and again. While the expectations for marriage increase, there is less religious and moral support to meet the strain. It can seem so much easier to look for new romance, rather than trying to rejuvenate the same with an all too familiar partner.

Issues of fidelity often arise. As Ginette Paris writes in *Pagan Meditations*, "Truth and honesty are among the highest of human qualities. But these virtues, like love, require reciprocity, without which they conspire in the victimization of the one who is honest." Paris goes on to say, "It is the most natural thing in the world for satisfied lovers to be faithful to one another, and without resentment. True fidelity is not promised, it exists." But why not *pledge one's troth* when it is also quite "natural" for married partners to wander. Why can't we deny ourselves at times? Is the marriage sacrament worth self-sacrifice?

Ever since Flaubert created Madame Bovary, adultery has been a central theme of the modern novel. Certainly the temptation to step outside the restrictions of the marriage bed is something most contemporary couples face, and this conflict between security and infidelity is explored in "The Bovary Bed." Here we are offered intense pictures of passionate love while we are also asked to reflect upon the substance of long-held relationships.

John Hawkes in his novel, *The Blood Oranges,* comes closest to describing corporeal pleasures with an almost Continental sensibility not typical of the American mind. Personally, I read him with relief, for his vision seems so nonjudgmental, and his main character, Cyril, is entirely ready to receive the blessings of Eros while continuing to cherish his most desirable wife.

Aphrodite, the goddess of love, often seems to be at odds with the head of the heavenly household, Hera, who rules over marriage, but Ginette Paris relates how both matrons and young married women would go to Aphrodite's temple in order to revive their husbands' ardor. "For sexuality to recover its color and magic," she writes, "it must be associated not with sin and darkness, but with pink and golden beauty, and with Aphrodite's civilizing power . . . Aphrodite assures the reciprocal pleasure of spouses that keeps them together, and without her the marriage remains cold and sterile."

The desire to secure and maintain true sensual love persists today; in fact this urge to find and keep a partner seems universally compelling, but because the idealized merging can never be fully realized, the impulse toward fusion often takes the form of an affair. Too often an inner sense of unity has not been found before it is sought in some outer way, and then the illusion is bound to fail.

This violation of the vows, so sweet at first, can suddenly sour in "The Broken Bed." The delusion of new love replacing the old shifts when the haze of projection wears off and harsh reality sets in. John Updike shows this most masterfully, displaying the heartbreak and disruption when there are children involved. Laurie Colwin writes, "Of all the terrible things in life, living with a divided heart is the most terrible for an honorable person."

There is a darker aspect reflected in the title to this anthology, for when the marriage itself is being unmade, torn apart, when love is no longer there—"Chaos is come again." And yet it seems that we must meet the challenge of these most difficult times, to encounter our deepest selves, our own inner marriage. Even children can no longer be protected from the painful shifts parents thrust upon them as their lives go through upheaval. When a marriage is broken and divorce ensues, it is often likened to major surgery for both parties involved. We limp and lunge through recovery, wondering at times: If marriages are made in heaven, can they be undone here on earth?

Maybe even after divorce the connection continues, but in a different way. Some say this is such a compressed time in history it is not surprising we often experience more than one marriage partner. Or perhaps life has become so speeded up that our desire for change simply mirrors a cultural franticness. Still, second marriages made in the more mature years have less to do with impulse and hormones, and more to do with true companionship.

What propels two people to come together, to stay together, or to make a new marriage for the second time? Hope can triumph over experience, as it does in the final section of this anthology, "The Forever Bed." Here love songs and stories rise to meet the optimism we all need to carry with us. Sometimes the simplicity of mature love can be disarming. Sharon Olds writes that "we are bound to each other with the huge invisible threads of sex, though our sexes themselves are muted, dark and exhausted and delicately crushed . . ." and in Raymond Carver's story, "What We Talk About When We Talk About Love," an old man who has been in a serious automobile accident is miserable because he can't see his wife through the eye-holes of his cast: "Can you imagine? I'm telling you, the man's heart was breaking because he couldn't turn his goddamn head and *see* his goddamn wife." It can make you wonder, in what unseeable ways a husband and wife are truly one.

With practice, the marriage bed can be wonderfully and wantonly unmade, over and over again, but it can be delicious when those white cotton linens are remade too. There is nothing quite so luxurious as the cool smell of wind-dried sheets, sinking into the plush of comforters and pillows, while awaiting the perfect partner.

—Laura Chester

PART I

THE NEWLYWED BED

A SHORT HISTORY OF SEX

GARY SOTO

"Hijo, this is the light switch. No pay you bill, no light, and you make babies with no light." This was Grandmother telling me about sex, or hinting about how sex works. If you don't pay up to the PG&E, then all there is to do at night is lie in bed and make love. This was my first introduction to cause and effect, how one thing leads to another. I was eleven, eating a peach from her tree and watching her water the lawn that was so green it was turning blue. Grandma turned the hose on me, said "Now you be a good boy and play." She squirted me as I ran around the yard with my jaw gripping the peach and my hands covering my eyes.

It was different with my mother, who broke the news about sex while folding clothes in the garage. "You get a girl pregnant, and I'll kill you." No logic there, just a plain simple Soto threat. I felt embarrassed because we had never talked about sex in the family. I didn't know what to do except to stare at the wall and an old calendar of an Aztec warrior eyeballing his girlfriend's breasts. I left the garage, got on my bike, and did wheelies up and down the street, trying my best to get run over because earlier in the week Sue Zimm and I had done things in Mrs. Hancock's shed. It was better, I thought, that I should die on my own than by my mother's hand.

But nothing happened. Sue only got fat from eating and I got skinny from worrying about the Russians invading the United States. I thought very little about girls. I played baseball, looked for work with a rake and poor-boy's grin, and read books about Roman and Greek gods.

During the summer when I was thirteen I joined the YMCA, which was a mistake—grown men swam nude there and stood around with their hands on their hips. It was an abominable exhibition, and I would have asked for my money back but was too shy to approach the person at the desk. Instead, I gave up swimming and jumped on the trampoline, played basketball by myself, and joined the Y "combatives" team, which was really six or seven guys who got together at noon to beat up one another. I was gypped there too. I could have got beaten up for free on my street; instead, I rode my bike three miles to let people I didn't even know do it to me.

But sex kept coming back in little hints. I saw my mother's bra on the bedpost. I heard watery sounds come from the bathroom, and it wasn't water draining from the tub. At lunchtime at school I heard someone say, "It feels like the inside of your mouth." What feels like that? I wanted to ask, but instead ate my sandwich, drank my milk, kicked the soccer ball against the backstop, then went to history, where I studied maps, noting that Russia was really closer than anyone ever suspected. It was there, just next to Alaska, and if we weren't careful they could cross over to America. It would be easy for them to disguise themselves as Eskimos and no one would know the difference, right?

In high school I didn't date. I wrestled for school, the Roosevelt Rough Riders, which was just young guys humping one another on mats. I read books, ate the same lunch day after day, and watched for Mrs. Tuttle's inner thighs above her miniskirt, thinking, "It's like the inside of your mouth." I watched her mouth; her back teeth were blue with shadows, and her tongue was like any other tongue, sort of pink. By then I wanted a girl very badly. Once almost had a girlfriend except she moved away, leaving me to mope around the school campus eating Spam sandwiches with the ugly boys.

My mother's bra on the bedpost, my sister now with breasts that I could almost see beneath her flannel nightgown. One night my brother bragged that he knew for sure it felt like a mouth and in fact was drippy like a marble coated with motor oil. In the dark I scrunched up my face as I remembered cross-eyed Johnny's sock of sweaty marbles, for which I had traded three bottles of red stuff from a chemistry kit.

I had to have a girl. I was desperate. I stuffed Kleenex in my pants pocket and went around with no shirt. I thought of Sue Zimm. But she was now lifting weights and looking more like a guy than a girl, which confused me. I was even more confused when George from George's Barber rubbed my neck and asked me how it felt. I told him it felt OK. He asked if I was going steady, and I told him that I sort of was, except my girl had moved away. He said that it was better that way because sometimes they carried disease you couldn't see for a long time until it was too late. This scared me. I recalled touching Sue when I was thirteen, and wasn't it true that she coughed a lot? Maybe something rubbed onto me. Biting a fingernail, I walked home very slowly, with a picture of a scolding priest playing inside my head. At home I noticed Mom coughing as she stirred a pot of beans. Fear ran its icy fingers up and down my back. I gave my mom the disease, I said to myself, and went to hide in my room and talk to God about becoming a priest.

Years passed without my ever touching a girl. My brother seemed to get them all, especially when we roomed together in college and he would bring them home. I was studying history then, things like, "In 1940 Britain invaded Tibet; in 1911 the first Chinese revolution began; about that time, people began to live longer because they had learned to wash their hands before eating." I would hover over a big book with few pictures while my brother and his girl went at it, howling so loudly that our cat would stir from sleep and saunter to the bedroom door and holler some meows herself.

I was twenty, the only guy left who went around eating Spam sandwiches in college, when I had my first girlfriend who didn't move away. I was a virgin with the girl whom I would marry. In bed I entered her with a sigh, rejoiced "Holy, holy" to my guardian angel, and entered her again with the picture of a tsk-tsking priest playing inside my head.

Twenty years, I thought. It's nothing like cross-eyed Johnny's sock of sweaty marbles. And I couldn't believe what it looked like. While my girl slept, I lowered myself onto an elbow and studied this peach mouth, squeeze thing, little hill with no Christian flag. Pussy was what they called it: a cat that meowed and carried on when you played with it very lightly.

LOVERS OUT OF THIS WORLD

Michael Benedikt

While these two otherwise really quite ordinary people who have just met are talking with one another, what are their eyes doing? These two otherwise really quite ordinary people are leaning forward and looking at each other with such intensity that it's somehow as if their eyes are doing almost all the listening! They speak, as we can already see, with a certain "Luminously Intense Fascination." Already, they are both almost "Out of This World." Already, their conversations seem mostly to consist of preparing vast, immensely intense, temptingly empty spaces, which the other person might just want to fill with something to say. So, increasingly, they both become what we might conventionally call "Mutually Involved." And somehow they both sense how their deepening feelings—which even at the very outset began with such wonderfully easy ecstasies—are continuing to grow and develop. Now, as they move closer, they are leaving this world as we know it! Now they look a whole lot more, even, as they listen—now their ears are doing almost all the talking. . . .

ESTHETIC NUPTIALS

I invited our favorite famous writer, who happens also to be a very close friend, to our wedding. To celebrate, he gets high and cuts up the manuscript of one of his most famous love poems, using a pair of scissors and a paper punch; then he throws it all over us in our hotel room, like confetti! And everybody considers us just one more nice, normal, average couple when I tell them that we spent the first night of our love in a hotel room, crawling around on our hands and knees.

THE ANSWER

Laura Chester

He couldn't decide if he should marry. He was already in his 40's and he'd never been married. People said that he'd be the perfect partner except for this flaw. Being a bachelor had become a stigma. But for the last couple of years he'd had this idea that he wanted to get married. He even spoke of it the first time we met, though he wasn't referring specifically to us.

"What do you think you want?" he asked.

I said I'd be happy with a committed weekend relationship. "I'm not saying I'm against marriage. I just don't believe in divorce."

But he thought he wanted a baby. Everybody else had a baby.

"Even if a child were conceived," I said, "we still wouldn't have to get married."

"Not with me, kid." He believed one got married first.

I began to wonder if he only wanted to get married because he thought that he should. Or if he did get married, would he only be trying it on to see how it felt? Maybe he had doubts about me—if I was the right woman.

He admitted to friends that he wasn't sure. One friend admitted to me this admission. That friend said that I should sit him down and ask *him* to get married.

"No way, José," I answered.

Still, one night I confronted him. "Do you think we'll ever get married?"

"I don't know," he said.

"What don't you know. If I'm the right one?"

"I don't know," he said.

"Well then, why don't you go ask God," I suggested.

He looked at me oddly. He was more likely to ask the cigarette he was smoking.

"Really," I smiled. "Just try it. Go on. Go in the other room and ask."

He got up slowly, then put out the cigarette and left the room.

I sat on the bed, thinking about what God would say to him. I imagined God would say, "Do you think you'll find anyone better? Of course not. So go ahead." I had to believe in that answer.

Suddenly he returned. He was also smiling.

"What did He say?" I asked.

"He said no."

"That's funny." I must have looked disappointed. "That's not what He told me."

"What did He say to you?"

"I guess I didn't really ask," I admitted. "I was only trying to overhear your conversation."

"But," he paused, "I still want to marry you."

I looked at him blankly.

"What do you say?" he asked.

"How can I say yes, if God said no?" I responded.

"He didn't really say No. I just made that up."

"So you didn't really ask?"

"I felt stupid," he admitted.

"That's all right. That's how you're supposed to feel. We *are* stupid."

"*I'm* not," he responded. And then he stood up. I thought he was going to leave. Maybe he had his answer and it was over.

"Where are you going?" I asked.

"In the other room."

"What are you going to do?"

He walked to the door and then looked at me. "I'm going to see if He changed His mind," he said.

AIR

Tom Clark

The sweet peas, pale diapers
Of pink and powder blue, are flags
Of a water color republic.
The soft bed, turned back,
Is a dish to bathe in them.
This early in the morning
We are small birds, sweetly lying
In it. We have soft eyes,
Too soft to separate the parts
Of flowers from the water, or
The angels from their garments.

BIOLOGICAL SUPREMACY

Biology still reigns supreme
In this zone around your hips
Where perception guides me
To perform what is no more than
The expected function after all
But let one thing be understood
I'd be dead if it wasn't for
The inspiration provided by your body
By which I don't mean information
For there are some things one can't know

They are of course the only things worth knowing
And it is the pursuit of these
On an everyday basis no less
Which makes life almost worth living

From: DURING THE REIGN OF THE QUEEN OF PERSIA

Joan Chase

She didn't think much of it at first, his still wanting to see her in the evenings, now riding out from the town, but she figured if it was worth it for him to travel that distance to sit and watch the fire, there wasn't any harm in it. He never did have much talk in him, even as a young man. He was out of the plain people, maybe shunned for something, folks suspected, though no one ever knew his past for sure. But Lil was seventeen and the mystery of Jacob's past was part of what intrigued her—she liked the different way he dressed, in shirts of home-dyed indigo and suspenders, and she liked his quaint old-fashioned manners, so at odds with his rough hard look. Tall and lean, he had straight dark hair falling to frame both sides of his face, and the little habit he had of tossing his hair back showed the strong bones clearly and his slanted, long-lashed eyes; and she began to want him in the way you want something you think will occupy you until Doomsday. The wanting felt like enough. There was no mother to warn her, and the other girls she knew were thrilled with Jacob too and envied her, though there was not a father or mother who would have sanctioned his attentions to their daughter. Lil did not desire the children that would come in a marriage; already she knew their demands well enough. But neither did she fancy the endless monotony of cooking for twenty farmhands every day while guarding herself against the teasing, fresh-mouthed married ones who, sensing her loneliness, determined to break her off and make use of her. Better that she should have her own man and the life he would bring her.

She did not deny it—Jacob drew her. He would sit with no words for her before the wood stove, watching her continually with his dark, dark eyes, and she began to feel his hunger, so that often she would get up to put more wood in the stove or busy herself at the sink, just to avoid his eyes and hide her trembling. Every night his eyes were watching, wanting her and letting her see it in him; but he wouldn't touch her, not so much as to let a hand graze hers, though when she would pass close beside him she would hear his breathing, harsh and quick. It nearly drove her wild and her mind came to dwell on him nearly every second. Sometimes, when she lifted up the handle of the stove to stir the wood, the glutted, ashy coals crumbled at the slight touch and something inside her seemed to fragment in the same way.

Lil would plot to forget him. During the day, going about her work, she would plan how she would be gone in the evening when he came. But she never was, and again she'd open the door to him, to his silent and steady need. It got so peculiar between them that neither of them said a word to the other through whole evenings. Lil would back against the wall when he entered and feel the exact dimensions of his body, the insistent presence of his nature. He would pass close to her, nearly touching her, his eyes locking on her, where they would stay fastened through whole evenings. Eons. She forgot time.

It took Hebbard Watson coming to court to change things, or else, Lil thought, they might have jumped together off a cliff to end it, both of them stubborn beyond belief. But Hebbard tied his horse by the gate a time or two, and although Jacob didn't even come to the door, his feelings were plain enough on his face as he stood outside and glared as if he wanted to strangle the horse. Then he took away in the direction of town without a further glance, though Lil was certain he'd known she watched from behind the parlor curtain. After a third evening of that, Lil was in the kitchen in the morning, peeling through a pail of early yellow apples, thinking about Jacob and his silent withholding, when she heard a commotion on the road. She went to the door and then out in the yard, wearing her flowered apron, her braids frayed with curl. Coming along was a wagon team of six horses driven by Jacob, who was so intent on managing things he didn't even glance up to see her, though they both knew she was there, the same as when they sat beside each other at the fire. The piano from her sister's house was strapped onto the wagon bed, swaddled with quilting and roped down to keep it steady. She watched it pass, slow and resounding, the wagon out of sight but the raised dust keeping its memory a little longer, almost like a song resonating, and Lil knew they would be married. It was the only semblance of a proposal that passed between them.

Married, they moved into rooms up over a store on the town's one street and in the secret dark Jacob touched her and moved himself in her, and though she got accustomed to it, a part of her was more aggravated by his touch than satisfied, and then it came to seem more invasion than touch, his need something he took care of, quick and by dark, by daylight no trace left, as though it had never happened between them. Lil felt resentment rising in her; his tacit denial shamed her, convinced her that he felt he stole something from her, was taking without asking. Every night, nearly, he turned to her and held her against him while, rapid and brutish, he moved in her. She began to be sick to her stomach nearly all day long. Afraid that it was a baby coming, dreading it, she lay under his heaviness, which blocked out any trace of light, and thought: Soon I'll be dead.

Then Jacob became more active in his cattle business. He left her alone, stayed away for days at a time, and Lil began going out to the church for prayer services or hymn sings, a little society one way to distract her mind from continual hating and grieving. Jacob didn't like going to church. He'd left his own religion but some of the teaching stayed with him, that fancy music mixed with religion was an abomination. Though he didn't try to stop her, a few times she'd seen him standing outside the church window staring in. Sometimes she was harmonizing with the schoolteacher and she felt it served Jacob right to see her with another man, for she had come to hate him for his neglect.

One night Lil watched him standing outside the church window for a long time. She trembled, knowing something was changing. When she got to their rooms, she felt certain of it, smelled the strong drink in the air though he stayed hidden and didn't answer when she called, "Jacob." She built up the fire because of her shivering, though that wouldn't touch the part that came from fear. She felt him watching her again. Waiting. Wanting her and still hiding it like a thief. She would give him something to want, and she began to remove her clothes, with the fire hot and dancing over the walls, shattering the shadowy places. Lil excited, knowing she was beautiful and that he had never seen her and that it would be a power over him and would cause something between them to change. The thought of it made her fumble over the layered items of winter clothing and her nipples stood erect, chafed by the fabric. It came into her mind that she would take his head in her two hands and place it against her breasts, each one in turn, press his mouth to suck on her, his tongue to lick her nipples. Wanting that all through her, she turned, fully naked, toward the doorway, where she heard his step.

By firelight all his need was finally visible in his face, what she'd longed to see. But there was such anger in it too that she tried to cover herself. When she saw the kindling hatchet raised in his hand, she thought that would be the end of it and part of her was glad, fire staining the blade red before blood. She couldn't get her breath even to scream. He brought the hatchet down then, on the piano, and twice more he struck, to leave it then, anchored in the wood, the piano vibrating as though it shrieked out and held to its voice long afterwards, as though it were her voice. Still she seemed to hear it, after he'd gripped her to bring her hard against him and then carried her to the bed. She couldn't take breath but repeated wordlessly: why didn't you, why didn't you?

THE MARRIAGE MADE IN HEAVEN

Sherril Jaffe

Ann dressed herself all in white. She had attended to the animals and the garden, and now she could head down to Abraham's. The moon was just rising as she reached the highway. It was clear to her that she and Abraham couldn't go on the way they had been going— although it had only been for two weeks. It was too clumsy to have two houses.

She loved her house and had thought that she would die there. She loved the peace and privacy of living in the country. She loved the pure sweet air, she loved to pick her fruit from the trees, and she loved to watch the sequence of flowers appear and disappear each year. Her house was more than a house. It had watched her life unfold. She was finally living in that house the way it wanted to be lived in and the heart of the house had opened. That house had become the world to her.

Now, Ann saw, it was nothing. She would gladly give it up and go to live with Abraham, even in the city.

She parked the car in front of his gate and quickly walked up the path to his cottage. Suddenly she was inside and his arms were around her. Some music was playing. Angels seemed to be singing.

Then he told her what he had been thinking. The separation was too painful.

"Yes," Ann said. She had been thinking the same. She would move to the city.

"I want you to marry me," Abraham said.

"Yes," Ann said. Although she had sworn many times she would never marry again. But this would be different. This would be a marriage made in heaven. And the angels sang.

ABRAHAM TELLS ANN HE LOVES HER

Many times a day Abraham would take Ann in his arms and hug her and kiss her and tell her he loved her. If he left the house for even a few minutes he would kiss her and tell her he loved her. He didn't need to tell her. She knew that he loved her. But the telling was a pleasure. And every day, also, he told her she was beautiful, and when he did she would go and sit in his lap and he would kiss her and tell her he loved her, and she told him she loved him again and again, for her love for him was always welling up and overflowing, and it was a pleasure to be able always to tell him, without embarrassment, how she loved him, without restraint, she loved him, without fear that her love wouldn't be returned. It *was* returned, over and over, and she never got tired of hearing it.

THE GLASS IS BROKEN

The wedding guests began to arrive. Friends and relations. The dead and dying. The cynical. The beaten. The lost. Those who lusted after power. Those who lusted after success. Those whose love had dried to dust. And they gathered from far and near. Even though the storm had begun to roar. The storm which was their lives began to toss. And it blew all about the house. And torrents of rain poured forth while inside all was aglow. All was aglow in the flickering firelight. Under the marriage canopy all was at peace. There Ann and Abraham joined hands, their little dog at their feet. Then William handed Abraham the ring, and Ann and Abraham promised to love each other forever and ever. Everyone looked on, but they just saw each other. And the glass was broken.

THE RECEPTION

Deborah Harding

Friends still say how lovely it was, the candlelight,
the sun setting over the Pacific, it's all
   a blur to me   I never saw the beauty—
Mom's whining about where to sit, didn't I make place cards,
did I know Steven's parents are ignoring her
   she never lets up— I'm at the head table now
some horseshoe type thing arranged so you can't
talk to anyone except whoever's on your right or left—
   When I look up, she's bombing towards me
across the dance floor while the photographer is taking
a picture of Steven and me kissing, the sun going down
   behind us over the golf course—
Anyway, she slaps both hands down on the table, says she
wants coffee, did I forget to tell the hostess, do they
   have decaf— I trudge back towards the kitchen
I think my train unhitches itself two or three times and I
keep tripping over the hem, which is dirty as hell by now—
   When I get there, the ladies are already wheeling out
carts with two hundred cups of coffee on them
so I go back to the table   try eating a crab puff
and here she comes again— how will she get all those
gifts to the car, do I think they have a dolly somewhere?
   We hadn't even cut the big mousse cake yet—
I thought the party was just starting and she's worried
about leaving— The band is playing so loud I can't hear anybody
not that one person comes up to congratulate us
   like we were royalty or something   like it wasn't OK
to cross over to our side of the dance floor—
   I was so lonely, Steven off mingling like we were supposed
to— I could see him out there getting kissed by relatives,

shaking hands with the men— I'm waiting for my Dad
or even his Dad to come for me,
    I guess mostly I wanted my Dad
so I keep waiting, the best man's telling me something
about his first cadaver at med school   then a couple I don't
    even know moves onto the floor— I want to tell them
go back, not yet you idiots, me and Steven
are supposed to have the first dance—
    the singer's wailing "Stand by Your Man"   I can hardly
swallow, but now it is time for the bride and groom dance
    so we go out there   Steven's cousin glaring at us,
    the one who tried to get me in bed that time when he
was away— she's out there doing voodoo on me . . .
    I'm staring into Steven's eyes, it's almost romantic
then he says his Mom has diarrhea, Grandad's pissed
'cuz nobody took a picture of him— Godfather Jimmy
cuts in, holds me so tight I swear I feel a hard-on pressing
into my thigh— Drum roll   time to cut the cake
Steven feeds me, I feed him, chunks of mousse plop on my gown
His uncle makes a toast   who knows what he said   things are
winding down now, just family, no one to throw my garter to
    so I slide it off   geez I'm not even on a balcony
or anything— fling it to Steven's little brother, big deal—
    Almost time to leave, here comes the cousin again
says how glad she is I'm finally part of the family—
it's all I can do to make it to the car, not in the mood now,
    dark out, as Steven gathers up my train like
something I should cherish.

THE SONG OF LOVE

Janet Hamill

Magnificent angel. in your white convulsive arms
I'm a delicate green bird of song
singing in praise of her cage. my ankles
lend themselves willingly to your slave bracelets

I'm a succulent pink dessert. the edible fruit
of a jungle flower. begging to be eaten
in your white convulsive arms
magnificent angel. I'm a dancing flame

clinging to your eyes of blue mirrored glass
my desire renews itself endlessly
in waves breaking over my anchored waist
waves that smell of fish and sweat

the intimate odors of a summer night
wrap around me. in your white convulsive arms
magnificent angel. I'm lifted up with moonlight bleaching my skin
to the measureless ocean in the stars

MARRIAGE

Amy Gerstler

Romance is a world, tiny and curved, reflected in a spoon. Perilous as a clean sheet of paper. Why begin? Why sully and crumple a perfectly good surface? Lots of reasons. Sensuality, need for relief, curiosity. Or it's your mission. You could blame the mating instinct: a squat little god carved from shit-colored wood. NO NO NO. It's not dirty. The plight of desire, a longing to consort, to dally, bend over, lose yourself . . . be rubbed till you're shiny as a new-minted utensil. A monogrammed butterknife, modern pattern or heirloom? It's a time of plagues and lapses, rips in the ozone layer's bridal veil. One must take comfort in whatever lap one can. He wanted her to bite him, lightly. She wanted to drink a quart of water and get to bed early. Now that's what I call an exciting date. In the Voudoun religion, believers can marry their gods. Some nuns wed Jesus, but they have to cut off all their hair first. He's afraid he'll tangle in it, trip and fall. Be laid low. Get lost. Your face: lovely and rough as a gravestone. I kiss it. I do.

In a more pragmatic age many brides' veils later served as their burying shrouds. After they'd paid their dues to Mother Nature, they commanded last respects. Wreaths, incense, and satin in crypts. In India, marriage of children is common. An army of those who died young marches through your studio this afternoon to rebuke you for closing your eyes to the fullness of the world. But when they get close enough to read what's written on your forehead, they realize you only did what was necessary. They hurriedly skip outside to bless your car, your mangy lawn, and the silver floss tree which bows down in your front yard.

His waiting room is full of pious heathens and the pastor calls them into his office for counseling, two by two. Once you caressed me in a restaurant by poking me with a fork. In those days, any embrace was a strain. In the picture in this encyclopedia, the Oriental bride's headdress looks like a paper boat. The caption says: "Marriage in Japan is a formal, solemn ceremony." O bride, fed and bedded down on a sea of Dexatrim, tea, rice, and quinine, can you guide me? Is the current swift? Is there a bridge? What does this old fraction add up to: you over me? Mr. Numerator on top of Miss Denominator? The two of us divided by a line from a psalm, a differing line of thinking, the thin bloodless line of your lips pressed together. At the end of the service, guests often toss rice or old shoes. You had a close shave, handsome. Almost knocked unconscious by a flying army boot, while your friends continued to converse nonchalantly under a canopy of mosquito netting. You never recognized me, darling, but I knew you right away. I know my fate when I see it. But it's bad luck to lay eyes on each other before the appropriate moment. So look away. Even from this distance, and the chasm is widening (the room grows huge), I kiss your old and new wounds. I kiss you. I do.

THE PREGNANT BRIDE

Larry Woiwode

Chris and Ellen were spending their honeymoon at a lodge in the Michigan woods, and this evening when the meal was finished, he uncovered the furniture in the main room and, under her supervision, began to scoot it back and forth over the board floor, from one corner of the enormous room to the other, arranging and rearranging it to suit her whims. There were several large pieces: three or four stuffed chairs, a plank banquet table, a daybed, a couch. The furniture rumbled and thundered over the floor, and it gave him a strange feeling to make so much noise, with no one present but her, in this big building so far from other human life. At last she was satisfied. He decided to add a touch of his own, and went to the piano and took the bearskin rug off its top. He carried it across the room and placed it where he felt it properly belonged, on the floor in front of the fireplace.

"Oh," she said. "We never put that down."

"Why's that?"

"Grandpa says we'd wear all the hair off. He wants everything preserved the way it was. He's very fastidious."

"Oh."

"Leave it if you want."

"No."

"I like it there," she said.

"No. Better not."

He carried the unwieldy thing back to the piano. She stretched out on the couch in front of the fireplace, turned on a floor lamp, and started leafing through one of the books from the library. He stared at her for a while, juggling the bearskin, then walked back with it and spread it on the floor. She gave him a curious look, and said, "I thought you decided not to put it there."

"I did. But we must, absolutely must, have it down for tonight."

"Why?"

"To use it," he said, and grinned.

She blushed and turned back to her book.

"It's in all the movies," he said.

He went to a wicker hamper next to the fireplace and picked out the thinnest twigs, pencil-size and smaller, snapped them into even lengths, and laid them across the andirons. He broke up more twigs of the same size and placed them in a crosshatch over the first layer. He repeated this procedure once more. He broke up larger, dowel-sized branches and laid them in a row over the little ones, and of these he also made a three-layer crosshatch. He put down a row of larger limbs that were sawed to length. He took up kindling the size of his wrist, nine pieces of it (an odd number being the best for a fire), and laid down five sticks, then laid the remaining four over the gaps he'd left between the first pieces. He took up a scroll of birch bark, tore it into strips, and made a pyramid of the strips on the floor of the fireplace, beneath the wood on the andirons. He lit a piece of newspaper, held it as flat as he could at the top of the fireplace, near the flue, and let it burn down until he had to release it. The orange and black papery ash hovered for a while above the wood, dipping down, winging up, and in a sudden swirl was sucked up the chimney. A good draft. He put a match to the birch bark and when the twigs, the branches, the limbs, and the sticks of kindling were lit and burning, reporting and spouting sparks, and the flames had begun to climb the chimney, he laid on three logs.

He sat on the bearskin rug and watched the flames, feeling his cheeks grow warm and his pants legs heat up over his shins. She rose from the couch and came and sat beside him. He lit a cigarette and smoked it slow, handing it to her for drags, and when it was smoked down he flipped it into the fire. She took him by the arm and they stared at the flames.

"What books did you check out?" he asked.

"The usual ones. Birds. Trees. Plants."

"No others?"

"No. Why?"

"I thought—" He shrugged his shoulders. "Birds, trees, bees"— he made a face and altered his voice to cover his uneasiness—"uh, duh, you know. Babies."

"Oh." She swung her legs around and lay down and put her head on his lap, placing her hands, clasped as in prayer, under her cheek. "I don't think about that."

"Why not? Shouldn't you?"

She lifted her shoulders and snuggled closer; she obviously didn't want to talk about it.

"What did the doctor say?"

"What doctor?"

"What doctor? The one I sent you to."

"Oh, him. Nothing much."

"He didn't give you any instructions?"

"About what?"

"*You* know." He was getting irritated.

"No. Nothing."

"Well, what did he say? He must have said something."

"Just that I should be myself, but go easy. Drink a lot of milk. No horseback riding. And that if nothing came up, I wouldn't have to see another doctor for about two months."

"That's it? It's that simple?"

"He did mention that most women aren't in the shape I'm in. He said I was very muscular."

"What did he mean?"

"Inside."

"Inside!"

"He said I have strong walls."

"He said *that?*"

"Yes."

"The bastard!"

Her mellow self-satisfied laughter matched the play of the flames. He lit another cigarette and smoked it down. He tossed it into the fireplace. He looked at her face and ran his hand over her hair, which was hot from the fire, and drew gold strands of it back from her cheek. He laid the back of his fingertips on her cheek and it seemed more hot (*her* temperature?) than her hair. Then he turned, easing her head onto the rug, and lay beside her. She moved against him. He kissed her, and for the first time he felt that he was married, that he was with a married woman, his wife, and he savored and prolonged each stage to fill himself with the experience, feeling the familiar shape of her mouth, teeth behind lips, the tongue, the curve of her rib cage and firm stomach, her hip, the strength of her legs, the cords in her inner thighs, and then the same curves with no clothes, the closer curves, the aroma of her skin, the feel and texture of it when she was ready, the taste, savoring that, her breasts aroused, one cool and one hot from the fire and both tipped up to him, their texture, tips, stretching out her arms to feel them taut against him, and he would enter for the first time, now, his wife, wet, the strong legs, walls, and then in a blossoming in his upper consciousness knowing she held his child, a life inside her, there, the nudge of muscle, that kiss, the light of the fire over her hair, her eyes, thighs rising, the points of her hair like stars, like Orion, Oh, love, love, Oh, El, Oh, love, "Oh, El."

"Yes, Chris, yes."

Holding him tight inside, she whispered, "That's the first time you've talked to me like that since we've been back together."

HOLD

David Giannini

A shadow
the texture of star moss
and lightly
you slip through
the placket of your dress
its wrinkled sun
on a tom-thumb lawn.
A lake the color of deep fern
and after swimming you shake off
its seed
after your moist strip
your face
like peeled birch
rubbed with oil.

Your breasts without tan
I moisten
your dark inland
open
I feel where the lake brushed
kiss where
the lake washed
the damp walls
around the warming pool
the wet stone
swelling and
hold (Hold) come around me now.

I GO BACK TO MAY 1937

Sharon Olds

I see them standing at the formal gates of their colleges,
I see my father strolling out
under the ochre sandstone arch, the
red tiles glinting like bent
plates of blood behind his head, I
see my mother with a few light books at her hip
standing at the pillar made of tiny bricks with the
wrought-iron gate still open behind her, its
sword-tips black in the May air,
they are about to graduate, they are about to get married,
they are kids, they are dumb, all they know is they are
innocent, they would never hurt anybody.
I want to go up to them and say Stop,
don't do it—she's the wrong woman,
he's the wrong man, you are going to do things
you cannot imagine you would ever do,
you are going to do bad things to children,
you are going to suffer in ways you never heard of,
you are going to want to die. I want to go
up to them there in the late May sunlight and say it,
her hungry pretty blank face turning to me,
her pitiful beautiful untouched body,
his arrogant handsome blind face turning to me,
his pitiful beautiful untouched body,
but I don't do it. I want to live. I
take them up like the male and female
paper dolls and bang them together
at the hips like chips of flint as if to
strike sparks from them, I say
Do what you are going to do, and I will tell about it.

THE NEWLYWED BED

THE WEDDING

Joy Williams

Elizabeth always wanted to read fables to her little girl but the child only wanted to hear the story about the little bird who thought a steam shovel was its mother. They would often argue about this. Elizabeth was sick of the story. She particularly disliked the part where the baby bird said, "You are not my mother, you are a *snort*, I want to get out of here!" Elizabeth was thirty and the child was five. At night, at the child's bedtime, Sam would often hear them complaining bitterly to one another. He would preheat the broiler for dinner and freshen his drink and go out and sit on the picnic table. In a little while, the screen door would slam and Elizabeth would come out, shaking her head. The child had frustrated her again. The child would not go to sleep. She was upstairs, wandering around, making "cotton candy" in her bone-china bunny mug. "Cotton candy" was Kleenex sogged in water. Sometimes Elizabeth would tell Sam the story that she had prepared for the child. The people in Elizabeth's fables were always looking for truth or happiness and they were always being given mirrors or lumps of coal. Elizabeth's stories were inhabited by wolves and cart horses and solipsists.

"Please relax," Sam would say.

At eleven o'clock every night, Sam would take a double Scotch on the rocks up to his bedroom.

"Sam," the child called, "have some of my cotton candy. It's delicious."

Elizabeth's child reminded Sam of Hester's little Pearl even though he knew that her father, far from being the "Prince of the Air," was a tax accountant. Elizabeth spoke about him often. He had not shared the 1973 refund with her even though they had filed jointly and half of the year's income had been hers. Apparently the marriage had broken up because she often served hamburgers with baked potatoes instead of french fries. Over the years, astonishment had turned to disapproval and then to true annoyance. The tax accountant told Elizabeth that she didn't know how to do anything right. Elizabeth, in turn, told her accountant that he was always ejaculating prematurely.

"Sam," the child called, "why do you have your hand over your heart?"

"That's my Scotch," Sam said.

Elizabeth was a nervous young woman. She was nervous because she was not married to Sam. This desire to be married again embarrassed her, but she couldn't help it. Sam was married to someone else. Sam was always married to someone.

Sam and Elizabeth met as people usually meet. Suddenly, there was a deceptive light in the darkness. A light that reminded the lonely blackly of the darkness. They met at the wedding dinner of the daughter of a mutual friend. Delicious food was served and many peculiar toasts were given. Sam liked Elizabeth's aura and she liked his too. They danced. Sam had quite a bit to drink. At one point, he thought he saw a red rabbit in the floral centerpiece. It's true, it was Easter week, but he worried about this. They danced again. Sam danced Elizabeth out of the party and into the parking lot. Sam's car was nondescript and tidy except for a bag of melting groceries.

Elizabeth loved the way he kissed. He put his hand on her throat. He lay his tongue deep and quiet inside her mouth. He filled her mouth with the decadent Scotch and cigarette flavor of the tragic middle class. On the other hand, when Sam saw Elizabeth's brightly flowered scanty panties, he thought he'd faint with happiness. He was a sentimentalist.

"I love you," Elizabeth thought she heard him say.

Sam swore that he heard Elizabeth say, "Life is an eccentric privilege."

This worried him but not in time.

They began going out together frequently. Elizabeth promised to always take the babysitter home. At first, Elizabeth and Sam attempted to do vile and imaginative things to one another. This was culminated one afternoon when Sam spooned a mound of pineapple-lime

Jell-O between Elizabeth's legs and began to eat. At first, of course, Elizabeth was nervous. Then she stopped being nervous and began watching Sam's sweating, good-looking shoulders with real apprehension. Simultaneously, they both gave up. This seemed a good sign. The battle is always between the pleasure principle and the reality principle, is it not? Imagination is not what it's cracked up to be. Sam decided to forget the petty, bourgeois rite of eating food out of one another's orifices for a while. He decided to just love Elizabeth instead.

"Did you know that Charles Dickens wanted to marry Little Red Riding Hood?"

"What!" Sam exclaimed, appalled.

"Well, as a child he wanted to marry her," Elizabeth said.

"Oh," Sam said, curiously relieved.

Elizabeth had a house and her little girl. Sam had a house and a car and a Noank sloop. The houses were thirteen hundred miles apart. They spent the winter in Elizabeth's house in the South and they drove up to Sam's house for the summer. The trip took two and one half days. They had done it twice now. It seemed about the same each time. They argued on the Baltimore Beltway. They bought peaches and cigarettes and fireworks and a ham. The child would often sit on the floor in the front seat and talk into the air-conditioning vent.

"Emergency," she'd say. "Come in please."

On the most recent trip, Sam had called his lawyer from a Hot Shoppe on the New Jersey Turnpike. The lawyer told him that Sam's divorce had become final that morning. This had been Sam's third marriage. He and Annie had seemed very compatible. They tended to each other realistically, with affection and common sense. Then Annie decided to go back to school. She became interested in animal behaviorism. Books accumulated. She was never at home. She was always on field trips, in thickets or on beaches, or visiting some ornithologist in Barnstable. She began keeping voluminous notebooks. Sam came across the most alarming things written in her hand.

Mantids are cannibalistic and males often literally lose their heads to the females. The result, as far as successful mating is concerned, is beneficial, since the subesophageal ganglion is frequently removed and with it any inhibition on the copulatory center; the activities of male abdomen are carried out with more vigor than when the body was intact.

"Annie, Annie," Sam had pleaded. "Let's have some people over for drinks. Let's prune the apple tree. Let's bake the orange cake you always made for my birthday."

"I have never made an orange cake in my life," Annie said.

"Annie," Sam said, "don't they have courses in seventeenth-century romantic verse or something?"

"You drink too much," Annie said. "You get quarrelsome every night at nine. Your behavior patterns are severely limited."

Sam clutched his head with his hands.

"Plus you are reducing my ability to respond to meaningful occurrences, Sam."

Sam poured himself another Scotch. He lit a cigarette. He applied a mustache with a piece of picnic charcoal.

"I am Captain Blood," he said. "I want to kiss you."

"When Errol Flynn died, he had the body of a man of ninety," Annie said. "His brain was unrealistic from alcohol."

She had already packed the toast rack and the pewter and rolled up the Oriental rug.

"I am just taking this one Wanda Landowska recording," she said. "That's all I'm taking in the way of records."

Sam, with his charcoal mustache, sat very straight at his end of the table.

"The variations in our life have ceased to be significant," Annie said.

Sam's house was on a hill overlooking a cove. The cove was turning into a saltwater marsh. Sam liked marshes but he thought he had bought property on a deep-water cove where he could take his boat in and out. He wished that he were not involved in the process of his cove turning into a marsh. When he had first bought the place, he was so excited about everything that he had a big dinner party at which he served *soupe de poisson* using only the fish he had caught himself from the cove. He could not, it seems, keep himself from doing this each year. Each year, the *soupe de poisson* did not seem as nice as it had the year before. About a year before Annie left him, she suggested that they should probably stop having that particular dinner party. Sam felt flimflammed.

When Sam returned to the table in the Hot Shoppe on the New Jersey Turnpike after learning about his divorce, Elizabeth didn't look at him.

"I have been practicing different expressions, none of which seem appropriate," Elizabeth said.

"Well," Sam said.

"I might as well be honest," Elizabeth said.

Sam bit into his egg. He did not feel lean and young and unencumbered.

"In the following sentence, the same word is used in each of the missing spaces, but pronounced differently." Elizabeth's head was bowed. She was reading off the place mat. "Don't look at yours now, Sam," she said, "the answer's on it." She slid his place mat off the table, spilling coffee on his cuff in the process. "*A prominent and——— man came into a restaurant at the height of the rush hour. The waitress was———to serve him immediately as she had———.*"

Sam looked at her. She smiled. He looked at the child. The child's eyes were closed and she was moving her thumb around in her mouth as though she were making butter there. Sam paid the bill. The child went to the bathroom. An hour later, just before the Tappan Zee Bridge, Sam said, *"Notable."*

"What?" Elizabeth said.

"Notable. That's the word that belongs in all three spaces."

"You looked," Elizabeth said.

"Goddamn it," Sam yelled. "I did not look!"

"I knew this would happen," Elizabeth said. "I knew it was going to be like this."

It is a very hot night. Elizabeth has poison ivy on her wrists. Her wrists are covered with calamine lotion. She has put Saran Wrap over the lotion and secured it with a rubber band. Sam is in love. He smells the wonderfully clean, sun-and-linen smell of Elizabeth and her calamine lotion.

Elizabeth is going to tell a fairy story to the child. Sam tries to convince her that fables are sanctimonious and dully realistic.

"Tell her any one except 'The Frog King,' " Sam whispers.

"Why can't I tell her that one?" Elizabeth says. She is worried.

"The toad stands for male sexuality," Sam whispers.

"Oh Sam," she says. "That's so superficial. That's a very superficial analysis of the animal-bridegroom stories."

"I am an animal," Sam growls, biting her softly on the collarbone.

"Oh Sam," she says.

Sam's first wife was very pretty. She had the flattest stomach he had ever seen and very black, very straight hair. He adored her. He was faithful to her. He wrote both their names on the flyleaves of all his books. They were married for six years. They went to Europe. They went to Mexico. In Mexico they lived in a grand room in a simple hotel opposite a square. The trees in the square were pruned in the shape of perfect boxes. Each night, hundreds of birds would come home to the trees. Beside the hotel was the shop of a man who made coffins. So many of the coffins seemed small, for children. Sam's wife grew depressed. She lay in bed for most of the day. She pretended she was dying. She wanted Sam to make love to her and pretend that she was dying. She wanted a baby. She was all mixed up.

Sam suggested that it was the ions in the Mexican air that made her depressed. He kept loving her but it became more and more difficult for them both. She continued to retreat into a landscape of chaos and warring feelings.

Her depression became general. They had been married for almost six years but they were still only twenty-four years old. Often they would go to amusement parks. They liked the bumper cars best. The last time they had gone to the amusement park, Sam had broken his wife's hand when he crashed head-on into her bumper car. They could probably have gotten over the incident had they not been so bitterly miserable at the time.

* * *

In the middle of the night, the child rushes down the hall and into Elizabeth and Sam's bedroom.

"Sam," the child cries, "the baseball game! I'm missing the baseball game."

"There is no baseball game," Sam says.

"What's the matter? What's happening!" Elizabeth cries.

"Yes, yes," the child wails. "I'm late, I'm missing it."

"Oh what is it!" Elizabeth cries.

"The child is having an anxiety attack," Sam says.

The child puts her thumb in her mouth and then takes it out again. "I'm only five years old," she says.

"That's right," Elizabeth says. "She's too young for anxiety attacks. It's only a dream." She takes the child back to her room. When she comes back, Sam is sitting up against the pillows, drinking a glass of Scotch.

"Why do you have your hand over your heart?" Elizabeth asks.

"I think it's because it hurts," Sam says.

Elizabeth is trying to stuff another fable into the child. She is determined this time. Sam has just returned from setting the mooring for his sailboat. He is sprawled in a hot bath, listening to the radio.

Elizabeth says, "There were two men wrecked on a desert island and one of them pretended he was home while the other admitted—"

"Oh Mummy," the child says.

"I know that one," Sam says from the tub. "They both died."

"This is not a primitive story," Elizabeth says. "Colorless, anticlimactic endings are typical only of primitive stories."

Sam pulls his knees up and slides underneath the water. The water is really blue. Elizabeth had dyed curtains in the tub and stained the porcelain. Blue is Elizabeth's favorite color. Slowly, Sam's house is turning blue. Sam pulls the plug and gets out of the tub. He towels himself off. He puts on a shirt, a tie and a white summer suit. He laces up his sneakers. He slicks back his soaking hair. He goes into the child's room. The lights are out. Elizabeth and the child are looking at each other in the dark. There are fireflies in the room.

"They come in on her clothes," Elizabeth says.

"Will you marry me?" Sam asks.

"I'd love to," she says.

Sam calls his friends up, beginning with Peter, his oldest friend. While they have been out of touch, Peter has become a soft contact lenses king.

"I am getting married," Sam says.

There is a pause, then Peter finally says, "Once more the boat departs."

It is harder to get married than one would think. Sam has forgotten this. For example, what is the tone that should be established for the party? Elizabeth's mother believes that a wedding cake is very necessary. Elizabeth is embarrassed about this.

"I can't think about that, Mother," she says. She puts her mother and the child in charge of the wedding cake. At the child's suggestion, it has a jam center and a sailboat on it.

Elizabeth and Sam decide to get married at the home of a justice of the peace. Her name is Mrs. Custer. Then they will come back to their own house for a party. They invite a lot of people to the party.

"I have taken out 'obey,' " Mrs. Custer says, "but I have left in 'love' and 'cherish.' Some people object to the 'obey.' "

"That's all right," Sam says.

"I could start now," Mrs. Custer says. "But my husband will be coming home soon. If we wait a few moments, he will be here and then he won't interrupt the ceremony."

"That's all right," Sam says.

They stand around. Sam whispers to Elizabeth, "I should pay this woman a little something, but I left my wallet at home."

"That's all right," Elizabeth says.

"Everything's going to be fine," Sam says.

They get married. They drive home. Everyone has arrived, and some of the guests have brought their children. The children run around with Elizabeth's child. One little girl has long red hair and painted green nails.

"I remember you," the child says. "You had a kitty. Why didn't you bring your kitty with you?"

"That kitty bought the chops," the little girl says.

Elizabeth overhears this. "Oh my goodness," she says. She takes her daughter into the bathroom and closes the door.

"There is more than the seeming of things," she says to the child.

"Oh Mummy," the child says, "I just want my nails green like that girl's."

"Elizabeth," Sam calls. "Please come out. The house is full of people. I'm getting drunk. We've been married for one hour and fifteen minutes." He closes his eyes and leans his forehead against the door. Miraculously, he enters. The closed door is not locked. The child escapes by the same entrance, happy to be freed. Sam kisses Elizabeth by the shower stall. He kisses her beside the sink and before the full-length mirror. He kisses her as they stand pressed against the windowsill. Together, in their animistic embrace, they float out the window and circle the house, gazing down at all those who have not found true love, below.

WIFE

Norman Fischer

Of all the women
    Of all the world
Delicate
    In their various encasings
Of body
    Of mind
This one
    Bent asleep before me
On the bed
    Is the one through whom all must be loved
As I have promised

PART II

THE HOT BED

FIRST KISS

Joan Logghe

Last week was our first kiss. We've been married eighteen years, really only seventeen, but I throw on a year for that kiss. He told me recently, We should go to a sex therapist. I asked why. Because you don't kiss me enough.

So I kissed him hard last week and I tasted, first, his mother. The time he threw the table over in a fight with her, because she brought to his attention all the wrongs of a dozen years in a mental list she'd kept. There was the time he was late for milking, how he read too much, the way he loved the work of Sigmund Freud, which she pronounced "Frood." We lived on the family dairy farm in Wisconsin in early marriage, and she'd relish telling me the crimes of his childhood; the time he cut the tail off the puppy, the time he and his brother crammed a cat in the mailbox. She wondered if I would have married this man if I'd heard about the boy he was.

I learned she used to tell her kids, The devil has got into you. I got it, in that kiss. Why he had a stutter as a child. He had such a blocked tongue that by high school he could barely speak in public and had no one to turn to but himself. He got a record of T. S. Eliot from the library and read aloud with it, recited until he learned elocution, alone on a Wisconsin dairy farm, practicing in the barn. His voice, ever after, has a moo in the vowels and a British accent when he reads me poems.

When you know somebody that deeply, so many bodies lie in the bed alongside. We need a king-sized bed to contain them. Our bed is full of farmland, two hundred acres including the back pasture. And you know, that is where the best sex always is, despite the scent of cows. The Jungians say that in bed there are always at least four people, invisible man and dark surly woman. But in our bed there is a herd—siblings and offspring, his parents, my parents, and the church, full of incense and Latin. My temple, so old it's got the history of God engraved in the bedsheets. It isn't a bed, it's a text, a Russian novel.

And so when I kissed him in our bed, that artifact of repeated love, I finally heard the words, all the lost words. I got the clinkers and the home runs that I never could catch. I got the ashamed red ones and the unexclaimed love words all in a kiss. I ate shame. His shame I could taste in crooked teeth no orthodontist ever saw. He was not perfect and I'd taught him that, too. I counted his not-perfects as a mother does the digits. Only I'm not his mother. Maybe it was then I separated from her.

When we fight he says, I want you to treat me like anyone else. I say, That's impossible. We're married.

He says, If we weren't, maybe we'd be good friends, maybe even lovers.

When I kissed him hard from on top, I got it, it clicked; boyhood, fall from the barn leaving a scar on his back. I smelled coffee his grandmother left on the stove all day. I felt the work ethic squeeze him tight for being a thinker, and then lambaste him for wasting time in bed. And I saw him riding the Ford tractor, plowing for corn with Freud propped in his lap.

By kissing, I begged, Drop down, love, into the heart and live here with me. Drop lower and lower into the deep river of sex and I'll kiss you more. Down out of your large skull, huge as Cro-Magnon, wide as acreage. I'll kiss you like last week when I didn't say a thing, but got a message in a bottle from across the vast ocean of marriage. That is my vow, our future.

From: BEAVER TALES

Elizabeth Hay

A Blood Indian tale. A man and a woman were camped on the shore of a lake and the man was always away hunting. In his absence a beaver came out of the water and made love to the woman. Day after day the beaver returned to her until she finally went away with him. The man came home. He looked for the woman and saw her trail going down to the shore. After a time she came up out of the water "heavy with child." She gave birth to a beaver, which she kept at the head of her bed in a bowl of water.

❉

I heard the splash. By the time I reached them he was sitting at the edge of the pond, cradling a woman between his legs.

They got up as I appeared, and we moved in the same direction to the same spot: a large slab of rock in the sun. I sat down with my daughter. He turned and smiled at us both, but especially the little girl. Is the young lady going swimming? he asked. The young lady is, but the old lady isn't. He laughed. Nor will this one, he said of the woman beside him. The woman wore shorts and a sleeveless shirt. Her hair was pulled back and held in place by a large clip. Her legs were scratched in several places, which made the skin look even whiter, more discolored, the veiny patches of middle age. She looked to be in her early forties.

He was tanned. His legs were very brown up to his shorts line, and paler from there to his briefs—all he was wearing. He was about fifty. European, from his accent, even more from his manner: the relaxed way he turned and smiled, the straight white teeth, the eyes, the charm.

I didn't notice his hands, or how much hair was on his chest—things I usually notice right away.

He swam again. The edge of the pond was muddy and rocky, deep with rotting leaves. Is it cold? I asked. Fresh, he answered. He felt his way gingerly before throwing himself out over the lily pads into deeper water.

While he was swimming I watched the woman. He had placed his faded cut-offs against the rock to soften it for her back. She rearranged them, leaned back for a moment, then sat up again and fished for a cigarette. She didn't look my way or watch him swim, even when he swam back towards her. She looked so unhappy. Her body had the loose, unmuscled quality of someone who watches what she eats but doesn't exercise. I imagined them in bed together—he so relaxed, she with that look of strain acquired over many years.

He came out of the water, climbed the rocky slope, put his wet hands on her thighs and stroked them. She twisted away, but laughed as she did so. I love you, he said. That's not a good enough excuse, she answered. Then he came around behind her and settled himself on the rock, pulling her between his legs. He lifted up the back of her blouse and pressed against her. She didn't resist as I had expected but leaned into the embrace.

I thought of him smelling of the lake, and her skin acquiring that smell. Of her tasting his skin, and tasting the lake. Of her hands, as they explored, exploring water. Where we were, in that woods with light breaking through evergreens, we seemed to be under water: something about the light, speckled on needle-deep ground, something liquid.

He did all this—pressing his wet cock against her back, wrapping his arms around her, kissing her neck—as I sat a few feet away. That seemed the most European thing of all.

After we left I imagined him going back to the car, stripping off his briefs, putting on his shorts, going the rest of the day without underwear. Was it that thought that made me shed my own? I walked naked under my sundress, the air lovely, soft, stroking.

※

When Samuel Hearne lived on the shores of Hudson Bay in the late 1700s, trading furs and exploring, he had, apparently, a number of Indian women as lovers. Hearne doesn't describe the women. He describes the beavers who were their pets. But by making mention of the women—they stayed in the fort all winter—he gave historians cause to write about his "harem."

Indian women, he wrote, nursed beaver orphans at the breast. They would nurse the kit until it was able to eat bark, about six weeks. He describes the women feeding the beaver dainties: rice and plum pudding. And the inordinate affection the beavers showed the women—playing in their laps, crying out when they left.

I was nursing the baby as I read. Lying on the bed, back against the headrest, I wore Alec's big flannel shirt and long underwear. The long underwear had several holes, an especially large one in the crotch. He sat down beside me and slipped his hand through the hole and began to stroke, warm hand on my vulva, and leaning over, he began to suck the other breast.

His sucking was so much more delicate than the baby's. He licked the tip, slid his tongue down the side, massaged the whole of my nipple with his mouth, took it between his teeth—and all the while his fingers were pushing and kneading, spreading me open, going inside. I reached for him, but with the baby on my breast could do little. He undid his fly himself—came into me through the same wide hole in the underwear—balancing so that he didn't disturb the baby. A homely bit of lovemaking.

✳

In a Cree tale a woman married to a pond speaks to her husband by the way she swims in him. There comes a time when there's no rain and the pond dries up. The woman sets off looking for her husband and, after many miles, finds him in a hole. She takes him home little by little in her hands.

✳

I know a woman who swam around an abandoned beaver lodge, entered it through the underwater passage, and climbed up onto the dry ledge inside. It was like a cathedral inside, she told me. Cathedral? An old barn—modifying her description but not losing the image of light drifting dimly through cracks.

For several mornings I got up early and paddled over to the beaver lodge. I heard them talking inside. Two large beavers patrolled behind me, swimming back and forth, about twenty feet away. The lodge was a mound of pale sticks piled up against a rock, a ghostly configuration between two balsam trees. A dead tree jutted up out of the water, and made the lodge easy to find. In fact there were two lodges fifteen feet away from each other, one much smaller than the other—still used. Sometimes beavers entered one, sometimes the other.

I try to remember the description that came to me when I heard the beavers talk—it was indeed as though their tongues had been removed, a low almost birdlike sound.

I ask him to lie on his belly, and reach between his legs with oily hands. He raises himself slightly on one hip and then I can massage his penis, upside down and backwards, pleased by the new perspective and reminded of Old Coyote Man.

Old Coyote Man saw a group of young women picking wild strawberries. Quickly he lay down under the earth and let only the tip of his penis protrude. One of the women saw this large berry and tried to pick it. She called to the other women, who came and pulled at it. It has deep roots, one of them said. They nibbled at it. It weeps, they said. It weeps milk.

More oil, and the thought of castoreum, the liquid in a beaver's scent glands, basis of perfume. The image of a beaver meadow—pungent with musk—of a fallen tree, leafy clearing, Alec's leg pressing up, and me riding it. This image of something male, something which shifts between animal and man—cock erect, or hanging long and low—the shift of myself into something else—this is the sort of loosening I love.

THE FAVORITE SLEEPER

Summer Brenner

every night
we bear down
into some dormant state
on the flats
of mats and beds

it is strange
the stoniness
the form of dream
that every night
we come again
to this repose
of working posture

like great animals
lying in the desert
we monstrously
fill up our sheets

like some plant
impinging on the white garden
we spring
again and again

we lie down
it is ridiculous
this sweetness
this sphinx

THE CORSET

Evan S. Connell

I think that you are, she had said, enunciating each word, unutterably disgusting. I think, to tell the honest truth, that never in my entire life have I heard such an inexpressibly vulgar suggestion. Just in case you care for my opinion, there it is. To think that any man would even propose such an idea, especially to his wife, which, just on the chance that you've forgotten, I happen to be, is, to put it in the simplest possible terms, unutterably disgusting.

Mosher shrugs. Okay, never mind. It was a thought, Alice.

What you did while you were in the Army, and the type of women who prey upon lonesome soldiers in foreign countries, or for that matter, how foreign women in other countries behave with their husbands, are things I'd just as soon not care to hear about. I don't know if I'm making myself clear. It simply does not concern me, first of all, and then too, I don't see why you keep harping on these things, as though I were merely some sort of concubine. I guess that's the word. To be perfectly frank, because certainly I've always wanted you to be frank with me whenever anything was bothering you about our relationship, and I'm sure you've always wanted me to express my feelings just as frankly, I appreciate the fact that you thought enough of me to mention it, but it's just so revolting, I mean, I honestly do not know quite what to say.

I thought it might be fun, says Mosher. Overseas the women would—

Fun! Did you say *fun?* When we've always had such a marvelous relationship? I can't understand you anymore. You've changed. We used to agree that we had the most beautiful relationship in the world, at least you said so every time I asked, but now I don't know whether to believe you or not. I should think you'd want to keep it the way it was. When two people sincerely respect each other they surely oughtn't to jeopardize their affiliation, do you think? A moment ago I could scarcely believe my ears. I never dreamed that you could be so—so—

Vulgar?

Exactly! Not by any stretch of the imagination.

Then you think it's an unreasonable request? asks Mosher after a pause. Listen, Alice—

What you did in Europe is one thing, and I try not to dwell on it, which is more than most wives would do, but now you're home and we ought to go on the way we did before.

Alice, it's a damned strange thing, says Mosher, that my own wife should know less about me than a whore on the Rue de la Paix.

For a moment she gazes at him. Then all at once she remarks: Tell me what you want. I love you, you must know that. I'll do anything on earth for you. Tell me specifically what would please you and I'll agree to do it, on the condition that it means preserving our relationship.

I don't want it that way! Mosher shouts, and bangs his fists together. Can't you understand? Oh my God, don't look so miserable, he adds. You look like I was getting ready to flog you.

That wouldn't surprise me. Nothing you do anymore could possibly surprise me. I don't know what's come over you. Honestly, I don't. You're a perfect stranger.

Mosher, enraged and baffled, lights a cigarette.

Smoking isn't good for you.

I know it isn't, I know, he says, puffing away.

You never listen to me.

Alice, he replies with a gloomy expression, I don't miss a word, not a word. Oh hell, I love you as you are. Don't change. You're probably right, we'll go on like we used to. I don't want you to change. Forget I said anything.

But you *do!* You do want me to change, and I've got to be everything to you, otherwise our—

Don't! Mosher groans, falling back on the bed. Don't keep calling the two of us a relationship, as though we were a paragraph in some social worker's report.

For better or worse, she says as though she had not heard him,

I've made up my mind to behave exactly like one of those European women. I'm quite serious. I mean that.

Mosher, rising on one elbow, gazes at his wife curiously.

I do mean it. I'm going to be every bit as depraved and evil as they are, you just watch!

What the hell's got into you? he demands. You're out of your mind. You're as American as Susan B. Anthony. Then he continues: But if you want to, fine. Go ahead.

What do I do first?

I don't know. Don't you?

No, this was your idea. Give me a suggestion.

Well, says Mosher uneasily, I'm a spectator, so to speak. I don't really know. He realizes that she has started to unbutton her blouse. What do you think you're doing? he asks. I mean, good God, it's three o'clock in the afternoon and the Haffenbecks are coming over.

I don't care, she says. I simply don't care about a thing anymore.

But wait a minute, Alice. We invited them for drinks and a barbecue, remember?

I don't care! I don't care about the Haffenbecks. And she takes off her blouse, asking: Shall I take off everything?

Oh, yes, yes, everything, everything, says Mosher absently, gazing at her shoulders. With his chin propped in his hands he watches her get undressed.

I really should have paid a visit to the beauty parlor this morning, she says. My hair is a fright.

The beauty parlor! he shouts. What the hell has a beauty parlor got to do with this? Life's too short for beauty parlors!

However, she's doing her best, he thinks, all for me, because she does love me and wants to please me, isn't that odd? She's not a bit excited, she's just ashamed and embarrassed, so I am too. He feels deeply touched that his wife is willing to debase herself for him, but at the same time he is annoyed. Her attitude fills him with a sense of vast and unspeakable dismay. In Europe, now, romping in a bedroom, there would be no stilted questions, no apologies or explanations, no pussyfooting about, no textbook psychology, nothing but a wild and fruitful and altogether satisfying game. Alice, though, after the first embrace, customarily looks to see if her clothing is torn or her hair has been mussed.

Why, he asks with a lump like a chestnut in his throat, do you wear that corset?

It isn't a corset, it's a foundation.

Mosher waves impatiently. Alice, I hate these Puritan bones. Those Boston snoods. You haven't the slightest idea how sick and tired I've become of Aunt Martha's prune-whip morals. Whenever I touch you while you're wearing that thing it's like I've got hold of a bag of cement. Didn't I ever tell you how much I hate that corset? Didn't you ever realize? I mean to say, I think of you as flesh and blood, but that freaking thing makes you look like a python that swallowed a pig. Why do you wear it? You have such a marvelous shape all by yourself. It would look wonderful to see you out in public without that damned corset.

I should think a man wouldn't want his wife to be seen on the street bulging at every seam.

Well, I would, says Mosher with great bitterness. I'd love it. Anyway, right now I want you to take that bloody thing off.

She does, with no change of expression; her eyes remain fixed on him rather like the eyes of a frightened tigress, bright and watchful and unblinking.

Do you love me because of this? she asks.

Because of what?

My figure.

Yes, he says earnestly, I certainly do. A moment later, to his amazement, a tear comes wandering down her cheek.

I hoped it was me you loved, she says, weeping a little more but holding her head high.

I should have been a monk, he thinks. I'd have a nice quiet cell with bread and porridge and books to read—it would all be so simple. On the other hand I wouldn't make a very successful monk. I know what I'd spend every day praying for.

You can leave those beads on, Alice, he says, I like the effect.

He gazes at her body with immense interest; it is as pale as a melon. In the undergloom of her belly, he thinks, a little bird has landed—a fierce little falcon with tawny wings. He lifts his eyes once more to her face and sees a lock of hair almost but not quite touching the lobe of her ear. She is as divine and inimitable and perfect as a snow crystal or an April leaf unfolding.

You mentioned some girl over there who was a dancer, who used to dance for the soldiers.

Oh yes, yes, and she was magnificent, Mosher answers. Her name was Zizi. She used to go leaping around like the nymphs on those Greek vases, and when she wriggled across the floor you'd swear she was made out of rubber. I never saw anything like it.

Well, look at me, says Alice. And to Mosher's astonishment she lifts both hands high above her head and turns a perfectly splendid cartwheel.

What do you think of *that?* she demands, on her feet once again, tossing her hair over her shoulders.

I didn't know you could turn a cartwheel, says Mosher. He sits up briskly, spilling cigarette ashes on the bed.

You haven't seen anything yet, she calls from the other side of the room, and bending backward until her palms are flat on the floor, she gives a nimble kick and is upside down.

I didn't know you could stand on your hands, says Mosher, looking at her in stupefaction. Even with your clothes on you never did that.

Does it please you?

I should say it does! Mosher replies.

Men are so peculiar. Why should you want me to do these things?

I don't know, Alice. Somehow it makes me love you all the more.

I simply cannot understand you, she remarks, and begins walking around the bedroom on her hands. Could your old Zizi do this?

I don't know, he mutters. I can't remember. You've got me confused. I don't think I ever saw anything in my life like this.

Not even in Paris?

Not even in Heidelberg. You look strange upside down, Alice. What else can you do?

Just then the doorbell rings.

Oh my word, she exclaims, that must be the Haffenbecks!

No doubt, says Mosher. Either it's the Haffenbecks or the police.

What on earth are we going to do?

I don't know, he replies, unable to stop staring at her. Who cares? Do you?

I suppose not, she answers, still upside down.

The corset is lying on the edge of the bed. Mosher picks it up, flings it out the window and, reclining comfortably, takes a puff at his cigarette.

Now, he commands, turn a somersault.

From: COUPLETS

ROBERT MEZEY

Mouths searching each other for minutes, years
Warmer and warmer, looking for the hidden word.

Arms and legs intertwined, skin sliding on skin,
The blood rushing joyously into its channels.

The breasts open their eyes in the darkness of palms,
The eyes widen at every little touch.

The fingers brush against the mouth of the womb
In the conversation of the deaf and blind.

Yoked by flesh, shaking, hollering praises,
They rise as one body to the opening.

The shining phallus erupts in a spray of stars
Flying into her night at tremendous speed.

If their eyes became the darkness, they would see,
Flaming in the darkness, their blowtorch auras.

Sperm on her lips, her hair, her eyes closed,
His whole body bathed in the odor of the garden,

Wet, motionless, barely breathing,
They fill slowly with the surrounding darkness.

From: THE CALCULUS OF VARIATION

Diane di Prima

Let me extol your body, the living flesh. The head is small, and turns in to the pillow. As the light turns, falling on your neck. One hand tucked out of sight. The living flesh. What darkness shimmers on your shoulder? Peace, like a child, the long white feet stretch out. Crusted with city dirt, the ankle bone/ streaked.

Gentle soft flesh, thickish about the middle. I slip an arm around you as you sleep. Soft in the middle, gentle, like a girl. Your son is tougher; your son's skin less smooth. LET ME PRAISE LIGHT THAT FALLS ON YOUR MORNING HAIR. Creeps up the edge of buildings, bare brick walls. And falls in pools on the flat tar roof outside.

What joy in the sounds of music, the kings of old/ made no sound richer than what Cecil makes. Playing with one hand on the blurred piano. There is laughter. I think of this. Your soft dull flesh. The variety between your world and mine. Your cock is limp between us. You breathe deep. The wind stirs dust and tar. The cat is stretching. I stroke your hip, the dip and spout of your pelvis.

Mornings are black and white ((oh yes, take sides)). Cat black and white, sheets, black slacks, and white shirt. Roof black, in the white air, like a mountaintop. Brick wall I look at, bathed in a golden light. Bright eyes of Milarepa. Laughing slits.

Clangor. The gongs. The children waking up. What joy we have here/ howls. The shrieks and cries. The names called out/ the shit rubbed in the hair. Black dog on the next roof barks amid green plants. Our cat comes to him, they both lie down. Your eyes, open like slits, the cloudy blue. You smile a little, your mouth tastes of morning.

* * *

The traffic moves through a cloud of sounds like waves. We wake every morning on another beach. The nervous horses dance in the busy streets. The hoods swing out, the cops/ also swing out. A slime like blood falls over everything. Red runs the river, the East River, red. A flame like hearts, like onehand Cecil music. The words John Wieners mumbled after shock. This hymn of joy we're making. Listen close.

My baby laid her head in my lap, she said "what will become of me?" She laughed, she did a dance. A shuffle, in her socks, in the living room. I sleep when I can, the swish of clothesline. The children jumping rope, the swish of traffic. Loud, joyous sounds from the pentecostal churches. Our bright, red car swung over the Brooklyn Bridge. Whom are they hanging where? The children, jumping

> Lady, lady, turn around
> Lady, lady, touch the ground
> Lady, lady, show your shoe
> Lady, lady, I love you . . .

What bright flesh/ turns in the morning air, an offering.

I come to the door of our room. You are still sleeping. The smell of roses hangs in the heavy air. The smell of tar, the musty smell of sheets.

In the high study, warm, I offer incense. My flesh a form of offering, consuming. The smell of musk, the smell of my own death. A formal grace, I turn in the small room. I smell your dream, joyous as shooting stars. We are on a train, outside of salt lake city. Joyous together in some kind of limbo . . .

※

To come to terms with this, the solstice past. The Darkening of the Light. My place & yours. That our acts should burn, our passions, our clear sight. Until the sun shall come to himself again.

So be it. We play this game of treachery. Of passions running out. Deceit. Of passion. Weeping children. Dripping skies. As if we weren't a single sheet of flame. One body. Fiery garment of the mother. That blows in any wind, the breath of Shiva. As if your ankle I take in my mouth, your sleeping hand, the black fur of the cat. Made something more than pictures on the wall. Shadows projected on a waving cloth. A drape whose folds run sideways.

LET ME DESTROY YOUR BODY, the living flesh. Come, cover it with mine. Our flesh becomes one flame. George, Cecil, Alan. Not many hands have touched as we have touched. Not many gestures cut in flame and stone. Beckon through aeons as our gestures beckon.

✳

POEM TO MY HUSBAND FROM MY FATHER'S DAUGHTER

Sharon Olds

I have always admired your courage. As I see you
embracing me, in the mirror, I see I am
my father as a woman, I see you bravely
embrace him in me, putting your life in his
hands as mine. You know who I am—you can
see his hair springing from my head like
oil from the ground, you can see his eyes,
reddish as liquor left in a shot-glass and
dried dark, looking out of my face,
and his firm sucking lips, and the breasts
rising frail as blisters from his chest,
tipped with apple-pink. You are fearless, you
enter him as a woman, my sex like a
wound in his body, you flood your seed in his
life as me, you entrust your children to that
man as a mother, his hands as my hands
cupped around their tiny heads. I have never
known a man with your courage, coming
naked into the cage with the lion, I
lay my enormous paws on your scalp I
take my great tongue and begin to
run the rasp delicately
along your skin, humming: as you enter
ecstasy, the hairs lifting
all over your body, I have never seen a
happier man.

From: CHIN MUSIC

JAMES McMANUS

Teresa can't help it. The churn in her brain has been flashing her back to a series of groaning and sweaty duets, complete with her and Raymondo's most private and personal code words and phrases and rules, to some things that she'd rather not dwell on right now but nonetheless can't quite phase out. It's perverse. Because the harder she struggles to keep certain episodes under, the quicker and fresher the mnemonic bytes effervesce.

For example. Either might balk at the outset, protesting they're GONNA BE LATE, since as often as not it begins as they're on their way out. Ray will be thoroughly naked, having just stepped from out of the shower, and into her own best silk panties will be all the further along she'll have got getting dressed. Somehow or other she'll wind up in front of him on their blue bedroom carpet in the midst of a strenuous set of her best FLEXIONES, making sure that her NIPPLES TOUCH CARPET each time, counting out loud to herself, pumping and straining and sweating. Raymondo JUST WATCHES. When she's done all she can, Raymondo goes to the second small drawer of her dresser and takes out two dice. One die is white, borrowed for keeps several years ago from Ray's uncle's Risk game. The other one's smaller, with more rounded corners, and red. (It was never real clear to her where this second die came from.) They call them ZEE LOGS. Raymondo caresses and rotates them between his huge palms, shakes them around in his fist, looks at her, blows on them, then rolls them out onto the carpet. The number of FLEXIONES she's managed times the number of pips showing on top of ZEE LOGS becomes the MAGIC NUMBER Raymondo will have to perform in order to COME OUT ON TOP. Her average is seven or eight, although when she's desperate to win she has managed as many as twelve. But even if she only does seven, Raymondo, who averages forty-five to fifty, will still have to roll craps or less to keep within striking distance. (One time he'd rolled an eleven after she had done seven and made it all the way up to seventy-three and a half before collapsing. He'd had to pitch that night too.) Once he has started his set, she SUPERVISES every last one very closely, making darn sure those hard concave cheeks DON'T START RISING—if they do they get SNAPPED with his towel—that his chest TOUCHES DOWN every time. He usually is still going strong till around thirty-five, but it's right around then that he starts getting shaky, his rear end STARTS RISING, and so on. SNAP SNAP! By forty his biceps are trembling, his face is all red, and he's gasping. If he fails, as he so often does, to SATISFACTORILY PERFORM THE MAGIC NUMBER, she's got him. WITHOUT HAVING TO BE TOLD, his big chest still heaving, Raymondo rolls over and lies on his back for his TREATMENT, throughout which he stays wholly SERVILE TO HER COY DISDAIN. The first thing she does is she SMOTHERS him by straddling his still-gasping face, propelling herself back and forth over his nose and his mouth and his chin, eventually torquing down to the max in order to keep him from talking or moving or breathing. And meantime, of course, his own NEW DIRECTION is completely IGNORED AND NEGLECTED. The most she'll consent to is lightly and dispassionately running the side of her thumb up and down it, maybe stroking it with her wrist or her palm, BUT THAT'S ALL. And meantime she's riding his face like she's busting a bronco, but harder, till her teeth start to chatter in fact, at which point d'orgue she will jerk off her panties, slide right back up onto his HARDON, continue. If either could take it, this could go on forever, but of course neither can, so it doesn't. When at last she is through with him, Raymondo, UNREQUITED CAMSHAFT and all, is sent back to the shower to cool himself off and get dressed—or whatever. Her reason? THE RULES. And besides. They're ALREADY LATE AS IT IS.

If, on the other hand, Raymondo sur*passes* the MAGIC NUMBER (ties, of course, go to the woman), then it's *she* who's in trouble. BUT NO ROUGH STUFF, she'll say, half kidding, half pleading. No use. WITHOUT FURTHER ADO she'll be DOWN ON HER KNEECAPS and SHLURPING. Raymondo's behavior might include anything from straightforwardly PROVIDING DIRECTION, caressing her ears with his palms, to grabbing her hair, barking out orders and curses, to wielding the infamous NIPPLEWHIP. It goes without saying that throughout this ordeal her own POOR UNMENTIONABLE gets no stimulation whatever, oral or otherwise. None. She's compelled by THE RULES to continue till she gets him to come, no matter how long he may take. They also provide that she KNOCK IT BACK GRATEFULLY, ALL OF IT, then lick off the series of AFTERSHOCKS. *Yum!*

For the most part these rules get adhered to. The one that gets broken most often, of course, is the one that provides that the loser be COOLLY NEGLECTED throughout the whole session. Her own biggest weakness is for sliding off Raymondo's cleft chin, shimmying down his sleek torso, then swinging around versy-arsy and giddying back up onto his ostensibly off-limits MOONBEAM, meanwhile, to make matters worse, greedily lapping his now comeslick features. DOMESTIC CRUDE city. It's so fun fun fun that 9.9 times out of ten she can't help it. Raymondo's most common transgression gets made in DIRECT RETALIATION, or so he will claim, for being INCISORED too hard, on the basis of which flimsy excuse he will gingerly remove MISTER MIKE from between her sharp choppers, shove her back down off her knee-caps, and pin her young ass to the carpet. Now she is *really* in trouble. For at this point he's got this quick, clever tackle-and-pulley maneuver whereby he forces her legs wide apart by scooping them up and then driving his body between them, shoving her thighs so far back in the process that her knees are on line with her shoulders, while at the same time he pinions her biceps beside her and hoists himself forward by pushing back down off her arms, yanking her torso in one direction while leaning down hard with his chest and his shoulders to double her back in the other. Wrenched open, raised up, defenseless, she hopes that he won't be TOO CRUEL. For Raymondo could sure go to town on her now, give her one real hard time, simply by using the same push-and-pull locomotion to jack up and stretch out her gash as to drive his hard cock down and in, tactically enhancing his thrust-to-weight ratio and at the same time providing for strategically deep penetration. If she's lucky, that is. Because most of the time he just holds her like this for a while, makes her wait, lets that wet helpless feeling soak in. It's her SENTENCE. She can protest all she wants about BREAKING THE RULES, but they both know she's way overmatched now: that the count's 0–2 and THE RULES have gone right out the window: that once she is caught in these hot ineluctable clutches he can tease her and zap her at will. One of his wickedest tricks at this stage is to jam her real slow for a bit, build up some rhythm, pretend that he's finding his stroke, and then suddenly stop and pull out. *O my God!* The soft pulsing void where his hardon just was drives her nuts, but all she can do now is tremble and writhe in short-circuit while he waggles its tip on her stomach, bastes up her thighs with her juices, and asks her HOW BAD DO YOU WANT IT. (She knows that she best keep her throes to a minimum now, but more often than not she just can't.) When she gives him no answer he bites on her nipples, calls her all sorts of lewd names, and jives her with more false alarms: and she *still* won't admit that she wants it. (She likes to make love with her husband, of course, in mature, more conventional manners, but she likes it much better when they fuck with each other, let things get strange and depraved, so it's sinful and painful and raunchy: like they're not really married or something.) When he's darn good and ready he'll stick it back in, lean on her thighs even harder, and then drill her and warp her and rock her, make her quiver and gasp with some extra firm jolts high and tight. Make her ache. Make her shake. Make her come and cry out once or twice, quaking all out of control. Then maybe he'll let up a little, allow her to shiver and shudder, perhaps even put up a (doomed, futile, wonderful) struggle, while he pulls it back out one more time and starts slipping and sliding the whole throbbing length of it upside her clit, back and forth, flaunting his stalwart control, changing speeds, seering her, zinging her, first very slowly, so lightly, so deftly, now faster, now harder, now sideways—by now she is begging him, pleading—or dangles it just out of reach, making her arch up her back even more just to touch it. In the end he will fuck her, of course, long and hard—till she thinks she can't take any more, till she feels like she'll stay fucked forever—but in the frantic and desperate condition in which he's already got her she really can't wait that much longer. She has to, however. She can't, but she has to. She has to.

In any event, whoever has done the most pushups, whoever has broken THE RULES, or even if the dice weren't used in the first place, when they're through with each other Raymondo invariably LIES AND BREATHETH ON HER FACE, and God does she love that. She does.

They do not have a name for this game, but sometimes just the thought of it can burn in Teresa's warm blood like cold powdered glass, and she'll either have to get the game started or, if Ray's not around, just stand there and brace herself, like she's doing right now, rubbing her knuckles and blushing, doing her darnedest to blot out his moonbeam, his breathing, his stubbly slippery frictiony chin, and his face, staring out hard into space, till it passes.

QUEEN

Anne Waldman

My sandpaper husband who
wears sackcloth when I don't behave
says Come sit on rattan, woman
Your will is as brittle as glass
Your mad mouth is untamable
& your heart is always in another country

Your ears are radar stalks
Your eyes magnetize yardmen
& when you sing you shake the house
AHHHHH   AHHHHH   AHHHHH
My wife is a burning house

My silky husband who tends the garden
whose arms shake like branches in a storm
complains I'm a slugabed on his time
He says Wake up woman of sleep & cream
Wake up & sweep back your flickering night-lids

Your hands are leopardesses
Your shins are Cadillacs
Your thighs are palaces of tears
When you weep the house rises
My wife is the Indian Ocean rising

My husband of sacred vows
has October weather in his voice

He says Come to bed, amorous woman
Your ancient desk is covered with leaves
Your tardy poem can't be coaxed
But will come to you like a Queen.

WHEN I SEE YOUR BREASTS I REMEMBER MY HEART'S DESIRE

Norman Fischer

When I see your breasts I remember my heart's desire the place I
want to go to in my dreams
Where all my hopes are completely realized and whatever it is I
want close to me is close to me and what I want pushed away from
me is far away
And I am not confused about anything never disappointed never
  dull
never at a loss functioning totally at full tilt all of the time
Your breasts so full and glorious in shape are the breasts I have
seen forever in my dreams and even deeper than my dreams
They are my two great hopes and they are my salvation my respite
from a cruel and fallen world
And they are also my two great fears I am afraid that you will at
some point leave me for another man or that there is something in
your life that is more important than me to you it is another man
isn't it?
So that when I see the outline of your body in the white nightgown
tonight before you go to bed with the lamp on on the table near
the bed so I can see through the nightgown and can make out
perfectly the calming satisfying shape of your breasts except they
are made more mysterious and even more beautiful by the softness
of the fabric
I am lost in this mountainous desire that can never be fulfilled
that aches wounded for you and will probably end up driving you
away
To him it will probably send you right into his arms
But I can't stop feeling it although it terrifies me
And also my hope is that someday my own life will come to a state
of completion I can imagine in a vague way what that would be like

although mainly what it feels like is a state somehow different
from the one I presently inhabit
And my second hope is that this state of completion involves you
we are complete together as intimate as water with water clouds
with clouds flowing in and out of each other
And when you turn your head as you are pinning up your hair and
lifting your arms up over your head in a gesture that is burned
into my mind as an eternal dreamtime image
And I see the outline of your neck and your breasts move higher
and change shape with the movement upward of your arms
Or when the light is a certain way and you are wearing the olive
grey turtleneck shirt I gave you for your birthday several years
ago
Or not that but you are wearing the salmon-colored low-neckline
dress the summer one and also a simple necklace of natural pearls
That accentuates your thick black hair which when worn down full
frames your face and neck so beautifully
Then I think I am going to fly apart with the centrifugal force
created by the pressure of grief within me
Caused by the impossibility of our actually being together in the
way I need you to be with me that kind of constancy and total
fusion
And I am like a woman in a red dress holding a calla lilly at a
funeral
Or a completely set holiday dinner table five minutes before it is
discovered that the guest of honor has suddenly died in a traffic
accident
Or the locker room of a high school football team during halftime
of the city championship game in which it will suffer a stunning
upset defeat
You look different on different days it's so confusing!
Sometimes your hair is short and blonde sometimes it is long and
red all its different colors of blue gold and yellow confused in a
dazzle in the sunlight
You are tall or often quite short and compact ethnic and dark
Scandinavian Russian black
I saw you this morning in my dream you were lovelier than ever and
I could see your breasts through the tee shirt you were wearing it

was you
But at the same time it was my mother when I was a little boy a
deep dream it was my own dream or was it the dream of the race of
all men imagining all women as mothers their breasts huge and
dripping with milk in a world in which there was no other food
and no way to get food other than love and no way to be worthy of
love and no way to keep love from eventually dissolving assuming
you could be worthy of it for a short time
I am wondering whether this passion I feel for you seems
undignified
And whether you can bear it for a single day more

IN THE BLOOD

Jonis Agee

When he had first gotten back, they felt new and strange to each other. It wasn't just that each was five years older, more worn and more certain about life now than in their earlier years. No, it was also the fact of where he had been and how far she had gone on, living in their house and raising their children alone, although for him she was still there as five years before. Somehow he was confident that the threads of feeling remained unbroken and attached as ever between them.

He imagined her body clean lined, though it had never been, and smooth, though she had always had scars and rough, bumpy patches of skin. She was uncomfortable and flattered.

When they made love, she imagined him entering the soft fine bodies of the women he must have known. She imagined him coming at them slowly, his dirty hands and face smudging their cleanness and mingling with their perfume. When he took off his clothes, she tried not to look at the fresh purple scars etched like insect trails along his legs. There had been a wound. A deep and hollow scar, white and strange, stood on one shoulder blade, and if she was not careful, her hand would slip into its cup as she smoothed the muscles on his back. Now she closed her eyes always when they made love. She could not stand the love eating into her like a dog not fed for too many days—this dog living in his eyes, becoming his eyes, the pitiable and the alien, some thirsty and hungry creature intent on feeding itself more than anything else, like the dog she had once accidentally locked in the garage for a weekend when she had gone away, the forgiveness and the starvation together she saw in its face on Monday morning. It had probably stopped howling after a day, when its throat had burned out. She could see the claw marks on the doors and the chewed edges of wood. His teeth had caught and torn the loose skin surrounding his gums. The blood, dried by then, matted the white hairs on his chin. In his frenzy he must have torn out several nails, because his paws were bloody too. And in his anguish of abandonment he had progressed to the diarrhea standing in pools on the concrete floor of the garage, when he must have been certain of his own death. But she had come back, had found him, and had taken him into the house for his food and water, and as he ate, she saw that look—too hungry for what she had offered it.

She felt him feeding on her breasts, biting softly and sucking, trying to drain her into his mouth, and she knew it was not enough. Even when he grew violent, while she lay on her stomach and he hammered himself into her buttocks, she knew that he was growing more afraid of the love he wanted. The only act he really allowed her was to let her use her mouth on him, and after he had emptied himself into her in that way, helpless to her comfort and succored by her tongue, releasing himself into the fear of her teeth, then he could be full. Sometimes he told her afterward that it was like walking down a forest trail, knowing that assassins were waiting for him, yet he could not keep from walking down the trail, smelling the urgent growth of vegetation, seeing the flowers and butterflies, and hearing the birds whose hasty cries could be the end.

She performed this act for him nightly after a while, and somehow it soothed him into his sleep. He could endure the days that way. His life became possible. Like the dog she had recovered from the garage, he became obedient and gentle. But always a little hunger lingered about his mouth, rested in his eyes.

It was two years later that they found out about the thing in his blood. They had gone on with their life, more than less comfortable, accepting the things that had happened, more or less. She sometimes felt tired at night and went to sleep immediately instead of making love with him. These nights he lay awake for hours, but he was beginning to forget the past. What he had lived through had become almost a familiar and comfortable fantasy on those nights of thinking. Often he found that just recalling it would give him an erection, which he would have to somehow dissolve before sleep. A couple of times he watched her sleeping, sometimes frowning, with her mouth slightly open and vulnerable to him at any moment he might choose. The slight pressing of a nipple against her nylon gown as she breathed in and out he would watch for a long time, the rhythm of its coming and going, until he ejaculated. And sometimes, when it was warm and she was in a deep sleep, her eyes fluttering behind the lids in dreaming, he would carefully draw back the covers and hold his penis over her breast or mouth.

Although the cancer in his blood required care from his physician, it didn't stop him from working, only made him tired and sometimes sick. But it also made him more sexual than ever. Now he wanted her all the time. As he lost weight, as he ate less, he grew more frantic about her love and her body. On the other hand, after the disease was discovered, she began to be afraid, even revulsed by the one act which could appease him. As if she now had to feed the dog from her own mouth, eat his fear, she could not bear on her tongue the liquid sex, filled, she imagined, with his blood and webbed with his sickness. She thought of how she had grown afraid of the dog, which, no matter how much she fed it, did not regain its weight. She eventually left the dog in the small wire cage at the Humane Society, panting from its starvation. Now her husband was like a dog let out of a cage, tracking her down, but as if her stomach were always full and bursting, she could not bear to open her mouth to him, and her body ached as if it had been filled with stones.

OLD TIMES NOW

Stephen Rodefer

My wife and I quite often make love in the car on long trips. While driving I mean. I mean usually the children are asleep, but if they're not it hasn't been too hard to avoid their apparent notice. I say apparent because you usually suspect they might well realize but for some reason or other just aren't letting on. I've often wondered if this wasn't some odd ability children have, a general busyness, half aware, that takes its energy from what is not in focus yet; or whether children aren't just more discreet than we give them credit for being. Either way it seems admirable behavior, and is certainly useful for everyone involved.

Of course if they are awake and playing it sets some practical limits on the way you can do it, but everything in the interest of variety seems a fair enough proposition. There are obviously as well the problems of visibility in the daytime. Really it's easier on the thruway. You don't have to pay so much attention to the driving and if you go generally between 50 and 60, passing cars don't have much chance to see anything I don't think. Though it is surprising how many people look back at you even though you're sure they can't know. They seem to sense something. An American habit perhaps, to think people still know when you're doing something amiss, even when they can't; as well as to have that feeling that something is going on even without evidence that it is. At any rate I automatically slow down as they pass, looking at them through my eyeballs.

Trucks and buses, anything that rides high, is what you would worry about obviously. But as I said, there's curiously very little problem, though I've never been stopped by a cop. But then passing through a toll booth has never been a serious interruption either. And every once in a while a brief conversation with Benjamin or Jesse, coming to lean over the front seat to ask what a soft shoulder is, is readily enough dispatched. Where the edge of the road, etc., so cars, go play, etc.

You can see how it's being done of course. Awkward fumbling to begin with. You only have your right hand you understand, but with a moving wife you can soon reach pretty far, she slouching over with her left arm around you and your right palm snailing down the back of her lap, under the elastic of her skirt and into the pants, your middle finger creasing through that straight crack to the wetness further on. I don't want to make it sound quick and determined, even planned. The slower the better, it's a luscious business and to each his own path.

Eventually she has you out, the kids are into their jabbering back of the back seat (it's a station wagon) and while she's opening your shirt and unbuckling your trousers, you're tipping the tips of your fingers with all the saliva that's flowing, and the old right hand can dive right back by now to the perfect place it just left, without bumping into anything. When the juices flow the motor abilities become more accurate and there is no sense of fumbling left.

You can see how snorked into the memory of this I'm getting, and if I go any further I won't be able to keep on typing, or if I could you wouldn't be able to keep reading, if you knew what was good for you. Maybe I better wrap it up.

Once she came four times, starting around Bakersfield, with some variation on the gearshift (floor), and we checked into the first motel in Arizona, to fall totally beyond at the fifth (hers not mine).

From: ROUGH STRIFE

Lynne Sharon Schwartz

Caroline and Ivan finally had a child. Conception stunned them; they didn't think, by now, that it could happen. For years they had tried and failed, till it seemed that a special barren destiny was pre-ordained. Meanwhile, in the wide spaces of childlessness, they had created activity: their work flourished. Ivan, happy and moderately powerful in a large foundation, helped decide how to distribute money for artistic and social projects. Caroline taught mathematics at a small suburban university. Being a mathematician, she found, conferred a painful private wisdom on her efforts to conceive. In her brain, as Ivan exploded within her, she would involuntarily calculate probabilities; millions of blind sperm and one reluctant egg clustered before her eyes in swiftly transmuting geometric patterns. She lost her grasp of pleasure, forgot what it could feel like without a goal. She had no idea what Ivan might be thinking about, scattered seed money, maybe. Their passion became courteous and automatic until, by attrition, for months they didn't make love—it was too awkward.

One September Sunday morning she was in the shower, watch-ing, through a crack in the curtain, Ivan naked at the washstand. He was shaving, his jaw tilted at an innocently self-satisfied angle. He wasn't aware of being watched, so that a secret quality, an es-sence of Ivan, exuded in great waves. Caroline could almost see it, a cloudy aura. He stroked his jaw vainly with intense concentration, a self-absorption so contagious that she needed, suddenly, to possess it with him. She stepped out of the shower.

"Ivan."

He turned abruptly, surprised, perhaps even annoyed at the in-terruption.

"Let's not have a baby anymore. Let's just . . . come on." When she placed her wet hand on his back he lifted her easily off her feet with his right arm, the razor still poised in his other, outstretched hand.

"Come on," she insisted. She opened the door and a draft blew into the small steamy room. She pulled him by the hand toward the bedroom.

Ivan grinned. "You're soaking wet."

"Wet, dry, what's the difference?" It was hard to speak. She began to run, to tease him; he caught her and tossed her onto their disheveled bed and dug his teeth so deep into her shoulder that she thought she would bleed.

Then with disinterest, taken up only in this fresh rushing need for him, weeks later Caroline conceived. Afterwards she liked to say that she had known the moment it happened. It felt different, she told him, like a pin pricking a balloon, but without the shattering noise, without the quick collapse. "Oh, come on," said Ivan. "That's impossible."

But she was a mathematician, after all, and dealt with infinitesimal precise abstractions, and she did know how it had happened. The baby was conceived in strife, one early October night, Indian summer. All day the sun glowed hot and low in the sky, settling an amber torpor on people and things, and the night was the same, only now a dark hot heaviness sunk slowly down. The scent of the still-blooming honeysuckle rose to their bedroom window. Just as she was bending over to kiss him, heavy and quivering with heat like the night, he teased her about something, about a mole on her leg, and in reply she punched him lightly on the shoulder. He grabbed her wrists, and when she began kicking, pinned her feet down with his own. In an instant Ivan lay stretched out on her back like a blanket, smothering her, while she struggled beneath, writhing to escape. It was a silent, sweaty struggle, interrupted with outbursts of wild laughter, shrieks and gasping breaths. She tried biting but, laughing loudly, he evaded her, and she tried scratching the fists that held her down, but she couldn't reach. All her desire was transformed into physical effort, but he was too strong for her. He wanted her to say she gave up, but she refused, and since he wouldn't loosen his grip they lay locked and panting in their static embrace for some time.

"You win," she said at last, but as he rolled off she sneakily jabbed him in the ribs with her elbow.

"Aha!" Ivan shouted, and was ready to begin again, but she quickly distracted him. Once the wrestling was at an end, though, Caroline found her passion dissipated, and her pleasure tinged with resentment. After they made love forcefully, when they were covered with sweat, dripping on each other, she said, "Still, you don't play fair."

"I don't play fair! Look who's talking. Do you want me to give you a handicap?"

"No."

"So?"

"It's not fair, that's all."

Ivan laughed gloatingly and curled up in her arms. She smiled in the dark.

That was the night the baby was conceived, not in high passion but rough strife.

She lay on the table in the doctor's office weeks later. The doctor, whom she had known for a long time, habitually kept up a running conversation while he probed. Today, fretting over his weight problem, he outlined his plans for a new diet. Tensely she watched him, framed and centered by her raised knees, which were still bronzed from summer sun. His other hand was pressing on her stomach. Caroline was nauseated with fear and trembling, afraid of the verdict. It was taking so long, perhaps it was a tumor.

"I'm cutting out all starches," he said. "I've really let myself go lately."

"Good idea." Then she gasped in pain. A final, sickening thrust, and he was out. Relief, and a sore gap where he had been. In a moment, she knew, she would be retching violently.

"Well?"

"Well, Caroline, you hit the jackpot this time."

She felt a smile, a stupid, puppet smile, spread over her face. In the tiny bathroom where she threw up, she saw in the mirror the silly smile looming over her ashen face like a dancer's glowing grimace of labored joy. She smiled through the rest of the visit, through his advice about milk, weight, travel and rest, smiled at herself in the window of the bus, and at her moving image in the fenders of parked cars as she walked home.

Ivan, incredulous over the telephone, came home beaming stu-

Part III

THE MARRIAGE BED

pidly just like Caroline, and brought a bottle of champagne. After dinner they drank it and made love.

"Do you think it's all right to do this?" he asked.

"Oh, Ivan, honestly. It's microscopic."

He was in one of his whimsical moods and made terrible jokes that she laughed at with easy indulgence. He said he was going to pay the baby a visit and asked if she had any messages she wanted delivered. He unlocked from her embrace, moved down her body and said he was going to have a look for himself. Clowning, he put his ear between her legs to listen. Whatever amusement she felt soon ebbed away into irritation. She had never thought Ivan would be a doting parent—he was so preoccupied with himself. Finally he stopped his antics as she clasped her arms around him and whispered, "Ivan, you are really too much." He became unusually gentle. Tamed, and she didn't like it, hoped he wouldn't continue that way for months. Pleasure lapped over her with a mild, lackadaisical bitterness, and then when she could be articulate once more she explained patiently, "Ivan, you know, it really is all right. I mean, it's a natural process."

LOVE POEM

Ron Padgett

We have plenty of matches in our house.
We keep them on hand always.
Currently our favorite brand is Ohio Blue Tip,
though we used to prefer Diamond brand.
That was before we discovered Ohio Blue Tip matches.
They are excellently packaged, sturdy
little boxes with dark and light blue and white labels
with words lettered in the shape of a megaphone,
as if to say even louder to the world,
"Here is the most beautiful match in the world,
its one and a half inch soft pine stem capped
by a grainy dark purple head, so sober and furious
and stubbornly ready to burst into flame,
lighting, perhaps, the cigarette of the woman you love,
for the first time, and it was never really the same
after that. All this will we give you."
That is what you gave me, I
become the cigarette and you the match, or I
the match and you the cigarette, blazing
with kisses that smoulder toward heaven.

THE ONE

Anselm Hollo

the one
long hair in my beard
                this morning
makes me smile:
                it's yours

FOR THE WOMAN WITH EVERYTHING

Geoffrey Young

With growing apprehension I thought about Margery's suggestion that I buy Laura a gun for Christmas. Would that be chic? Gun-related accidents in otherwise normal homes produced statistics of national disgrace, as did crimes of passion. And to read in the papers the occasional account of pistol-whipped children was truly upsetting. Still, looking at our life together, and in spite of the distressing paucity of tenderness on all sides lately, I deemed it orderly, respectful, a vessel worthy of the launch.

Was Margery just projecting onto Laura her own desire for a gun? Her knowledge of radical theater tactics was inspiring. Or was this gun suggestion in response to an off-color joke about tacos I had earlier told the Print Center staff at their Christmas party? Margery didn't think it funny, in fact she looked confused, real consternation on her face. Shortly after the laughs faded I noticed she faded from the room. When she returned I remember thinking, she has re-grouped her considerable forces in order to study the enemy from behind the blind of a newly adjusted composure. From this observation I gleaned the deduction that Laura needed a gun to protect herself and her sex from a man like me. Ah, Margery *was* being clever!

I drove to the sporting goods store and browsed the hardware. I chose a .22 Browning automatic pistol. It was lovely, especially if you appreciate carved walnut handles, and oily reflections from a gunmetal blue barrel. Along the underside of the barrel were printed the legend and the patent number of this classy little piece. The butt fit perfectly in my hand, and an unmistakable warmth rose to my finger's tip as I squeezed the trigger, ever so lightly, click. Perhaps yes.

And Laura would be excited by the originality of my gift, as well as vaguely threatened by its bravado. She would be eager to tell her family and friends. Her eyes would narrow slightly, and the set of her jaw would soften as she volunteered this new information over the phone to Gloria, to Catherine, to her parents, to Nicole, to Bob. And I could hear Michael's crazed laugh change from hilarity at the image of Laura brandishing a real "peashooter," to nervous distress at the more problematic image of me brandishing it. His son Nathan would not be safe in our house, etc. I imagined Laura's straining to hear whatever minute spasm of shock surfaced in her friends' initial reactions. This would make her happy, but happy with a quizzical expression on her face. And I could eavesdrop the chat that would follow, hearing theoretical conjecture, their armchair attempts to get at my intention (which I would refuse to discuss), and perhaps more importantly the subtextual symbolic meaning lying parallel to the shining pistol, but in some other plane. All this for $162.50, without holster.

I found myself so disoriented, however, at the threshold of this purchase, that I committed the unforgivable sin of saying to the clerk, "Throw in a box of those silver bullets, too." He winced slightly, then worked up a half smile that did no more than reveal an utter exhaustion with seasonal good cheer.

Quickly I tightened up, and reached for my checkbook. Yes, a kind of intimacy would be restored to our life at home, some drastic spiritual charge felt lingering over this revolver like love. The presence of the gun in either of our hands would be a firm reminder to follow the golden rule, no matter how dark the night, or horrible the imagined crime. The gun would unite us, just as the atomic bomb threads all nations together on the same global charm bracelet.

But where was the checkbook? Had I left it in the car? I pulled a measly eleven dollars cash from my wallet, said "fuck" under my breath, then trying to figure what to do, explained to the clerk, "Uh, I can't pay for it right now, my wife must have the checkbook." He stood in the uniform light near the cash register, staring over at me as if I were a cardboard cutout of a man, someone who looked just like me, but who lacked essential human definition.

"Listen, I'll be back, I have to get that gun," I promised him. He saw the arms and legs of the figure begin to back slowly out of the store, when in disgust he turned away, to a burning cigarette.

Outside. Providence? I asked myself. I hadn't gotten the key in the ignition when I flung the car door open and ran back in the store. But I went directly away from the gun counter, moving left- past racks of athletic footwear, to a row of multi-colored jogging suits in small, medium, and large. Under them, into an unfolded pile, I reached, and grabbed a pair of medium-size navy blue "sweat pants" marked 5.95, paid for them with the ten dollar bill, and walked out, knowing how much comfortable wear she would get from them, soft, relaxed in the crotch, and easy to get off.

Selections From: IN BED

Kenneth Koch

MORNINGS IN BED

Are energetic mornings.

*

SNOW IN BED

When we got out of bed
It was snowing.

*

MARRIED IN BED

We'll be married in bed.
The preachers, the witnesses, and all our families
Will also be in bed.

*

ORCHIDS IN BED

She placed orchids in the bed
On that dark blue winter morning.

*

ANGELIC CEREMONY IN BED

Putting on the sheets.

*

THEATRICAL BED

Exceeded expectations
And received applause.

*

COURTSHIP IN BED

"Please. Tell me you like me."
"How did you get in this bed?"

*

LET'S GO TO BED

When the tree
Is blossoming. It will be
A long time
Before it is blossoming again.

*

ADVANCE BED

Advance arm. Advance stairs. Advance power.
Advance bed.

*

CHILD BED

You had two babies
Before we met.

*

ORCHIDS IN BED

She placed orchids on the bed
On a dark red winter afternoon.

*

ENEMIES IN BED

Enemies sleep in separate beds
But in the same part of the city.

*

SUMMER

The bed lies in the room
The way she lies in the bed.

*

ZEN BED

I can't get to bed.
Show me the bed and I will show you how to get to it.

*

SNOW IN BED

When we get out of bed
There is no more bed.

*

MARRIED IN BED

We did not get married
In bed.

*

SHOWER BED

For her engagement they gave her a shower
And for her marriage they went to bed.

*

STREAM BED

In the stream bed
The snails go to sleep.

*

PHILOSOPHY OF BED

A man should be like a woman and a woman should be like an
   animal
In bed is one theory. Another is that they both should be like beds.

*

MALLARMÉ'S BED

An angel came, while Mallarmé lay in bed,
When he was a child, and opened its hands
To let white bouquets of perfumed stars snow down.

*

DAY BED

When I loved you
Then that whole time
Was like a bed
And that whole year
Was like a day bed.

*

DENIED BED

We were not in bed
When summer came.

*

SNOW IN BED

Vanishing snowflakes, rooftops appearing
And sidewalks and people and cars as we get out of bed.

From: FULL OF LIFE

John Fante

There was also this passionate need for her. I had it from the first time I saw her. She went away that first time, she walked out of her aunt's house where we had met at tea, and I was no good without her, absolutely a cripple until I saw her again. But for her I might have lived out my life in other streams—a reporter, a bricklayer—whatever was at hand. My prose, such as it was, derived from her. For I was always quitting the craft, hating it, despairing, crumpling paper and throwing it across the room. But she could forage through the discarded stuff and come up with things, and I never really knew when I was good, I thought every line I ever wrote was no better than ordinary, for I had no way of being sure. But she could take the pages and find the good stuff and save it, and plead for more, so that it became habitual with me, and I wrote as best I could and handed her the pages, and she did a scissors-and-paste job, and when it was done, with a beginning and middle and end, I was more startled than seeing it in print, because at first I couldn't have done it alone.

Three years of this, four, five, and I began to have some notions about the craft, but they were her notions, and I never gave much thought to the others who might read my stuff, I only wrote it for her, and if she had not been there I might not have written it at all.

She didn't care to read me while she was pregnant. I brought her sequences from the script and she was not interested. That winter in her fifth month I wrote a short story and she spilled coffee on it—an unheard-of thing, and she read it with yawning attention. Before the baby she would have taken the manuscript to bed with her and spent hours pruning and fixing and making marginal notes.

Like a stone, the child got between us. I worried and wondered if it would ever be the same again. I longed for the old days when I could walk into her room and snatch up some intimacy of hers, a scarf or a dress or a bit of white ribbon, and the very touch had me reeling around, croaking like a bullfrog for the joys of my beloved. The chair she sat upon before the dressing table, the glass that mirrored her lovely face, the pillow upon which she laid her head, a pair of stockings flung to launder, the disarming cunning of her silk pants, her nightgowns, her soap, her wet towels still warm after her bath: I had need for these things; they were a part of my life with her, and the smear of lipstick made no difference, for the red had come from the warm lips of my woman.

Things were changed around there now. Her gowns were specially contrived, with a big hole in front through which leered the bump, her slips were impossible sacks, her flat shoes were strictly for the rice fields, and her blouses were like pup tents. What man could take such a gown and crush it to his face and shudder with the old familiar passion? Everything smelled different too. She used to use some magic called Fernery at Twilight. It was like breathing Chopin and Edna Millay, and when its fragrance rose from her hair and shoulders I knew the flag was up and that she had chosen to be pursued. She didn't use Fernery at Twilight anymore: something else was substituted, a kind of Gayelord Hauser cologne, reeking of just plain good health, clean alcohol and simple soap. There was also the odor of vitamin tablets, of brewer's yeast and blackstrap molasses, and a pale salve to soothe her bursting nipples.

Lying in bed, I used to hear her slushing around, and wonder what was happening to us. I smoked in the darkness and moaned in the belief that she was driving me into another woman's arms. No, she didn't want me anymore, she was forcing me to another woman, a mistress. But what mistress? For years I had been retired from the jungle where bachelors prowled. Where was I to find another woman, even if I wanted one? I saw myself skulking about on Santa Monica Boulevard, drooling at free women in dark, offbeat saloons, sweating out clever dialogue, drinking heavily to hide the stark ugliness of such romances. No, I could not be unfaithful to Joyce. I didn't even want to be unfaithful, and this worried me too. For was it not something of a custom for men to be unfaithful to their wives during confinement? It happened all the time out at the golf club: I heard it from all the guys. Then what was wrong with me? Why wasn't I on the town, chafing for forbidden joys? And so I lay there, trying to coax up a flicker of that flame for strange fruit. But there was none.

LYING UNDER A QUILT

Rachel Hadas

Twilight; a drowsy dim
haven of thick repose
and half the journey done,
we sleepily suppose.
Hidden in either self,
memories lodge in lips,
creased into secret cells;
we're quiet, touching hips,

lying under a quilt,
catted on either flank,
our little boy asleep
on the other side of the wall,
and summer still ungroomed,
bugs in the bushy grass,
rain hanging undecided
whether or not to fall.

I see you—shining islands
haloed with sheer desire!
Unearthly mauve and crimson
sculptings of upper air!
I swoop, I solo float,
I sacrifice it all
for color beyond thought,
gesture, ineffable!

Through empyrean brilliance
our son is cast, a shadow
growing up exiled, empty

of what no one but me
or you can give him. You.
You too were left behind!
My arms are empty. Flailing
I thrash, make up my mind,

clip the wide-flung wings
and fall down the bright air
which speaks to me in light:
Come dive me, plunge me, here.
My purifying fire
gilds all you hope to be,
to travel, to discover,
and everything you've done.

       Again my breast
hardens. Milk comes down.
As constant dripping wears away a stone
so I am hard and softened, bottleful
of riches, magical
and always out of reach
till need uncorks me.

NORTH

Lyn Lifshin

children were wanted

were always close
to their parents'

skin even during
fucking. nobody

put the baby down

except to dip male
babies in the

wind and snow
to make them strong

then close to
the nipple again

BOSS DRAIN

Geoffrey Young

Out of the domestic bed where he lies
mute finger to lips
she steps to put her blue bathrobe on

turning to say through red teary eyes
Don't I look pretty
don't I look real good

He hadn't been looking so he did
She didn't look pretty
she didn't look real good

She was always wrong

PARALLEL BARS

It gets bad and then it gets worse
and then the bottom falls out
but then it gets better, even great, you think
you're there, but then it goes sour, totally alone, hurting,
but it comes back, new breath, friends again,
it's the best it's been in months,
really clicking, it's heaven and then
just about the time you think it's going to stay heaven,
it gets bad, and then it gets worse, and then
the bottom falls out, will it ever get better? and then
it does, it's even great, you blink an eye

and it goes sour, vicious, destructive,
but it comes back, new breath, friends again,
it's the best it's been in months, really clicking,
it's heaven, and then just about the time
you think it's going to stay heaven

From: A COUPLE CALLED MOEBIUS

Carol Bergé

The father, guilty and innocent, moves about the house near the kitchen, carpentering, smoothing, polishing, moving about with his rabbit-beaver stained teeth in the big apartment or in the big advertising agency. His place, his shell, his pride. While the mother moves about the big apartment, cleaning, cleaning, cleaning, endlessly washing, sponging, rubbing, mopping, folding, soaping, polishing, sorting, opening, closing, wrapping, dishing, portioning, fastening, freezing, bottling, pouring, shifting, unwrapping, rewrapping, corking, slicing, grating, blending, mixing, ladling, dicing, slicing, grating, testing, moving, moving, moving. . . . Talking on the phone to her friends, reading recipes, talking to her house-helper, to her children, to her husband.

At the end of the day, the wife and the husband are still awake. They sit at the kitchen table with cups of coffee. Have been married for ten years. Have slept in the same bed for ten years. Have had sex together for ten years, had marital relations, have made love, have had intercourse, have never fucked, have been in rooms near their kitchen table but never on it, never on the kitchen floor in a flurry of excitement, always on their bed, never at the edge of their bed, never with some clothing on, never in the middle of the day, always in either of two usual positions, never the variations, never feeling each other till they came, never taking it in the ass, never with the loving mouths, always hidden from their own sight and from the sight of the lover. Not to be discussed. I do not want to know. It is not nice. We do not. Now they sit in their kitchen at the end of the day, it is quiet, the kitchen fan hums softly at the window drawing the air out, she has swept the floor, wet-mopped it, started the dishwasher, it hums at her right, a harder sound than the fan. He has eaten dinner out with his art director, they have accomplished a gratifying amount of work on a certain account, so he has eaten dinner at Pen and Pencil, he reports to her what they ate, but not before she tries to guess, knowing his favorite luxury meal: two very dry martinis, pâté de maison, filet mignon, baked potato, poire hélène, no, he says, went to the P&P, kept it simple, bourbon and branch, tried their chicken, wasn't any damn good, too dry. O too bad, she says. What'd *you* do today, he asks. Not much, she says, it was kind of . . . What do you mean, kind of, he says. O not much, she says, just my way of putting it, that feeling, you know, one of those kind of nothing days, Elsie came in, took the kids out, I had lunch with Sherry, you know, nothing much. Sometimes I just feel like, you know, just taking off and disappearing, she tells her husband, without looking at him. O you don't have to take off to do that, baby, he says, smiling. O boy you're in a lousy mood, she says, I didn't say that to aggravate *you*, you know . . . I just mean. I was just. Feeling like. I don't know what. Getting the hell. Out or something. Something. Sure, he says. Sure you do, baby. It's a tough life for you isn't it. All depends on who's living it, she says. Maybe it's a lot tougher than it looks to you from there. Maybe even tougher than Sherry's, and from what she told me today, she's having it pretty rough lately. Yeah, I'll bet, he says, there's a broad who really has it rough all right. Her old man makes even more dough than I do. Must be hitting fifty grand easy. What the fuck she have to complain about this time?

THE PROMISE

Toi Derricotte

I will never again
expect too much of you. I have
found out the secret of marriage:
I must keep seeing your beauty
like a stranger's, like the face
of a young girl passing on a train
whose moment of knowing illumines
it—a golden letter in a book.
I will look at you in such
exaggerated moments, lengthening
one second and shrinking eternity
until they fit together like man and wife.
My pain is expectation:
I watch you for hours sleeping, wanting
you to roll over
and look me in the eye;
my days are seconds of waiting
like the seconds between the makings
of boiling earth and sweating rivers.
What am I waiting for if not
your face—like a fish rising
to the surface, a known
but forgotten expression that
suddenly appears—or like myself,
in a strip of mirror, when, having
passed, I come back to that image
hoping to find the woman
missing. Why do you think I sleep
in the other room, planets away,
in a darkness where I could die solitary,

an old nun wrapped in clean white sheets?
Because of lies I sucked
in my mother's milk, because
of pictures in my first grade reader—
families in solid towns as if
the world were rooted and grew down
holding the rocks, eternally;
because of rings in jewelers' windows
engraved with sentiments—*I love you
forever*—as if we could survive
any beauty for longer than just after . . .
So I hobble down a hall
of disappointments past where
your darkness and my darkness have
had intercourse with each other.
Why have I wasted my life
in anger, thinking I could have more
than what is glimpsed in recognition?
I will let go, as we must
let go of an angel called
back to heaven; I will not hold
her glittering robe, but let it
drift above me until I see
the last shred of evidence.

GOOD TIMES

Lydia Davis

What was happening to them was that every bad time produced a bad feeling that in turn produced several more bad times and several more bad feelings, so that their life together had become crowded with bad times and bad feelings, so crowded that almost nothing else could grow in that dark field. But then she had a feeling of peace one morning that lingered from the evening before spent sewing while he sat reading in the next room. And a day or two later, she had a feeling of contentment that lingered in the morning from the evening before when he kept her company in the kitchen while she washed the dinner dishes and then later talked to her in bed about this and that. If the good times increased, she thought, each good time might produce a good feeling that would in turn produce several more good times that would produce several more good feelings. What she meant was that the good times might multiply perhaps as rapidly as the square of the square, or perhaps more rapidly, like mice, or like mushrooms springing up overnight from the scattered spore of a parent mushroom which in turn had sprung up overnight with a crowd of others from the scattered spore of a parent, until her life with him would be so crowded with good times that the good times might crowd out the bad as the bad times had by now almost crowded out the good . . .

NEXT DOOR

Tobias Wolff

I wake up afraid. My wife is sitting on the edge of my bed, shaking me. "They're at it again," she says.

I go to the window. All their lights are on, upstairs and down, as if they have money to burn. He yells, she screams something back, the dog barks. There is a short silence, then the baby cries, poor thing.

"Better not stand there," says my wife. "They might see you."

I say, "I'm going to call the police," knowing she won't let me.

"Don't," she says.

She's afraid that they will poison our cat if we complain.

Next door the man is still yelling, but I can't make out what he's saying over the dog and the baby. The woman laughs, not really meaning it, *"Ha! Ha! Ha!,"* and suddenly gives a sharp little cry. Everything goes quiet.

"He struck her," my wife says. "I felt it just the same as if he struck me."

Next door the baby gives a long wail and the dog starts up again. The man walks out into his driveway and slams the door.

"Be careful," my wife says. She gets back into her bed and pulls the covers up to her neck.

The man mumbles to himself and jerks at his fly. Finally he gets it open and walks over to the fence. It's a white picket fence, ornamental more than anything else. It couldn't keep anyone out. I put it in myself, and planted honeysuckle and bougainvillea all along it.

My wife says, "What's he doing?"

"Shh," I say.

He leans against the fence with one hand and with the other he goes to the bathroom on the flowers. He walks the length of the fence like that, not missing any of them. When he's through he gives Florida a shake, then zips up and heads back across the drive-way. He almost slips on the gravel but he catches himself and curses and goes into the house, slamming the door again.

When I turn around, my wife is leaning forward, watching me. She raises her eyebrows. "Not again," she says.

I nod.

"Number one or number two?"

"Number one."

"Thank God for small favors," she says, settling back. "Between him and the dog it's a wonder you can get anything to grow out there."

I read somewhere that human pee has a higher acid content than animal pee, but I don't mention that. I would rather talk about something else. It depresses me, thinking about the flowers. They are past their prime, but still. Next door the woman is shouting. "Listen to that," I say.

"I used to feel sorry for her," my wife says. "Not anymore. Not after last month."

"Ditto," I say, trying to remember what happened last month to make my wife not feel sorry for the woman next door. I don't feel sorry for her either, but then I never have. She yells at the baby, and excuse me, but I'm not about to get all excited over someone who treats a child like that. She screams things like *"I thought I told you to stay in your bedroom!"* and here the baby can't even speak English yet.

As far as her looks, I guess you would have to say she's pretty. But it won't last. She doesn't have good bone structure. She has a soft look to her, like she has never eaten anything but donuts and milk shakes. Her skin is white. The baby takes after her, not that you would expect it to take after *him*, dark and hairy. Even with his shirt on you can tell that he has hair all over his back and on his shoulders, thick and springy like an Airedale's.

Now they're all going at once over there, plus they've got the hi-fi turned on full blast. One of those bands. "It's the baby I feel sorry for," I say.

My wife puts her hands over her ears. "I can't stand another minute of it," she says. She takes her hands away. "Maybe there's something on TV." She sits up. "See who's on Johnny."

I turn on the television. It used to be down in the den but I brought it up here a few years ago when my wife came down with an illness. I took care of her myself—made the meals and everything. I got to where I could change the sheets with her still in the bed. I always meant to take the television back down when my wife recovered from her illness, but I never got around to it. It sits between our beds on a little table I made. Johnny is saying something to Sammy Davis, Jr. Ed McMahon is bent over laughing. He is always so cheerful. If you were going to take a really long voyage you could do worse than bring Ed McMahon along.

"Sammy," says my wife. "Who else is on besides Sammy?"

I look at the TV guide. "A bunch of people I never heard of." I read off their names. My wife hasn't heard of them either. She wants to know what else is on. " 'El Dorado,' " I read. " 'Brisk adventure yarn about a group of citizens in search of the legendary city of gold.' It's got two and a half stars beside it."

"Citizens of what?" my wife asks.

"It doesn't say."

Finally we watch the movie. A blind man comes into a small town. He says that he has been to El Dorado, and that he will lead an expedition there for a share of the proceeds. He can't see, but he will call out the landmarks one by one as they ride. At first people make fun of him, but eventually all the leading citizens get together and decide to give it a try. Right away they get attacked by Apaches and some of them want to turn back, but every time they get ready the blind man gives them another landmark, so they keep riding.

Next door the woman is going crazy. She is saying things to him that no person should ever say to another person. It makes my wife restless. She looks at me. "Can I come over?" she says. "Just for a visit?"

I pull down the blankets and she gets in. The bed is just fine for one, but with two of us it's a tight fit. We are lying on our sides with me in back. I don't mean for it to happen but before long old Florida begins to stiffen up on me. I put my arms around my wife. I move my hands up onto the Rockies, then on down across the Plains, heading south.

"Hey," she says. "No Geography. Not tonight."

"I'm sorry," I say.

"Can't I just visit?"

"Forget it. I said I was sorry."

The citizens are crossing a desert. They have just about run out of water, and their lips are cracked. Though the blind man has delivered a warning, someone drinks from a poisoned well and dies horribly. That night, around the campfire, the others begin to quarrel. Most of them want to go home. "This is no country for a white man," one says, "and if you ask me nobody has ever been here before." But the blind man describes a piece of gold so big and pure that it will burn your eyes out if you look directly at it. "I ought to know," he says. When he is finished the citizens are silent: one by one they move away and lie down on their bedrolls. They put their hands behind their heads and look up at the stars. A coyote howls.

Hearing the coyote, I remember why my wife doesn't feel sorry for the woman next door. It was a Monday evening, about a month ago, right after I got home from work. The man next door started to beat the dog, and I don't mean just smacking him once or twice. He was beating him, and he kept beating him until the dog couldn't even cry anymore; you could hear the poor creature's voice breaking. It made us very upset, especially my wife, who is an animal lover from way back. Finally it stopped. Then a few minutes later, I heard my wife say, "Oh!" and I went into the kitchen to find out what was wrong. She was standing by the window, which looks into the kitchen next door. The man had his wife backed up against the fridge. He had his knee between her legs and she had her knee between his legs and they were kissing, really hard, not just with their lips but rolling their faces back and forth one against the other. My wife could hardly speak for a couple of hours afterwards. Later she said that she would never waste her sympathy on that woman again.

It's quiet over there. My wife has gone to sleep and so has my arm, which is under her head. I slide it out and open and close my fingers, considering whether to wake her up. I like sleeping in my own bed, and there isn't enough room for the both of us. Finally I decide that it won't hurt anything to change places for one night.

I get up and fuss with the plants for a while, watering them and moving some to the window and some back. I trim the coleus, which is starting to get leggy, and put the cuttings in a glass of water on the sill. All the lights are off next door except the one in their bedroom window. I think about the life they have, and how it goes on and on, until it seems like the life they were meant to live. Everybody is always saying how great it is that human beings are so adaptable, but I don't know. A friend of mine was in the Navy and he told me that in Amsterdam, Holland, they have a whole section of town where you can walk through and from the street you can see women sitting in rooms, waiting. If you want one of them you just go in and pay, and they close the drapes. This is nothing special to the people who live in Holland. In Istanbul, Turkey, my friend saw a man walking down the street with a grand piano on his back. Everyone just moved round him and kept going. It's awful, what we get used to.

I turn off the television and get into my wife's bed. A sweet, heavy smell rises off the sheets. At first it makes me dizzy but after that I like it. It reminds me of gardenias.

The reason I don't watch the rest of the movie is that I can already see how it will end. The citizens will kill each other off, probably about ten feet from the legendary city of gold, and the blind man will stumble in by himself, not knowing that he has made it back to El Dorado.

I could write a better movie than that. My movie would be about a group of explorers, men and women, who leave behind their homes and their jobs and their families—everything they have known. They cross the sea and are shipwrecked on the coast of a country which is not on their maps. One of them drowns. Another gets attacked by a wild animal, and eaten. But the others want to push on. They ford rivers and cross an enormous glacier by dog sled. It takes months. On the glacier they run out of food, and for a while there it looks like they might turn on each other, but they don't. Finally they solve their problem by eating the dogs. That's the sad part of the movie.

At the end we see the explorers sleeping in a meadow filled with white flowers. The blossoms are wet with dew and stick to their bodies, petals of columbine, clematis, blazing star, baby's breath, larkspur, iris, rue—covering them completely, turning them white so that you cannot tell one from another, man from woman, woman from man. The sun comes up. They stand and raise their arms, like white trees in a land where no one has ever been.

SONNET

Lewis Warsh

If I turn into you
By force of habit, dint
Of luck, or just
Normally, as the occasion warrants
Not romantically, but because
Sifting through myself, I find
I'm thinking your thoughts, and you mine,
So it's possible both to inhabit
The body that sleeps beside you
And the concise fragments of the person
You thought you were, part in-
decision, part desire, part heavenly
Love, or all these things
Scattered over the earth, like sparks.

WANTING ALL

Alicia Ostriker

> More! More! is the cry of a mistaken soul,
> less than All cannot satisfy Man.
> —William Blake

Husband, it's fine the way your mind performs
Like a circus, sharp
As a sword somebody has
To swallow, rough as a bear,
Complicated as a family of jugglers,
Brave as a sequined trapeze
Artist, the only boy I ever met
Who could beat me in argument
Was why I married you, isn't it,
And you have beaten me, I've beaten you,
We are old polished hands.

Or was it your body, I forget, maybe
I foresaw the thousands on thousands
Of times we have made love
Together, mostly meat
And potatoes love, but sometimes
Higher than wine,
Better than medicine.
How lately you bite, you baby,
How angels record and number
Each gesture, and sketch
Our spinal columns like professionals.

Husband, it's fine how we cook
Dinners together while drinking,

How we get drunk, how
We gossip, work at our desks, dig in the garden,
Go to the movies, tell
The children to clear the bloody table,
How we fit like puzzle pieces.

The mind and body satisfy
Like windows and furniture in a house.
The windows are large, the furniture solid.
What more do I want then, why
Do I prowl the basement, why
Do I reach for your inside
Self as you shut it
Like a trunkful of treasures? *Wait,*
I cry, as the lid slams on my fingers.

PART IV

❦

THE BOVARY BED

From: THE BLOOD ORANGES

John Hawkes

Love weaves its own tapestry, spins its own golden thread, with its own sweet breath breathes into being its mysteries—bucolic, lusty, gentle as the eyes of daisies or thick with pain. And out of its own music creates the flesh of our lives. If the birds sing, the nudes are not far off. Even the dialogue of the frogs is rapturous.

As for me, since late boyhood and early manhood, and throughout the more than eighteen years of my nearly perfect marriage, I always allowed myself to assume whatever shape was destined to be my own in the silken weave of Love's pink panorama. I always went where the thread wound. No awkward hesitation, no prideful ravaging. At an early age I came to know that the gods fashion us to spread the legs of woman, or throw us together for no reason except that we complete the picture, so to speak, and join loin to loin often and easily, humbly, deliberately. Throughout my life I have never denied a woman young or old. Throughout my life I have simply appeared at Love's will. See me as small white porcelain bull lost in the lower left-hand corner of that vast tapestry, see me as great white creature horned and mounted on a trim little golden sheep in the very center of Love's most explosive field. See me as bull, or ram, as man, husband, lover, a tall and heavy stranger in white shorts on a violet tennis court. I was there always. I completed the picture. I took my wife, took her friends, took the wives of my friends and a fair roster of other girls and women, from young to old and old to young, whenever the light was right or the music sounded.

✳

The sun was setting, sinking to its predestined death, and to the four of us, or at least to me, that enormous smoldering sun lay on the horizon like a dissolving orange suffused with blood. The tide was low, the smooth black oval stones beneath us were warm to the flesh, we could hear the distant sounds of the three girls playing with the dog behind the funeral cypresses. Fiona, wearing a pale lemon-colored bra and pale lemon-colored briefs for the beach, and I in my magenta trunks as sparse and thick and elastic as an athletic supporter, and Hugh in his long-sleeved cotton shirt and loose gray trunks like undershorts, and Catherine dressed in her faded madras halter and swimming skirt and shorts—together we sat with legs outstretched, soles of our feet touching or nearly touching, a four-pointed human starfish resting together in the last vivid light of the day.

No one moved. Without calculation, almost without consciousness, Fiona lay propped on her elbows and with her head back, her eyes closed, her tense lips gently smiling. Even Catherine appeared to be sunk in a kind of worried slumber, aware somehow of the thick orange light on her knees. Prone bodies, silence hanging on the children's voices and scattered barking of their old black dog, the empty wine bottles turning to gold. All of us felt the inertia, suspension, tranquillity, though I found myself tapping out a silent expectant rhythm with one of my big toes while Hugh's narrow black eyes were alert, unresting, I noticed, and to me revealed only too clearly his private thoughts. But the small black oval stones we lay on were for us much better than sand. Our beach, as we called it, was a glassy volcanic bed that made us draw closer together to touch toes, to dream. With one hand I was carelessly crushing a few thin navy-blue seashells, making a small pile of crushed shell on my naked navel. And yet it was the sun, the sun alone that filled all our thoughts and was turning the exposed skin of all four bodies the same deepening color. The lower the sun fell the more it glowed.

I felt someone's foot recoil from mine and then return. Even the tiny black ringlets in Hugh's beard were turning orange. I could hear the powdery shells collecting in the well of my belly and I realized that all four of us were together on a black volcanic beach in the hour when fiercely illumined goats stand still and huddle and the moon prepares to pour its milk on the fire.

"Cyril. We don't have to go back yet, do we?"

I glanced at Fiona, heard the matter-of-fact whisper and saw that her expression had not changed, that her lips had not moved. But rolling onto one hip, propping myself on one elbow, brushing away crushed shells with a hasty stroke of one hand, I saw also that there was movement in the curve of her throat and that the sun had saturated one of her broad white shoulders. And before I could answer, Fiona giggled. My sensible, stately, impatient, clear-bodied wife giggled, as if in a dream a small bird had alighted on her belly. Giggled for no reason apparently, she whose every impulsive gesture was informed with its own hidden sense, and at the sound Hugh became suddenly rigid, Catherine opened her eyes. I knew what to do.

In silence, while the sun flushed us most deeply and unrecognizably with orange light, I got to my knees beside Fiona, who did not move, and with a flick of my hand untied the silken strings of her pale lemon-colored halter, those thin silken cords knotted in a bow behind her bent neck and curving back, and then with a few more skillful movements removed altogether Fiona's little lemon-colored bra. Then I folded this the briefest of all Fiona's half-dozen bathing bras, stuck it for safekeeping inside one of my empty shoes, and flowed back slowly into my former position on the hot rocks.

Understandably perhaps, for the first few moments Catherine and even Hugh could not bear to look. I myself hardly dared to look. But then I heard a sound like a finger scratching inside Hugh's throat and our three heads turned furtively, shyly, violently or calmly in my wife's direction. And Fiona's eyes, I saw, were open. We said nothing, Fiona was looking straight at the sun and smiling. But had she wanted me to expose her breasts, I wondered, for Hugh's sake or mine? Or was the exposure purely my own idea and something that entered her consciousness and gave her pleasure only after I had touched her, untied the strings? I could not know. But I knew immediately that it was a good idea.

Fiona's breasts were not large. Yet in the sun's lurid effulgence they glistened, grew tight while the two nipples turned to liquid rings, bands, so that to me Fiona's two firm breasts suddenly became the bursting irises of a young white owl's wide-open eyes, and when in the next moment she giggled again, again apparently without reason, those bright naked eyes, breasts, recorded the little spasms of pleasure that, otherwise unseen, were traveling down Fiona's chest and neck and arms.

"Baby, can't we just stay like this forever?"

We heard the words, we watched the very motion of Fiona's speech in her lips and breasts. In mouth and breasts my wife was singing, and despite the possibility of another unexpected giggle, which no doubt would be accompanied by another small eruption of rolling or bouncing in the lovely breasts as well as a slight twisting in the slope of the shoulders, despite all this or perhaps because of it the preciousness of what Fiona said maintained the silence, prevented the rest of us from talking. I could see the thin white edge of Fiona's teeth between the slightly parted lips, the voice was soft and clear, the naked orange breasts were unimaginably free, her eyes were partially open. Even in the silence she was singing, and the rest of us were listening, watching.

Then suddenly Hugh began to scratch viciously at himself beneath the loose gray shorts, and Catherine moved. With a brief flashing sensation of regret, it occurred to me that she was about to climb heavily, angrily to her feet and leave. She too could hear that in the distance the children were beginning to quarrel, beginning to tease the dog. But I was wrong, and she merely drew herself slowly out of her supine state, raised her back and lifted up her long heavy legs and sat upright with her thighs pressed together on the black rocks and her knees bent and her strong calves crossed at the ankles.

And then Hugh spoke. Stopped scratching himself and spoke, while Catherine's unreadable eyes met mine and I smiled, allowed my large right orange hand to lie comfortably where my upper thighs, which were about twice the girth of even Catherine's thighs, joined in special harmony the inverted apex of my own magenta briefs for the beach.

"That's it. All these years you've been castrating him!"

On this occasion it was hardly what I thought he would say. Was this the extent of the private thoughts I had been watching all this time in his black eyes? But then I laughed, because Hugh had been staring all this time at the bare breasts of my wife and because he was thin and because despite the ringlets of his beard and curls of black hair across his forehead he was nonetheless wearing the long gray shapeless bathing trunks and the white cotton collarless shirt with the right sleeve pinned up with one of Catherine's large steel safety pins. Perhaps he did not enjoy the sight of Fiona as much as I did, or would not admit that he did. Nonetheless, that he could lie in my shadow and stare at my wife as he was in fact staring at her, and then pronounce what he had just pronounced, aroused in me new admiration for so much craft, for so much comic design.

"Cyril is virile, baby. He really is."

The absolute certainty of the soft voice which in timbre matched the curve of Fiona's throat, the pleasing brevity of the assertion, the mild sex-message of the accompanying giggle, which was more than the giggle of a mere girl, the fact that Fiona still had not moved but lay back on her elbows with one slender leg raised at the knee and her breasts falling imperceptibly to either side—at that moment I could not have loved Fiona more or felt more affection for my courageous, self-betraying Saint Peter, as I had come to call Hugh mentally whenever our quaternion reached special intensity or special joy.

Suspension, suffusion, peace for the four of us on that black beach. But it was all beginning to pass, I knew, and still I waited, now hearing the older girl shouting at the smaller girls behind the funeral cypresses. Shifting a little, growing mildly impatient myself, I waited, wondering if this momentary idyll would pass before the rose and golden metallic threads could begin to spin our separate anatomies forever into the sunset scene, would come to a sudden conclusion, incomplete, unbalanced. What was the matter with Hugh? Why was he not holding up his end?

I could understand Hugh's affected lack of gratitude, could enjoy his efforts to conceal his feelings on seeing Fiona without her bra. And of course Hugh could not possibly know that I was well aware of the fact that he had already seen Fiona's naked breasts, had already held her breasts in his good hand, so that in taking off her halter I knew full well that I was violating no confidence and was merely extending naturally the pleasures of a treat already quite familiar to the two of us. And I realized also that Hugh did not know that already I was as familiar with Catherine's naked breasts as he was with Fiona's, so that the baring of Catherine's breasts would be no surprise for me. Was he then thoughtless? Selfish? Without even the crudest idea of simple reciprocity? Certainly he must have known that it was up to him, not me, to unfasten Catherine's overly modest halter and take it off. What was holding him back? Could he not see that Catherine herself was puzzled, uncomfortable? Could he deliberately mean to embarrass his wife and to tamper with the obviously intended symmetry of our little scene on the beach? Hugh was unmusical, but I had hoped I could count on him for at least a few signs of romantic temperament. After all, how could any man love my wife and yet fail to appreciate simple harmonious arrangements of flesh, shadow, voice, hair, which were as much the result of Fiona's artistry as of mine. But perhaps I had been wrong. Perhaps Hugh had no eye for the sex-tableau.

I yawned, glanced at the finely muscled music of Fiona's breathing, began crushing another pile of shells. Back at the villas one of the smaller girls was now shrieking distantly in short monotonous bursts of pain.

And then, nearly too late, Catherine acted on her own behalf, brought herself to do what Hugh should have done, and out of feelings of exclusion or possibly pleasure or more likely irritable retaliation, managed to complete the picture that Hugh had almost destroyed. She frowned, tightened her lips, took a short breath and, crooking her elbows so that her bent arms became the rapidly moving wings of some large bird, reached behind her back and quickly, without help, unfastened her halter and pulled it off. It was an awkward, rapid, determined, self-sufficient gesture of compliance, and I was proud of her. And even though in that first moment of exposure she looked as if she wanted nothing more than to cross her arms and conceal beneath the flesh of her arms the flesh of her breasts, still she sat up straight and kept herself uncovered. I was proud of her.

And though I had already known what we would see when she finally bared herself, could visualize to the last detail the surfaces of Catherine's nakedness, still it pleased me to see the round rising breasts and the nipples that resembled small dark rosebuds tightly furled, and to see all this, not at night in their villa, but here at sunset on the polished black stones born of the volcano's chaotic fire.

How long would we manage to preserve this balance of nudity? For how long would we be allowed to appreciate the fact that the nude breathing torsos of these two very different women simply enhanced each other? I could not know. But here, at least, was the possibility of well-being, and though Catherine sat with eyes averted and arms straight and the large halter half-wadded, clutched, in one large hand in her lap, still at that moment I found myself tingling with the realization that Hugh's wife had acted deliberately and in large part for me. And now, this instant, if Catherine had been able, say, to cup her breasts in her hands with Fiona's thoughtless exhilaration, might not the sight of Catherine be as stimulating as that of Fiona? Then again, wasn't the naturalness of Catherine's slight lingering discomfort exactly as stimulating as the naturalness of my own wife's erotic confidence? I smiled, I found that the ball of my right foot was pressed gently to the solid front of one of Catherine's knees, I heard Fiona giggling and saw that Hugh's blue-gray ankle was now trapped, so to speak, between both of Fiona's energetic feet, and again I began to hope that I had not overestimated Hugh after all.

But rolling onto my hands and knees, getting to my feet with a cheerful groan, lumbering to cut off the oldest girl who was running toward us out of the cypresses and shouting for Catherine, and stopping her and displaying friendliness and knowing that when I turned to wave I would see distant gestures of busy hands fastening big and little halters once again into place—still I could only smile and do a few dancing bear steps for the angry child, because no sex-tableau was ever entirely abortive and because ahead of us lay an unlimited supply of dying suns and crescent moons which Fiona, and Catherine too, would know how to use.

A MYTHOLOGICAL SUBJECT

Laurie Colwin

It is often to the wary that the events in life are unexpected. Looser types—people who are not busy weighing and measuring every little thing—are used to accidents, coincidences, chance, things getting out of hand, things sneaking up on them. They are the happy children of life, to whom life happens for better or worse.

Those who believe in will, in meaning, in intentionality, who brood, reflect, and contemplate, who believe there are no accidents, who are born with clear vision or an introspective temperament or a relentless consciousness are quite another matter.

I am of the former category, a cheerful woman. The first man who asked me to marry him turned out to be the perfect mate. It may be that I happily settled for what came my way, but in fact my early marriage endured and prospered. As a couple we are even-tempered, easy to please, curious, fond of food and gossip. My husband Edward runs his family's import business. We have three children, all away at school. We are great socializers, and it is our chief entertainment to bring our interesting friends together.

Of our set, the dearest was my cousin Nellie Felix. I had known her as a child and was delighted when she came to New York to live and study. After all, few things are more pleasing than an attractive family member. She was full of high spirits and emotional idealism. What would become of her was one of our favorite topics of conversation.

In her twenties she had two dramatic love affairs. These love affairs surprised her: she did not think of herself as a romantic, but as someone seeking honor and communion in love. Her idealism in these matters was sweet and rather innocent. That a love affair could lead to nothing stumped her. When she was not seriously attached she was something of a loner, although she had a nice set of friends.

At the age of thirty Nellie fell in love with a lawyer named

Joseph Porter. He was lovable, intelligent, and temperamental enough to make life interesting. With him Nellie found what she had been looking for, and they were married. Nellie believed in order, in tranquillity, in her household as a safe haven, and she worked harder than even she knew to make sure she had these things. She taught three days a week at a women's college an hour outside New York. Her students adored her. She and Joseph expanded their circle, and eventually they had a child, an enchanting daughter named Jane. They lived in a town house and their life was attractive, well organized, comfortable, and looked rather effortless.

But Nellie did not feel that it was effortless. She had so ardently wanted the life she had, but she felt that she had come close to not having it; that her twenties had not been a quest for love but a romantic shambles; that there was some part of her that was not for order and organization but for chaos. She believed that the neat and tidy surfaces of things warded off misery and despair, that she had to constantly be vigilant with everything, especially herself. She once described to me a fountain she had seen on her honeymoon in the close of the Barcelona Cathedral. It was an ornamental fountain that shot up a constant jet of water. On top of this jet bobbled an egg. This seemed to Nellie a perfect metaphor to express the way she felt about her life. Without constant vigilance, self-scrutiny, accurate self-assessment, and a strong will, whatever kept the egg of her life aloft would disappear and the egg would shatter. She knew the unexamined life was not worth living. She never wanted to do things for the wrong reason, or for no reason or for reasons she did not understand. She wanted to be clear and unsentimental, to believe things that were true and not things that it consoled her to believe. When her colleague Dan Hamilton said to her: "You're very rough on me," she said: "I'm rougher on myself, I promise you."

My husband and I introduced Nellie to Dan Hamilton. We had been planning to get the Porters and the Hamiltons together for some time, but the Hamiltons were hard to pin down. Miranda Hamilton was a designer whose work frequently took her abroad. Dan was a historian. Once every three or four years he would produce a popular and successful book on some figure in colonial history. Over the years these books had made him rich, and he had become a sort of traveling scholar. Now that their three sons were grown up and married they had more or less settled down in New York. Dan had taken a sabbatical from writing and was the star appointment at Nellie's college—all the more reason to bring the two couples together.

They got along famously. My husband and I looked down from our opposite ends of the table flushed with the vision of a successful dinner party. How attractive they all looked in the candlelight! Joseph, who was large, ruddy, and beautifully dressed, sat next to Miranda. They were talking about Paris. Miranda wore her reddish hair in a stylish knot. She was wiry and chic and smoked cigarettes in a little black holder. Nellie sat next to Dan. Her clothes, as always, were sober and she looked wonderful. She had straight ashy hair that she pulled back off her face, and hazel eyes full of motion and expression. Dan, who sat next to her, was her opposite. As Nellie was immaculate and precise, Dan looked antic and boyish. He had a mop of curly brown, copper, and grey hair, and he always looked a little awry. His tie was never quite properly tied, and the pockets of his jackets sagged from carrying pipes and books and change in them. He and Nellie and my husband were being silly about some subject or other at their end of the table, and Nellie was laughing.

Over coffee it was discovered that Nellie and Dan shared the same schedule. Dan said: "In that case I ought to drive you up to school. I hate to drive alone and the trains are probably horrible." At this Miranda gave Dan a look which Nellie registered against her will. She imagined that Dan was famous for loving to drive alone and that he was teasing Miranda by flirting.

But the idea of being driven to school was quite heavenly. The trains *were* awful. The first week of Dan and Nellie's mobile colleagueship was a great success. They talked shop, compared notes on faculty and classes and family. Dan knew some of the people who had taught Nellie at college. The time, on these trips, flew by.

After two weeks Nellie became uneasy about the cost of gas and tolls and insisted on either paying for them or splitting them. Dan would not hear of this so Nellie suggested that she give him breakfast on school days to even up the score. Dan thought this was a fine idea. Nellie was a good plain cook. She gave Dan scones, toasted cheese, sour cream muffins, and coffee with hot milk. On Thursdays when they did not have to be at school until the afternoon they got into the habit of having lunch at Nellie's. They sat in the kitchen dining off the remains of last night's dinner party.

A million things slipped by them. Neither admitted how much they looked forward to their rides to school, or their breakfasts or their unnecessary Thursday lunches. Nellie told herself that this arrangement was primarily a convenience, albeit a friendly one.

One stormy autumn night, full of purple clouds and shaking branches, Nellie and Dan sat for longer than usual in front of Nellie's house. They were both restless, and Nellie's reluctance to get out of the car and go home disturbed her. Every time she got set to leave, Dan would say something to pull her back. Finally she knew she had to go, and on an unchecked impulse she reached for Dan's hand. On a similarly unchecked impulse, Dan took her hand and kissed it.

What happened was quite simple. Nellie came down with the flu—no wonder she had felt so restless. She canceled her classes and called Dan to tell him. He sounded rather cross, and it was clear he did not like to have his routines interrupted.

On Thursday she was all recovered, but Dan turned up in a terrible mood. He bolted his breakfast and was anxious to get on the road. Once they hit the highway he calmed down. They discovered that both Miranda and Joseph were away on business and that Jane was on an overnight school trip. They decided to stop for dinner at the inn they always passed, to see if it was any good.

That day Nellie felt light and clear and full of frantic energy. She taught two of the best classes she had ever taught, but she was addled. She who never lost anything left her handbag in her office and her class notes in the dining commons. Although she and Dan usually met in the parking lot, they had arranged to meet in front of the science building, but both kept forgetting what the plan was, necessitating several rounds of telephone calls.

Finally they drove through the twilight to the inn. The windows were made of bull's-eye glass, and there were flowers on the sideboard. Nellie and Dan sat by the fireplace. Neither had much in the way of appetite. They talked a blue streak and split a bottle of wine.

Outside it was brilliantly clear. The sky was full of stars, and the frosty, crisp air smelled of apples and woodsmoke. Dan started the car. Then he turned it off. With his hands on the steering wheel he said: "I think I've fallen in love with you and if I'm not mistaken, you've fallen in love with me."

It is true that there is something—there is everything—undeniable about the truth. Even the worst true thing fills the consciousness with the light of its correctness. What Dan said was just plain true, and it filled Nellie with a wild surge of joy.

It explained everything: their giddiness, their unwillingness to part, those unnecessary lunches and elaborate breakfasts.

"My God," she said. "I didn't mean for this to happen." She knew in an instant how much care she had been taking all along— to fill her conversation with references to Joseph and Jane, to say "us" and not "me," not to say any flirtatious or provocative thing. How could she have not seen this coming? Falling in love is very often not flirtatious. It is often rather grave, and if the people falling in love are married the mention of a family is not so much a banner as it is a bulletproof vest.

They sat in the cold darkness. Someone looking in the window might have thought they were discussing a terminal illness. Nellie stared at the floor. Dan was fixated on the dashboard. Neither said a word. They were terrified to look at one another—frightened of what might be visible on the other's face. But these things are irresistible, and they were drawn into each other's arms.

They drove home the long way through little towns and villages. Nellie sat close to Dan, who kept his arm around her and drove with one hand, like a teenage boy. At every stop sign and red light they kissed each other. Both of them were giddy and high. They talked and talked—like all lovers worth their salt they compared notes. They had dreamed and daydreamed about each other. They recited the history of their affections: how Dan had once come close to driving the car off the road because he was staring at Nellie one afternoon; how the sight of Dan with his shirttail out had brought Nellie near to tears she did not understand, and so on.

With their families away they had the freedom to do anything they liked but all they did was to stand in Nellie's kitchen and talk. They never sat down. When they were not talking they were in each other's arms, kissing in that way that is like drinking out of terrible thirst. Twice Nellie burst into tears—of confusion, desire, and the terrible excess of happiness that love and the knowledge that one is loved in return often brings. Nellie knew what she was feeling. That she was feeling it as a married woman upset her terribly, but the feeling was undeniable and she did not have the will to suppress it. They stood on opposite sides of the kitchen—this was Nellie's stage direction—and discussed whether or not they should go to bed. They were both quite sick with desire but what they were feeling was so powerful and seemed so dangerous that the idea of physical expression scared them to death.

Very late at night Nellie sent Dan home. In two separate beds in two separate places, in Nellie's house and Dan's apartment, separated by a number of streets and avenues, these two lovers tossed and ached and attempted to sleep away what little of the night remained to them.

The next morning Nellie woke up exhausted and keen in her empty house. When she splashed water on her face to wake herself up she found that she was laughing and crying at the same time. She felt flooded by emotions, one of which was gratitude. She felt that her life was being handed back to her, but by whom? And from where?

Alone in her kitchen she boiled water for tea and thought about Dan. For a moment he would evaporate and she could not remember what had passed between them. She drank her tea and watched a late autumn fly buzz around the kitchen. When it landed on the table, she observed it. The miraculous nature of this tiny beast, the fact that it could actually fly, the complexities and originality of things, the richness of the world, the amazing beauty of being alive struck Nellie full force. She was filled up, high as a kite. Love, even if it was doomed, gave you a renewed sense of things: it did hand life back to you.

But after a certain age, no joy is unmitigated. She knew that if she did not succeed in denying her feelings for Dan her happiness in his presence would always mix with sadness. She had never been in love with anyone unavailable, and she had never been unavailable herself.

Her heart, she felt, was not beating properly. She did not think that she would take a normal breath until she heard from Dan. When the telephone rang, she knew it was him.

"May I come and have breakfast with you?" he said. "Or do you think it's all wrong?"

Nellie said: "It's certainly all wrong but come anyway."

This was their first furtive meeting. Friday was not a school day: they were meeting out of pure volition. If Joseph asked her what she had been up to she could not say casually: "Dan Hamilton stopped by." It might sound as innocent as milk, but they were no longer innocent.

The sunlight through the kitchen windows suddenly looked threatening. The safe, tidy surfaces suddenly looked precarious and unstable. Her life, the life of a secure and faithful wife, had been done away in an instant, and even if she never saw Dan Hamilton again it was clear that something unalterable had happened to her. She could never again say that she had not been tempted. She felt alone in the middle of the universe, without husband or child, with only herself. Surely at the sight of Dan everything would fall into place and everything would be as it had been a day ago. She would see that Dan was her colleague and her friend, and that a declaration of love would not necessarily have to change everything.

But as soon as she saw him from the window she realized that a declaration does in fact change everything and that Dan was no longer just her colleague and friend. They could not keep out of each other's arms.

"I haven't felt this way since I was a teenager," said Dan. Nellie didn't say anything. She *had* felt this way since she was a teenager.

"It feels sort of heavenly," Dan said.

"It will get a little hellish," Nellie said.

"Really?" said Dan. "It's hard to believe."

"I've felt this way a couple of times," said Nellie. "Back in the world of childhood when everyone was single and nothing got in the way of a love affair. You could spend your every minute with the one you loved. You could have the luxury of getting *tired* of the one you loved. You had endless time. This is the grown-up world of the furtive, adulterous love match. No time, no luxury. I've never met anyone on the sly."

"We don't have to meet on the sly," said Dan. "We're commuters."

"I don't think you realize how quickly these things get out of hand," Nellie said.

"I'd certainly like to find out," said Dan, smiling. "Can't we just enjoy our feelings for a few minutes before all this furtive misery comes crashing down on us?"

"I give it an hour," said Nellie.

"Well, all right then. Let's go read the paper. Let's go into the living room and cozy up on the couch like single people. I can't believe you actually went out this morning and got the paper. You must have it delivered."

"We do," said Nellie.

"We do, too," said Dan.

Miranda was due back the next day, and Joseph in the early evening. Dan and Nellie stretched out on the couch in the sunlight and attempted to browse through the paper. Physical nearness caused their hearts to race. Adulterous lovers, without the errands and goals and plans that make marriage so easy, are left horribly to themselves. They have nothing to do but be—poor things.

"Here we are," said Nellie. "Representatives of two households, both of which get the *Times* delivered, curled up on a couch like a pair of teenagers."

They did not kiss each other. They did not even hold hands. The couch was big enough for both of them, with a tiny space between. They kept that space between them. Everything seemed very clear and serious. This was their last chance to deny that they were anything more than friends. Two gestures could be made: they would become lovers or they would not. It seemed to Nellie a very grave moment in her life. She was no longer a girl with strong opinions and ideals, but a mortal woman caught in the complexities of life. Both Nellie and Dan were silent. Once they were in each other's arms it was all over, they knew, but since falling in love outside of marriage is the ultimate and every other gesture is its shadow, when they could bear it no longer they went upstairs to Nellie's guest room and there became lovers in the real sense of the word.

Of all the terrible things in life, living with a divided heart is the most terrible for an honorable person. There were times when Nellie could scarcely believe that she was the person she knew. Her love for Dan seemed pure to her, but its context certainly did not. There was not one moment when she felt right or justified: she simply had her feelings and she learned that some true feelings make one wretched; that they interfere with life; that they cause great emotional and moral pain; and that there was nothing much she could do about them. Her love for Dan opened the world up in a terrible and serious way and caused her, with perfect and appropriate justification, to question everything: her marriage, her ethics, her sense of the world, herself.

Dan said: "Can't you leave yourself alone for five seconds? Can't you just go with life a little?"

Nellie said: "Don't you want this to have anything to do with your life? Do you think we fell in love for no reason whatsoever? Don't you want to know what this means?"

"I can't think that way about these things," Dan said. "I want to enjoy them."

Nellie said: "I have to know everything. I think it's immoral not to."

That was when Dan had said: "You're very rough on me."

Any city is full of adulterers. They hide out in corners of restaurants. They know the location of all necessary pay telephones. They go to places their friends never go to. From time to time they become emboldened and are spotted by a sympathetic acquaintance who has troubles of his or her own and never says a word to anyone.

There are plain philanderers, adventurers, and people seeking revenge on a spouse. There are those who have absolutely no idea what they are doing or why, who believe that events have simply carried them away. And there are those to whom love comes, unexpected and not very welcome, a sort of terrible fact of life like fire or flood. Neither Nellie nor Dan had expected to fall in love. They were innocents at it.

There were things they were not prepared for. The first time Nellie called Dan from a pay phone made her feel quite awful— Joseph was home with a cold and Nellie wanted to call Dan before he called her. That call made her think of all the second-rate and nasty elements that love outside marriage entails.

The sight of Nellie on the street with Jane upset Dan. He saw them from afar and was glad he was too far off to be seen. That little replica of Nellie stunned him. He realized that he had never seen Jane before: that was how distant he and Nellie were from the true centers of each other's lives. He was jealous of Jane, he realized. Jealous of a small daughter because of such exclusive intimacy.

When Nellie ran into Dan with his middle son Ewan at the liquor store one Saturday afternoon, it had the same effect on her. Both she and Dan were buying wine for dinner parties. Both knew exactly what the other was serving and to whom. This made Nellie think of the thousands of things they did not know and would never know: that family glaze of common references, jokes, events, calamities—that sense of a family being like a kitchen midden: layer upon layer of the things daily life is made of. The edifice that lovers build is by comparison delicate and one-dimensional. The sight of the beloved's child is only a living demonstration that the one you love has a long and complicated history that has nothing to do with you.

They suffered everything. When they were together they suffered from guilt and when apart from longing. The joys that lovers experience are extreme joys, paid for by the sacrifice of everything comfortable. Moments of unfettered happiness are few, and they mostly come when one or the other is too exhausted to think. One morning Nellie fell asleep in the car. She woke up with a weak winter light warming her. For an instant she was simply happy—happy to be herself, to be with Dan, to be alive. It was a very brief moment, pure and sweet as cream. As soon as she woke up it vanished. Nothing was simple at all. Her heart felt heavy as a weight. Nothing was clear or reasonable or unencumbered. There was no straight explanation of anything.

Since I saw remarkably little of Nellie, I suspected something was up with her: she was one of those people who hide out when they are in trouble. I knew that if she needed to talk she would come to see me and eventually she did just that.

It is part of the nature of the secret that it needs to be shared. Without confession it is incomplete. When what she was feeling was too much for her, Nellie chose me as her confidante. I was the logical choice: I was family, I had known Nellie all her life, and I had known Dan for a long time, too.

She appeared early one Friday in the middle of a winter storm. She was expected anyway—she and I were going to pick up Jane later in the afternoon, and then my husband and I, Nellie, Joseph, and Jane were going out for dinner.

She came in looking flushed and *fine*, with diamonds of sleet in her hair. She was wearing a grey skirt, and a sweater which in some lights was lilac and in some the color of a pigeon's wing. She shook out her hair, and when we were finally settled in the living room with our cups of tea I could see that she was very upset.

"You look very stirred up," I said.

"I am stirred up," said Nellie. "I need to talk to you." She stared down into her tea and it was clear that she was composing herself to keep from crying.

Finally she said: "I'm in love with Dan Hamilton."

I said: "Is he in love with you?"

"Yes," said Nellie.

I was not surprised at all, and that I was not surprised upset her. She began to cry, which made her look all the more charming. She was one of those lucky people who are not ruined by tears.

"I'm so distressed," she said. "I almost feel embarrassed to be as upset as I am."

"You're not exempt from distress," I said. "You're also not exempt from falling in love."

"I wanted to be," she said fiercely. "I thought that if I put my will behind it, if I was straight with myself I wouldn't make these mistakes."

"Falling in love is not a mistake."

She then poured forth. There were no accidents, she knew. That she had fallen in love meant something. What did it say about herself and Joseph? All the familiar emotional props of girlhood—will, resolve, a belief in a straight path—were gone from her. She did not see why love had come to her unless she had secretly—a secret from herself, she meant—been looking for it. And on and on. That she was someone who drew love—some people do, and they need not be especially lovable or physically beautiful, as Nellie believed—was not enough of an explanation for her. That something had simply happened was not an idea she could entertain. She did not believe that things simply happened.

She talked until her voice grew strained. She had not spared herself a thing. She said, finally: "I wanted to be like you—steady and faithful. I thought my romantic days were over. I thought I was grown up. I wanted for me and Joseph to have what you and Edward have—a good and uncomplicated marriage."

It is never easy to give up the pleasant and flattering image other people have of one's own life. Had Nellie's distress not been so intense, I would not have felt compelled to make a confession of my own. But I felt rather more brave in the face of my fierce cousin: I was glad she was suffering, in fact. I knew she divided the world into the cheerful slobs like me and the emotional moralists like herself. A serious love affair, I thought, might take some of those sharp edges off.

I began by telling her how the rigorousness with which she went after what she called the moral universe did not allow anyone very much latitude, but nonetheless, I was about to tell her something that might put her suffering into some context.

"I have been in love several times during my marriage," I said. "And I have had several love affairs."

The look on her face, I was happy to see, was one of pure relief.

"But I thought you and Edward were so happy," she said.

"We are," I said. "But I'm only human and I am not looking for perfection. Romance makes me cheerful. There have been times in my life when I simply needed to be loved by someone else and I was lucky enough to find someone who loved me. And look at me! I'm not beautiful and I'm not so lovable, but I'm interested in love and so it comes to find me. There are times when Edward simply hasn't been there for me—it happens in every marriage. They say it takes two and sometimes three to make a marriage work and they're right. But this had nothing to do with you because I picked my partners in crime for their discretion and their very clear sense that nothing would get out of hand. I can see that an affair that doesn't threaten your marriage is not your idea of an affair, but there you are."

This made Nellie silent for a long time. She looked exhausted and tearstained.

"One of the good things about this love affair," she said, "is that it's shot my high horse right out from under me. It's a real kindness for you to tell me what you've just told me."

"We're all serious in our own ways," I said. "Now I think you need a nap. You look absolutely wiped out. I'll go call Eddie and tell him to meet Joseph and then when you wake up we can plot where we're going to take Jane for dinner."

I gave her two needlepoint pillows for her head, covered her with a quilt, then went to call my husband. When I got back I sat and watched my cousin sleeping. The sleety, yellowish light played over her brow and cheekbones.

She was lying on her side with her hand slightly arched and bent. Her hair had been gathered at her neck but a few strands had escaped. She looked like the slain nymph Procris in the Piero di Cosimo painting *A Mythological Subject*, which depicts poor Procris who has been accidentally killed by her husband Cephalus. Cephalus is a hunter who has a spear that never misses its mark. One day he hears a noise in the forest, and thinking that it is a wild beast, he takes aim. But it is not a beast. It is Procris. In the painting a tiny jet of blood sprays from her throat. At her feet is her mournful dog, Lelaps, and at her head is a satyr, wearing the look of a heartbroken boy. That picture is full of the misery and loneliness romantic people suffer in love.

The lovely thing about marriage is that life ambles on—as if life were some meandering path lined with sturdy plane trees. A love affair is like a shot arrow. It gives life an intense direction, if only for an instant. The laws of love affairs would operate for Nellie and Dan: they would either run off together, or they would part, or they would find some way to salvage a friendship out of their love affair. If you live long enough and if you are placid and easygoing, people tell you everything. Almost everyone I know has confessed a love affair of some sort or another to me.

But I had never discussed my amours with anyone. Would Nellie think that my affairs had been inconsequential? Certainly I had never let myself get into such a swivet over a man, but I had made very sure to pick only those with very secure marriages and a sense of fun. Each union had been the result of one of the inevitable low moments that marriages contain, and each parting, when the right time came to part, had been relatively painless. The fact was, I was not interested in love in the way Nellie was. She was interested in ultimates. I remembered her fifteen years ago, at twenty-three, rejecting all the nice, suitable young men who wanted to take her out for dinner and in whom she had no interest. She felt this sort of socializing was all wrong. When my husband and I chided her, she said with great passion: "I don't want a social life. I want love, or nothing."

Well, she had gotten what she wanted. There she lay, wiped out, fast asleep, looking wild, peaceful, and troubled all at the same time. She had no dog to guard her, no satyr to mourn her, and no bed of wildflowers beneath her like the nymph in the painting.

What a pleasant circumstance to sit in a warm, comfortable room on an icy winter's day and contemplate someone you love whose life has always been of the greatest interest to you. Procris in the painting is half naked, but Nellie looked just as vulnerable.

It would be exceedingly interesting to see what happened to her, but then she had always been a pleasure to watch.

FEELING NORMAL

Gary Soto

I'm unrepentant on a park bench. For every attractive woman who passes, two bad thoughts knock on my forehead and enter, lie down and frolic with a bold nakedness that scares me. It's lunchtime, the sun half-hidden behind clouds but bright enough to do tricks to my senses, and the women, some alone, some in pairs, some in packs, are so beautiful that tears, like a leaky faucet, drip inward. They're unobtainable and, because of that, more desirable, mysterious, dangerous—all the qualities a man builds into what he can't have.

I only have to glance at the woman across form me, glance and look away, and the knocking begins. Her knees are pink, her cheeks pink, her nails a shade of pink, and so it must be that behind her career woman's clothes—the little gray pinstripe suit—she must be pink. Gray and pink. I like those colors, and black too, the color of her briefcase, which winks a yellow light on the brass latches each time she opens it to ruffle through papers. I have to wonder to myself, is that the signal? Would she like me to get up and move closer to her, sit, right next to her? The latches wink, go dead, wink again.

On lunch break she's taking in the sun, no doubt tired of closed-in office smells of Xerox machines and typewriters and greasy phones. Maybe she's a lawyer, an accountant perhaps, someone in merchandising. Whatever she does she seems happy to be outside eating her lunch. She has already finished her sandwich and is now enjoying her peach. She takes a small bite, chews, and runs a slow tongue across her teeth, which seem also to wink with the noontime light. What would Freud say about that? What would my mother say, a young woman like that chewing so lasciviously?

But how should I approach her? What would I say? Hello, this is Mr. Irresistible. Yes, I am an Aries. Pink and gray are my favorite colors. My BMW is in the shop. I could tell her, "I'm from Fresno!" which would lead smoothly right into my saying that they grow peaches there and that the one she is eating is probably from my hometown, was in fact picked by someone I know. Who would ever guess that we had something in common?

Love can start harmlessly, over lunch for instance, and grow into hand-holding walks and dinner. Maybe we can go out tomorrow night, try the Emerald Garden, yet another new Vietnamese restaurant on California. And the Lumiere is just down the street from there. We can see a movie, see ourselves in the movie: I'm the lead actor in a wheelchair, some unfortunate fellow who was pushed under a train by a psychotic; she's the nurse on the night shift whose real interest is not the sick but literature, and she is, in fact, 13 units away from a second degree, this time in English. Together we fall for one another, but not after some jealous rage at a restaurant. I stir my bread pudding into mush when she hints that she has been married before, two times in fact, OK, if you really want to know the truth, three times; she smacks my face when I mention an old love has better teeth.

But I'm going to meet this woman. I've been working out at the Y, and I'm sweaty, sour as a dirty sock, and generally bad to look at. I'm also hungry for lunch, and married, and a father to a great child who's learning about Europe this week. Why should I ruin myself, and others? And what right does this other woman have to enter my life and cause havoc? Shouldn't a single woman know better? And the truth of the matter is that I have to hurry home: jog a little, walk; jog a little, walk. I have to answer a letter and start the stew my wife expects when she comes home, tired of the office smells she endures daily. If it weren't for the sun, none of this enticement would happen. It would be too dreary for these women to leave their workplace ten minutes early and return ten minutes late. They would not swagger by in tight skirts, each new skirt more beautiful. Neither would bad thoughts knock on my forehead, enter and frolic on all fours. No brass latches would wink and tell me "Go ahead, make a fool of yourself, and tell me you're an unmarried Aries with money and kindness and humor and health." And that would be too bad.

From: EMPIRE

RICHARD FORD

He followed Sergeant Benton into the lounge car, which was smoky.
The snack bar was closed. Padlocks were on each of the steel cabinets. Two older men in cowboy hats and boots were arguing across
a table full of beer cans. They were arguing about somebody named
Heléna, a name they pronounced with a Spanish accent. "It'd be a
mistake to underestimate Heléna," one of them said. "I'll warn you
of that."

"Oh, fuck Heléna," the other cowboy said. "That fat, ugly bitch.
I'm not afraid of her *or* her family."

Across from them a young Asian woman in a sari sat holding an
Asian baby. They stared up at Sergeant Benton and at Sims. The
woman's round belly was exposed and a tiny red jewel pierced her
nose. She seemed frightened, Sims thought, frightened of whatever
was going to happen next. He didn't feel that way at all, and was
sorry she did.

Sergeant Benton led him out into the second, rumbling vestibule,
tiptoeing across in her stocking feet and into the sleeping car where
the lights were turned low. As the vestibule door closed, the sound
of the moving train wheels was taken far away. Sergeant Benton
turned and smiled and put her finger to her lips. "People are sleeping," she whispered.

Marge was sleeping, Sims thought, right across the hall. It made
his fingers tingle and feel cold. He walked right past the little silver
door and didn't look at it. She'll go right on sleeping, he thought,
and wake up happy tomorrow.

At the far end of the corridor a black man stuck his bald head
out between the curtains of a private seat and looked at Sims and
Doris. Doris was fitting a key into the lock of her compartment door.
The black man was the porter who'd helped Marge and him with
their suitcases and offered to bring them coffee in the morning. Ser-

geant Benton waved at him and went "shhhh." Sims waved at him, too, though only halfheartedly. The porter, whose name was Lewis, said nothing, and drew his head back inside the curtains.

"Give me your tired, right?" Doris said, and laughed softly as she opened the door. A bed light was on inside, and the bed had been opened and made up—probably, Sims thought, by Lewis. Out the window he could see the empty, murky night and the moon chased by clouds, and the ground shooting by below the grass. It was dizzying. He could see his own face reflected, and was surprised to see that he was smiling. *"Entrez vous,"* Doris said behind him, "or we'll have tomorrow on our hands."

Sims climbed in, then slid to the foot of the bed while Doris crawled around on her hands and knees reaching for things and digging in her purse behind the pillow. She pulled out an alarm clock. "It's twelve o'clock. Do you know where your kids are?" She flashed Sims a grin. "Mine are still out there in space waiting to come in. Good luck to them, is what I say." She went back to digging in her bag.

"Mine, too," Sims said. He was cold in Doris's roomette, but he felt like he should take his shoes off. Keeping them on made him uncomfortable, but it made him uncomfortable to be in bed with Doris in the first place.

"I just couldn't stand it," Doris said. "They're just other little adults. Who needs that? One's enough."

"That's right," Sims said. Marge felt the same way he did. Children made life a misery and, once they'd finished, they did it again. That had been the first thing he and Marge had seen eye to eye on. Sims put his shoes down beside the mattress and hoped they wouldn't start to smell.

"Miracles," Doris said and held up a pint bottle of vodka. "Never fear, Doris is here," she said. "Never a dull moment. Plus there's glasses, too." She rumbled around in her bag. "Right now in a jiffy there'll be glasses," she said. "Never fear. Are you just horribly bored already, Vic? Have I completely blown this? Are you antsy? Are you mad? Don't be mad."

"I couldn't be happier," Sims said. Doris, on her hands and knees in the half-light, turned and smiled at him. Sims smiled back at her.

"Good man. Excellent." Doris held up a glass. "One glass," she said, "the fruit of patience. Did you know I look as good as I did when I was in high school. I've been told that—recently, in fact."

Sims looked at Doris's legs and her rear end. They were both good-looking, he thought. Both slim and firm. "That's easy to believe," he said. "How old *are* you?"

Sergeant Benton narrowed one eye at him. "How old do you think? Or, how old do I look? I'll ask that."

She was taking all night to fix two drinks, Sims thought. "Thirty. Or near thirty, anyway," he said.

"Cute," Sergeant Benton said. "That's extremely cute." She smirked at him. "Thirty-eight is my age."

"I'm forty-two," Sims said.

Doris didn't seem to hear him. "Glass," she said, holding up another one for him to see. "Two glasses. Let's just go on and have a drink, what do you say?"

"Great," Sims said. He could smell Doris's perfume, a sweet flowery smell he liked and that came from her suitcase. He was glad to be here.

Doris turned and crossed her legs in a way that stretched her skirt across her knees. She set both glasses on her skirt and poured two drinks. Sims realized he could see up her skirt if the light in the compartment was any better.

She smiled and handed Sims a glass. "Here's to your wife," Doris said. "May sweet dreams descend."

"Here's to that," Sims said and drank a gulp of warm vodka. He hadn't known how much he'd wanted a drink until this one was down his throat.

"How fast do you think we're going now?" Doris said, peering toward the dark window where nothing was visible.

"I don't know," Sims said. "Eighty, maybe. I'd guess eighty."

"Hurtling through the dark night," Doris said and smiled. She took another drink. "What scares you ought to be interesting, right?"

"Where've you been on this trip?" Sims said.

Sergeant Benton pushed her fingers through her blond hair and gave her head another shake, then sniffed. "Visiting a relative," she said. She stared at Sims and her eyes seemed to blaze at him suddenly and for no reason Sims could see. Possibly this was a sensitive subject. He would be happy to avoid those.

"And where're you going? You told me but I forgot. It seems like a long time ago."

"Would you like to hear a little story?" Sergeant Benton said. "A recent and true-to-life story?"

"Sure." Sims raised his vodka glass to toast a story. Doris extended the bottle and poured in some more, then more for herself.

"Well," she said. She smelled the vodka in her glass, then pulled her skirt up slightly to be comfortable. "I go to visit my father, you see, out on San Juan Island. I haven't seen him in maybe eight years, since before I went in the Army—since I was married, in fact. And he's married now himself to a very nice lady. Miss Vera. They run a boarding kennel out on the island. He's sixty something and takes care of all these noisy dogs. She's fifty something. I don't know how they do it." Doris took a drink. "Or why. She's a Mormon, believes in all the angels, so he's more or less become one, too, though he drinks and smokes. He's not at all spiritual. He was in the Air Force. Also a sergeant. Anyway, the first night I get there we all eat dinner together. A big steak. And right away my father says he has to drive down to the store to get something, and he'll be back. So off he goes. And Miss Vera and I are washing dishes and watching television and chattering. And before I know it, two hours have gone by. And I say to Miss Vera, 'Where's Eddie? Hasn't he been gone a long time?' And she just says, 'Oh, he'll be back pretty soon.' So we pottered around a little more. Each of us smoked a cigarette. Then she got ready to go to bed. By herself. It was ten o'clock, and I said, 'Where's Dad?' And she said, 'Sometimes he stops and has a drink down in town.' So when she's in bed I get in the other car and drive down the hill to the bar. And there's his station wagon in front. Only when I go in and ask, he isn't there, and nobody says they know where he is. I go back outside, but then this guy steps to the door behind me and says, 'Try the trailer, hon. That's it. Try the trailer.' Nothing else. And across the road is a little house trailer with its lights on and a car sitting out front. And I just walked across the road—I still had on my uniform—walked up the steps and knocked on the door. There're some voices inside and a TV. I hear people moving around and a door close. The front door opens then and here's a woman who apparently lives there. She's completely dressed. I'd guess her age to be fifty. She's younger than Vera anyway, with a younger face. She says, 'Yes. What is it?' and I said I was sorry, but I was looking for my father, and I guessed I'd gotten the wrong place. But she says, 'Just a second,' and turns around and says, 'Eddie, your daughter's here.'

"And my father came out of a door to the next room. Maybe it was a closet, I didn't know. I didn't care. He had his pants on and an undershirt. And he said, 'Oh hi, Doris. How're you? Come on in. This is Sherry.' And the only thing I could think of was how thin his shoulders looked. He looked like he was going to die. I didn't even speak to Sherry. I just said no, I couldn't stay. And I drove on back to the house."

"Did you leave then?" Sims said.

"No, I stayed around a couple more days. *Then* left. It didn't matter to me. It made me think, though."

"What did you think?" Sims asked.

Doris put her head back against the metal wall and stared up. "Oh, I just thought about being the other woman, which I've been that enough. Everybody's done everything twice, right? At my age. You cross a line. But you can do a thing and have it mean nothing but what you feel that minute. You don't have to give yourself away. Isn't that true?"

"That's exactly true," Sims said and thought it was right. He'd done it himself plenty of times.

"Where's the real life, right? I don't think I've had mine, yet, have you?" Doris held her glass up to her lips with both hands and smiled at him.

"Not yet, I haven't," Sims said. "Not entirely."

"When I was a little girl in California and my father was teaching me to drive, I used to think, 'I'm driving now. I have to pay strict attention to everything; I have to notice everything; I have to think about my hands being on the wheel; it's possible I'll only think about this very second forever, and it'll drive me crazy.' But I'd already thought of something else." Doris wrinkled her nose at Sims. "That's my movie, right?"

"It sounds familiar," Sims said. He took a long drink of his vodka and emptied the glass. The vodka tasted metallic, as if it had been kept stored in a can. It had a good effect, though. He felt like he could stay up all night. He was seeing things from the outside, and nothing bad could happen to anyone. Everyone was protected. "Most people want to be good, though," Sims said for no reason. Just words under their own command, headed who-knows-where. Everything seemed arbitrary.

"Would you like me to take my clothes off?" Sergeant Benton said and smiled at him.

"I'd like that," Sims said. "Sure." He thought that he would also like a small amount more of the vodka. He reached over, took the bottle off the blanket and poured himself some more.

Sergeant Benton began unbuttoning her uniform blouse. She knelt forward on her knees, pulled her shirttail out, and began with the bottom button first. She watched Sims, still half smiling. "Do you remember the first woman you ever saw naked?" she said, opening her blouse so Sims could see her white brassiere and a line of smooth belly over her skirt.

"Yes," Sims said.

"And where was that?" Sergeant Benton said. "What state was that in?" She took her blouse off, then pulled her strap down off her shoulder and uncovered one breast, then the other one. They were breasts that went to the side and pushed outward. They were nice breasts.

"That was California, too," Sims said. "Near Sacramento, I think."

"What happened?" Sergeant Benton began unzipping her skirt.

"We were on a golf course. My friend and I and this girl. Patsy was her name. We were all twelve. We both asked her to take off her clothes, in an old caddy house by the Air Force base. And she did it. We did too. She said we'd have to." Sims wondered if Patsy's name was still Patsy.

Sergeant Benton slid her skirt down, then sat back and handed it around her ankles. She had on only panty hose now and nothing beyond that. You could see through them even in the dim light. She leaned against the metal wall and looked at Sims. He could touch her now, he thought. That was what she would like to happen. "Did you like it?" Sergeant Benton asked.

"Yes, I liked it," Sims said.

"It wasn't disappointing to you?"

"It was," Sims said. "But I liked it. I knew I was going to." Sims moved close to her, lightly touched her ankle, then her knee, then the soft skin of her belly and came down with the waist of her hosiery. Her hands touched his neck but didn't feel rough. He heard her breathe and smelled the perfume she was wearing. Nothing seemed arbitrary now.

"Sweet, that's sweet," she said, and breathed deeply once. "Sometimes I think about making love. Like now. And everything tightens up inside me, and I just squeeze and say *ahhhh* without even meaning to. It just escapes me. It's just that pleasure. Someday it'll stop, won't it?"

"No," Sims said. "That won't. That goes on forever." He was near her now, his ear to her chest. He heard a noise, a noise of releasing. Outside, in the corridor, someone began talking in a hushed voice. Someone said, "No, no. Don't say that." And then a door clicked.

"Life's on so thin a string anymore," she whispered, and turned off the tiny light. "Not that much makes it good."

"That's right, isn't it?" Sims said, close to her. "I know that."

"This isn't passion," she said. "This is something different now. I can't lose sleep over this."

"That's fine," Sims said.

"You knew this would happen, didn't you?" she said. "It wasn't a secret." He didn't know it. He didn't try to answer it. "Oh you," she whispered. "Oh you."

Sometime in the night Sims felt the train slow and then stop, then sit still in the dark. He had no idea where he was. He still had his clothes on. Outside there was sound like wind, and for a moment he thought possibly he was dead, that this is how it would feel.

Sergeant Benton lay beside him, asleep. Her clothes were around her. She was covered with a blanket. The vodka bottle was empty on the bed. What had he done here? Sims thought. How had things exactly happened? What time was it? Out the window he could see no one and nothing. The moon was gone, though the sky was red and wavering with a reflected light, as though the wind was moving it.

Sims picked up his shoes and opened the door into the corridor.

The porter didn't appear this time, and Sims closed the door softly and carried his shoes down to the washroom by the vestibule. Inside, he locked the door, ran water on his hands, then rubbed soap on his face and his ears and his neck and into his hairline, then rinsed them with water out of the silver bowl until his face was clean and dripping, and he could stand to see it in the dull little mirror: a haggard face, his eyes red, his skin pale, his teeth gray and lifeless. A deceiver's face, he thought. An adulterer's face, a face to turn away from. He smiled at himself and then couldn't look. He was glad to be alone. He wouldn't see this woman again. He and Marge would get off in a few hours, and Doris would sleep around the clock.

Sims let himself back into the corridor. He thought he heard noise outside the train, and through the window to the vestibule he saw the Asian woman, standing and staring out, holding her little boy in her arms. She was talking to the conductor. He hoped there was no trouble. He wanted to get to Minot on time and get off the train.

When he let himself into Marge's roomette, Marge was awake. And out the window he saw the center of everyone's attention. A wide fire was burning on the open prairie. Out in the dark, men were moving at the edges of the fire. Trucks were in the fields and high tractors with their lights on, and dogs chasing and rumbling in the dark. Far away he could see the white stanchions of high-voltage lines traveling off into the distance.

"It's thrilling," Marge said and turned and smiled at him. "The tracks are on fire ahead of us. I heard someone outside say that. People are running all over. I watched a house disappear. It'll drive you to your remotest thoughts."

"What about *us?*" Sims said, looking out the window into the fire.

"I didn't think of that. Isn't that strange?" Marge said. "It didn't even seem to matter. It should, I guess."

The fire had turned the sky red and the wind blew flames upwards, and Sims imagined he felt heat, and his heart beat faster with the sight—a fire that could turn and sweep over them in a moment, and they would all be caught, asleep and awake. He thought of Sergeant Benton alone in her bed, dreaming dreams of safety and confidence. Nothing was wrong with her, he thought. She should be saved. A sense of powerlessness and despair rose in him, as if there was help but he couldn't offer it.

"The world's on fire, Vic," Marge said. "But it doesn't hurt anything. It just burns until it stops." She raised the covers. "Get in bed with me, sweetheart," she said, "you poor thing. You've been up all night, haven't you?" She was naked under the sheet. He could see her breasts and her stomach and the beginnings of her white legs.

He sat on the bed and put his shoes down. His heart beat faster. He could feel heat now from outside. But, he thought, there was no threat to them, to anyone on the train. "I slept a little," he said.

Marge took his hand and kissed it and held it between her hands. "When I was in my remote thoughts, you know, just watching it burn, I thought about how I get in bed sometimes and I think how happy I am, and then it makes me sad. It's crazy, isn't it? I'd like life to stop, and it won't. It just keeps running by me. It makes me jealous of Pauline. She makes life stop when she wants it to. She doesn't care what happens. That's just a way of looking at things. I guess I wouldn't want to be like her."

"You're not like her," Sims said. "You're sympathetic."

"She probably thinks no one takes her seriously."

"It's all right," Sims said.

"What's going to happen to Pauline now?" Marge moved closer to him. "Will she be all right? Do you think she will?"

"I think she will," Sims said.

"We're out on a frontier here, aren't we, sweetheart? It feels like that." Sims didn't answer. "Are you sleepy, hon?" Marge asked. "You can sleep. I'm awake now. I'll watch over you." She reached and pulled down the shade, and everything, all the movement and heat outside, was gone.

He touched Marge with his fingers—the bones in her face and her shoulders, her breasts, her ribs. He touched the scar, smooth and rigid and neat under her arm, like a welt from a mean blow. This can do it, he thought, this can finish you, this small thing. He held her to him, her face against his as his heart beat. And he felt dizzy, and at that moment insufficient, but without a memory of life's having changed in that particular way.

Outside on the cold air, flames moved and divided and swarmed the sky. And Sims felt alone in a wide empire, removed and afloat, calmed, as if life was far away now, as if blackness was all around, as if stars held the only light.

From: THE PERPLEXING HABIT OF FALLING

Rosemarie Waldrop

Your arms were embracing like a climate that does not require being native. They held me responsive, but I still wondered about the other lives I might have lived, the unused cast of characters stored within me, outcasts of actuality no stranger than my previous selves. As if a word should be counted a lie for all it misses. I could imagine my body arching up toward other men in a high-strung vertigo that scored a virtual accompaniment to our real dance, deep phantom chords echoing from nowhere though with the force of long acceleration, of flying home from a lost wedding. Stakes and mistakes. Big with sky, with bracing cold, with the drone of aircraft, the measures of distance hang in the air before falling in thick drops. The child will be pale and thin. Though it had infiltrated my bones, the thought was without marrow. More a feeling that might accompany a thought, a ply of consonants, an outward motion of the eye.

✳

Many questions were left in the clearing we built our shared life in. Later sheer size left no room for imagining myself standing outside it, on the edge of an empty day. I knew I didn't want to part from this whole which could be said to carry its foundation as much as resting on it, just as a family tree grows downward, its branches confounding gravitation and gravidity. I wanted to continue lying alongside you, two parallel, comparable lengths of feeling, and let the stresses of the structure push our sleep to momentum and fullness. Still, a fallow evening stretches into unknown elsewheres, seductive with possibility, doors open onto a chaos of cul-de-sacs, of could-be, of galloping off on the horse in the picture. And whereto? A crowning mirage or a question like What is love? And where?

Does it enter with a squeeze, or without, bringing, like interpretation, its own space from some other dimension? Or is it like a dream corridor forever extending its concept toward extreme emptiness, like that of atoms?

SIGNS OF DEVOTION

Maxine Chernoff

While Dave was away and I was asleep, a sniper fired two shots on our block. The next morning a neighbor child found bullets under Carla and Stanley Penn's magnolia. Harmless as snails, they hadn't come close to a house. The police theorize that it was a prankster. I must confess I wasn't that sniper, though I wish I were as I wipe off the counter, as I slip off my tee shirt, as Jeff entangles me with his sensitive nerves. I mention the sniper because he signals a change in my relationship with Dave. I used to be afraid to go to bed before my husband was home. For seventeen years, I listened to my tight heartbeat drumming like a toy until I worried him through the door. Something terrible might happen that I might have prevented awake.

Jeff is my first lover, Dave's visiting cousin. After Jeff's marriage failed, he decided to make a tour of all the states he'd never visited. His old Datsun contains souvenirs for Billy: deerskin Indian moccasins from Nebraska, a doll face made of dried apples from Iowa, and a plastic bust of Abraham Lincoln, mole and all, from Springfield, Illinois. Leonora, his ex, has taken little Billy back to Hattiesburg, where she'll live with her mother until they can't stand each other. Leonora's a muralist and needs big walls to keep her happy. I don't think she'll find what she needs in Hattiesburg.

Jeff's sitting on the couch reading the *Journal of Psychomotor Disorders*. When he relaxes, he slouches like laundry. When he slouches, he resembles Dave. "Listen to this," he'll say, and read me a paragraph on facial tics. He'll exaggerate the details, and if I consent to watch, act them out with precision. I pretend that I'm enthused. It makes things work more smoothly.

Whenever the phone rings, it's Irene, who uses her radar to call at the worst moments.

"Hi, Irene," I say.

"I'll be late again," Dave replies.

"Call when you'll be on time. It'll save your firm money."

Dave's seeing Donna. She's a cost accountant with turquoise contact lenses and a wet smile. She used to come to family gatherings with Glen, who's British. She'd get a lot of attention showing him off.

"Say *laboratory*," she'd tell him. "Say *aluminum*."

He'd do exactly as she asked. When Glen's mom died of emphysema and he returned to Birmingham last fall, Donna stopped visiting us. I thought it was unfair that she should feel unwelcome without Glen, so I called her.

"This is hard to believe," she said. "Dave claimed you knew."

When I finally understood her meaning, I reeled around the kitchen feeling myself diminished to a dark hot stone. For months when people spoke, I wondered how they could see me.

Dave doesn't know that Donna told me. He's so cordial that I've begun to feel relieved when he's away. Dave attends sales meetings in the Amazon, at resorts with pineapple-shaped swimming pools. He brings me lizard-skin bags he buys duty-free at the airport. In rooms furnished with mahogany antiques rowed down the river by natives, Dave sleeps with Donna. I can picture them buried under the covers, the air conditioner tweeting. I wonder if Donna thinks about me anymore. At home Dave and I sleep in tense shifts, bumper cars passing in the night.

The first time Jeff fell asleep on our couch, his mouth was an O. His hands, folded in front of him like a diver's, were stiller than hands. He looked like Daniel taking a nap ten years ago, or the little boy I saw in the park asleep under a checkered picnic blanket. When Daniel was small, I used to perform this test: I'd raise his hand above his head, then let it drop. It would fit back in place without disturbing his sleep. He has a pure heart, my sister Irene used to say. Jeff is twenty-nine, too old to seem like a child.

Three days ago, I was sitting on the floor watching Jeff sleep. When he sensed that I was there, he reached over and pulled me on top of him. At first I wondered if he'd done it unconsciously, dreaming that I was Leonora. I thought of those country songs where one or the other says the wrong name in bed.

"What time is it?" he asked after he was inside me.

"Dave's away," I said. "Danny's at school till four."

He dug his head into my hair and said, "Jerri, you're terrific."

It was as simple as that.

The phone rings again. It's really Irene, older than me by twelve years. Irene thinks that Jeff's a nice boy. Her own husband, Clark, left Irene when she was still young. I remember sitting in my mother's house. From the hi-fi in the front room, I could hear Bobby Darin singing "Mack the Knife." Chain-smoking in the kitchen, Irene was telling my mother about Clark. I watched the ash on her cigarette drop onto the green Formica tabletop and thought about Clark's hair. Can elaborately styled hair predict bad character? I considered asking Irene, but she looked too miserable to bother with me. She'd been crying and her eyes were nearly swollen shut. Around her eyes little plateaus of hives had formed.

After Irene left, my mother smoked a rare cigarette. She inhaled like she wanted to swallow the world. Then she began a cleaning frenzy that culminated in defrosting the refrigerator and throwing out the wedding cake top she'd been saving for them. Thinking Irene still might want to keep it, I saved it in my room for a few weeks. When I showed it to Irene, she said, "Dog food."

Irene's worked for years as a secretary to the president of the roofers' union. She attends theater, plays bingo, and talks endlessly to me. She's pieced together a life from others' leftovers: She works for a man whose wife ran off to Scotland with the union treasurer. Her theater companions are widows who call themselves by their husbands' names, Mrs. John Merllman, Mrs. Norman DeBianca. She plays bingo at an old people's home, cheating to make herself lose. Irene's never been wise about capital. My dad called Clark a jack-of-no-trades. When air-conditioning spread, Clark considered refrigeration, but he moved slower than industry. Besides, there was a place for him in Dad's firm. Soon Dad died and Cress Industries was found to be insolvent. Some evidence pointed to Clark's having mishandled the books. After he took off, there were a few letters, and on their third anniversary, a monkey-faced bank made of a coconut with Irene's name etched on it.

Irene gave the bank to Daniel when he was little. He keeps it on his dresser. He's home now, studying in his room with the door bolted. When he was younger, he'd tie a rope to the chair to assure his privacy. Once, I opened the door and upset the chair.

"Expecting terrorists?" I asked him.

"I'm expecting my rights," he countered.

How could I argue?

Daniel's thirteen. Tall for his age, blue-eyed, he has Dave's easy charm and icy way of turning it off. Alone in the bedroom, he's singing along to his radio earphones. His voice is high, sweet even in mimicry. He excels in math and science and hangs Black Hole posters all over his room where I once hung Natalie Wood.

Now I say good-bye to Irene, knowing she'll remember something later and call back.

"Did you hear anything more about the sniper?" she asks before hanging up.

"It happened because I was asleep."

"I don't get it. Was it one of your crazy students?"

My job demands that I be perfectly literal, steady as concrete, since I teach disturbed children. No humor, puns, asides. I finish a joke, lose speed, return to normal gear; they race ahead, overtake me, crash at a curve. Most of the time I give simple orders in an emotionless voice: "Put down that ruler, Tanya. Rulers are for measuring, not for striking other children."

Alex sets fires, but he's careful to choose self-limiting objects. He has burnt towels in a washroom, containing them in a sink. Once, he set fire to a window shade, burning it down to the circular drawstring where the flames stopped, nowhere to spread. The other children I teach are sullen and quiet twelve-year-olds, each with a diagnosis. We're most successful with delinquents like Craig. His minor life of crime is absorbed in building a defense against the biters, the kickers, the glass breakers.

In the morning Dave says hello. I no longer wake up when he gets into bed. Just before the alarm rings, he could walk in, undress and slip under the sheets, and I wouldn't know he hadn't slept with me. But this morning I can tell by the way he ignores the newspaper that he's had a bad night and that he wants to talk.

"I got in after one," he explains. "Wouldn't you know that as soon as I open the door the phone rings? It's for Daniel. I shout up the stairs to him. I ask him why he's up so late."

"What's it your business?" Daniel calls down.

"So I count to ten, Jerri, and decide not to kill him. I'll do something useful. I go outside and dig up some holes to plant the new rosebushes, but I feel stupid digging at two in the morning so I come inside and take a shower. Jeff's up too. He pours me a big glass of milk and we talk about when we were kids. He remembers us playing *The Count of Monte Cristo* in his yard in Spokane. I don't remember reading it, but he says I stood on the porch stairs and acted like the director."

"You're best at that," I tell him.

"Say something to Daniel this morning. He listens to you."

But Daniel's asleep when I'm ready to leave, and our garden looks like it's barely survived a meteor shower.

Rays of sun filtering through the leaded glass windows of the Shedd Aquarium intersect at the coral reef in the lobby. I'm in charge of Alex, the pyromaniac. Since my job will be easy in an aquarium, I relax as he presses his cheek to the huge convex glass of the coral reef. He shouts in pretended terror when a saw-nosed shark brushes past his face. Following him from room to room, I put my hand on his windbreaker when he allows me. Sometimes he brushes me away with a fly-flicking motion neither of us is supposed to acknowledge.

In the room of smaller tanks we now enter, the angelfish seem suspended in water. Only their undulating antennae indicate life. "They're shaped like triangles," I tell Alex, remembering how Daniel liked to distinguish the form of objects when he was younger. Alex drums his long fingers, nails bitten to the quick, against the glass. The fish aren't bothered.

"They like you," I tell him.

Inside their display a tiny ceramic diver stretches his hand in front of me. He's pointing outside of the tank. Water bubbles from his head. In the next tank two lamprey eels poke their rubbery heads out of a clay cylinder. Alex's laugh is so strong that I'm embarrassed by my own weak silence. Running from display to display, the carpeted floor absorbing his steps, Alex is the only moving object in the room of slow water-breathers. He lunges toward the angelfish, which never move. He darts to the eels, bobbing to their own ungainly rhythm. He shoots out into the hallway to press his face against the reef. Angelfish, eels, reef is his path all morning. Back at school Alex hands me a picture he's drawn, two angelfish facing each other, silver with black stripes, perfect triangles.

That evening Daniel stays at a friend's. The daily paper has dropped the sniper story though the local paper still claims he's at large.

"I wouldn't be surprised if the guy isn't a terrorist," Irene says.

"How do you know it's not a woman?"

I pour a bath, climb in and lean my head back on the clammy porcelain. In walks Jeff holding two tall gin and tonics on a tray.

"I don't drink." I smile.

He pours mine into the water. "Bathtub gin," he says. "May I join you?" He's already taken off his shoes. He's unbuttoning his shirt.

"Can I meet you later?" I ask.

This time Jeff's carrying teacups and some generic sandwich cookies I often give Daniel for lunch. I think of a cat I had when we lived in California that used to bring me dead wading birds, egrets and herons, as signs of devotion. I think of telling Jeff about her, but knowledge is only a complication.

"It's hard to believe I'll be leaving soon."

"Right."

"Too bad I can't stay."

"Let's not talk," I say, stirring my tea with a cookie. Then we both laugh without really knowing why.

As soon as Jeff leaves, I'll speak to Dave. I'll tell him it doesn't matter what he does with Donna. There's so much trouble in the world that a little more confusion can't hurt. If Dave tells me I'm generous, I'll leave him. If he knows to be quiet, maybe I'll let him stay.

From: ADULTERY

ANDRE DUBUS

In the winter and into the spring when snow melted first around the trunks of trees, and the ice on the Merrimack broke into chunks that floated seaward, and the river climbed and rushed, there was a girl. She came uninvited in Christmas season to a party that Edith spent a day preparing; her escort was uninvited too, a law student, a boring one, who came with a married couple who were invited. Later Edith would think of him: if he had to crash the party he should at least have been man enough to keep the girl he crashed with. Her name was Jeanne, she was from France, she was visiting friends in Boston. That was all she was doing: visiting. Edith did not know what part of France she was from nor what she did when she was there. Probably Jeanne told her that night while they stood for perhaps a quarter of an hour in the middle of the room and voices, sipping their drinks, nodding at each other, talking the way two very attractive women will talk at a party: Edith speaking and even answering while her real focus was on Jeanne's short black hair, her sensuous, indolent lips, her brown and mischievous eyes. Edith had talked with the law student long enough—less than a quarter of an hour—to know he wasn't Jeanne's lover and couldn't be; his confidence was still young, wistful, and vulnerable; and there was an impatience, a demand, about the amatory currents she felt flowing from Jeanne. She remarked all of this and recalled nothing they talked about. They parted like two friendly but competing hunters after meeting in the woods. For the rest of the night—while talking, while dancing—Edith watched the law student and the husbands lining up at the trough of Jeanne's accent, and she watched Jeanne's eyes, which appeared vacant until you looked closely at them and saw that they were selfish: Jeanne was watching herself.

And Edith watched Hank, and listened to him. Early in their marriage she had learned to do that. His intimacy with her was private; at their table and in their bed they talked; his intimacy with men was public, and when he was with them he spoke mostly to them, looked mostly at them, and she knew there were times when he was unaware that she or any other woman was in the room. She had long ago stopped resenting this; she had watched the other wives sitting together and talking to one another; she had watched them sit listening while couples were at a dinner table and the women couldn't group so they ate and listened to the men. Usually men who talked to women were trying to make love with them, and she could sense the other men's resentment at this distraction, as if during a hand of poker a man had left the table to phone his mistress. Of course she was able to talk at parties; she wasn't shy and no man had ever intentionally made her feel he was not interested in what she had to say; but willy-nilly they patronized her. As they listened to her she could sense their courtesy, their impatience for her to finish so they could speak again to their comrades. If she had simply given in to that patronizing, stopped talking because she was a woman, she might have become bitter. But she went further: she watched the men, and saw that it wasn't a matter of their not being interested in women. They weren't interested in each other either. At least not in what they said, their ideas; the ideas and witticisms were instead the equipment of friendly, even loving, competition, as for men with different interests were the bowling ball, the putter, the tennis racket. But it went deeper than that too: she finally saw that. Hank needed and loved men, and when he loved them it was because of what they thought and how they lived. He did not measure women that way; he measured them by their sexuality and good sense. He and his friends talked with one another because it was the only way they could show their love; they might reach out and take a woman's hand and stroke it while they leaned forward, talking to men; and their conversations were fields of mutual praise. It no longer bothered her. She knew that some women writhed under these conversations; they were usually women whose husbands rarely spoke to them with the intensity and attention they gave to men.

But that night, listening to Hank, she was frightened and angry. He and Jeanne were watching each other. He talked to the men but he was really talking to her; at first Edith thought he was showing off; but it was worse, more fearful: he was being received and he knew it and that is what gave his voice its exuberant lilt. His eyes met Jeanne's over a shoulder, over the rim of a lifted glass. When Jeanne left with the law student and the invited couple, Edith and Hank told them goodbye at the door. It was only the second time that night Edith and Jeanne had looked at each other and spoken; they smiled and voiced amenities; a drunken husband lurched into the group; his arm groped for Jeanne's waist and his head plunged downward to kiss her. She quickly cocked her head away, caught the kiss lightly on her cheek, almost dodged it completely. For an instant her eyes were impatient. Then that was gone. Tilted away from the husband's muttering face, she was looking at Hank. In her eyes Edith saw his passion. She reached out and put an arm about his waist; without looking at him or Jeanne she said goodnight to the law student and the couple. As the four of them went down the walk, shrugging against the cold, she could not look at Jeanne's back and hair; she watched the law student and wished him the disaster of bad grades. Be a bank teller, you bastard.

She did not see Jeanne again. In the flesh, that is. For now she saw her in dreams: not those of sleep which she could forget but her waking dreams. In the morning Hank went to his office at school to write; at noon he and Jack ran and then ate lunch; he taught all afternoon and then went to the health club for a sauna with Jack and afterward they stopped for a drink; at seven he came home. On Tuesdays and Thursdays he didn't have classes but he spent the afternoon at school in conferences with students; on Saturday mornings he wrote in his office and, because he was free of students that day, he often worked into the middle of the afternoon, then called Jack to say he was ready for the run, the sauna, the drinks. For the first time in her marriage Edith thought about how long and how often he was away from home. As she helped Sharon with her boots she saw Jeanne's brown eyes; they were attacking her; they were laughing at her; they sledded down the hill with her and Sharon.

When she became certain that Hank was Jeanne's lover she could not trust her certainty. In the enclosed days of winter she imagined too much. Like a spy, she looked for only one thing, and she could not tell if the wariness in his eyes and voice were truly there; making love with him she felt a distance in his touch, another concern in his heart; passionately she threw herself against that distance and wondered all the time if it existed only in her own quiet and fearful heart. Several times, after drinks at a party, she nearly asked Jack if Hank was always at school when he said he was. At home on Tuesday and Thursday and Saturday afternoons she wanted to call him. One Thursday she did. He didn't answer his office phone; it was a small school and the switchboard operator said if she saw him she'd tell him to call home. Edith was telling Sharon to get her coat, they would go to school to see Daddy, when he phoned. She asked him if he wanted to see a movie that night. He said they had seen everything playing in town and if she wanted to go to Boston he'd rather wait until the weekend. She said that was fine.

In April he and Jack talked about baseball and watched it on television and he started smoking Parliaments. She asked him why. They were milder, he said. He looked directly at her but she sensed he was forcing himself to, testing himself. For months she had imagined his infidelity and fought her imagination with the absence of evidence. Now she had that: she knew it was irrational but it was just rational enough to release the demons: they absorbed her: they gave her certainty. She remembered Jeanne holding a Parliament, waiting for one of the husbands to light it. She lasted three days. On a Thursday afternoon she called the school every hour, feeling the vulnerability of this final prideless crumbling, making her voice as casual as possible to the switchboard operator, even saying once it was nothing important, just something she wanted him to pick up on the way home, and when he got home at seven carrying a damp towel and smelling faintly of gin she knew he had got back in time for the sauna with Jack and had spent the afternoon in Jeanne's bed. She waited until after dinner, when Sharon was in bed. He sat at the kitchen table, talking to her while she cleaned the kitchen. It was a ritual of theirs. She asked him for a drink. Usually she didn't drink after dinner, and he was surprised. Then he said he'd join her. He gave her the bourbon, then sat at the table again.

"Are you having an affair with that phony French bitch?"

He sipped his drink, looked at her, and said: "Yes."

The talk lasted for days. That night it ended at three in the morning after, straddling him, she made love with him and fell into a sleep whose every moment, next morning, she believed she remembered.

She had slept four hours. When she woke to the news on the radio she felt she had not slept at all, that her mind had continued the talk with sleeping Hank. She did not want to get up. In bed she smoked while Hank showered and shaved. At breakfast he did not read the paper. He spoke to Sharon and watched Edith. She did not eat. When he was ready to leave, he leaned down and kissed her and said he loved her and they would talk again that night.

All day she knew what madness was, or she believed she was at least tasting it and at times she yearned for the entire feast. While she did her work and made lunch for Sharon and talked to her and put her to bed with a coloring book and tried to read the newspaper and then a magazine, she could not stop the voices in her mind: some of it repeated from last night, some drawn up from what she believed she had heard and spoken in her sleep, some in anticipation of tonight, living tonight before it was there, so that at two in the afternoon she was already at midnight and time was nothing but how much pain she could feel at once. When Sharon had been in bed for an hour without sleeping, Edith took her for a walk and tried to listen to her and said yes and no and I don't know, what do you think? and even heard most of what Sharon said and all the time the voices would not stop. All last night while awake and sleeping and all day she had believed it was because Jeanne was pretty and Hank was a man. Like any cliché, it was easy to live with until she tried to; now she began to realize how little she knew about Hank and how much she suspected and feared, and that night after dinner which she mostly drank she tucked in Sharon and came down to the kitchen and began asking questions. He told her he would stop seeing Jeanne and there was nothing more to talk about; he spoke of privacy. But she had to know everything he felt; she persisted, she harried, and finally he told her she'd better be as tough as her questions were, because she was going to get the answers.

Which were: he did not believe in monogamy. Fidelity, she said. You see? he said. You distort it. He was a faithful husband. He had been discreet, kept his affair secret, had not risked her losing face. He loved her and had taken nothing from her. She accused him of having a double standard and he said no; no, she was as free as she was before she met him. She asked him how long he had felt this way, had he always been like this or was it just some French bullshit he had picked up this winter. He had always felt this way. By now she could not weep. Nor rage either. All she could feel and say was: Why didn't I ever know any of this? You never asked, he said.

It was, she thought, like something bitter from Mother Goose: the woman made the child, the child made the roof, the roof made the woman, and the child went away. Always she had done her housework quickly and easily; by ten-thirty on most mornings she had done what had to be done. She was not one of those women whose domesticity became an obsession; it was work that she neither liked nor disliked and, when other women complained, she was puzzled and amused and secretly believed their frustration had little to do with scraping plates or pushing a vacuum cleaner over a rug. Now in April and May an act of will got her out of bed in the morning. The air in the house was against her: it seemed wet and gray and heavy, heavier than fog, and she pushed through it to the bathroom where she sat staring at the floor or shower curtain long after she was done; then she moved to the kitchen and as she prepared breakfast the air pushed down on her arms and against her body. *I am beating eggs*, she said to herself, and she looked down at the fork in her hand, yolk dripping from the tines into the eggs as their swirling ceased and they lay still in the bowl. *I am beating eggs.* Then she jabbed the fork in again. At breakfast Hank read the paper. Edith talked to Sharon and ate because she had to, because it was morning, it was time to eat, and she glanced at Hank's face over the newspaper, listened to the crunching of his teeth on toast, and told herself: *I am talking to Sharon.* She kept her voice sweet, motherly, attentive.

Then breakfast was over and she was again struck by the seductive waves of paralysis that had washed over her in bed, and she stayed at the table. Hank kissed her (she turned her lips to him, they met his, she did not kiss him) and went to the college. She read the paper and drank coffee and smoked while Sharon played with toast. She felt she would fall asleep at the table; Hank would return in the afternoon to find her sleeping there among the plates and cups and glasses while Sharon played alone in a ditch somewhere down the road. So once again she rose through an act of will, watched Sharon brushing her teeth (*I am watching . . .*), sent her to the cartoons on television, and then slowly, longing for sleep, she washed the skillet and saucepan (*always scramble eggs in a saucepan*, her mother had told her; *they stand deeper than in a skillet and they'll cook softer*) and scraped the plates and put them and the glasses and cups and silverware in the dishwasher.

Then she carried the vacuum cleaner upstairs and made the bed Hank had left after she had, and as she leaned over to tuck in the sheet she wanted to give in to the lean, to collapse in slow motion face down on the half-made bed and lie there until—there had been times in her life when she had wanted to sleep until something ended. Unmarried in Iowa, when she missed her period she wanted to sleep until she knew whether she was or not. Now *until* meant nothing. No matter how often or how long she slept she would wake to the same house, the same heavy air that worked against her every move. She made Sharon's bed and started the vacuum cleaner. Always she had done that quickly, not well enough for her mother's eye, but her mother was a Windex housekeeper: a house was not done unless the windows were so clean you couldn't tell whether they were open or closed; but her mother had a cleaning woman. The vacuum cleaner interfered with the cartoons and Sharon came up to tell her and Edith said she wouldn't be long and told Sharon to put on her bathing suit—it was a nice day and they would go to the beach. But the cleaning took her longer than it had before, when she had moved quickly from room to room, without lethargy or boredom but a sense of anticipation, the way she felt when she did other work which required neither skill nor concentration, like chopping onions and grating cheese for a meal she truly wanted to cook.

Now, while Sharon went downstairs again and made lemonade and poured it in the thermos and came upstairs and went down again and came up and said yes there was a little mess and went downstairs and wiped it up, Edith pushed the vacuum cleaner and herself through the rooms and down the hall, and went downstairs and started in the living room while Sharon's voice tugged at her as strongly as hands gripping her clothes, and she clamped her teeth on the sudden shrieks that rose in her throat and told herself: *Don't: she's not the problem*; and she thought of the women in supermarkets and on the street, dragging and herding and all but cursing their children along (one day she had seen a woman kick her small son's rump as she pulled him into a drugstore), and she thought of the women at parties, at dinners, or on blankets at the beach while they watched their children in the waves, saying: *I'm so damned bored with talking to children all day—no*, she told herself, *she's not the problem.* Finally she finished her work, yet she felt none of the relief she had felt before; the air in the house was like water now as she moved through it up the stairs to the bedroom, where she undressed and put on her bathing suit. Taking Sharon's hand and the windbreakers and thermos and blanket, she left the house and blinked in the late morning sun and wondered near-prayerfully when this would end, this dread disconnection between herself and what she was doing. At night making love with Hank she thought of him with Jeanne, and her heart, which she thought was beyond breaking, broke again, quickly, easily, as if there weren't much to break anymore, and fell into mute and dreary anger, the dead end of love's grief.

In the long sunlit evenings and the nights of May the talk was sometimes philosophical, sometimes dark and painful, drawing from him details about him and Jeanne; she believed if she possessed the details she would dispossess Jeanne of Hank's love. But she knew that wasn't her only reason. Obsessed by her pain, she had to plunge more deeply into it, feel all of it again and again. But most of the talk was abstract, and most of it was by Hank. When she spoke of divorce he calmly told her they had a loving, intimate marriage. They were, he said, simply experiencing an honest and healthful breakthrough. She listened to him talk about the unnatural boundaries of lifelong monogamy. He remained always calm. Cold, she thought. She could no longer find his heart.

At times she hated him. Watching him talk she saw his life: with his work he created his own harmony, and then he used the people he loved to relax with. Probably it was not exploitative; probably it was the best he could do. And it was harmony she had lost. Until now her marriage had been a circle, like its gold symbol on her finger. Wherever she went she was still inside it. It had a safe, gentle circumference, and mortality and the other perils lay outside of it. Often now while Hank slept she lay awake and tried to pray. She wanted to fall in love with God. She wanted His fingers to touch her days, to restore meaning to those simple tasks which now drained her spirit. On those nights when she tried to pray she longed to leave the world: her actions would appear secular but they would be her communion with God. Cleaning the house would be an act of forgiveness and patience under His warm eyes. But she knew it was no use: she had belief, but not faith: she could not bring God under her roof and into her life. He waited her death.

Nightly and fearfully now, as though Hank's adulterous heart had opened a breach and let it in to stalk her, she thought of death. One night they went with Jack and Terry Linhart to Boston to hear Judy Collins. The concert hall was filled and darkened and she sat in the sensate, audible silence of listening people and watched Judy under the spotlight in a long lavender gown, her hair falling over one shoulder as she lowered her face over the guitar. Soon Edith could not hear the words of the songs. Sadly she gazed at Judy's face, and listened to the voice, and thought of the voice going out to the ears of all those people, all those strangers, and she thought how ephemeral was a human voice, and how death not only absorbed the words in the air, but absorbed as well the act of making the words, and the time it took to say them. She saw Judy as a small bird singing on a wire, and above her the hawk circled. She remembered reading once of an old man who had been working for twenty-five years sculpting, out of a granite mountain in South Dakota, a 563-foot-high statue of Chief Crazy Horse. She thought of Hank and the novel he was writing now, and as she sat beside him her soul withered away from him and she hoped he would fail, she hoped he would burn this one too: she saw herself helping him, placing alternate pages in the fire. Staring at the face above the lavender gown, she strained to receive the words and notes into her body.

She had never lied to Hank and now everything was a lie. Beneath the cooking of a roast, the still-affectionate chatting at dinner, the touch of their flesh, was the fact of her afternoons ten miles away in a New Hampshire woods where, on a blanket among shading pines and hemlocks, she lay in sin-quickened heat with Jack Linhart. Her days were delightfully strange, she thought. Hank's betrayal had removed her from the actions that were her life; she had performed them like a weary and disheartened dancer. Now, glancing at Hank reading, she took clothes from the laundry basket at her feet and folded them on the couch, and the folding of a warm towel was a manifestation of her deceit. And, watching him across the room, she felt her separation from him taking shape, filling the space between them like a stone. Within herself she stroked and treasured her lover. She knew she was doing the same to the self she had lost in April.

There was a price to pay. When there had been nothing to lie about in their marriage and she had not lied, she had always felt nestled with Hank; but with everyone else, even her closest friends, she had been aware of that core of her being that no one knew. Now she felt that with Hank. With Jack she recognized yet leaped into their passionate lie: they were rarely together more than twice a week; apart, she longed for him, talked to him in her mind, and vengefully saw him behind her closed eyes as she moved beneath Hank. When she was with Jack their passion burned and distorted their focus. For two hours on the blanket they made love again and again, they made love too much, pushing their bodies to consume the yearning they had borne and to delay the yearning that was waiting. Sometimes under the trees she felt like tired meat. The quiet air which she had broken in the first hour with moans now absorbed only their heavy breath. At those moments she saw with detached clarity that they were both helpless, perhaps even foolish. Jack wanted to escape his marriage; she wanted to live with hers; they drove north to the woods and made love. Then they dressed and drove back to what had brought them there.

This was the first time in her life she had committed herself to sin, and there were times when she felt her secret was venomous. Lying beside Terry at the beach she felt more adulterous than when she lay with Jack, and she believed her sun-lulled conversation was somehow poisoning her friend. When she held Sharon, salty and cold-skinned from the sea, she felt her sin flowing with the warmth of her body into the small wet breast. But more often she was proud. She was able to sin and love at the same time. She was more attentive to Sharon than she had been in April. She did not have to struggle to listen to her, to talk to her. She felt cleansed. And looking at Terry's long red hair as she bent over a child, she felt both close to her yet distant. She did not believe women truly had friends among themselves; school friendships dissolved into marriages; married women thought they had friends until they got divorced and discovered other women were only wives drawn together by their husbands. As much as she and Terry were together, they were not really intimate; they instinctively watched each other. She was certain that Terry would do what she was doing. A few weeks ago she would not have known that. She was proud that she knew it now.

With Hank she loved her lie. She kept it like a fire: some evenings after an afternoon with Jack she elaborately fanned it, looking into Hank's eyes and talking of places she had gone while the sitter stayed with Sharon; at other times she let it burn low, was evasive about how she had spent her day, and when the two couples were together she bantered with Jack, teased him. Once Jack left his pack of Luckies in her car and she brought them home and smoked them. Hank noticed but said nothing. When two cigarettes remained in the pack she put it on the coffee table and left it there. One night she purposely made a mistake: after dinner, while Hank watched a ball game on television, she drank gin while she cleaned the kitchen. She had drunk gin and tonic before dinner and wine with the flounder and now she put tonic in the gin, but not much. From the living room came the announcer's voice, and now and then Hank spoke. She hated his voice; she knew she did not hate him; if she did, she would be able to act, to leave him. She hated his voice tonight because he was talking to ballplayers on the screen and because there was no pain in it while in the kitchen her own voice keened without sound and she worked slowly and finished her drink and mixed another, the gin now doing what she had wanted it to: dissolving all happiness, all peace, all hope for it with Hank and all memory of it with Jack, even the memory of that very afternoon under the trees. Gin-saddened, she felt beyond tears, at the bottom of some abyss where there was no emotion save the quivering knees and fluttering stomach and cold-shrouded heart that told her she was finished. She took the drink into the living room and stood at the door and watched him looking at the screen over his lifted can of beer. He glanced at her, then back at the screen. One hand fingered the pack of Luckies on the table, but he did not take one.

"I wish you hadn't stopped smoking," she said. "Sometimes I think you did it so you'd outlive me."

He looked at her, told her with his eyes that she was drunk, and turned back to the game.

"I've been having an affair with Jack." He looked at her, his eyes unchanged, perhaps a bit more interested; nothing more. His lips showed nothing, except that she thought they seemed ready to smile. "We go up to the woods in New Hampshire in the afternoons. Usually twice a week. I like it. I started it. I went after him, at a party. I told him about Jeanne. I kept after him. I knew he was available because he's unhappy with Terry. For a while he was worried about you but I told him you wouldn't mind anyway. He's still your friend, if that worries you. Probably more yours than mine. You don't even look surprised. I suppose you'll tell me you've known it all the time."

"It wasn't too hard to pick up."

"So it really wasn't French bullshit. I used to want another child. A son. I wouldn't want to now: have a baby in this."

"Come here."

For a few moments, leaning against the doorjamb, she thought of going upstairs and packing her clothes and driving away. The impulse was rooted only in the blur of gin. She knew she would get no farther than the closet where her clothes hung. She walked to the couch and sat beside him. He put his arm around her; for a while she sat rigidly, then she closed her eyes and eased against him and rested her head on his shoulder.

From: MARRY ME

John Updike

When they first began to make love, she had felt through his motions the habitual responses his wife must make; while locked in this strange man's embrace she struggled jealously against the outline of the other woman. On her part she bore the impress of Richard's sexual style, so that in the beginning four contending persons seemed involved on the sofa or in the sand, and a confused, half-Lesbian excitement would enclose her. Now these blurs were burned away. On the brightening edge of the long June day that followed the third night they had ever spent together, Jerry and Sally made love lucidly, like Adam and Eve when the human world was of two halves purely. She watched his face, and involuntarily cried out, pierced by the discovery, "Jerry, your eyes are so sad!"

The crooked teeth of his grin seemed Satanic. "How can they be sad when I'm so happy?"

"They're *so* sad, Jerry."

"You shouldn't watch people's eyes when they make love."

"I always do."

"Then I'll close mine."

Oh Sally, my lost only Sally, let me say now, now before we both forget, while the spark still glitters on the waterfall, that I loved you, that the sight of you shamed my eyes. You were a territory where I went on tiptoe to steal a magic mirror. You were a princess married to an ogre. I would go to meet you as a knight, to rescue you, and would become instead the dragon, and ravish you. You weighed me out in jewels, though ashes were what I could afford. Do you remember how, in our first room, on the second night, I gave you a bath and scrubbed your face and hands and long arms with the same methodical motions I used on my children? I was trying to tell you then. I was a father. Our love of children implies our loss of them. What a lazy lovely naked child you were, my mistress and momentary wife; your lids were lowered, your cheek rested on the steaming sheet of bathwater. Can I forget, forget though I live forever in Heaven among the chariots whose wheels are all eyes giving God the glory, how I saw you step from a tub, your body abruptly a waterfall? Like a man you tucked a towel about your woman's hips, and had me enter the water your flesh had charmed to a silvery opacity. I became your child. With a drenched blinding cloth that searched out even the hollows of my ears, you, my mother, my slave, dissolved me in tender abrasions. I forgot, sank. And we dried each other's beaded backs, and went to the bed as if to sleep instantly, two obedient children dreaming in a low tent drumming with the excluded rain.

*

Later she wondered how she could have been so blind, and blind so long. The signs were abundant: the sand, his eccentric comings and goings, his giving up smoking, his triumphant exuberance whenever Sally was at the same party, the tender wifely touch (this glimpse had stung at the time, to endure in Ruth's memory) with which Sally on one occasion had picked up Jerry's wrist, inviting him to dance. Jerry's obsession with death the spring before had seemed to her so irrational, so unreachable, that she dismissed as also mysterious his new behavior: his new timbre and strut, his fits of ill temper with the children, his fits of affection with her, the hungry introspective tone he brought to their private conversations, his insomnia, the easing of his physical demands on her, and a new cool authority in bed, so that at moments it seemed she was with Richard again. How could she have been so blind? At first she thought that, having gazed so long at her own guilt, she mistook for an afterimage what was in truth a fresh development. She admitted to herself, then, what she could never admit to Jerry, that she did not think him capable of it. . . .

Jerry asked for a divorce on a Sunday, the Sunday after a week in which he had been two days in Washington, and had returned to her in an atmosphere of hazard, on a late flight. There had been a delay, the airlines were jammed up, and she met plane after plane at LaGuardia. When at last his familiar silhouette with its short hair and thin shoulders cut through the muddled lights of the landing field and hurried toward her, her heart surprised her with a groveling gladness. Had she been a dog, she would have jumped and licked his face; being only a wife, she let herself be kissed, led him to the car, and listened as he described his trip—the State Department, a hurried visit to the Vermeers in the National Gallery, his relative lack of insomnia in the hotel, the inadequate gifts for the children he bought at a drugstore, the maddening wait in the airport. As the city confusion diminished behind them, his talking profile, in the warm vault of the car, shed its halo of wonder for her, and by the time they crackled to a stop in their driveway, both felt tired; they had chicken soup and bourbon and fumbled into a cold bed. Yet afterward this homecoming of his was to seem enchanted, a last glimpse of solid headland before, that rainy Sunday afternoon, she embarked on the nightmare sea that became her habitat.

In the morning, she and the children went to the beach. Jerry wanted to go to church. The summer services began at nine-thirty and ended at ten-thirty. She did not think it fair to the children to make them wait that long, especially since the pattern of the summer days was to dawn clear and cloud over by noon. So they dropped him off in his good suit and drove on.

The clouds materialized earlier than usual; little upright puffs at first, like puffs of smoke from a locomotive starting its run around the horizon, then clouds, increasingly structural and opaque, castles, continents that, overhead, grew as they moved, keeping the sun behind them. Waiting for the gaps of sunshine between the clouds was a game for the beach mothers. The clouds blew eastward, so their eyes scouted the west, where a swathe of advancing gold would first ignite the roofs of the cottages on Jacob's Point; then the great green water tower that supplied the cottages would be liberated into light, and like an arrived Martian spaceship the egg of metal on its stilts would glow; then like an onrushing field of unearthly wheat the brightness would roll, in steady jerks like strides, up the mile of sand, and overhead the sun would burn free of the struggling tendrils at the cloud's edge and skyey loops of iridescence would be spun between the eyelashes of the mothers. On this Sunday morning the gaps between the clouds closed more quickly than usual and by eleven-thirty it was clearly going to rain. Ruth and the children went home. They found Jerry sitting in the living room reading the Sunday paper. He had taken off his suit coat and loosened the knot of his tie, but his hair, still combed flat with water, made him look odd to Ruth. He seemed distracted, brittle, hostile; he acted as if they personally had consumed the few hours of beach weather there would be that day. But often he was irritable after attending church.

She took the roast out of the oven and all except Jerry ate Sunday dinner in bathing suits. This was the one meal of the week for which Jerry asked grace. As he began, "Heavenly Father," Geoffrey, who was being taught bedtime prayers, said aloud, "Dear God . . ." Joanna and Charlie burst into giggling. Jerry hurried his blessing through the interference, and Geoffrey, eyes tight shut, fat hands clasped at his plate, tried to repeat it after him and, unable, whimpered, "I can't *say* it!"

"*Amen,*" Jerry said and, with stiff fingers, slapped Geoffrey on the top of his head. "Shut *up.*" Earlier that week the boy had broken his collarbone. His shoulders were pulled back by an Ace bandage; he was tender all over.

Swallowing a sob, Geoffrey protested, "You said it too *fast!*"

Joanna explained to him, "You're stupid. You think you're supposed to say grace after Daddy."

Charlie turned and a gleeful taunting sound, "K-k-k," scraped from the roof of his mouth.

The insults were coming too fast for Geoffrey to absorb; he overflowed. His face blurred and crumpled into tears.

"Jerry, I'm amazed," Ruth said. "That was a sick thing to do."

Jerry picked up his fork and threw it at her—not at her, over her head, through the doorway into the kitchen. Joanna and Charlie peeked at each other and their cheeks puffed out in identical smothered explosions. "Goddamn it all," Jerry said, "I'd rather say grace in a pigpen. You all sitting here stark naked."

"The child was trying to be good," Ruth said. "He doesn't understand the difference between grace and prayers."

"Then why the fuck don't you teach him? If he had any decent even half-ass Christian kind of a mother he'd know enough not to interrupt. *Geoffrey,*" Jerry turned to say, "you *must* stop crying, to make your collarbone stop hurting."

Stunned by his father's unremittingly angry tone, the child tried to enunciate a sentence: "I—I—I—"

"I—I—I—" Joanna mocked.

Geoffrey screamed as if stabbed.

Jerry stood and tried to reach Joanna to slap her. She shied away, upsetting her chair. Something about her expression of terror made Jerry laugh. As if this callous laugh released all the malign spirits at the table, Charlie turned, said "Crybaby," and punched Geoffrey in the arm, jarring his collarbone. Before the child could react, his mother screamed for him; Charlie shouted, "I forgot, I forgot!" Wild to stop this torrent of injury at its source, Ruth, still holding the serving spoon, left her place and moved around the table, so swiftly she felt she was skating. She swung the hand not holding the spoon at Jerry's face. He saw it coming and hid his face between his shoulders and hands, showing her the blank hairy top of his skull, with its helpless amount of gray. His skull was harder than her hand; she jammed her thumb; pain pressed behind her eyes. Blindly she flailed, again and once again, at the obstinate lump of his cowering head, unable with one hand, while the other still clutched the serving spoon, to claw her way into his eyes, his poisonous mouth. The fourth time she swung, he stood up and caught her wrist in midair and squeezed it so hard the fine bones ground together.

"You pathetic frigid bitch," he said levelly. "Don't touch me again." He gave each word an equal weight, and his face, uncovered at last, showed a deadly level calm, though flushed—the face of a corpse, rouged. The nightmare had begun.

PART V

THE BROKEN BED

THERE'S AN OLD . . .

Bobbie Louise Hawkins

There's an old Texas saying that I think I may be the only one who remembers it.

It goes "I've enjoyed just about as much of this as I can stand."

It's a magic formula that lets you head for the door past all the frenzy of any minute now it's going to get significant. It's a way to say that whatever you had in mind this ain't it. It lets you stop eating slop that needs a palate and a vocabulary.

I've enjoyed just about as much of this as I can stand.

LOVE TOO LONG

Barry Hannah

My head's burning off and I got a heart about to bust out of my ribs.
All I can do is move from chair to chair with my cigarette. I wear
shades. I can't read a magazine. Some days I take my binoculars and
look out in the air. They laid me off. I can't find work. My wife's
got a job and she takes flying lessons. When she comes over the
house in her airplane, I'm afraid she'll screw up and crash.

I got to get back to work and get dulled out again. I got to be a
man again. You can't walk around the house drinking coffee and
beer all day, thinking about her taking her brassiere off. We been
married and divorced twice. Sometimes I wish I had a sport. I bought
a croquet set on credit at Penney's. First day I got so tired of it I
knocked the balls off in the weeds and they're out there rotting,
mildew all over them, I bet, but I don't want to see.

Some afternoons she'll come right over the roof of the house and
turn the plane upside down. Or maybe it's her teacher. I don't know
how far she's got along. I'm afraid to ask, on the every third night
or so she comes in the house. I want to rip her arm off. I want to
sleep in her uterus with my foot hanging out. Some nights she lets
me lick her ears and knees. I can't talk about it. It's driving me into
a sorry person. Maybe Hobe Lewis would let me pump gas and sell
bait at his service station. My mind's around to where I'd do nigger
work now.

I'd do Jew work, Swiss, Spanish. Anything.

She never took anything. She just left. She can be a lot of
things—she got a college degree. She always had her own bank account. She wanted a better house than this house, but she was patient. She'd eat any food with a sweet smile. She moved through
the house with a happy pace, like it meant something.

I think women are closer to God than we are. They walk right
out there like they know what they're doing. She moved around the

house, reading a book. I never saw her sitting down much, unless she's drinking. She can drink you under the table. Then she'll get up on the spot of eight and fix you an omelet with sardines and peppers. She taught me to like this, a little hot ketchup on the edge of the plate.

When she walks through the house, she has a roll from side to side. I've looked at her face too many times when she falls asleep. The omelet tastes like her. I go crazy.

There're things to be done in this world, she said. This love affair went on too long. It's going to make us both worthless, she said. Our love is not such a love as to swell the heart. So she said. She was never unfaithful to me that I know. And if I knew it, I wouldn't care because I know she's sworn to me.

I am her always and she is my always and that's the whole trouble.

For two years I tried to make her pregnant. It didn't work. The doctor said she was too nervous to hold a baby, first time she ever had an examination. She was a nurse at the hospital and brought home all the papers that she forged whenever I needed a report. For example, when I first got on as a fly in elevated construction. A fly can crawl and balance where nobody else can. I was always working at the thing I feared the most. I tell you true. But it was high pay out there at the beam joints. Here's the laugh. I was light and nimble, but the sun always made me sick up there under its nose. I got a permanent suntan. Some people think I'm Arab. I was good.

When I was in the Navy, I finished two years at Bakersfield Junior College in California. Which is to say, I can read and feel fine things and count. Those women who cash your check don't cause any distress to me, all their steel, accents and computers. I'll tell you what I liked that we studied at Bakersfield. It was old James Joyce and his book *The Canterbury Tales.* You wouldn't have thought anybody would write "A fart that well nigh blinded Absalom" in ancient days. All those people hopping and humping at night, framming around, just like last year at Ollie's party that she and I left when they got into threesomes and Polaroids. Because we loved each other too much. She said it was something you'd be sorry about the next morning.

Her name is Jane.

Once I cheated on her. I was drunk in Pittsburgh. They bragged on me for being a fly in the South. This girl and I were left together in a fancy apartment of the Oakland section. The girl did everything. I was homesick during the whole time for Jane. When you get down to it, there isn't much to do. It's just arms and legs. It's not worth a damn.

The first thing Jane did was go out on that houseboat trip with that movie star who was using this town we were in in South Carolina to make his comeback film. I can't tell his name, but he's short and his face is old and piglike now instead of the way it was in the days he was piling up the money. He used to be a star and now he was trying to return as a main partner in a movie about hatred and backstabbing in Dixie. Everybody on board made crude passes at her. I wasn't invited. She'd been chosen as an extra for the movie. The guy who chose her made animalistic comments to her. This was during our first divorce. She jumped off the boat and swam home. But that's how good-looking she is. There was a cameraman on the houseboat who saw her swimming and filmed her. It was in the movie. I sat there and watched her when they showed it local.

The next thing she did was take up with an architect who had a mustache. He was designing her dream house for free and she was putting money in the bank waiting on it. She claimed he never touched her. He just wore his mustache and a gold medallion around his neck and ate yogurt and drew houses all day. She worked for him as a secretary and landscape consultant. Jane was always good about trees, bushes, flowers and so on. She's led many a Spare That Tree campaign almost on her own. She'll write a letter to the editor in a minute.

Only two buildings I ever worked on pleased her. She said the rest looked like death standing up.

The architect made her wear his ring on her finger. I saw her wearing it on the street in Biloxi, Mississippi, one afternoon, coming out of a store. There she was with a new hairdo and a narrow halter and by God I was glad I saw. I was in a bus on the way to the Palms House hotel we were putting up after the hurricane. I almost puked out my kidneys with the grief.

Maybe I need to go to church, I said to myself. I can't stand this alone. I wished I was Jesus. Somebody who never drank or wanted nooky. Or knew Jane.

She and the architect were having some fancy drinks together at a beach lounge when his ex-wife from New Hampshire showed up naked with a single-shotgun gun that was used in the Franco-Prussian War—it was a quaint piece hanging on the wall in their house when he was at Dartmouth—and screaming. The whole bar cleared out, including Jane. The ex-wife tried to get the architect with the bayonet. She took off the whole wall mural behind him and he was rolling around under tables. Then she tried to cock the gun. The policeman who'd come in got scared and left. The architect got out and threw himself into the arms of Jane, who was out on the patio thinking she was safe. He wanted to die holding his love. Jane didn't want to die in any fashion. Here comes the nude woman, screaming with the cocked gun.

"Hey, hey," says Jane. "Honey, you don't need a gun. You got a hell of a body. I don't see how Lawrence could've left that."

The woman lowered the gun. She was dripping with sweat and pale as an egg out there in the bright sun over the sea. Her hair was nearabout down to her ass and her face was crazy.

"Look at her, Lawrence," said Jane.

The guy turned around and looked at his ex-wife. He whispered: "She was lovely. But her personality was a disease. She was killing me. It was slow murder."

When I got there, the naked woman was on Lawrence's lap. Jane and a lot of people were standing around looking at them. They'd fallen back in love. Lawrence was sucking her breast. She wasn't a bad-looking sight. The long gun lay off in the sand. No law was needed. I was just humiliated. I tried to get away before Jane saw me, but I'd been drinking and smoking a lot the night before and I gave out this ninety-nine-year-old cough. Everybody on the patio except Lawrence and his woman looked around.

But in Mobile we got it going together again. She taught art in a private school where they admitted high-type Negroes only. And I was a fly on the city's first high-rise parking garage. We had so much money we ate out even for breakfast. She thought she was pregnant for a while and I was happy as hell. I wanted a heavenly blessing—as the pastors say—with Jane. I thought it would form the living chain between us that would never be broken. It would be beyond biology and into magic. But it was only eighteen months in Mobile and we left on a rainy day in the winter without her pregnant. She was just lean and her eyes were brown diamonds like always, and she had begun having headaches.

Let me tell you about Jane drinking punch at one of the parties at the University of Florida where she had a job. Some hippie had put LSD in it and there was nothing but teacher types in the house, leaning around, commenting on the azaleas and the evil of the administration. I never took any punch because I brought my own dynamite in the car. Here I was, complimenting myself on holding my own with these profs. One of the profs looked at Jane in her long gown, not knowing she was with me. He said to another: "She's pleasant to look at, as far as *that* goes." I said to him that I'd heard she was smart too, and had taken the all-Missouri swimming meet when she was just a junior in high school. Another guy spoke up. The LSD had hit. I didn't know.

"I'd like to stick her brain. I'll bet her brain would be better than her crack. I'd like to have her hair falling around my honker. I'd love to pull on those ears with silver loops hanging around, at, on, above—what is it?—*them.*"

This guy was the chairman of the whole department.

"If I was an earthquake, I'd take care of her," said a fellow with a goatee and an ivory filter for his cigarette.

"Beauty is fleeting," said his ugly wife. "What stays is your basic endurance of pettiness and ennui. And perhaps, most of all, your ability to hide farts."

"Oh, Sandra!" says her husband. "I thought I'd taught you better. You went to Vassar, you bitch, so you wouldn't say things like that."

"I went to Vassar so I'd meet a dashing man with a fortune and a huge cucumber. Then I came back home, to assholing Florida and you," she said. "Washing socks, underwear, arguing with some idiot at Sears."

I met Jane at the punch bowl. She was socking it down and chatting with the librarian honcho who was her boss. He was a

Scotsman with a mountain of book titles for his mind. Jane said he'd never read a book in thirty years, but he knew the hell out of their names. Jane truly liked to talk to fat and old guys best of all. She didn't ever converse much with young men. Her ideal of a conversation was when sex was nowhere near it at all. She hated all her speech with her admirers because every word was shaded with lust implications. One of her strange little dreams was to be sort of a cloud with eyes, ears, mouth. I walked up on them without their seeing and heard her say: "I love you. I'd like to pet you to death." She put her hand on his poochy stomach.

So then I was hitting the librarian in the throat and chest. He was a huge person, looked something like a statue of some notable gentleman in ancient history. I couldn't do anything to bring him down. He took all my blows without batting an eye.

"You great bastard!" I yelled up there. "I believed in You on and off all my life! There better be something up there like Jane or I'll humiliate You! I'll swine myself all over this town. I'll appear in public places and embarrass the shit out of You, screaming that I'm a Christian!"

We divorced the second time right after that.

Now we're in Richmond, Virginia. They laid me off. Inflation or recession or whatever rubbed me out. Oh, it was nobody's fault, says the boss. I got to sell my third car off myself, says he. At my house, we don't eat near the meat we used to, says he.

So I'm in this house with my binoculars, moving from chair to chair with my cigarettes. She flies over my house upside down every afternoon. Is she saying she wants me so much she'd pay for a plane to my yard? Or is she saying: Look at this, I never gave a damn for anything but fun in the air?

Nothing in the world matters but you and your woman. Friendship and politics go to hell. My friend Dan three doors down, who's also unemployed, comes over when he can make the price of a six-pack.

It's not the same.

I'm going to die from love.

TO HAVE & TO HOLD

Christine Schutt

I have accidents in the Fifth Avenue kitchen—cuts, falls, scaldings. What could I be thinking of when I scissor through a plugged cord? My sleeve catches fire on the burner, and all I do is watch its crinkling into nothing. Fast as paper, it burns, filling the kitchen with a stink of burnt hair, my hair, and that is what finally makes me run for the salt, the smell of me catching fire.

Worse things happen in the kitchen—my husband tells me he is in love with someone else, and what do I do? I go out and buy he- and she-gerbils to make us feel more like a family.

I hate the gerbils. Nothing about them is cute; they twitch and gnaw. The animals live in a plastic, night-glow cage set next to the stove, because this kitchen is small, even if it is on Fifth Avenue, and here they scrabble and play and shred their tray paper—dirty animals that eat their own tails.

The girl was the first at it. One morning I found her dragging her rump through the shavings, scooting around the cage, past the boy. His tail was whole; hers was stubbed, pink, wet-looking. I saw her dizzying chase of it. I thought, maybe this is a mating ritual, maybe this is natural. What do I know? Except a few days later, some of the boy's tail was missing; now both of these cannibals are nearly tailless.

This eating has nothing to do with making baby gerbils. I don't think they even like one another. When the gerbils escape from their cage, and they escape every night, squiggling through a gnawed-away part, I never find them huddling. I might find the boy under the sink, the girl near the warm and coiled back of the refrigerator. I catch them up with a dishcloth; I can't stand to touch these silly savages—who could?—especially since they started eating themselves.

I want to know why my husband picked this woman to love, this woman who has been in my kitchen, who once helped me dry the silverware. This woman my husband loves is always, always on my mind here in the kitchen, where she once hugged me good-bye in her fur and pearls. I split open the coals of feeling to feel the buckle on her belt heat up in my hand. I touch her skirt and the stitched spine of her high heels. I am in a kind of hurry. I snatch at her nylons, her bag. Her bag is the color of toffee; I could eat it, I could gnaw off the clip to where the lining riffles with the scent of her, perfume and pennies and lipstick. Would she want to trade her clothes for my kitchen? Does she want babies?

The Fifth Avenue kitchen is so bright and clean. My husband says the counters are still gritty with cleanser. He says the food's embarrassed to be seen.

I admit it, I am driven. Last thing I do each night is wash my floor. One of the reasons the gerbils are such a problem is that they are so ridiculously dirty.

I should get out of the kitchen.

I should set the gerbils free.

I should let the scrub pads rust and the inky vouchers stain the counters. I should mess up.

My husband says the fridge door reads like an advertisement. He says the door is not a bulletin board. He says, Why don't you get a datebook, act like other people?

I thought that's what I was doing—acting like other people. So much space glinting off the white dune of Fifth Avenue, I thought, other people must want this, but not, it seems, the woman my husband wants. She, he says, wants to pitch her umbrella elsewhere.

Where?

I am standing here with the gerbils, who are loose again and scrabbling over my bare feet.

There is broken glass on the floor.

I can't help what happens.

The kitchen is sprung like an army knife, and I am in a hurry.

I have thrown open the window and am moving fast to catch these gerbils with only my hands. First the girl, who is trembling and trying to nip me, I swing her by the leg and out the window, she is gone. Then I make for the boy, hiding in a corner.

I think he thinks he is safe; he doesn't move. Lost, pointless, filthy boy.

I toss him underhand—just like rice.

DRIVE, IT SAID

Geoffrey Young

I was in love with a song, kept blurting it out, didn't know the words, maybe something about gazing at stars, I do that too, the constellations like old friends, but I might have been in a hot desert wearing snowshoes, the song would not let me go, I was like someone in love, that was the name of the tune in fact, I played it on the trumpet for the ghost of Kenny Dorham, even missing the highest note out of respect for Kenny's "flat on his ass" style, this song was leading me to something, wasn't it? There was no love in my life, or there *was* love, children are loves, brothers and sisters and old friends are love, even the dog is love, but when the fire in the hearth goes out there's no love, no love served at the table, time to get up, time to leave; my candor is true even if my art is grave. Certainly there was no feeling of new love, no baptismal lifeblood romance excitation stirring up the emotions, the months plodding by, celibate eternities curiously bearable, like an experiment in sensory deprivation these months would go on the soul's résumé, though I didn't feel noble, strong or medieval. Rather sad and exhausted, it's hard to swallow a family, tough to cling to what is no longer there. I could ask for a show of hands here, yes, I could ask for a show of hands.

Hollow at the center of the chest, my lungs, and underneath a shirt, my heart hurt. It was a constant pain, it wasn't painful, it was ponderous, I felt closer to everybody on the street, to the people I didn't know, the disfigured and halt, the guy with the huge goiter on his neck standing with his little dog on the storefront sidewalk, I felt tender toward the scruffy kids in the neighborhood whose fathers were in jail or drunk, people who'd gone through it, or were about to, it hurt to see them, one big unhappy family starring everyone. I was poised on that point where measurement fails, the body clamped in on itself, bruised, the little light pleasures of taste and sound were difficult to endure, hard to put two or three thoughts together, reason through an essay, move from sofa to chair, and back, finally standing up to wolf down a sandwich, single people always eat standing up at the sink, just as love compels me to this dialect, says "take a walk, drive around neighborhood, look at houses," their stiff faces, their colors, their porches, if any, glass in windows divided into panes, smoke from chimneys, formal snowshovels. So much was up in the air, so many moments I'd turn to a last falling leaf, or a dashing cat, and want to speak, say "What's up?" or "Where are the boys?" Elements of an unraveling tale written by squirrels in the circular sockets of a brain, I was eager for duties, for the demands of a job, contact with real people around a real table, I am literal, lived in, to think out loud is not to say much until it's written, give me a life in turmoil so I can feel what size brushstrokes will convey its portrait, the set of jaw, eyes the way the painter saw them, slipping. Homemade tapes accompanied my long commutes, driving was music, music never sounded more fundamental, like a dictionary come alive, it entered bodily, it was purposeful direction, all touch and go. I didn't know any teenage girls flipping out, didn't have to include that sound. Sometimes silence and the humming car would take on the shape of domestic anger's impossible heavy life injustice, no one to blame, not even myself, or the culture, a vicious spear thrust into the shell of an alien other, it hit me, I closed up around it, a sea anemone. Why do we hold on to the pain, perform heroic measures to sustain an embalmed identity? Why not melt into it and notice a sea gull's beak?

Or I would begin to flirt with desire for the very change I feared, to be free of the rasps, to be on my own again, be my own boss, make my own clichés, hang my own pictures, dial my own information, less security, but more adventure, less friction, more desire, click the lights off, knock back the heat and slip upstairs to read late into the night, a light that disturbs no one, a few pillows behind the back, a notebook on the nightstand, you can see me here, I'm covered from head to toe, it's an 18th-century classic, it's a copy of *Tears on My Pillow*, it's the neo-wave of the present, I'm wide awake, there's so much to read, so many sentences to speak out loud, words to prowl.

* * *

The bedside clock ticks, it's a different tune, it sings, "Take care of yourself and get plenty of rest," then sleep like a sponge drops, sops up awareness, involuntary muscular jerks unkink the self, a distant voice whispers, "Take the night off, Lonesome. You can't just have these emotions, you gotta pay for 'em." I was like someone in love falling asleep alone, but only like, there was no one there but memory, but fear, cold mornings the sun would tip through the east-facing windows and arrive on my skin all but extinguished, the light bouncing off the snow was a screaming vitamin, and curious people would tour the little house, it was amusing, I didn't own it, things began to fill it, tables on loan, sofa too, I'd be self-conscious, apologize for the bow in the shelves containing the poetry books, made 'em myself, the rooms so small my eyes could travel the spines, I could jump out of bed and reach a volume of my choice and be back under the covers before the mattress knew I'd left. Sometimes I think everything I know I've learned from poems, then I wake up, I see whole rooms exactly as they were, filled with paintings, I think I'm still in them, the Malevitch room at the Stedelyk in Amsterdam, it's a space station on the trajectory of abstract painting, I sit back down and watch it orbit, it's supreme.

My dreams these mornings weren't spectacular, some revenge, some lust, but the big gnawing fact relentless and obsessive was there to greet me at dawn, a broken record, a tape loop, in the video version the fact planted its green flag in my face, I was its imagery's victim, even as the credits went rolling by, our distant vows went back into the can for the next night's showing, beginning middle and end, finito, history, join the club. I bought a TV set and played the remote buttons like a thumb piano, it broke the silence, it lit the walls, and at dusk I'd say to myself, as I reached for the lamp, "Light the first light of evening," in stentorian tones, or "His gorgeous self-pity." So much for darkness then, but the darkness was only more apparent in the lamplight, I couldn't see where I was going, the body, my own, the room like a cage, moving from chair to sofa, legs tucked up under for warmth, a blanket, a magazine, I was eighty-five years old, I was fifteen, a manuscript was my afghan, a pile of mail, then the hop-up adrenaline of a phone call, let's have another show of hands here, you've been there too, it's ringing just for you, the minuscule bag of groceries, silent rice, passing moments passing, sponged whiteness of stove, sink, all the books filed away, the rug unwalked on, records in alphabetical order, a new ribbon, a stack of envelopes, the liquid paper crust that fell as white dots swept into the trash, I was puttering, not paralyzed, I was waiting, I remembered hitchhiking through Bulgaria with a Lebanese guy in a two-door sedan, and stopping to share cigarettes in a village off the main road. People suddenly materialized, we were surrounded, they looked at our clothes, we exchanged furtive smiles, kidded with the children, then out of nowhere a woman advances, hands us a just-baked loaf of bread, it's big and round and solid and warm and we are immediately touched, we thank them, I shake the woman's hand, it is callused and rough, her eyes are light brown, they are filled with amber lines that seem to spin, while my hands are soft, I'm bookish, I'll sleep tonight on the floor of the train station in Sofia, use my bookbag for a pillow, be up early fully dressed still and away, is there still a crust of that bread? Later picked up in Yugoslavia by a Persian driving a truckload of rugs to Munich, you want to hear about this guy? I believe my senses, I finally had to escape from him in Vienna, completely unstrung me, he was single-minded devotion, we shared five words in English and that's all. One night at a truck stop outside Belgrade, about midnight of a moonless starry night, we stopped to eat, he propositioned our blond waitress, we finished the meal, and she followed us out to the truck, got in between us, we drove a mile down the road, pitch-black. He pulled to the side and stopped. He grabbed a blanket from the cab, they got out, they disappeared into the featureless landscape. Is this the freebooting life of adventure so ably described in the *Tropic of Cancer?* Was I next? Could one say No, in Serbo-Croatian? Is there a God? I can't see them out there. Then just as suddenly as the truck had stopped, and they'd gotten out, she was back, alone, she was furious, she grabbed her jacket from the cab, she was livid, her light summer dress fit her perfectly, she slammed the cab door and took off walking down the highway, back to her truck stop. What had my Persian rug trucker done to earn her disapproval? It was a precipitate disaster. He got back to the truck, threw the blanket in the cab, shrugged his shoulders, and off we drove into the night, there were borders to cross, spring flood-waters rushing off the Alps to admire. But by the time we got to

Vienna, after some harrowing driving routines in dense traffic, some lane-changing leaps of faith that only a true son of Allah's compassionate protection could have gotten away with, he finally pulled off onto a side street, it was about eight o'clock, we stopped, he said, "Girls" (that was one of the five words we shared), and smiled, reached under the front seat, brought out a razor, a mug with soap, a brush, some cold water from a bottle, and a filthy hand towel, and proceeded to lather up the soap for his evening shave, daubing cold water on his bristly dark beard, and glancing over at me as if to indicate, What an Evening We'll Have! But listening to him pull that dull razor across his cold scraped cheeks I nearly gagged, he was really scraping, nicking chin and cheek, his towel on the seat I wouldn't even touch. I had to cut, jam, no time to get sick, I thanked him for the lift, he looked surprised, I was abandoning him! Where was my sense of fun? I grabbed my bag, opened the cab door, swung down, waved once, and took off walking down the city street, it was meant to be, back on my own two feet, and all aboard for the night train to Munich, I was on it, now it's the next day, it's two in the afternoon and I've just eaten a bratwurst and drunk a beer, I turn a corner and nearly bump into the only person I know in all of Germany, a girlfriend named Brigitte Gapp with a Marilyn Monroe–like birthmark on a pale cheek, dark hair, big bright smile, I go crazy, this is serendipity writ large, Jung's magic synchronicity, we fall into each other's arms, we stare, the only person I know, how account for it? The mind entertains a wisdom that the body can't understand.

People would say it takes a year, maybe two, there was money on the table, there were things, what was spoiled needed division, a few rounds of letterhead legality meetings on creamy stationery, the feints and dodges, the disclosures, the aggressive silence, the screaming meemies, the three-piece options expert, the comma that allows, insists, demands another term, something must follow the end of the world, this one here, the oil burner clicks on, these words cost money, it was happening to other people too, it was commonplace, you could join a group and discuss it, commiserating phone calls from old friends long since lost track of, the word spreads, a postcard from a woman in New York wanting to meet, we've mutual friends, let's have a drink, there's one in Stockbridge, you could drive down together, a movie nut uptown, I'd really like her, the chorus chorused, she's just breaking up with, this is the network speaking, it's an erotic universe of random strangers coupling, the matchmakers were lighting up, they closed the cover before striking, life could resume, don't hesitate, change your sheets, act like someone in love would act, get that bounce back into your step, kid, talk funny again, and all so nice and young. *Quel* sequence. It's typical though, isn't it? There's more variety in a crisis, more sense of drama in the pain of a social hello, to be on the crest of a breaking wave, but would you get smashed to the sand and ground up, or ride it for all it's worth into a new life, stolen like fire from the gods one burning finger at a time? Drive, it said, digitalized, accessed, therapied, the talk in every cafe on Main Street. This is our human universe, the glue on a chipped cup, this end that signals a new beginning is the cheapest gas in town. I drink it myself.

THE RIGHT SKATES

Laura Chester

The hand of the famous artist was warm when I met him, but then it was also freezing cold outside. I had written him a fan letter about his recent exhibition, and sent along a book of my own. I think he must have liked the photo on the dust jacket, because he called me immediately, all fired up, and invited me down to the city.

I didn't dare say—I don't really look like that, but suggested we meet at this gallery—the sculptor was a woman friend of mine, and the show was delightful—long, sculpted sticks that had been painted and bent into an airborne dimension.

I felt lively yet relaxed walking around the space, reading the names of the pieces.

"The titles don't matter," the famous artist said. He was almost twenty years older—lanky, severe. "I like this work," he added.

The sculpture reminded me of the arrows of Artemis, of giant ice-fishing hooks. I was pleased he could appreciate the work of a woman, a sure sign of a confident man.

I could have lingered for a while, but he wanted to get going. The heat inside the gallery was making him tired. He had already invited me for Indian food, a little place right around the corner. I'd brought a bottle of champagne. "To celebrate," I said. My husband was getting married.

I know I should say, ex-husband, but that doesn't sound natural. I don't believe in divorce, even if I was the one who left him.

Earlier in the week, I'd gone out and bought a pair of ice skates. It had been a cold, snowless winter, and if I was going to live in this climate, I figured, I should at least be equipped. I bought a pair of black leather figure skates, men's 9's, but when I reached the pond where my husband was meeting me with our ten-year-old son, I discovered both skates were for the right foot. "Can you believe this?" I said to him, though weirder things have happened.

They wanted me to come to their wedding. In fact his sister had asked specifically if she and her family could stay with me. "She can stay," I told him, "whether I'm around or not. But I might be in Siena for the *Palio*. Are you going to take a honeymoon this time?"

Suddenly I felt overwhelmed, and walked over to this bridge where water was leaking, forming stalactite shapes. My son skated over and looked up at me, "Are you crying, Mom?"

"No," I lied. "My skates don't fit."

"Do you want me to push you?" He was such a feeling child and I said yes, and let him push me, though I didn't really want to be shoved across the ice.

My husband offered to let me use his ice skates, and I accepted. We wore the exact same size, but they were hockey skates and didn't have sharp edges. I felt like they could slip out from beneath me. They didn't have those teeth on the front to help you stop, and I didn't want to fall and break something.

The famous artist had age on his mind. He was trying to figure out how old I was by asking me the ages of my children, the year I was pregnant in Paris. I found him very attractive—similar to the looks of my ex-husband actually, and I didn't mind that he was older. I let him order dinner, but he didn't drink, so I'd left the champagne in my car.

I was feeling high anyway, cheerful, alert. I had purposefully tried to look beautiful. This man had been on my mind, even in my dreams. I was amazed that he had responded to my fan note. Now he seemed to be feeling the situation out. He didn't want to fall on ice either.

I told him that I'd had this dream. He was walking through a gallery, an opening full of people, and he had waved at me. I was asked to read "the marriage of true minds," then discovered that all my clothes were lined with poetry. All I had to do was open up and read. I realized this was quite an invention, for I could even go to the bathroom and read poetry in my underpants. "What do you think it means?" I asked.

"I'm sure I don't know, but it sounds pretty good." He went on to describe the different dishes as he knew them—the dry, clay-baked tandoori chicken, the juicier creamed spinach with lamb. I said that I could eat anything, dying for a beer. I was tired of living alone.

THE BROKEN BED

I was still very close to my husband, talked to him on the phone at least once a day, but I also got along very well with the woman he was now marrying. We genuinely liked each other. Perhaps I should have minded that she was not at all jealous. She had given me a lambskin cover for my bike seat at Christmas, and I'd given her real turquoise earrings. It would seem odd if I refused to celebrate their marriage, when I was actually glad that she was the one. I'm sure it would be different if I had a partner. I could hobble across the ice, half gliding, but I'd rather not.

I couldn't tell if this famous man was interested in me. There were moments when his eyes lit up, when my thinking brushed up against his. "I grew up in a home where beauty was essential," I told him. "Every painting, each object—it all becomes part of you. Most people pull away from beauty, don't you think? Because they're afraid they might feel something. Pain for instance. But artists have to enter in a state of dilation."

"Yes," he said, in complete agreement. "Though it's sad, most painters squeeze the juice out of their work. They're afraid of appearing sentimental. It can take courage to make something beautiful," he said. "It's more acceptable these days to get ugly."

Whatever he created at this point in his career would undoubtedly be applauded, but still, I could see he continued wrestling with the medium, trying to make it new. I wasn't sure if I should go to the wedding.

The globed lights had come on all around the pond, and our son was skating the periphery. "All our friends would be wondering how I felt, I don't know. I just think it would give you more freedom if I wasn't there." It might also make me very sad.

"Well, you're invited," my husband said, explaining it away. "That was then, and this is now." But everything past still seemed present to me. Even the future was contained in this moment—we just couldn't see the entire panorama, the ribbon that surrounded our lives.

A year ago I saw a psychic who described a tall, married man, older, with glasses and a prominent nose, as if she could actually *see* him. Now I wondered if it was this artist, who fit the description. He was still married, though his wife had left him for a woman less than six months ago.

"It seems that women usually leave men," I said. "Men only leave a marriage if there's something else lined up."

"That's because men associate marriage with the mother," he answered. "And when it's over, believe me, it's almost like death."

I wasn't sure why I felt so comfortable with this man. Most women would feel intimidated, but it seemed as if I almost knew him. He was familiar in this unfamiliar way.

"Do you miss her?" I asked.

"Not at all."

I wondered if this was true. Even though I didn't want my husband back in bed with me, I certainly missed something we'd had— a feeling of wholeness, of skating together, arms linked, feet gliding in tandem.

He asked me if he could have his skates back if I was just going to stand there, shivering. "Sure," I said, and wobbled across the frozen grass to the car. His girlfriend had not shown up. She was making chicken soup because our older son was sick. She was better at mothering than I was, and I was grateful that she cared for my children in my absence.

When my husband put on the skates he was suddenly taller. The famous man *was* taller, and I liked his bony looks, his eyes, when he took off his glasses and left a generous tip. "I hope you enjoyed that. Ready to go?"

He had invited me to stay at his loft—"I've got plenty of room," and though I knew I shouldn't impose, my other city friends were either sick or on vacation, and it was true, he had the entire top floor of this building. One half of it was studio space. Enormous new works were up on the walls—they were like a cross between painting and sculpture. Each canvas had a different object pressing from behind, creating a subtle bulge. I wondered if anything would happen.

I knew men liked me in that way, but I hadn't slept with anyone in over seven months. I'd been writing so much it didn't seem to matter. There were always men interested, hanging around, but for some reason, recently, I hadn't been tempted, and felt like something big was approaching my life. At least that's what I told myself.

As soon as we walked into his living space, the telephone rang. He didn't have an answering machine. He wasn't going to have a machine stand in for him, I guess. "That was my friend," he said, after he had spoken. He didn't elaborate so I didn't ask. Maybe his conscience was getting the better of him. "Do you mind if we don't make a fire?" Having a fireplace was a luxury in New York, and he was almost out of wood. He was not making a move to be romantic.

But the huge space needed warming. "Oh can't we?" I begged.

Once it was lit, he admitted how much he enjoyed watching it, how he didn't do enough for pleasure.

I said, "Pleasure is something we must serve," as if she were a goddess and the fire an offering.

My ex-husband once called me *"la femme de ma vie,"* introducing me to a well-known French poet while his girlfriend was standing right there. It was a slip that slipped by because of the language, but I was flattered, not just the mother of his children.

I wondered if I should tell my husband about the dream I'd had. We were driving together—he was at the wheel and I was sitting very close to him. I kissed him on the cheek and said, *You can never be replaced.* When I woke up, I found myself sobbing.

The next morning I called home and my youngest son answered, informing me, "Dad's getting married. He bought her a ring." I wondered if he had paid for it himself this time.

I said to my son, "Oh, I'm glad! Aren't you?"

"I don't know," he said, honestly.

And I felt myself falling.

"Do you want a divorce?" I asked the artist.

"I don't like to think of anything ending," he said. His statements seemed to contradict, but I could accept that. He went on about the suicide rate for men after divorce, how they didn't fare well. "Most women are relieved."

"Maybe at first," I answered. "A false euphoria."

"I was always wrapped up in my painting." He seemed disconcerted, as if he didn't have much time, and I wondered if he wanted to work that very evening.

He no longer seemed all fired up, just tired, and even the logs had quickly settled. The loft was chilly and too big. I pulled an Indian blanket up over me as I lay back on the sofa, while he sat in his chair. He looked as if he had rested there throughout a very long marriage. He yawned, though it was only ten o'clock. He said that he got up early. That he liked to start painting by seven.

"You can shower." He stood up and showed me the bathroom, got a pillow for the couch. "When you wake," he added, "I'll make you a nice breakfast." He stooped to check the coals. "You're a good fire maker."

"I should be," I answered, "I'm a fire sign."

"Oh, when?" he wanted to know.

"April thirteenth."

"That's *my* birthday." He seemed astounded, as if he owned the date. But I was not so surprised. We were just like that pair of right skates, too similar to be of any use to each other.

"I'm all fire and air. No water anywhere. No earth," I explained, as if I were a female Icarus, flying a bit too high and close to the sun.

He seemed disenchanted, ready for bed. "So is there anything you'd like?" he asked, meaning cider or a magazine.

"I'd like to be *always* in love," I responded.

"Yes," he smiled. "We need that, don't we." He said good night then without giving me a hug, and as soon as he closed the door on the far side of the room, I felt an immense loneliness descending.

The fire had almost burned itself out. It was hardly giving off light or heat. I turned off the lamp and sat in the darkness, wide awake. Then I heard him in his bedroom, talking to someone on the phone. I got up and walked closer, listening for a moment. "I don't care if it's been a year, I just want to see you."

I had this terrible feeling that my presence, my company, had made him feel even more desperate.

I sat back down on the sofa in the darkness, as if I had fallen on the slick, black ice, way out in the middle of nowhere. I could feel the sure cold slowly entering my body, but I did not try to move or make a sound.

SEPARATING

John Updike

The day was fair. Brilliant. All that June the weather had mocked the Maples' internal misery with solid sunlight—golden shafts and cascades of green in which their conversations had wormed unseeing, their sad murmuring selves the only stain in Nature. Usually by this time of the year they had acquired tans; but when they met their elder daughter's plane on her return from a year in England they were almost as pale as she, though Judith was too dazzled by the sunny opulent jumble of her native land to notice. They did not spoil her homecoming by telling her immediately. Wait a few days, let her recover from jet lag, had been one of their formulations, in that string of gray dialogues—over coffee, over cocktails, over Cointreau—that had shaped the strategy of their dissolution, while the earth performed its annual stunt of renewal unnoticed beyond their closed windows. Richard had thought to leave at Easter; Joan had insisted they wait until the four children were at last assembled, with all exams passed and ceremonies attended, and the bauble of summer to console them. So he had drudged away, in love, in dread, repairing screens, getting the mowers sharpened, rolling and patching their new tennis court.

The court, clay, had come through its first winter pitted and windswept bare of redcoat. Years ago the Maples had observed how often, among their friends, divorce followed a dramatic home improvement, as if the marriage were making one last strong effort to live; their own worst crisis had come amid the plaster dust and exposed plumbing of a kitchen renovation. Yet, a summer ago, as canary-yellow bulldozers gaily churned a grassy, daisy-dotted knoll into a muddy plateau, and a crew of pigtailed young men raked and tamped clay into a plane, this transformation did not strike them as ominous, but festive in its impudence; their marriage could rend the earth for fun. The next spring, waking each day at dawn to a sliding sensation as if the bed were being tipped, Richard found the barren tennis court—its net and tapes still rolled in the barn—an environment congruous with his mood of purposeful desolation, and the crumbling of handfuls of clay into cracks and holes (dogs had frolicked on the court in a thaw; rivulets had evolved trenches) an activity suitably elemental and interminable. In his sealed heart he hoped the day would never come.

Now it was here. A Friday. Judith was reacclimated; all four children were assembled, before jobs and camps and visits again scattered them. Joan thought they should be told one by one. Richard was for making an announcement at the table. She said, "I think just making an announcement is a cop-out. They'll start quarreling and playing to each other instead of focusing. They're each individuals, you know, not just some corporate obstacle to your freedom."

"O.K., O.K. I agree." Joan's plan was exact. That evening, they were giving Judith a belated welcome-home dinner, of lobster and champagne. Then, the party over, they, the two of them, who nineteen years before would push her in a baby carriage along Fifth Avenue to Washington Square, were to walk her out of the house, to the bridge across the salt creek, and tell her, swearing her to secrecy. Then Richard Jr., who was going directly from work to a rock concert in Boston, would be told, either late when he returned on the train or early Saturday morning before he went off to his job; he was seventeen and employed as one of a golf-course maintenance crew. Then the two younger children, John and Margaret, could, as the morning wore on, be informed.

"Mopped up, as it were," Richard said.

"Do you have any better plan? That leaves you the rest of Saturday to answer any questions, pack, and make your wonderful departure."

"No," he said, meaning he had no better plan, and agreed to hers, though to him it showed an edge of false order, a hidden plea for control, like Joan's long chore lists and financial accountings and, in the days when he first knew her, her too copious lecture notes. Her plan turned one hurdle for him into four—four knife-sharp walls, each with a sheer blind drop on the other side.

All spring he had moved through a world of insides and outsides, of barriers and partitions. He and Joan stood as a thin barrier between the children and the truth. Each moment was a partition, with the past on one side and the future on the other, a future containing this unthinkable *now*. Beyond four knifelike walls a new life for him waited vaguely. His skull cupped a secret, a white face, a face both frightened and soothing, both strange and known, that he wanted to shield from tears, which he felt all about him, solid as the sunlight. So haunted, he had become obsessed with battening down the house against his absence, replacing screens and sash cords, hinges and latches—a Houdini making things snug before his escape.

The lock. He had still to replace a lock on one of the doors of the screened porch. The task, like most such, proved more difficult than he had imagined. The old lock, aluminum frozen by corrosion, had been deliberately rendered obsolete by manufacturers. Three hardware stores had nothing that even approximately matched the mortised hole its removal (surprisingly easy) left. Another hole had to be gouged, with bits too small and saws too big, and the old hole fitted with a block of wood—the chisels dull, the saw rusty, his fingers thick with lack of sleep. The sun poured down, beyond the porch, on a world of neglect. The bushes already needed pruning, the windward side of the house was shedding flakes of paint, rain would get in when he was gone, insects, rot, death. His family, all those he would lose, filtered through the edges of his awareness as he struggled with screw holes, splinters, opaque instructions, minutiae of metal.

Judith sat on the porch, a princess returned from exile. She regaled them with stories of fuel shortages, of bomb scares in the Underground, of Pakistani workmen loudly lusting after her as she walked past on her way to dance school. Joan came and went, in and out of the house, calmer than she should have been, praising his struggles with the lock as if this were one more and not the last of their long chain of shared chores. The younger of his sons, John, now at fifteen suddenly, unwittingly handsome, for a few minutes held the rickety screen door while his father clumsily hammered and chiseled, each blow a kind of sob in Richard's ears. His younger daughter, having been at a slumber party, slept on the porch hammock through all the noise—heavy and pink, trusting and forsaken. Time, like the sunlight, continued relentlessly; the sunlight slowly slanted. Today was one of the longest days. The lock clicked, worked.

He was through. He had a drink; he drank it on the porch, listening to his daughter. "It was so sweet," she was saying, "during the worst of it, how all the butchers and bakery shops kept open by candle-light. They're all so plucky and cute. From the papers, things sounded so much worse here—people shooting people in gas lines, and everybody freezing."

Richard asked her, "Do you still want to live in England forever?" *Forever:* the concept, now a reality upon him, pressed and scratched at the back of his throat.

"No," Judith confessed, turning her oval face to him, its eyes still childishly far apart, but the lips set as over something succulent and satisfactory. "I was anxious to come home. I'm an American." She was a woman. They had raised her; he and Joan had endured together to raise her, alone of the four. The others had still some raising left in them. Yet it was the thought of telling Judith—the image of her, their first baby, walking between them arm in arm to the bridge—that broke him. The partition between his face and the tears broke. Richard sat down to the celebratory meal with the back of his throat aching; the champagne, the lobster seemed phases of sunshine; he saw them and tasted them through tears. He blinked, swallowed, croakily joked about hay fever. The tears would not stop leaking through; they came not through a hole that could be plugged but through a permeable spot in a membrane, steadily, purely, end-lessly, fruitfully. They became, his tears, a shield for himself against these others—their faces, the fact of their assembly, a last time as innocents, at a table where he sat the last time as head. Tears dropped from his nose as he broke the lobster's back; salt flavored his cham-pagne as he sipped it; the raw clench at the back of his throat was delicious. He could not help himself.

His children tried to ignore his tears. Judith, on his right, lit a cigarette, gazed upward in the direction of her too energetic, too sophisticated exhalation; on her other side, John earnestly bent his face to the extraction of the last morsels—legs, tail segments—from the scarlet corpse. Joan, at the opposite end of the table, glanced at him surprised, her reproach displaced by a quick grimace, of forgive-ness, or of salute to his superior gift of strategy. Between them, Mar-garet, no longer called Bean, thirteen and large for her age, gazed from the other side of his pane of tears as if into a shopwindow at something she coveted—at her father, a crystalline heap of splinters and memories. It was not she, however, but John who, in the kitchen, as they cleared the plates and carapaces away, asked Joan the question: *"Why is Daddy crying?"*

Richard heard the question but not the murmured answer. Then he heard Bean cry, "Oh, no-oh!"—the faintly dramatized exclamation of one who had long expected it.

John returned to the table carrying a bowl of salad. He nodded tersely at his father and his lips shaped the conspiratorial words "She told."

"Told what?" Richard asked aloud, insanely.

The boy sat down as if to rebuke his father's distraction with the example of his own good manners. He said quietly, "The separation."

Joan and Margaret returned; the child, in Richard's twisted vision, seemed diminished in size, and relieved, relieved to have had the bogieman at last proved real. He called out to her—the distances at the table had grown immense—"You knew, you always knew," but the clenching at the back of his throat prevented him from making sense of it. From afar he heard Joan talking, levelly, sensibly, reciting what they had prepared: it was a separation for the summer, an experiment. She and Daddy both agreed it would be good for them; they needed space and time to think; they liked each other but did not make each other happy enough, somehow.

Judith, imitating her mother's factual tone, but in her youth off-key, too cool, said, "I think it's silly. You should either live together or get divorced."

Richard's crying, like a wave that has crested and crashed, had become tumultuous; but it was overtopped by another tumult, for John, who had been so reserved, now grew larger and larger at the table. Perhaps his younger sister's being credited with knowing set him off. "Why didn't you *tell* us?" he asked, in a large round voice quite unlike his own. "You should have *told* us you weren't getting along."

Richard was startled into attempting to force words through his tears. "We *do* get along, that's the trouble, so it doesn't show even to us—" *That we do not love each other* was the rest of the sentence; he couldn't finish it.

Joan finished for him, in her style. "And we've always, *especially*, loved our children."

John was not mollified. "What do you care about *us?*" he boomed. "We're just little things you *had.*" His sisters' laughing forced a laugh from him, which he turned hard and parodistic: "Ha ha *ha.*" Richard and Joan realized simultaneously that the child was drunk, on Judith's homecoming champagne. Feeling bound to keep the center of the stage, John took a cigarette from Judith's pack, poked it into his mouth, let it hang from his lower lip, and squinted like a gangster.

"You're not little things we had," Richard called to him. "You're the whole point. But you're grown. Or almost."

The boy was lighting matches. Instead of holding them to his cigarette (for they had never seen him smoke; being "good" had been his way of setting himself apart), he held them to his mother's face, closer and closer, for her to blow out. Then he lit the whole folder—a hiss and then a torch, held against his mother's face. Prismed by his tears, the flame filled Richard's vision; he didn't know how it was extinguished. He heard Margaret say, "Oh stop showing off," and saw John, in response, break the cigarette in two and put the halves entirely into his mouth and chew, sticking out his tongue to display the shreds to his sister.

Joan talked to him, reasoning—a fountain of reason, unintelligible. "Talked about it for years . . . our children must help us . . . Daddy and I both want . . ." As the boy listened, he carefully wadded a paper napkin into the leaves of his salad, fashioned a ball of paper and lettuce, and popped it into his mouth, looking around the table for the expected laughter. None came. Judith said, "Be mature," and dismissed a plume of smoke.

Richard got up from this stifling table and led the boy outside. Though the house was in twilight, the outdoors still brimmed with light, the lovely waste light of high summer. Both laughing, he supervised John's spitting out the lettuce and paper and tobacco into the pachysandra. He took him by the hand—a square gritty hand, but for its softness a man's. Yet, it held on. They ran together up into the field, past the tennis court. The raw banking left by the bulldozers was dotted with daisies. Past the court and a flat stretch where they used to play family baseball stood a soft green rise glorious in the sun, each weed and species of grass distinct as illumination on parchment. "I'm sorry, so sorry," Richard cried. "You were the only one who ever tried to help me with all the goddam jobs around this place."

Sobbing, safe within his tears and the champagne, John explained, "It's not just the separation, it's the whole crummy year, I *hate* that school, you can't make any friends, the history teacher's a scud."

They sat on the crest of the rise, shaking and warm from their tears but easier in their voices, and Richard tried to focus on the child's sad year—the weekdays long with homework, the weekends spent in his room with model airplanes, while his parents murmured down below, nursing their separation. How selfish, how blind, Richard thought; his eyes felt scoured. He told his son, "We'll think about getting you transferred. Life's too short to be miserable."

They had said what they could, but did not want the moment to heal, and talked on, about the school, about the tennis court, whether it would ever again be as good as it had been that first summer. They walked to inspect it and pressed a few more tapes more firmly down. A little stiltedly, perhaps trying now to make too much of the moment, Richard led the boy to the spot in the field where the view was best, of the metallic blue river, the emerald marsh, the scattered islands velvety with shadow in the low light, the white bits of beach far away. "See," he said. "It goes on being beautiful. It'll be here tomorrow."

"I know," John answered, impatiently. The moment had closed.

Back in the house, the others had opened some white wine, the champagne being drunk, and still sat at the table, the three females, gossiping. Where Joan sat had become the head. She turned, showing him a tearless face, and asked, "All right?"

"We're fine," he said, resenting it, though relieved, that the party went on without him.

In bed she explained, "I couldn't cry I guess because I cried so much all spring. It really wasn't fair. It's your idea, and you made it look as though I was kicking you out."

"I'm sorry," he said. "I couldn't stop. I wanted to but couldn't."

"You *didn't* want to. You loved it. You were having your way, making a general announcement."

"I love having it over," he admitted. "God, those kids were great. So brave and funny." John, returned to the house, had settled to a model airplane in his room, and kept shouting down to them, "I'm O.K. No sweat." "And the way," Richard went on, cozy in his relief, "they never questioned the reasons we gave. No thought of a third person. Not even Judith."

"That *was* touching," Joan said.

He gave her a hug. "You were great too. Very reassuring to everybody. Thank you." Guiltily, he realized he did not feel separated.

"You still have Dickie to do," she told him. These words set before him a black mountain in the darkness; its cold breath, its near weight affected his chest. Of the four children, his elder son was most like a conscience. Joan did not need to add, "That's one piece of your dirty work I won't do for you."

"I know. I'll do it. You go to sleep."

Within minutes, her breathing slowed, became oblivious and deep. It was quarter to midnight. Dickie's train from the concert would come in at one-fourteen. Richard set the alarm for one. He had slept atrociously for weeks. But whenever he closed his lids some glimpse of the last hours scorched them—Judith exhaling toward the ceiling in a kind of aversion, Bean's mute staring, the sunstruck growth of the field where he and John had rested. The mountain before him moved closer, moved within him; he was huge, momentous. The ache at the back of his throat felt stale. His wife slept as if slain beside him. When, exasperated by his hot lids, his crowded heart, he rose from bed and dressed, she awoke enough to turn over. He told her then, "Joan, if I could undo it all, I would."

"Where would you begin?" she asked. There was no place. Giving him courage, she was always giving him courage. He put on shoes without socks in the dark. The children were breathing in their rooms, the downstairs was hollow. In their confusion they had left lights burning. He turned off all but one, the kitchen overhead. The car started. He had hoped it wouldn't. He met only moonlight on the road; it seemed a diaphanous companion, flickering in the leaves along the roadside, haunting his rearview mirror like a pursuer, melting under his headlights. The center of town, not quite deserted, was eerie at this hour. A young cop in uniform kept company with a gang of T-shirted kids on the steps of the bank. Across from the railroad station, several bars kept open. Customers, mostly young, passed in and out of the warm night, savoring summer's novelty. Voices shouted from cars as they passed; an immense conversation seemed in progress. Richard parked and in his weariness put his head on the passenger seat, out of the commotion and wheeling lights. It was as when, in the movies, an assassin grimly carries his mission through the jostle of a carnival—except the movies cannot show the precipitous, palpable slope you cling to within. You cannot climb back down; you can only fall. The synthetic fabric of the car seat, warmed by his cheek, confided to him an ancient, distant scent of vanilla.

A train whistle caused him to lift his head. It was on time; he had hoped it would be late. The slender drawgates descended. The bell of approach tingled happily. The great metal body, horizontally fluted, rocked to a stop, and sleepy teenagers disembarked, his son among them. Dickie did not show surprise that his father was meeting him at this terrible hour. He sauntered to the car with two friends, both taller than he. He said "Hi" to his father and took the passenger's seat with an exhausted promptness that expressed gratitude. The friends got into the back, and Richard was grateful; a few more minutes' postponement would be won by driving them home.

He asked, "How was the concert?"

"Groovy," one boy said from the back seat.

"It bit," the other said.

"It was O.K.," Dickie said, moderate by nature, so reasonable that in his childhood the unreason of the world had given him headaches, stomachaches, nausea. When the second friend had been dropped off at his dark house, the boy blurted, "Dad, my eyes are killing me with hay fever! I'm out there cutting that mothering grass all day!"

"Do we still have those drops?"

"They didn't do any good last summer."

"They might this." Richard swung a U-turn on the empty street. The drive home took a few minutes. The mountain was here, in his throat. "Richard," he said, and felt the boy, slumped and rubbing his eyes, go tense at his tone, "I didn't come to meet you just to make your life easier. I came because your mother and I have some news for you, and you're a hard man to get a hold of these days. It's sad news."

"That's O.K." The reassurance came out soft, but quick, as if released from the tip of a spring.

Richard had feared that his tears would return and choke him, but the boy's manliness set an example, and his voice issued forth steady and dry. "It's sad news, but it needn't be tragic news, at least for you. It should have no practical effect on your life, though it's bound to have an emotional effect. You'll work at your job, and go back to school in September. Your mother and I are really proud of what you're making of your life; we don't want that to change at all."

"Yeah," the boy said lightly, on the intake of his breath, holding himself up. They turned the corner; the church they went to loomed like a gutted fort. The home of the woman Richard hoped to marry stood across the green. Her bedroom light burned.

"Your mother and I," he said, "have decided to separate. For the summer. Nothing legal, no divorce yet. We want to see how it feels. For some years now, we haven't been doing enough for each other as, making each other as happy as we should be. Have you sensed that?"

"No," the boy said. It was an honest, unemotional answer: true or false in a quiz.

Glad for the factual basis, Richard pursued, even garrulously, the details. His apartment across town, his utter accessibility, the split vacation arrangements, the advantages to the children, the added mobility and variety of the summer. Dickie listened, absorbing. "Do the others know?"

"Yes."

"How did they take it?"

"The girls pretty calmly. John flipped out; he shouted and ate a cigarette and made a salad out of his napkin and told us how much he hated school."

His brother chuckled. "He did?"

"Yeah. The school issue was more upsetting for him than Mom and me. He seemed to feel better for having exploded."

"He did?" The repetition was the first sign that he was stunned.

"Yes. Dickie, I want to tell you something. This last hour, waiting for your train to get in, has been about the worst of my life. I hate this. *Hate* it. My father would have died before doing it to me." He felt immensely lighter, saying this. He had dumped the mountain on the boy. They were home. Moving swiftly as a shadow, Dickie was out of the car, through the bright kitchen. Richard called after him, "Want a glass of milk or anything?"

"No thanks."

"Want us to call the course tomorrow and say you're too sick to work?"

"No, that's all right." The answer was faint, delivered at the door to his room; Richard listened for the slam that went with a tantrum. The door closed normally, gently. The sound was sickening.

Joan had sunk into that first deep trough of sleep and was slow to awake. Richard had to repeat, "I told him."

"What did he say?"

"Nothing much. Could you go say good night to him? Please."

She left their room, without putting on a bathrobe. He sluggishly changed back into his pajamas and walked down the hall. Dickie was already in bed, Joan was sitting beside him, and the boy's bedside clock radio was murmuring music. When she stood, an inexplicable light—the moon?—outlined her body through the nightie. Richard sat on the warm place she had indented on the child's narrow mattress. He asked him, "Do you want the radio on like that?"

"It always is."

"Doesn't it keep you awake? It would me."

"No."

"Are you sleepy?"

"Yeah."

"Good. Sure you want to get up and go to work? You've had a big night."

"I want to."

Away at school this winter he had learned for the first time that you can go short of sleep and live. As an infant he had slept with an immobile, sweating intensity that had alarmed his babysitters. In adolescence he had often been the first of the four children to go to bed. Even now, he would go slack in the middle of a television show, his sprawled legs hairy and brown. "O.K. Good boy. Dickie, listen. I love you so much, I never knew how much until now. No matter how this works out, I'll always be with you. Really."

Richard bent to kiss an averted face but his son, sinewy, turned and with wet cheeks embraced him and gave him a kiss, on the lips, passionate as a woman's. In his father's ear he moaned one word, the crucial, intelligent word: "*Why?*"

Why. It was a whistle of wind in a crack, a knife thrust, a window thrown open on emptiness. The white face was gone, the darkness was featureless. Richard had forgotten why.

SONNET

Bernadette Mayer

A thousand apples you might put in your theories
But you are gone from benefit to my love

You spoke not the Italian of Dante at the table
But the stingy notions of the bedded heterosexual

You cursed and swore cause I was later
To come home to you without your fucking dinner

Dont ever return su numero de telefono it is just this
I must explain I dont ever want to see you again

Empezando el 2 de noviembre 1980-something I dont love you
So stick it up your ass like she would say

I'm so mad at you I'm sure I'll take it all back tomorrow
& say then they flee from me who sometime did me seek

Meanwhile eat my existent dinner somebody and life
C'mon and show me something newer than even Dante

INTIMACY

Raymond Carver

I have some business out west anyway, so I stop off in this little town where my former wife lives. We haven't seen each other in four years. But from time to time, when something of mine appeared, or was written about me in the magazines or papers—a profile or an interview—I sent her these things. I don't know what I had in mind except I thought she might be interested. In any case, she never responded.

It is nine in the morning, I haven't called, and it's true I don't know what I am going to find.

But she lets me in. She doesn't seem surprised. We don't shake hands, much less kiss each other. She takes me into the living room. As soon as I sit down she brings me some coffee. Then she comes out with what's on her mind. She says I've caused her anguish, made her feel exposed and humiliated.

Make no mistake, I feel I'm home.

She says, But then you were into betrayal early. You always felt comfortable with betrayal. No, she says, that's not true. Not in the beginning, at any rate. You were different then. But I guess I was different too. Everything was different, she says. No, it was after you turned thirty-five, or thirty-six, whenever it was, around in there anyway, your mid-thirties somewhere, then you started in. You really started in. You turned on me. You did it up pretty then. You must be proud of yourself.

She says, Sometimes I could scream.

She says she wishes I'd forget about the hard times, the bad times, when I talk about back then. Spend some time on the good times, she says. Weren't there some good times? She wishes I'd get off that other subject. She's bored with it. Sick of hearing about it. Your private hobby horse, she says. What's done is done and water under the bridge, she says. A tragedy, yes. God knows it was a tragedy and then some. But why keep it going? Don't you ever get tired of dredging up that old business?

She says, Let go of the past, for Christ's sake. Those old hurts. You must have some other arrows in your quiver, she says.

She says, You know something? I think you're sick. I think you're crazy as a bedbug. Hey, you don't believe the things they're saying about you, do you? Don't believe them for a minute, she says. Listen, I could tell them a thing or two. Let them talk to me about it, if they want to hear a story.

She says, Are you listening to me?

I'm listening, I say. I'm all ears, I say.

She says, I've really had a bellyful of it, buster! Who asked you here today anyway? I sure as hell didn't. You just show up and walk in. What the hell do you want from me? Blood? You want more blood? I thought you had your fill by now.

She says, Think of me as dead. I want to be left in peace now. That's all I want anymore is to be left in peace and forgotten about. Hey, I'm forty-five years old, she says. Forty-five going on fifty-five, or sixty-five. Lay off, will you.

She says, Why don't you wipe the blackboard clean and see what you have left after that? Why don't you start with a clean slate? See how far that gets you, she says.

She has to laugh at this. I laugh too, but it's nerves.

She says, You know something? I had my chance once, but I let it go. I just let it go. I don't guess I ever told you. But now look at me. Look! Take a good look while you're at it. You threw me away, you son of a bitch.

She says, I was younger then and a better person. Maybe you were too, she says. A better person, I mean. You had to be. You were better then or I wouldn't have had anything to do with you.

She says, I loved you so much once. I loved you to the point of distraction. I did. More than anything in the whole wide world. Imagine that. What a laugh that is now. Can you imagine it? We were so *intimate* once upon a time I can't believe it now. I think that's the strangest thing of all now. The memory of being that intimate with somebody. We were so intimate I could puke. I can't imagine ever being that intimate with somebody else. I haven't been.

She says, Frankly, and I mean this, I want to be kept out of it from here on out. Who do you think you are anyway? You think you're God or somebody? You're not fit to lick God's boots, or anybody else's for that matter. Mister, you've been hanging out with the wrong people. But what do I know? I don't even know what I know any longer. I know I don't like what you've been dishing out. I know that much. You know what I'm talking about, don't you? Am I right?

Right, I say. Right as rain.

She says, You'll agree to anything, won't you? You give in too easy. You always did. You don't have any principles, not one. Anything to avoid a fuss. But that's neither here nor there.

She says, You remember that time I pulled the knife on you?

She says this as if in passing, as if it's not important.

Vaguely, I say. I must have deserved it, but I don't remember much about it. Go ahead, why don't you, and tell me about it.

She says, I'm beginning to understand something now. I think I know why you're here. Yes. I know why you're here, even if you don't. But you're a slyboots. You know why you're here. You're on a fishing expedition. You're hunting for *material*. Am I getting warm? Am I right?

Tell me about the knife, I say.

She says, If you want to know, I'm real sorry I didn't use that knife. I am. I really and truly am. I've thought and thought about it, and I'm sorry I didn't use it. I had the chance. But I hesitated. I hesitated and was lost, as somebody or other said. But I should have used it, the hell with everything and everybody. I should have nicked your arm with it at least. At least that.

Well, you didn't, I say. I thought you were going to cut me with it, but you didn't. I took it away from you.

She says, You were always lucky. You took it away and then you slapped me. Still, I regret I didn't use that knife just a little bit. Even a little would have been something to remember me by.

I remember a lot, I say. I say that, then wish I hadn't.

She says, Amen, brother. That's the bone of contention here, if you hadn't noticed. That's the whole problem. But like I said, in my opinion you remember the wrong things. You remember the low, shameful things. That's why you got interested when I brought up the knife.

She says, I wonder if you ever have any regret. For whatever that's worth on the market these days. Not much, I guess. But you ought to be a specialist in it by now.

Regret, I say. It doesn't interest me much, to tell the truth. Regret is not a word I use very often. I guess I mainly don't have it. I admit I hold to the dark view of things. Sometimes, anyway. But regret? I don't think so.

She says, You're a real son of a bitch, did you know that? A ruthless, coldhearted son of a bitch. Did anybody ever tell you that?

You did, I say. Plenty of times.

She says, I always speak the truth. Even when it hurts. You'll never catch me in a lie.

She says, My eyes were opened a long time ago, but by then it was too late. I had my chance but I let it slide through my fingers. I even thought for a while you'd come back. Why'd I think that anyway? I must have been out of my mind. I could cry my eyes out now, but I wouldn't give you that satisfaction.

She says, You know what? I think if you were on fire right now, if you suddenly burst into flame this minute, I wouldn't throw a bucket of water on you.

She laughs at this. Then her face closes down again.

She says, Why in hell *are* you here? You want to hear some more? I could go on for days. I think I know why you turned up, but I want to hear it from you.

When I don't answer, when I just keep sitting there, she goes on.

She says, After that time, when you went away, nothing much mattered after that. Not the kids, not God, not anything. It was like I didn't know what hit me. It was like I had *stopped living*. My life had been going along, going along, and then it just stopped. It didn't just come to a stop, it screeched to a stop. I thought, If I'm not worth anything to him, well, I'm not worth anything to myself or anybody else either. That was the worst thing I felt. I thought my heart would break. What am I saying? It did break. Of course it broke. It broke, just like that. It's still broke, if you want to know. And so there you have it in a nutshell. My eggs in one basket, she says. A tisket, a tasket. All my rotten eggs in one basket.

She says, You found somebody else for yourself, didn't you? It didn't take long. And you're happy now. That's what they say about you anyway: "He's happy now." Hey, I read everything you send! You think I don't? Listen, I know your heart, mister. I always did. I knew it back then, and I know it now. I know your heart inside and out, and don't you ever forget it. Your heart is a jungle, a dark forest, it's a garbage pail, if you want to know. Let them talk to me if they want to ask somebody something. I know how you operate. Just let them come around here, and I'll give them an earful. I was there. I served, buddy boy. Then you held me up for display and ridicule in your so-called work. For any Tom or Harry to pity or pass judgment on. Ask me if I cared. Ask me if it embarrassed me. Go ahead, ask.

No, I say, I won't ask that. I don't want to get into that, I say.

Damn straight you don't! she says. And you know *why*, too!

She says, Honey, no offense, but sometimes I think I could shoot you and watch you kick.

She says, You can't look me in the eyes, can you?

She says, and this is exactly what she says, You can't even look me in the eyes when I'm talking to you.

So, okay, I look her in the eyes.

She says, Right. Okay, she says. Now we're getting someplace, maybe. That's better. You can tell a lot about the person you're talking to from his eyes. Everybody knows that. But you know something else? There's nobody in this whole world who would tell you this, but I can tell you. I have the right. I *earned* that right, sonny. You have yourself confused with somebody else. And that's the pure truth of it. But what do I know? they'll say in a hundred years. They'll say, Who was she anyway?

She says, In any case, you sure as hell have *me* confused with somebody else. Hey, I don't even have the same name anymore! Not the name I was born with, not the name I lived with you with, not even the name I had two years ago. What is this? What is this in hell all about anyway? Let me say something. I want to be left alone now. Please. That's not a crime.

She says, Don't you have someplace else you should be? Some plane to catch? Shouldn't you be somewhere far from here at this very minute?

No, I say. I say it again: No. No place, I say. I don't have anyplace I have to be.

THE BROKEN BED

211

And then I do something. I reach over and take the sleeve of her blouse between my thumb and forefinger. That's all. I just touch it that way, and then I just bring my hand back. She doesn't draw away. She doesn't move.

Then here's the thing I do next. I get down on my knees, a big guy like me, and I take the hem of her dress. What am I doing on the floor? I wish I could say. But I know it's where I ought to be, and I'm there on my knees holding on to the hem of her dress.

She is still for a minute. But in a minute she says, Hey, it's all right, stupid. You're so dumb, sometimes. Get up now. I'm telling you to get up. Listen, it's okay. I'm over it now. It took me a while to get over it. What do you think? Did you think it wouldn't? Then you walk in here and suddenly the whole cruddy business is back. I felt a need to ventilate. But you know, and I know, it's over and done with now.

She says, For the longest while, honey, I was inconsolable. *Inconsolable*, she says. Put that word in your little notebook. I can tell you from experience that's the saddest word in the English language. Anyway, I got over it finally. Time is a gentleman, a wise man said. Or else maybe a worn-out old woman, one or the other anyway.

She says, I have a life now. It's a different kind of life than yours, but I guess we don't need to compare. It's my life, and that's the important thing I have to realize as I get older. Don't feel *too* bad, anyway, she says. I mean, it's all right to feel a *little* bad, maybe. That won't hurt you, that's only to be expected after all. Even if you can't move yourself to regret.

She says, Now you have to get up and get out of here. My husband will be along pretty soon for his lunch. How would I explain this kind of thing?

It's crazy, but I'm still on my knees holding the hem of her dress. I won't let it go. I'm like a terrier, and it's like I'm stuck to the floor. It's like I can't move.

She says, Get up now. What is it? You still want something from me. What do you want? Want me to forgive you? Is that why you're doing this? That's it, isn't it? That's the reason you came all this way. The knife thing kind of perked you up, too. I think you'd forgotten about that. But you needed me to remind you. Okay, I'll say something if you'll just go.

She says, I forgive you.

She says, Are you satisfied now? Is that better? Are you happy? He's happy now, she says.

But I'm still there, knees to the floor.

She says, Did you hear what I said? You have to go now. Hey, stupid. Honey, I said I forgive you. And I even reminded you about the knife thing. I can't think what else I can do now. You got it made in the shade, baby. Come *on* now, you have to get out of here. Get up. That's right. You're still a big guy, aren't you. Here's your hat, don't forget your hat. You never used to wear a hat. I never in my life saw you in a hat before.

She says, Listen to me now. Look at me. Listen carefully to what I'm going to tell you.

She moves closer. She's about three inches from my face. We haven't been this close in a long time. I take these little breaths that she can't hear, and I wait. I think my heart slows way down, I think.

She says, You just tell it like you have to, I guess, and forget the rest. Like always. You been doing that for so long now anyway it shouldn't be hard for you.

She says, There, I've done it. You're free, aren't you? At least you think you are anyway. Free at last. That's a joke, but don't laugh. Anyway, you feel better, don't you?

She walks with me down the hall.

She says, I can't imagine how I'd explain this if my husband was to walk in this very minute. But who really cares anymore, right? In the final analysis, nobody gives a damn anymore. Besides which, I think everything that can happen that way has already happened. His name is Fred, by the way. He's a decent guy and works hard for his living. He cares for me.

So she walks me to the front door, which has been standing open all this while. The door that was letting in light and fresh air this morning, and sounds off the street, all of which we had ignored. I look outside and, Jesus, there's this white moon hanging in the morning sky. I can't think when I've ever seen anything so remarkable. But I'm afraid to comment on it. I am. I don't know what might happen. I might break into tears even. I might not understand a word I'd say.

She says, Maybe you'll be back sometime, and maybe you won't.

THE BROKEN BED

This'll wear off, you know. Pretty soon you'll start feeling bad again. Maybe it'll make a good story, she says. But I don't want to know about it if it does.

I say good-bye. She doesn't say anything more. She looks at her hands, and then she puts them into the pockets of her dress. She shakes her head. She goes back inside, and this time she closes the door.

I move off down the sidewalk. Some kids are tossing a football at the end of the street. But they aren't my kids, and they aren't her kids either. There are these leaves everywhere, even in the gutters. Piles of leaves wherever I look. They're falling off the limbs as I walk. I can't take a step without putting my shoe into leaves. Somebody ought to make an effort here. Somebody ought to get a rake and take care of this.

OUR FIRST SUMMER

Marie Harris

At a deepening
of the Isinglass River
I lie down in stones and tea-colored water.
I think: be careful; do not say
Home.
The bones of that word mend slowly.

LUCY ORTIZ

Miriam Sagan

Lucy Ortiz backs her blue Hyundai out of its spot in front of the state library and keeps going. A line of cars is parallel-parked along Don Gaspar in front of the Bataan Building and the eternal flame burning under a cottonwood in remembrance of those New Mexicans forced on a death march in such a hot and sticky place. The blue Hyundai keeps going until it stops with its back fender neatly rammed into the door of an old station wagon. Too late, Lucy hits the brakes and then puts her head down on the steering wheel in an attitude of prayer.

Lucy Ortiz has not been looking where she is going. She has been thinking instead of Joe Senior, her no-good soon-to-be-ex-husband, her husband she has loved so long and faithfully. Joe Senior has been two-timing her again. He has been two-timing her at the Thunderbird Motel on Cerrillos Road. It is not a nice motel. Lucy likes a nice motel as well as anyone. She likes the Best Western in Carlsbad, where she has gone on a librarians' tour of the radioactive-waste facilities. The radioactive-waste will be stored in salt mines sunk deep in the flat earth. These salt deposits have not moved in half a billion years. Lucy Ortiz thought marriage was forever. Unlike her mother and grandmother, she even expected to be happy. And now Joe Senior has hurt her where no man should hurt a woman. He has hurt her in her dark Spanish pride and in her dark Spanish name: Lucille Baca Serna Ortiz. She wishes she had brothers so they could kill him.

Lucy Ortiz gets out of her car and goes to inspect the damage. The damage is not extensive. The station wagon was already old, chipped, and dented. Lucy's car has only added a bruise the size of her hand. Lucy looks at the dent blankly. Then she looks at the owner of the dent, a tall ordinary enough Anglo guy, all boots and blondish mustache. Lucy touches the Virgin of Guadalupe key chain inside her purse for spiritual aid and bursts into tears. She is still thinking about Joe Senior stretched out on one of the ratty orange bedspreads at the Thunderbird Motel.

"Hey, it's not that bad," he says.

Lucy Ortiz looks down because her eyes are full of tears. She sees her own feet—nice, slightly plump feet in a pair of sheer pantyhose and a librarian's sensible summer sandals with closed toes so as not to upset the patrons. Granted, the shoes are red and have slightly too much heel, but underneath, her toenails are modestly painted mauve. Her feet are planted in the dirt. Visitors might call it earth and remark on its spiritual healing qualities, but to Lucy it is dirt, red dirt, chicken-pecked dirt, cholla cactus dirt, prickly pear dirt, dirt dirt.

"I bet it won't even cost fifty dollars to fix," he says. "Even if you have to pay it against the deductible, it's nothing to cry about."

Lucy Ortiz sobs openly.

"Okay, look," he says, "I won't even bother to get it fixed. That door is pretty dented anyway. I won't even file."

The tears run down her face.

"Come on," he says, "I'll take you to lunch. You eat lunch, don't you? I can't stand to see a pretty woman cry."

Lucy gives him the chilly look of her conquistador forebears and of her paternal grandmother, who was the meanest woman in two counties. "Lunch?"

"Lunch. Like a sandwich. A beer. Chili. Like eating."

"I'm getting divorced," says Lucy Ortiz.

"Oh . . . that," he says. "Well, divorced or married, you still have to eat."

"Where are we going?" asks Lucy.

"I thought maybe to Dave's Not Here. We'll take my car. I'll drive," he adds magnanimously.

Dave's Not Here smells of hamburgers, green chili, lemonade, a week of sunshine. Not adobe chic—the salt, pepper, and ketchup sit right on the table. Like half the restaurants in town it was once part of a coke deal. But the *federales* had caught Dave. When the new owners—formerly, a feminist vegetable Co-op—bought the place, Dave was in jail in El Paso and his creditors were banging on the door. Hence the name—Dave's Not Here.

At Dave's the linoleum is clean and the chocolate cake is as big as the dark side of the moon. Lucy studies the menu even though she knows it by heart. She wants fried onions on her hamburger, but can she eat onions on a date? Does it count as a date if you have sideswiped the guy? Does it count as a date if you haven't had sex with anyone besides your husband in seventeen years?

The guy across the table thinks this is a date. He is even telling her his name, that he works as a surveyor, and that right now he is working for Sandia Pueblo on a boundary line dispute. He listens as Lucy talks about her two children and her job as a state librarian. It turns out they both like hiking and unexcavated archaeological sites—potsherds and bits of volcanic glass. Lucy eats her hamburger as if she were a normal person. She eats her onions because she realizes this is not a date. She hates all men everywhere and could never marry her luncheon companion because he is not Catholic. Then she agrees to go walking with him in the back country at Bandelier next Saturday. That will not be a date either. She is just being nice because she backed into his car.

After lunch the surveyor drops Lucy back at her car. She knows that should she ever overcome her revulsion for handsome men with mustaches and kiss him or even go to bed with him, it would not be a date, because her heart is broken. She decides to take the rest of the day off and call in sick. Divorce has made her sick. She gets into her car, which she loves. It is spotlessly clean. Joe Senior gave her one of those little hand vacuums two Christmases ago, during that good year after he'd stopped sleeping with his secretary and before he'd started sleeping with the family dentist. She loves the vacuum cleaner and uses it weekly.

Just a few miles from her house Lucy is forced to stop by a flooded arroyo. An arroyo is the bed that temporary water makes in a dry place. Three hundred and sixty-four days a year it is dry, but today it is running fast, brown with muddy foam, and carrying the carcass of a cottonwood tree.

Lucy Ortiz stands in the red New Mexico mud. There is no way she can cross the arroyo. She has been married practically her whole life. Lucy Ortiz reaches down and picks up a handful of dirt. Experimentally she squeezes it between her fingers, then she puts a small daub on her cheek. It feels both warm and cool, like kissing a baby.

She rubs a little across her chin and opens her mouth as if she is going to eat some. She unbuttons first the top button of her white rayon blouse and then the next. She takes off her blouse and white bra and begins to cover her breasts with mud. She takes off her tailored purple skirt until she is standing in just her taupe pantyhose and her red shoes. She begins to smear mud over her belly, covering the stretch marks from pregnancy.

Mud trickles under the elastic of her pantyhose. Now Lucy Ortiz slips down the elastic band. The pantyhose begin to run as she tears off one foot, then the other. She covers her ankles, knees, and thighs with mud. She stands stark naked, covered with mud, in the middle of the New Mexico afternoon, between her car and the flooding arroyo. But she is still a sensible woman. She will not throw herself in the arroyo. She will not believe that death is as easy as taking off her pantyhose. She reminds herself that she was not a virgin when she married Joe Senior, despite the long white veil. She will wash in the water of the arroyo and put on her skirt and drive home barefoot the long way round. She will make tortillas by hand and cook beans for her children. She will marry the next man who asks her. She will be a good wife, but not yet. She stands naked, her thirty-seven-year-old body covered in mud that trickles down her breasts and thighs. She isn't crying. She isn't thinking about her no-good ex-husband. Lucy Ortiz is thinking that she isn't the kind of woman who is easy to fool twice.

HURT BOOKS

Edra Ziesk

I know I shouldn't be spending my whole life thinking about Joe and how to get him to come back, but I can't help it. Nothing else really interests me. I've talked to Joe about it and he says it isn't healthy. He says I should go out and get myself a full-time job, then I'd be too busy to think about him and I'd also have a retirement plan and some medical coverage. This is basically Joe's solution to everything, but as I've told him about four thousand times, I'm only twenty-seven. I'm not interested. Besides, I like the job I have. I only have to work three days a week, which gives me time to do other things, even though right now that's mostly thinking about Joe. I'm a secretary to a psychiatrist. I feel secure working in a shrink's office, though it's not the kind of security Joe's talking about. It's like it makes me immune from contracting any kind of mental illness myself. The office is quiet, it's like a club or a library with dark floor-to-ceiling bookcases and green leather chairs. I sit in the waiting room behind a glass-topped mahogany desk that's so large it makes me feel like a child whose feet don't touch the floor. I answer the phone and type Dr. Friedman's notes off a transcribing machine with earphones that look like the paws of small animals. I have a lot of time to think about Joe. I got used to my life being Joe and me—we were married for four and a half years. My life is still Joe and me; being divorced hasn't really changed that. Sometimes I see him doing stuff that's already happened. Like it's the night before he moved out more than a year ago. Joe's standing in our living room looking out the window, even though there's nothing to see in the dark except the lit-up red-pink apartment across the way where, for years, a man wearing only boxer shorts stood at his window and watched us.

"I'm really going to miss this place," Joe says. His voice is low and he speaks without inflection. There's a light on in the kitchen;

it makes the skin of Joe's back look yellow and luminous. I can see the slightly darker alley that travels the length of his spine.

"It's a dump," he says, meaning the apartment. I look up at the large cornflake-shaped strips of paint unrolling from the steam pipe. "But I'm really going to miss it." He pauses. "When I move out," he says. I can hear him forcing himself to use those words and other words—divorce, separate, split, go. When we used to say them about other people, they seemed only tinged with distant menace; now they detonate inside him, leaving his insides stewed and bloodied. I watch myself watching Joe, not knowing what to say. I am the one who decided he should leave; who decided our life, which had felt as safe as a used nest, had suddenly closed up around me. Needing to be by myself felt urgent. I didn't know that as soon as he moved out I would start to want him back.

There's a mantelpiece clock in Dr. F's office, the kind where the slow gold works are visible under a domed crystal. Today—it's a Tuesday—Joe's going out of town. His flight was at 10:40. All day I've been looking at the clock and thinking: now he's leaving for the airport, now he's sitting on the plane. I am ghosting through his life. I can feel the weight of his legs dropping down into the seat; the knobby hardness of his pelvic bones. When he looks out the window, I can see the delicate red threads in the whites of his eyes.

I turn on an all-news radio station every twenty-two minutes, which is how long it takes them to give you the world. They don't say anything about a plane crash. I go home after work and sit on the bed hoping Joe will call. I asked him to, so I'd know he was safe. He got pissed off. "Listen," he said, "we aren't married, you don't have to worry about it anymore." I think he might call anyway. I've always been his check-in point. I sit with my legs crossed and examine the crease behind my knee. The TV is on in the living room. I can make out the commercials because the volume goes up. The rest of the time I just hear an undercurrent of sound like the distant rumble of trucks. I'm jittery and wired. I pick up the phone a few times to make sure it's working, but I'm afraid Joe will be calling me right at that second, so I hang up. I get furious at the phone for not ringing. This is what it would feel like if Joe had died, I tell myself. I start to get breathless and panicky. I get myself some brandy and flip through the TV stations, but I can't stand being this far from the phone, as if the few feet between the living room and the bedroom puts an extra unbearable distance between us. I go back inside and sit on the bed in the same cross-legged position. It makes me a little calmer. I think about calling up every hotel in Los Angeles until I find the one Joe's staying at. That makes me a little calmer too. I wonder how many hotels there are in L.A. I fall asleep with my clothes and all the lights on. The brandy is on the floor next to the bed. When I wake up, a cloud of alcohol blooms up out of the glass.

On Saturday morning the phone rings. "Hi," Joe says. It sounds like two words. On the second, his voice goes up. He's surprised that I'm home. I'm out a lot. I walk around, hang out in bars, so I'll have to spend as little time as possible by myself in the apartment. Joe thinks I'm out with friends, some mysterious collection I've acquired since he moved out. "Like who?" I say. I don't have many friends. I got used to it being just the two of us.

"How ya doing?" Joe says. I hear a chair creak, as if he is settling back.

"Where are you?" I say.

"Home." Home. The word hangs there: home, what place is that? I've never been to the apartment Joe lives in now or seen his furniture, what he has on the walls, the views from his windows. It sounds like a setback, that he has begun to call that place home. "So," I say. "How was the trip?"

"Oh, boring," he says and yawns, as if to prove this. "Same old shit. You know how those conventions are." I do know. We used to work in the same place, this small advertising agency that wouldn't take soap or cigarette or fast-food accounts. I left when we got married—they have this rule about married couples, and everyone knew it was Joe who'd be staying. It was okay, though, since I wanted to do other things. I thought I might try to be a writer. I had a teacher in college who said I had a writerly eye but lacked discipline. Joe said that pretty much summed me up.

"Jackie," he says. "Don't think I'm nuts or anything, but were you *over* here or something lately?"

"Over there?" I say. "You mean your apartment?" I feel odd, as if he found out about this plan I have of going to sit on his front stoop some night, waiting for him to come home.

"Listen to this, this is the weirdest thing," Joe says. "Remember those little books you used to make me?"

"Books?" I say.

"Books. You know. Those drawings?" I used to hide notes when Joe went out of town, in his toiletry case, in the pockets of his shirts. They were small books made out of folded sheets of blue or white Xerox paper. I illustrated them with stick figures of myself—a skinny long-legged person with a mess of wild-looking curly hair. I wrote little stories, stuff the person was up to when Joe went away. In one, she cried so much she filled up two buckets with briny water which she saved to make cucumber pickles. In another, she strapped herself to the underbelly of Joe's plane with leather belts.

"Yeah?" I say.

"Well, I get down to L.A., I'm putting my shit in the bathroom, and I find one."

"Really?" I say. I am pleased this is what Joe has called to tell me. It makes me hopeful. My cheeks feel as pink as cherries. "I wonder how that got there. Osmosis?" I know it's an old note I probably once stuck in his toilet case and he forgot about. I can picture how the red Pentel I used to draw it has bled, turning pink and blurred from the wetness of his toothbrush. "What'd it look like?" I say. "Describe it." I'm sitting on a kitchen stool next to the phone. I look down at my bare thighs spreading across the seat.

"Well, it was you—you know, that stick person—strewing flowers all over the bed or something. You're standing on the bed," he says.

"Yup," I say. "Sounds like me."

"On the outside it says, 'The person who's here wishes to inform the person who's there . . .' and on the inside . . ." I hear him unfolding the paper. It sounds stiff and cracked and old. Sadness shoots through me, quick and delicate, like a feathery crack in an eggshell. It gets my attention. " 'That she hates sleeping alone,' " Joe is saying, " 'and so has decided to turn the bed into a garden.' "

"Not *strewing* flowers," I say. "*Watering* them! And at the bottom it says, 'Consider this fair warning. I miss you, come home,' right?"

"Yeah," Joe says. His voice is low. It is flat and sad and unbearable, as if he has caught himself doing some futile thing.

THE BROKEN BED

"Joe," I say, "it's still true. I miss you. More." I draw the sentence out. I can feel him slipping away, like a fast-moving silvery fish.

"Don't start this stuff, okay? What's the point? What's done is done." I try to think of something to say, a way to argue with him, but all I can think of are other little clichés: a stitch in time, a bird in the hand. To Joe, the divorce was huge and catastrophic, like a flood or an earthquake, against which he had no defense. Now it is over. He wants to put it all behind him. He wants—he has told me a hundred times—to get on with it and says I should do the same. If I cry, tell him I wish he would come back, he won't call me for days; if I call him he'll speak in curt sentences and stick to general subjects like sports or the news in the paper. "Look," he says, "let me go, I have stuff to take care of. I haven't even unpacked yet, everything smells like an airport. I'll talk to you next week."

"Next week is your birthday!" I say, trying to keep him on the phone. He'll be thirty-one. "Let's get together and have drinks— notice I put an s on that. On me."

"On you! You don't have two nickels to rub together!"

"I have enough. For drinks."

"Let me see how it goes," Joe says.

"Work, you mean?" I sound too eager. I know he does not mean work. He means if he can take it, being around me, even on neutral territory. "I'd really like to see you," I say. I realize I am sitting here with my fingers crossed.

I buzz Dr. F on the intercom as soon as I know her last patient has left because I see him go out through the side door on Seventy-eighth Street. Dr. F shows her patients out through the side so they won't have to run into each other in the waiting room, their eyes hopping all over like furtive rabbits. I ask her if it's okay if I take a long lunch. I've been trying to buy Joe a birthday present for three days.

I go into Barnes & Noble. They're paving the sidewalk out front and you can only get in or out by walking single file across a raised plank that has too much give and bounces back against you. Everyone crosses it with a loopy, goofy step, looking like cartoon characters.

It's cool inside. There's a crowd of prep-school teenagers hanging out, talking in clear loud voices that sound rude and jarring in a bookstore. The girls are wearing pastel tank tops and dangling earrings made out of beads. I start looking through a table where there's a sign that says "Hurt Books." It's a random collection, in no order. The books cost $1.98. Their covers have small flaps torn in them and are blurred from overhandling. I keep twisting my head from side to side so I can read the titles. I see one called *The Mick* by Mickey Mantle. It jumps right out at me. Mickey Mantle is Joe's all-time favorite hero. One year I gave him a Mickey Mantle key chain. It had a picture of Mantle in a round plastic disc the size of the face of a child's watch. I bought it in a store that sold antique campaign buttons and sports memorabilia. I gave it to Joe in a necklace box. "Oh, wow," he said when he opened it. He sounded awed. "This is the best gift anybody ever gave me." He held the key chain up to the light and looked at it as if it were made out of deep-colored lustrous stones.

Out of nowhere there's this great rolling pain inside me, as intense and as sudden as a fall caused by an invisible slick of ice. It makes me jump back and take two steps away from the table. Everything's mined. There is no thing that has not somehow touched or passed through or surrounded Joe and me during our marriage, and everything—book titles, colors, the heat—everything hurts. I leave the store without buying anything.

It's two days after Joe's birthday. I'm in the coffee shop where I go for lunch every day and eat things with no nutritional value. Today I am having pound cake that came wrapped in a piece of matted plastic and iced tea made from henna-colored powder with sugar and lemon flavoring already mixed in. It leaves a metallic aftertaste.

I didn't send Joe a birthday card. They all seemed tastelessly cheerful. Some didn't have enough space to write anything; some, the blank ones, had too much space. I'd either have to go on and on or leave a large white or blue or salmon-colored gap. My idea was to call Joe and talk him into letting me buy him that drink, but when he heard it was me, all the juice ran out of his voice and I barely got out "Happy birthday" before he hustled me off the phone.

Today, before lunch, I went to a card store. I got a card with a bunch of clocks on the outside, all set at different times like in an airport or a war room. On the inside it said, "I didn't miss your birthday. I got confused." The left side of the card was blank. I decided to draw one of those picture notes. I got out a blue pen. At the top I wrote, "A Dance for Your Birthday," then I started drawing the wild-haired stick figure doing dance steps. She twirled around. She did splits and leaps and cartwheels. When I drew her in a handstand, I turned the card upside down so the twisty curls would fly in the right direction. One of the countermen came over and cocked his head to see what I was doing. "Oooh," he says. "Very bee-you-tee-ful!" I slapped my hand down on the card. The spoon in my iced tea glass jumped.

I was up to the last picture. I was going to draw the little stick figure holding a bouquet of flowers out in front of her with a "Happy Birthday" streamer trailing down. The counterman came back to serve the people sitting next to me. He had a line of large and small dishes up his arm. There was a strong mixed smell of stew and the counterman's sweat. I wanted to get out of there. I wanted to get the card in the mail so I could start thinking about Joe receiving it. I could picture him smiling, starting to melt down, even though I know Joe basically thinks my sending him cards now is like some kind of booby prize. So I rushed the last drawing. I didn't do the hair right, which I drew with three or four squiggly strands like cooked fusilli on either side of this round moon face, and I realized when I finished it that the picture looked like a girl in a dress, holding a bouquet, wearing a veil. It looked like a bride. Forget it, I told myself. Even I knew there was no way I could send Joe a card with a picture of a stick person who was supposed to be me dressed like a bride on it.

So I tore it up. I threw it away in the wire trash can on the corner instead of leaving it on my plate where, I was sure, the counterman would pick it up and paste it back together. I decided I'd go back to Barnes & Noble and buy *The Mick*. I ran the eight blocks to the bookstore. The new sidewalk out front was dry and they'd taken the plank away. I went to the Hurt Books section and started scanning titles but I didn't see it, so I walked around to the other side of the table for a different perspective. I went through the books slowly, one at a time, flipping my fingers along the spines. It wasn't here—I couldn't believe it. For a second I couldn't move. I stood there, my hand hovering above the books as if I was about to bless them. I felt like I'd lost this one chance: if I could just have the right thing to give Joe, everything would be okay. Except, at the same time I'm thinking it, I'm aware of this other thought, right at the edge of my consciousness: that it didn't make any difference. Joe wasn't going to come back.

But I wouldn't let myself think about it. I left the store. By the time I hit the street I had a reserve plan, Plan B. Tonight, after work, I'd go downtown and check out the Barnes & Noble on Eighteenth Street. They'd have it. That store is fucking humongous. They have everything.

PART VI

THE FOREVER BED

I WAS BORN TO SPEAK YOUR NAME

Tom Clark

I knew the tune
It was my song
Even before you came along
Yet only then did I perceive its meaning

This *you* I wished for
This desired Other of whom
I spoke so glowingly in poems
I never knew its name

When I lifted its arms up
I noticed tiny wings
That's all I knew
The rest was Muselike
Anonymous this "you"

So I guess those poems
Were like phonecalls to the future
I think I had your number
Knew what I was looking for
Even before I found it
In the face directory

And luckiest of all
Your human substance
Was life's loveliest
Far as I could see

As if I'd placed
Bones and skin
Together in a dream
You were put together that way
But I wouldn't let it go to my head if I were you

LOVE SONG

Theodore Enslin

Though we have travelled far
we have not reached
the mountains.
                    Mons Veneris,
the mountain of love,
is as far from us now
as when we set out fresh
in the early morning.
Now we are tired, and feel old.
The only things worth looking at
are the mountains:
                    Love's
and a few others,
catching the late flame of the sun,
almost down,
                    behind us.

THE FOREVER BED

233

From: GERALD'S PARTY

ROBERT COOVER

"Somehow," she said now, gazing around wearily (she was standing in front of me, easing her shoes off: I hadn't seen her come up),
"parties don't seem as much fun as they used to." She sat down
beside me, curling under my arm, the one I could still move, and
tucked her feet up. "It's almost as though the parties have started
giving us instead of us giving the parties . . ." She loosened my shirt,
lay her head sleepily against my chest. "It gives me a . . . funny
feeling . . ."

"Yes . . ."

"Still, I guess it's worth it . . ."

The woman in Greece had said something much like that about
making love. She'd had an appetite for the unusual, the perverse
even, and I too was pretty jaded in those days, frustrated by the
commonplaces of sex, bored with all its trite conventions—the state
of the art, so to speak—and so in need of ever greater novelty, ever
greater risktaking, in order to arouse myself to any kind of performance. What worked for her—and thus for us both—was to be unexpectedly violated in a more or less public place, the key to a
successful orgasm being not so much the setting or the use of force
as the element of surprise. It was a kind of essential trigger for her—
like having to scare someone out of her hiccups. Thus, I might walk
her through public parks, churches, department stores, taunting her
with exotic possibilities while yet denying her, only to jump on her
back in the busy hotel lobby while asking for the key. Or I might
arrange a night out at some mysterious destination, coax her into
dressing up elaborately, then get her out of the hotel, hail a taxi—
and suddenly violate her on the sidewalk just as she was stepping
into the cab. I don't know why I thought that pitful of decayed
atrocity victims would work. Perhaps because it seemed so unlikely.
But nothing happened. In fact it was a disaster. We got filthy, she

hurt her back on the bones, got her nose bloodied, I cracked my elbow, we were both choking with dust, and when it was over—or rather, when there was no point in going on—she told me just to leave her alone and go away. I never saw her again, my last vision of her being sprawled out there in the—"*Ouch!*"

"Sorry, Gerald, is something . . . ?" She had been stroking me through the trousers and had caught the place where Jim had nicked me. She opened my trousers carefully, eased my shorts down. "Oh, I see . . ." She licked it gently, then took the crown into her mouth, coating it with warm saliva. "Bat's a bad bwuise, too," she observed, touching my tummy, then let her mouth slide gradually down the shaft. I reached for the hem of her dress and she shifted her hips, turning her knees toward the back of the couch.

There was a sudden crash, the whole house shook—I lurched away, reared up—and then a scraping, another crash, a rumble, something rolling in the street. She closed her mouth around my penis again, curled her hands behind my hips, tugged at the back of my trousers.

"But . . . my god, what *was* that—?!"

"Pwobabwy Chawwey puwwing out ubba dwibe . . ."

"Ah . . ." She eased my trousers down below my hips—outside, there was another crunch, the distant squealing of tires—then pulled them away from between my thighs. She put my hand back on the hem of her dress. There was a tag there, I noticed, stamped by the city police department. "Wewacsh, Gewawd," she whispered. I liked the pushing of her tongue against the consonants and, surrendering to that, slid down toward her knees. "Tell me again . . ."

"Wewacsh, Gewawd . . . ?"

"Yes . . . good . . ." It all comes down to words, as I might have argued with Vic. Or parts of them. "Is this a new dress?"

"Yeumf," she said, working my trousers down to my ankles: I lifted out foot one and raised it to the couch. "Do woo wike it?"

"Right now, it's in my way . . ."

"You say the nicest things, Gerald," she sighed, taking her mouth away. She located the fastener, unhooked it, pushed at the skirt: I pulled it away and, stretching forward, eased it past her feet. "What are you doing with pancake makeup on the back of your neck?" she asked.

"I don't remember."

I tugged at her panty girdle, stretching it down past her soft hips, and she took my penis in her mouth again, warming it all over, closing one hand tenderly around my testicles. She kneaded them softly, pulling them toward her as though gently pumping them, sliding her other hand around to stroke my buttocks, finger my anus. Only one arm worked for getting her clothes off her: I left the dead one between her legs for the time being and she squeezed her thighs around it. "Just . . . a minute . . ." The panties and stockings came off in a tangle. I ran my tongue slowly up her leg from her calf, past her knee, and up the inside of her thigh: she spread her legs and, as I nosed into her vulva, lifted the top one over my head. "Mmmmf!" She had her finger up my anus now and was sucking rhythmically, her mouth full of foamy saliva like a warm bubble bath. I had found the nub of her clitoris with the tip of my tongue and now worked against it as though trying to pry it open. I reached round from behind, dipped my fingers into her moist vagina, pushed one of them up her rectum—"*Ouch!*" she cried, letting my penis go.

"Sorry . . ." I pushed my nose deeper between her thighs to have a closer look: her anus was drawn up in a tight little pucker, inflamed and cracked, slightly discolored as though rubbed with ashes. "How did you—?"

"You know. The police." She paused, holding my penis by the root. Perhaps she was studying it. Or simply reflecting.

I pressed my chin against the hood of her clitoris, gazing thoughtfully at her crinkled anus, remembering now her position on the butcherblock (as though being changed, I'd thought as they lowered her), her thighs stretching back, belly wrinkling, tiny little red lines running down her cheeks. "What . . . what's an exploding sausage . . . ?" I asked uneasily.

"Oh, Gerald!" She laughed and wagged my penis playfully. "Don't you know a joke when you hear one?"

"Ah . . ." I stroked her buttocks gently as my penis returned to its soothing bath, rubbing my chin rhythmically against her pubic knoll. Like veined marble, they'd seemed to me at the time, as I remembered, something like that, though now they sparkled with a kind of fresh dewy innocence (it was the kind of feeling I had between my own legs now) under the bright overhead light. She was beginning to grind vigorously against my chin, thighs cuffing my ears, so I moved my mouth back over her rosy lips, dipping my tongue into their warm mushy depths—I was aswim in warm mushy depths, we were both—

"Say, uh . . . where the hell *is* everybody?" someone asked. I peered up between my wife's convulsing thighs, my own hips bucking against the cushions: it was Knud, standing bleary-eyed over us, rubbing the back of his neck. "Crikey!" he muttered, his voice phlegmy with sleep. "You'll never believe the dream I just had!"

"Everybody's gone home, Knud," I gasped, my chin sliding now in the dense juices beneath it.

"Hunh?" He frowned at his empty wrist. My wife had stopped pumping her head up and down the shaft of my penis, but she was still sucking at it rhythmically and stroking it with her tongue, marking time, as it were, her throbbing clitoris searching for my mouth. "Even Kitty? Jeez, what time is it?"

"*Everybody's* gone, Knud. It's *late.*"

"Holy cow, I must have slept through the whole goldarn party," he rumbled, still staring at his wrist. He yawned, belched. "Boy! What a dream, though!" My wife's hips had stopped pitching. She held my testicles and one buttock firmly, but had let my penis slide past her teeth into one cheek. "I was like in some kind of war zone, see, only everyone was all mixed up and you didn't know who was on your side—"

"Not now, Knud," my wife panted, letting me go and twisting round to look up at him. Her buttocks spread a bit, giving me a clearer view of Knud: he was puffy-eyed and rumpled, tie undone, shirttail out, pants damp and sticky, and he looked like he needed a shave.

"No, listen, it was a lot longer. And really weird. Since you couldn't be sure who anybody was, see, just to be safe you naturally had to kill everyone—right? Ha ha! You wouldn't *believe* the blood and gore! And all in 3-D and full color, too, I kid you not! I kept running into people and asking them: 'Where *am* I?' They'd say: 'What a *loony,*' or something like that—and then I'd chop their heads off, right?"

"Please, Knud—?"

He glanced down at my penis withering in my wife's hand, at

her buttocks flattening out in front of my face. "Oh, right . . . sorry . . ." He gazed around at the living room, running his hand through his snarled hair. "Say, do you remember, was I wearing a watch when I came here tonight?"

"Well . . ." my wife began tentatively, raising herself up on one elbow, and I cut in: "I can't remember, Knud."

He seemed to accept that. He squinted up at the lights on the ceiling for a moment, yawning. "Kitty been gone long?"

"No, you can probably catch her." I was beginning to feel my wife's weight: I gave a little push and she lifted herself off my face. "Don't get up," Knud insisted. "I can find my own way out." He stumbled away, stuffing his shirttail in. My wife, sitting up, let her hand fall idly on my hip. We could hear Knud peeing noisily in the toilet bowl. It was a lonely sound, but not so lonely as the silence all around it. "At least it's working," my wife said. She picked up her stockings and panty girdle, toweled between her legs with them. "Hey, thanks," said Knud from the doorway. "See you at the next one."

"Flush it, please, Knud!" my wife called, but he was already out the door. "Oh well." I curled around her from behind, hugging her close, and she patted my hip with sleepy affection. My penis nuzzled between her cheeks. It felt good there. It was something to think about. "Do you notice a kind of chill in here?" she murmured sleepily.

"Well, all the windowpanes are out," I said. I ran my hand along her thigh where it met the couch. "We could try the TV room now that Knud's vacated it . . ."

She smiled, a bit wearily, then took my good hand and pulled me to my feet. I kicked off the trousers, still tangled around one foot, and, holding hands, we stepped out from under the tented drapes and linens into the glare and wreckage of what was once our living room. She drew close to me suddenly, pressing her naked hip against mine. I was feeling it, too. As though the house had not been emptying out so much as filling up. The windows, stripped bare and paneless, seemed to crowd in on us, letting the dark night at their edges leak in like some kind of deadly miasma. Hugging each other's waists, we picked our way barefoot through the shards of broken pots and glassware, the food squashed into the carpet, the chalk outlines and bent cocktail skewers. The wall next to the dining room doorway was splattered and streaked with a mince pie someone must have thrown, and even that, innocent as it was, seemed to add to our feelings of apprehension and melancholy.

The wall above the dining room sideboard was eloquently vacant, the picture hooks sitting on it like a pair of pinned insects. Bottles lay tipped like fallen soldiers, liquor still, amazingly enough, gurgling from one of the open mouths. "What exactly happened to Vic?" my wife whispered.

"He . . . got shot . . ."

"He makes you think of Tania's painting, doesn't he? The one with the eyes . . ."

"Well . . ."

I tugged her on into the TV room. We seemed safer in here somehow. Maybe because the lights were softer ("Our antique lamps are missing," she remarked quietly as though in explanation) or because the drapes were still on the windows and the furniture more or less where it ought to be. Or just the soothing blueness of the walls. I could feel my wife's hip soften and I too seemed to walk less stiffly, my knees unlocking, my scrotum sliding back into place. Snow played on the TV screen, making a scratchy noise like a needle caught on the outer lip of a record, but I didn't want to turn it off. It was company of sorts. "I'll put a cassette on," I said, letting go her waist, and she sat down on the sofa to wait. "Don't be long, Gerald," she yawned.

I couldn't seem to find any of our old tapes, but there were plenty of new ones scattered about to choose from. "How about 'The Ancient Arse'?" I proposed, reading the labels. "Or 'Cold Show at the Ice Palace'—or here's one: 'The Garden Peers.' "

"I think that's *pee*-ers. I've seen that one. I don't want to see it again." Ah. I understand now. "Below the Stairs," "Butcherblock Blues," "Party Time," "Life's Mysterious Currents," "The Host's Hang-up," they all fell dismally into place. "Candid Coppers." "Some Dish." "Special Favors." I felt defeated even before I'd begun. There were tears in my eyes and a strange airy tingling on my exposed behind, like a ghostly remembrance of cold knuckles. I shuddered. "Put on 'Hidden Treasure,' " my wife suggested, unbuttoning her blouse and jacket.

I searched through the pile of cassettes, intent on doing my best, getting through it somehow, but my appetite had faded. "It . . . it will never be the same again," I muttered, my throat tight.

"Tsk. You said that the last time, Gerald. After Archie and Emma and . . ."

"Yes, well . . ." It was true, I'd all but forgotten. "But Ros, Vic, Tania . . ."

"Roger, Noble . . ."

"Yes, that's right, Roger . . ."

"Fiona . . ."

"Fiona—?" I took off the cassette labeled "The Wayward Finger," and inserted "Hidden Treasure," rewound it to the beginning, punched the "Play" button, wishing it were all so easy as that.

"Yes, that was why Cyril was so upset." She was completely naked now, stretched out on the sofa, hands behind her head, eyes half-closed, scratching the bottom of her foot with one toe. "How do you think Peg found out?"

"Found out what?" I took off my shirt, folded it neatly over the back of the sofa, stalling for time. On the TV, my mother-in-law was getting Mark into his pajama bottoms. "That's better," she was saying. Mark was holding Peedie, which now had one of Sally Ann's patches sewn on its underside. "HOT TWOT," it said.

"Well, she was pregnant."

"Peg was?"

"No, Fiona." I sat down beside her and stroked her thighs, pushing into the warm place between her legs, but my heart wasn't in it. Mark, on the television screen, was asking: "What's a 'twot,' Gramma?" Behind him, his bedroom door was all smashed in. "That's the whole point, Gerald. Didn't you notice? It was very obvious."

"It's a . . . a faraway place," my mother-in-law was explaining. "A kind of secret garden . . ."

"I'm not sure I saw her all night," I said. Maybe it was the scar, cold and bluish in the light from the flickering TV image, that was bothering me. I looked around, spied one of her aprons hanging over the edge of the games table.

"Is it always hot, Gramma?"

"But you heard Peg carrying on when she left—she was telling everybody!"

"No, it's warm. Like a bed. Now you crawl up into yours there, young man."

"I guess I missed that." I brought the apron over: "Listen, do you mind—?"

"But then that's why everyone was feeling so sorry for Cyril after." She raised her hips so I could tie the apron on. "Will I ever go there someday?" Mark was asking. "You know, to lose them both in one night . . ."

"Both—?"

"It seems inevitable, child . . ."

"Yes—my goodness, Gerald, where *were* you?" I slid my hand up under the apron: yes, this was better. There was a faint stirring at last between my legs, which my mother-in-law appeared to be overseeing from the TV screen, her face marked by a kind of compassionate sorrow mixed with amusement. "Tell me a story about it, Gramma," Mark was pleading sleepily, as she led him to the bed. "You missed just about everything!"

"About what?" she asked.

"You know, the Twot," said Mark, as my hand reached my wife's pubis. I let my fingers scratch gently in the hair there, while my thumb slid between her thighs and curled into her vagina. "Well, once upon a time," she began, lifting Mark onto the bed, and I too lifted slightly, then let her down again. "You know . . . sometimes, Gerald . . . ," she sighed, closing her hands gently over mine, . . . "it's almost as if . . ." "There was a young prince . . ."

". . . you were at a different party . . ."

"Was his name Mark?"

I edged closer to my wife's hips, my thumb working rhythmically against the ball of my index finger ("Oh yes . . . good . . ."), and she took my wilted organ in her hand. On the television screen, my mother-in-law was tucking Mark in. "All right then, a young prince named Mark—but get down under the covers, or I won't tell it."

I pushed my thumb as deep as it would go, while at the same time stretching my fingers up her belly, her pubis thrusting at me under the apron, closing around my thumb, her own hand (my mother-in-law had already launched Prince Mark out on his "unique adventure," but Mark wanted to know: "Where's his mommy and daddy? Is he a orphan?") stroking me with a gentle but insistent cadence, slowly helping me forget what I'd been sticking out from under the games table a moment ago when I'd reached for her apron: a foot, wrapped in a plastic bag, one toe poking out. Its nail painted. Cherry red. "No, he was the little boy of Beauty and the—her husband . . ." my mother-in-law was saying, as the prospect of orgasm swelled in my mind like a numbing intuition. I gazed down at my wife, her hair unrolled now and loose about her pale shoulders, her thin lips parted, nostrils flared, and thought I could hear Ros whispering: *Oh yes, let's!*

Oh no . . .

". . . But he was a big boy now and it was time to leave home and seek his own fortune . . ."

I was frightened and wanted to stop ("We are in it, Gerry, we cannot get out of it," I seemed to hear Vic mumble right outside the door—had he moved somehow?!), but my wife was blindly pulling me toward her, spreading her legs, the apron wrinkling up between us, and my genitals, it seemed, were quite willing to carry on without the rest of me. "We can only stand up to it or chicken out . . ."

What? Vic—?

"Was the Beast nice now?"

"Oh yes, yes . . . !" my wife was gasping.

"Most of the time . . ."

I'd let go my thumbhold on her pubic handle and, twisting my hand around, my mouth sucking at a breast now (ah, what was it I *really* wanted? I didn't want to think about it . . .), had slid my handful of fingers down there instead, my bodily parts separating out like a houseful of drunken and unruly guests, everybody on his own. She tugged still at that most prodigious member, the host, as it were ("He paused at the edge of the Enchanted Forest: it was dreary and dangerous and . . ."), pumping it harder and harder, her other hand grasping my testicles like a doorknob: she gave them a turn, opened, and, going up on my knees as though to offer my behind to the invading emptiness ("And . . . dark?" asked Mark fearfully, hugging his Peedie under the blankets), mouth still at her breast, I crossed over between her legs.

THE UNMADE BED

"Yes . . . !"

"Hurry, Gerald!"

"I'm afraid, Gramma!"

There was a congestion now of fingers and organs, a kind of rubbery crowding up around the portal ("But he was not alone," my mother-in-law was explaining in an encouraging voice), but then she slipped her hands out to snatch at my buttocks, yanking them fiercely toward her as though to keep them from floating away like hot-air balloons—perhaps I'd been worrying about this, I felt like I was coming apart and falling together at the same time—and as her legs jerked upward ("Little Prince Mark was protected by his faithful companion Peedie the Brave Rabbit . . ."), I dropped in through the ooze as though casting anchor. *This*, I was thinking with some excitement, and with some bewilderment as well—what *is* this "we" when the I's are gone?—is my *wife!*

TRUE LOVE

Sharon Olds

In the middle of the night, when we get up
after making love, we look at each other
in total friendship, we know so fully
what the other has been doing. Bound to each other like
soldiers coming out of a battle,
bound with the tie of the birth-room, we
wander down the hall to the bathroom, I can
hardly walk, we weave through the dark
soft air, I know where you are
with my eyes closed, we are bound to each other with the
huge invisible threads of sex, though our
sexes themselves are muted, dark and
exhausted and delicately crushed, the whole
body is a sex—surely this
is the most blessed time of life,
the children deep asleep in their beds like a
vein of coal and a vein of gold
not discovered yet. I sit on the
toilet in the dark, you are somewhere in the room, I
open the window and the snow has fallen in a
deep drift against the pane, I
look up into it, a
world of cold crystals, silent and
glistening so I call out to you and you
come and hold my hand and I say
I cannot see beyond it! I cannot see beyond it!

THE HEART STUMBLES IN DARKNESS

Nathaniel Tarn

Anxious at every moment of his life, without fail.
Each time, as if he were on the brink of an abyss.
At every moment, lapsing a step into the darkness.
That cavern where consciousness seems to vegetate,
a hollow prison full of dark steps, trip and fall.
"If I could only bury my face in her body — invade
her, hang out for some time as in the sacred river
of salvation bathed in waters as cool as their own
definition, come out on the other side of herself,
like the word having its being in the world, *then*,
I could know that single moment free of it, again,
that moment would spread out everywhere and assume
all time, to home in purified, recovered, reborn."
Little but the week has gone by in his divine city
where men still hear of salvation; the narcissi on
his desk are still pungent and send him, all night
messages of self-pleasure — yet, already he misses
her odors where she sits on the world and makes it
human for him to adopt, be reborn into, as if from
a lifelong death, fear, that companion at his side
walking with deliberate slowness, the black beast,
in pace with him, stalling the outcome of the sun.

BODY

Robert Creeley

Slope of it,
hope of it—
echoes faded,
what waited

up late inside
old desires
saw through
the screwed importunities.

This regret?
Nothing's left.
Skin's old,
story's told—

but still touch,
selfed body,
wants other,
another mother

to him, her
insistent "sin"
he lets in
to hold him.

Selfish bastard,
headless catastrophe.
Sans tits, cunt,
wholly blunt—

fucked it up,
roof top, loving cup,
sweatered room,
old love's tune.

Age dies old,
both men and women cold,
hold at last no one,
die alone.

Body lasts forever,
pointless conduit,
floods in its fever,
so issues others parturient.

Through legs wide,
from common hole site,
aching information's dumb tide
rides to the far side.

WHAT WE TALK ABOUT
WHEN WE TALK ABOUT LOVE

Raymond Carver

My friend Mel McGinnis was talking. Mel McGinnis is a cardiologist, and sometimes that gives him the right.

The four of us were sitting around his kitchen table drinking gin. Sunlight filled the kitchen from the big window behind the sink. There were Mel and me and his second wife, Teresa—Terri, we called her—and my wife, Laura. We lived in Albuquerque then. But we were all from somewhere else.

There was an ice bucket on the table. The gin and the tonic water kept going around, and we somehow got on the subject of love. Mel thought real love was nothing less than spiritual love. He said he'd spent five years in a seminary before quitting to go to medical school. He said he still looked back on those years in the seminary as the most important years in his life.

Terri said the man she lived with before she lived with Mel loved her so much he tried to kill her. Then Terri said, "He beat me up one night. He dragged me around the living room by my ankles. He kept saying, 'I love you, I love you, you bitch.' He went on dragging me around the living room. My head kept knocking on things." Terri looked around the table. "What do you do with love like that?"

She was a bone-thin woman with a pretty face, dark eyes, and brown hair that hung down her back. She liked necklaces made of turquoise, and long pendant earrings.

"My God, don't be silly. That's not love, and you know it," Mel said. "I don't know what you'd call it, but I sure know you wouldn't call it love."

"Say what you want to, but I know it was," Terri said. "It may sound crazy to you, but it's true just the same. People are different, Mel. Sure, sometimes he may have acted crazy. Okay. But he loved me. In his own way maybe, but he loved me. There was love there, Mel. Don't say there wasn't."

Mel let out his breath. He held his glass and turned to Laura and me. "The man threatened to kill me," Mel said. He finished his drink and reached for the gin bottle. "Terri's a romantic. Terri's of the kick-me-so-I'll-know-you-love-me school. Terri, hon, don't look that way." Mel reached across the table and touched Terri's cheek with his fingers. He grinned at her.

"Now he wants to make up," Terri said.

"Make up what?" Mel said. "What is there to make up? I know what I know. That's all."

"How'd we get started on this subject, anyway?" Terri said. She raised her glass and drank from it. "Mel always has love on his mind," she said. "Don't you, honey?" She smiled, and I thought that was the last of it.

"I just wouldn't call Ed's behavior love. That's all I'm saying, honey," Mel said. "What about you guys?" Mel said to Laura and me. "Does that sound like love to you?"

"I'm the wrong person to ask," I said. "I didn't even know the man. I've only heard his name mentioned in passing. I wouldn't know. You'd have to know the particulars. But I think what you're saying is that love is an absolute."

Mel said, "The kind of love I'm talking about is. The kind of love I'm talking about, you don't try to kill people."

Laura said, "I don't know anything about Ed, or anything about the situation. But who can judge anyone else's situation?"

I touched the back of Laura's hand. She gave me a quick smile. I picked up Laura's hand. It was warm, the nails polished, perfectly manicured. I encircled the broad wrist with my fingers, and I held her.

"When I left, he drank rat poison," Terri said. She clasped her arms with her hands. "They took him to the hospital in Santa Fe. That's where we lived then, about ten miles out. They saved his life. But his gums went crazy from it. I mean they pulled away from his teeth. After that, his teeth stood out like fangs. My God," Terri said. She waited a minute, then let go of her arms and picked up her glass.

"What people won't do!" Laura said.

"He's out of the action now," Mel said. "He's dead."

Mel handed me the saucer of limes. I took a section, squeezed it over my drink, and stirred the ice cubes with my finger.

"It gets worse," Terri said. "He shot himself in the mouth. But he bungled that too. Poor Ed," she said. Terri shook her head.

"Poor Ed nothing," Mel said. "He was dangerous."

Mel was forty-five years old. He was tall and rangy with curly soft hair. His face and arms were brown from the tennis he played. When he was sober, his gestures, all his movements, were precise, very careful.

"He did love me though, Mel. Grant me that," Terri said. "That's all I'm asking. He didn't love me the way you love me. I'm not saying that. But he loved me. You can grant me that, can't you?"

"What do you mean, he bungled it?" I said.

Laura leaned forward with her glass. She put her elbows on the table and held her glass in both hands. She glanced from Mel to Terri and waited with a look of bewilderment on her open face, as if amazed that such things happened to people you were friendly with.

"How'd he bungle it when he killed himself?" I said.

"I'll tell you what happened," Mel said. "He took this twenty-two pistol he'd bought to threaten Terri and me with. Oh, I'm serious, the man was always threatening. You should have seen the way we lived in those days. Like fugitives. I even bought a gun myself. Can you believe it? A guy like me? But I did. I bought one for self-defense and carried it in the glove compartment. Sometimes I'd have to leave the apartment in the middle of the night. To go to the hospital, you know? Terri and I weren't married then, and my first wife had the house and kids, the dog, everything, and Terri and I were living in this apartment here. Sometimes, as I say, I'd get a call in the middle of the night and have to go in to the hospital at two or three in the morning. It'd be dark out there in the parking lot, and I'd break into a sweat before I could even get to my car. I never knew if he was going to come up out of the shrubbery or from behind a car and start shooting. I mean, the man was crazy. He was capable of wiring a bomb, anything. He used to call my service at all hours and say he needed to talk to the doctor, and when I'd return the call, he'd say, 'Son of a bitch, your days are numbered.' Little things like that. It was scary, I'm telling you."

"I still feel sorry for him," Terri said.

"It sounds like a nightmare," Laura said. "But what exactly happened after he shot himself?"

Laura is a legal secretary. We'd met in a professional capacity. Before we knew it, it was a courtship. She's thirty-five, three years younger than I am. In addition to being in love, we like each other and enjoy one another's company. She's easy to be with.

"What happened?" Laura said.

Mel said, "He shot himself in the mouth in his room. Someone heard the shot and told the manager. They came in with a passkey, saw what had happened, and called an ambulance. I happened to be there when they brought him in, alive but past recall. The man lived for three days. His head swelled up to twice the size of a normal head. I'd never seen anything like it, and I hope I never do again. Terri wanted to go in and sit with him when she found out about it. We had a fight over it. I didn't think she should see him like that. I didn't think she should see him, and I still don't."

"Who won the fight?" Laura said.

"I was in the room with him when he died," Terri said. "He never came up out of it. But I sat with him. He didn't have anyone else."

"He was dangerous," Mel said. "If you call that love, you can have it."

"It was love," Terri said. "Sure, it's abnormal in most people's eyes. But he was willing to die for it. He did die for it."

"I sure as hell wouldn't call it love," Mel said. "I mean, no one knows what he did it for. I've seen a lot of suicides, and I couldn't say anyone ever knew what they did it for."

Mel put his hands behind his neck and tilted his chair back. "I'm not interested in that kind of love," he said. "If that's love, you can have it."

Terri said, "We were afraid. Mel even made a will out and wrote to his brother in California who used to be a Green Beret. Mel told him who to look for if something happened to him."

THE FOREVER BED

251

Terri drank from her glass. She said, "But Mel's right—we lived like fugitives. We were afraid. Mel was, weren't you, honey? I even called the police at one point, but they were no help. They said they couldn't do anything until Ed actually did something. Isn't that a laugh?" Terri said.

She poured the last of the gin into her glass and waggled the bottle. Mel got up from the table and went to the cupboard. He took down another bottle.

"Well, Nick and I know what love is," Laura said. "For us, I mean," Laura said. She bumped my knee with her knee. "You're supposed to say something now," Laura said, and turned her smile on me.

For an answer, I took Laura's hand and raised it to my lips. I made a big production out of kissing her hand. Everyone was amused.

"We're lucky," I said.

"You guys," Terri said. "Stop that now. You're making me sick. You're still on the honeymoon, for God's sake. You're still gaga, for crying out loud. Just wait. How long have you been together now? How long has it been? A year? Longer than a year?"

"Going on a year and a half," Laura said, flushed and smiling.

"Oh, now," Terri said. "Wait awhile."

She held her drink and gazed at Laura.

"I'm only kidding," Terri said.

Mel opened the gin and went around the table with the bottle.

"Here, you guys," he said. "Let's have a toast. I want to propose a toast. A toast to love. To true love," Mel said.

We touched glasses.

"To love," we said.

Outside in the backyard, one of the dogs began to bark. The leaves of the aspen that leaned past the window ticked against the glass. The afternoon sun was like a presence in this room, the spacious light of ease and generosity. We could have been anywhere, somewhere enchanted. We raised our glasses again and grinned at each other like children who had agreed on something forbidden.

"I'll tell you what real love is," Mel said. "I mean, I'll give you a good example. And then you can draw your own conclusions." He poured more gin into his glass. He added an ice cube and a sliver of lime. We waited and sipped our drinks. Laura and I touched knees again. I put a hand on her warm thigh and left it there.

"What do any of us really know about love?" Mel said. "It seems to me we're just beginners at love. We say we love each other and we do, I don't doubt it. I love Terri and Terri loves me, and you guys love each other too. You know the kind of love I'm talking about now. Physical love, that impulse that drives you to someone special, as well as love of the other person's being, his or her essence, as it were. Carnal love and, well, call it sentimental love, the day-to-day caring about the other person. But sometimes I have a hard time accounting for the fact that I must have loved my first wife too. But I did, I know I did. So I suppose I am like Terri in that regard. Terri and Ed." He thought about it and then he went on. "There was a time when I thought I loved my first wife more than life itself. But now I hate her guts. I do. How do you explain that? What happened to that love? What happened to it, is what I'd like to know. I wish someone could tell me. Then there's Ed. Okay, we're back to Ed. He loves Terri so much he tries to kill her and he winds up killing himself." Mel stopped talking and swallowed from his glass. "You guys have been together eighteen months and you love each other. It shows all over you. You glow with it. But you both loved other people before you met each other. You've both been married before, just like us. And you probably loved other people before that too, even. Terri and I have been together five years, been married for four. And the terrible thing, the terrible thing is, but the good thing too, the saving grace, you might say, is that if something happened to one of us tomorrow, I think the other one, the other person, would grieve for a while, you know, but then the surviving party would go out and love again, have someone else soon enough. All this, all of this love we're talking about, it would just be a memory. Maybe not even a memory. Am I wrong? Am I way off base? Because I want you to set me straight if you think I'm wrong. I want to know. I mean, I don't know anything, and I'm the first one to admit it."

"Mel, for God's sake," Terri said. She reached out and took hold of his wrist. "Are you getting drunk? Honey? Are you drunk?"

THE FOREVER BED

253

"Honey, I'm just talking," Mel said. "All right? I don't have to be drunk to say what I think. I mean, we're all just talking, right?" Mel said. He fixed his eyes on her.

"Sweetie, I'm not criticizing," Terri said.

She picked up her glass.

"I'm not on call today," Mel said. "Let me remind you of that. I am not on call," he said.

"Mel, we love you," Laura said.

Mel looked at Laura. He looked at her as if he could not place her, as if she was not the woman she was.

"Love you too, Laura," Mel said. "And you, Nick, love you too. You know something?" Mel said. "You guys are our pals," Mel said.

He picked up his glass.

Mel said, "I was going to tell you about something. I mean, I was going to prove a point. You see, this happened a few months ago, but it's still going on right now, and it ought to make us feel ashamed when we talk like we know what we're talking about when we talk about love."

"Come on now," Terri said. "Don't talk like you're drunk if you're not drunk."

"Just shut up for once in your life," Mel said very quietly. "Will you do me a favor and do that for a minute? So as I was saying, there's this old couple who had this car wreck out on the interstate. A kid hit them and they were all torn to shit and nobody was giving them much chance to pull through."

Terri looked at us and then back at Mel. She seemed anxious, or maybe that's too strong a word.

Mel was handing the bottle around the table.

"I was on call that night," Mel said. "It was May or maybe it was June. Terri and I had just sat down to dinner when the hospital called. There'd been this thing out on the interstate. Drunk kid, teenager, plowed his dad's pickup into this camper with this old couple in it. They were up in their mid-seventies, that couple. The kid—eighteen, nineteen, something—he was DOA. Taken the steering wheel through his sternum. The old couple, they were alive, you understand. I mean, just barely. But they had everything. Multiple fractures, internal injuries, hemorrhaging, contusions, lacerations, the works, and they each of them had themselves concussions. They were in a bad way, believe me. And, of course, their age was two strikes against them. I'd say she was worse off than he was. Ruptured spleen along with everything else. Both kneecaps broken. But they'd been wearing their seat belts and, God knows, that's what saved them for the time being."

"Folks, this is an advertisement for the National Safety Council," Terri said. "This is your spokesman, Dr. Melvin R. McGinnis, talking." Terri laughed. "Mel," she said, "sometimes you're just too much. But I love you, hon," she said.

"Honey, I love you," Mel said.

He leaned across the table. Terri met him halfway. They kissed.

"Terri's right," Mel said as he settled himself again. "Get those seat belts on. But seriously, they were in some shape, those oldsters. By the time I got down there, the kid was dead, as I said. He was off in a corner, laid out on a gurney. I took one look at the old couple and told the ER nurse to get me a neurologist and an orthopedic man and a couple of surgeons down there right away."

He drank from his glass. "I'll try to keep this short," he said. "So we took the two of them up to the OR and worked like fuck on them most of the night. They had these incredible reserves, those two. You see that once in a while. So we did everything that could be done, and toward morning we're giving them a fifty-fifty chance, maybe less than that for her. So here they are, still alive the next morning. So, okay, we move them into the ICU, which is where they both kept plugging away at it for two weeks, hitting it better and better on all the scopes. Se we transfer them out to their own room."

Mel stopped talking. "Here," he said, "let's drink this cheapo gin the hell up. Then we're going to dinner, right? Terri and I know a new place. That's where we'll go, to this new place we know about. But we're not going until we finish up this cut-rate, lousy gin."

Terri said, "We haven't actually eaten there yet. But it looks good. From the outside, you know."

"I like food," Mel said. "If I had it to do all over again, I'd be a chef, you know? Right, Terri?" Mel said.

He laughed. He fingered the ice in his glass.

"Terri knows," he said. "Terri can tell you. But let me say this.

THE FOREVER BED

255

If I could come back again in a different life, a different time and all, you know what? I'd like to come back as a knight. You were pretty safe wearing all that armor. It was all right being a knight until gunpowder and muskets and pistols came along."

"Mel would like to ride a horse and carry a lance," Terri said.

"Carry a woman's scarf with you everywhere," Laura said.

"Or just a woman," Mel said.

"Shame on you," Laura said.

Terri said, "Suppose you came back as a serf. The serfs didn't have it so good in those days," Terri said.

"The serfs never had it good," Mel said. "But I guess even the knights were vessels to someone. Isn't that the way it worked? But then everyone is always a vessel to someone. Isn't that right, Terri? But what I liked about knights, besides their ladies, was that they had that suit of armor, you know, and they couldn't get hurt very easy. No cars in those days, you know? No drunk teenagers to tear into your ass."

"Vassals," Terri said.

"What?" Mel said.

"Vassals," Terri said. "They were called vassals, not vessels."

"Vassals, vessels," Mel said, "what the fuck's the difference? You knew what I meant anyway. All right," Mel said. "So I'm not educated. I learned my stuff. I'm a heart surgeon, sure, but I'm just a mechanic. I go in and I fuck around and I fix things. Shit," Mel said.

"Modesty doesn't become you," Terri said.

"He's just a humble sawbones," I said. "But sometimes they suffocated in all that armor, Mel. They'd even have heart attacks if it got too hot and they were too tired and worn out. I read somewhere that they'd fall off their horses and not be able to get up because they were too tired to stand with all that armor on them. They got trampled by their own horses sometimes."

"That's terrible," Mel said. "That's a terrible thing, Nicky. I guess they'd just lay there and wait until somebody came along and made a shish kebab out of them."

"Some other vessel," Terri said.

"That's right," Mel said. "Some vassal would come along and

spear the bastard in the name of love. Or whatever the fuck it was they fought over in those days."

"Same things we fight over these days," Terri said.

Laura said, "Nothing's changed."

The color was still high in Laura's cheeks. Her eyes were bright. She brought her glass to her lips.

Mel poured himself another drink. He looked at the label closely as if studying a long row of numbers. Then he slowly put the bottle down on the table and slowly reached for the tonic water.

"What about the old couple?" Laura said. "You didn't finish that story you started."

Laura was having a hard time lighting her cigarette. Her matches kept going out.

The sunshine inside the room was different now, changing, getting thinner. But the leaves outside the window were still shimmering, and I stared at the pattern they made on the panes and on the Formica counter. They weren't the same patterns, of course.

"What about the old couple?" I said.

"Older but wiser," Terri said.

Mel stared at her.

Terri said, "Go on with your story, hon. I was only kidding. Then what happened?"

"Terri, sometimes," Mel said.

"Please, Mel," Terri said. "Don't always be so serious, sweetie. Can't you take a joke?"

"Where's the joke?" Mel said.

He held his glass and gazed steadily at his wife.

"What happened?" Laura said.

Mel fastened his eyes on Laura. He said, "Laura, if I didn't have Terri and if I didn't love her so much, and if Nick wasn't my best friend, I'd fall in love with you. I'd carry you off, honey," he said.

"Tell your story," Terri said. "Then we'll go to that new place, okay?"

"Okay," Mel said. "Where was I?" he said. He stared at the table and then he began again.

"I dropped in to see each of them every day, sometimes twice a day if I was up doing other calls anyway. Casts and bandages, head to foot, the both of them. You know, you've seen it in the movies. That's just the way they looked, just like in the movies. Little eye-holes and nose-holes and mouth-holes. And she had to have her legs slung up on top of it. Well, the husband was very depressed for the longest while. Even after he found out that his wife was going to pull through, he was still very depressed. Not about the accident, though. I mean, the accident was one thing, but it wasn't every-thing. I'd get up to his mouth-hole, you know, and he'd say no, it wasn't the accident exactly but it was because he couldn't see her through his eye-holes. He said that was what was making him feel so bad. Can you imagine? I'm telling you, the man's heart was break-ing because he couldn't turn his goddamn head and *see* his goddamn wife."

Mel looked around the table and shook his head at what he was going to say.

"I mean, it was killing the old fart just because he couldn't *look* at the fucking woman."

We all looked at Mel.

"Do you see what I'm saying?" he said.

Maybe we were a little drunk by then. I know it was hard keeping things in focus. The light was draining out of the room, going back through the window where it had come from. Yet nobody made a move to get up from the table to turn on the overhead light.

"Listen," Mel said. "Let's finish this fucking gin. There's about enough left here for one shooter all around. Then let's go eat. Let's go to the new place."

"He's depressed," Terri said. "Mel, why don't you take a pill?"

Mel shook his head. "I've taken everything there is."

"We all need a pill now and then," I said.

"Some people are born needing them," Terri said.

She was using her finger to rub at something on the table. Then she stopped rubbing.

"I think I want to call my kids," Mel said. "Is that all right with everybody? I'll call my kids," he said.

Terri said, "What if Marjorie answers the phone? You guys, you've heard us on the subject of Marjorie? Honey, you know you don't want to talk to Marjorie. It'll make you feel even worse."

"I don't want to talk to Marjorie," Mel said. "But I want to talk to my kids."

"There isn't a day goes by that Mel doesn't say he wishes she'd get married again. Or else die," Terri said. "For one thing," Terri said, "she's bankrupting us. Mel says it's just to spite him that she won't get married again. She has a boyfriend who lives with her and the kids, so Mel is supporting the boyfriend too."

"She's allergic to bees," Mel said. "If I'm not praying she'll get married again, I'm praying she'll get herself stung to death by a swarm of fucking bees."

"Shame on you," Laura said.

"Bzzzzzzz," Mel said, turning his fingers into bees and buzzing them at Terri's throat. Then he let his hands drop all the way to his sides.

"She's vicious," Mel said. "Sometimes I think I'll go up there dressed like a beekeeper. You know, that hat that's like a helmet with the plate that comes down over your face, the big gloves, and the padded coat? I'll knock on the door and let loose a hive of bees in the house. But first I'd make sure the kids were out, of course."

He crossed one leg over the other. It seemed to take him a lot of time to do it. Then he put both feet on the floor and leaned forward, elbows on the table, his chin cupped in his hands.

"Maybe I won't call the kids, after all. Maybe it isn't such a hot idea. Maybe we'll just go eat. How does that sound?"

"Sounds fine to me," I said. "Eat or not eat. Or keep drinking. I could head right on out into the sunset."

"What does that mean, honey?" Laura said.

"It just means what I said," I said. "It means I could just keep going. That's all it means."

"I could eat something myself," Laura said. "I don't think I've ever been so hungry in my life. Is there something to nibble on?"

"I'll put out some cheese and crackers," Terri said.

But Terri just sat there. She did not get up to get anything.

Mel turned his glass over. He spilled it out on the table.

"Gin's gone," Mel said.

Terri said, "Now what?"

I could hear my heart beating. I could hear everyone's heart. I could hear the human noise we sat there making, not one of us moving, not even when the room went dark.

NOW THAT I AM NEVER ALONE

Tess Gallagher

In the bath I look up and see the brown moth
pressed like a pair of unpredictable lips
against the white wall. I heat up
the water, running as much hot in as I can stand.
These handfuls of water over my shoulder—how once
he pulled my head against his thigh and dipped
a rivulet down my neck of coldest water from the spring
we were drinking from. Beautiful mischief
that stills a moment so I can never look
back. Only now, brightest now, and the water
never hot enough to drive that shiver out.

But I do remember solitude—no other
presence and each thing what it was. Not this raw
fluttering I make of you as you have made of me
your watch-fire, your killing light.

LEGACY

Laurie Duesing

The new man sends 3 cans of tuna,
a brown bag of filberts and a letter.
When I am ready, he writes, we will hunt
chanterelles in Oregon. Fish in Alaska.

The label on the tuna says Bumble Bee
and large yellow insects nestle their bodies
in bright flowers. I am 40 years old.
The man I love died 9 weeks ago.

In every room of my house I can see
at least one photograph of him. In the one
I look at now he sits sidesaddle
on his motorcycle, smiling at me.

He was always in motion. But since he died,
I can't stop moving. I am looking
for his body, backlit by the sun. I walk
out to the yard filled with plants

he gave me. Gladiolas spray peach and magenta
into the air. See what you've done,
I say. Nothing can keep me from it.
Everything you gave me is in bloom.

A MIRACLE

After you'd been killed, you often walked up
behind me and rested your hands on my shoulders.
That was no miracle. Neither was the fact I'd catch
you in peripheral glance pacing the living room,
your right arm crooked over your head,
fingers raking your thick dark hair.
Nor the mornings I found the garage door open
your tools rearranged on the cement floor.
I knew you'd never leave me, something the physician
who would not let me hold your dead hand
failed to understand. He was trying to separate
the living woman from the dead man and did not know
the living and the dead never let go.
Simply because they don't have to.
So when I lift your green T-shirt from the drawer
to feel your body's smells or when you speak
to me in my dreams, never think I am ungrateful.
But even with the sweetness of nothing, flesh longs
for its kind. The next time your spirit walks
the house, if you'd stop, hold still
and let me come to you, hold your hand in mine,
that, my love, would be a miracle.

A WONDERFUL WOMAN

ALICE ADAMS

Feeling sixteen, although in fact just a few months short of sixty, Felicia Lord checks into the San Francisco hotel at which her lover is to meet her the following day. Felicia is tall and thin, with the intense, somewhat startled look of a survivor—a recent widow, mother of five, a ceramicist who prefers to call herself a potter. A stylish gray-blonde. Mr. Voort, she is told, will be given the room next to hers when he arrives. Smiling to herself, she then follows the ancient wizened bellboy into an antique elevator cage; once inside, as they creakingly ascend, he turns and smiles up at her, as though he knows what she is about. She herself is less sure.

The room to which he leads her is a suite, really: big, shabby-cozy living room, discreetly adjoining bedroom, large old-fashioned bath, on the top floor of this old San Francisco hotel, itself a survivor of the earthquake and fire, in an outlying neighborhood. All in all, she instantly decides, it is the perfect place for meeting Martin, for being with him, in the bright blue dazzling weather, this sudden May.

San Francisco itself, connected as it is with Felicia's own history, has seemed a possibly dangerous choice: the scene of her early, unlikely premarital "romance" with Charles, her now dead husband; then the scene of holiday visits from Connecticut with the children, treat zoo visits and cable-car rides, Chinese restaurants; scene of a passionate ill-advised love affair, and a subsequent abortion—all that also took place in San Francisco, but years ago, in other hotels, other neighborhoods.

Why then, having tipped the grinning bellboy and begun to unpack, silk shirts on hangers, silk tissue-papered nightgowns and underthings in drawers, does she feel such a dizzying lurch of apprehension? It is too intense in its impact to be just a traveler's nerves, jet lag. Felicia is suddenly quite weak; she sits down in an easy chair next to the window to absorb the view, to think sensibly about her situation, or try to. She sees a crazy variety of rooftops: mansard, Victorian curls, old weathered shingles and bright new slate. Blue water, paler sky, green hills. No help.

It is being in love with Martin, she thinks, being "in love," and the newness of Martin Voort. I've never known a farming sailor before, and she smiles, because the words don't describe Martin, really, although he owns some cranberry bogs, near Cape Cod, and he builds boats. Charles was a painter, but he was rich (Martin is not rich) and most of his friends were business people. Martin is entirely new to her.

And at my age, thinks Felicia, and she smiles again, a smile which feels tremulous on her mouth.

"Wonderful" is the word that people generally have used about Felicia. She was wonderful with Charles, whose painting never came to much, although he owned a couple of galleries, who drank a lot. Wonderful to all those kids, who were a little wild, always breaking arms or heads.

Her lover—a Mexican Communist, and like Charles a painter, but a much better painter than Charles—Felipe thought she looked wonderful, with her high-boned face, strong hands and her long, strong voluptuous body. She was wonderful about the abortion, and wonderful too when he went back to his wife.

Felicia was wonderful when Charles died, perfectly controlled and kind to everyone.

Wonderful is not how Felicia sees herself at all; she feels that she has always acted out of simple—or sometimes less simple—necessity.

Once married to Charles, and having seen the lonely, hollow space behind his thin but brilliant surface of good looks, graceful manners, skill at games—it was then impossible to leave him; and he couldn't have stood it. And when the children had terrible coughs, or possible concussions, she took good care of them, sometimes staying up all night, simply because she wanted them well, and soon.

During the unanesthetized abortion, she figured out that you don't scream, because that would surely make the pain much worse, when it is already so bad that it must be happening to someone else, and also because the doctor, a Brazilian chiropractor in the Mission District, is hissing, "Don't make noise." And when your lover defects, saying that he is going back, after all, to his wife in Guadalajara, you don't scream about that either; what good would it do? You go back to your husband, and to the clay pots that you truly love, round and fat or delicately slender.

When your husband dies, as gracefully as he lived, after a too strenuous game of tennis, you take care of everything and everyone, and you behave well, for your own sake as well as for everyone else's.

Then you go to visit an old friend, in Duxbury, and you meet a large wild red-haired, blue-eyed man, a "sailor-farmer," and you fall madly in love, and you agree to meet him for a holiday, in May, in San Francisco, because he has some boats to see there.

She is scared. Sitting there, in the wide sunny window, Felicia trembles, thinking of Martin, the lovely city, themselves, for a long first time. But supposing she isn't "wonderful" anymore? Suppose it all fails, flesh fails, hearts fail, and everything comes crashing down upon their heads, like an avalanche, or an earthquake?

She thinks, I will have to go out for a walk.

Returned from a short tour of the neighborhood, which affords quick beautiful views of the shining bay, and an amazing variety of architecture, Felicia feels herself restored; she is almost her own person again, except for a curious weakness in her legs, and the faintest throb of blood behind one temple, both of which she ascribes to fatigue. She stands there for a moment on the sidewalk, in the sunlight, and then she re-enters the hotel. She is about to walk past the desk when the bellboy, still stationed there, waves something in her direction. A yellow envelope—a telegram.

She thanks him and takes it with her into the elevator, waiting to open it until she is back in her room. It will be from Martin, to welcome her there. Already she knows the character of his gestures: he hates the phone; in fact, so far they have never talked on the telephone, but she has received at least a dozen telegrams from Martin, whose instructions must always include: "Deliver, do not phone." After the party at which they met he wired, from Boston to Duxbury: HAVE DINNER WITH ME WILL PICK YOU UP AT SEVEN MARTIN VOORT. Later ones were either jokes or messages of love—or both: from the start they had laughed a lot.

This telegram says: DARLING CRAZY DELAY FEW DAYS LATE ALL LOVE.

The weakness that earlier Felicia had felt in her legs makes them now suddenly buckle; she falls across the bed, and all the blood in both temples pounds as she thinks: I can't stand it, I really can't. This is the one thing that is too much for me.

But what do you do if you can't stand something, and you don't scream, after all?

Maybe you just go to bed, as though you were sick?

She undresses, puts on a pretty nightgown and gets into bed, where, like a person with a dangerously high fever, she begins to shake. Her arms crossed over her breast, she clutches both elbows; she presses her ankles together. The tremors gradually subside, and finally, mercifully, she falls asleep, and into dreams. But her sleep is fitful, thin, and from time to time she half wakes from it, never at first sure where she is, nor what year of her life this is.

A long time ago, in the early forties, during Lieutenant (USN) Charles Lord's first leave, he and Felicia Thacher, whom he had invited out to see him, literally danced all night, at all the best hotels in town—as Felicia wondered: Why me? How come Charles picked me for this leave? She had known him since childhood; he was one of her brother's best friends. Had someone else turned him down? She had somewhat the same reactions when he asked her to marry him, over a breakfast glass of champagne, in the Garden Court of the Palace Hotel. Why me? she wondered, and she wondered too at why she was saying yes. She said yes, dreamily, to his urgent eyes, his debonair smile, light voice, in that room full of wartime glamour, uniforms and flowers, partings and poignant brief reunions. Yes, Charles, yes, let's do get married, all right, soon.

A dream of a courtship, and then a dream groom, handsome Charles. And tall, strong-boned, strong-willed Felicia Thacher Lord.

Ironically, since she had so many, Felicia was not especially fond of babies; a highly verbal person, she was nervous with human creatures who couldn't talk, who screamed out their ambiguous demands, who seemed to have no sense and who often smelled terrible. She did not see herself as at all a good mother, knowing how cross and frightened she felt with little children. Good luck (Charles's money) had provided her with helpful nurses all along to relieve her of the children, and the children of her, as she saw it. Further luck made them all turn out all right, on the whole. But thank God she was done with all that. Now she liked all the children very much; she regarded them with great fondness, and some distance.

Her husband, Charles, loved Felicia's pregnancies (well, obviously he did), and all those births, his progeny. He spoke admiringly of how Felicia accomplished all that, her quick deliveries, perfect babies. She began to suspect that Charles had known, in the way that one's unconscious mind knows everything, that this would be the case; he had married her to be the mother of his children.

"I have the perfect situation for a painter, absolutely perfect," Charles once somewhat drunkenly declared. "Big house, perfect studio, money for travel, money to keep the kids away at school. A wonderful kind strong wife. Christ, I even own two galleries. *Perfect.* I begin to see that the only thing lacking is talent," and he gave a terrible laugh.

How could you leave a man in such despair?

Waking slowly, her head still swollen with sleep, from the tone of the light Felicia guesses that it must be about midafternoon. Eventually she will have to order something to eat, tea or boiled eggs, something sustaining.

Then, with a flash of pain, Martin comes into her mind, and she begins to think.

She simply doesn't know him, that's half the problem, "know" in this instance meaning able to predict the behavior of, really, to trust. Maybe he went to another party and met another available lady, maybe someone rather young, young-fleshed and never sick or tired? (She knows that this could be true, but still it doesn't sound quite right, as little as she knows him.)

But what does FEW DAYS mean to Martin? To some people a week would be a few days. CRAZY DELAY is deliberately ambiguous. Either of those phrases could mean anything at all.

Sinkingly, despairingly, she tells herself that it is sick to have fantasies about the rest of your life that revolve around a man you have only known for a couple of months.

Perfectly possibly he won't come to San Francisco at all, she thinks, and then: I hate this city.

When the bellboy comes in with her supper tray, Felicia realizes for the first time that he is a dwarf; odd that she didn't see that before. His grin now looks malign, contemptuous, even, as though he recognizes her for what she now is: an abandoned woman, of more than a certain age.

As he leaves she shivers, wishing she had brought along a "sensible" robe, practical clothes, instead of all this mocking silk and lace. Looking quickly into the mirror, and then away, she thinks, I look like an old circus monkey.

She sleeps through the night. One day gone, out of whatever "few days" are.

When she calls to order breakfast the next morning, the manager (manageress: a woman with a strong, harsh Midwestern accent) suggests firmly that a doctor should be called. She knows of one.

Refusing that suggestion, as firmly, politely as she can, Felicia knows that she reacted to hostility rather than to concern. The manageress is afraid that Felicia will get really sick and die; what a mess to have on their hands, an unknown dead old woman.

But Felicia too is a little afraid.

Come to think of it, Felicia says to herself, half-waking at what must be the middle of the afternoon, I once spent some time in another San Francisco hotel, waiting for Felipe, in another part of town. After the abortion.

She and Felipe met when he had a show at one of Charles's galleries; they had, at first tipsily, fallen into bed, in Felipe's motel (Charles had "gone to sleep") after the reception; then soberly, both passionately serious, they fell in love. Felipe's paintings were touring the country, Felipe with them, and from time to time, in various cities, Felicia followed him. Her excuse to Charles was a survey of possible markets for her pots, and visits to other potters, which, conscientiously, she also accomplished.

Felipe was as macho as he was radical, and he loved her in his own macho way, violently, with all his dangerous strength. She must leave Charles, Charles must never touch her again, he said. (Well, Charles drank so much that that was hardly an issue.) She must come with him to Paris, to a new life. All her children were by then either grown or off in schools—why not?

When they learned that she was pregnant he desperately wanted their child, he said, but agreed that a child was not possible for them. And he remembered the Brazilian chiropractor that he had heard about, from relatives in San Francisco.

The doctor seemingly did a good job, for Felicia suffered no later ill effects. Felipe was kind and tender with her; he said that her courage had moved him terribly. Felicia felt that her courage, if you wanted to call it that, had somewhat unnerved him; he was a little afraid of her now.

However, they celebrated being together in San Francisco, where Felipe had not been before. He loved the beautiful city, and they toasted each other, and their mutual passion, with Mexican beer or red wine, in their Lombard Street motel. Then one afternoon Felipe went off alone to visit a family of his relatives, in San Jose, and Felicia waited for him. He returned to her very late, and in tears: a grown man, broad-backed, terrifically strong, with springing thick black hair and powerful arms, crying out to her, "I cannot—I cannot go on with you, with our life. They have told me of my wife, all day she cries, and at night she screams and wakes the children. I must go to her."

Well, of course you must, said Felicia, in effect. If she's screaming that's where you belong. And she thought, Well, so much for my Latin love affair.

And she went home.

And now she thinks, Martin at least will not come to me in tears.

Martin Voort. At the end of her week in Duxbury, her visit to the old school friend, Martin, whom in one way or another she had seen every day, asked her to marry him, as soon as possible. "Oh, I know we're both over the hill," he said, and then exploded in a laugh, as she did too. "But suppose we're freaks who live to be a hundred? We might as well have a little fun on the way. I like you a lot. I want to be with you."

Felicia laughed again. She was secretly pleased that he hadn't said she was wonderful, but she thought he was a little crazy.

He followed her home with telegrams: WHEN OH WHEN WILL YOU MARRY ME and ARRIVING IN YOUR TOWN THIS FRIDAY PREPARE.

And now, suppose she never sees him again? For the first time in many months (actually, since Charles died) Felicia begins to cry, at the possible loss of such a rare, eccentric and infinitely valuable man.

But in the midst of her sorrow at that terrible possibility, the permanent lack of Martin—who could be very sick, could have had a stroke: at his age, their age, that is entirely possible—though grieving, Felicia realizes that she can stand it, after all, as she has stood other losses, other sorrows in her life. She can live without Martin.

She realizes too that she herself has just been genuinely ill, somewhat frighteningly so; what she had was a real fever, from whatever cause. Perhaps she should have seen a doctor.

However, the very thought of a doctor, a doctor's office, is enough to make her well, she dislikes them so; all those years of children, children's illnesses and accidents, made her terribly tired of medical treatment. Instead she will get dressed and go out for dinner, by herself.

And that is what she does. In her best clothes she takes a cab to what has always been her favorite San Francisco restaurant, Sam's. It is quite early, the place uncrowded. Felicia is given a pleasant side table, and the venerable waiters are kind to her. The seafood is marvelous. Felicia drinks a half-bottle of wine with her dinner and she thinks: Oh, so this is what it will be like. Well, it's really not so bad.

Returned to the hotel, however, once inside her room she experiences an acute pang of disappointment, and she understands that she had half-consciously expected Martin to be there; Martin was to be her reward for realizing that she could live without him, for being "sensible," for bravely going out to dinner by herself.

She goes quickly to bed, feeling weak and childish, and approving neither her weakness nor her childishness, not at all.

Sometime in the middle of the night she awakes from a sound sleep, and from a vivid dream; someone, a man, has knocked on the door of her room, this room. She answers, and he comes in and they embrace, and she is wildly glad to see him. But who is he? She can't tell: Is it her husband, Charles, or one of her sons? Felipe? Is it Martin? It could even be a man she doesn't know. But, fully awake, as she considers the dream she is saddened by it, and it is quite a while before she sleeps again.

The next morning, though, she is all right: refreshed, herself again. Even in the mirror, her face is all right. I look like what I am, she thinks: a strong healthy older woman. She dresses and goes downstairs to breakfast, beginning to plan her day. Both the bellboy and the manager smile in a relieved way as she passes the desk, and she smiles back, amiably.

She will see as much of San Francisco as possible today, and arrange to leave tomorrow. Why wait around? This morning she will take a cab to Union Square, and walk from there along Grant Avenue, Chinatown, to North Beach, where she will have lunch. Then back to the hotel for a nap, then a walk, and dinner out—maybe Sam's again.

She follows that plan, or most of it. On Union Square, she goes into a couple of stores, where she looks at some crazily overpriced clothes, and buys one beautiful gauzy Indian scarf, for a daughter's coming birthday. Then down to Grant Avenue, to walk among the smells of Chinese food, the incense, on to North Beach, to a small Italian counter restaurant, where she has linguine with clam sauce, and a glass of red wine.

In the cab, going back to the hotel, she knows that she is too tired, has "overdone," but it was worth it. She has enjoyed the city, after all.

An hour or so later, from a deep, deep sleep she is awakened by a knocking on her door, just as in her dream, the night before.

Groggily she calls out, "Who is it?" She is not even sure that the sound has been real; so easily this could be another dream.

A man's impatient, irritated voice answers, "It's me, of course."

Me? She is still half asleep; she doesn't know who he is. However, his tone has made her obedient, and she gets out of bed, pulling her robe about her, and goes to the door. And there is a tall, red-haired man, with bright blue eyes, whom of course she knows, was expecting—who embraces her violently. "Ah, Martin," she breathes, when she can.

It is Martin, and she is awake.

The only unfamiliar thing about his face, she notes, when she can see him, is that a tooth is missing from his smile; there is a small gap that he covers with his hand as soon as she has noticed. And he says, "It broke right off! Right off a bridge. And my dentist said I'd have to wait a week. How could I send you a telegram about a goddamn dentist? Anyway, I couldn't wait a week to see you."

They laugh (although there are tears somewhere near Felicia's eyes), and then they embrace again.

And at last they are sitting down on the easy chairs near the window, next to the view, and they are quietly talking together, making plans for the rest of that day and night.

SELVES

Madeline Tiger

Then when you came back, nervous,
stepping out of night,
I saw only the millefleurs walls,
the rose carpet darkening,
the white sheets sprayed with flowers,
the pillows softly propped.
I had drawn the shades,
hung my strewn clothes, closed
both closet doors, dimmed the lights
of the whole house, so when you came up
after all those weeks we saw
only ourselves, directly, so
when we opened the bed and turned
to each other we saw nothing but
our pale forms, our ideal
selves. And we took these wild
we took these dark,
these shadows—
gentle old buck, old doe, simple
and more human than the forest
of hidden mirrors allows.
We, entering, then, accepting
blindness, met each other
at the center of earth, and heaven
grew around us like the unknown
morning. In the morning
there were no reflections.
We moved away
from where we had touched
unspoken things

THE FOREVER BED

273

and I sealed the place
where my blood moves
into the shape of praise.
There is no marriage
in such a story,
and no end to this,
except a warning
about the beast in the courtyard,
about naming, holding
what is afraid, about no one
taming the other.

IN DREAM

David Ignatow

I died and called for you,
and you came from a distance,
hurrying but impassive. You
looked long and steadily
at my face, then left and strode
back into the distance, rapidly
growing smaller to the eye. You
vanished, but where I lay
I could hear your voice
low and quick, urging me
to awaken to the sunrise
at the window of the bedroom
where we slept together. I
rose up and followed you
into the distance, and there
heard the laughter and wit
with which we had spent
our days together. Then silence,
and I knew we both were dead,
for you had spoken to me
in death, as only the dead
could do, and so at last
we were together.

ON WAKING

Laura Chester

I reared up and saw my matching half, and laughed the laugh gods love, when human pain has passed, and the barn doors slide to a warmer state of mind, the kind you get when your Man comes home, when you find you're not alone anymore on this hard earth in white December—pipes that froze are running now with water—stationed in the desert, but now he's made it back, following the whinny of the one sweet call which is his name I say out loud. I rise to meet his face, his fur, receive his sure advances, and when he enters through my sleeping hair— We both entwine and laugh the laugh gods love to hear. When we awake, my long long arms will wind around him, warm *and* warm. A lovely morning on our dish will come. Just like the big doors kiss on barns.

THE IVY CROWN

William Carlos Williams

The whole process is a lie,
     unless,
          crowned by excess,
it break forcefully,
     one way or another,
          from its confinement—
or find a deeper well.
     Anthony and Cleopatra
          were right;
they have shown
     the way. I love you
          or I do not live
at all.
Daffodil time
     is past. This is
          summer, summer!
the heart says,
     and not even the full of it.
          no doubts
are permitted—
     though they will come
          and may
before our time
     overwhelm us.
          We are only mortal
but being mortal
     can defy our fate.
     We may
by an outside chance
     even win! We do not

                    look to see
jonquils and violets
          come again
                    but there are,
still,
          the roses!
Romance has no part in it.
          The business of love is
                    cruelty which,
by our wills,
          we transform
                    to live together.
It has its seasons.
          for and against,
                    whatever the heart
fumbles in the dark
          to assert
                    toward the end of May.
Just as the nature of briars
          is to tear flesh,
                    I have proceeded
through them.
          Keep
                    the briars out,
they say.
          You cannot live
                    and keep free of
briars.
Children pick flowers.
          Let them.
                    Though having them
in hand they have
          no further use for them
                    but leave them crumpled
at the curb's edge.
At our age the imagination
          across the sorry facts
                    lifts us

THE UNMADE BED

to make roses
            stand before thorns.
                        Sure
love is cruel
            and selfish
                        and totally obtuse—
at least, blinded by the light,
            young love is.
                        But we are older,
I to love
            and you to be loved,
                        we have,
no matter how,
            by our wills survived
                        to keep
the jeweled prize
            always
                        at our fingertips.
We will it so
            and so it is
                        past all accident.

Copyright Acknowledgments

"A Wonderful Woman" is taken from *To See You Again* by Alice Adams. Copyright © 1981 by Alice Adams. Reprinted by permission of Alfred A. Knopf Inc.

"In the Blood" is taken from *Bend This Heart* by Jonis Agee. Copyright © 1989 by Jonis Agee. Reprinted by permission of Coffee House Press.

"Lovers Out of This World" by Michael Benedikt. Copyright © 1991 by Michael Benedikt. Used by permission of the author.

"Esthetic Nuptials" is taken from *Mole Notes* by Michael Benedikt. Copyright © 1971 by Michael Benedikt. Originally published by Wesleyan University Press. Reprinted by permission of the author.

Excerpt from *A Couple Called Moebius* by Carol Bergé. Copyright © 1972 by Carol Bergé. Originally published by Bobbs-Merrill. Reprinted by permission of the author.

"The Favorite Sleeper" is taken from *From the Heart to the Center* by Summer Brenner. Copyright © 1977 by Summer Brenner. Originally published by The Figures. Reprinted by permission of the author.

"Intimacy" is taken from *Where I'm Calling From* by Raymond Carver. Copyright © 1986, 1987, 1988 by Raymond Carver. Reprinted by permission of Atlantic Monthly Press.

"What We Talk About When We Talk About Love" is taken from *What We Talk About When We Talk About Love* by Raymond Carver. Copyright © 1981 by Raymond Carver. Reprinted by permission of Alfred A. Knopf Inc.

Excerpt from *During the Reign of the Queen of Persia* by Joan Chase. Copyright © 1983 by Joan Chase. Reprinted by permission of HarperCollins Publishers.

"Signs of Devotion" by Maxine Chernoff. Copyright © 1992 by Maxine Chernoff. Used by permission of the author.

"The Right Skates" is taken from *Bitches Ride Alone* by Laura Chester. Copyright © 1991 by Laura Chester. Originally published by Black Sparrow Press. Reprinted by permission of the author.

"The Answer" and "On Waking" are taken from *In the Zone* by Laura Chester.

Copyright © 1988 by Laura Chester. Originally published by Black Sparrow Press. Reprinted by permission of the author.

"Biological Supremacy" is taken from *Paradise Resisted: Selected Poems 1978–1984* by Tom Clark. Copyright © 1984 by Tom Clark. Reprinted by permission of Black Sparrow Press.

"I Was Born to Speak Your Name" and "Air" are taken from *When Things Get Tough on Easy Street* by Tom Clark. Copyright © 1972 by Tom Clark. Originally published by Black Sparrow Press. Reprinted by permission of the author.

"A Mythological Subject" is taken from *The Long Pilgrim* by Laurie Colwin. Copyright © 1981 by Laurie Colwin. Reprinted by permission of Alfred A. Knopf Inc.

"The Corset" is taken from *Saint Augustine's Pigeon* by Evan S. Connell. Copyright © 1980 by Evan S. Connell. Reprinted by permission of North Point Press.

Excerpt from *Gerald's Party* by Robert Coover. Copyright © 1985 by Robert Coover. Reprinted by permission of Linden Press.

"Body" by Robert Creeley. Copyright © 1992 by Robert Creeley. Used by permission of the author.

"Good Times" by Lydia Davis. Copyright © 1992 by Lydia Davis. Used by permission of the author.

"The Promise" is taken from *Captivity* by Toi Derricotte. Copyright © 1989 by Toi Derricotte. Reprinted by permission of the University of Pittsburgh Press.

Excerpt is taken from *Calculus of Variation* by Diane di Prima. Copyright © 1972 by Diane di Prima. Originally published by Eidolon Editions. Reprinted by permission of the author.

Excerpt from *Adultery and Other Choices* by Andre Dubus. Copyright © 1977 by Andre Dubus. Reprinted by permission of David R. Godine, Publisher.

"Legacy" and "A Miracle" by Laurie Duesing. Copyright © 1992 by Laurie Duesing. Used by permission of the author.

"Love Song" is taken from *From Near the Great Pine* by Theodore Enslin. Copyright © 1988 by Theodore Enslin. Originally published by Spoon River. Reprinted by permission of the author.

Excerpt from *Full of Life* by John Fante. Copyright © 1952, 1988 by John Fante. Reprinted by permission of Black Sparrow Press.

"Wife" and "When I See Your Breasts I Remember My Heart's Desire" by Norman Fischer. Copyright © 1992 by Norman Fischer. Used by permission of the author.

Excerpt from "Empire" is taken from *Rock Springs* by Richard Ford. Copyright © 1987 by Richard Ford. Reprinted by permission of Atlantic Monthly Press.

"Now That I Am Never Alone" by Tess Gallagher first appeared in *The New Yorker*. Copyright © 1990 by Tess Gallagher. Reprinted by permission of the author.

"Marriage" is taken from *Bitter Angel* by Amy Gerstler. Copyright © 1990 by Amy Gerstler. Reprinted by permission of North Point Press.

"Hold" is taken from *3* by David Giannini. Copyright © 1986 by David Giannini. Originally published by Longhouse Press. Reprinted by permission of the author.

"Lying Under a Quilt" is taken from *A Son from Sleep* by Rachel Hadas. Copyright © 1987 by Rachel Hadas. Reprinted by permission of University of New England Press.

"The Song of Love" is taken from *Nostalgia of the Infinite* by Janet Hamill. Copyright © 1991 by Janet Hamill. Originally published by Ocean View Books. Reprinted by permission of the author.

"Love Too Long" is taken from *Airships* by Barry Hannah. Copyright © 1978 by Barry Hannah. Reprinted by permission of Alfred A. Knopf Inc.

"The Reception" by Deborah Harding. Copyright © 1992 by Deborah Harding. Used by permission of the author.

"Our First Summer" by Marie Harris. Copyright © 1992 by Marie Harris. Used by permission of the author.

Excerpts from *The Blood Oranges* by John Hawkes. Copyright © 1970, 1971 by John Hawkes. Reprinted by permission of New Directions Publishing Corporation.

"There's an Old . . ." is taken from *Almost Everything* by Bobbie Louise Hawkins. Copyright © 1982 by Bobbie Louise Hawkins. Originally published by Long River Books. Reprinted by permission of the author.

"Beaver Tales" by Elizabeth Hay. Copyright © 1992 by Elizabeth Hay. Used by permission of the author.

"The One" by Anselm Hollo first appeared in *The Coherences* published by Trigram Press. Copyright © 1968 by Anselm Hollo. Reprinted by permission of the author.

"In Dream" is taken from *New and Collected Stories 1970–1985* by David Ignatow. Copyright © 1986 by David Ignatow. Reprinted by permission of University Press of New England.

"The Marriage Made in Heaven," "Abraham Tells Ann He Loves Her," and "The Glass Is Broken" are taken from *The Unexamined Wife* by Sherril Jaffe. Copyright © 1983 by Sherril Jaffe. Originally published by Black Sparrow Press. Reprinted by permission of the author.

Selections from "In Bed" is taken from *Days and Nights* by Kenneth Koch. Copyright © 1982 by Kenneth Koch. Originally published by Random House, Inc. Reprinted by permission of the author.

Excerpt from "The Ache of Marriage" is taken from *Poems 1960–1967* by Denise Levertov. Copyright © 1964 by Denise Levertov Goodman. Used by permission of New Directions Publishing Corporation.

"North" is taken from *Leaving South* by Lyn Lifshin. Copyright © 1977 by Lyn Lifshin. Originally published by Red Dust. Reprinted by permission of the author.

"First Kiss" by Joan Logghe. Copyright © 1992 by Joan Logghe. Used by permission of the author.

Excerpt from *Chin Music* by James McManus. Copyright © 1985 by James McManus. Originally published by Grove Press. Reprinted by permission of the author.

"Sonnet" is taken from *Sonnet* by Bernadette Mayer. Copyright © 1990 by

Bernadette Mayer. Originally published by Tender Buttons. Reprinted by permission of the author.

Excerpt from "Couplets" is taken from *Evening Wind* by Robert Mezey. Copyright © 1987 by Robert Mezey. Reprinted by permission of University of New England Press.

"Poem to My Husband from My Father's Daughter" is taken from *The Dead and the Living* by Sharon Olds. Copyright © 1983 by Sharon Olds. Reprinted by permission of Alfred A. Knopf Inc.

"I Go Back to May 1937" is taken from *The Gold Cell* by Sharon Olds. Copyright © 1987 by Sharon Olds. Reprinted by permission of Alfred A. Knopf Inc.

"True Love" by Sharon Olds. Copyright © 1992 by Sharon Olds. Used by permission of the author.

"Wanting All" is taken from *The Imaginary Lover* by Alicia Ostriker. Copyright © 1986 by Alicia Ostriker. Reprinted by permission of the University of Pittsburgh Press.

"Love Poem" is taken from *Triangles in the Afternoon Sun* by Ron Padgett. Copyright © 1979 by Ron Padgett. Originally published by SUN. Reprinted by permission of the author.

Excerpts in the Foreword from *Pagan Meditations* by Ginette Paris. Copyright © 1986 by Ginette Paris. Reprinted by permission of Spring Publications.

"Old Times Now" is taken from *One or Two Poems from the White World* by Stephen Rodefer. Copyright © 1976 by Stephen Rodefer. Originally published by Duende. Reprinted by permission of the author.

"Lucy Ortiz" by Miriam Sagan. Copyright © 1992 by Miriam Sagan. Used by permission of the author.

"To Have & to Hold" by Christine Schutt. Copyright © 1992 by Christine Schutt. Used by permission of the author.

Excerpt from *Rough Strife* by Lynne Sharon Schwartz. Copyright © 1980 by Lynne Sharon Schwartz. Reprinted by permission of HarperCollins Publishers.

"A Short History of Sex" and "Feeling Normal" are taken from *Lesser Evil* by Gary Soto. Copyright © 1988 by Gary Soto. Originally published by Arte Publico Press, University of Houston. Reprinted by permission of the author.

"The Heart Stumbles in Darkness" is taken from *Seeing America First* by Nathaniel Tarn. Copyright © 1989 by Nathaniel Tarn. Originally published by Coffee House Press. Reprinted by permission of the author.

"Selves" by Madeline Tiger first appeared in *Zone 3*, vol. IV. No. 2, 1989. Copyright © 1989 by Madeline Tiger. Reprinted by permission of the author.

Excerpt from *Marry Me* by John Updike. Copyright © 1971, 1973, 1976 by John Updike. Reprinted by permission of Alfred A. Knopf Inc.

"Separating" is taken from *Problems and Other Stories* by John Updike. Copyright © 1975 by John Updike. Reprinted by permission of Alfred A. Knopf Inc.

"Queen" is taken from *Skin Meat Bones* by Anne Waldman. Copyright © 1985 by Anne Waldman. Originally published by Coffee House Press. Reprinted by permission of the author.

COPYRIGHT ACKNOWLEDGMENTS

"The Perplexing Habit of Falling" is taken from *Lawn of Excluded Middle* by Rosemarie Waldrop. Copyright © 1991 by Rosemarie Waldrop. Originally published by Tender Buttons. Reprinted by permission of the author.

"Sonnet" is taken from *Blue Heaven* by Lewis Warsh. Copyright © 1978 by Lewis Warsh. Originally published by The Kulchur Foundation. Reprinted by permission of the author.

"The Wedding" is taken from *Taking Care* by Joy Williams. Copyright © 1981 by Joy Williams. Reprinted by permission of Random House Inc.

"The Ivy Crown" is taken from *Collected Poems 1939–1962 Volume Two* by William Carlos Williams. Copyright © 1962 by William Carlos Williams. Reprinted by permission of New Directions Publishing Corporation.

Excerpt from *What I'm Going To Do, I Think* retitled, "The Pregnant Bride" by Larry Woiwode. Copyright © 1966, 1967, 1968, 1969 by Larry L. Woiwode. Reprinted by permission of Farrar, Straus and Giroux, Inc.

"Next Door" is taken from *In the Garden of the North American Martyrs* by Tobias Wolff. Copyright © 1981 by Tobias Wolff. Reprinted by permission of The Ecco Press.

"Boss Drain," "For the Woman with Everything," and "Parallel Bars" by Geoffrey Young first appeared in *Subject to Fits*. Copyright © 1980 by Geoffrey Young. Originally published by The Figures. Reprinted by permission of the author.

"Drive, It Said" by Geoffrey Young first appeared in *New American Writing 2*, edited by Maxine Chernoff and Paul Hoover. Copyright © 1987 by Geoffrey Young. Reprinted by permission of the author.

"Hurt Books" by Edra Ziesk. Copyright © 1992 by Edra Ziesk. Used by permission of the author.

P9-CEJ-901

Also by Robert Coover

THE ORIGIN OF THE BRUNISTS
THE UNIVERSAL BASEBALL ASSOCIATION, J. HENRY WAUGH, PROP.
PRICKSONGS & DESCANTS (short fictions)
A THEOLOGICAL POSITION (plays)
THE PUBLIC BURNING
A POLITICAL FABLE
SPANKING THE MAID

Gerald's
Party

A Novel by

Robert Coover

Linden Press
Simon & Schuster
New York 1986

A *portion of the novel appeared previously in* Anteus *under the title*
The Interrogation.

This novel is a work of fiction. Names, characters, places and incidents
are either the product of the author's imagination or are used
fictitiously. Any resemblance to actual events or locales or persons,
living or dead, is entirely coincidental.
Copyright © 1985 by Robert Coover
All rights reserved
including the right of reproduction
in whole or in part in any form
Published by Linden Press/Simon & Schuster
A Division of Simon & Schuster, Inc.
Simon & Schuster Building
Rockefeller Center
1230 Avenue of the Americas
New York, New York 10020
LINDEN PRESS/SIMON & SCHUSTER and colophon
are trademarks of Simon & Schuster, Inc.
Designed by Levavi & Levavi
Manufactured in the United States of America

1   3   5   7   9   10   8   6   4   2

Library of Congress Cataloging in Publication Data
Coover, Robert.
Gerald's party.

I. Title.
PS3553.O633G47   1986   813'.54   85-15901
ISBN 0-671-60655-7

168546
Flagstaff Public Library
Flagstaff, Arizona

Coover,
Robert

For John Hawkes, who, standing beside me in a dream one night long ago, long before we'd become friends, and remarking upon another author's romanticization of autumn (there seemed to be hundreds of them actually, stooped over, on the endless tree-lined streets before us), observed wistfully: "It's so true, people still do that, you know, count the dead leaves. Ten, nine, eight, seven, six, five, three, four . . ."

Nyone of us noticed the body at first. Not until Roger came through asking if we'd seen Ros. Most of us were still on our feet—except for Knud who'd gone in to catch the late sports results on the TV and had passed out on the sofa—but we were no longer that attentive. I was in the living room refilling drinks, a bottle of dry white vermouth for Alison in one hand (Vic had relieved me of the bourbon), a pitcher of old-fashioneds in the other, recalling for some reason a girl I'd known long ago in some seaside town in Italy. The vermouth maybe, or the soft radiance of the light in here, my own mellowness. The babble. Or just the freshening of possibility. My wife was circulating in the next room with a tray of canapés, getting people together, introducing newcomers, snatching up used napkins and toothpicks, occasionally signaling to me across the distance when she spotted an empty glass in someone's hand. Strange, I thought. The only thing on my mind that night in Italy had been how to maneuver that girl into bed, my entire attention devoted to the eventual achievement of a perfectly shared climax (I was still deep into my experimental how-to-do-it phase then), and yet, though no doubt I had succeeded, bed and unforgettable climax had been utterly forgotten—I couldn't even remember her face!—and all I'd retained from that night was a vision of the dense glow of candlelight through a yellow tulip on our restaurant table (a tulip? was it possible?), the high pitch of a complicated family squabble in some alleyway billow-

ing with laundry hung out like bunting, the girl's taste for anchovies and ouzo, and my own exhilarating sense of the world's infinite novelty. Not much perhaps, yet had it not been for love, I knew, even that would have been lost. I passed among my guests now with the bottle and pitcher, sharing in the familiar revelations, appraisals, pressing searches, colliding passions, letting my mind float back to those younger lighter times when a technically well-executed orgasm seemed more than enough, feeling pleasurably possessed—not by memory so much as by the harmonics of memory—and working my way through the congestion meanwhile ("She was great in *The House of the Last Hymen*," someone remarked, and another, laughing, said: "Oh yeah! Is that the one about the widow and the pick?" No, I thought, that was *Vanished Days . . .*) toward a young woman named Alison: not only, uniquely, a vermouth drinker—thus the bottle in my hand—but virtually the sole cause and inspiration for the party itself. Alison. Her name, still fresh to me, played teasingly at the tip of my tongue as I poured old-fashioneds for the others (and not a pick but—): "A little more?"

"Thanks, Gerry! You know, you're the only man I know who still remembers how to make these things!"

"Ah well, the ancient arts are the true arts, my love."

"Like poison, he means. Take my advice and stick with the beer."

"More in the fridge, Dolph, help yourself. Naomi—?"

"What? Oh yes, thank you—what is it?"

I poured, glancing across the busy room at Alison, now profiled in a wash of light cast by the hanging globes behind her—like a halo, an aura—and I knew that, crafted by love, that glow of light would be with me always, even if I should lose all the rest, this party, these friends, even Alison herself, her delicate profile, soft auburn hair ("Ouch, Dolph! Stop that!"), the fine gold loops in her small ears—

"Hey, golly! That's enough!"

"Oops, sorry, Naomi . . . !"

"Steady!" shouted Charley Trainer, charging up to lick at her dripping hand. "Yum!"

"What is this, some new party game?"

"Ha ha! Me next, Ger!"

I heard the doorbell ring, my wife's greetings in the hall. Sounded like Fats and Brenda, but my view was blocked by the people pushing in and out of the doorway: Knud's wife Kitty gave Dickie a hug and he ran his hands between her legs playfully, Yvonne looking wistful,

her husband Woody shaking the hand of an old man who said: "In Babylonia, y'know, they used to drown folks for sellin' beer too cheap— we visited the holes they dipped 'em in!"

"Love the ascot, Gerry! Très chic! Cyril and Peg here yet?"

"Yes, I think so. In the dining room maybe. Old-fashioned?"

"Mine's a stinger."

"Ha ha! don't kid me!" someone butted in, crowding up behind me.

"I can show you pictures."

"Try it and see!"

Laughter rose lightly above the drone of music and chatter, then ebbed again, throbbing steadily as a heartbeat, as people pressed close, parted, came together again, their movements fluid, almost hypnotic, as though (I thought in my own inebriate and spellbound state) under some dreamy atavistic compulsion. I squeezed, myself compelled, past a group of serious whiskey drinkers hustling a painted-up redhead with pickaninny pigtails (Ginger: one of Dickie's girls), ignoring their disappointed glances at the vermouth bottle in my hand, and made my way toward Alison (Kitty, flushed and happy, crossed left of me, just as Patrick in immaculate green passed right, someone singing "It's No Wonder" on the hi-fi), feeling the excitement of her as I drew near.

The glow, profile, it was different now, yet overlaid as though stereoscopically by the way I'd seen her just before. And by that earlier time across the dimming auditorium. We'd met a few weeks earlier in a theater lobby during intermission. Friends of friends. We'd exchanged passing reflections on the play, and Alison and I had found ourselves so intimately attuned to each other that we'd stopped short, blinked, then quickly, as though embarrassed, changed the subject. Her husband had given me his card, my wife had said something about getting up a party, I'd said I'd call. On the way back to our seats, passing down parallel aisles, Alison and I had exchanged furtive glances, and I'd been so disturbed by them that the play was over before I'd realized that I'd not seen or heard any of the rest of it: only by asking my wife her opinion of the last act did I learn how it came out. Now Alison's glance, as I pressed up beside her at last and refilled her glass with vermouth, was not furtive at all, even though there were several other people standing around, watching us, waiting for refills of their own: she was smiling steadily up at me, her eyes (so they seemed to me just then) deep brown puddles of pure desire . . .

"Somehow," I said pensively, holding her gaze, seeking the thought

that might connect us to that heightened moment at the theater, "I feel as though all this has happened before . . ."

"It's an illusion, Gerald," she replied, her voice smooth, round, almost an embrace, my name in her mouth like a cherry. She reached into the old-fashioneds pitcher for an ice cube without taking her brown eyes off me. There was a peculiar studied balance in her stance that made me think of those girls in advertisements out on the decks of rushing yachts, topless, their bronzed breasts sparkling with sea spray, hair unfurling, legs spread wide and rigid in their tight white denims like cocked springs—though tonight in fact she was wearing a green-and-gold silk charmeuse dress of almost unbelievable softness. The peculiar thing about love, I thought, gazing deeply into those beckoning pools of hers which yet reflected my own gaze, the reflected gaze itself a reflection of that first numbingly beautiful exchange (that night at the theater she'd been wearing a Renaissance-styled suit of cinnamon panne velvet with a white ruffled blouse, the ruffles at the cuffs like foliage for the expressive flowering of her hands, her auburn hair, now loose, drawn then to her nape by an amber clasp), is that one is overwhelmed by a general sense of wanting before he knows what it is he wants—that's why the act, though like all others, seems always strange and new, a discovery, an exploration, why one must move toward it silently, without reason, without words, feeling one's way . . . "You know, I'll bet you're the sort of man," she said, as though having come to some sort of decision, her voice gloved in intimacy and, yes, a kind of awe (I felt this and drew closer), "who used to believe, once upon a time, that every cunt in the world was somehow miraculously different."

"Yes—ah, yes, I did!" I glanced up from her gaze: we were alone. Our thighs were touching. "Hot *what—?*" someone hooted behind me, and I thought, this may not turn out quite as I'd imagined after all. My wife, in the next room, pointed, her hand high above her head, at Tania's empty glass. Tania, smiling broadly over the faces between us, held it up like a signpost. "Each one a . . . a unique adventure." Alison was licking the ice cube before dropping it into her glass of vermouth, and, watching her, I seemed to remember the ice wagons that used to call at my grandmother's house, the heavy crystallized blocks that had to be chopped up (this memory was soothing), the ice chips in the truck beds, the little girl next door . . . "But I was young then . . ."

"Ah, but it's true, Gerald!" She smiled, sucking coyly on the cube. It sparkled like a fat gem between her lips. She let it ooze out like a slow birth and drop—*plunk!*—into her vermouth. "Each one *is* . . ."

And just then Roger came through, interrupting everybody, asking if we'd seen Ros.

I understood Roger's anxiety, I'd witnessed it many times before. Roger loved Ros hopelessly—loved her more no doubt than the rest of us loved anything in the world, if love was the word—and he was, to his despair, insanely jealous of her. He'd found her, as though in a fairy tale, in a chorus line, a pretty blonde with nice legs and breasts, a carefree artless manner, and an easy smile (yet more than that, we'd all been drawn to her, her almost succulent innocence probably, and a kind of unassuming majesty that kept you in crazy awe of her, even in intimacy—during my own moments with her, I'd found myself calling her Princess), and he'd been overwhelmed at his good fortune when she took him to bed with her the same night he met her. That there might be others who shared in his fortune, he could hardly believe; in fact, to the best of his ability, he chose *not* to believe it, which was the beginning of his grief. Instead, he pursued her with the relentless passion of a man with a mission, striving to fill up her nights so there'd be no room for others, begging her to marry him, and because in the end you could persuade her to do just about anything, she did. And went right on living as she always had, barely noticing she'd even changed her address. Poor Roger. She loved him of course: she loved all men. He was still in law school at the time and had difficulty finding the money for them to live on. Eager to help, she took a job as a nude model for a life-drawing class in a men's prison, and nearly drove him mad. She'd plan a big surprise for him, take him out to dinner, joined by another man who'd pick up the bill and offer to drive Roger back to the library after. She returned to the theater, to acting, unable to stay away, and so then neither could he, doing his studying in the back rows during rehearsals, almost unable to see the texts through his tears. Backstage, of course, her thighs were pillowing cast, crew, and passing friends alike, but Roger wasn't even aware of that—just the scripted on-stage intimacies were enough to plunge him into all the desolation he could bear.

So when he came through now with that look of rage and terror and imminent collapse on his face, breaking up conversations, shouting over the music, demanding to know if we'd seen Ros, I smiled pa-

tiently and—though in fact I couldn't remember having seen her since the moment they'd arrived—said, "I think she's in the kitchen with my wife, Roger."

"No, she's not!" he cried, turning on me. The light gleamed on his damp face almost as if he were drawing it to him. "I've just come from there!"

Some people were still dancing out in the sunroom, or conversing in remote corners, slipping off to the toilet or wherever, but most of us in here were by now watching Roger. Our relative silence made the music—oddly romantic, nostalgic (a woman was singing about mirrors and memory)—seem to grow louder. I remember Roger's law partner Woody stepping forward as though to offer consultation, then shrugging, turning away, as a woman sighed. Parties are clocked by such moments: we all knew where we were in the night's passing when Roger's anguish was announced. He glanced fearfully from face to face (Dickie, leaning against a doorframe near Vic's daughter Sally Ann, winked and cast an appraising eye on Alison beside me), then down at the floor. Roger turned pale, his eyes widening. We all looked down: there she was, sprawled face-down in the middle of the room. She must have been there all the time. "Ros—!!" he gasped and fell to his knees.

Alison touched my arm, pressed closer. I could almost feel the warmth of her breath through my shirt. "Is she all right?" she whispered.

I opened my mouth to speak, perhaps (as though obliged) to reassure her, but just then Roger turned Ros over. Ros's front was bathed with blood—indeed it was still fountaining from a hole between her breasts, soaking her silvery frock, puddling the carpet. I could hardly believe my eyes. I had forgotten that blood was that red, a primary red like the red in children's paintboxes, brilliant and alive, yet stagy, cosmetic. Her eyes were open, staring vacantly, and blood was trickling from the corners of her mouth. Roger screeched horribly, making us all jump (some cried out, perhaps I did), and threw himself down upon her, covering her bubbling wound with his own heaving breast.

Alison's hip had slid into the hollow above my thigh, as though, having pushed past me for a moment to see, she was trying now to pull back and hide inside me. It felt good there, her hip, but I was wondering: How has it got so hot in here? Who turned up the lights? Is this one of Ros's theatrical performances? I glanced inquiringly up at Jim.

Jim was staring down in surprise at Ros like everyone else, his thick square hand on the back of his head, his professional instincts momentarily enthralled. Roger screamed again—"Ros! Ros, *what have you done?!*"—releasing Jim from his stupor: he knelt, felt her wrists, her throat, peered under Roger at the wound, closed the girl's eyes, concern clouding his face, actually darkening it as though (I thought) in closing Ros's eyes, some light in the room has been put out. Alison trembled slightly and reached behind her to touch my hand: the thought had not been wholly mine (a responsive tremor made my head twitch), but hers as well. Jim looked up at me, his coarse gray hair falling down over one eyebrow. "She's dead, Gerry," he said. "She seems to have been stabbed to death."

I looked around at the shocked faces pressing in, but I couldn't see her: she must have gone to the kitchen. Even in this crowd of friends, squeezed up against Alison, I felt alone. The house was silent except for the upbeat wail, oddly funereal, of the show tune playing on the hi-fi. Roger shrieked—"*No! No! No!*"—and someone turned the music down. "What's happening?" Tania cried, and pushed through the jam-up in the doorway. Jim, standing now, was wiping his bloody hands with a white handkerchief. I saw that his sleeves were rolled up, yet seemed to remember him kneeling beside Ros in his suit jacket still. Memories, I realized (recalling now the sudden gasps, the muttered expletives of disbelief, the cries rushing outward from the body through the door like a wind: "*It's Ros! She's been killed!*"), always come before the experiences we attach them to. Comforted somehow by this insight, I brushed past Alison's hips, bumped gently by each firm buttock, and went to the kitchen, looking for my wife.

She was at the counter, decorating a tray of cold cuts with little sprigs of fresh parsley. She wore a brown apron with purple-and-white flowers on it and held a butcher knife in her left hand. There was no blood on it, but it startled me to see it in her hand just the same. Perhaps she'd been slicing the roast beef with it. "Ros has been murdered," I said.

My wife looked up in alarm—or maybe the alarm had been there on her face before she turned it toward me. "Oh no! Where—?"

"In the living room," I said, though I wasn't sure that was what she'd meant by the question. I was having trouble breathing. She stared past my shoulder toward the door, her mouth open, little worry lines crossing her forehead. There were plates and glasses in the sink

behind her, but the counter was wiped clean. I wondered if she wanted me to hug her reassuringly or something. But I had these things in my hands. "What . . . what do you think we ought to do?" I asked.

With difficulty, she pulled her gaze back to me. "I don't know, Gerald," she said softly, touching her cheek with the back of the hand holding the knife. "Probably we should call the police."

"Yes. Yes, of course," I said, and went back out front, thinking of my wife with a butcher knife in one hand and a bouquet of parsley in the other, and trying to remember the special telephone number for emergencies.

But Alison's husband was using the phone. He was murmuring secretively into the mouthpiece, his head ducked, a sly grin on his thin bearded face. I tried to interrupt him but he waved me away without even looking up, puckering his mouth as though blowing a kiss into the phone and chuckling softly. "Listen," I cried, "there's been a murder!"

"Yes, I know," he said coldly, putting the receiver down. "I've just called the police." I was troubled by the way he stared at me. It occurred to me that I knew almost nothing about him: only his name and address on a white card.

I followed him back into the living room where Roger was still carrying on pathetically over Ros's corpse. Tania had knelt beside him and was trying to console him, draw him away from the body, but he was beyond her reach. Beyond anybody's. He was wild with grief, looked a terror, his front now as bloody as Ros's. His face seemed twisted, as if a putty mask were being torn away from it, and people watching him were twisting up, too. Vic's girlfriend Eileen had apparently fainted and was lying on the gold couch. Jim was sitting by her, holding one wrist, slapping her face and her palms gently, while Dickie at the end of the couch, keeping her shoes away from his bright white pants and vest, held her legs up so the blood would flow to her head. Vic flung what was left of his drink up her nose and that brought her to with a snort, but she went on lying there, whimpering softly to herself. Vic said something about "a stupid cunt," and Jim said: "Take it easy, Vic. She's had a severe shock."

The contrast was there for everyone to see: Roger and Ros, Vic and Eileen. It seemed to bring a kind of ripeness to the room. Alison gripped her husband's hand tightly and stared over at me as though

in supplication, but what was it she wanted? I felt lost and confused, a stranger inside my own house. I did, however, remember now the special phone number for emergencies. Her husband, watching me, withdrew his hand from hers to smooth down the fine black hairs of his beard. "There's nothing we can do until the police come," I said at last. Alison seemed helped by this: she sighed, her slender shoulders relaxing slightly, and turned to gaze compassionately across the room at Eileen on the couch. Her dark hair fluttered wispily, as though filmed in slow motion, as she turned her head, and I thought: I understand myself better because of this woman. This was true of my wife, too, of course.

Tania, still trying to comfort Roger, was now completely bespattered with blood herself. "Oh my god, Gerry!" she cried, showing me her bloody dress, her dark expressive eyes full of dismay and sorrow (I felt my own eyes water: I bit down on my lip), her nostrils flaring. *"This is terrible!"*

Roger, as though in response, suddenly tilted far back, clutching his face with bloody hands, and let forth an awful howl, scaring us all, then pitched back down upon Ros's ruptured breast, still amazingly spouting fresh blood.

Eileen at that same moment cried out. We looked up. Vic was standing over her at the couch, his legs spread, elbows out, the back of his thick neck flushed, and the way she was curled up with one arm flung over her drawn face, I had the impression Vic had just struck her. Dickie had backed away, clearly wanting no part of it. When our eyes met for a moment, I frowned in inquiry, and Dickie, tugging at the ivory-buttoned cuffs of his plaid jacket, shrugged wearily in reply. "No . . . !" Eileen sniveled.

"We've got to be patient!" I said sharply, but no one appeared to be listening. Even Alison was distracted. Her husband was studying a Byzantine icon depicting the torture of a saint, a curious piece my wife had bought at an auction. Mr. and Mrs. Draper came in and began to discuss it with him. He turned away. I felt there was something I should be doing, something absolutely essential, but I couldn't think what it might be. It didn't matter: I'd had the same sensation many times before—just a little while ago in the kitchen, for example—and knew it for what it was: the restless paralysis that always attends any affront to habit.

Not always had I read this feeling rightly, I should say. There was

the terrible night, for example, of our first son's stillbirth. Little Gerald. I'd been by my wife's side throughout the daylong ordeal that preceded it, holding her hand through the ferocious pain that was tearing her apart: a small fineboned woman exploding with this inner force growing increasingly alien to her as it struggled, though we did not yet suspect this, against its own strangulation, having tried, its cord twisted, to breathe too soon—oh, how I'd loved her then, loved her delicacy, her courage, her suffering, her hopes, even the fine cracks disfiguring her belly, the veins thickening in her legs, her swollen teats, fierce grimace, cries of pain. It had been Jim who had suddenly guessed the truth and rushed her into the delivery room. But too late, the child was dead. Afterward, drugged, she'd slept. "It's all so unreal," I'd said, contemplating the wreckage of so much natural violence, "so unbelievable . . ." Jim had given me a sedative to take and, wrapping one arm around me, said I should go home, get some rest, come back early in the morning. Leaving the hospital, then, I'd had this same feeling: that there was something important I should be doing, but I couldn't think what. Halfway home, dreading the emptiness there, still a bit awed and frightened, I'd thought of a woman I'd been seeing occasionally during the final months of my wife's pregnancy, and it had occurred to me that she too must be needing solace, understanding, and needing too the opportunity to be needed in this calamity, needed by me, even if only this last time (yes, it was probably the last time), and I'd supposed that this must be the important thing I had to do, that thing I couldn't put my finger on. And so, full of sorrow and distress and compassion, I'd gone by. But I'd been wrong. She'd been shocked, disgusted even. "My god, have you no feelings at all?" she'd cried, still only half awake, her face puffy from sleep and her hair loose in front of her eyes. "That's—that's just it," I'd explained, tried to, love (I'd supposed it was love, for someone) thickening my tongue. "I need someone to talk to and I thought—" "Christ, Gerry, go find a goddamn shrink!" she'd shot back, and slammed the door. I'd gone on home, feeling sick with myself (what kind of filth are we made of, I'd wondered miserably, nauseated by my own flesh, its dumb brutalizing appetites and arrogant confusions), and had found my mother-in-law waiting for me there: she'd come to help with the new baby and she was all smiles. It was like a strange nightmare memory: my mother-in-law smiling . . .

I looked up from Ros's corpse and saw Jim's wife, Mavis, standing

there like something hung from a hanger, locked in a helpless stupor, her soft red mouth agape, her eyes puffy and staring. I knew how she felt: Ros was like her own daughter, or so she often said. Jim was clearly shaken, too, but had the defenses of his profession: right now, playing the family doctor, he was counseling Vic's daughter Sally Ann. Sally Ann wore, as usual, a white shirt open down the front and knotted at the waist, and tight faded blue jeans with a heart-shaped patch sewn over her anus that said, "KISS ME." She'd painted her eyes and lashes to appear grown-up, but had only made herself look more a child. Earlier, Dickie had been moving in on her, but now she was alone with Jim. Maybe they were talking about her father: Vic was sitting heavily on the couch, his large shaggy head in his hands, Eileen stretched out limply behind him, looking less alive than Ros. Jim smiled gently and Sally Ann sighed petulantly and looked away. Tania's nephew Anatole was hovering furtively at the outer edge of their conversation, a look on his tense angular face that seemed to say: I *told* you this would happen! But then, he always had that kind of look on his face.

His aunt, still on the floor beside Roger and the body, had sunk back on her heels, her half-lens spectacles dangling on a chain around her neck, her celebrated vitality utterly drained away. The crowd of people around her watched as she rubbed her eyes with the tips of her long bloodstained fingers, pressed her lips together, and looked up at Mavis beside her. Mavis seemed to be trying to speak. She slumped there over Tania, staring bleakly, working her soft mouth fitfully around some difficult word, her squat pillowy body otherwise lifeless. Anatole, noticing this, tugged at Jim's arm, but Jim was still reasoning patiently with Sally Ann and appeared not to notice. Patrick, taking a seeming interest in Jim's counsel, had joined them, sidling close to Anatole, a tumbler of vodka and grapefruit juice—Patrick's famous "salty bitch"—in one hand, French cigarette in the other. Sally Ann glanced over at me suddenly, her eyes flashing, then stamped her foot and left the room. Beyond them, I could see Alison, alone, her head down: was she crying? "Who . . . ?" Mavis finally managed to blurt out, and the other conversations in the room died away. Jim looked toward his wife at last, then away again, focusing on the doorway leading in from the hall. Someone in red moved past it. "Wh-who . . . ?" It was the question, I knew, that had been quietly worming through us all. Patrick took a nervous puff on the cigarette held like a dart be-

tween the tips of his fingers, watching Mavis now over Anatole's shoulder. Dolph came in with a can of beer in his hand and popped it open. Jim was talking with Mr. and Mrs. Draper, nodding his head in agreement as Mr. Draper gesticulated broadly. I had the feeling he was describing some kind of pyramid or temple. Mavis's plump white arms hung limply at her sides, palms out. She lifted her head slowly and we waited for her question. I felt people crowding up behind me like mustered troops. Or a theatrical chorus. Somebody was chewing potato chips in my ear. Vic stood up. "*Who—?*"

The front doorbell rang.

"Ah! they're here!" I exclaimed, and went to answer it, greatly relieved. The thick clusters of guests parted, murmuring, as I passed through. I could hear Roger moaning behind me, Tania speaking gently with Mavis. Old Mr. Draper stepped forward and clutched my forearm with his gnarled white hand, surprisingly powerful. He tipped his head back to peer down his lumpy nose at me and said: "There's someone at the door, son!"

"I know . . ."

There were people filling up the hallway, too, watching expectantly. I'd forgotten we'd asked so many. I could see my wife trying to squeeze in from the dining room, wiping her hands on the bib of her flowered apron. "Can you get it, Gerald?" she pleaded from the back of the hall.

"Yes," I called over the heads between us as the bell rang again. "Don't worry, it's all right!"

Dickie, stepping out of the downstairs toilet, still zipping up, seemed incongruously amused by this exchange. The tank refilled noisily behind him. He glanced up at Vic's daughter Sally Ann, staring down at me from the staircase landing over his head, her tanned belly pressed against the balustrade. "Hey," he grinned, fingering the buttons on his white vest, "it's free now."

"Never mind," she snapped and continued up the stairs, switching her fanny huffily.

My wife backed away toward the dining room, looking momentarily defeated, lost in the crowd. Mrs. Draper, standing near me, touched my sleeve and said: "She's so pale, the poor dear. She needs a little sunshine." The Drapers, complete strangers to me, had been belaboring everyone all night with tales of their retirement-age tourist travels, such a tonic, they'd said, and I'd found myself wondering ear-

lier if my party might be part of some package tour they'd bought. But it was true, we hadn't had a holiday in years . . .

The bell rang a third time and I reached hastily for the doorknob, only to discover I was still carrying the bottle of vermouth and pitcher of old-fashioneds. I looked around for some place to set them down, but the door opened and a tall moustachioed man in a checkered overcoat and gray fedora entered, followed by two uniformed policemen. "May we come in?" he asked politely, but more as a statement of fact than a question: he was already in.

"Of course. I'm sorry, I was just—"

"Inspector Pardew," he explained with a slight nod of his head. "Homicide." He removed his gloves carefully, finger by finger, tucked them in his pockets, unbuttoned his overcoat. The two officers watched us impassively, but not impolitely. They were armed but their weapons were holstered and the holsters fastened. The taller one carried photographic equipment and what looked like a paintbox, cables and cords looped over his narrow shoulders; the short one had a toolkit and a tripod. "Now, I understand there has been a murder . . ."

"Yes, a girl—"

"Ah." He slipped out of his overcoat, reached for his fedora, gazing thoughtfully at Dickie's girl Ginger, who had just, as though prodded from behind, stepped up beside me. "Of course . . ."

Ginger, under his steady gaze, kept shifting her weight nervously from foot to foot, fumbling at my elbow to keep her balance. Her long lashes seemed almost to click metallically when she blinked them and her pickaninny-style pigtails quivered like little red Martian antennae.

Inspector Pardew handed his coat and hat to me, but, glancing away from Ginger, saw that my hands were full. This caused him to frown briefly and study my face. There was something incisive and probing about every move he made, and his gaze chilled and reassured me at the same time. I tried to explain: "I was serving drinks. I-I'm the host and I—" But he stopped me with an impatient flick of his hand, a disinterested smile. He folded his coat on the seat of a hall chair, placed his fedora on top of it, smoothed down the few hairs he had left on the top of his head, and, still wearing his white silk scarf, strode on into the living room, his thumbs hooked in his vest pockets.

The hallway emptied out as the others, rapt, curious, followed him in, some circling through the dining room to get there ahead of the

rest. Ginger, made awkward by her own self-consciousness, picked out her steps behind the others as though negotiating a minefield. Or maybe it was just the exaggerated height of her glittering red stiletto heels that made her walk that way. The two police officers paused in the doorway to watch her go. It was hard not to watch. She wore an alarmingly eccentric costume which seemed to be hand-sewn from printed kerchiefs of Oriental design, intricately multicolored but primarily in tones of mauve, crimson, emerald, and gold. They were stretched tight in some places, hung loose and gaping in others. Sort of like Ginger herself. Dickie called her a walking paradox: "More cunt inside than body out, Ger. Fucking her's like pulling a prick on over your condom." I watched, too ("What's within's without," as Tania would say, "without within . . ."), but when I looked back at the policemen, a faint smile on my face, it was me they were staring at. Nothing malevolent about their stare, but something was clearly bothering them. They bulked large and alien in the living room doorway, their brass buttons and leather straps stranger to me than Ginger's kerchiefs, their noses twitching, and though nothing was said, it felt like an interrogation. I found myself running over the night's events in my mind as though hunting for dangerous gaps in the story (but it was the gaps I seemed to remember, the events having faded), my smile stiffening on my face. It was like crossing a border: what might they look for? what might they find?

But then Roger started bellowing wildly again and, touching their hands to their holsters, they whirled around and, in a crouch, the tall one bobbing on a leg that seemed shorter than the other, left me.

I released a long wheezing sigh, aware that I'd been holding my breath for some time. My arms ached with the weight of the bottle and pitcher, and I could feel sweat in my armpits and on my upper lip. Tania's husband Howard came down the stairs behind me. "What's going on, Gerald?" he asked softly, looking a little flushed, his hand at the knot of his red silk tie.

"Ros has been murdered," I said. I felt like I'd just been the victim of something. Or might have been.

"Is that so . . . !"

I went into the dining room to leave the vermouth and old-fashioneds on the sideboard with the rest of the drinks. I noticed that all the ice in the pitcher of old-fashioneds had melted and, recalling Alison licking the ice cube, shuddered at the world's ephemerality. I looked at

my hands as if to see time falling through them like water. My wife came in with the cold cuts. "Can you move that empty tray, Gerald?" she said.

"It was the police," I told her, my voice catching in my throat. "They're in looking at Ros now."

She nodded. She seemed paler than usual and her hands were taut, the blue veins showing. I thought of her stubborn taciturn mother upstairs and wondered whether my wife, drifting prematurely into sullen stoicism, was a victim of her genes, her mother, or of me. I took the empty tray away and she set the cold cuts down, cautiously, as though afraid they might leap from her hands. There were four different kinds of cold cuts, laid out in perfect rows, lapped like roof tiles and spaced with parsley and sliced tomatoes. Perhaps I should find someone to be with her. "Don't bother Mother just yet," she said, as though reading my mind. "There's no need to upset her, and there's nothing she can do."

"No," I agreed. It felt like a recitation, and I remembered something my grandmother, a religious woman, had once said about freedom. "Besides, Mark's just getting settled down and . . ."

She nodded again, leaning over the cold cuts as though studying a dummy hand in bridge, her slender nape under the tightly rolled hair (free to do what we must, my child, she'd said with her sweet clenched smile, free to do what we must) sliced by the thin pallor of the fluorescent light from the kitchen behind her. "You'd better go back in there, Gerald," she said without looking up. "You might be needed."

Once, somewhere, long ago, I recalled, her nape had shone that way from the light of the moon: was it on the Riviera? during a transatlantic cruise? The memory, what was left of it, saddened me. It's not enough, I thought, as I left her there—it's beautiful, but it's just not enough.

On the way back in, I passed Vic coming out. He looked terrible, his large-boned face ashen and collapsed, thick hair snarled, eyes damp, movements clumsy, his blue workshirt sweaty. "You already out?" he asked sourly, poking an empty whiskey bottle at me. I pointed toward the sideboard, clustered round now with other guests (through the door into the TV room I could see Dickie arguing with Charley Trainer's wife Janny: "Me? You're crazy!" he shouted—she was biting her little pink lip and there were tears starting in the corners of her mascaraed eyes, but she continued to stare straight at him), and again

found myself with something in my hand, this time the empty tray. I seem to be having trouble letting go of things tonight, I said to myself (to Vic I said, "Down below, on the left . . ."), and set the tray down behind the antique prie-dieu. "What a fucking mess," Vic grumbled, and gave the doorjamb a glancing blow as he bulled through. I didn't think he was drunk: it was still early and Vic could hold his liquor. It was more like some final exasperation.

In the living room, Inspector Pardew, ringed round by a crowd of gaping faces, was crouching beside Ros's body, examining the wound, while the two officers, their criminalistic gear beside them, held Roger up a few feet away. Roger was apparently in a state of shock, eyes crossed, head lolling idiotically on his bloodstained chest, legs sagging outward at the knees like an unstrung puppet's. One side of him hung lower than the other, due to the mismatched sizes of the two policemen supporting him, adding to the poignancy of his grief. Tania, who was now kneeling by Mavis, watched Roger with concern. Mavis was sitting lotuslike in the spot where before she'd been standing, her legs apparently having ceased to hold her up. She stared dull-eyed at Ros's corpse, but seemed to be gazing far beyond it. It was as though, in her quiet matronly way, she had guessed something that none of the rest of us had become aware of yet, and the knowledge, as visions have been known to do, had struck her dumb. Ros's wound had at last stopped flowing, but the blood seemed almost to be spreading on its own: through the carpet under Mavis's bottom to Roger's feet, up the shoes and uniforms of the two policemen, down Tania's front and Kitty's knees, even turning up on Jim's white shirt, Michelle's cheek, the Inspector's drooping moustache.

"Ah!" the Inspector exclaimed now. "What's this—?!"

He asked for a pair of tweezers and the women scrambled about, looking for their handbags. Naomi, another of Dickie's entourage, a bigboned girl over six feet tall with naturally flushed cheeks and long blond hair clasped at the nape, lurched forward impulsively and emptied out her shoulderbag all over the floor: compacts, cigarettes, lipstick, earrings and bracelets and spare hairclasps, postcards, safety pins, a handkerchief, combs and coins, birth-control pills, antacids, ticket stubs, zippers and buttons, a driver's license, body and hair sprays, maps, matches, tampons and timetables, thread, newspaper clippings, breath sweeteners, photographs, chewing gum, a ladies'

switchblade, addresses, tranquillizers, credit cards, hormone cream, shopping lists, a toothbrush, candy bars, a dog-eared valentine, flashlight, vial of petroleum jelly, sunglasses, paper panties, and little balls of hair and dust all tumbled out—even a tube of athlete's foot ointment, a half-completed peckersweater, one knitting needle, and one of my Mexican ashtrays—but no tweezers. "I'm just *sure* I had some," she insisted, scratching around at the bottom of her bag, turning it upside down and shaking it. My wife, I knew, kept a pair in the upstairs bathroom, and I wondered if I should go get them. "I have a fingernail file," offered Mrs. Draper. Tania stood with a grunt, putting her spectacles on and fishing through her pockets, but then Patrick produced a silver pair from his keyholder.

The Inspector studied Patrick skeptically a moment, squinted down his nose at the tweezers, then with a shrug bent over the body once more, his white scarf falling over Ros's breasts like theater curtains. Jim knelt beside him, observing critically. Working with meticulous care, the Inspector extracted what looked like a bloody hair, or a thread maybe, from Ros's wound. He held it up to the light a moment, then sandwiched it carefully between two glass slides he'd been carrying in his pocket. Watching him, I had a sudden recollection of my biology teacher in high school, fastidiously tugging on a pair of transparent rubber gloves, finger by finger, before dissecting for us the fetus of a pig. The gloves, I remembered, had made his hands look as wet and translucent as the pickled fetus, and when he'd had them on, what he'd said was, "All right, boys and girls, ready for our little party?"

Dickie came in, but without Janice, and stepped up beside me, toothpick in his teeth, hands stuffed in the pockets of his crisp white pants. He looked harassed, chewing fiercely on his pick. It was ironic to see him so unsettled by a person as simple as Janice Trainer—even Chooch, her husband, liked to say that under all that makeup there was nothing but a doublejointed flytrap on a broomstick, and most people supposed he was being generous. "Hey, Ger, what the hell's going on?" he whispered around the toothpick.

"Pardew is examining the body."

"No, I mean, what's Naomi doing down there on her hands and knees with her shit all over the floor?"

"*Sshh!*" Howard admonished. Others were glaring.

Indeed it had become very quiet. The Inspector, bending closely,

was probing the wound again with Patrick's tweezers (Patrick, flushing, winced, his teeth showing), and there was an attentive stillness, almost breathless, in the room. Jim stood with a frown on his square face, troubled about something. Is the hole the empty part in the middle, Daddy, Mark once asked me, or the hard part all around? I didn't know the answer then and I didn't know it now. Distantly, I could hear the thuck of darts hitting the dart board down in the rec room. Almost like the ticking of a slow clock. The chopping of ice. The bib of Ros's bloodstained frock was in the Inspector's way: he pulled part of it aside and one white breast slid free.

Whereupon Roger starting screaming wildly again, shattering the silence and making us all jump. Patrick squeaked and dropped his drink, Mavis groaned, and Tania cried, "Oh my god!" sinking to her knees again.

Roger, eyes starting as though to fly from their sockets, struggled desperately to reach Ros's body, the two police officers hanging on, grappling for balance and handholds, their veins popping. "Kee-rist!" hissed Dickie between his teeth, and Naomi, picking up her things, dropped them again. One of the officers lost his hat and the other stumbled once to his knees, but they managed to subdue Roger and pin him back against a wall. "Easy now, fella, easy!" gasped the shorter one, pressing his knee into Roger's bloodsoaked groin, then, glancing at me over his shoulder, he shook his head as though sharing something privately with me and blew his cheeks out.

Inspector Pardew, absorbed in his examination, noticed little of it. Using the glass slides as a makeshift magnifying glass, he peered closely at the wound, poking and probing, muttering enigmatically from time to time. He picked Ros's breast up once by the nipple to peer under and around it, but he seemed disinterested in the breast itself—if anything, it was an obstacle to him. I couldn't get my eyes off it. Ros was famous for her breasts, and seeing the exposed one there now, so soft and vulnerable, its shrunken nipple looking like a soft pierced bruise, pecked fruit, I felt the sorrow I'd been holding back rise like hard rubber in my throat. I glanced up and found Alison watching me, tears running down her cheeks. She smiled faintly, and it was a smile so full of love and understanding that for a moment I could see nothing else in the room, not even Roger in his despair or poor drained Ros, such that when I heard the Inspector ask, shouting over Roger, "How long ago did this happen?" I realized that it was at

least the second time he had asked it and that he was looking straight at me.

"I-I can't remember," I stammered hoarsely. I looked at my watch but I couldn't see the dial.

"Here, use mine," said Dickie.

"Wait a minute—!" barked Pardew, rising.

Dickie smiled, shrugged, took his watch back. I rubbed at my eyes: there were tears in them.

"Hey! Where's Sally Ann?" shouted Vic, blundering in. He seemed to be asking Eileen, who was sitting up now, face buried in her hands, looking distraught, and I was invaded by the same feeling I'd had earlier with Alison: that all this had happened before. But then it went away as Sally Ann appeared in the doorway and said: "What do you want, Dad?" I glanced across the room at Alison, still watching me, damp-eyed and gently smiling, looking almost fragile now in her soft satiny dress with its slashed sleeves, its frail silken folds. She touched the glass of vermouth to her lips. No, I thought, as Vic grunted ambiguously and shoved his way out of the room again, I hadn't really had that feeling with Alison before. I'd only wished to.

"The *time*," the Inspector was insisting. "This is *important*—!"

"How long," I asked, turning to him, not really thinking about what I was saying, my mind on an earlier Alison, playful and mischievous, now nearly as remote to me as that girl from Italy (and I recalled now from that night, as though my memory were being palpated, the splatter of a pot on a cobbled street, a wail, something about gypsies in another country, and the way the girl's pubic hair branched apart like brown bunny ears: discoveries like that were important then), "does it take ice to melt in a pitcher?"

"Ice?" exclaimed the Inspector, genuinely astonished.

"I'm sorry. What I mean is—"

"*Ice*—?!"

"When you came in," I tried to explain, "I was—"

"Ah yes," interrupted the Inspector, "so you were." He drew a large Dutch billiard pipe and tobacco pouch from his pockets. Roger's ravings had subsided to a soft whimper, and he'd sagged lopsidedly into the arms of the policemen once more. The tall one stared at me coldly, leaning on his short leg, a dark line of sweat staining the collar of his shirt. The short one had unbuttoned his blue coat, and his shirtfront, stretched over his bulging low-slung belly, was soaked with

Flagstaff Public Library
Flagstaff, Arizona

blood. He nodded me back to the Inspector, who asked: "I wonder . . . has the murder weapon been found?"

"No," I replied. He peered at me closely, one finger in the bowl of his pipe like an accusation. Inexplicably, I felt my face reddening. "We left her exactly—"

"Yes, yes, I'm sure." He lifted his gaze to the ceiling as though studying something there, and involuntarily, the rest of us looked up as well. Nothing to see: a plain white ceiling, overlapping circles of light cast on it by the various lamps in the room. In some odd way, in its blankness, it seemed to be looking down on us, dwarfing us. I wondered, staring at it, if Alison might not be thinking the same thing—or, knowing I'd be having such thoughts, refuting me: there *is* no audience, Gerald, that's what makes it so sad. Hadn't I said much the same thing the night we met: that the principle invention of playwrights was not plays or actors but audiences? "Curious . . . ," mused the Inspector. He was gazing down at Ros again. As though directed, so then did we. Her breast was covered by the frock once more, but now her legs seemed farther apart, the silvery skirt riding halfway up her stockinged thighs, and she had some kind of apparatus stuck in her mouth. An X-ray unit maybe. "You'd think a girl like her . . ." He paused thoughtfully, zipping up the tobacco pouch. What had he meant? There was a heavy stillness in the room, broken only by Roger's muffled sob, a low hum (the hi-fi? or that thing in Ros's mouth?), and the labored breathing of the two police officers. Inspector Pardew sighed as though in regret, then looked up at me: "But excuse me, you were speaking of an ice pick, I believe . . ."

I started. "No . . . ice!" It was a cheap trick. Not to say a complete absurdity. And yet (I was finding it hard to catch my breath), hadn't I just been . . . ? "There—there was ice in the pitcher I was carrying when you—"

"Of course." He smiled, making an arch pretense of believing me. He tamped the tobacco into the bowl of his pipe, returned the pouch to his pocket, withdrew a lighter. "So you've said . . ."

"You think she might have been killed with an ice pick, do you?" I shot back, though I felt I was blustering, inventing somehow my own predicament. Where did all this come from?

"I don't know," he replied, tucking the pipe in his mouth, watching me closely. Behind him, Jim was shaking his head at me. Most of the others simply looked amazed. Or distracted. "Do you?"

"We—we don't even *have* an ice pick, Inspector," I replied. This seemed more sensible, but I still felt like I had lost my place somehow. "Our refrigerator has an automatic unit which—"

"One moment!" cried Pardew, his attention drawn suddenly to something at the other side of the room. "Unless I am very much mistaken, we shall find what we are looking for in that white chair over there!" Pocketing his unlit pipe, he strode over to it, guests parting to form a corridor. We all saw it now: something glinting just behind the cushion at the back, red stains on the creamy velvet. "Aha!" he exclaimed as he lifted the cushion. I half-expected him to produce an ice pick from under it, absurd as that seemed, but there was only a knife. I recognized it: it was my wife's butcher knife. Just as I'd seen it in the kitchen. "It's been wiped clean, I see," he observed, picking it up with a handkerchief from his trousers pocket. "But there are streaks on it still of something like blood . . . !"

Distantly, in another room, half lost in shadows, I saw my wife, slipping back toward the kitchen again. She was gazing tenderly at me over the heads of our guests, through the bluish haze of cigarette smoke and what seemed almost like steam (I wiped my brow with a shirtsleeve), looking more serene than I'd seen her for months. Yet pained, too, and a bit forlorn. Love is *not* an art, Gerald, she had once shouted at me in rare anger but common misunderstanding: *It is a desperate compulsion! Like death throes!* "What? What did you say?" I asked.

The Inspector was holding the knife up in front of my face. The handkerchief in which he cradled it was wrinkled and discolored, clotted with dried and drying mucus. "I said, do you recognize it?"

"Yes, it's ours." I looked up into his penetrating gaze. "It's from our kitchen."

"I see . . . and who would have access—?"

"Anybody. It hangs on a wall by the oven."

"Hmmm." He stared down at the knife, lips pursed, twisting one end of his moustache meditatively—then he arched his brows and, handing the knife to Anatole, blew his nose in the handkerchief. Anatole studied the knife skeptically, weighed it in his palm, tightened his fingers around the handle, tested the cutting edge with his thumb, and then, while the Inspector stared absently into his filthy handkerchief, passed it on to Patrick, crowding in at his elbow. Patrick jumped. Someone said: "Is that it?" Patrick, panicking, held it at arm's length

between thumb and forefinger as though it might contaminate him. He pushed it toward the distracted Inspector, back at Anatole who shrugged it off, then thrust it at Dickie. Laughing, Dickie tossed it up in the air, caught it by the handle, wiped the blade on the seat of Patrick's green trousers ("Naughty boy!" squeaked Patrick, twisting about, trying to see over his hip where Dickie had wiped), and handed it on to Charley Trainer, who had just come in with his wife, Janice, she still looking a bit weepy. Charley said: "What is it, huh, some kinda joke?"

And so it went around the room, passing from hand to hand as though seeking recognition, approval, community, and as I watched, it suddenly and finally came home to me: Ros, our own inimitable Ros, was dead. All those breathless hugs: gone forever. And now everything was different. Fundamentally different. I felt as though I were witnessing the hardening of time. And the world, ruptured by it, turning to jelly.

"Tell me," said Inspector Pardew, looking up from his handkerchief, "is your wife here?"

"Yes, of course, in the kitchen—but she had nothing to do with this!"

"Who said she did?" asked the Inspector, eyeing me narrowly. He stuffed the wad of yellowed handkerchief back in his pocket. The knife was still moving like a message around the room. It reached Tania on the floor, who explored it dreamily with both hands, her eyes closed. "All the same, we'd better interview her," said the Inspector to his assistants, nodding toward the back of the house.

"Yessir," said the shorter one, as the Inspector set up a tripod, unwrapped some film. "Can you handle him, Bob?"

The tall one, Bob, nodded grimly and gave an extra twist on Roger's arm, but just then Tania opened her eyes, lifted her spectacles onto her nose, and, frowning curiously at the knife in her hands, leaned over and touched its tip to Ros's wound. "*WrraAARGHH!*" screamed Roger and broke free.

"Oh no—!"

"*Stop him!*" somebody shouted.

The two policemen managed to cut him off from the body, but they were unable to lay hold of him. He lurched violently about the room in a wild whinnying flight, blind to all obstacles, slapping up against walls and furniture, tangling himself in curtains, leaving not

mere fingerprints behind but whole body blotches, and howling insanely as he went. People tried to duck out of his way, but he slammed into them just the same, knocking them off their feet, sloshing them with Ros's blood, making them yell and shriek and lash out in terror. I saw Mavis tip backward on her round bottom, her thick white legs looping gracefully over her head like surfacing porpoises. Some guy behind her crashed into the fireplace in a cloud of dust and ashes, still holding his drink aloft, big Louise slipped on Ros's blood, Howard hit the wall like a beanbag, spectacles flying. Roger was a man possessed. The police chased him, stumbling through the wreckage, knocking down what Roger missed, but there was no catching him. Glasses were spilling and smashing, tables tipping, potted plants splattering like little bombs, lamps whirling, camera gear flying like shrapnel; someone screamed: *"Get down! Get down!"* I was glad my wife was well out of it, but I was afraid for Alison. She was standing in the middle of the uproar as though chained there, her eyes locked on mine, the tears drying on her cheeks, her smile fading. And then I couldn't see her anymore as Roger pitched suddenly toward Ros again, tripped over Tania ducking the wrong way, and fell upon Naomi, who was trying desperately in the confusion to get everything back in her bag again. Naomi squealed as she sprawled under his weight and all her stuff went flying again. Before the police could reach him, Roger was back on his feet, half-galloping, half-flying through a flurry of paper and toilet gear, plowing into Patrick, caroming off big Chooch Trainer, whose eyes popped and crossed at the force of the blow, and sending Woody and Yvonne, who'd just come in with fresh drinks in their hands, scrambling back through the door again on their hands and knees.

"Hey, listen, Ger, do me a favor," whispered Dickie in my ear as we watched all this (Anatole and Janice were just being knocked over like toy soldiers, Anatole's black jacket and Janny's pink skirt billowing behind their fall like lowering flags), "tell that silly slit to get off my case, will you?"

I looked up at him (the short officer was clomping about furiously, his foot caught in the toolbox), standing tall and trim in his white vest and trousers, dark plaid sports jacket, blue tie, his blond hair swept back with care, a cool half-smile on his lips, yet a kind of loose panic in his eyes. "Who, you mean—?" And just then Roger hit me. I felt the blood spray up my nose like wet rust and I crumpled to the

floor under a creature moist and cold as a slug, but with roaring breath and flailing crablike limbs, and massive with its own furious but mindless energy. It was some kind of monster I was grappling with, not Roger, and the sheer bloody reality of it terrified me. Maybe I was even screaming. I saw the police grab at him, but he leaped away, kneeing me in the stomach, and they fell on me instead. The short cop's hat had slipped down over his eyes, and in his blindness he seized my wrist, threw me over onto my face, and twisted my arm up to my neck, nearly breaking it. *"Hey!"* I cried, and something cold and hard knocked up behind my ear.

"Hold it, Fred!" gasped the other one. *"It's the host!"*

"Wha—?" The officer on top of me, snorting and blowing, leaned toward my face, pushing his hat up with the barrel of his pistol. *"Whoof*—sorry, fe—*fah!*—fella!" he wheezed, letting go my arm. His face was smeared with blood and sweat like warpaint and his shirtfront had popped its buttons, his blood-red belly pushing out in front of him like a grisly shield. He holstered the gun he had pressed to my head. "I thought it was the—*poo!*—bereaved!"

Roger had got as far as Inspector Pardew, who was holding him calmly away from Ros's body with one hand, while brushing irritably at the specks of blood on his white scarf and three-piece suit with the other, muttering something about "a stupid waste of energy." He frowned impatiently at the two policemen and, abashed, they got off me and (the short cop kicked the toolkit off his foot, there was a clatter of wrenches, glass cutters, and hammers, Kitty exclaiming: "Knud will never believe this!") took hold of Roger, dragging him away, still screaming, into the next room. I sat up, massaging my twisted arm. My head was ringing, and there was a sullen pain deep in my stomach where Roger had kneed me. The others were picking themselves up, mumbling, coughing (Janny, snuffling, said: "Where's my shoe?"), surveying the damage.

"Jesus! Remind me not to ask you any more favors!" groaned Dickie in my ear. "That one fucking near killed me!"

He sat beside me, wiping his face with his shirttail, his bright white vest and trousers peppered with blood as though riddled with punctures. His redheaded girlfriend Ginger, who had somehow kept her feet through it all, now fell down. I saw Alison in a corner, straightening her tights under the softly drawn folds of her skirt. Her husband seemed not to be around, had apparently missed it all. Had I seen him

stroll disdainfully out when Roger launched forth? Or perhaps he'd gone before. Alison looked so vulnerable. I wanted to touch her, be touched, and just thinking about that eased the pain some. "She sure has a sweet ass on her," acknowledged Dickie, following my gaze. "Tight and soft at the same time, like bandaged fists." As though to model it for us, Alison turned her back and smoothed her silk skirt down. I sighed. Between us, in debris and rubble, Ros lay like a somber interdict. "Reminds me of a dancer I used to know who could pull corks with hers. Who is she anyhow, Ger?"

"People we met," I said noncommittally. Dickie had energy, but no subtlety. He was like an artisan who had the craft, but no serious ideas, and what he didn't finish, he often spoiled. "What do you think's the matter with Naomi?" I asked.

We watched her, looking utterly stricken, go hobbling out of the room taking little baby steps, clutching her skirts tight around her knees, her shoulderbag spilled out behind her. "Christ," Dickie muttered, struggling to his feet, "she must've shit her pants!" And he followed her out.

Across the room, near the fireplace, Tania's husband, Howard, held his spectacles up for me to see: both lenses cracked. Like everyone else, he was splattered all over with blood, making him look like his red tie had sprung a leak. The indignant expression on his flushed face seemed to suggest that he blamed me for the broken lenses.

"Now then, one thing I don't understand," insisted Inspector Pardew calmly, one hand at the knot of his tie as though to draw himself erect: "Why did you speak of an ice pick?"

"Not an ice pick," I replied wearily, looking up at him from the floor. "Ice." Even as I spoke, my words seemed, like the punchline to one of Charley Trainer's shaggy dog stories, stupid, yet compulsory. Something Tania had once said about art as the concretizing of memory lurked like a kind of nuisance (we'd been talking about her "Ice Maiden" and the paradoxes of the "real") at the back of my mind, back where it was still throbbing from the revolver's knock on the skull. I hoped both would go away at the same time. The knife was nowhere to be seen, though it could have been anywhere amid all that wreckage. "I was trying to get at the time, working backward . . ."

"Gerald was serving drinks," Alison said, coming over through the clutter to stand above me. Her voice was clear and musical, and it mellowed somewhat the Inspector's expression. She let her hand fall

softly into my hair, her silk dress caressing my ear like a blown kiss. Legs passed my head, moving toward the dining room. "Did you ever notice how blood *smells?*" someone whispered. "It was about an hour ago."

"Ah, that's better!" The Inspector reached into his vest pocket and pulled out a fob watch. Beyond him, Mavis lay on her belly still, staring vacantly, Tania kneeling beside her, speaking softly into her ear. Smashed film gear lay scattered around them, the tripod's legs bent double at the joints like broken ski poles. I rose achingly to my feet, helped by Alison. The touch of her hands on me was wonderfully comforting. My wife's fat friend Louise passed us on her way toward the back of the house, disapproval darkening her face like a bruise. The Inspector, his chin doubling, stared down at the body (I was thinking about Ros again, those gentle body massages she loved to give and receive between orgasms, the way she held your face in both her hands when she kissed you, even in greeting, and the soft silky almost phantasmal touch of her finger as she slipped it dreamily up your anus), idly winding his fob watch; then, pocketing it, he looked up and said: "I'm afraid I'm going to have to ask everyone to turn their watches in to me, if you don't mind." I sighed when Alison took her hands away, and in response she smiled. Her nose and cheeks were freckled with blood, and there were larger spots between her breasts, but she wore them gracefully, like beauty marks. "Come along, hurry it up, please!"

My own watch was on an expansion band and simply slipped off, but Alison's band was a complicated green leather affair with three different buckles. "Here, let me help," I said, taking her hand in mine. A warm flush of nostalgia swept over me as, like a boy again with bra hooks, I fumbled with the buckles, her fingers teasing my wrists, her free hand falling between our thighs.

I wanted to hold on to this moment, but Pardew interrupted it. "I'll need someone to collect them," he said. I knew he was looking at me, and I smiled apologetically at Alison. Her eyes seemed to be penetrating mine, reading feverishly behind them, while her free hand stroked the inside of my thigh as though scribbling an oath there. Or an invocation. "And I'll want those of all the people outside this room as well."

"Allow me," offered Mr. Draper, stepping in behind us from the dining room with a roast-beef sandwich in his bony fist, and Alison

took her hand away. "I may not be good for much, old as I am, heh heh, but takin' up collections is one thing I can still execute, as you might say." To my embarrassment, he turned to Alison and presented her with his sandwich, softly mangled at one end. "Here, hold this for me, will you, dear?" he said. "Can't seem to get these new choppers through the durned thing." He saw me staring and clacked his teeth once for me as a demonstration. "Store teeth, y'know," he explained wistfully, removing his suit jacket and rolling up his sleeves. "Perils of a long life, son, nothin' works like it used to." And he winked meaninglessly, snapping his braces.

"Thanks, Mr. Draper," I said, handing him our watches.

"My pleasure, sir!" He strapped mine on his arm, dropped Alison's into a pocket of his baggy trousers, then went off on his rounds, gathering watches onto his arms and into his pockets, greeting everyone boisterously: "I'll take your watches, please! At my age, I need all the time I can get!" Followed by a mechanical chuckle like some kind of solemn ratification. Ame-heh-heh-heh-hen.

"I'm sorry," I said to Alison, trying to disassociate myself from him, "I've never seen him before tonight." Certainly he was out of place here, he and his wife both. I supposed my wife had invited them. "The old fellow's been badgering me all night to look at some snapshots from his tourist travels. I think he's a bit—"

"I know, I've seen them all." She smiled, but when I reached for her hand, she pulled it away. Absently, she began eating the old man's sandwich. Dolph came by with a can of beer in one hand, gazing at something across the room, and Alison winced, bumping me with her hip. She reached into her teeth and pulled out a little piece of string. "Tell me about her, Gerald. The girl . . ."

"Ros?" I looked down at the body. Inspector Pardew was chalking out an outline of her. It occurred to me that she'd been jostled somewhat during Roger's recent rampage. One arm and leg had shifted and her head was tilted a different way. Did that matter? Exposed film plates lay beside her like last words and the apparatus had fallen out of her gaping mouth. "She was an actress. Not a very good one. Her problem was, she could never be anyone on stage but herself. Mostly she was in chorus lines or shows where they needed naked girls with good bodies." Roger seemed to have quieted down. "Did you see *Lot's Wife*, by any chance?"

"No, I don't think so." She chewed, watching me closely, eager, it

seemed, merely to hear me speak, no matter what about. The Inspector, having completed his chalk outline of the corpse and some of the stuff around it—including, I noticed, some of the junk that had fallen out of Naomi's bag and out of the toolbox—was now moving Ros's limbs about as though looking for something under them. Mr. Draper's croaky old voice could be heard out in the hallway, saying: "Watches, please! Take time off! Thank you, thank you! Your time is my time! Yeh heh heh . . ."

"She had the title role, probably her best part, one of them anyway. She'd been getting little but walk-ons before then, back row of the chorus, even nonparts like one of Bluebeard's dead wives or the messenger at the door who never enters, and mainly because Roger blew up such a storm whenever something a little more adventurous came along. So when the chance came to do *Lot's Wife*, she could hardly turn it down." I felt as though I were shaping the words for her, rounding them, smoothing them, curling them in over the little gold loops: and that she felt them there, sliding in, caressing her inner ear, and that it made her breathe more deeply. "The play was a kind of dionysian version of the Bible story in which, after being turned to salt and abandoned by Lot, she was supposed to get set upon by ecstatic Sodomites, stripped, stroked, licked from top to bottom, and quite literally reimpregnated with life. At the end, Lot returns, sees his mistake, repents, and joins the Sodomites, now no longer as her husband of course, but just one of her many worshipers, which is supposedly an improvement for him."

"And Roger, I take it, was not so wise."

"I'm afraid not—of course, Lot probably had some help from the director."

"Roger had not seen the script."

"Oh, he'd seen it all right," I smiled. "That was exactly the problem."

Pardew was down on his hands and knees now, fishing about under Ros's skirt with the tweezers. He had filter papers in one hand, empty pillboxes, tape, and a pick glass on the floor beside him. Alison watched him a moment, distracted, the last bite of her sandwich held out absently like a coin about to be dropped in a meter. The two policemen had returned and the short one was holding Ros's limbs in various positions at the Inspector's instructions, while he nosed around. The other was making sketches of the scene. They seemed a bit subdued.

Alison turned back to me, her face softened by a momentary sorrow. "The problem—?"

"He turned up at the first rehearsal with a gun at his head, saying he'd pull the trigger if she didn't leave the play and come home with him, and since Ros couldn't say no, that's what she did."

"Turned back. Like Lot's wife, after all." She popped the last bite in. I saw a neat row of gleaming white teeth sunk into red flesh, crisp green lettuce, dark rye painted with yellow mustard. If even that arouses me, I thought, I'm pretty far gone . . . "Yet you said—?"

"Well, the author refused to let the play go on without her. He insisted she'd inspired him to write it, a dream he'd had or something, and she had to play the lead. So they talked Ros into having Roger temporarily committed. Because of the suicide attempt. For his own good, they said, and it probably was."

"Until the show closed."

"That's right. Ros visited him every day in the ward to cheer him up, never told him she was in the play, and he never asked."

"An old trouper, after all. And so," she added, not wryly, just sadly, staring down at her hands, "everybody lived happily ever after." She brushed the crumbs away, tongued a bit of sandwich from her teeth. For some reason I thought: Am I forgetting something? What I remembered was an old beggar in Cadiz who did tricks with coins. His last trick always was to stack as many coins on his tongue as people would put there, then swallow them. Or seem to. I made some remark at the time about "pure theater" and the woman I was with said: "I know a better trick but it is not so practical." The old fellow climaxed his act by belching loudly and producing a paper note in "change," and the truth about the woman was that she was mistaken. "And was the play a success?"

"It had a good run."

In fact, she packed them in. But mainly because they invited the audience to join in, and the same crowd kept coming back night after night to lick the salt. True believers. Her breast, I saw, had fallen out of the dress again. It seemed less important now. The Inspector, peeling down one stocking, had found a run, which he peered at now through his pick glass. "There's another good one here at the back, Chief." Alison touched my hand. "You loved her very much."

"Yes. Along with a thousand other guys." I watched Pardew and his two assistants tugging her dead weight this way and that, watched her breast and head flop back and forth together as though in protest

at the mockery of it, thinking: How quiet it has grown! I lowered my voice: "She had something . . . very special . . ."

"I might have guessed," Alison said. She was grinning. "Unique, I think you said before . . ."

I smiled, leaning toward her touch. "Mm, but hers *really* was, you see," I said, brushing at the specks of blood on Alison's nose, letting the truth slip away now, or at least that kind of truth, letting myself be led, "and not just in the eye, so to speak, of the beholder . . ."

"Ah, poor Gerald!" she laughed. "When will you ever learn?"

She stifled her laughter: people were staring at us. Even the police had glanced up from the body. She covered her mouth, forced a solemn expression onto her face, peeked up at me guiltily. She waited until the others had looked away again ("Calipers, please," the Inspector muttered), then whispered: "But it was her breast that made you want to cry."

I nodded, conscious of Alison's own breasts, tender and provocative under the soft silken folds of her dress, the nipples rising hard now like excited little fingers, seeming to reach through the bloodstains in the delicate jacquard pattern as though to point hopefully beyond. "Her sex was a secret, known only to millions, her dark side, you might say . . . her buried treasure . . ." No longer: the police had their noses down there now, arguing about something. Her thighs had been pulled apart and the curled tip-ends of little straw-colored pubic hairs could be seen fringing the legbands of her panties. For some reason, it was making me dizzy. The glossiness of her panties or something. "But her . . . her breasts," I continued, taking a deep breath, forcing my gaze away (somewhere a toilet flushed; down in the rec room, the darts players were still at it), managing to draw myself back to Alison's eyes once more, "her breasts were her public standard, what we knew her by . . ." The placid depths of Alison's eyes calmed me. I felt certain that everything was going to be all right. Somehow. "Her innocence and her light, you might say. The good white flag she flew." I smiled as our legs met: she touched her throat. "Flags . . ."

"In the dark and dangerous land of make-believe," whispered Alison, not so much completing my thought for me as marrying her thought to mine in a kind of voluptuous melodrama.

"Yes . . . yes, that's it . . ."

There was something truly extraordinary about Alison's eyes. Some-

times they seemed to penetrate my head as though copulating with it like a man, and then as quickly they'd go soft, almost opaque, inviting me in. Or they'd suddenly seem to pick up light from somewhere and cast it twinkling back at me, suggestively, mischievously—then just as suddenly withdraw it again, hide it, daring me to come and look for it. "Bewitching . . ."

"Pardon?"

"Your eyes, Alison . . ."

"Ah, that must be the wormwood." She grinned. There was a simple gaiety in them again, and I could feel her releasing me.

"Wormwood?"

"The vermouth. That's where the name comes from."

"I always thought it was just some kind of wine, I didn't know I was giving you wormwood—"

"Oh yes. The flowers anyway. And sweetflag root and cinchona bark and coriander seeds and sandalwood—shall I go on?"

"I take it you're trying to tell me something."

"Mmm, after that sandwich—"

"I'll be right back," I said and lightly touched her hip. "Don't move."

"*Nobody* moves!" barked the Inspector, glancing sharply up at me from under Ros's skirt. "Nobody leaves this house without my permission!"

"I'm not—it's only—just an errand," I stammered. "The dining room . . ."

Pardew studied me closely a moment, hooded by Ros's silver skirt like a monk. He stroked his thick moustache, glanced thoughtfully at Alison, then nodded and returned to his work, snipping through the legband of Ros's panties now with a tiny pair of manicure scissors. He made two crosswise cuts, an inch or two deep, then peeled away the little flap of silk as though easing a stamp from an envelope. Jim came in with his black bag and handed the Inspector a probe with a light on the end of it, and the others in the room pressed closer. The Inspector looked up at me and frowned: "Off you go, then!"

Something, as I turned away, was worrying me, something just at the edge of my vision. The way Ros's stockings had been rolled down to her ankles like doughnuts maybe, making her seem pinioned, the stark face-powder whiteness of her bare thighs under their silvery canopy, the shadows beyond, Jim shaking down a thermometer. . . . Or

was it that tube of lipstick I'd noticed, its greasy red tip extended as though in sudden excitement, lying not far from Mavis in the chalked outline of one of my wife's fallen plants like a child's crayon on a coloring book drawing? Or Tania, scrambling out of Roger's way a moment ago, still clutching the—?

"Boy, they sure tore up jack in here," remarked Daffie in the doorway: one of Dickie's girls, regal tonight in her sleek indigo sheath. Her drink looked like pink lemonade, but I knew it to be straight gin tinted with juice from the maraschino cherries jar. "Your whole house looks like it's suffering from violent nosebleed, Ger."

"Well, it just goes to show," I said vaguely.

"You mean never hire a lip as an interior decorator?" She smiled, drawing deeply on a small black cigarillo. Over her shoulder, just inside the dining room, I could see Dolph's burry head with its bass clef ears, and beyond him a crowd of people jammed up around the food and drink. At the sideboard, under one of his wife Tania's paintings (a conventional subject, "Susanna and the Elders," yet uniquely Tania's: a gawky self-conscious girl stepping over a floating hand mirror into a bottomless pit, gazing anxiously back over her shoulder at a dark forest crowding up on her—no elders to be seen, yet *something* is watching her), Howard was stirring up a fresh pitcher of martinis. I was afraid he might use up all the dry vermouth, but Daffie had taken a gentle grip on my forearm, holding me back. "You know, Ger," she said softly, smoke curling off her lower lip as she spoke, "there's something funny about those cops."

"What's that, Daffie?"

"Scratching around in Ros's drawers like that," she said. Daffie was a model, one of the best, but in the soft-focus photos you never saw the worry lines, the dark hollows under her eyes, the nervous twitching of her nostrils. "I don't know, but it's, well—it's like they've been there before."

"They're professionals. They've seen a lot of murders."

"No, I mean . . ." She hesitated, withdrew her hand, took a stiff jolt of iced gin. "I want you to do me two favors, Ger."

"Sure, Daffie. If I can . . ."

"One, tell that pint-sized ham-fisted ape behind me to stop messing around behind the scenes," she said loudly, Dolph's ears reddening like dipped litmus paper as he disappeared around the corner, "and two . . ." She leaned close, touched my arm again, lowered her

husky voice: "Be careful, Ger . . . ." Then, bracing herself, her elbows tucked in, she drifted on into the living room (both the Inspector and the short cop, Fred, had their heads under Ros's skirt now, Bob standing by with a test tube), moving with exaggerated elegance as though to demonstrate for me her sobriety. What she showed me, though, was a backside splattered head to foot with blood, a split skirt, and tights laddered from cheek to heel like torn curtains.

Most of the people in the dining room were crowded around the chafing dish on the table, spearing miniature sausages out of a barbecue sauce that bubbled lazily over a low blue flame. Squeezing through them on my way to the sideboard, Daffie's warning still echoing in my ear, I was reminded (I felt flushed through by fear as though it were a sudden passion) of a night at the theater when we went backstage to see Ros after a play. On that occasion, too, I'd been cautioned, but by my wife, who, seeing Roger standing guard at Ros's door and looking utterly demented, had clutched my arm, whispered her warning ("Be careful . . ."), shouted at Roger to give Ros our love and blown him a kiss, and then had dragged me away through the frothy bustle of actors and their friends and hangers-on and on out the backstage exit. I'd thought she'd seen something more specific than Roger's monstrous but by then familiar affliction—and indeed perhaps she had, for what she'd said when we got outside was: "I sometimes get the feeling, Gerald, that the world is growing colder and colder." Having just watched a corny but loving play about a houseful of prostitutes with an innocent virgin and old-fashioned boy-meets-girl romance on their hands, I'd wanted to say that, yes, and Ros was the flame at which all chilled men might well warm themselves; but instead, sensing my wife's deep disquiet, what I'd come out with was: "You think Roger's going crazy?" "No," she'd replied, drawing me close to her as we came out onto the street, pressing her cheek against my shoulder, "what scares me is I think he's going sane."

I greeted Howard at the sideboard and, noticing that the pitcher of martinis he was stirring was only about half full, asked him (the flush had passed; I thought: a passion, yes, but passion's passion) how the vermouth was holding out, but before he could answer, his wife's nephew Anatole, hovering crowlike beside him, shot me a dark long-lashed glance and asked bluntly, his voice breaking: "How much longer are you going to put up with this horseshit?" Then he glared at his tumbler of bourbon and ginger ale as though discovering some-

thing trenchant there and, flinging back his long black hair with a toss of his head, promptly drank down most of it.

"The vermouth's not the *problem*, Gerald!" his uncle Howard snapped. "But there's no *ice* and the *gin* is all gone!" He seemed unusually peevish. His cracked specs maybe. Behind them, when he looked up at me, his eyes appeared broken up and scattered like little cubist exercises, and probably the world seen through them looked a bit that way as well.

I laid a consoling hand on his shoulder. "Don't worry, Howard, there's ice in the kitchen and more gin down here below. Excuse me, Anatole." I knelt for the gin, and the boy jerked backward, thumping up against Vic, just coming for a refill of his own. Vic swore, Anatole stammered an apology, and Howard said: "And *someone's* stolen the fruit knife for the *lemons!*" Looking up, I saw then that he'd been using his scout knife. His hands, stained and soiled, were trembling.

"Those three dicks probably borrowed it," said Vic sourly, his speech beginning to slur. "I think they're in there now, trying to peel Ros's cunt with it."

Anatole laughed, took a nervous puff on his French cigarette, and said: "That's just it, those stupid turds can't see what they're looking straight at!"

"I'm afraid the whole fucking species has much the same problem, son," Vic growled, cocking one shaggy eyebrow at Anatole. "Like bats in daylight, we can't even see when we're pissing on ourselves." Vic was a hardnosed guy with a spare intellect, but he had a weakness for grand pronouncements, especially with a few shots under his belt. I handed him a new bottle of bourbon, pushed the cabinet door shut with my knee, poured a wineglass full of vermouth for Alison, and then, on reflection, one for myself as well.

"Here's a good one," said Anatole. He was reading the cocktail napkins Kitty and Knud had given us, which were decorated with the usual party gags based on lines like "Please don't grind your butts into the carpet," or "Thou shalt not omit adultery." The one he showed us was of a policeman frisking a girl bankrobber. He had her face up against the wall, her skirt lifted and her pants pulled down (as though on cue, the cop with the test tube limped in, pushing people aside, and snatched the salt away from Mrs. Draper, went bobbing out again), from which heaps of banknotes were tumbling out, and what he was saying was: "Now, let's get to the bottom of this!"

"Tell me," said Vic, plunging his fist into Howard's martini pitcher for a couple of ice cubes, Howard sputtering in protest, "where do you think the cop got that line? Did it come natural to him as a simple horny human, or did it get thrust on him somehow?"

Anatole flushed, a nervous grin twitching on his thin lips. "You mean about free will or—?"

"I mean, has he emptied his own incorrigibly shitty nature into the vacuum of an occupation here, or has the job and society made him, innocent at birth, into the crude bullying asshole that he's become?"

"I-I don't know . . . I guess a little of both—"

"Just as I thought," grunted Vic, "another goddamn liberal." And he turned away as though in contempt, sucking the ice cubes, squinting down at some of the other cocktail napkins, held at arm's length.

Anatole, badly stung, looked to Howard for support, but his uncle, absently stirring the martinis, was distracted, his head bent toward the TV room where several couples were necking. Ah. Probably the true cause of his bad temper: I'd interrupted his little spectacle. Howard the art critic. At the far wall, Charley Trainer's wife, Janice, was in a stand-up clinch with some guy whose back was to us, her arms wrapped around his neck schoolgirl-style, her pink skirt rucked up over her raised thigh. Our eyes met for a moment and what I saw there, or thought I saw, was terror. "I guess I'll get something to eat," Anatole muttered clumsily and slouched off toward the dining table, looking gangly and exposed. "I'm feeling drunk or something . . ."

Ginger was over there, jabbing clumsily at the sausages in the chafing dish with a toothpick. She caught the tip end of one, lifted it shakily toward her little comic-book "O" of a mouth. It fell off. As she bent over, stiff-legged above her heels, to pick it up, Dolph stepped up behind her and, as though by accident, his eyes elsewhere, let his cupped palm fall against her jutting behind. Anatole saw this, spun away, found himself moving on through the doorway into the living room, puffing shallowly on his cigarette stub.

"You were pretty hard on him, Vic."

"He's all right. But he's all style and no substance. He needs to grow up." Ginger rose, holding painfully with her fingertips the hot sausage, furry now with dust and lint. She looked around desperately for some place to put it, finally gave up and popped it in her mouth, then brushed at her rear end as though flicking away flies. "Isn't she the one that cunt-hungry fashion plate brought here tonight?"

"One of them." Dolph took his hand away and (Vic, moving like an aging lion, now stalked off into the TV room, flinging open doors, peering behind furniture) rubbed his nose with it. Poor Dolph. Bachelorhood, since his break-up with Louise, had not sat well on him. Ginger blew out her cheeks around the hot sausage and bobbed up and down on her high heels, her halo of carroty little pigtails quivering around her heart-shaped face like nerve ends.

"Hey," I said when Vic returned (Howard had left us, taking up a position over near the dining table where he still had a view into the TV room, his fractured lenses aglitter with myriad reflections of the candles on the table), "fatherhood doesn't last forever, you know."

"She's a fucking innocent, Gerry, and I'm telling you, if that cocksucker gets his filthy hands on her, so help me"—he ripped a wadded-up cocktail napkin apart in demonstration—"I'll tear his balls off!"

I believed him. It was what made Vic more than just an armchair radical: he could kill. "I'll get some more ice," I said, taking the bucket along with me, dumping the empty bottles in it, and Vic called after me: "If you see Sally Ann, damn it, tell her I want to talk to her. Right now!" Alison's husband came through just then with Roger's law partner Woody and his wife, Yvonne, and as I passed them I heard them laugh together behind me. All three were carrying croquet mallets: had they been playing out there in the dark?

Louise stood up suddenly when I entered the kitchen, almost as though I'd caught her at something. She'd been squeezed in at the breakfast bench, watching my wife whip up what looked like an avocado dip—or perhaps helping with some of the chopping: there was a little cheese board and knife in front of her—and she nearly took the buttons off the front of her dress trying to jump out of there.

Patrick, halving a grapefruit at the counter with a small steak knife, exclaimed: "My goodness, Louise! I felt that all the way over here!"

"You don't have to leave, Louise," I said, raising my voice as the dishwasher thumped suddenly into its wash cycle. "I've only come for some ice and mix."

"Let her go, Gerald," my wife called out, getting to her feet. "She's just eating up all my potato chips anyway."

"Are you still making more food?" There was a huge platter of freshly prepared canapés on the counter, empty tuna cans and cracker boxes scattered about, dip mix packets, bread from the freezer, the wrappers still frosty, home-canned pickles and relishes up from cellar,

smoked oysters on toast squares. And something was cooking in the oven. "I thought you had everything ready *before* the party."

"So did I. But it's all going so fast." Louise glanced suspiciously past the bucket of empty bottles I was carrying to the two full wineglasses in my other hand, as without a word but accompanied by the splashy grind of the dishwasher, she shifted heavily toward the dining room. "Did you notice how many sausages were left in the chafing dish?"

"Not many. Should I turn the flame off?"

"No, I've got more." She went to the refrigerator and brought out a ceramic bowlful, bumping the door closed with her hips. "Louise, would you mind?" she called, stopping her at the door.

"My, what cute little weenies," Patrick remarked as Louise, flushing, took the bowl from my wife's hands.

"Can I fix you a drink before you go, Louise?" I called, but averting her face darkly, she backed out through the dining room door without replying. "What's the matter with *her?*"

"She was badly bruised in there," my wife said, speaking up over the dishwasher. She brought the avocado dip over and set it on the butcherblock worktable in the middle of the room, under the big fluorescent lamp, and I thought of Alison again, that play we'd seen. "Don't you notice? Everything that happens," she'd said that night, "happens where the light is." "Didn't you see her face?"

"Ah, was that a bruise . . . ?" I poked my nose in the fridge: about a dozen cans of beer left—Dolph must be drinking them six at a time. They were squeezed in there among dishes and dishes of prepared foods, tins of sardines, anchovies, pimentos, bags of sliced and chopped vegetables, pâtés, and dozens of sausages and wrapped cheeses.

"She said Roger bumped her cheek with his elbow," my wife explained over her shoulder, pulling hot bread out of the oven, hurrying it gingerly to the butcherblock.

"I'm afraid her *face* isn't *all* that's bruised," Patrick announced archly. "It's a good thing for you this house has firm foundations!"

"Now, Patrick," my wife scolded playfully (her busy hands, slender, a bit raw, stirred dips, arranged biscuits and crackers, sliced bread), winking at me as I dragged a case of beer up to the fridge, "she's not *that* heavy!"

"My dear," declared Patrick, one hand on his hip, the other holding his glass up as though in a toast, "I had already fallen when Louise

went down, and when she hit the floor *I skidded three feet in her direction!*"

My wife laughed and waggled an admonishing finger. "Patrick, you're a scandal!" Patrick, looking smug, lit up one of his French cigarettes, and she put a saucepan of water on to boil.

"By the way," I said, realizing that this had been bothering me for sometime now—in fact since I'd talked to Daffie—"where did they take Roger?" This last was shouted out in relative silence, as the dishwasher timer suddenly clicked over, and it made my wife and Patrick start. Frightened me, too, in a way. They turned away. I lowered my voice. "I, uh, didn't see him in the dining room."

"They took him into your study," my wife explained. She put a lid on the saucepan, staring at it as though estimating its contents. "They said the TV bothered them."

"Really?" I pulled the cold beers forward, packing the warm cans in at the back. "I don't even think it's on."

"Knud was watching something."

"He fell asleep."

"You know, he told me a really *weird* story tonight," said Patrick, sucking up some of the crushed ice from his salty bitch.

"Knud?"

"No, Roger, of course. Before the—before . . ."

Shoving things around to make room for the beer, I discovered at the back an old bottle of tequila, still about a third full. Must have been in there for years.

"He said he came home one night and Ros was gone."

"Nothing weird about that. The weird thing was to find her home. Say, how long's it been since we were last in Mexico?"

"Eight and a half years, Gerald—but don't interrupt. Tell us about the story, Patrick. What happened . . . ?"

"Well, it's very peculiar," said Patrick, stubbing out his cigarette, his bright eyes squinting from the smoke, his voice losing some of its mincing distance, mellowing toward intimacy. "He said he arrived home from the office late one night and Ros was gone, but there in her place, sitting in a chair by the window, was a strange old lady. Roger said the only word for her was 'hag.' An old hag. She had long scraggly white hair, wild piercing eyes, a hunched back, and she was dressed in pitiful old rags. He said he felt a strange presentiment about her as though he were in the presence of some dreadful mystery. He

asked her why she'd come, and she replied that she'd been told he was a great lawyer and could help her in her misfortune. She claimed to possess a fabulous wealth which she wished to share with all the world, but which had been taken away from her by a wicked and spiteful son and locked in a secret vault. Moreover, her son was seeking to have her declared mentally insane and put away, and she wanted Roger to force the son to release the fortune for the benefit of all and to prevent her unjust incarceration. Well! Roger said he understood immediately that it was a parable she'd been speaking, one meant for him alone, *he* was the selfish son, and his treasure—well, he told the strange old woman that though he sympathized with her plight he was unable to do as she asked. 'For shame!' hissed the old woman. 'You'll burn in hell for your lack of charity!' Mortified by his own weakness, he buried his head in his hands, and when he looked up again the hag was gone. He ran to the door and found Ros, lying in a swoon in the corridor outside, her hair loose and wild, her clothes torn."

"In a swoon—?"

"That's what he said. You should have seen his eyes when he told us! He said he carried her into the bedroom, fearing for her very life. He sat up with her all night, weeping buckets, kissing her feverishly, pleading for her forgiveness, until at last she came around. He begged her to tell him all that had happened, but she said she couldn't remember a thing since she'd left the bank that afternoon."

We were both staring at Patrick in silence when the dishwasher popped suddenly into its rinse cycle, making us all jump. I laughed. My wife said: "It must have been a dream, don't you think, Gerald?"

Even over the noisy churning of the dishwasher, we could hear Mr. Draper's booming voice on the other side of the door: "*Yes, heh heh, you might say I've got a lot of time on my hands!*" Patrick started up uneasily. "Probably," I said. "Or maybe a play Ros was in . . ."

"*Time, heels! Yeh heh heh!*"

"Do you think they'll *keep* my tweezers?" Patrick asked anxiously, tugging his cuffs down over his wrists, his eye on the door. "They're real silver!"

"Speaking of silver, I forgot to tell you, we're invited to Cyril and Peg's big anniversary party," my wife said, peeking into the kettle of water. The way she held the lid made me think of the Inspector hooded by Ros's skirt.

"Are they here yet?"

"A-a gift from my mother—!"

"Cyril and Peg? I think so." She poked around in the refrigerator and found a carton of eggs. "Didn't they come with Fats and Brenda?"

"It's Old Man Time here, soaks! I mean, folks!" Mr. Draper sang out jovially, bumping in through the door, and Patrick slipped stealthily out behind him. Mr. Draper wore wristwatches chockablock up both arms like sleeves of armor and his pants bagged low, their thin suspenders stretched tight, weighted down by his deep bulging pockets. "Come along now, heh heh, no present like the time!"

My wife, using a ladle, dropped the last of the eggs into the boiling water, checked her watch, then peeled it off and handed it to him. "Mine was your first, Mr. Draper," I said, showing him my empty wrist.

"Call me Lloyd, son! You—oops, nearly forgot!" The old man reached into his hip pocket and pulled out the butcher knife the Inspector had found. "Iris said to return this to you."

"Why, thank you, Lloyd. Looks like it needs a good washing." As she turned to put it in the sink, our eyes met. "Are you all right, Gerald?" she asked, smiling at me as she might at our young son.

"Yes, only I-I keep forgetting things . . ."

"Wasn't there someone else here when I came in?" asked Mr. Draper, peering over his spectacles, just as Dolph came thumping in for another beer.

"He left," said my wife, turning her bottom away from Dolph as he passed. She winked at me.

"Christ, have I got a thirst!" Dolph exclaimed, swinging open the refrigerator door.

"Gerald just put some in, Dolph."

"Cold ones to the front," I said. It was coming back to me, the knife, loose in the room like a taunt, then someone reaching for it, picking it up . . .

Dolph pulled a beer out and popped it open, took a long guzzle, all the while holding the door agape.

"Excuse me, sir," smiled Mr. Draper, coming forward (yes, Naomi, Naomi picking it up and putting it in her bag, Mrs. Draper making her take it out again—it must have been just before Roger hit me). "It's time—"

"You already got mine, Dropper," grumped Dolph, wiping his

mouth with his sleeve (and some big woman, fallen among my wife's potted plants, greenery in her hair like laurel, a silly look on her face as though she'd just remembered something she wished she'd forgot). "That one with the gold band halfway up your arm—don't lose it!" He belched and the dishwasher shut down. "That's better!"

"Time is never lost," Mr. Draper declared, lifting his chin so as to peer grandly down over his long warty nose, "only mislaid!"

"Jesus, what a night," wheezed Dolph, ignoring the old man. He shook his burry head as though in amazement, hauled out another beer. "It's starting to look like a goddamn packing house in there, Gerry!"

My wife blushed, wiped her hands on her checkered apron. "I'll go tidy up in a minute, Dolph."

"Is this guacamole?" Mr. Draper asked at the butcherblock.

The two glasses of vermouth sat there, pools of pale green light on the maple top beside the dark pudding of mashed avocado. Like two halves of an hourglass. I hurried over to the fridge, filled the bucket with ice. "You're right, Gerry," Dolph said, watching me ("Well, it has avocados in it," my wife was explaining, "but it's not as spicy— would you like to try some?"), "you sure as hell couldn't stab anybody with *that* thing."

"Yes indeed, ma'am—if you have a spoon. I don't think I can chance those crispy things. New store teeth, you know." He grinned sheepishly and pushed them halfway out of his mouth at her.

Dolph squeezed his empty can double and tossed it in the bin, then, belching voluminously, popped the other one open. "I'll take that bucket in for you, Gerry."

"Thanks, Dolph. Oh, hey—this bottle of tonic, too."

Mr. Draper smacked his lips generously. "A real treat, senyoretta!" he beamed. She smiled again, but less buoyantly. Her courage was slipping, and I could see the anxiety and weariness crowding back. "But I must fyoo-git!" He lifted his manacled arms: "Time, like they say, hangs heavy—yeh heh heh!" And he left us, Dolph having preceded him without farewell.

"Are you fyoo-gitting, too?" my wife asked, her apron twisted up in her hands.

"Well, duty," I said, picking up the two glasses.

"Someone . . ." She hesitated, staring at her hands. "Someone said there was a valentine."

"What? A valentine?"

"In Naomi's bag."

"Ah, well, what *didn't* she have in there! Even our—"

"They said it was from you."

"From *me!* What, a valentine to Naomi?" I didn't know whether to laugh or be offended. But she seemed to be trembling, so I set the glasses down and took her in my arms. "Hey, has Louise been working on you again?"

She turned her head into my chest, wrapped her arms around my neck. At least, I was thinking, she didn't ask about the cock sock. "Gerald, I'm afraid . . ."

"Come on, *you're* my only valentine. You *know* that," I said, and lifted her chin to kiss her.

But there was a sudden rush of chattery laughter as the door whumped open and in came Charley Trainer with Woody's wife, Yvonne, and a tall skinny man he introduced as Earl Elstob. We pulled apart. I recognized Earl by the mismatched pants and sports jacket, green socks and two-toned penny loafers, as the guy who'd been in a clinch with Charley's wife in the TV room a little while ago. What I hadn't seen before was the awesome overbite that nearly hid his chin from view. One of Charley's insurance prospects no doubt; he often brought them to parties to soften them up.

"Hey!" boomed Charley affably, wrapping his free arm around my wife's waist; the other carried glasses and a half bottle of scotch. "*Hey!*"

My wife, getting out a fresh handtowel, said, "Goodness! I've got so much to do!" and Earl Elstob, grinning toothily, asked us if we knew what a constipated jitterbug was. Charley Trainer har-harred and lumbered over to the fridge for some ice cubes. He grabbed ahold of two, and a half dozen fell out. "You're lookin' beautiful!" he said to the room in general, and Yvonne, a huge splotch of blood over the left side of her face, thrust her empty glass out and cried: "You goddamn *right!*"

My wife picked up the avocado dip and offered it around, Charley slopping half of it out on the floor with his first dip. He stooped with a grunt to wipe it up with his fingers, hit his face on the edge of the bowl in my wife's hands, came up with a green blob over his right eye like some kind of vegetable tumor. "What izziss stuff anyhow?" he asked, licking his fingers. Big Chooch they called him back in his college football days: Choo-Choo Trainer, last of the steamroller fullbacks. In those days he could sometimes be stopped but rarely brought

down; now, any time after happy hour, you could tip him over with your little finger.

"One who can't *jit!*" Earl Elstob hollered out, just as my mother-in-law came in, looking down her nose at so much noise, to get cookies and milk for Mark. Charley backed out of her way, crunching ice cubes underfoot, and bumped into the cabinets, sending things clattering around inside.

"There's some vanilla pudding for him in there, Mother," my wife said, exchanging a cautionary glance with me. "Behind the bean salad."

"Mark's still not asleep?" I asked. Yvonne seemed to be crying.

"Not *yet!*" my mother-in-law snapped, giving me a fierce penetrating look which had more in it than mere reproach. She slammed the refrigerator shut, snatched down a box of candies from the cupboards, and, jaws clenched, planted a button of chocolate in the middle of the little bowl of pudding—*fplop!*—like some kind of immutable judgment.

Charley Trainer, staring down at it, suddenly went limp and morose, his thick jowls sagging. "That poor damn kid . . . ," he muttered tearfully, the avocado dip now slipping down over his eyebrow as though he were melting, and my wife shook her head at him, her finger at her lips.

Charley stared at her foggily, failing to understand, opened his mouth to speak, and my wife, in desperation, grabbed up the dip again: "Charley! A little more . . . ?" Yvonne stifled a sob.

"But . . . but I *loved* her—!"

"We all did, Charley. Here . . ."

I had a catch in my own chest and felt suddenly I had to get out of here (Mavis over the body, working her jaws: it was like trying to turn a key in a stiff lock, my chest felt like a stiff lock)—but as I grabbed up the glasses and turned to go, Tania came bursting in, her bangles jangling, holding her bloodsoaked dress out away from her body as though it were hot soup spilled there, crying: "My god, look at this! What am I going to *do?*"

My mother-in-law took one glance and replied matter-of-factly: "It should be soaked in a chloride-of-lime solution. If that doesn't work, try salts of sorrel."

"Protein soap will do just as well," my wife said, turning the fire off under the boiling eggs. "Just a minute and I'll get you some, Tania."

Her mother sniffed scornfully and paraded out with the milk and

pudding, her chin high, old dark nylons whistling in deprecation, Earl Elstob holding the door for her, while slurping at his drink. "One who—huh! *shlup!*—can't jit?" he repeated hopefully. Yvonne had buried her face in her hands, her short straight hair, rapidly going gray, curtaining her face. It was the first time I'd seen her break down since the day she first learned about her breast cancer.

Tania picked up the steak knife Patrick had used to cut his grapefruit, touched the point with her fingertip. "Janny was crying, too," she said, peering up at Charley over her half-lens spectacles.

"Janny's not very flexible," Charley rumbled apologetically, wiping away the green dip in his eye.

Yvonne lifted her head, flicked her hair back from her face (I saw now that the eyelash on the side splashed with blood was thickly clotted and her penciled eyebrow was erased: it looked like that side of her face was disappearing), blew her nose and wailed: "God gave me a blue Louie, Charley!"

"Well, give'm one *back*, Yvonne! God-*damn* it!"

Tania had discovered and examined the cheese knife on the breakfast table, and was now poking through the silverware and utensils drawers. My wife glanced up anxiously from the sink where she was draining the water off the eggs. "Is there something you need, Tania?"

"Yes," said Tania, closing a drawer, while Charley staggered around the room dropping cubes in drinks and on the floor and pouring scotch, "maybe I *will* rinse this dress out."

"The soap's up in the bathroom," my wife said, running cold water over the eggs. "In the cabinet under the sink, or else the linen cupboard—Gerald, could you look for it? It's in a blue box . . ."

"Sure . . ." A whiff of herbs rose to my nose from the cool sweating glasses in my hands, and that now-familiar sense of urgency washed over me again. "As soon as I—"

"Is that my wife's drink?" It was Alison's husband, standing behind me in the doorway, one hand in his jacket pocket, the thumb pointed at me like a warrant, the other holding a meerschaum pipe at his mouth. "She's been *waiting* . . ."

"Ah! Yes, I was just—"

"Two of them? Well . . ." He clamped the pipe in his teeth, took both glasses as though, reluctantly, claiming booty. "I'll see that she gets them."

"Now, *there* goes a pretty man!" exclaimed Yvonne as the door

slapped to, and Earl Elstob, as though suddenly inspired, asked: "Say, huh! yuh know the best way to find out if a girl's ticklish?" Charley was fishing about in the refrigerator and things were crashing and tinkling in there. He came out with that bottle I'd noticed earlier, dragging dishes and beer cans with it, and, holding it at arm's length, stared quizzically at the label, then shrugged and poured some in his glass of scotch. "He looks like Don the Wand!"

"Juan?"

"Yeah, or the Scarlet Pippin—Pimple—what the hell—?"

"Hey!" Charley laughed, waggling the bottle. "Y'know why the—?"

"Pimpernel," my wife said.

Tania took my arm. "C'mon, Gerry. Let's go get cleaned up."

"No, wait!" Charley rumbled. "Jussa—ha ha!—jussa goddamn minute! Why'da Mexican push his wife till she—hruff! haw!—fell offa cliff?"

"Uh, that's sorta—*shlup!*—like a shotgun weddin'," Earl yucked, sucking.

"Check on the toilet paper while you're up there, Gerald!" my wife called as Tania, her arm wrapped in mine, pulled me through the door, whispering: "There's something I have to show you, Gerry—something strange!"

"You know, huh, a case of wife or—"

"What *cli-iii-iif-fff?*" howled Yvonne.

"*And handtowels!*"

"No—haw haw!—*wait* . . . !"

As we pushed through the people around the dining table, making our way toward the hall, Tania said, "Just a sec," and reached in to inspect some knives and skewers, her dress rustling as it brushed others. Over by the sideboard, Alison, discussing Tania's painting with Mrs. Draper, pointed up at something, then adopted "Susanna's" pose, one hand down in front, the other, holding the vermouth, at her breast, and looked back over her shoulder. Our eyes met and she smiled brightly, dropping the pose as though, still Susanna, exposing herself. She raised her fresh glass of vermouth at me, invited me over with a jerk of her head. "(*In a moment!*)" I mouthed silently, pointing at Tania's broad back (she was slipping something into the pockets of her dress), then blew her a kiss just as her husband, who'd been standing in the TV room doorway, turned around, fitting his pipe into

his mouth. He froze for a second, teeth bared around the tooth-white pipe, staring at me, and I wiped my lips with the hand with the kiss in it as though I had something hot in my mouth. Alison looked puzzled. Her husband lit up thoughtfully in the shadows behind her.

"Hey, these horseradish meatballs are terrific, Ger! Is there any more of the dip?"

"Uh . . . probably. In the kitchen, Talbot. Ask my wife." Earlier, Iris Draper had remarked on the dimness of the light in here, the relative brightness of the rooms around, comparing it to some mantic ceremony or other she'd come across in her tourist travels, and though at the time I'd found her chatter about "secret chambers" and "illumination mysteries" naively pedantic, now as I gazed at the candlelit faces of my friends gathered around the table (Alison had been drawn back to the painting by Iris and her husband, and now seemed glowingly mirrored there)—bruised, crumpled, bloodied—it all seemed strangely resonant. "What's the matter with your ear, Talbot?"

"Hit the goddamn fireplace with it."

"Whew! Did you show that mess to Jim?"

"Yeah, he had to put three stitches in. Hurt like hell. Good excuse to soak up more anaesthetic, though—oh oh, the old ball-and-chain's calling. I was supposed to bring her one of these fancy whatchamacallits in the seashells. See ya in a minute." I noticed one of Ginger's kerchiefs on the floor where he'd been standing and stooped to pick it up, also some toothpicks, spoons, a mustard knife, parsley sprigs, and a ripped-up cocktail napkin. The joke on the napkin, when I pieced it together, was of a frightened young suitor, his knees knocking together, asking a towering irate father with fumes rising from his head: "May I have your d-d-daughter's hole in h-handy matrimony, s-sir?"

Someone's breast was touching my elbow. "Hi, Gerry."

"Hey, Michelle." Her breast burrowed into the crook of my arm as if seeking shelter. "You all right?"

"I think so. Awful, wasn't it?"

"What happened to the fucking scotch, Ger?"

"Charley's got it in the kitchen."

"Is he sober enough to be trusted with it?"

"I don't know, Noble—but there's more down there in the cabinet."

"Listen." He leaned close, dead eye toward us, good one keeping watch. There was something not quite clean about Noble's breath.

"Chooch's wife knows something," he whispered, and Michelle backed off a step.

"Janny? She doesn't know the time of day."

Noble shrugged, his lids heavy. "Maybe. But she's been talking to the cops. I think she's naming names. I'd check it out if I were you." He took Ginger's fallen kerchief from my hand, casually popped his false eyeball into it, and knotted it up.

"Come on," said Tania, taking my hand. Across the room (Michelle "oh'ed" as Noble, squinting, unknotted the kerchief and showed it to be empty), Alison and her husband were moving parallel with us toward the living room, and again we found ourselves exchanging furtive glances. What had she said that night we met? I'd been speaking of the invention of audiences, theater as a ruse, a game against time. "Yes," she'd said, smiling up at me over the ruffles at her throat (I gave Tania's hand a little squeeze, as I'd no doubt squeezed my wife's hand that night at the theater), "and that's why the lives of actors, thought frivolous, are essentially tragic, those of the audience, comic."

The short policeman, the one called Fred, pushed in from the front room, blocking my view of her. At the table, he picked out three or four forks, held them up (Noble was prying his eyelid open, revealing the false eye back in place, gold backside out: Michelle gasped), chose one and turned to go, but got stopped by Woody, Roger's law partner. They huddled for a moment, watched closely by Tania's husband, Howard, standing stockstill against the wall, his broken lenses twinkling, and it looked to me, before I lost sight of them, like Woody gave the cop some money.

"Who's that playing darts downstairs?" Tania asked in the hallway.

"I don't know." I was still thinking about Noble, his pocked face dark with apprehension: Ros had told me he'd been brutal to her once. Down below, the darts could still be heard striking the board, but the conversation, if any, wasn't carrying up the stairs. "Cyril and Peg maybe."

Tania considered this, twining the laces of her peasant dress around one finger. Noble had tried to shove the handle of a hairbrush up her bottom, she'd said, apparently as part of yet another amateur magic trick, and when it wouldn't go, he'd beat her with the other end of it. In the doorway into the living room ("I'm not a prude, Gerry," Ros had declared, "but it didn't even have round edges—what was he so

mad about?"), Jim was swabbing Daffie's elbow with a ball of soaked cotton, Anatole and Patrick watching. Daffie made some remark to Anatole that made him blush, then looked up and winked at me.

"Curiously," Tania said, fluttering her arm in a kind of salute at her nephew as she passed, "Peg was just talking about Ros. She said she'd always been a little jealous of her because, in spite of the crazy life Ros led, she was never unhappy, as far as anyone could tell, while Peg, talented, well-educated, orderly, comfortably married to Cyril for over twenty-four years now and never a serious quarrel or a single infidelity, could not truly claim to have been happy a single day of her life. It seemed so unfair, she said, like all the things you get born with and can't help." Tania paused at the foot of the stairs to look back at me, one hand, knobby with heavy jeweled rings, resting on the banister, and I thought of Ros, bouncing goofily down a broad ornate staircase in a play in which she was supposed to be a stately middle-aged matron, descending to receive the news of the death of her husband, whom she herself had poisoned. "But then one day Peg saw Ros in a terrible state, all in a frazzle and close to tears, and the cause of it was simply that Ros was trying to learn her lines for a new play, something she always found almost impossible. She said it was a revelation, not about Ros, but about herself: she said she'd never see her own marriage in quite the same way again!" Tania's dark eyes crinkled with amusement as she thought about this, her lower lip caught in her bright white teeth, then she said: "The wound—it wasn't made by that knife, you know. It was more like a puncture than a gash . . ."

"Yes, that's how it looked to me, too."

From the stairs as we climbed them, I could see over Jim and Daffie and their audience into the living room, where Inspector Pardew seemed to be demonstrating something to his two assistants. Ros was out of sight, but her chalked outline, blood-drenched at the heart, was clearly visible, ringed about by the legs of watchers-on. Things still looked pretty smashed up and scattered in there, but from this angle the peculiar thing was the complex arrangement of chalked outlines, which reminded me of the old star charts with their dot-to-dot drawings of the constellations.

On the landing, in front of another of her paintings, Tania paused and raised her spectacles to her nose. "Look," she said. It was a painting of "The Ice Maiden," an extraordinary self-portrait in glacial greens and crystalline blues, viewed as though from the surface of

an icy mountain lake. The Ice Maiden—Tania—was swimming up toward the viewer, her dramatic highboned face distorted with something between lust and terror, a gold ring deep in the throat of her gaping mouth, her right arm stretched out, sapphire-ringed finger reaching toward the hand of an unseen swimmer, like Adam's toward God's in all those European paintings. Behind her—below her—swirling up from the buried city streets of her childhood through a fantastic tapestry of crystal ice: blind frozen images from her other paintings up to then—"The Thief of Time," "The Dead Boy," our "Susanna," the tortured "Saint Valentine" with his bloody erection, the orgiastic couples of "Orthodoxy" and the dancing "Unclean Persons," "The Executioner's Daughter" in her pratfall, the pettifogging privy councilors holding a meeting on "Gulliver's Peter," plus a number I didn't know—and one of these, a woman poised in astonishment, had had her face scratched out.

"My god!" I cried. "Who's done this—?!"

"It's what I wanted to show you."

"It's—it's *terrible!*" I touched the scarred area.

"Gives you a funny feeling, doesn't it? Like somebody's made a hole in the world . . ."

"But then that girl, I was never sure—it was *Ros,* wasn't it?"

Tania nodded. "It wasn't a very good likeness. I did it from memory and from other sketches."

"Do I know the painting it's from?"

"No, I never finished it." She seemed to think about this for a moment, staring at the obliterated face, as though, like the Ice Maiden, being sucked down into it. "Did you ever see that play, *Bluebeard's Secret,* the one—"

"Yes, Ros had a bit part. Or nonpart. It was the only reason we went to see it. I . . . well, I guess I didn't—"

Tania smiled. "I know. All that self-indulgent melodrama, phony symbolism, pompous huffing and puffing about free will and necessity—just a lot of sophomoric mystification for the most part and a few bare bosoms. But I came away from it with an idea for a painting, Gerry—more than an idea: it was like some kind of compulsion, a desperate, almost violent feeling. A painting is like that sometimes. It can start from the most trivial image or idea and suddenly, like those monsters in the movies, transform itself and overwhelm you. That's what happened to me with 'Bluebeard's Chambers.' I came home with

nothing more than the idea of doors, the color blue from the lights they used, and Ros. And yet—"

"But she hardly—"

"I know, that was the point. Part of it. I meant to have a lot of doors in my painting, doors of all sizes, some closed, some partly open, some just empty doorframes, no walls, but the various angles of the doors implying a complicated cross-hatching of different planes, and opening onto a great profusion of inconsistent scenes, inconsistent not only in content but also in perspective, dimension, style—in some cases even opening onto other doors, mazes of doors like funhouse mirrors—and the one consistent image was to be Ros. As you see her there." As she spoke I could feel the surge of excitement she must have felt as the idea grew in her, filling her out, as though her brain, sixth sense organ, were being erotically massaged. I loved this power she had: to be excited. It was a kind of innocence. "Only from all angles, including above and below, sometimes in proportion with the scene around her, sometimes not, sometimes only a portion of her or perhaps strangely distorted in particulars, yet essentially the same basic pose, a being dispossessed of its function. And as she disappeared into her own multiplicity, Bluebeard himself, though not present in the painting except in the color, would hopefully have emerged as the unifying force of the whole." She sighed tremulously. "But I couldn't handle it. Too many doors at once, you might say." It was like a tide ebbing. Her voice softened. "And Ros was not just fidgety—she was almost fluid. Never the exact pose twice—even twice in the same minute. But the colors were good, and eventually they led me to this one, a painting I'd been wanting to try for years." She stared now at her own image, beautiful, yet frightening in its intensity. "I think now if I tried again . . . the 'Bluebeard,' I mean . . ."

She didn't finish, but I felt I knew: she'd try scratching the faces of all the Ros figures, just as it was here. "Why not, Tania? Maybe you're ready for it now."

She smiled wanly, curling a few strands of her black hair around one long pointed fingernail, painted a deep magenta. "It's so late, Gerry . . ." In reflex, I glanced at my empty wrist. Below us, people were arguing noisily about what they'd seen or heard before the discovery of Ros's body, and I heard my own name mentioned. Tania touched my arm. "Come on. We've come this far, we might as well wash these stains out."

As we started up, I found myself thinking of that town in Italy again, a staircase, the hotel probably where I took that girl with the bunny-ear pubes—no, wait: some city to the north. Paris. Yes, a walk-up ("I think of him, you know," Tania was saying, she was apparently talking about Bluebeard still, "as a man who wished to share all he had with the world . . . but could not . . ."), bare bulb on the landing. Over an Algerian restaurant on the Left Bank. Then who was I with? Oddly it seemed like Alison. But later, on the bidet—

"Sometimes I think art's so cowardly, Gerry. Shielding us from the truth . . ."

"Well . . . assuming the truth's worth having . . ." We'd had this conversation before. Vic's daughter Sally Ann slouched against the banister at the top of the stairs, watching us.

"In other words, scratching that face out was the same thing in the end as painting it in . . ."

"No, Tania, the one takes talent, genius, the other—"

"Ah! But you don't say which!"

There was a new patch on Sally Ann's blue jeans, just over the crotch—the first thing I saw, in fact, as we climbed past her—that said "SWEET MEAT" in bright fleshy colors. She was slumped against the rails, body arched, rolling a cigarette. Or maybe a joint. "Hey, your father's looking for you," I said, and then, because she was staring so intently at me, I poked my finger in her bare navel and added: "Deli Belly."

She jumped back, dropping her handiwork down the stairs. "Oh, Gerry, that's stupid!" She slapped at my hand, then pranced on down to the landing.

"Someone's got a crush on you, Gerry," Tania observed.

"I always did have more luck with poets than painters," I sighed, and stooped to pick up another of Ginger's kerchiefs on the top stair. In Paris, climbing, I was carrying some books with plain green jackets, a print bought from a stall along the Seine, and I stooped for . . . for . . . a coin? a ring? a button maybe, a brass or silver button . . .

The bathroom door was closed. I started to knock, but Tania with her customary lack of ceremony walked on in. "Well, *that's* pretty," she declared, and turned on the ventilator fan. Dickie was in there, cleaning Naomi's bottom over the toilet. She was straddling the thing, bent over and facing the wall, skirt hiked, elbows resting on the water

tank. Dickie looked very unhappy, smoking self-defensively with one hand, dabbing clumsily at her big hindend with the other. His shirtsleeves were rolled up, his plaid jacket hanging on the doorhook. "Hey, Ger! Just in time!" he cried, flinging his butt into the paperclogged stool. I saw he'd used up all the toilet paper on the roller and a box of tissues besides. "*You're* the host, *you* can wipe her goddamn ass!"

"No, thanks, you're doing fine," I protested, but he was already washing up. Yes, the restaurant smells below, the creaky climb, the bare bulb, the bidet—but cold water. And a smaller fanny, plump but like a little pink pear, softly creased by the bidet lips, not two big melons like this—ah! my wife's!

"I'm so *embarrassed*," Naomi said. I was directly behind her, down on my haunches by the linen cupboard, reaching for more toilet paper (these genuflections, these child's-eye views!), and her voice seemed to be coming out of her high looming behind. "I've never done anything like this before—you know, poohed at a party. But I was so scared—!"

"It was what you'd call a moving experience, Nay," said Dickie, reaching for a towel. I found Tania's protein soap down there as well. Only it was in a white box with blue lettering, not a blue box. I noticed a worn wooden handle behind the soap and grabbed it up—an old ice pick! *Where had this come from—?!* "Christ! Even the goddamn towels are covered with shit!"

Dickie came over to get a clean one from the cupboard and I shoved the thing out of sight, covering it up hastily with the nearest cloth to hand. It was uncanny, I hadn't seen one in years—as best I could remember, the last time was at my grandmother's house when I was still a boy—it was almost as though . . .

"What you need is a bidet in here," Tania said, sprinkling soap into the tub and churning the water up with her hands.

"*What—?!*" I gasped. Naomi's bottom reared above me, seeming to watch me with a suspicious one-eyed stare, pink mouth agape below as though in astonished disbelief.

"A bidet. It's what they're for, you know, washing bottoms."

"Yes, sure, but oddly I-I was just thinking about—"

"Can you beat that," said Dickie, tossing the towel over Naomi's bent back. "I always thought they were for cooling the beer in." He leaned close to the mirror, scraped at a fleck of blood in front of his

golden sideburns. "Oh, by the way, Ger, I don't know if you saw what's left of the poor bastard on the way up, but Roger's no longer with us, you know."

"*Roger—?!*" It was like a series of heavy gates crashing shut, locks closing like meshing gears. I stumbled to my feet.

"*I knew it!*" gasped Tania, clutching her arms with wet hands.

Dickie unzipped his white trousers and tucked his shirttails in, frowning at the bloodstains on his vest. I braced myself on the cupboard shelves. "But . . . but who—?"

He raised his eyebrows at me in the mirror as though to say I already knew. And I did. "They used croquet mallets," he said with a grimace, zipping up. "The grand fucking round, Ger—it was awful."

"But did you see it? Couldn't you do anything about it?"

Dickie, framed in lights, smiled enigmatically. I recalled now the thud of the policemen's blows, the shrieks, the thrashing about, the sudden stillness: we all knew what they were going to do when they took Roger out of the room. Maybe I'd even been told . . .

"Dickie asked them to stop it," Naomi said from behind her bottom. "But they didn't pay any attention to him, it was like they couldn't even hear him, maybe because of the screaming, they were like standing on his head all the time. And we couldn't stay, I was starting to . . . to poop again . . ."

Dickie turned his cuffs down, buttoned them, adjusted his tie. "Woody said the cops were claiming self-defense," he said, pulling a hair off the fly of his pants. He touched the top of his head, took out a comb.

Tania turned off the taps, got slowly to her feet, using the tub for support. "Self-defense. Yes . . . maybe it was . . ." Tears filmed her big dark eyes. She'd been with me in the hallway when the two of them arrived tonight, Ros radiant, all smiles, Roger jittery as usual, trying to swallow down his panic as Ros went bouncing off into the living room, hugging everybody—it seemed so long ago! Like some kind of ancient prehistory, utterly remote, lost, an impossible past . . . "He was the most dangerous thing in the world, after all. A child . . ."

"Hullo, folks! It's your ole ticker taker!" shouted Mr. Draper, pushing heavily in, his glittering arms held out like a robot's. "Just pass the time, please, any old time! Yeh heh heh!"

Dickie, carefully combing his fine blond hair back over the thin spot on top, grunted, slipped off his all-gold wristwatch, and, still

checking himself in the mirror, held it out to Mr. Draper: just then, one of the light bulbs surrounding the mirror sputtered and went out.

"Hey!" Dickie exclaimed, his arm outstretched, watch waggling at the end of it as though on the same circuit as the bulb.

"Everything I've painted so far," Tania sighed, staring down at her dress, hands clutching her laces, "is shit . . ."

"Could you slide it on there for me, son? Can't bend my doggone arms anymore!"

Once, during a thunderstorm, when the lights had gone out suddenly, my son had asked: "Which is real, Daddy? The light or the dark?" "The light," I'd replied, just as my wife, entering behind me, had said: "The dark." Then, as now, I'd felt inexplicably guilty of something I couldn't define. I found a new bulb on the second shelf, then pushed the linen cupboard door shut behind me, leaned against it.

"Which . . . if I am what I've painted . . ."

"My watch was in my shoulderbag," said Naomi, sniffling. "I'm sorry . . ."

"Now, now, child, don't cry over lost time! When you get as old as me, you'll—say! looks like you folks need a plumber there!"

"I'm going to fix it in a minute, Mr. Draper." He peered at me over his spectacles as though discovering me for the first time. I was thinking about my wife still. What had she said about the TV? I couldn't remember. But I felt somehow I shouldn't leave her alone too long. I held up my arm shakily, as Tania, beside me, began undoing the laces of her dress. "You've already--"

"Yep, I've got yours, son, I know. I may have lost most everything else, but I still got my marbles. And Lloyd's the name, lad, or is your memory lettin' *you* down in your old age?" He chortled drily and winked, then gazed pensively at Naomi's backside. "Y'know, a curious thing happened to my wife and me in the catacombs of Calcutta—"

"You can't have love *or* art without the imagination, but it's dangerous," Tania murmured, removing her half-lens reading glasses and setting them on the edge of the tub. "Roger said that . . ." He had also explained to me once that, in the theater, when business was bad it was *brutal*, and when it was good it was: *murder*.

Talbot's wife Wilma came in just then, asking if we had any aspirin. "For Talbot," she explained, peering at herself in the mirror over Dickie's shoulder. "His ear's hurting him so much, I'm afraid the dope's going to drink himself silly, and you all know how, when Tal-

bot's looped, it's goodbye—why, hello there, Lloyd! My, you've got quite a collection!"

"Oh, it's not *my* collection! No, I'm—heh heh!—I'm not *keepin'* time, I'm just, as you might say, hangin' on to it for the *time bein'!*"

Dickie, still primping, stepped aside to let me at the medicine cabinet. I caught a glimpse of myself in the mirrored door before I swung it open, and I was shocked at how rumpled and bloody I looked—and how natural it seemed . . .

"Oh, Lloyd," Wilma was saying, "you do pop out with the wittiest things! You ought to be on television! I was just talking to your wife, and she said how you had everybody on the bus out to the pyramids just in stitches about mummies and mommies and—"

"In *stitches*, did you say—?"

"Oh my goodness! It must be catching!" She fussed at her perm, which had come undone in places, loose curls poking out like released springs.

"Don't you mean *all wound up?* Yeh heh heh!"

In the cabinet, my wife's manicure set lay scattered on the bottom shelf. The tiny curved scissors were gone. The tweezers, too, for that matter. And was that a bloody hair—? No . . . no, a piece of red thread. I was overwrought. Dickie puffed his chest and smoothed down his vest, then reached for his plaid jacket.

"I've lost touch," Tania muttered. She gazed sorrowfully down at Naomi straddling the toilet and pursed her lips. "I've got to get back to landscapes again . . ."

"You know, by coincidence Talbot and I were just discussing yesterday, Lloyd, the idea of touring the—just give me the whole bottle, Gerry. If I can tranquillize the jerk maybe I'll have a little fun myself for a change—we were just saying we maybe ought to visit Africa and the Middle East next year, so we must get together! You and Iris can tell us what to take, the good places to eat, nightclubs—Dickie, where are you going? I didn't mean to chase you out!"

"Don't leave me, Dickie!" Naomi begged.

"The most important thing about Africa and the Middle East," Lloyd Draper was saying, "is that they're two different places . . ."

"Dickie, *please!* What am I going to *wear?*"

"Go as you are, Nay, you'll have them rolling at your feet!"

"And of course it depends on what you're keen on. Some folks like the cities, some the countryside, some the resorts."

"But what if it all starts *up* again—!"

"Didn't I see some disposable underthings in your shoulderbag, dear?" Wilma asked.

"I'm a temples-and-tombs man myself, though Iris goes more for the arts and crafts."

"*Were* there?"

"Paper panties, Dickie, a package of them," I called, unscrewing the dead bulb. "You can't miss them, they're all chalked out—"

"You can send Howard up with them, Dickie," Tania shouted. In the mirror, I saw her, her laces loosened, emptying her pockets onto the bathtub ledge. "I have to talk to him anyway!"

"All wound up! Lloyd, however do you do it? Say, wasn't that absolutely horrid about poor Roger! I just heard about it on the way up!" I unwrapped the new bulb and screwed it in, feeling it pop alight under my fingertips. That hole in Tania's painting. All along I'd been supposing Roger might have done it. Now I didn't think so. "They say he was very brave, but as I told Talbot, such bravery, Talbot, we can do without! If they want to ask you anything, you just—but then there's nothing to worry about really, Talbot always makes a good impression in interviews, heaven knows he's had enough practice! Are you leaving us, Lloyd?"

"Yes, eh, I'm afraid I mustn't take any more time—or rather, I *must!*" He chuckled, but his heart wasn't in it. His arms and pants as he lumbered out seemed suddenly to be hanging a couple of inches lower.

"Dear me, it seems I'm chasing everybody away tonight!" I took the towel off Naomi's back, hung it on the rod by the basin, tossed all the other towels into the clothes hamper. "Close the door, please," she begged, "it's bad enough without everybody—" "Oh, I'm sorry, dear. My, you're the very model of patience!"

"With Dickie, you have to be."

Wilma checked herself quickly in the mirror, turned away in disappointment, fumbling in her handbag for makeup. "Do you think those policemen down there know what they're doing?" she asked idly, uncapping a tube of lipstick. "Well, I suppose they do." One night I was backstage talking with Ros in front of her mirror (she liked it best when she could do her lips in a cherry red), when an actor came rushing in, leaned over her shoulder, popped her breasts out of her costume, and kissed them with loud sucking smacks, crying: "Yum! I

just *love* them!"—then dashed out again, shouting: "Two minutes, sweetheart!" She reached over, flushed with excitement, took my face in both her hands, and whispered: "Wait for me, Gerry!"—then gave me her breasts to kiss, tucked them in, and rustled out. But she never came back. Not that night. It was a long way from the stage to her dressing room and, as often happened, she just didn't get that far.

"Before you start that, Gerry," Tania grunted, "could you help me off with this damned dirndl? It's a bit tight through the middle."

Of course, if I'd been more patient . . .

"Still, poor Roger! Wasn't it frightful, I still can't get over it!"

. . . But in those days I believed in energy and ingenuity: that there was nothing beautiful in the world but what you worked for.

"Do you think the visit of that old witch had anything to do with it?"

"What witch?"

Which was a long time ago . . .

"I think it's snagged on my bra!" Tania called from inside her skirts, as I tugged on them. I could almost hear Ros giggling under there, trying to guess who was behind her by feeling between his legs. Ah, Ros . . . I was beginning to choke up again. "At the back!" I pushed my hand up under the heavy material and unhooked the bra clasp: her full black-nippled breasts tumbled out of their straitjacket like a landslide and Tania was free. "Thanks, Gerry!" she gasped, and shook the dress out. "This damn thing's worse than a corset!"

"It's beautiful, though," sighed Wilma. "Wherever did you get it, Tania? No, don't tell me! I'd look as plain in something like that as I do in this. Why is it that no matter how much I spend I always come out looking like a hostess for a ladies' club?"

Tania fastened her bra back on, hiking her heavy breasts into the cups, then knelt to spread her dress into the soapy water. I was struck by all the color on her face and down into her neck, against the sudden vulnerable milkiness of her naked back, its soft flesh (I was thinking of age, time, loss—Ros's giggle like a hollow terrifying echo now—and the fruitless efforts to rise above them) deeply imprinted by the checks and crosses of the waistband and bra straps. I unrolled some toilet paper, took a preliminary swipe at Naomi's behind as though to fight back. "I feel so ashamed," she said. "Dickie shouldn't have left you to do this—"

"No, it's all right."

"It's a crime," complained Wilma, patting at her hairdo. "Even this movie star mirror doesn't help!"

There was a sharp knock on the door and I opened it, the pad of soiled toilet paper in my hand. It was my wife's mother. "Mark needs to use the bathroom," she said testily.

"Sure. Tell him to come on in."

"Not while *you're* in there!" She glared angrily past my shoulder at the three women.

"Then why don't you take him downstairs?"

"Can't do that. There's a dead person down there."

"Ah, you . . . you know, then. I'm sorry . . ." She stood there, rigid in her implacable distrust and isolation. I knew it was hard for her here, I wanted to reach out to her, make her feel at home, but she shrank from all such gestures as though to avoid defilement. "All right then. Just a minute."

"Hurry, Daddy! *I can't wait!*" my son called from behind her.

"I'm just going anyway," said Wilma, squeezing past us. She rattled the aspirin bottle: "Gotta give Talbot his fix. Hello there, Mark— say, that's a handsome sweatshirt! You look like Little Boy Blue! Remember me? Auntie Wilma? No?"

"What am I going to *do?*" Naomi whimpered. "I can't go out there like this! And if I let my skirt down it'll get all dirty—!"

Tania dried her hands on a large bathtowel, then wrapped it around herself like an Indian blanket. I retrieved the used handtowel from the clothes hamper. "Here, put this between your legs, Naomi—I'll hold it for you, just let your skirt fall over it . . ." She straightened up, towering over me as I crouched to hold the towel in place: a big girl.

"Can I come in now?"

"Not yet!" said my mother-in-law as the skirt fell.

"That's it—now hold on to it, both sides . . . !" She clapped her hands front and back and I came out from under the skirt. Even standing, I had to look up to her.

"Please tell him not to take too long," Naomi pleaded softly as we stepped out, Tania wrapped in her towel, Naomi strutting stiff-legged, feet wide apart like a mechanical soldier, holding her tummy and behind. "I feel so stupid . . . !"

My son rushed past us, one hand inside his pajama pants, followed by my mother-in-law, straight-backed and icily silent. "Don't flush it!

It's all stopped up—!" The door slammed shut on my warning, and I could hear her snapping the lock into place. At the same moment, across the hall, the door to her room snapped open, and Woody's cousin Noble came out, tie loose around his neck, buttoning his shirt-cuffs, heading for the bathroom. "It's busy," I said, and Noble, looking somewhat distant, his good eye as dull as his bad one, nodded and moved on downstairs.

Tania had meanwhile started telling me about Roger and the bad time she'd had when he found out about Ros posing for her—"There were just the two of us women in a closed studio, but he couldn't bear the thought of other men even seeing Ros's naked image—when he came storming over, he didn't even knock, Gerry, he just smashed the door down!"—but I was only able to follow part of it, my eye caught now by Alison. She was with a group of people down on the landing—her husband, Wilma, Lloyd Draper weighted with watches, Woody, Noble still doing himself up, and a handsome dark-suited woman I didn't know but remembered from Roger's rampage (the dignity of her fall, even as her pendant rose to strike her on the nose)—and maybe they'd all been looking at Tania's painting before, or simply had run into each other there on the landing by chance (her husband shook hands now with Noble), but just as I spied her there, she turned, smiled suddenly at discovering me, and then, watching her husband (he was being introduced to the woman beside her, as Lloyd Draper clumped heavily on down the stairs), tossed me a kiss by kissing her hand, putting it behind her back and flipping it up at me from her rear. "As it happened, the day he came to wreck my studio, Ros wasn't even there. Howard was up on a little pedestal, posing for me in a pink leotard as a privy councilor, and he nearly died of shock and mortification when Roger came crashing in."

"I should imagine . . ."

Woody had something he was showing to everybody, and as they all leaned closer to see it, or perhaps to sniff at it ("I haven't been able to get him to pose for me since . . ."), Alison slipped away and came hurrying up the stairs, her hair flowing, her breasts bouncing gently in their silken pockets. "I've been looking all over for you!" she whispered. She took my hand, pulled me urgently into the darkened sewing room doorway (or what we called the sewing room), out of sight from those below, and kissed me. There was an incredible taste of something like herbs and mountain air, and a strange feeling, almost

of a lost memory, swept over me—but just for a moment: laughter rattling up from below broke in on us. She glanced back over her shoulder, as I licked my lips. "He has a piece of that girl's underwear."

"What?"

"That man down there. The lawyer? He has a piece from her panties."

"Woody?"

"I saw them cutting them up. I thought the policeman—the main one with the moustache—had something in mind. But apparently he forgot and the pieces started getting passed around. Like souvenirs or something . . ."

"Ah, that explains . . ."

"I've heard a thousand stories about her tonight." What I was thinking about was the money. And what Ros once said about time and love. "You're right, you certainly weren't the only one . . ." She turned back and gazed up at me as though pained by something, then, unfastening a middle button, ran her hand inside my shirt. "When it's like a river," Ros had said, "it scares me. What I want it to do is just *ooze*." There was a faint rustling in the sewing room darkness beyond us, a couple, perhaps more than one. I saw something red, a dress probably, and a glimmer of flesh. Alison's mouth opened under mine and I closed my eyes, let my free hand slide down to grip one supple buttock. She kissed me, tonguing my lips apart, murmured into my mouth: "They killed her husband, Gerald. It was terrible."

"I know. I heard. I'm still not completely over it." Behind me, Naomi was telling Tania about her childhood, her mother's cruelty and the cruelty of all her mother's lovers.

"Didn't you expect it?" Alison whispered, licking my lips.

"I guess I did. That's not what upset me. It was—"

"Learning something you already knew—you said that during the intermission that night we met."

I recognized now the source of that feeling I'd had since she came up the stairs. She stroked my chest gently, and I (I peeked past the doorframe—Noble was into another act down there now, making his cigarette vanish, then, with a bulge of his false eye, reappear from inside his mouth, now lit at both ends) pulled her closer to me, curled my hand around both firm cheeks, amazed at the familiarity of them. I disbelieved in fate, hated plays and novels whose plots were governed by it, but now, with Alison's silky bottom filling my hand like

an idea the mind . . . Naomi was telling Tania about being tied up and locked all day in a closet without a potty, then getting whipped with a belt for wetting on her mother's pink suede pumps. Alison nibbled at my throat.

"But it was more than that even," I whispered into her ear, a gold loop glinting there like a wish. Or a promise. I heard somebody grunt hoarsely in the sewing room shadows, then a soft stifled whimpering sound. Alison found a nipple, drew a gentle circle around it as though inscribing a target. "I think what struck me was not so much learning something I already knew, as the sudden recognition that in fact it *had* to be *learned*."

Alison gasped softly, her bottom flexing in my grip as though to squeeze my hand, and looked up at me, her brown eyes swimmingly wide in a kind of awe, excitement, wonder. Her fingers tugged at my nipple. "That's funny! I was just thinking the—!"

The bathroom door banged open behind us and my son came bounding out, calling my name—I let go of Alison and turned, squatting (my shirt jerked against her hand, a button ripped), just in time to catch him up. "Good night!" he shouted, giving me a big kiss. There was a large white "SUPERLOVER" emblazoned on his sweatshirt.

"Good night is right, chum! You know what time it is?"

"Daddy, do I look like Little Boy Blue?"

"Well, you don't look much like Red Ridinghood, do you?"

"But Little Boy Blue's a *little* boy!"

"Not really. They just put that in the poem to make it sound better. He doesn't like it either." Naomi, still holding on to the two ends of the towel through the skirt, rocked stiffly back and forth on her way back into the bathroom. "And you know, it wouldn't hurt you to imitate Boy Blue and go crawl under—"

"That's a funny lady! Does she always walk that way?"

"I don't think so. She must have got wound up too tight."

"Daddy . . . ?"

"Yes?"

"Daddy, somebody's broke all my soldiers!"

"What—?" Why did that startle me so? "Hey, don't cry!"

"They took all the *heads* off! All my *best ones*! From the *Waterloo*!"

"Easy, pal! We'll get new ones! Here, wipe your eyes with this . . ."
My mother-in-law was glaring impatiently down on us, her arms folded.

Alison ran her fingers into the hair above my nape. "I'll see you in a few minutes," she murmured, and Mark smiled up at her through his tears.

"Not you, mister!" I said, getting to my feet and handing him over to his grandmother. "You're off to bed!"

He blinked, surprised. "You look scary, Daddy!" he exclaimed, backing away.

"We've been playing monsters," I laughed, and made a face.

"Can I play?"

"Not yet. When you grow up." I winked at my mother-in-law, but she turned her head away, her lips pinched shut.

"Oh gosh, help!" Naomi called from the bathroom. "I've dropped part of it!"

I turned to touch Alison's fingertips in farewell, but she was already at the head of the stairs. She waggled her hand behind her back and waved at someone down on the landing, and I heard my son's door slam. The heads?

In the bathroom, Tania was sliding open the shower curtain which my mother-in-law had apparently drawn shut. "Like variations on a theme or something," she said, and Naomi, in some distress, replied: "Well, that's exactly the problem! It seemed so unfair!"

"Here, let me help." I knelt and reached up under her skirt to hold the towel against her buttocks, but it had dropped down in front and I accidentally stuck my finger in her vagina. "Oop, sorry, Naomi . . ." I found the loose end. "Okay, now pull your skirt up, I've got it . . ."

She hiked her skirt and, gripping it with her elbows, straddled the toilet stiffly once more. "Ouch," she complained as she leaned low onto the watertank, keeping her rear high so the skirt wouldn't fall back over it. "I think it's getting hard!"

"Heavens!" exclaimed Tania, casting a professional eye upon the sight. "Red, green, brown, yellow—what have you been eating tonight, Naomi?"

"Just what was out on the table."

"Look, there's even a little piece of string!"

"It's a shame to wash it away," I said, dipping the dirty towel under the hot water faucet in the sink. "Maybe we ought to frame it and hang it on the wall." A monster: yes, I was: there was blood at the edge of my mouth.

Tania, smiling, knelt to her task, wrapped still in the bathtowel, which slowly loosened as she squeezed and kneaded the dress. My grandmother, rolling out pie dough, would tell me stories about the wilderness, about the desperate, almost compulsive struggle against it as though it were some kind of devil: "We had to domesticate it, now look what we got for it." I could still see her old hands, dusted with flour, gnarled around the handgrips of the wooden rolling pin, her thin wrinkled elbows pumping in and out as she talked. Once she'd told me the story of a man in love with his own reflection who went out ice-fishing one day and drowned himself. She'd said it was her cousin. Tania held the sudsy dress up to study it. "By the way, Naomi, where did you get this switchblade?"

"Switchblade?" I touched my throat: a tiny red toothmark.

"It was in your shoulderbag."

"Golly, I don't know—I don't know *half* the things in that bag!"

"My favorite Mexican ashtray, too!" I scolded, turning away from the sink and clapping the hot towel against her backside. Naomi oohed gratefully. "And, say, what's this about a valentine?"

"Did I have a valentine in there, too?"

"Somebody said it was from me."

"Did you give me a valentine?"

"No, dummy, that's just the point." I took the compress away: it seemed to be softening up. I rinsed the towel out and applied it again, molding it to the curves of her moony cheeks. "What I want to know is who *was* it from?"

"Honest, I don't understand a thing you're saying. I don't think I ever got a valentine in my whole life." She sighed tragically. "Except once, a long time ago. And then it was more like giving it than getting it." She shuddered at the recollection. Or maybe at the chill when I took the towel away for another rinse. "My mother let one of her men friends spank me. It wasn't the only time, but this time she didn't even pretend I'd done anything wrong. Mother said it was a valentine, for him or for me, I don't know which she meant, but he could slap it until it was bright red, a little bright red heart. They laughed and laughed all the time they smacked it."

"That's what I like," said Tania, "a happy ending." She had a painting by that name, the darkest, most depressing piece she'd ever done, her vision of the lust for survival. "A cartoon," she called it.

"Well, it was so . . . so humiliating!" Naomi's bottom did seem

to be blushing at the memory, but mainly it was the warmth that was turning it rosy. "And there were others—an old man, I remember, who used a thing he called his 'stinger,' and another one—"

Tania laughed, pushing the dress under. "All these family stories! They remind me of my own father the day he gave me my first box of paints." She lifted her dress out of the water to examine it, her arms bubbly with pink suds up to the elbows. " 'Tatiana,' he said, 'there are no lies in the world, so everything you paint will be true. But not everything will be beautiful.' " She glanced at me over her pale fleshy shoulder, then plunged her dress back into the ruddled suds once more.

"Ow," said Naomi, trying to peer past her bunched-up skirt at her behind, "it feels all prickly now like when you skin your knees!"

"It's a little raw. I wonder if we still have any baby oil around . . . ?" There was none in the medicine cabinet or on the shelves below the sink, but I found half a bottle at the back of the linen cupboard: thus life provides these little markers, I thought—then closed the door quickly. I'd nearly forgotten. How was I going to get that thing out of here? Should I even try? And what would I do with it? In my palm, the oil felt like sweat. I spread oil on one buttock, my mind racing through the house like a scanner (the clothes basket at the bottom of the chute? the loose floorboard in my mother-in-law's room? the deep freeze?), then puddled out another palmful for the other one.

"Actually, spankings and valentines go together," Tania remarked. "Saint Valentine was himself whipped before they beheaded him, and the Church has got a special kick out of beating lovers ever since."

"Beheaded—?" gasped Naomi. Her buttocks clenched, and I thought of Alison, the way her hips had flexed in my grip, and a wave of anxiety swept over me. It was as though something were rushing down upon me which I wasn't ready for, and I remembered my own mother, hurtling down a ski slope toward a broad bulge of mud—we'd hit an unusual dry spell that winter, and the snow had got worn off in places; the rest of us could ski round the muddy patches, but my mother still hadn't progressed beyond the snow plow. We could see her streaking down a ridge toward the big glistening mud patch, a sickly smile on her face, and there was nothing we could do. "Sit down! Sit down!" my father had cried, but she just kept coming, her eyes getting bigger and bigger. And then suddenly she'd stopped. I didn't remember the

fall, I must have looked away, but it was terrible, and she was in the hospital for a long time afterward. It was not only our last ski trip. It was the last time we ever went anywhere as a family.

"Well," said Tania with a sigh (of course, I could simply turn it over to the police—why did that seem so impossible?), "they had to chop *something* off . . ."

I rubbed the baby oil into those big cheeks, bigger than my own, thinking back on my son when he was tiny, his little bottom like two fat knuckles, narrow and pointed, his life still simple then, his memories wholly utilitarian and unfocused. Now . . . One of his drawings was stuck up on the wall over the clothes hamper. It was a picture of a castle with a war going on, blood and flags flying, bodies scattered like jacks. There was a big figure up on top that was presumably Daddy. He had a long thing hanging down between his legs which Mark said was for killing the bad guys, and he was throwing somebody off the ramparts. Mark said sometimes the picture made him laugh and sometimes it made him afraid, but he wouldn't tell me who it was that was getting thrown off. "The only Saint Valentine story I remember," I said, dribbling a little more oil into my hand and spreading it into the creases of the thighs and the furrow between her cheeks (I could feel her muscles relax as I worked the oil in—her tummy sagged and her thighs gaped a little as though her pelvis had distended), "was how he restored the sight of a blind girl."

"That's nice . . ." she whispered. I oiled the surface of her anus in little circles as though polishing a button (perhaps, I was thinking, recalling my son's question, it's neither the hard part nor the empty part, but something in between), then pushed my fingertip in, twisting it gently; she groaned and squeezed her cheeks together in pleasure and gratitude as I pulled it out: "I—*oh!*—like stories like that . . ."

"Yes, well, naturally both she and her father got converted, and so consequently got *their* heads chopped off, too, bright eyes and all."

"Yuck! Why'd you have to go and *spoil* it?"

"Ah, well, who's to judge him?" Tania sighed. She was wearing pink suds now all the way to her armpits. "Probably, like all of us, he only wanted company . . ."

I capped the oil, set it aside, then gave Naomi's buttocks one final vigorous rub, making them gleam rosily, buffing away their playing-card pallor. If I could get that thing out of the house, I thought, I could bury it in the garden. "You like that girl, don't you, the one

with the pretty hair . . . ?" she asked softly, her voice jiggly from the massage.

"How's that?"

"You were-her thi-hi-hinking about her ju-hust now, I-hi-hi could tell-ll-ll . . ."

"Actually I was thinking about all those pee-hee-heople downstairs, and what they're going to do-hoo-hoo to me if I don't get back down there." This was a lie. I *was* thinking about Alison. She was all I'd been thinking about all night. Except for Ros of course. I spread the excess oil around the sides of Naomi's hips and down her thighs, gave her cheeks a final slap, straightened up. And my wife. "There! that should—"

"You want to make love to her, don't you, Geoffrey?"

"Gerry." I wrung out the towel, tossed it in the hamper, washed up.

"Gerry . . ." Naomi seemed to have grown fond of her position, or maybe she was falling asleep. Her voice was just a drowsy murmur. "How would your wife feel about it?"

I glanced at Tania in the mirror, her broad back to me like a stone tablet. A soft sympathetic stone tablet. "She wouldn't like it." I wiped my hands, combed my fingers through my hair. "I'll go get something for you to wear, Naomi."

But when I opened the door, there was Howard kneeling down behind it, his eye where the keyhole had been—the package of paper panties hit the floor. He snatched at them. "I-I'm sorry, I, eh, just dropped—they slipped . . ."

"Is that you, Howard?" Tania called, and he popped erect as though on wires. She wrapped herself in the bathtowel, pulled the door on open. "Well! *look* at you!"

He stood there in the doorway holding the package of panties in his chubby fist, weaving slightly, knees bent, a silly smile on his flushed blood-flecked face, one shirttail out, red silk tie dangling loose. "I just—hic!—brought these—this, you see. Dickie, eh . . ." He thrust the package at me, but it had been opened and what reached me was only the cellophane wrapping: the panties lay in a soft heap at his feet. Tania picked them up, glanced at them curiously, then handed them to me with a wink. "Howard, Howard!" she clucked, tucking in his shirttail. He giggled idiotically. "You've popped all your buttons!"

"Here, Naomi, Howard's—Naomi? *Hey!*"

She started up with a snort, blinking her eyes, her skirt slipping

down her shiny bottom. "Oh . . ." I could hear Tania asking her husband for his scout knife: "Which one's the leather punch, Howard?" Naomi smiled sleepily, leaned her head on my shoulder, looping her arms softly around my neck. "Can you help me," she yawned, "just one more time?"

"You're a big girl, Naomi, you can—"

"Please, Geoffrey? I always split these things . . ."

I knelt with a sigh and, clumsily, one hand braced on my back, the other on the sink, she pushed her feet through the legholes. I could see it was going to be a tight fit. "Are these your size, Naomi?"

"How should I know?"

Tania opened the linen cupboard. Maybe she was looking for some place to hide Howard's knife. There was nothing I could do about it—the panties were caught halfway up Naomi's thighs and had to be inched the rest of the way. "You'd think the oil would help," I complained, one eye on Tania.

"Your wife, ahem, asked me to tell you, Gerald, she needs some things from the top shelf of the pantry and—burp!—can't find the ladder." The ladder was *in* the pantry, but never mind, I understood. Naomi lifted her skirt out of the way, as I tugged at her flesh, pushed at the band. "I think we're almost there, Naomi . . . easy now!"

"Mmf! Whoo—thanks!" she gasped, helping me at the crotch. Howard's head was twitching from trying to look at Naomi and not look at her at the same time, making his thick fractured spectacles flutter with reflected light and his pink jowls wobble. "Now, just so I don't have to bend over . . . !"

"Also, eh, something about food stuck in the freezer, and the garbage was filling up and, well, she seemed . . ."

"Yes, all right, Howard, tell her—"

"You know, it's funny," Naomi interrupted, "but these pants feel like they've already been worn by someone."

Tania smiled; Howard was gone.

Naomi wiggled her hips to let the skirt drop. "Maybe I *could* do something to help, Geoffrey—I mean, if you want to see that girl. Like, you know, I could go talk to your wife for a while maybe, or get her to go to the basement with me and play darts or something . . ."

"It's too dangerous, Naomi," I said, wiping my hands. "She throws a wild dart. Anyway, I don't see why you—"

"Love!" she said with a kind of sweet breathless tremor in her voice.

"It should have a chance, wherever and whenever it appears. It's so rare . . . and wonderful!"

Tania snorted. "Roger once told me he thought love was the most evil thing in the world—and seeing what he got out of it, you can hardly argue with him."

"Oh golly—!"

"Don't bring up Roger, Tania, I've just got her all cleaned up."

Tania smiled wanly, leaning back against the linen cupboard, wrapped in her towel like a desert mystic, the tip of my ascot peeking out between her feet. I glanced up at her face, but it told me nothing. "It was that day he came breaking into my studio. Once he'd calmed down, we had a long talk together. He knew what was happening to him . . ."

"But that wasn't love, that was something . . . something *crazy!*"

"He told me he used to believe, before he met Ros, that love was a kind of literary invention, that people wouldn't fall in love at all if they didn't read about it first. He said he always thought that we learned our lines about love, as it were, from fairy tales, then went out in the world and acted them out, not even knowing why it was we had to do it. But he said he forgot all that when he met Ros, forgot everything. He said she left him completely stupid, an illiterate, a wolf-child, a man utterly without a past, she invented him where he stood—it was as if he'd been concussed, suffered some kind of spectacular fusing of his entire nervous system, reducing it to the simple synchronous acivity and random explosions of a newborn child."

"I can understand that," said Naomi softly, staring at me. "It's great . . ."

"He was terrified. He said it wasn't that he needed to possess her, it wasn't even selfishness, not in the way one would think. And he didn't feel protective, didn't feel kind or generous toward her, didn't especially want her to be happy or successful or feel fulfilled—it was something much more immediate than that, something much more frightening, it was something almost *monstrous* . . . !"

"Oh my . . . !" Naomi fled, holding her tummy, brushing past Vic's girlfriend Eileen, who had just come in behind us, looking dazed still, one whole side of her face now swollen and turning blue.

"You'd think, after such a colorful childhood," I said, wiping the sink, then tossing the towel in with the others (yet I, too, was thinking about love), "she'd be a bit more calloused."

Tania laughed drily. "My god, Gerry, I knew the girl's parents. Her father was a teacher and poet, her mother a musician, played the viola, gentlest people in the world. I'm sure Naomi's never had a real spanking in her life. Not that she couldn't use one . . ." Eileen set her empty glass down on the rim of the basin, stared at us bleakly for a moment as though trying to place us, then dropped the seat of the toilet, lifted her limp skirt, pushed her pants down to her knees, and sat to pee. "Or maybe she's at the wrong party . . ."

"It's blocked, Eileen," I said. I noticed that my electric razor was missing. Not (Tania was staring down at her dirndl in the tub of suds, lost in thought, it was as good a moment as any) in the linen cupboard either. "You should use the one downstairs."

"Somebody's in there," she replied dully. "I think it's Janice Trainer and some guy." I hung fresh towels on the racks, got out a washcloth and soaked it in cold water. Eileen looked down at her shoes and, peeing disconsolately, said to them: "I'm sorry . . ."

"Here, Eileen, hold this against your face."

"It's so sad," she said, "and there's nothing we can do about it." She blew her nose in the washcloth. "And the worst thing is, I don't feel a thing. That's what's horrible. They're both killed and I don't feel a thing."

"You feel sad."

"I felt sad when I came here." She'd left the door open: Alison didn't seem to be around, but the sewing room light was on. I felt vaguely frightened and wanted her close to me again. Eileen twisted her finger in her cotton drawers, looked up at me. "Your wife was asking for you, Gerry."

"I know. I'm going."

"Gerry, do me a favor," Tania said, stopping me just as I stepped out the door.

"It's . . . it's not over, you know," Eileen murmured softly behind her, posted there as above some deep abyss. Her urine had dwindled, but now it started up again, rattling against the clog of paper like a disturbing thought.

"I'm worried about Mavis. Something about that look on her face. I can't get it out of my mind. Check on her for me, will you?"

"Sure, Tania. Should I—?"

But something she'd seen past my shoulder had made her frown

suddenly and close the door. I turned to look: the two uniformed officers were coming up the stairs. Nobody in the sewing room now except Sally Ann and Dickie. My mother-in-law's room was locked. The policemen had paused on the landing, hats tipped back, arguing about something around mouthfuls of food: it seemed to be about which sandwich was whose, but the party noises from below drowned them out. In the sewing room (little Gerald's room actually—left more or less as it was ever since the stillbirth, the walls still a bright green, decals on all the furniture and closet doors, only a couch and a sewing machine added), Sally Ann was trying to thread a needle, and Dickie, cuddling behind her, had reached around and pushed his hand down inside her jeans. She glanced up, saw me watching, pulled his hand out as though to kiss it, and stabbed it with the needle. As the policemen started up the stairs again, alerted by Dickie's yell, I decided it might be a good moment to get changed. Also I needed time to think. Too much was happening too fast and I was beginning to feel like my mother on that ski slope, sit down, sit down.

"Can't you tell them to be a little more quiet?" my mother-in-law scolded, standing sentinel at the doorway of my son's room.

I smiled at her, then edged past a stack of dirty plates and crumpled cocktail napkins into our bedroom and closed the door.

The room was quiet, hushed almost, lit only by the dense yellow glow cast by the bedside lamp, and I felt the jitteriness ebb away. I crossed the room to draw the curtains shut, catching a glimpse of myself in the wall mirror as I passed it. Hmm. Once I'd cleaned up, I should go say good night to Mark again so he wouldn't carry that face into his sleep with him. Unless, of course (recalling Naomi's valentine), he needed it.

Tania's "Susanna and the Elders" had hung where the mirror was until something she said one night made us move it to the dining room. Her husband, Howard, writing on a painter he disliked, had called his work "bedroom art," meaning too private and self-indulgent. I'd argued that all good art, being a revelation of the innermost self, and thus a kind of transcended dream, was "bedroom art," but Howard would have none of it. "This widespread confusion of art and dreams is a romantic fallacy," he'd said, "derived from their common exercise of the brain's associative powers—but where dreams protect one's sleep, art disturbs it." Tania had agreed: "I don't paint in bed-

rooms, I don't even *think* about painting in bedrooms, and I certainly wouldn't hang one of my paintings in one, any more than I'd go to a party in haircurlers and pajamas." So we'd put the mirror there and moved "Susanna" down to the dining room (admittedly, we'd hung it in the bedroom in the first place for no better reason than that the forest colors went well with the curtains and russet-canopied four-poster), and truth to tell, it did seem to take on more power down there.

Tania and Howard had arrived with Anatole tonight just minutes before Roger and Ros—in fact, I was still taking their coats when I heard Ros laughing on the porch—so we were all there in the hallway together for a moment, a moment that now in retrospect seemed almost magical. Ros had given each of us a big hug (I remembered Anatole blushing and staring at the ceiling as she smashed her breasts against him, Howard adjusting his spectacles knocked askew) and announced she'd just got a new part in a play—I'd had the impression at the time that it was news to Roger as well, and dismaying news at that—and then off she'd gone, the last time I'd seen her alive, best I could remember, to pass her hugs around. Ros was a great hugger. She always made you feel, for about five seconds, like you were her last friend on earth and she'd found you in the nick of time, and now, as I searched through the clothes hanging in the closet for something to wear, I found myself remembering all her hugs like one composite one: not a girl hugging, but hugging, girl-shaped. I picked out some soft linen slacks and a rust-colored open-collared wrap-tie shirt, tossed them over the back of a chair. Have to change shoes too. And socks: I was wearing blue.

Ros sometimes asked us, if we were visiting her backstage, to help her change costumes. I say "us": I was seldom lucky enough to have her all alone. And anyway, somehow you were never really quite alone with Ros even when there wasn't anyone else around. But it didn't matter. One of the best times I ever had with her, in fact, was the day I arrived to find a photographer there shooting stills. I was married by then and so was she, so we'd seen each other only rarely, but her greeting was the same as if we'd been actively lovers. That is to say, exactly as it always was. What the photographer was after were simple straightforward publicity stills of Ros in rapture, but whenever she tried to *act* ecstatic, she always looked like she had a fly up her nose. The photographer said he'd be glad to help her work up the real thing

himself, but he wasn't loose enough, as he put it, to shoot pix and jism at the same time, so he asked me if I'd do him the favor of pulling Ros's trigger for her. For the sake of art, he added with a professional grin. I protested—weakly, as Ros had just thrown her soft arms around me and given me another breathless hug: oh yes! let's!—that my wife had slightly less magnanimous notions about art and duty, and I couldn't take the risk of an uncropped photo turning up somewhere. Ros, of course, didn't understand this at all, but the photographer, a married man thrice over, thought about it for a moment, then suggested: why not wear a mask? So we got the keys to the costume trunks, locked ourselves in a rehearsal room where they had some colored lights, mirrored walls, and a few loose props, and enjoyed an enchanted hour of what I came to think of as an erotic exploration of my own childhood. I was severally a clown, a devil, a scarecrow, skeleton, the back half of a horse, Napoleon, a mummy, blackamoor, and a Martian. I played Comedy to Ros's Tragedy, Inquisitor to her Witch, Sleeping Beauty to her Prince Charming, Jesus Christ to her Pope. Sometimes the mirrored images actually scared or excited me, altered my behavior and my perception of what it was I was doing, but Ros was just the same, whether as a nymph, a dragon, an old man or the Virgin Mary: in short, endlessly delicious. The photographer occasionally joined in—just to keep his hand steady, as he put it—and once we balled her together without masks, dressed only in red light and jesters' bells. I probably learned more about theater in that hour or so—theater as *play*, and the power of play to provoke unexpected insights, unearth buried memories, dissolve paradox, excite the heart—than in all the years before or since. After the third orgasm, it all became very dreamlike, and if I didn't have a set of prints locked away down in my study to prove that it actually happened, I probably wouldn't believe it myself. I enjoyed no particular costume so much as the strange sequence of them—a kind of odd stuttering tale that refused to unfold, but rather became ever more mysterious and self-enclosed, drawing us sweetly toward its inner profundities—but from the photographer's viewpoint, the best was probably one of the simplest, a variation on Beauty and the Beast in which Ros wore only a little strip of diaphanous white cheesecloth and I dressed up in a gorilla suit. He said her astonished expression as she gazed up at the monstrous black hairy belly with a little white pecker poking out was exactly what he'd been looking for.

I smiled, feeling grateful. My bruises hurt less. I felt I could stay here forever, wrapped round by memory and the soft light and fabrics of my bedroom; but then I heard my mother-in-law scolding someone out in the corridor. I sighed, kicked my shoes off, peeled off the socks, removed my belt and laid it over the chairback with the clean clothes, lowered my trousers (all that blood in the crotch, hers: I shuddered, pained by this sad final gift), and had one leg out when Vic's daughter came in. "Hey, I'm changing, Sally Ann!"

"That's all right, don't mind me—I just want to sew this patch on." She peeked back out into the hallway (I heard someone protesting, something like a scuffle on the stairs—what I read on Sally Ann's hindend was "SEAT OF BLISS"), then eased the door shut. "Everywhere else, there's always somebody *bothering* me."

She padded barefoot across the room to my wife's dressing table, pausing there to admire her navel in the mirror. I'd pulled my trousers back up, partly to hide the erection I had from thinking about Ros, and stood holding them. "Come on, I've got a houseful of guests! I've got to get dressed and—"

"Well, go ahead, for goodness' sake," she said with an ingenuous smile, studying my open fly, "don't let *me* stop you!" She turned her back to me, pushed her blue jeans down, her little bikini pants getting dragged along with them. She stepped out of her jeans, very slowly pulled her panties back up, then sat down on the dressing-table stool, her little bum stuck out like she was trying to get rid of it. "I mean, we *do* know what men and women *look* like, *don't* we, Gerry?" She laid her blue jeans across her lap, took up her needle and thread as though conducting me with a baton. I noticed now the two whiskey glasses on the dressing table, the half-eaten sandwich, open jar of petroleum jelly, smelled the alien perfumes, the sweat and smoke. Even here then. . . . "Look, I won't even *watch* if that's what's bothering you," she added, gazing at me mischievously in the dressing-table mirror.

"Have it your own way," I said, turning my back on her. I saw now that the bed had been rumpled, the covers tossed back over loosely. I lifted them: there was a bloodstain on the sheet, a small brown hole burned by a cigarette, coins, crumbs, a wet spot, and someone's false eyelashes. Well . . . and the lamp's yellow glow: it came from one of my wife's nighties, draped over it.

I removed my trousers and tossed them on the bed, feeling funda-

mentally deceived somehow, just as Sally Ann said "Ow!" and came prancing over to show me her thumb, which she said she'd pricked with the needle. "Kiss it for me, Gerry," she groaned, squeezing up behind me, her voice schoolgirl-sultry.

"Now, see here, damn it—!" I snapped, whirling around, and the ice pick, wrapped in my ascot, fell out of my shirt on the floor at our feet.

"Gerry—! My gosh!" she squeaked, stepping back, still holding her pricked thumb up with its tiny bead of blood.

"It's not mine," I said lamely. "It just . . . turned up . . ."

She squatted to pick it up. "It's so—so *sexy!*" she gasped, stroking it gently. She wound it up carefully in the ascot once more and handed it back to me. "I'll never tell, Gerry!" she whispered gravely and, standing on her tiptoes, threw her arms around my neck and kissed me. "Cross my heart!" I tried to twist away, but she held on to my nape with one small warm hand, pointing down at the hard bulge in my shorts with the other: "See, you *do* like me, Gerry! I felt it pushing on my tummy—you can't hide it!"

"Don't be silly, it gets that way by its—"

"Can I see it?"

"What? No, of course not!" I pried her hand away from my neck.

"Please, Gerry!" She blushed, her worldly pretensions evaporating. "I've never really, you know, seen one . . ." She touched the tip of it gingerly through the cotton. "Not . . . not sticking up like that . . ."

"Don't kid me, Sweet Meat, I've read your ads."

"Don't make fun of me, Gerry. I was . . . all that was just for you. You're so experienced, I thought you'd . . ." She ducked her head, sucking at her pricked thumb. "I was just showing off . . ." Her knotted shirt gaped, showing the firm little bubbles inside with their pink points like new pimples. I could hide it inside one of my wife's hatboxes, I thought. Or her boot maybe, a sewing basket . . . "I feel so dumb . . ." She leaned against me, putting one arm around my waist, pulling my shorts down with the other.

"Hey—!"

She started back in amazement, holding on to the shorts. "Wow! Is that supposed to go in . . . in me?" she gasped, cradling it in both hands. "Doesn't it, you know . . . hurt?"

"Only when you swallow," I said drily, tugging at my shorts with my free hand, trying to back away.

"Wait, Gerry!" She held the shorts down firmly with one hand, clutching my rigid member with the other. "I'm not as dumb as you think, honest—but in all the pictures they showed us at school, it was always hanging down like a lump of taffy, I never saw one all stiff like this!"

Maybe it was so; but her curiosity both angered and saddened me and I thought again of my walk that night through the laundry-laden streets of that seaside town in Italy: what a fool I was! "Sally Ann, please . . ."

"But look—there's the penis and there's the scrotum, right? And the scrotum contains the epididymus, the seminiferous, uh, some-things, and the vas deferens, which I can just feel, I think, at the back . . ." The illusion of novelty, that old shield against time: her fingers stepped tentatively between my thighs like a traveler in a strange city, excited by the possibility of the next turning, poor child . . . "At school, we girls called it the 'vast difference' . . ."

"Very funny." She pushed the shorts down further, thrusting her hand deeper, maneuvering my penis with the other like a lever—and in truth I felt like some kind of antiquated machine, a museum piece, once an amazing invention, the first of its kind, or thought to be, now seen as just another of time's ceaseless copies, obsolete, worthless except as a child's toy, disposable. I regretted my sarcasm.

"And then the perannum—"

"Perineum."

"The perineum, the anus, the—may I try to feel the prostate, Gerry?" She held my organ gently now, the tip of it resting in her bared navel, as her finger probed speculatively up my rectum, and I thought: yes, the vast difference: a schoolgirl's titter was what it was worth. Yet: maybe that was enough . . . "It's all so soft and squishy and—"

"SALLY ANN!" roared Vic as he came crashing in, the door slamming back against the wall with a bang, his face pale with rage and anxiety.

Startled, she jerked her finger out—*ffpop!*: "*Yow*—!"

"Oh, Dad!" she groaned. "For crying out loud . . . !"

"*If that goddamn sonuvabitch—!*"

"Daddy, stop it! You're making a scene!"

"Holy smoke . . . !" I wheezed, touching my anus gingerly: yes, it was still there.

Vic blinked, looked around blearily. "Oh, hullo, Gerry. Sorry. I

thought—well, I didn't see that bastard around anywhere, and . . ."

"Really! You'd think it was the Middle Ages!" She sighed petulantly, then, sniffing her finger, tipped my penis up for one last glimpse of it from the underside: "It's all goosebumpy," she murmured, sliding the foreskin up and down, "just like the neck of an old turkey!"

"Sally Ann, your father—"

"I can take care of myself!"

"Goddamn it, you don't *know* that guy, baby!" Vic insisted, stumbling heavily about the room. He looked like a runner who'd just finished a mile and was trying to keep from falling over.

Sally Ann groaned, gave me a sympathetic grimace and a final squeeze, let go at last, as Vic fell heavily on the stool. I pulled my shorts up, caressing away the twinge in my anus. "*Now*, you've just sat down on my *jeans!*"

"Sorry," he muttered, standing again, his eyes averted.

"You're drunk, Daddy, and you don't know what you're doing," Sally Ann scolded, tugging her jeans on. Vic had turned his back momentarily, drinking deeply, so I stuffed the ascot and ice pick under the mattress. There was something else under there already—a meat skewer? More picks? "I'm not a child, you know!"

"You coulda fooled me," Vic grumbled, and wiped his mouth with his sleeve. His blue workshirt, half unbuttoned and bloodstained, was sweaty at the back.

"Oh, Daddy, you're such a pain," Sally Ann said, checking herself in the dressing-table mirror, pressing one hand against her flat tanned belly, untying and loosely reknotting her shirt when she saw me watching; but it was her mortality, not her childish flirtations, that I saw there. Something Tania had once said about mirrors as the symbol of consciousness or imagination. Maybe we'd been talking about her painting of "Saint Lucy's Lover," the one with all the eyes. It had started, I remembered, with one of her little parables on wisdom, her painterly belief in immersion, flow, inner vision, as opposed to technique, structure, reason. Just as mirrors, she'd said, were parodies of the seas, themselves symbols of the unconscious, the unfathomable, the formless and mysterious, so were reason and invention mere parodies of intuition. What one might expect from Tania. What impressed me at the time, however, was her definition of parody: the intrusion of form, or death (she equated them), into life. Thus the mirror, as parodist, did not lie—on the contrary—but neither did it

merely reflect: rather, like a camera, it *created* the truth we saw in it, thereby murdering potentiality. Sally Ann, watching me curiously through it, had clutched the collars of her shirt and tugged them closed as though chilled. "What . . . what's the matter . . . ?"

I gazed at her mirrored image, unable to see her shadowed back between us. A great pity welled up in me. "You are too willful . . ."

"You can goddamn well say that again!" growled Vic, looking up. "Now the rest of the night I want you downstairs where I can—"

"Oh, pee!" she pouted, clenching her little fists to her sides. "Both of you can kiss my elbow!"

Vic lunged at her: "Why, you little—!" But she was out the door. He stood there glaring furiously for a moment, his broad sweat-darkened shoulders hunched; then the strength seemed to go out of him and he sank down again on the dressing-table stool. I sat on the edge of the bed to pull the clean socks on, tie my shoes, and relieve the tingling between my cheeks. I was thinking still about death and parody and mirrors and the essential formlessness of love (my mother-in-law appeared in the doorway, glared at us, and snapped the door shut), and about how I might explain it all to Alison. And then: how she'd gaze up at me . . . "You keep a bottle up here somewhere? Under the mattress or something?"

"You might find some hair tonic in one of those drawers . . ." And so what about marriage then, Gerald? Just another parody? I seemed to hear Alison ask me that.

Vic grunted. His face was in shadows, but his shaggy white hair was rimmed with light right down into his sideburns. He spied the two glasses on the dressing table, sniffed them, chose one, dumped the cubes from his own glass into it. I transferred the things from the pockets of the old pants to the new, shocked again at the obscenity of the bloodstains (and how had I come to pocket a can-opener, this medicine dropper, these shriveled oysters and bumpy little marbles?), then threaded my belt through the linen loops. "Jesus, what am I going to do, Gerry?"

"I don't know, do you ever just talk to her?"

"Talk to her! What the fuck about? My father was a happy-go-lucky tough-ass illiterate coal miner, hers is a sour bourgeois overeducated drunk—what could we possibly have in common? Hell, she understands my old man better than I can understand either of them!"

"That figures."

"Come on, don't get supercilious with me, pal—!"

"I only meant—"

"You meant what we all know: love blinds. I ruined myself as a thinker the day I knocked up my wife. I haven't been worth stale piss ever since." I couldn't argue with him. He hadn't written a thing since Sally Ann was about six years old, and had slacked off long before that. But I didn't believe it was that simple. It's one thing to reduce the world to a mindless mechanism, another to live in it. Flow had surprised him, offended him, dragged his feet out from under him. Even now, as he reared up and paced the room restlessly, he seemed to slip and weave. "Let me tell you something about my old man. Just because he could belt the shit out of you, he thought he was tough. And smart. The sonuvabitch was full of cocky aphorisms, proverbs— he had the secret. And you know what it was? Power. This cringing yoyo, who spent his whole life slaving away down in the nation's ass- hole when he wasn't in the breadlines, believed in power like kids believe in fairy godmothers. He still does. Still talks tough and acts smart and lies there in his goddamned hospital bed in the old folks' home waiting to be blessed with it. With Sally Ann, on the other hand, it's experience. Spoiled, naive, unable to grasp anything more complicated than a goddamned confession magazine, a girl who wouldn't recognize the real world if it rolled over her, and what she believes in—guides her whole life by—is experience!"

"What are you trying to tell me, Vic?"

"That I *know* what my fucking problem is, goddamn you—but what burns my ass is that I can't seem to do anything about it!"

"Well, you're coming around in your old age . . ."

"What, to paradox? Hell, no, I've always accepted that—I just don't make a religion out of it like you do, that's all."

I took a sip at the drink Vic had turned down: something between a Manhattan and a gin rickey. Awful. Against the light: lipstick smears on the far rim. Full lips. Cherry red. "And what do you sup- pose Eileen believes in, Vic?"

He sighed, finished off his drink, chewed an ice cube. "I can't im- agine. Ecstasy maybe? Belly laughs?"

"You're awfully hard on her—why do you even go out with her?"

"She's got a comfortable hole I can use. And when I'm done I can go away and she doesn't complain."

"Is that fair?"

"I don't know. I don't think about it."

I shook my head. "I don't think I could enjoy it that way."

"Well, you're more considerate than I am. You give parties, I don't."

"Maybe the trouble, Vic, is that you've never been in love."

His sour laughter boomed out. "No, you silly shit, you're right—I've loved, god-*damn* I've loved, but *in* love is one fucking place I've never been! Except . . ." He paused, sobering some, ran his broad hand through his hair. "Except once maybe . . ." He leaned against a bedpost, his craggy face softening.

"Anyone I know?"

He sighed, rubbed his jaw, lurched away from the bedpost. "Yeah."

I drank in silence while he paced. He was clearly in pain. Not Eileen's kind of pain, sullen and stoic: it was more disturbing than that. He seemed riven by it, his stride broken, his vision blocked, and I thought: Yes, I've known all along—Eileen on the couch, Vic standing over her, his back to the rest of us, his neck flushed, fists doubled . . . "Ros," I said.

He nodded. "It was right after my wife and I broke up." His voice was husky, and as though to cover, he cleared his throat and sucked up another cube to chew. "I needed somebody quick and easy," he said, the words crunched with ice. "No complications."

"Like Eileen."

"Like Eileen. Only it didn't turn out that way." He sighed: more like a groan—then dropped onto the stool as though undermined. He sat there, his back bent, elbows on his knees, staring mournfully into his empty glass. "We ran into each other at a political rally. Roger was defending some prisoners who'd rioted down at the jail—"

"I know. I read about it."

He grunted. "For some reason, he'd dragged Ros along. Probably afraid to leave her on her own anywhere. The rally was held on the steps of the courthouse, and those of us who were organizing the thing were up on the porch, under the colonnade, facing the crowd. I was pressed up against Ros when we first arrived, and pretty soon we found ourselves holding hands and asses and finally all but jerking each other off—Jesus, I was horny! We must've excited everybody within thirty yards of us!"

"Where was Roger?"

"Up front with all the main characters. He was pretty nervous about

her as usual, but though he kept craning his head around, he couldn't really see anything—except for the flush on Ros's face and the way she twitched around." He paused, licking idly at the melting ice, his thick brows knitted. "You sure you want to listen to this?"

"Yes . . ."

"It's not just a cheap cocksman's brag—I mean . . ."

"I know."

He leaned forward again, staring off through the far wall. "She was wearing a soft woolen skirt, lambswool maybe. I never notice women's clothes, but I know every goddamn thing she had on that day. By feel anyway. I don't remember for sure what color the skirt was—a greenish plaid, I think—but I'll never forget what it felt like to grip her cunt through it." The fingers of his right hand closed around his knee. "A fat furry purse, a little soft bristly stuffed animal that you stroked between the ears—Christ, I'm getting a hard-on just thinking about it!" He scratched his crotch, sucked up a cube, spat it back again. Tears glinted in the corners of his eyes. I screwed the lid on the petroleum jelly. "Anyway, it came my turn to speak, and I whispered to Ros before I left her how fucking unhappy I was, and how much I needed something human to happen to me. She was waiting for me when I'd finished—I don't know what I said out there, but it must have been good, taut and hard and nothing wasted, my whole body working on the message, as it were—and when I got back she pulled me gradually behind the others and finally on into the building, smiling toward Roger all the while. She knew the courthouse pretty well, I guess because of having to go there with Roger a lot. She hurried me up some stairs, down a corridor, through an empty courtroom and into a little cloakroom where the judges' robes were hung. We could hear the speeches and chanting and applause from in there, so we were able to time it pretty close. Or I could anyway. I don't think it mattered to her. Probably we weren't up there more than ten or fifteen minutes, but thinking back on it I feel I spent the best half of my life in that cloakroom, and I left enough seed in Ros and all over those fucking robes to turn a desert green! Jesus! I knew it was crazy, adolescent, unreal, but I didn't care. I came down out of the goddamn building about three feet off the ground! It's too bad we weren't storming the fucking barricades that day, I could've died a happy man!" He smiled broadly, thinking about this, and for a moment, a glow of warmth and innocence lighting up his craggy face, he looked like a different

man. Then the skepticism returned, the sour shrewdness, the weariness: he glanced up at me to see how I was taking it, shrugged at my sobriety (oh, I knew it, knew what she could do, knew what I'd lost, what we'd all lost), set his glass down. "It was so goddamn beautiful, Gerry . . ."

"Yes . . ."

"Fucked me up politically though. My head was useless, she blew a hole right through it. No will. Everything was body." He seemed, guiltily, to savor the thought. I was thinking about that old joke of Charley's: making it stand up in court . . . "A weird kind of connection. For me anyhow. The illusion of . . . owning time . . ."

"I know. We have the past, we have the future, but what we never seem to be able to get ahold of is the present."

"Yeah, well, the present is in the hands of a very few." I could see his jaws grinding under the heavy sideburns.

"Have you seen a lot of her?"

He peered up at me under his shaggy gray brows, his eyes damp, then back down at his empty glass. "We met a few times afterward, but as you know, with Roger it's not easy. And it was against my principles, in ruins as they were by then, to fuck another man's wife, so finally I got enough self-control back to bring an end to it. The fucking anyway. I still wanted to be around her whenever I could, even if I had to exercise my imagination a little and get my rocks off in a substitute. I mean, no offense, but Ros was pretty much the reason I came here tonight. Just to be . . . well . . . and now . . ." He bit his lip, reared up, and began stalking around the room again, rubbing his face with one thick hand, breathing heavily. *"They're using a goddamn fork on her down there, Gerry!"* he cried.

"A fork—?!"

"Those fucking cops!" He smashed his fist into the wall. I recalled now that view I'd had into the living room over the heads of Daffie and Jim and the others, Inspector Pardew on the floor on his knees, reaching back over his shoulder toward his two assistants like a surgeon asking for a scalpel. Vic whirled around suddenly and bulled out, fists clenched, slamming past some people just outside the door: Dolph and Talbot spun back against the wall, Charley Trainer fell on his arse, his scotch flying, a woman giggled nervously. *"Beautiful!"* exclaimed Charley from the floor, his face dripping whisky, and the woman, a rolypoly lady I didn't know but judged from her rouged

cheeks, colorful print dress, bloodied broadly at the belly, short socks and loafers (why did I think of her in a garden?) to be Mrs. Earl Elstob, tittered again.

There was a crash down on the landing and somebody cried out.

"Jesus, what was that?" Dolph asked thickly, bumping up against the back of the fat lady, who looked surprised and moved away.

"Maybe he forgot about the stairs," Talbot said, and licked his palm. His bandaged ear made him look like he was growing a second head.

I gave Charley a hand getting to his feet, hauling him up out of the dirty dishes. He'd sat square in a plateful of Swedish meatballs, but he didn't seem to care. "Physical contact—I *love* it!" he declared, weaving, and flung his arm around me, the bottle of scotch at the end of it thumping heavily against my shoulder. "You're a wunnerful guy, Big G!" He belched sentimentally, his eyes crossed, and Dolph echoed him more prosaically.

"I heard that one before," said Talbot stupidly. They looked like bloated parodies of horny teenagers, papier-mâché caricatures from some carnival parade, and for a moment they seemed to be wearing their mortality on their noses like blobs of red paint: yes, we're growing old, I thought, and felt a flush of warmth for them.

I started to pull away, but Charley hugged me tight, the neck of the whisky bottle pressing up cold and wet under my ear. "Hey, I *love* this fella!" he exclaimed to the fat lady, and she commenced to giggle. "Honess t'god, Gladys, he's my oldess 'n bess friend! He's a—he's a *prince!*"

"Oh you!" she tee-heed, her face flushed and blood-flecked.

"No, *s'true*, Gladys! He's a real goddamn *prince!* And I wanna tell ya something—!"

Oh oh. "Listen, Charley, no kidding, I—"

"Charming," said Dolph drily, a bit slow in his beery distance. "Prince Charming."

"Pleased, I'm sure," giggled Gladys, holding out a reddish hand, and Talbot, taking it, said: "And this is our fairy godmother, Prince. Make a wish—*any* wish!"

"I wish I had another beer," said Dolph quietly, his face flattening out, and Charley, laughing loosely and dragging me lower as his knees sagged, said: "No, wait a minute! Ha ha! This'll kill ya! We were out inna country, see—"

"Keep it clean," admonished Talbot, holding a small patch of silk to his nose. He sniffed and, winking, offered me the scrap: I turned away, clamped still in Charley's grip. Distantly, I could hear Woody's wife, Yvonne, complaining loudly and drunkenly.

"I *awways* keep it clean, Tall-Butt, you *know* that!" Charley was rumbling, drooling a bit at the corners of his mouth. "I soak it three times a day in hot borax, beat it on Saturdays, 'n hang it out to air on Sundays—how clean can ya *get*? No, cross my heart—ask Gladys here, she's *seen* it!"

"Oh my!" she gasped as the others yukked it up. "I've . . . I've never been to a party like this before!"

"Firss time fr'evrything, my love!" Charley declared, the dark pouches of his left eye flexing in a drunken wink. "I'll drink to that!" said Talbot confusedly, and Charley, staring at us quizzically, mouth adroop and eyes rheumy, asked: "Whawere we talkin' about? Hunh? God-*damn* it, men!"

"The . . . the prince . . . ?" whispered Gladys.

" '*Ass* it! You got it! By God, Gladys, you *got* it!" He slumped toward her, pulling me with him (once in a film when the heroine said her lover took her breath away, Charley's wife Janny had sighed wearily and said she knew just how the lady felt, and I thought of her now, blanched with the terror of some knowledge, as though—could this be it?—as though hugged once too often . . .), resting his empty glass on her big round shoulder. Down below, Yvonne was hollering something about the sky falling in. "You got it," he growled, "*an' I want it!*"

She squealed again, clapping a pudgy hand to her mouth, and the big soft mounds of her bosom bobbled with giggling, watched glassily by Dolph and Talbot. Charley winked at me, hugging me close, but behind all the clowning I saw a soggy sadness well up in his blue eyes, a plea: help me! it's terrible, old buddy, but this is all I can do . . . !

"I think your wife's about to bust a vessel down there," Dolph put in, crumpling his beer can and dropping it in the hallway clothes hamper. "She asked me to tell you—"

"Yes, I know."

"You got a goddamn mess downstairs, you wanna know the truth," Charley declared, frowning drunkenly down his nose at me. "We come up here t'get away from it all, Earl's sister here'n Doll-Face'n ole Tall-Butt'n me—all us birds of a feather, we gotta, you know, go

flock together!" Talbot grinned sheepishly, glancing toward the head of the stairs, Dolph's ears turned red (he pulled a spare can of beer out of his back pocket as though in self-defense), Gladys looked blank. " 'N hey! we'd be honored t'have yer company, you ole scut-licker, if you careta join us—?"

"Thanks, but I have to go see what my wife—"

"Woops, I feel rain, boys!" Charley hollered, ducking, as Dolph popped the beer open, and I was able to squeeze out from under his arm at last. "We better get under *cover!*" There was a slap, a nervous titter, something about age and beauty, while ahead of me, Yvonne: "Just break the goddamn thing off, Jim, and throw it away—what the hell do I need it for anyway?"

"C'mon back, Ger, when you get a chance! Awways room for one more!"

The mess in the hall seemed to be worsening—not just the dirty plates and glasses (picking my way through it, I was reminded of a similar occasion, stepping gingerly by moonlight through the wreck-age of an ancient ruin somewhere in Europe, I was there with some woman, she was Czech, I think, though she said she was French), but pits and crusts, ashes, butts, napkins, toothpicks: I stuffed ten glasses full of debris and picked them up with my fingers in their mouths (I'd been experimenting around a lot and felt the need for tradition, something stable—but the ruin was a terrifying cul-de-sac, capriciously dangerous in the moonlight, and the woman's sudden wheezing appe-tite for oral sex scared the blazes out of me; afterward, so I was told, she threw herself down a well), paused a moment to listen at my son's door. My mother-in-law was reading to him: ". . . endeavoring to appear cheerful, sat down to table, and helped him. Afterward, thought she to herself, Beast surely has a mind to fatten me before he eats me, since he provides such plentiful entertainment . . ." The way she read it, it sounded like a Scripture lesson—no wonder Mark had been telling us lately he didn't like fairy tales. As I listened to her re-count the trials of beauty in a world of malice and illusion, I was re-minded of my own grandmother's bedtime stories, variations mostly on a single melancholy theme: that people are generally better off not getting what they think they want most in this world. For her, the Beast's miserable enchantment would have been paradise compared to the Prince's eventual regret.

Yvonne howled with pain and swore fiercely. "Take a grip on some-

thing," I could hear Jim grunting, and Yvonne bellowed again: "*Waaah! Woody—? Where's Woody?!*"

I rushed toward the stairs, worried suddenly about my wife—how long had I been gone? what were the police thinking about that?—and crashed into Alison's husband, just stepping out of the bathroom: two glasses slipped from my fingers and exploded on the floor. "Oops, sorry!" I exclaimed, shaken.

"It's occupied," he replied flatly, touching his beard. I caught just a glimpse of the drawn shower curtains and what looked like my wife's apron on a hook as he pulled the door firmly shut behind him (probably I should call a plumber, you could smell it all the way out here) and waited for me to precede him down the stairs. If in fact he meant to follow.

"It's okay, Yvonne," some woman urged (I'd already turned toward the stairs, as though compelled, as though following some dancestep pattern laid out in footprints on the floor), and Yvonne cried: "*Okay—?! What the hell do you mean it's okay?!*"

My knees flexed involuntarily on the top step: it was (like a sudden wash of color, the fall of a memory scrim) the ski slope again—not now the one on which my mother fell (Yvonne lay sprawled on the landing, one foot sticking out at an angle under Jim's seat as he bent over her, worried onlookers pressed around), but the recurrent ski slope of my dreams, impossibly sheer, breathtaking, ambiguously crosshatched, disasters at the base: my tip (watched always by rows of dark spectators and now as though pushed from behind) into oblivion . . . "Yvonne—!"

"Gerry!" Yvonne cried, looking up at me (they all looked up, Iris Draper, Howard, that woman I'd seen with Noble, Anatole, Daffie, Ginger, as though I were something painted on the ceiling—all but Jim, now gripping Yvonne's foot by its heel and instep). "They're *after* me, Gerry!" The dark side of her face, bruised and bloodied, glistened with tears (the skis were off, I was walking down stairs again), but the eye looked dead: it was the near side alone that seemed to be speaking to me: "They're taking me away by *pieces!*" As she said this, Jim pulled steadily against Daffie on the leg, twisting it inward (the toes had been sticking out at ninety degrees), actually stretching the leg as though indeed trying to screw it off, and there was a harsh grating sound—"*Yowee! Lord love a duck, Jim!*" she yelped and her free leg kicked out, catching Ginger in the back of

the knees and making her sit abruptly, her narrow rump thumping the stair with a crisp little knock. *"Use a little grease!"*

"That's got it, I think," Jim grunted, holding her foot with one hand and wiping his brow with the other. The grating sound echoed in my head like the faint harmonic of some lost memory. Jim pushed her skirt back to study the symmetry of the two legs, and I thought of Ros again, a game we used to play which we called "Here's the church, here's the steeple . . ." I was breathing heavily. "All right, let me have those splints, son . . ."

Anatole, down a few steps behind him, handed him a pair of croquet stakes, the spikes still muddy. I knelt next to them, bracing myself on the glasses I was carrying. "It was Vic," Daffie panted, squatting alongside ("Oh, Gerry," Ros would say, "did we? I just don't remember!"), and Anatole said: "He was after the cops." I could hear his stomach gurgling; he didn't look all that well. "He ran straight into the living room and grabbed the fork away from them—!"

"The *fork*—! What was he, *starving* or something?" Yvonne squawked, her head resting now in the lap of Noble's friend. Ginger unpinned a kerchief from one shoulder and handed it to Jim, searched her body for another. Over our heads, Howard and Mrs. Draper seemed to be arguing about Tania's painting of "The Ice Maiden," Iris finding it too unskillful and farfetched. "If that's all he wanted, why the hell didn't he ask? Do I look like the resisting type?"

Daffie, leaning over the railing ("But of *course* there's distortion," Howard was insisting, "there's *always* distortion!"), called out: "Hey, Nay, is that a fresh drink? Bring it up here like a good old dog! We got an avalanche victim who needs it bad!"

"I wouldn't," said Jim. He was tying Yvonne's two legs together with Ginger's kerchiefs. "She's probably got some fever, a drink could make her sick."

"Make me *sick!* Oh boy! That's a good one!" Yvonne hooted. "Just *look* at me! *Sick* would be a goddamn *improvement!*"

I looked through the railings and saw Alison in the hallway gazing up at me. She glanced past my shoulder, pursed her lips, then beckoned me with a faint little nod and disappeared from view, replaced by Kitty, rushing past, clutching her shirt front together, a flushed grin on her face. Ginger, perched awkwardly on two steps, her ankles wobbling above the stiletto heels, had meanwhile bent over and run her hand between her knees and up the back of her skirt: she smiled suddenly, her little red pigtails bobbing, and whipped another kerchief

out, then grabbed her rear as though it were all falling apart back there, crossed her eyes, and tottered bowlegged down the stairs, past Naomi coming up. "It's just too ambitious," Iris Draper said flatly (I glanced into the cluster of glasses under my hands, disconcerted suddenly by the sense of being anchored outside time: I jerked my fingers out of them), and Howard sighed with disgust.

"Gosh, what *happened?!*" asked Naomi, staring wide-eyed at Yvonne's bandages. She leaned down to offer Yvonne her drink, provoking a disapproving sigh from Jim, and there was a sound like a paper sack being popped, then a slow soft tear. Naomi smiled sheepishly at me and shrugged, and Yvonne said: "Thanks, honey, you just saved an old lady from a fate worse than life!" She tossed the drink back as Jim, nose twitching, asked: "What's in that thing?"

"I don't know," Naomi said. "I just found it."

"Yum!" wheezed Yvonne. "Pure bourbon!"

"Smells like a salad."

Below us, Dickie laughed, and Daffie, saddened by her glance over the railing ("But please," Howard was arguing, "there's not arts *and* crafts, there's only art *or* crafts!"), said: "Roger once told me a funny thing. He said all words lie. Language is the square hole we keep trying to jam the round peg of life into. It's the most insane thing we do. He called it a crime. A fucking crime."

"You mean he . . . he thought it was a crime to be insane?" Naomi gasped, looking distressed, and Yvonne, smacking her lips, declared hoarsely: "My oh my! That oughta put some chest on my hair!"

The woman cradling Yvonne's head winced and exchanged a sorrowful glance with Jim, who said: "The thing now is to get you more comfortable. Here, son, you're young and strong, you take that side and I'll—can you manage the legs, Gerry?"

"Sure," I said as the doorbell rang. "Ah . . ."

Jim glanced up from under Yvonne's right arm, a shock of gray hair in his eyes. "That may be the ambulance . . ."

"Ambulance?"

"The police wanted an autopsy on Ros." Anatole, under the other arm, looked startled and annoyed. Jim pivoted toward the foot of the stairs just as Woody appeared there, coming in from the back. The doorbell rang again. "They said here and now, but I told them this was not the place for it . . ."

"*Woody!*" Yvonne wailed, breaking into the tears she'd been holding back.

I nodded and set her feet down gently. "Thanks, Jim. Just a minute, I'll let them in."

"Where've you *been,* for chrissake?!"

"I'm sorry, I was in conference," her husband said, hurrying up the steps with his cousin Noble. As they brushed past me, Noble took a last impatient drag, then flicked his cigarette butt over the railing (Patrick, below, ducked, glaring—behind him: a line of people at the toilet door). "I just heard—are you all right?"

"All *right?!* Are you *crazy?*" She was bawling now, all bravura swept away in the sudden flood. Wilma had started for the door, but hesitated when she saw me coming, turned to check herself in the hallway mirror instead. "It's gonna take three goddamn *trips* just to get all of me *home,* Woody! *Baw haw haw!* How can I be *all right?!*"

"She's had a rough time," the woman who'd been holding her said, her voice sharp, and Woody, behind and above me, muttered something apologetic about an interrogation: "I'm sorry, the police needed help opening some drawers—I think they're on to something . . ."

"It's the ambulance," I explained to Wilma's reflection, but when I opened the door it wasn't. It was Fats and Brenda.

"Ta-*daa-aa-ah!*" Fats sang out, his arms outspread like a cheerleader's, a big grin on his face, and Brenda, squeezed into a bright red pants suit, did a little pirouette there on the porch, one hand over her head, and, snapping her gum, asked: "Hey, am I beautiful? Am I beautiful?"

"But . . . what are you guys doing out there?" I asked in confusion.

"I give up, man," Fats replied, rolling his eyes and thrusting a bottle in a paper bag at me. "What are *you* guys doin' in *there?*"

"But I thought—I thought you'd already—"

"Sorry we're late, lover," Brenda said breathlessly, pushing in and pecking my cheek ("She's too *heavy* for him," Patrick was complaining through the banister rails), "but it took—hi, Wilma!—it took me an hour to get into this goddamn pants suit!"

"It's gorgeous!" Wilma exclaimed, holding her breasts. "Where'd you ever—?"

"And I got so turned on *watchin'* her," Fats rumbled with a grin, unzipping his down jacket, "that I made her get *out* of it again!"

"Which was damn near as hard as getting *in*—God help me if I—*pop!*—have to pee!"

"Never mind, I can't wear pants anyway," Wilma sighed ruefully, turning back to the mirror and giving her hair a pat. "The last time I tried it, Talbot said I reminded him of an airbag."

"Gettin' *in*," Fats admitted, jabbing a stiff thick finger at us ("Or maybe it was Archie who told me that . . . ," Wilma mused), "it was pretty hard, okay." The finger drooped: "But gettin' out . . ."

"Or Miles . . ."

"Listen," I broke in, "you have to know, something terrible has—"

"What? Do I hear somebody at the dartboard?" boomed Fats, tossing his jacket on the chair over the Inspector's overcoat: the fedora (now dented as well as spotted, I noticed) fell brim-up to the floor. Above us, glasses, kicked, clattered and tumbled. "Lemme at 'em!"

"Talbot likes to do it with mirrors," Wilma added, turning away from her reflection. Fats, over her shoulder, was slicking down his pate, someone was hammering on the toilet door: "The police are here, Brenda. Ros has been—"

"*Hey*, baby!" Fats boomed out over our heads. "Whatta they *done* to you?!"

"It's been a helluva ballgame, Fats!" Yvonne declared from half-way down the stairs, her arms around Jim and Anatole, Woody carrying her bound legs, Noble cradling the middle: "Don't let it sag, Noble!" Jim gasped. Patrick's face was screwed up, his body tense, as though sharing the burden.

"He says it makes him feel like a movie star," Wilma explained to no one in particular. "It only makes me feel depressed."

"Well, old Fats is here now, honey—you just point out the bad asses who *done* this to you!"

"Easy!" puffed Jim as they reached the bottom, crunching glass underfoot, and Michelle came over to see what was going on. Up on the landing, Alison's husband was expounding on something to Howard and Mrs. Draper, pointing into the depths of the Ice Maiden's mouth.

"Say, Gerry, your wife—"

"Yes, yes, I know, Michelle—"

"Wait a minute, what's all that *red* stuff all over everybody?" Brenda cried.

"It's just what it looks like," said Wilma. "Wait'll you see the living room . . ."

"All I can say," said Noble darkly (Daffie, stepping down, turned

her back to the hallway mirror, presenting us with a mocking before-and-after contrast that seemed almost illusory: a time trick that Tania might have used), "is it had better come out!"

The downstairs toilet door opened just then: and it wasn't Janice Trainer who emerged, but the short cop, shirttails dangling, still struggling with his buttons: "Awright, *awright!* Christ!" he muttered, his face flushed, and ducked into the living room.

"Blood always does . . ."

"They still won't give them back to me," Patrick was whispering to Woody. Woody nodded, grunting sympathetically: "See me about it later, Patrick. We'll see what we can do."

"Roger went crazy," Michelle explained to Fats, but he wasn't listening: "Here, man, you ain't lookin' so good," he said, taking over from Anatole. "How 'bout lettin' ole Fats have a cuddle now?"

Anatole, starkly pale, gave up his burden gladly, and as they carted Yvonne off to the living room ("I'm okay! Send me in again, coach! I'm not finished yet!" she was declaiming), he turned to Brenda and said, his breath catching: "That woman was there when they killed him. He gave her something."

"Who, sweetie?" Brenda asked, smiling up at him (Patrick, behind the boy's shoulder, bristled). "Killed who?" She blew a teasing bubble, popped it, sucked it in.

"It was nothing," Daffie shrugged. She held her elbow cradled in her palm, cheroot dangling before her face. "I saw it. He gave her a small gold earring, that's all."

I started. "What kind of—?"

But the phone rang and Daffie went to answer it. "Who?"

"*Bren!*" Fats bellowed from the living room. "*It's Ros! Our little Ros! She's DEAD!*"

"*What? Ros—?!*" she cried and went running in there in her tight red pants (there was a thump, a curse): "*Oh NO—!!*"

The tall officer appeared, scowling, in the doorway, leaning on his short leg, and Daffie with the phone said: "It's for your boss, kiddo."

"Fucking bastard," muttered Anatole under his breath, and Michelle whispered: "I once had a dream about something like this."

Howard came down, his hips swiveling with drunkenness, and announced petulantly: "The upstairs toilet is blocked, Gerald!"

"I know, don't flush it. I'm going to call a plumber. As soon as the phone's free."

"Only it was at the art school, a boy who'd been painting me—he was dead but he kept on painting and I couldn't get away . . ."

"Have you seen Talbot, Howard? I can't find him anywhere."

Inspector Pardew now stood in the living room doorway, thumbs hooked in his vest pockets under the drapery of his white silk scarf, his impeccability marred only by the dark stains and chalk dust on the knees of his trousers. He gazed thoughtfully at Wilma, then at each of us in turn. Anatole brushed past him, thumping his shoulder (the Inspector seemed not to notice, his eye falling just then on his overturned fedora), and Patrick followed nervously, making little whimpering noises probably meant as apologies. "It was so strange," Michelle was saying softly, "but then it suddenly became a movie we were all watching. Only I still didn't have any clothes on. I wanted to get out of the movie theater before the lights came up, I was so afraid . . ."

Pardew picked up his fedora, smoothed out the dent, brushed it on his sleeve, and, glancing casually at the label of Fats' jacket, placed his hat on top of it. He seemed all the while covertly interested in Michelle's description of her attempt to push, naked, past all the people in the movie house of her dream ("I kept hearing them all laugh, but every time I turned around, they'd be like gaping statues, fixed in some kind of awful terror—and the scary thing about it was I couldn't find any aisles . . . !"), ignoring Daffie behind him, holding the phone at her crotch like a dildo and blowing smoke at the back of his head. "Is that for me?" Iris Draper asked, leaning over the banister, her spectacles dangling on a golden chain, and Wilma said: "That reminds me of the time Talbot took me to a professional wrestling match, and Wolfman threw Tiny Tim, who weighed about five hundred pounds, right in our laps." Yes, the trouble with ritual, I thought, is that it commits you to identifying the center (Pardew, staring at the front door, seemed momentarily nonplussed), which is—virtually by its own definition—never quite where or what you think it is . . .

"But then I was in the film again that I'd been watching and I was crying over the dead boy, yet all the time I felt like I had to go the bathroom . . ."

"I know what you mean, dear! When Tiny Tim came crashing down—"

"Yes, yes," Inspector Pardew was saying (he had the phone now and Daffie had vanished), "I'm doing everything I can." Howard,

hands outspread for balance, wobbled past us into the dining room, muttering something about "that stupid boy," and Michelle, taking my arm, her hand like gossamer, whispered: "It's so eery down here without any music. It makes everybody feel lost or something . . ."

"Put something on if you like," I said.

"Well, because it's very complicated," Pardew barked. Ginger crossed behind him, tiptoeing springily toward the toilet, her red pigtails trembling, kerchief tails lifting and dipping. She tried the door but it was locked. "Yes, yes . . . in her chambers. Just an agonal phenomenon probably. We'll get prints later. No, that's smashed up."

"Do you think it—it would be all right?"

"Sure, Michelle, why not?" I touched her hand gently: so frail, yet the knuckles were sharp and hard. I was thinking of Susanna in Tania's painting, that fixed artificial way she stood, and then Alison, miming it, the puzzled look on her face—and now Michelle, who'd posed for the painting in the first place, soft beside me, so light, almost wraithlike, yet brittle: a sequence, as it were, of interlocking figures, "Susanna" a kind of primal outline, like Pardew's pale chalk drawings on my living room floor (he glanced up at me, phone at his ear, and I heard the cries from in there: such an emptiness under them, yes, music might help), for the subsequent incarnations . . . "Something quiet."

"It's a problem of dynamics, you see. She was a blonde and—what? How should I know?" Pardew turned and, picking his nose, watched absently as Ginger pressed an ear against the toilet door, both hands pinched between her thighs, mouth puckered, kerchiefs dangling loosely like bits of laundry. "No, she was married. Probably. Yes, of course I did, but we got nothing from him we could use."

A kerchief fluttered to the floor, and Ginger, her thin legs tensed above her high stilletto heels, bent stiffly to pick it up just as Earl Elstob banged out of the toilet, wiping his shoes on his pantlegs: "Woops!" he exclaimed as the door batted her behind and sent her flying. He watched her bellyflop and, eyes agoggle, pink mouth pertly agape, skid across the hall, then he looked up, blinked, and grinned toothily. "Hey, uh, didja hear about the ole lady who—*shlup!*—backed into the airplane propeller?"

"Well, I *know* it's too bad," the Inspector snapped, scowling at his fingertip as he turned away, "but it can't be helped!"

Michelle pulled me on toward the living room, saying something

about my being forgiven (I was worried about this: where had the time gone?), or someone wishing to be forgiven. "What's that?"

"Fiona. She told me all about it."

"She did?"

"Well, a dipping refractometer maybe, if you have one—we can see what's going down here . . ."

"She said she knows how upset you were that night and she should have been more understanding, but her own guilt feelings made her fly off the handle like that." Elstob's got the word for it all right, I thought, as we stepped into the front room (he was yuk-yukking dopily behind us, helping Ginger back up on her spiky stilts, the Inspector meanwhile describing someone as a "spoiled weak-willed ladies' man with a propensity for dare-deviltry and an inflated ego" and outlining his equipment needs): all these violent displacements, this strange light, these shocked and bloodied faces—it was as though we'd all been dislodged somehow, pushed out of the frame, dropped into some kind of empty dimensionless gap like that between film cuts, between acts . . .

"Waah! I'm getting reamed by those goddamn posts, Jim!"

"It's your big ass, Yvonne, it's too heavy!" Noble grunted.

"It's *terrible*, Bren! I can't *believe* it!"

"Hang on, we'll get you braced up."

People stood in hushed awkward clusters, gripping drinks, cigarettes, crushed napkins, watching Yvonne get settled noisily onto the couch, or Fats and Brenda keening unabashedly over Ros's body in the far corner, or just staring at the people drifting uneasily in and out of the room. The blood, drying, seemed to have sunk back slightly from the surface of things, giving them another dimension. Like visual echoes, hints of hidden selves. It was almost as if (footprints had trampled Ros's outlines, disturbing the contours, laying down around them tracks of checks and arrows, a patina of graying chalkdust) the room had *aged* somehow . . . "She knows it was never meant as unkind—if anyone was being cruel that night, she said, she was—but under the circumstances, you know, after what had just happened, where you were coming from and all, and then with your penis moving inside her and her face, wet, on your cheek, almost like something had been skipped over, well, suddenly she—"

"What in the world are you talking about, Michelle?"

"You know, Fiona. She was telling me about the night you—"

"*Yipes!*" Yvonne yelled, jerking upward against her bindings and swatting reflexively at Jim, who, with help from Noble and the woman he was with, was trying to push an extension leaf from our dining table under her: "There's *slivers* in that goddamn thing, Jim!"

"Don't be silly, I'm sliding it *under* the cushions."

Alison and her husband appeared in the dining room doorway: they seemed to be arguing about something, but he was smiling. The two policemen went out past them, then came in again through another door.

"Well, then, something's *biting* me, I—OWW!"

"Aha," said Jim, reaching under her and pulling out a shard of broken glass, stained with blood, part of a microscope slide maybe ("How could this be *happenin'*?!" Fats was weeping, Brenda hugging him, Woody squatting beside them offering counsel, or perhaps just telling them what he knew: "It's *crazy!*" "Oh my *god*, Fats!"), and Yvonne shrieked: "Yah—is that blood *mine*—?!"

"I don't think so . . ."

"Fiona said it was sort of like going from one room to the other without using the door," Michelle whispered, leaning on my arm (Alison was gone again), "but she didn't mean to—"

"Well, you've got it all wrong!" I snapped angrily, turning on her (poor girl—I hadn't even been listening), as Yvonne cried out: "Honest to god, Jim, I think you guys pulled a fast one on me! This isn't my *body!*"

Startled, Michelle took her hand away, and I saw my wife in the sunroom watching us, a broom in her hands like a flagpole, Louise squatting fatly in front of her with a dustpan (and yes, I was aware now that much had been done: tables and chairs had been righted, debris cleared away, plants repotted—there were even fresh bowls of peanuts and rice crackers here and there, clean cloths on some of the tables). "Well, I don't know, Gerry, it's what she *said*. Anyway, she's here somewhere, you can ask her yourself."

"Fiona—? But I'm sure we didn't—"

"I never had this gray hair! And where did this fat *ass* come from?"

"I think she came with Gottfried."

"Gottfried—?" But, with a cautioning glance past my shoulder, she'd slipped away. I turned ("Fats! Look! Somebody's stolen her rings!" Brenda cried, as Woody, suddenly interested in a bowl of black

olives on a lamp table, left them, whereupon the tall cop, Bob, appeared in the doorway, one hand on his holster, his eyes asquint, lips tensed; then he relaxed and dipped out again) and kissed my wife on the cheek. She was wearing a blue-and-white apron now with red hearts for pockets, a mauve-and-crimson kerchief around her hair. "I was just looking for you," I said ("How come all the hard parts are flopping around now and the nice soft parts have gone hard? Eh, Jim?"), and brushed at a streak of dirt near her eye. "Someone said you needed me . . ."

"Oh no," she smiled, stooping to pick up a mashed tamale. She seemed amused, surprised even, but her voice betrayed her. She cleared her throat. "Louise is helping." As though on cue, Louise came lumbering up behind, but as I turned to thank her, she veered away, rolling off toward the back of the house ("Hell of a surgeon you are! You left me the rotten tit and took all the rest! I'm not *me* anymore!") with her dustpan and bag of garbage. My wife dropped the tamale bits in a pocket, stared at the brown smudges on her fingertips, then wiped them on her apron. "The upstairs toilet is stopped up."

"I know. I'm sorry." I watched her as she untied the kerchief from around her hair and stuffed it in one of the red hearts in the apron, the brilliant kerchief making the heart seem dull. There was a thick smell of chili and warm chocolate. "I'm going to call a plumber, but right now the police are using the phone."

"Have you been into your study . . . since they . . . ?"

"I had to get something *off* my *chest*, he told me! Make a *clean breast* of it, he says!"

"No, but I heard. Poor Roger. It's terrible."

"The worst was the way they talked to him about Ros."

"Now, hell, it's the only *dirty* thing I got *left!*"

"Woody said that they made people come in and confess to things in front of him. Awful things." Over in the glow of our carmine-shaded table lamp, Woody now offered a black olive to Patrick, Anatole slumping, hand to stomach, into the white easy chair beside them like a frail shadow. "The only thing harmless in this world," Roger had once said—we'd been speaking enviously about Dickie's success with women, Roger had remarked gloomily that for him it would not be success but a catastrophe, and I'd said: "We're not talking about affairs, Roger, emotional engagements, just harmless anonymous sex," and he'd burst out in dry laughter, tears in the corners of his eyes, re-

peating my phrase—"is death." "And they . . . they showed him the photos . . ." Alison had just reappeared. She and her husband had joined Fats and Brenda at the body and were exchanging introductions, Brenda smiling and weeping at the same time, Fats rubbing his big nose, shaking his head sadly. "They want to . . . to talk to me now, Gerald. An interview, they said . . ."

"Yes, I'm sure . . ."

They all gazed down at Ros, their faces crinkling with pain at the sight. I felt my own cheeks pinching up around my nose. I was with Fats and Brenda the night they went to see *Lot's Wife:* they'd both stepped forward when the audience was invited up, and Ros had welcomed them to her body like old friends, their faces smoothed out then by a kind of glazed rapture. But theater, I thought, as the four of them raised their heads almost in unison, is *not* a communion service. No, a communion service may be theatrical, but to perceive theater as anything *other than* theater (I was talking to Alison now, she was smiling eagerly up at me, her auburn hair falling back from her slender throat) is to debase it. "So what did Michelle have to say?"

"What—?"

My wife sighed. "You were talking together when I—"

"Ah, yes, nothing—a dream she had . . ."

"I might have guessed." She touched her brow lightly with the back of her hand and, leaning slightly on her broom as though to steer herself by it, gazed off across the room. "Why is it that people always tell you their dreams, Gerald?"

"I don't know. Maybe they think I don't have any of my own." I tried to recapture the thought I'd just had about the debasement of theater, but to my annoyance I'd lost the thread. I didn't remember much of Michelle's dream either. "It was about being trapped in a movie house without exits."

"Did she have any clothes on?"

Alison's husband had left the room, but Dickie, Wilma, and others had joined the little group around Ros. Brenda, her jaws snapping vigorously at the gum, admired Dickie's white vest, showed off her pants suit. Alison looked around—for me, I felt sure—but her view was blocked (there was something I wanted to tell her about this, something I'd been thinking about all night) by Jim, who was talking quietly in the middle of the room with Howard and Noble's girlfriend. Jim rolled his sleeves down and buttoned them, lit a cigarette,

glanced up at me. "Listen, I really am sorry—but, well, I needed a moment to myself. You understand. Alone." My wife hooked her free arm in mine. I wanted to tell her about Tania, about the damaged "Ice Maiden" and Eileen's premonitions, Mark's headless soldiers, the blood on our bedsheets, what I'd found in the linen cupboard—but she seemed unusually fragile just at that moment, twisting her wedding ring on her finger as though to screw up her flagging courage, so what I said was: "Mark's fine . . ."

"Yes . . . He said you were playing monsters with Uncle Dolph and some silly lady who said he was little."

"Wilma, he meant."

"Was Dolph with Wilma?"

"No, but . . ."

"Peg said it wouldn't last. I guess she was right." She sighed. "I wish they were still together."

"You mean Wilma—?"

"Louise and Dolph."

"Ah." I had the peculiar sensation, briefly, that this conversation was both unlikely (Jim showed the tall cop the shard of glass he'd found: the officer shook his head and handed it back) and, word for word, one we'd just been having a few moments before. Of course, all conversations were encased in others, spoken and unspoken, I knew that. It was what gave them their true dimension, even as it made their referents recede. It was like something Alison had said to me about the play we were seeing that night we met—or rather, not about the play itself, but the play-within-the-play, in which the author's characters had taken on the names of the actors playing them ("self-consciousness reified," Alison had called it—or perhaps she'd been reading from the program notes: I watched her now as she scratched at something on the bare flesh of her chest between the silken halters of her dress, overseen approvingly by Dickie, Jim and the cop having parted between us like curtains) and then had improvised a sketch based on what had supposedly happened to them that day out in the so-called real world: "If that's what life is, Gerald, just a hall of mirrors," she'd mused, blowing lightly on her cup of intermission coffee, the tender V of her chin framed in ruffles and brown velvet like an Elizabethan courtier's, "then what are we doing out here in the lobby?" "I don't know," I said (Alison was laughing now at some remark of Dickie's—he was pointing at his own behind—and her husband, re-

joining them with drinks for Fats and Brenda, licked his fingers and smiled with them), "they never seemed very happy."

"Who, Yvonne and Woody?"

"No . . ." I realized that she had changed the subject and had just been telling me about Yvonne's crying jag, brought on by Earl Elstob's joke about the retired brassiere salesman who liked to keep a hand in the business (my wife said: the brassiere salesman who wanted to keep working but had already retired): "She couldn't stop, it just kept pouring out, so she'd gone running upstairs to be by herself, and she'd just reached the top when Vic hit her and knocked her right back down again."

"She seems almost to be seeking out her own catastrophes," I said, though I wasn't sure the line was my own. "Vic was upset about Sally Ann. I'm sure he meant no harm."

"That's what you always say." She tipped her head against my shoulder, the broom handle cradled in the crook of her far elbow, index fingers linked. She yawned. "But why did he want the fork?"

"Well, and Ros, too, of course."

"I feel I should know what you mean, Gerald," my wife said after a moment, lifting her head and unlatching her fingers to tug briefly at her bra strap, "but I don't."

The doorbell rang and the tall officer, unsnapping his holster, bobbed out into the hall. "I'll get it," I said, starting to disengage myself, but before I could move, a tall woman in a frilly black gown came swooping in like a huge bird, trailing feathery chiffon wisps, her hands clasped at her breast: one of Ros's actress friends, the one who'd played the Madame in the bordello play and Nancy Cock in *The Mother Goose Murders*, though she'd once been an opera singer. "I came over just as soon as I heard!" she cried breathlessly. "Where *is* she?"

"You mean Ros? She's—"

"Good God! I'd never have recognized her!" she gasped, staring in amazement at Yvonne on the couch. Yvonne, speechless for once and equally amazed, stared rigidly back as though into a mirror. "*Ros!* What have they *done* to you—?!" She threw herself on Yvonne, who now found her voice and used it for screaming blue murder, Jim dragging the woman off and redirecting her.

"*NOW she's broke the OTHER one!*"

"Easy, Yvonne. You're all right . . ."

"*Waahhh!*"

"*Ros, love! It's me, Regina!*" the woman wailed, pitching herself, arms outflung, through the people around the body (Fats' face was screwing up again as though to cry, and Brenda, gum in her teeth, was grimacing) and—though she seemed frantically to be trying to arrest herself in midair—on down on Ros: there was a windy rattling sound and Ros's head bounced up off the floor briefly, then hit it again, jaw sagging slackly at an angle. "*Oh Christ, no!!*" Regina rasped, stepping on her dress and tearing it in her haste to scramble to her feet. She looked around desperately and found herself staring at Anatole, slowly going green in the white chair, lips pulling back, his eyes agog with a horror reflecting her own. Then she clutched her mouth and ran teary-eyed out of the room: "Nobody *told* me she was *dead*—!" she gurgled as she passed.

"My goodness! Poor Regina!" my wife whispered, drawing closer. "I hope she makes it to the bathroom!" Ros lay wide-eyed and gaping as though frozen in perpetual astonishment, truer than any she could ever have play-acted, her limbs now disjointedly akimbo, her wound thick and dark between her breasts. "I just like to be looked at," she used to say. I could hear the sweet childish lilt in her voice. "Do you thing they're . . . they're simply going to leave her there . . . ?"

"No, Jim has called an ambulance," I said, a catch in my throat. Alison, following Regina's flight, had—as though cued by the folk music starting up softly around us—discovered me at last: the pained shock on her face gave way to a gentle sadness, and she turned to her husband and took his hand. I felt my own shoulders relax as, not unlike mockery, the stringed instruments behind me tensed and slackened. I gave my wife a little reassuring hug and said: "Don't worry, it'll be here soon."

"Sometimes I feel I hardly knew her. Ros, I mean. She seemed so obvious, there was always something so direct, so *immediate* about her—and yet . . ."

"Well, maybe that's all there was."

"How can you say that, Gerald? Even bare skin is a kind of mask . . ." Dickie, never one to patronize melodrama, had, even while Regina was still clawing the air helplessly in her grim descent, left the group around the body, but they were joined now by Noble and his girlfriend. Noble, fresh drink in his hand and cigarette dangling in his thick lips, seemed almost intentionally to scuff through

the chalked outlines as he wandered over, to kick at objects on the floor. "Don't you remember? *You* told me that the night we went to see that awful incest play about Jesus and his family."

"The Beatitudes, you mean . . ." She was right, of course, and it was true. Noble turned his glass upside down, making Brenda gasp, but nothing poured out; then he took a long slow drink.

"It's that kind of openness, *directness,* that's the hardest to understand, to really *know.*" Alison glanced up at me and seemed about to make some gesture or other (Noble had just turned his empty glass over, pouring what seemed like pitchers of whiskey out on Ros and the floor), but just then the tall officer returned, blocking my view of her, and told Anatole to get out of the easy chair. He was threatening him, or so it seemed, with a pair of scissors. Anatole grumbled but dragged himself weakly to his feet, and Brenda, watching him, said something that made Fats laugh and turn his head to watch. "It was what you said about amateurs and professionals, how it was easy to see how people *learned* their parts, but the mystery was the part that *wasn't* learned, the *innerness,* the—what did you call it?" Lloyd Draper clumped through in all his golden armor: "Time passes!" he called out with a kind of leaden cheerfulness. Reflexively I glanced again at my naked wrist, reminded of Alison's slender hand when I stripped her watch from it, that mischievous grin under her freckled nose (I was recalling my thoughts about blocked views now, the special chanciness of live theater, the uniqueness of each spectator's three-dimensional experience, the creative effort, as in life, to see past sight's limits, all those things I'd wanted to talk to her about), the taut excitement of her body as her finger circled my nipple, its pad brushing it lingeringly across the top, the nail in turn underscoring it as though to italicize it with some gentle ambivalent threat . . .

"Gerald . . . ?"

"Ah, the . . . the innateness?"

"Yes. What's in the sack?"

"I don't know, a bottle of something. Fats brought it." I handed it to her, and she peered inside, saying: "Fats? But I thought they'd already . . . ?" I had apparently missed seeing the short cop, Fred, leave the room, but he entered from the dining room now with a freshly made sandwich, just as his gimpy partner, tugging his cap brim down over his brow, went lurching out: they collided in the doorway, the sandwich popping out of Fred's hand onto the floor, and Bob,

backing up with his scissors uplifted like a sword, stepped in it with his short leg (there was distant applause: the folk album was a recording from a live theatrical performance), squirting catsup and mustard out over the carpet. I felt my wife wince as his foot came down. "I hope we have enough food," she murmured. Alison was distracted by Brenda and Anatole. "Everyone seems to have starved himself before coming tonight, and those two are the worst of all." Bob scraped the mess off his boot on the rung of a chair, as, out in the hall, the doorbell rang again.

"Oh no, not more . . . !"

"Maybe that's the ambulance."

"I've got everything for moussaka, I think. And I could fix some eggrolls and chicken wings . . ."

"Can I help clean up?" asked Naomi, rushing up with an ashtray full of cigarette butts and olive pits. She cast me a meaningful glance (I could hear new voices out in the hallway, loud and insistent, and there were quick bursts of light) and dropped the ashtray. "Woops!"

"Oh, Naomi! I just *cleaned* in here!"

"Honest, I'm all thumbs!" She squatted to gather up the litter, smiling at me and nodding toward Alison.

My wife knelt in front of her, reaching toward a little constellation of spilled pits ("You know, I think I'm beginning to like other people's parties better than my own," she sighed), then paused, her hand outstretched, sniffing curiously.

"I'll see who it is," I said, pulling away (someone was shouting: "As if it weren't bad enough—!"), just as Soapie, an old acquaintance of ours from the city newspaper, painstakingly seedy in his sweaty press hat, black horn-rimmed spectacles, tweed sports jacket and frayed tennis shoes, came striding in with his photographer Leonard: "There she is, Leonard! Beautiful! Looks like she's screaming or something! Don't miss that bottle of pills! Or—wow!—the pinking shears!" He greeted Woody and Patrick—"No, hold it! Just like that! Got it, Leonard?"—then waved at Noble, slapped Fats on his paunch ("Howzit goin', champ?" "Not so dusty, Soap . . ."), lit a smoke, watching Alison slip around behind Woody and Patrick, aimed Leonard at Brenda. "Holy moley, Yvonne!" he cried. "What kinda party games you been playing? Leonard, get a picture of that mess!"

"Get my good side, Leonard! The *back* one!"

Leonard, dipping and twisting, fired away, Soapie instructing. Some

ducked, some smiled painfully, others turned away as though to ig- nore the newsmen. Behind me, over the simple throbbing chords on the hi-fi, I could hear my wife laugh and say: "Darts! Goodness, Na- omi, I don't know which end you throw at the target!"

"Whoo-eee," exclaimed Soapie, rubbing his finger along a blotch on the wall and tasting it, as Leonard crouched for a shot, through legs, of the soles of Ros's feet, "this is the real stuff! Did she get it with her socks down like that?"

"No, she—"

"She just got a part in some new play, didn't she? I heard that somewhere—something about a rapist who turns out to be the Presi- dent or God or the Pope maybe, I forget which—"

"She said it was about a private eye who—"

"Yeah, you think there's any connection, Ger?"

"You mean with the murder?"

"Not likely, hunh? *Nothing* private about our gal Ros, right? I'll never forget that toyland musical where she was a limp puppet with strings tied to her bazongas, but nothing else! What was it—?"

"*The Naughty Dollies' Night*—"

"Right! Sensational! Just so long as she didn't have to act, eh? Why was she carting around all this junk, by the way?"

"Well, actually that's not—"

"I mean, like *pipe* cleaners? Wacko!" He scratched out a note, his cigarette between his teeth like a blowgun. "Best ever, though, was that pillar-of-salt thing—remember that, Leonard?"

Leonard licked the thick brush under his nose and rolled his eyes, then focused again on Yvonne, who, pulling some strands of stiff gray hair under her nose, said: "What would you say to a pillar of blood blisters, Leonard?"

"Yummy," Soapie remarked absently, watching Brenda put her arm around a wobbly Anatole, Howard trying to hide himself in the shad- ows of the drapes. Soapie picked up a fallen ashtray, stubbed his butt out in it, then tossed the ashtray over in a pile of swept-up debris, fished his pack out for another smoke. I saw we didn't have to worry about how to get the stains out in the white easy chair: they'd been cut out. "This where you found her?"

"No, more like . . ." Suddenly we were all looking around on the floor. "Here!" I said, pointing down to her chalk outline. It was al- most completely trampled away, a ghost drawing.

"Are you kidding?" argued Noble. "That's where I was standing."

"She was over—here!" said Wilma, pointing down at another outline, this one of Ros spread-eagled. "Here's the place!" Yvonne stretched round in her bindings, trying to see, winced, sat back hurt and frustrated. I was afraid she might start crying again. "Then what about this one?" Fats asked, standing over a third, and Lloyd Draper, disencumbered now of his timepieces, came in and, thumbs hooked in his red suspenders, pointed down at yet another, this one of Ros curled up, near the foot of Yvonne's couch. "Here's where she was, young fella, the poor thing."

Soon everyone was arguing about this, moving around the room from outline to outline as though on a guided tour, plumping for one chalk outline or another, even Dickie, winking at me and grinning around a toothpick, pointing at the place where Roger had knocked me down. "You can see the bloodstains here at the heart."

Yvonne reached out and took my hand, slipping something into it. "Listen, do me a favor, Gerry," she whispered ("So what, they've all got bloodstains!"): a small gold loop, an earring . . .

"Sure, Yvonne—"

"Whatever happens, just don't let them take me away!"

"But no one's—"

"Please?" She squeezed my hand, held it tight, her own hand trembling. "Promise?"

"Of course I promise. But nobody's going to—"

"I love you, Gerry," she whispered, while around us the argument raged on: "Her legs were together! Like this one!" "No, apart! Here!" "You *care* . . ."

"Do you like this one better, Leonard? Okay? Then, let's get started!" By a kind of vote, they'd chosen the one chalk drawing I knew to be impossible, for, until Roger had knocked it over running wild, our brass coffee table had stood there. Now, Soapie instructing, Fats, Woody, his cousin Noble, and Alison's husband began shifting the body. "*Easy—!*"

"Jesus, she's so fucking *cold!*" Noble complained, letting go and wiping his hands on his trousers, and Lloyd, patting him on the shoulder, took over for him. "That's right, old man," grumped Noble, "it's more in your line."

"Really? In a *swoon?*" his girlfriend asked, fingering her medallion, and Patrick, commanding a small group with his tale of Roger and the old hag, nodded gravely: "That's what he said."

"You've got it all wrong," Brenda butted in (she was clinging to

Anatole, or maybe holding him up), and Patrick went red, his eyes narrowing. "You always overdramatize, Patrick."

"By the way, Yvonne," I whispered, rubbing the little golden earring gently between my fingers (I'd just, averting my gaze from the resettling of poor Ros, caught a glimpse of Alison past the bent back of her husband: she'd also turned away and was now watching the tall police officer, Bob, scrape dried blood off the walls into little pillboxes, and I thought, captured once more by the illusion of pattern: What love shares with theater is the poetry of space . . .), "who's that woman who came with Noble? I missed her name when—"

"Who, Cynthia?" Yvonne hollered out, and the whole room seemed to stiffen. "With that one-eyed pig? Come *on*, Gerry, give the lady credit—that's my husband's new mistress!"

"Oh, I'm sorry—!"

"Sorry? What's to be sorry?" What had Tania said earlier about Yvonne? I should have been listening. The earring seemed to be dissolving between my fingers like a melting coin. "I mean, what the hell, you can't blame him—who wants to poke his little whangdoodle in me and catch a goddamn cancer?" Her voice was breaking. "Right, Soapie?"

"Right," replied Soapie absently, tipping his hat back and lighting up. "Okay, that looks terrific—don't worry about the stockings, just leave them down like that, it's a nice touch. So what do you think, Leonard?"

Yvonne had burst into tears again, and Cynthia, holding her hand, cradled her head against her stomach. "I'm so goddamn miserable, Cynthia!"

"I know. It's okay . . ."

"Reminds me of a sailor I once saw clapped in bilboo-boots," Lloyd Draper drawled, staring down his long lumpy nose from the foot of the couch.

"Hey, Ger!" Soapie called, arm outstretched. "Come over here a minute!"

"Iris and me were in Singapore at the time, thought bilboos had gone out of fashion, but nothing does really. Let an idea come into the world and you're stuck with it till the cows come home, seems like."

"You weren't here! You didn't see him! How do *you* know what he said?" Patrick cried, becoming a bit hysterical as Brenda linked her

plump fingers with Anatole's and smiled icily back at him, grinding her jaws.

Soapie guided me around behind Ros's body, then stepped back (something cracked under his sneakered foot, he kicked it aside: glass, it glittered) to peer at me through a frame made by his thumbs and index fingers: "That's it, Ger, just—no, turn a little to the right, *your* right!" While Soapie focused on me through his fingers (I tightened the ties on my rust-colored shirt which had fallen loose, the earring pressed to the hollow of my palm with two oily fingers), Leonard knelt behind my ankles shooting Ros's profile against the lights. "Okay, good—now where's your wife?"

Michelle, hands crossed at her shoulders and elbows tucked in, danced alone in the sunroom now, swaying trancelike to the whining nervous music. "I guess she's gone back to the—"

"That's okay, never mind." Soapie pulled Alison away from her husband to stand beside me. "Just need a warm body." Her husband went over to watch Leonard, who was setting up a tripod about fifteen feet away, the tall cop complaining: "Somebody has stepped on my X-ray unit . . . !" "I'm telling you, Patrick, I *know*. I was the one who sent that old lady *to* him! She's a welfare client of mine." Brenda popped her gum, Patrick bit his lip; Anatole, looking confused, gazed through both of them, letting himself be fondled. "No, not like tin soldiers—relax, you two! More like you're talking or joking about something!"

Woody started to slip away, but Soapie clutched his sleeve and guided him behind Alison, jostling her slightly, so that, having tried not to, we touched.

"Excuse me," I said, clearing my throat, but Alison was looking the other way: yes, the left one was missing.

"I feel so exposed," she muttered between her teeth, tugging at the green silk sash at her waist.

"Hey, Doc—?"

"I can see now why the old lady came away convinced that Roger had a goddamn screw loose!" Brenda laughed behind us, and Patrick hissed: "That's stupid!"

"Well, he wasn't stupid," Wilma said, "he certainly wasn't."

"Somebody's going to *pay* for this," the cop swore as he limped past us, and Anatole said: "Can I sit down again?"

Jim had come over and, directed by Soapie, had removed his jacket

once more and rolled up his shirtsleeves. He plugged the stethoscope into his ears, knelt down in front of Ros: "Like this?"

"You got it, Doc—but sit back so's you don't block the view! And here—let's open her up in front like you're listening to her heart or something."

"Jesus, Soapie! Do we need that?"

"Leonard needs it. Flesh keeps him awake. Besides, how else will all her fans recognize her?" Leonard pretended to doze off until the breast appeared, then perked up and started fiddling with his camera with jerky speeded-up motions. "Barfo! What did they ram in there, a steam drill?"

"It wasn't that large before," said Jim, glaring up at Bob, who was back with a miniature vacuum cleaner, sucking dust samples up through little filter papers from cuffs, hems, pockets, shoes: I closed my fist around the golden earring. "*Someone's* made it *worse*." His gray hair lifted and fell as Bob's vacuum sweeper passed over it.

I heard the thin rattle of applause again, as Soapie plumped up the shrunken breast by pulling the cloth tight under it: Michelle, alone in the sunroom, no longer danced but stood impaled as it were by her own trance, eyes closed, clutching her shoulders as though trying to hold herself in. "Okay, the rest of you people back there: step in closer, come on, crowd around—!"

"What? Are we having our picture taken?"

"Hey, leave a little room for ole Fats!"

"You know, it's curious," I murmured, "we've had that painting in the dining room hanging there for years, and only tonight did I notice for the first time that Susanna was wearing gold loops in her ears . . ."

Alison caught her breath, glanced up. "I've got to see you," she whispered, letting the hand between us curl around my thigh for a moment, as the others pushed up around us. I wanted to show her what I had in my hand (I was sure it was in there, though in fact I'd lost the feel of it), but we were ringed round with spectators. "As soon as this is over . . ."

"I look such a fright," Wilma was protesting, primping nervously at my shoulder. "But then I guess that's nothing new."

Photos, Tania believed (Soapie had pulled the shades off some lamps, bent others up to aim the light at us, using Cynthia and Alison's husband to hold the shades in position), did not preserve the

past, they only distorted it. Memory, left alone, even as it purged and invented, was always right. Photography could only be defended, she felt (I understood this, recalling the collection of old postcards my grandmother used to let me play with as a child), as a fantastic art form.

"Okay, we're getting there!" Soapie dropped his butt on the carpet, ground it out with his heel. "Why's it getting so cold in here?" Yvonne, left to herself, wanted to know. "Howard? Come out from behind those drapes! Don't be shy, press up in there—say, what's wrong with that kid?"

"He's not feeling so great, Soapie."

"Well, hold him up!"

"This reminds me of the time Archie took me to one of his high school reunions," Wilma said.

"I've told you, Patrick, they're yours," Woody was murmuring just behind my ear. "If you want them, take them. You're perfectly within your rights."

"Only I ended up in their group photo somehow and Archie didn't."

Bob came over, pulled a thermometer out of a hole in Ros's side I hadn't noticed before, and left the room, scowling at it. Alison had felt me flinch and now gave a little squeeze. "They couldn't get it into her behind," she whispered, "there was something in there. They had to punch a hole through to her liver."

"Ah . . ." Was this what I'd wanted to know?

Jim, sighing, put an adhesive strip on the hole and covered it with a loose tatter of her dress. "We oughta get Cyril and his goatee into this picture," somebody remarked, and Wilma said: "Did you know Peg had a tattoo?"

"Come *on* now, frenzied neighbors," Soapie called out, "let's show a little *life* there! We don't wanna make our readers have to guess which one's the victim!"

"A little red heart—right where you usually get your flu shots . . ."

"What's that about Cyril?"

"My old corpus delicious isn't good for much anymore, but—heh heh—if you need another bystander—"

"Not that badly, old-timer. But I tell you what, if you can find one of those cops for me—" Anatole burped ominously. "Woops! Hang on, kid! Are we ready, Leonard?"

"Who, Fiona—?"

Jim stood, unlocked his knees, and paced around in a little circle. "Foot went to sleep," he explained apologetically.

"Hold it, Leonard! Fats, stop crossing your eyes like that! You got no respect!"

"You mean the one with the big nose?"

"*Sshh!* She's around here somewhere!"

"Are you ready, Doc?"

"That's really hard to believe!"

"Whoa, look what's just blowed in! Get in here, gorgeous, and show these amateurs how it's done!" It was Regina, leaning in the doorway behind Leonard, gripping the doorjamb, looking drained as though she might have coldcreamed her face and just wiped it off. Her black hair and costume were limp, her lips still drooling. Slowly she lifted her head and found herself staring directly at Anatole, staring helplessly back. Briefly they reflected each other, gasping, eyes watering, hands sliding upward to clutch at their gaping mouths—then Anatole, swallowing hard against the bubbling sounds in his throat, lurched forward, falling over Ros's body (*"Unf!"* Jim grunted), picked himself up and staggered out of the room, hand to mouth, Regina having just, with a muffled gargle, preceded him. "Hey, you clowns, come *back* here!" exclaimed Soapie, his press hat flying, as Leonard struggled with his tipped camera, and Brenda asked: "Who *is* that boy anyhow?"

"Tania's nephew."

"Oh yeah?" She cracked her gum. "*Cute!*"

"Awright, just straighten the knees out where he hit her, Doc," Soapie shouted (I heard a hissed whisper: "*Bitch!*"), "we haven't got all night." I glanced into my hand: yes, it was still there. I held it between my fingertips, letting my palm air out, recalling the little magic shows I used to do for my grandmother with coins and cards and little balls. The trick, always, depended on distraction, a lesson, as it were, in the way the world worked. Lloyd Draper had returned meanwhile with the short cop in tow, Fred now carrying a big steaming slice of pizza in both hands, and Soapie, flicking away the cigarette he'd just lit up, pulled Fred over to join us around the body. "Here by the head maybe . . . yeah, that's—listen, gimme that garbage! Now, one step back . . . right, hold it! That's terrific!"

"Should I have my gun out maybe?"

"What do you think, Leonard?" Soapie asked around a mouthful of

pizza, his head cocked (behind the lights, the doorbell rang again), and Fats said: "Say, is there eats?"

"Yeah, all right, why not?" Soapie mused, handing the rest of Fred's drippy pizza to Leonard. Leonard folded it up and stuffed it all in his mouth, then wiped his hands on Yvonne's bindings ("Psst! Do me a favor, Leonard," she whispered, "go get me a drink!") and, oozing oily juices from under his scruffy clump of moustache, bent down (he bugged his eyes at her and winked: "Ah, you're a nut case, Leonard," she grumped) behind his viewfinder again. "Come on, let's get a hump on, Soap, while there's still some groceries left!" Fats whined, and Soapie said: "No, don't point that wart remover at the body, sarge! What kinda sense does *that* make? Aim it more toward Ger there!"

"Hey—!"

"I got the safety on," Fred assured me with a wink.

"Talbot! Come on in here! You can take the kid's place—make room for him there, Bren!"

"How 'bout if we move this tab in round the table and do a little *in*-terior *dec*-oratin' at the same time?" Fats suggested hopefully.

"At least you might tuck your shirt in," sniffed Wilma as Talbot wobbled over, a dippy smile on his face. He had his own jacket on, but the pants he was wearing now—agape at the waist and baggy at the ankles—were mine.

I glanced down at Alison, feeling vaguely apologetic, and caught her looking up at me. She blushed. "I was thinking about that play we saw," she whispered, "what you said that night about happy endings . . ."

Talbot, weaving blowzily in front of us and accompanied by a nimbus of sweat and bathpowder, belched. He seemed puzzled by the sight of Ros's body at his feet, Fred's upraised revolver. He braced himself on Jim's shoulder and lifted his feet high over Ros's body, as though straddling a fence. Alison, leaning back against me to make room, scratched furtively at the back of my thigh, her hair aglow with a light that was almost magical—except that it came from the lamp her husband, lost in the shadows behind it, was beaming at her. Talbot stumbled into our midst, peered blearily up at me. "Your can's leakin' all over the goddamn place," he announced loudly, and Patrick whispered: "*Now?*"

"It's as good a time as any," said Woody.

"Stinks, too."

"I know, I'm going to call a plumber, Talbot," I said, excited by Alison's hand, her pressing thigh, her toe on mine beneath the body: I squeezed the earring in my palm, recalling for some reason the wetness of that beggar's tongue as he stacked the coins. A kind of unappeasable hunger . . . "As soon as we're done here—"

"Oh yeah, the plumber. Met him on the stairs when I was comin' down."

"What?"

"Okay, lazy gents, let's watch the little birdie!"

"*Love* to! Pull it out there where we can see it, Talbot!"

"You saw a plumber—?"

"Cockadoodle-*doo!*"

"*Talbot*—!"

"That's putting your best halffoot forward, Talbot," Yvonne cawed, as Soapie went on, Leonard beginning to click away: "Come on, everybody halo around there, squeeze up—you're not paying attention, Ger! I've never seen you like this! Give us a hug or a smooch or something! Talbot's got the idea—what's the matter with the rest of you lot? This *is* a goddamn party, isn't it—Pat, where are you going?"

"I-I'll be right back—!"

"That's *disgusting*, Talbot!"

"Oh, it's not so bad," Brenda laughed, smacking her gum (Wilma, leaning toward Talbot in an effort to help him zip his spreading fly, had jostled us, and as I gripped Alison's buttock for support, she gasped and said: "I'll meet you by the cellar stairs!"), "but there's one over there that beats it!"

We turned to look at Earl Elstob, his hand in Michelle's blouse, an erection pushing his pants out in front of him like a plow—we all laughed, even Woody: a peculiar little barking noise—but I was wondering at the strange intense beauty of this charge between us, brief, sudden, even (we knew this, it lent poignancy, passion, to our furtive touches) ephemeral, yet at the same time somehow ageless: a cathectic brush, as it were, with eternity, numbing and profound . . .

"Don't laugh at him, it may be a tumor!"

"Terrific!" exclaimed Soapie as Leonard cranked and fired at us. "You got it now! Ha ha! Hold it!"

Fred, grinning over his shoulder at Elstob, had lowered his gun, but now he raised it again. "You'd be doing your little ball-and-chain a fa-

vor," he said, holding the smile for Soapie, but staring ominously at me, "if you told her to stop interfering with our investigation."

"Interfering?" Alison was stroking my finger as though trying to peel back a foreskin.

"How can you even *see* me, Soapie, past that wad on Talbot's ear?"

"Yeah, sweeping up, moving things, covering up the evidence—it can get her in a lotta trouble." I started to explain (Janny had appeared in the doorway, her pink skirt creased horizontally and makeup smeared, holding something up), but Woody was distracting the cop, muttering something in his ear about the protection of forensic evidence; to give him room (but I was thinking about my wife, how to get a message to her), I leaned toward Alison's breast. "He *what—?!*" roared Fred.

"I think Janny's got something for you," Talbot mumbled. I saw it now: the ice pick, my ascot knotted around the tip—in reflex, I jerked away from Alison. She too pulled back in alarm: "What—what's the matter?"

"Whoa! Hold the horses!" Soapie shouted. Janny was picking her way past the lights and camera, waggling the pick and ascot like a little flag. "Only a couple more!"

"No—!"

But it was Fred who broke up the picture-taking, leaping past us to smash Patrick in the face with the butt of his gun just as he was leaning into the pile of scattered criminalistic gear in the corner. *"Hey!"* Lamps tipped, Soapie shouted something at Leonard, Patrick screamed (*"[Not in here, Janny!]"* I mouthed, backing off), Fats seized the cop by his collar and pulled him away.

"A-a gift from my m-mother . . . !" Patrick bawled, his lip split, blood streaming from his nose and mouth as though a pipe had burst.

"Now, what'd you go and do that for?" Fats wanted to know, his big arm around Fred's throat (I'd managed to get several people between me and Janny, but she came on, smiling dimly, holding the pick high): then Bob came rocking in, cocked revolver in an extended two-handed grip, shouting: *"FREEZE!"* and Fats let go. "Awright, awright, I can take a hint . . ."

The two officers pried the tweezers out of Patrick's clenched fist, then dragged him out, still blubbering bloodily, Bob covering us with his revolver. "Stupid little nance," Noble grumbled in the doorway, watching them go, and we all relaxed: I was on the move again.

"*Here*, Gerry!" Janny called, circling wide around Ros's abandoned body in her stocking feet as I ducked behind Leonard. "We *found* it! It was under the *bed!*"

I scowled at her and shook my head, I was nearly at the door, but there she was, passing the pick on to me like a relay baton—what could I do? I grabbed it and tucked it inside my shirt. "Thanks! I-I was just looking for it!"

She smiled wanly, a little breathlessly, her face a blank (had someone put her up to this? I glanced over at Talbot: Wilma was fussing with his clothes and he grinned dopily at me over her bent back), then suddenly, spying something past my shoulder, she yanked me back against the wall, threw her arms around my neck, straddled my thigh, and kissed me, her greasy mouth yawning, in undisguised panic. "It's that horrible Earl Elstob," she breathed. "Stick your finger in me, Gerry—*quick!*"

"Eh, huh! Can I cut in?"

"Can't you see we're busy?" Janny panted, her thigh twitching mechanically between my legs as though pumping a treadle. "Well, nothing works like it used to, old-timer," Soapie was saying a few feet away, while across the room, Fats, giving Woody some money, seemed momentarily stunned: "Who, *Roger*—?" Janny's tongue dipped in and out of my ear like a swab. "You can't find his lower lip, Gerry!" she gasped. "It's like kissing only half a mouth! I felt like I was falling over the *edge* of something!"

Brenda was holding a little handkerchief of some kind to her nose, her eyes watering. She offered it to Howard ("I mean, French-kissing him is worse than painting a *ceiling*, Gerry!"), but he shrank back, Fats clutching her elbow in pained alarm: "They *killed* him, Bren!" "Oh *no!* Not Roger—!" And then, as they rushed out past Noble (the doorbell was ringing), someone on the stairs shouted down: "You the guy who lives here?" He was leaning over the railing to peer in at us in the living room, a bulky man in cap and overalls, monkey wrench in his fist, the name STEVE stitched over his pocket. There were new voices in the hallway, the slap and bang of doors.

I eased Janny away. "Yes . . . ?"

"Well, I can't do much with the stool, mister, I didn't bring the right tools—but it's easy to see what's fouling up your tub."

"The tub? But I didn't know it was—"

"Yeah, some poor broad just took her last drink in it."

"What?" I felt the pick slip, pinched it nervously against my ribs with my elbow. People were passing between us, greeting each other, pulling off wraps, asking about Ros ("In here!" one of them shouted, a woman in a yellow knit dress), there was a lot of confusion. "Who . . . ?" But I knew, yes, even before Anatole came tumbling down the stairs behind the plumber, wheyfaced and woebegone, I knew—and the others knew, too, knew something, for there was a sudden awestruck silence as at the raising of a baton. Even the comings and goings had stopped, the greetings, the music, the footsteps, the whisper of clothing against clothing had stopped. There was only, in another room somewhere, the solitary clink of a fork against a dish.

"*Uncle Howard!*" Anatole cried.

We all turned to look: Howard was in the middle of the room, alone, down on his plump haunches alongside Ros, his hand under her silvery skirt; he gaped back at us, aghast, seemingly transfixed there in an intersection of beamed lamps, his cracked spectacles aglitter with a confusion of tiny lights as though his eyes were bursting. "My god, what are you *doing*, Howard—?!" a woman asked.

His mouth worked but all that came out was a little squeak. A flush, seeming to rise from the well of his dangling tie, flooded up through his throat and into his cheeks, crept behind his eyes and into his scalp. "My, ah . . . tiepin!" he managed to stammer at last. "I . . . eh . . . dropped—"

"*It's Aunt Tania, Uncle Howard! She's dead!*"

A sudden spasm jerked Howard's lips back into a terrible clenched grin, the flush draining away as though some plug had been pulled—then he fainted and, anchored by the hand still locked in Ros's thighs, fell over her body, Leonard's flashgun popping.

There was a pause, then a rush for the stairs, people shouting, crying, swearing. The plumber, catching my eye as they clambered past him, shrugged apologetically. "Christ! When did all this happen?" somebody asked behind me, and Soapie said: "That's it, Leonard! That's our story!"

"We're not exactly sure, there's an Inspector here from Homicide trying to work it out now."

"Notch it!"

"Woody—?"

I stood, rooted in turmoil, clasping the ice pick to my breast like precious treasure and staring down at my feet, invaded by a fearful

sense of some kind of ultimate déjà vu. I was standing, I saw, in one of the police team's chalk drawings of Ros, the fetal one: what had Tania said about primal outlines? Life, she'd said (I seemed to see her again, kneeling at the tub, her arms scabbed with pink suds, peering at me over her pale turned shoulder as though to offer me something: love perhaps, or a vision of it), was nothing but a sequence of interlocking incarnations, an interminable effort to fill the unfillable outline. Yes, vague chalk drawings, that's what genetic codes were, the origin of life: questions with no answers, just endless inadequate guesses. Art, she believed, attempted to reproduce not the guesses, but the questions; this was how beauty differed from decoration—or indeed from truth, in her father's sense of the word—which was why Tania always claimed that, contrary to the common opinion, she was in fact a realist. But art was therefore dangerous: the heart of beauty was red-hot (she'd once tried, in that notorious self-portrait, to paint this heat directly) and it could burn your eyes out, sear your flesh away. Like she said tonight: "Something almost monstrous . . ."

"Jesus, did they both die like that?" someone asked behind me. "It's like a goddamn fairy tale!"

"No, you don't understand . . ."

"Gerald . . . ?"

I looked up, meeting my wife's gaze. There was, as always, a touch of worry in her eyes, a touch of uncertainty: even as she smiled it was there, though now she wasn't smiling. In her arms she carried a bundle of dirty clothes, and I saw that she had changed aprons again. This one was an icy blue with pink pears and yellow apples in it. "Where did everybody go?" Yvonne wanted to know. "Cynthia . . . ?" "It's Tania," I said, swallowing. "She's dead."

"I know." She turned to look at the people on the stairs, holding the soiled laundry in her arms like a gift received but still unopened. She shuddered and the sleeve of my bloodstained shirt dropped and wagged from her bundle like a spotted tail. "Can you get his finger out of there, Jim?" someone asked behind me. "I don't know, I think she's getting hard." She touched a hand to her brow, gazing past me: a towel uncoiled as though to slip away, a blue sock fell to the floor, someone's underwear, a handkerchief, all falling—I stopped to scoop it up for her. It lay scattered in and around Ros's outline like conjectural apprehensions of form, like Mark's drawings of Christmas trees (yes, I felt myself in a child's world down here, disassociated, unseen:

it slid out from under my shirt like a duty shed and I folded my soiled shorts around it): even a pillowcase: had she been changing the bedding? "Thank you, Gerald. I thought I'd do a load . . . before we got too far behind . . ."

"Whose handkerchief is this?" It was almost too filthy to pick up: I pinched it by one corner, dropped it loosely on top.

"His." She nodded back over her shoulder toward my study. Daffie had paused to speak to Anatole, now lying on the stairs, staring blankly out through the railings, and Noble, passing, whispered something in her ear. She threw her glass of pink gin at him. "Gerald, they've got Patrick in there now. I'm afraid."

I kissed her forehead, clasping a hand to each shoulder: "Don't worry, I'll go check on him," I said, and stepped by her, freeing myself from Ros's outline as I did so. "I *believe* it," someone said as I pressed through the jostle in the doorway toward the downstairs toilet (Daffie was rubbing her arm where Noble had struck her and she exchanged a commiserating glance with me), "but there's one goddamn thing I just don't understand . . ."

"Wait, don't go in there," Woody cautioned, touching my arm. "They're using it for a darkroom." He glanced back over his shoulder, just as Cynthia came out of my study. "Everything okay?"

She nodded, businesslike. "I loaned him my calculator, which should help, but he still has a long way to go." She handed Woody a gold watch which he pulled on, then she took his arm, looked up at me. "I'm sorry if we caused you any embarrassment in there—?"

"No, it was my—"

"How's Patrick?" Woody interrupted, placing a hand over hers, a hand stubbier than her own.

"You'd be surprised. He has a split lip, some bruises, he's going to be pretty sore—but I think he's fallen in love."

"Patrick—?" I couldn't help smiling, and she returned it: I thought of teachers I'd had, bank managers, a doctor who treated me once for trenchmouth in Rouen. A man in lilac and gray passed us, muttering something about "a good run" or "cut one." "I mean, is anyone noticing?" he asked.

"They discovered a set of photos of the girl—the victim—being raped by some man in disguise. It's true, I've seen a couple of them—they're pretty offensive, and there's even a dagger or something in one

of them. The only clue to the rapist's identity, it seems, is his exposed genitalia, so they're taking measurements, checking for peculiar marks, scars, circumcision, and so on, as you might expect." My smile was gone. She watched me serenely. "Anyway, when they took hold of your friend's member, it erected on them. This enraged one of the officers for some reason and he struck it with his nightstick. Quite firmly, I must say—you may have heard the scream."

"Aha," smiled Woody. The photos: had someone just been telling me . . . ?

"The Inspector reprimanded the officer and apologized to your friend, even patting him on the shoulder as he put his bruised organ away—then he returned the tweezers to him and with that the little fellow simply melted, started telling them everything he knows. When I left, it was something about a fabulously wealthy old woman who presumably came to Roger with what was a kind of parable about love and jealousy, if I understood it correctly."

"Close enough. I remember the day Roger came into the office with that stupid story," Woody said, shaking his head. "He was very talented, Roger. Sometimes, in a courtroom, he could be downright brilliant, an artist in his way. But he was too ego-centered ever to make a really good lawyer."

"I always had the feeling it was his *loss* of ego that got him into trouble," I said, recalling Tania's account of Roger concussed by love.

"Maybe." Woody pursed his lips like a skeptical prosecuting attorney confronting a dubious plea. It was almost as though he were preparing a case against his ex-partner. "But maybe ego *is* absence, that bottomless hole in the center that egomaniacs like Roger keep throwing themselves into."

Cynthia, on his arm, her gaze steady, seemed neutral, but there was something disquieting about her, too. Something odd. Now, fingering her medallion, she turned to Woody and said: "If we're going up to see the body, we should do it soon, before Yvonne starts missing us."

"I know—but first, damn it, there's something I have to . . ." He glanced toward the study, his face clouded, just as Fats and Brenda, in tears, holding each other up, came staggering out. "God, it's *awful*, Bren!" "I can't believe it! Did you see his *eyes*—?" "Gerry, listen, could you do me a small favor?"

"Sure, Woody, only first I—"

He laid a hand on my shoulder, leaned close. Through the doorway

into the dining room, I caught a glimpse of Alison with Dickie, his arm around her, both of them laughing—she didn't seem to see me. "Would you go in there with me? I'd really appreciate it . . ."

"Well . . ." I looked around. What was it my wife had wanted? Something from the freezer, a stepladder, fruit knife? I couldn't remember. There was a lot of activity on the stairs and I could feel it inside myself like a kind of abdominal turmoil. Alison, I saw, had both hands at her ear, her head tipped toward them—what? My hand was empty: *I must have dropped it!* Dickie smiled and she gave him a little kiss on his cheek. "I've got a lot to do, Woody—my wife . . ." Woody was gazing at me intently, as though through me, more than just an appeal somehow. "But, I suppose, if you really—"

"Thanks, Gerry. I knew I could count on you. We'll be right back, Cyn."

"That's right, it nearly slipped my mind," Cynthia said, as Woody pulled me away. "The police were talking about your wife. I'm not sure—I think they found something in the laundry."

"The laundry—! But I just left her!"

"Well, I don't know when," she called back over her shoulder.

"I really don't have much time, Woody," I insisted, though by now it was too late, we were already at my study door.

I blinked, drew back, bumping into Woody in the doorway. I was almost unable to believe what I saw in there. Everything had been turned inside out. The desk drawers and filing cabinets had been broken open and emptied out on the floor, books dumped from the shelves. The walls, seen only insubstantially through the haze of pipesmoke and shadows (the lamps had been moved about, it was hard even to get my bearings), were smeared now with what was no doubt blood, most of the pictures torn away so violently there were holes in the plaster. There were sketches of the crime pinned up in their stead, procedural charts and instructions, a diagram of what looked like an amusement-park maze. They'd set up a lot of strange equipment, turning the place into a kind of crime lab with test tubes and burners, sieves, calipers, inkpads and rollers, odd measuring gadgets—even now the tall cop, Bob, sat at a microscope holding up between his fingers what looked like a piece of bloody flesh—ah no, the swatch he'd cut out of our white easy chair . . . Fred, wearing translucent rubber gloves, worked at a hot plate. He seemed to

be boiling up some kind of soup. Photographs hung from strung-up lines like dance decorations, and brightly tagged objects—I saw knives, drinking glasses, an ax, swimming trunks, Mark's paintbox, knotted-up pantyhose, a tin of anchovies, pillboxes and specimen bottles, a black-striped croquet ball, a pink shoe—lined the swept-out bookshelves like museum exhibits. I had the feeling my whole house was reinventing itself. "What have you done—?!" I gasped, and Woody said: "Here he is."

Inspector Pardew looked up from his paperwork. He sat at my desk behind a heap of watches, calculator in hand and dead pipe in mouth, Patrick hunched nearby, hands between his legs, muttering something about "the woman in red." The Inspector looked me over carefully, passed a folded bill to Woody. "Very well."

"Let me know if you need any help, Gerry," Woody whispered in my ear. "We'll be upstairs."

"Hey, wait a minute, I thought you—!"

"*Here!* Just *look* at this!" Inspector Pardew commanded, holding up a little heart-shaped watch on a gold chain. In his other hand, I saw, he now held Alison's watch with its three opened buckles, the straps dangling from either side of its digital face like green plaited locks, the numbers blinking between them like a part. "I tell you, time is *not* a toy!"

"Actually, I was only, uh, passing by, I have to get back to—"

"It is *not* a mere *decoration!*"

"It certainly is *not!*" echoed Patrick, scowling at me like a judge. His mouth where Fred had hit him was puffed up and purple, and there was a big bloody gap just under his nose that made him look like he was metamorphosing into a frog or something. Woody was gone, vanished in that moment that Alison's watch had distracted me, and the short cop, tracking through the correspondence and check stubs, travel brochures, books, photos, and old newspaper clippings that littered the floor, had moved over between me and the door. He wore his rubber gloves still, white powder down his front. I seemed to have trouble thinking clearly, my mind confused by all this . . . this confusion.

"It is the very *content* and *shape* of the world," Pardew was saying. "Look! This one doesn't even have a *face!* It doesn't have *hands!* It's like a theater marquee, reflecting nothing but our pathetic *vanity!*"

Turning back to him, I now saw, past Fred's abandoned hot plate,

what I hadn't seen before: Roger, sprawled upside down in the far corner like a broken doll, limbs akimbo, legs listing against the walls as though he'd slid down from the ceiling, his right leg bent sideways at the knee, forming a kind of aleph of the whole. His face was smeared with blood, his hair matted with it, his eyes below the gaping mouth starting minstrellike from their sockets. I gaped my own mouth (I was thinking suddenly about Tania, what she'd said: "Like a new-born child . . . !") to suck in air. "Are you just—just *leaving* him there—?!"

"*Time*," Pardew was insisting, wagging the heart-shaped watch at me (I'd turned just in time to see him hurl Alison's watch behind him as though it were contaminating him: "It's a *mockery!* A *corruption!*"), "we're talking about *time!*" With a sweep of his other hand, his white silk scarf fluttering about his neck as though in awe and wonder, he indicated the glittering mound of watches on the desk, and it was then, noticing a heavy ring he wore with a large red stone in it, that I realized what it was that had seemed odd about Cynthia just now: her rings. She had been wearing four of them, all uncharacteristically ostentatious, on one hand, none on the other. "It's the *key* to it all, it *always* is, the key to *everything!*"

"Yes, pay attention, Gerald."

The Inspector sighed, sat back, nodded at Fred. "If you don't mind, please," he said to Patrick.

"But I haven't finished telling you about—!"

"I know, we'll discuss it later. Now I have to speak with this gentleman."

"But I'll be quiet! I won't be in the way! I *promise!*"

"Sergeant . . . ?"

"Please! Wait! My tweezers!" Patrick cried, fumbling in his pocket as Fred took his arm.

"I gave them back to you."

"Yes, but—" He fished them forth, thrust them at Pardew. There were tears welling up in his eyes. "There was a little silver chain—it's not *there* anymore!"

"Oh, I see. Well, you'll have to fill out a claim form," the Inspector said, his moustaches lifting and falling with a dismissive smile as he handed the tweezers back. Bob was stapling a tag to the patch from our easy chair. "We'll leave one with you before we go."

Patrick hesitated, tugged at by Fred in his dusty rubber gloves, then

plunged recklessly forward and planted a wet crimson kiss on Pardew's cheek. "Thank you!" he burbled, his split lip bleeding afresh, as Fred collared him. "You're so . . . so *kind!*"

The Inspector winced faintly, narrowing his eyes at Fred, and the policeman led Patrick away, still twittering and squeaking, holding himself as he hobbled along. "In the old days," Pardew muttered icily, "we used to strip perverts like that in the middle of winter and scourge them in the marketplace." He caught my frown and added: "Well, a long time ago, of course. That old gent was telling me . . ." He touched his cheek, glanced at his fingertips. "Do you perhaps have a handkerchief I could borrow?"

"Sure, here, I won't—"

"Thank you." He folded it into a little pad, dabbed at his cheek with it as though at a wound. "Your wife took mine. Said she'd wash it for me." Bob looked up at us from his microscope, lip between his teeth like a thought he might be chewing on, then (the alarm went off on one of the wristwatches in Pardew's heap: he located it, depressed the button that turned it off) bowed his head again. "Does your wife usually do the laundry during a party?"

"Sometimes. It depends. Why do you ask?"

He shrugged, staring at the stained handkerchief, then refolded it and applied it to his cheek again. "I'm interested in patterns. And the disruption of patterns. That's my job. I solve crimes. Do you understand?"

I nodded. I was trying to be civil, but his bluntness and cold piercing gaze made civility seem like evasion. I felt unfairly singled out, he at my desk, I before it as though at a dressing down, but when I turned away from him, there was only poor battered Roger staring back, the preoccupied cop at his microscope (he was working now with a piece of material from the heap of rumpled clothing at his feet, and as I watched him bend to his lens, I thought of my wife at the kitchen stove, lifting the pan lid to peer in at the boiling water—I realized I should have gone over right then and taken her in my arms, but the moment was gone, what had been done could not be undone— or rather, undone done—and I felt a flush of sorrow penetrate my chest, spread, pulsing, through my body, and leak away like time itself, like hope, like Being, that great necromantic illusion . . .), close-ups of Ros's corpse hanging from the line, the room upended and strewn with the debris of my dislodged past. What they'd done here re-

minded me of a line Ros once had to deliver in a film called *The Invasion of the Panty Snarfers*: "When they stuck their noses in, it felt like everything just changed its shape!" Pardew waited still. Watching. "I mean, patterns, and, uh, crime—murder—as . . . you know . . ." I was struggling. The Inspector narrowed his eyes: I supposed I was an open book. "A . . . disturbance of things, and so—"

"Not necessarily. On another scale, this party of yours is the true disturbance. Maybe all conventions are, all efforts at social intercourse." He sighed, and sighing, seemed more human. There was still a trace of blood on his cheek where Patrick had kissed him, but he'd ceased rubbing at it. "Since I was a child, I have been troubled by, let's call it the irrational, and have been trying to find an order, a logic, behind what is given to us as madness and disorder. That hidden commonality, you see. Well, I have been in homicide a very long time now, and I can tell you, the more I run into all the surface codes and structures—as we say in the business—that people invent for themselves, the more it seems to me that the one common invariant behind them all is, quite frankly, *murder itself!*"

I felt he was confiding in me and I smiled politely, hoping only to get out of here. What I'd thought was a maze, I saw now, was only a diagram of the brain, showing the consequences of injury to the various parts. "That's interesting, but I don't believe anyone here could possibly—"

"*What? What—?! You think I can't see what's going on here?*" he roared, bolting up out of his chair in a sudden rage that sent me staggering back a step. "I *live* in the *filth* of the world! I live at the *heart* of absolute *evil* and *degradation!* It's my *profession*, and certain things I am *good* at! I have an *eye* for them! Hatred, for example! No matter how deeply it is buried, I can *see* it! Lust, doubt, fear, greed: I can see these things like color painted on people's faces, washed into their movements, their words, and believe me, this place is *screaming* with it!"

"It—it's only a party—!" I protested.

"*Only!* Do you think I'm *blind?* You've got drug addicts here! You've got perverts, anarchists, pimps, and peeping toms! Adulterers! You've got dipsomaniacs! You've got whores, thugs, thieves, atheists, sodomists, and out-and-out lunatics! There isn't *anything* they wouldn't do!" He seemed almost to have grown. He was rigid, powerful—yet his hand was trembling as he picked up a piece of paper. "In this world,

nothing—*nothing*, I tell you—is ever wholly concealed! I *know* what's in their sick stinking hearts!"

"But—!"

"Look at this! It's a drawing of the murder scene! Only it was drawn *before the murder!* We can *prove* this! Somebody was planning this homicide all along! You see? Somebody here, *in this house!* Down to the *last vile detail*—except that they apparently meant to strike her in the womb instead of the breast—at least that must be the true *meaning* of the crime—you can see here the blood, the hideous weapon between her legs. There's the killer standing over her. *Gloating!* One interesting thing: he's bearded. That might be a clue or it might not, of course. It might be a disguise, for example, or some fantasy image of the self, a displacement of some kind . . ." He was calming some and, reluctant to stir him up again, I was tempted to let him have his "bearded murderer." But then he added: "And beside him, this horned figure, his diabolical accomplice, you might say, *his own evil conscience!*"—and I felt obliged to interrupt.

"I'm afraid that's the, uh, Holy Family."

"The what?" He looked pained, his eyes widening as he stared at me, as though I might have just grown horns myself and struck him.

"It's the Christmas scene. You know, the manger and all that. My son drew it for nursery school."

He slumped back into his chair, staring at the drawing in disbelief. "But—all this *blood*—!"

"There was a childbirth documentary on television the week before that we all watched. Not surprisingly, my son put the two things together. The 'weapon' is the baby and the 'killer's' the father, and that, eh, 'diabolical accomplice' is a cow."

The Inspector seemed momentarily deflated, his moustaches drooping, and I was sorry I had had to be the one to tell him. "It's terrible," he said. He turned the drawing over, applied a self-adhesive label to the back, and scribbled something on it. "It might be worse than I thought. Your son's name?"

"His—? Mark, of course, but—"

"Age?"

"He's four, almost five now, but he—"

"Did you or your wife ever have syphilis?"

"No!"

He handed the drawing to Bob, who asked: "Should we get stats?"

"Probably a good idea."

"Wait a minute! What are you—?"

"Now as regards the missus and her laundry," the Inspector continued icily, turning back to me. I watched Bob add a few notes of his own to the label on Mark's drawing, then put it on the shelf beside a crushed beer can and what looked like part of a truss. "She's been a busy little lady."

"Well . . ." It was a mistake, I sensed, to be too frank with this man. Yet, it was difficult to conceal anything from him either. "She likes things clean, if that's what you mean."

"I'm afraid it's not as simple as that. Let me show you something." He nodded Bob over. The policeman picked up some jockey shorts lying near his feet, brought them to Pardew. "She was just stuffing these into the washing machine when we stopped her. She pretended surprise, of course. Or perhaps she was really surprised. You can see that there is blood on them. Very close to that of the victim, I might say."

"Yes, but everybody—"

"And feces, which we haven't yet identified"—he sniffed meditatively—"as well as oil and alcohol stains, what might be lipstick, the usual. Or so we thought. But then, under the microscope, we discovered a fleck of old blue paint and a—"

"Blue?"

He smiled flickeringly. Bob, watching us, scratched out a note. "Mmm, or green, gray, something like that, and a touch of rust. Curious, isn't it? Of course, blood, paint, rust—just a pair of dirty shorts, you might say. But we found something else. Look: do you see that hole? Well! You'll agree, only one instrument could make a perforation like that! If we find the weapon that did it, we'll have our . . . our perpetrator . . ."

I knew there was something I should be doing, or saying (at my feet lay a photo of Ros on her back, dressed in a pith helmet and gunbelt, and sucking off a tiger that crouched over her, lapping at her sex with a huge rough tongue—how did we do that? I couldn't remember, but I did remember the one we shot with Ros as the tiger: that one scared me to this day . . .), but before I could get my thoughts in order (some vague sense of entrapment: I was trying to play back the recent exchanges), Fred came back in behind me with a fresh sandwich and Howard: "We caught him with his thumb in the old pud-

ding," Fred reported around a half-chewed mouthful, and the Inspector raised his brows at me as though to say: Haven't I just told you so?

Howard, sagging flabbily in Fred's grip—shirttails out, broken glasses hooked over one ear and the tip of his pink nose, thin gray-blond hair falling loosely over his brow like a lowered scrim—held his stained finger up in front of his nose, trying to focus his weak eyes on it. "Something . . . spesh . . . ," he mumbled and put it in his mouth. Fred clipped him ferociously behind the ears, kicked him in the belly as he hit the floor.

"Stop!" I protested. "You've got to understand—he just lost his *wife*—!"

Fred whirled round on me, whipping out his nightstick, sandwich clamped in his jaws, Bob unsnapped his holster, elbow crooked behind his back. "All right, all right," said Pardew, "that will do!" The cops eased up, their hunched shoulders dropping, backs straightening, though they continued to watch me with narrowed eyes. Howard gurgled miserably into the carpet at my feet, his horn-rimmed spectacles crushed once and for all beneath him. Poor Howard. I understood what the others could not: that there was nothing mischievous or prurient about what he had done, that for him it was simply a matter of aesthetic need. He was an art critic. A good one. He had to *know*.

On a signal from Pardew, Bob and Fred hauled Howard to his feet and dragged him, weak-kneed and drooling, over to their work area. "The important thing," the Inspector was saying, his finger in his nose, "is to keep your eyes open, to miss nothing, not just to look, but to *see*—true percipience is an art, but you must work at it, it's the first thing you learn in this game." He fished a long string of mucus from his nose like a snail from its shell and laid it in my handkerchief. His two assistants were taking caliper measurements of Howard's head and face. "I've solved crimes with my ears, my mouth, even my toes and the seat of my pants, but mostly I've solved them up here. In the old conk."

"Well, he's got the thick lips and swollen eyelids, all right," Fred was saying, putting the last of the sandwich in his mouth and mumbling around it, "but the hair's too thin and the jaw's not right."

"How about bumps?"

"It's a little like sorting out the grammar of a sentence," the Inspector went on. He was studying the string of mucus in my handkerchief. "You have the object there before you and evidence at least of the

verb." He folded the mucus into the handkerchief and handed it back to me. "But you have to reach back in time to locate the subject. I say, *locate*—"

"Ah, you can keep it, I have—"

"*Take it!*"

"What about the left one?" Bob was asking, and Fred, chewing, said: "Definitely different from the right."

"It—he is what I came in here to tell you about," I said, and wiped my hands on my shirt. Fred had grabbed a hank of Howard's hair and jerked his head forward: "Crikey, look! He's wearing somebody's flopper-stoppers!" "Fucking weirdo." Fred plucked a strand of hair, scraped some dirt from Howard's ear, made him spit on a glass slide, while Bob scratched away in a notepad, muttering to himself. "It's about his wife, you see—she's up in the bathtub, we just—"

"*One thing at a time!*" The Inspector rapped his briar pipe smartly against the ashtray. "*We're scientists here, not sightseers!*"

"Say, speaking of your old chamber of commerce," Fred put in over his shoulder (they had pulled Howard over to the inkpad and roller and were undoing his pants), "you got a real problem up there!"

"I know. There's a plumber—"

"Come on, apeshit, stand up straight!" Bob growled, kneeing Howard in the butt.

"Or *if* sightseers," the Inspector added thoughtfully, fitting the empty pipe into his mouth, "then sightseers of a very special kind."

"Pardon?"

"Is that a hernia scar?" Bob asked.

Fred leaned closer. "Looks like it."

"I mean, sightseers not of place, but of time." Pardew picked up some watches from the pile and began laying them out in single file. "We tend to think of time as something that passes by," he said around his pipe, "a kind of endless flow, like a river, coming out of nowhere and going into nowhere, with space the theater in which this drama of pure process is acted out, as it were." When he ran out of room on the desk, he added five or six watches at a forty-five degree angle to the last one, turning it into a kind of checkmark. "But what if it's the other way around? What if it's the world that's insubstantial, time the immovable stage for its ghostly oscillations? Eh?" The checkmark had become an arrow. From my perspective it was pointed from right to left.

"I'll tell you one thing," said Fred, "that ain't the one in the photos."

"And *if* it's a stage," the Inspector continued, picking up a large gold pocketwatch and pointing to its face, "*if* it's there in its entirety, the script all written, so to speak, a kind of cyclorama which seems to move only because we, like these hands here, move *through* it, then it should be possible, if we could just overcome our perceptual limitations, to visit any *part* of it, including the *no-longer* and the *not-yet!*" He was jabbing at these places on the watch, and it brought to mind a play Ros was in called *Vanished Days*, the one in which, having poisoned her husband, she descended the stairs to receive the news of his death. "This idea first came to me—and you can imagine the potential consequences for criminalistics!—when I was working on the case of the West Indian omphaloclast, wherein I ran into the problem of the exact—what are you smiling about?"

"I'm sorry. I was thinking of . . ."

"You wouldn't think it was funny if you'd been one of his victims!"

"No . . ." At the first rehearsal, she'd come bouncing down the stairs and crossed over to the guy who'd brought the news, reached into his pants, and given him a twist that had sent him yowling and stumbling into the wings. "No, no, Ros!" the director had shouted. "You're supposed to grab up the *clock* and wind it!" Or such at least was the legend. One of them. . . .

"He actually cut them out and *ate* the bloody things!" As though finding it distasteful, the Inspector took the cold pipe out of his mouth. "The point was, I couldn't pin down the exact moment when it happened. I could not even *imagine* it! One moment the knife was *outside* the flesh"—he demonstrated this, using his pipestem against his stomach—"and then it was *inside:* but what was that moment in between when it was *neither?*" I too could not imagine this. I could not even make the effort. Ros was wholly on my mind again, and I could recall only the poignancy of her hugs, the taut silkiness of the flesh around her own navel, the rich juicy flow that filled my mouth as her clitoris stabbed my tongue, and now (in another version, of course, it was not a clock, but—)— "*Stabbed!*" he cried. "What does it *mean?* If we say, he, the murderer, *is stabbing* her, there are at least twenty ways of verifying it, but if we say he . . ." I had started violently with his first word, thinking I must have been talking out loud, and now he watched me intently. "Is something—?"

"No! Sorry, I . . . I was just thinking about your idea of time . . ."
Trying to anyway. I couldn't seem to concentrate. The two policemen
were putting Howard's shoes back on. His crushed spectacles stared
up at me from the carpet beside a roadmap of Provence and a torn
zipper. "A stage, you said, a kind of space—like a fourth dimension—"

"Not fourth—*first!*"

"Yes, well, I mean the idea of events just being there, waiting for
us, like stations we keep pulling into—"

"That's correct. Crimes, for example . . ." He peered up at me
over his handlebar moustache and white silk scarf, his pate gleaming
in the subdued light. He had returned his pipe to the ashtray and
seemed to be shuffling watches like cards. We were alone, his two
assistants having hauled Howard from the room, feet first, like an old
sack. "*Murders* . . ."

"And—and their solutions." It was very quiet. Fred's soup bubbled.
Roger, fallen on his neck, stared at us vacantly. I lowered my voice.
"Or not: the failure to solve them. Also there waiting. Which would
make us just passive observers, and you seem, well . . . more *willful*
than that . . ."

"On the contrary. Will, free or otherwise, is just as much a hallucination as flowing time is, or change or meaning. Detectives, like
criminals, are born, not made, for even the social forces that might be
said to shape them are also part of their birthright. When we in the
trade speak, for example, of the 'perpetrator' of a crime, we are really
speaking not of this or that actor like some character in a play, but
rather of certain innate traits and tendencies borne by various individuals like seed, like wavelengths, like the properties of theorems—my
curiosity, for instance, or your solicitude and hedonism."

"I don't think that's—"

"Don't take offense. I'm merely trying to say that I am swept along
by the seeming restlessness of matter like everyone else. My investiga-
tive labors may define me, but they do not account for my success.
Indeed, my most famous solutions to crimes have come to me quite
unexpectedly, like gifts. Visions. I use science as a discipline, but only
to prepare myself as a vessel for intuition. This is the secret of all great
detective work, I might say, and the most important clues, therefore,
are not facts, but rather what you might call 'impressions of radiance'—
like my rather luminous apprehension here tonight of some unspeakable crime-within-a-crime, some dalliance, as it were—or so I feel—

with *oblivion itself!*" He watched me with that same close intensity as before, and I felt my mouth twitch involuntarily into a half-smile.

"But then—"

He looked away as though dismissing me, concentrating instead on his watches, enlarging upon his diagram: he was crossing his arrow now with a perpendicular row. "I don't know what it is that perceives these things. I don't feel any personal identity—any 'I' or 'me'—I feel simply that I stand at a crossroads on this map of time—that I *am* a crossroads, that we *all* are—do you follow?" He glanced up, transfixing me with the vehemence of his gaze. "I realize that it is not easy, that it takes an exceptional mind . . ." I chose not to contradict him, but as he returned to his display, sliding the watches from the arrow's leading edge into the middle, adding others to form a kind of field, fretted with straps and chains and buckles, I recalled a history teacher we once had who accused us of "attending to the head of the arrow to the neglect of its tail"—which at the time we all took as a dirty joke. "What I want—*all* I want, really—is to *see time!*" He hovered tensely above the field of watches, his hands outspread as though to scoop them all up, seeming almost to tremble with greed—and indeed they did give an illusion, all ticking, clicking, or pulsing away, of a plenitude. "Yes . . ." He concentrated on them, his eyes narrowing. "Now . . ." Beads of perspiration appeared on his brow and the top of his head. I, too, concentrated, afraid to move. "Eeny," he intoned gravely, his hands quivering rigidly in fiercely contested restraint, "meeny, miny . . ." He reached, as though through some dense magnetic storm, for a watch. "*Mo!*" My wife's.

"Hey, look, Leonard! It's our old buddy Nigel!" Soapie shouted from the doorway, blowing in like a sudden gale: the Inspector stiffened momentarily as though buffeted, then sat back, folding his arms. Fred and Bob, who had dragged Howard out, now dragged him in again: "Excuse us, Chief—they wanta restage this guy's examination so as to get some photos." Pardew, his brow damp, nodded his permission, watching Soapie warily as the reporter kicked through the papers on the floor in his tattered sneakers, picked up a Mexican rattle—a dried gourd that looked like a tattooed testicle—and shook it, peered into Bob's microscope, and sniffed specimen bottles, the two policemen meanwhile hauling Howard, his feet trailing behind him, over to the work area and opening him up again. Soapie tested a magnet out on a row of needles and probes, then on Leonard's crotch—Leonard

rolled his eyes, still firing away, his feet seeming to lift off the floor and fall back again—finally on the display of watches on the desk between Pardew and me. "What's old shortcake trying to palm off on you here, Ger?" Soapie laughed as a watch jumped to his magnet. He pocketed the watch and magnet and, admiring the photos hanging from the line, lit up a cigarette, Leonard's flashgun popping away the while like magnesium bubbles. "So whaddaya got, Nige? Who done it?"

"We have several leads," replied the Inspector frostily, "but we are still pursuing our inquiries."

"Yeah? Well, what about fatty here with the red tie and inky ding-dong?"

"What about him?"

"You know, abusing the habeas corpus like that, like maybe he was returning to what you might call the scene of the crime—and then, he's obviously banged to the bung—"

Inspector Pardew leaped to his feet. "We are not jumping to any half-baked conclusions! We are not peddling headlines here—we are seeking the *truth!*"

"Awright, awright, calm down—!"

"Holistic criminalistics *rejects* these narrow localized cause-and-effect fictions popularized by the media! Do you think that poor child in there died because of some arbitrary indeterminate and random act? Oh no, *nothing* in the *world* happens that way! It is just by such simple atavistic thinking that we fill our morgues and prisons, missing the point, solving nothing!" Pardew stormed about the room, waving his arms. Soapie whipped out his notebook. "Murder, like laughter, is a muscular solution of conflict, biologically substantial and inevitable, a psychologically imperative and, in the case of murder, death-dealing act that *must* be related to the *total ontological reality!*"

"Hold up, hold up!" cried Soapie, scribbling away frantically, hat tipped back and cigarette between his teeth. "Jesus! How do you spell 'interterminant'?"

"This death tonight was a violent but dynamically predetermined invasion of what we criminologists call a self-contained system of ritually proscribed behavior in which the parts are linked by implacable forces and the behavior of the whole is *precisely* defined by the laws of social etiology—and I *assure* you, we are *not* going to be pressured by any *hack scandalmongers* into abrogating our broader *responsibili-*

ties and jumping to unwarranted and even irrelevant parochial *conclusions!*"

"Whoa-ho-ho!" laughed Soapie, his pencil waggling frantically across the pad in his hand. "Violent total antilogical, uh, irreverent system . . . whew! I don't know what any of this malarkey's about, Nigel, by golly, but it should knock 'em out on the funny pages!" He dotted a few *i*'s, flicked his butt away, and, slapping his notebook shut, nodded at Leonard, who had been photographing the Inspector's bristly tirade through a foreground of test tubes and beakers. "C'mon, Leonard, let's go get a coupla skin shots of these impeccable faucets, and then have us something to eat. Ger's old lady puts out a handsome spread."

"Stick around," Fred urged, coming back in with Bob, the two of them having just dumped Howard outside the door, "this one's next!"

"Nah," grinned Soapie, winking at me. "He's old hat."

"*Those shameless egotistical frauds!*" shrieked the Inspector when the two newsmen had left, and then, in a fit of decompressed rage, he began to beat his head against the far wall. "*Filthy bloated mythomaniacs who feed like dogs off the excrement of their own vile lies!*" I thought this might be a good moment to slip away, but before I could make my move, the Inspector whirled around and cried: "*Seize him!*"

"No, *wait—!*" But they had already grabbed me, twisted my arm behind my back, and were highstepping me over to their work area, my feet barely touching the floor. "*Don't—!*"

"Easy, pal!"

"We don't want to have to get rough!"

The Inspector, who was striking his temples with his fists and groaning something about "dark fissures of the soul" and "massive spiritual deformity," now threw a sheaf of photographs on the table in front of me and, jabbing a tremulous finger at the erected penis that Ros, dressed as a telephone operator, was holding in her ear, cried: "Whose *is* that?!"

"I-I don't know," I stammered, mine being the one she was speaking into.

"And *that!!*" he demanded, pointing now at Ros's pumping fist in a photo of the *Pietà*, then at one of Little Miss Muffet with what looked like a lamb under her skirt: "And *this!!*"

"Actually, uh, that one's from a show, I believe—a publicity still— *The Mother Goo—*"

"*What are you trying to hide?*" he screamed, banging his fists on the table, making the photos fly.

Bob tightened his grip on my arm, Fred whipped out his nightstick. "*Nothing!*"

"Nothing? *Nothing?* Then how do you explain *this?!*" he cried, flinging a valentine onto the table.

"Where did you find that?" I gasped. It was one I had given my wife long ago—I recognized the "honeymoon hotel" with its heart-shaped shutters, a private joke: there'd been a heart-shaped hole in the door of the outhouse we'd had to use . . .

"Next to the body!"

"Ah, that must be the one Naomi—"

"We *know* what it is! Do you take us for *fools?* Do you *deny* you knew the victim?"

"Of course not! She's—"

"She's *dead!* I *know* that! But I need to know *how!* And *when!* Now for the last time: what have you *seen?* Eh? *What have you heard?*"

Bob tightened his grip again; Fred, still wearing the dusty rubber gloves, grabbed my belt with one hand, brought the nightstick crashing down on the table with the other—"*Dickie!*" I yelped. It was all I could think of. I could hardly breathe. I felt like I'd reflexed my testicles all the way into my ribcage. "Somebody said—!"

"Dickie?"

They eyed me narrowly. I felt betrayed by my own desperation, ashamed of the outburst. I swallowed. "Actually—"

"That the lily-dip in the white ducks?" grunted Bob behind my back.

"Yes," I squeaked, "but I only . . . Mrs. Trainer said—"

Fred shook his head. "Nothing there, Chief. We checked him out. Double on-tonder."

"*What—?!* More *lies?!*" I felt relief, even as Bob threw his free arm around my throat, half-strangling me. "I tell you, I can't *stand* lies! They turn our consciousness to *rot* and *putrefy the spirit!*" He waved a photo in front of my face of a round-helmeted cop being buggered by a masked superhero: "Now, who *is* that?"

Bob squeezed, arching my back, and all I could see was the ceiling. Fred, sucking in wind, drew his arm back. "I . . . I can *explain—!*"

"Explain? *Explain?!*" the Inspector raged. The ceiling seemed to be pulsating and a chemical pungency filled the air. "*Open him up!*"

"*No, just a minute!*" I gasped. I groped for my buckle—"In the end, Gerry," my father used to say, "we *reach* for the inevitable"—and Fred took his hand away. "I'll . . . I'll do it . . ."

They seemed to accept this. Fred lowered his stick. Bob loosened his grip slightly, though he kept his arm around me. "Awright," he growled, "*out with it!*"

The three of them pressed round, boxing me in. We were all breathing heavily. On the wall in front of me they'd tacked up their charts for spectrochemical analysis: they looked like indictments, columnar and menacing, with something penciled in across the top. I studied it without seeing it, my hands at my buckle. I might as well get it over with, I thought. Who knows, I might not even be recognized. But I didn't believe it. I felt betrayed somehow. A kind of inconsolable dismay swept over me, and a loneliness, as I reached, my eyes misting over (I'd had dreams like this: some final crowded-up demand, my will erased), for my zipper.

Bob and Fred backed off, laughing. The Inspector, too, relaxed, laid a restraining hand on mine. "That's all right," he said quietly. "We know it's not you. We showed your wife the photos and she said definitely not."

"We were just kidding," said Fred.

"Ah . . ." My heart was still in my throat. I wiped my eyes. The penciled-in notation on the chart read: "Never confuse the objective with the subjective sections of the protocol." It sounded like a line from a play.

"Naturally, we would appreciate any help you could give us," said Pardew, filling his pipe from a small saclike pouch. I settled back. I'd been standing on my toes all this time, and somehow this had added to my sense of isolation and vague nameless guilt.

Bob had limped away to switch off the lamp on the microscope, shutting down the show there, and now gathered up some little boxes, plastic bags, and tools. "Shall I knock the teeth out before we bag her up," he asked, "or save it till later?"

"Might as well do it now. What about the cast?"

"The stuff's ready," said Fred at the hot plate, stirring (I could hear music now, conversations, people shouting on the stairs: where had they been before?). "You want the whole chest or just—?"

"All of it." The Inspector tamped the tobacco into the bowl with his little finger. He seemed to be studying one of the odd inky prints

the cops had taken. I was still having trouble breathing, and I wasn't sure my knees were going to hold me: at such times I resented my gentility, yet understood that often as not it had spared me worse. "Be sure to get the angle of penetration."

"I'll help with that, Fred," said Bob, tucking his tools in his armpit.

"Careful, it's hot . . ."

"I want to thank you for coming in," Pardew said as they left. He settled his pipe in under his drooping moustaches (I heard a glass break, laughter, someone said: "Don't try to explain . . ."), fumbled in his pockets. "It's been good to have someone to talk to, someone who understands . . ."

"Well, I only—"

He smiled. "You've been more help than you know. Got a match?"

"No, sorry . . ." I slapped my ribs pointlessly.

He poked about the shelves, the worktable, finally lit his pipe from a Bunsen burner. I mopped my brow with the handkerchief I realized too late had been the one used by the Inspector, thinking (not for the first time at a party like this): I should make better use of my time than this. "Like all intellectual pursuits," he said around start-up puffs (there seemed to be a growing agitation outside, as though to set off the deep stillness here in my study), "this is a lonely and thankless profession, a daily encounter with depravity, cruelty, and sudden—"

Fred burst in, looking sweaty, his eyes popping: *They're trying to take the body away!* he cried, then rushed out again.

"*What—?!*" the Inspector roared, rearing up, his moustaches bristling.

"It's probably only the ambulance men," I offered, but he pushed me aside and strode out in the wake of his assistant, his fists clenched and jaws set, white scarf fluttering.

People—some of whom I didn't even know—were piling down the stairs, thumping out of the kitchen, rushing for the living room where there was a great commotion. "*Stop them!*" they cried. "*Oh my god!*" "He was using a hammer on her *mouth!*" In the middle of the room, two white-jacketed men and Jim were trying to lift Ros's body onto a stretcher, but the two police officers, grabbing a limb each, had engaged them in a kind of grisly tug-of-war. "*The Inspector*—grunt!—*says she stays!*"

"*Sorry, pal! We got orders!*"

"*Oof!*"

"*Do* something, Gerry! I can't *take* this!"

Talbot and Fats and some guy in a gray chalkstriped suit with a lilac shirt (he was familiar, I'd seen him somewhere before) were already trying to do something, struggling clumsily with the two policemen ("Talbot! You come out of there right this minute!" Wilma
fussed from the sidelines), and Pardew now stepped into the melee
on the other side, straddling one of Ros's arms (her hands were
wrapped now in plastic bags, I saw, her feet as well, and her front was
splotched with drying plaster as though someone had hit her with
a custard pie), a long finger jabbed at Jim's lapel: "I must warn you
that any further interference will be viewed as *a criminal breach of
the law!*"

"I'm *not* interfering, damn you, I'm *trying* to—"

But just then Vic strolled in ("Oh boy! look out!" squawked
Yvonne, "it's the Grim Raper!"), walked serenely up to Fred in time
to the dance tune playing on the hi-fi, and chopped him—*kthuck!*—
in the back of the neck: "*Yow!* Crikey, you didn't have to do *that!*"
Fred howled, crumpling.

Bob let go of the body, whipped out his revolver, backed off in a
crouch: "*Anybody move—!*"

Vic smiled, showing his teeth, then turned and walked nonchalantly
away toward the dining room, his back to the cop. It was so quiet you
could hear ice clinking somewhere in an empty glass. "Jeez," Fred
whimpered, all curled up on the floor, hands behind his head (Jim,
also ignoring the drawn weapon, knelt to examine his neck), "we're
only doing our job, for cripe's sake!"

"He's going to go too goddamned far if he doesn't watch out," Noble grumbled to Eileen, standing listlessly by. "What?" she asked absently, and picked up Vic's drink, which he'd left behind. Bob fired,
shattering the glass: Noble threw himself down heavily behind the
couch, and someone screamed, but Eileen seemed not to notice what
had happened, staring in bruised puzzlement at her dripping hand
and what was left of the glass. "Give that boy a silver dollar!" Yvonne
applauded from the couch, and Talbot in his drunken stupor (Wilma
seemed to be feeding him aspirin by the spoonful) joined in, slapping his hands together loosely like a trained seal. "I'm sorry," Eileen
said, and Fats, watching Bob warily, lit up a thick black cigar. "Or
maybe . . . maybe I'm not sorry . . ."

"Please," I urged, but no one seemed to be listening. I felt locked into one of Pardew's space-time configurations, where the only thing moving was my perception of it. The Inspector had knelt beside Jim and the injured officer (Jim was fitting him with a kind of neckbrace, using a pillow from the couch and attaching it with a woman's garter belt—might have been my wife's), and Bob, covering us with his gun, now loped over to join them, leaving the two ambulance men free to carry on with removing Ros's corpse. But even as they heaved the body onto the stretcher (so light: she seemed almost to float, her torso rising and falling airily), Regina appeared in the doorway with her friends Zack Quagg, the playwright-director, and the actor Malcolm Mee, Quagg with his famous purple cape pulled on over a white unitard, Malcolm in faded blue jeans and a striped sailor shirt. Quagg was normal enough (not that my wife thought so: once in a performance he had stepped down into the audience and slapped her face with a dead fish), but Mee always struck me as dangerously homicidal. Just the parts he tended to play maybe, but his cold glassy stare and the scar on his cheek always sent a chill down my spine. Regina, hand to mouth and face averted, was pointing across the room at Ros, long white finger quivering, and Quagg, following it, swept into the room, his eyes ablaze. "What kinda two-bit tank show *is* this?" he cried, shoving the ambulance men aside. "That's my *star!*"

"Hey, wait a minute—!"

"Get these greaseballs *outa* here!" Quagg yelled, swinging wildly, but before he could hit anything, Fats locked him in a bearhug: "Whoa! *Cool* it, Zack!"

"Whose company you *in*, Fats?" Quagg grunted, as Talbot staggered blearily away from Wilma and threw himself at everybody: Mee, his face icily deadpan, lashed out with a whistling left hook and knocked him cold. Anatole was there too now, thin and pale in his all-black get-up, Earl Elstob grinning stupidly at his elbow with his fists cocked. On the hi-fi, somebody was singing something about "needing someone to talk to," and I thought: maybe it would help if I just changed the record. "The doc wants her tucked away outa the lights, Zack—it's no *good* for her here!" Fats gasped around his cigar, and the woman in yellow came up and kicked him in the shins. "OW!"

I stepped forward to explain, somewhat disquieted by the odd sensation of walking through a grid of intersecting vectors, just as Bob

sprang up out of his half-crouch next to Fred, swinging the butt of his pistol: he'd have got me had not Ginger at that same moment crossed between us, wobbling on her high heels and holding the tattered remains of her costume together with both hands, and short-circuited the cop, who fell between her legs like trapped game. I ducked and they struck Anatole in their fall, propelling him into a scuffle between Mee and one of the ambulance men ("Stop that! Stop that!" I could hear Patrick shrieking over the uproar). Ginger, when she hit the carpet with Bob on her, squeaked airily as though getting her noise button squeezed, the officer cursing when his head knocked bonily on hers. "Yuh huh," said Earl Elstob, stumbling over Talbot, tangled up in Quagg's cape. Dolph wandered in sleepily, wearing one of my ski sweaters and opening a beer can: "Christ, what's been going *on* down here?" Leonard, who'd been taking cheesecake shots of Daffie straddling the back of an easy chair as though horsed over it, turned away to get one of Ginger with her eyes crossed, lips puckered, and skinny legs straight up in the air like spiky red signposts, Bob between them seemingly humping away, but really just trying, in vain, to get his short leg under him. Daffie slid off the chair, walked over (Noble from behind the couch was telling someone to shut up), and kicked the cop in the face, and his gun went off again, shooting the cigar out of Fats' mouth.

"*Wha—?!*" Fats exclaimed, feeling the bulb of his nose speculatively, and some guy in the doorway threw his hands up and whooped: "Hey, I like the *pitch!*" I recognized him: the actor who'd played the wind-up sergeant-major in Quagg's soft-core production of *The Naughty Dollies' Nightmare.* Gudrun the makeup artist and a plump actress in a toga and a pair of oversize rubber galoshes, worn like slapshoes, crowded up behind him. Knud's wife, Kitty, shouting something about official rape, had meanwhile leaped on the cop between Ginger's legs and was pulling on his ears, and now Earl Elstob, seemingly misreading everything, jumped on Kitty, pushing her skirt up. "Can you use some talent, Zack?" hollered the actor, as he elbowed in.

"Yeah," shouted Quagg, trying to wrest the stretcher grips away from the man in the lilac shirt, "but first get the word out, Jacko: Ros has been ragged! Go call Hoo-Sin and Vachel and get them over here! And anyone else you can think of!"

"I'll do it!" said Regina, appearing in the doorway at the actor's elbow, and, released, he came bounding over, eyes aglitter and a smile

on one side of his mouth—*"Ha ha! Hold up the exits!"* he howled—
and flung himself at the lilac-shirted man.

Brenda, bending over to drag Elstob off Kitty (she'd let go the
cop's ears and was struggling to keep her underpants on), suddenly
yelped, spun around, and laid into Patrick. *"You little creep!"* she
screamed, her fists flying.

"It wasn't me!" he blubbered, his split mouth bleeding anew, as
Dolph slipped away (I felt Alison near me again and wondered if she
understood, relative stranger here though she herself was, what was
happening, and if that was why she'd drawn close to me again), sipping beer. Mee, standing on Anatole's face ("Can't somebody *do*
something?" Wilma was wailing: Talbot was under there somewhere,
too), seemed to be strangling one of the ambulance men—the other
one had tackled Quagg and they had fallen over Ros, her plastic-
mittened extremities flopping, her face masked in chipped plaster
which bearded her throat and chest as well, and I felt (as a soft belly
pressed up against my buttocks) newly sorrowed: "It's almost sad,"
she used to say after oral sex, "that it tastes so good."

"That's enough!" someone cried. "You don't know what you're
doing!"

"Someone should go get Cyril!"

"Hold the bimbo down, Malcolm, while I—"

"Wait a minute! I—*unff!*—I got an idea!"

The word "crepitus" came to me just then, the word I'd been trying to recall since I'd first seen Yvonne on the landing (they were
talking about her now, the punch-up was slackening and there were
negotiations under way), and with it came a general sense of loss that
embraced Ros, Tania, Yvonne, my mother and grandmother, life itself in its fleeting brevity, its ruthless erosions. Yes, I thought as arms
encircled my waist, a hand slid under my shirt (Bob was getting to his
feet at last, using Ginger's legs for crutches, exposing the fat little red
purse between them: it was expanding and contracting rhythmically
like someone chewing), it's true: love is indeed, as a woman once
whispered to me (from our balcony we could hear mullahs in minarets
singing the sun down: the setting, coming back to me now like a fragrance in the air, was ripe for such sentiments), the tragic passion—not
for her reasons of course (she had just left her husband to spend a
strange, fleeting, but beautiful week with me in Istanbul, which was
perhaps, though I'd forgotten it until now, the most beautiful week

of my life), but because of its ultimate inadequacy: for all its magic, love was not, in this abrasive and crepitant world, enough. And was that, I wondered as one gentle hand caressed my nipple, the other burrowed below my belt (Ros had been abandoned and with her the free-for-all as well, people were picking themselves up, groaning, laughing—"Hoo-*eee!* that was a real dingdong!"—and the ambulance men, breathing heavily, had turned their attentions to Yvonne: "Sure, why not? They told us to—*whoof!*—pick up a body, but they—*gasp!*—didn't say which!"), the source of its strangely powerful appeal: its own tragic inadequacy? The question itself was resonant with passionate implications, tragic or otherwise, but even as I turned to share them (out of the corner of my eye I glimpsed my son Mark, one of my ski caps down around his ears, eating things off the floor, my mother-in-law dragging him over toward me, something clutched in her white fist), Yvonne cursing raucously, screaming for help, Jim distracted by his efforts to bring Talbot around, I realized that it was not vermouth I'd been smelling (Alison in fact was watching me from the dining room doorway, looking somewhat startled), but bubble gum. "Damn it, Sally Ann, this is no time for adolescent vamping!" I exclaimed, tearing her hands away. "People are hurt here! Your own father—!"

"Oh, crumbs, Gerry! Stop treating me like a child! I mean, I only want to make love with you—is that so awful?"

"I just won't have it!" my mother-in-law snapped, glaring at Sally Ann's hands on my belt. She held up the ice pick like a denunciation: "He was playing with *this!*"

"Ah—!"

"I'll take it," said Sally Ann quietly, dropping it in her shirt. There was a patch now over the breast pocket that said: "HANDS OFF UNLESS YOU MEAN BUSINESS." I glanced over at Alison, but she was watching the ambulance men, a pained look in her eyes.

"Where did it come from, Daddy?"

"I-I'm not sure . . ." Fred was turning round and round, trying to get used to his neckbrace; at his feet, the Inspector was tying a plastic bag around Ros's head. "Hey, man, what gig you working here?" Quagg wanted to know. "What's that you're eating, son?"

"Hormone tablets," my mother-in-law replied icily, speaking up to be heard over Yvonne's bawling as the ambulance men stretchered her away. "And before that it was some kind of *foot* ointment!"

"No, hey, I *like* it, it's *got* something!"

"Ow, what happened?" Talbot moaned, then coughed and gagged. Jim was holding something to his nose. "Who did I hit?"

"All you hit was that young man's fist with your silly face," sniffed Wilma. "And then the floor."

"Hard, though—right? *Hard!* Ooohh . . . !"

"Take another whiff of this," Jim said, and Talbot snorted and gagged again.

"*Gerry*—? Do something! *Help me!*" I caught just a glimpse of the terror on her stricken face ("You know what I hate most, Gerald?" my mother once exclaimed—maybe the expression on Yvonne's face had made me think of it—"What I really hate is *having a good time!*") as they squeezed her through the door into the hall, past the new arrivals pressing in. "Man, somebody really chewed up the scenery in here!" one of them said: Scarborough, Quagg's lugubrious baggy-eyed set designer. He looked around as though measuring the space.

"If this is a party, Daddy, why aren't there any balloons?"

"Yeah, there was some guy went crazy, Scar . . ."

"*I'll be good! I won't complain!*"

"I didn't realize it would hurt so much," Anatole whimpered, holding his mouth as though to keep his teeth from falling out.

"Here, try this, Mark," Sally Ann suggested, picking up one of the condoms Naomi had dropped earlier in the evening. Alison had vanished, and in her place Ginger was just wobbling out of the room on her high red heels, her pigtails bent askew, the cheeks of her narrow behind peeping out through gaps in her costume, looking carpet-burned, others drifting away as well.

"Whoo! After all that excitement, I think I'm gonna hafta go out back and—*wurp!*—table a motion!"

Mark puffed futilely into the condom, then handed it back to Sally Ann. "The hole's too big."

"*What—?!*" Brenda cried.

The tall cop was crawling around on his hands and knees. "I lost her goddamn teeth," he grumped.

"It's also fun to fill them up with water," Sally Ann whispered conspiratorially, "and drop them like bombs!" Mark grinned, his eyes lighting up under the woolly fringes of the ski cap, and my mother-in-law said: "That's not clean! It was on the floor!" She looked up at me accusingly. "Daddy, who's the lady in the bathtub?"

"No one, pal—now you get to bed." I took his hand and led him toward the door, Brenda crying behind me: "Oh no! My god, where's Fats? *Fats?!*" just as Yvonne in the hallway in front of us ("Last Year's Valentine" was playing on the hi-fi, a silly nostalgic song about time and loss, and it reminded me somehow of something Tania had once said to me about the way language distorts reality: "I know we can't survive without it, Gerry, probably we even need all those fictions of tense embedded in the goddamn grammar—but art's great task is to reconcile us to the true *human* time of *the eternal present*, which the child in us *knows* to be the *real* one!"—which was why, paradoxically, she had always defended abstraction as the quintessence of realism) cried: "*Woody—?!*"

"Fats said he was flyin' light," someone said. "I think he went to put on the nosebag."

"*Fats—?!*" Brenda cried, charging off toward the dining room. "You won't *believe* it!"

"Don't let them take me away, Woody! *Please!*"

Woody and Cynthia were standing on the stairs a step or two below the landing, holding hands in their underwear, Woody in stolid boxer shorts and ribbed undershirt, Cynthia in a heavily cross-strapped brassiere and old-fashioned umbrella-shaped lace drawers, seemingly stunned into a kind of grave compassionate silence. "*Cyn—?!* Christ all Jesus, *don't just stand there!*" There were tears in Cynthia's eyes now as she took Woody's stubby hand in both of hers (their heavy ornamentation made her hands now seem more overdressed than ever), sliding partway behind him and nuzzling her pale cheek against his bare dark-tufted shoulder. "*Help me! WOODY—?!*"

"Daddy, why is the lady all tied up? Did she do something bad—?"

"No, son, she—"

"*Gerry?!*" Yvonne wailed, spying me past the others, her eyes raw, her gray hair stringy and wild. She had grabbed onto the front doorjamb, and the ambulance men were now prying her hands loose. "Goddamn it, Gerry, you *promised—!*"

"I-I'll get Jim," I offered (and there was another thing about my mother: you could have anything she had, she was utterly unpossessive, thought of nothing in the world as exclusively her own—but she never, ever—this came to me now, and I felt, oddly as if for the first time, the unfairness of it—gave anyone any presents), but before I could let go of my son's hand, Charley Trainer came tumbling noisily

down the stairs, my bathrobe stretched tight around his flab, shouting: "*Whuzz happenin'? Whuzz goin' on downair?*"

"*Charley! It's me! Help!*" Yvonne bawled from the front porch even as the door swung shut behind her, her voice disappearing as though into a tunnel, and Charley yelled: "*Hole on, Yvonne! God-DAMN it! Ole Chooch is comin'!*" But his knees started to cave about halfway down to the landing and there was no negotiating the right-angle turn there—Woody and Cynthia ducked, clinging to each other, as he went hurtling past behind them, smacking the banister with his soft belly and somersaulting on over the railing to the floor below: "*Pp-FOOOFF!*" he wheezed mightily as he landed on his back (I'd managed to jerk Mark out of the way just in time), bathrobe gaping and big soft genitals bouncing between his fat legs as through hurling them to the floor had been his whole intent. "Ohh, shit!" he gasped (Mark was laughing and clapping, my wife's mother shushing him peevishly), lying there pale and, except for the aftershock vibrations still rippling through his flaccid abdomen, utterly prostrate: "*Now wha've I done . . . ?!*"

"Careful, just lie still a moment," Jim cautioned, kneeling by his side and palpating gently his neck and collarbone, while above them Cynthia was saying (Woody seemed to be putting yet another ring on one of her fingers): "Woody, you shouldn't . . ."

"Who the hell was runnin' innerference?" Charley groaned, as Jim reached under and ran his hand slowly down his broad back.

The phone rang, but as I turned to answer it, Fats and Brenda, tears streaming down their cheeks, came blundering through from the dining room, making us all fall back. "Oh my *god*, Brenda," Fats, stuffing the last half of a cheese-dog in his jaws, cried as he stumbled over Charley's upturned feet ("Unf! Get his goddamn nummer, coach!"), "this is too *much!* Not *Tania*—!" And then, picking himself up, he staggered on up the stairs behind her, Woody and Cynthia pressing up against the banister to let them by. "Yeah," somebody was saying into the phone ("Woops! Damn!" Woody muttered as the ring slipped through the railings and hit the floor near Charley—"Gerry, could you pass that up to me?"), "it's Ros! A cold curtain, man—that's it, gone dark! You comin' over?"

"Hey, Ger," Charley moaned softly as I dug under his ear for the ring: it was elaborately worked with a heavy stone, somehow familiar, "I'm in trouble."

"Right, Hoo-Sin's already here—just this minute walkin' on," the guy on the phone was saying, out of sight now behind all the people gathering around, concerned about Charley, who still lay flat out, motionless, my bathrobe twisted around his thick torso like a bit of rind. "Is it his heart?"

"Has to be—he's *all* heart, ole Chooch . . ."

"But I don't *wanna* go! I wanna see Unca Charley do it again!"

"And Gudrun, Prissy Loo, the Scar . . ."

"You'll be okay, Charley," I said, handing the ring up to Woody ("Great—and bring Benedetto," said the guy on the phone, "we'll *need* a groaner!"), "Jim's here, he—"

"Naw, I mean—didn' Tall-butt tell ya?" He was nearly crying, his eyes puffy, his nose purple. "I juss found out . . . the reason ya can't take it with ya . . ."

"Ah," said Jim, pausing thoughtfully in his trek down Charley's spine.

". . . Is cuz *it* dies before *you* do!"

"He's got a slipped disc," Jim said. "We need to double his knees back and see if we can pop it back in place." "Oh my! let *me* help!" exclaimed Patrick, getting a laugh, just as Lloyd Draper stepped up and remarked down his nose: "See here now, looks like you've had a little tumble, young fella!"

"Since Ros died, Ger, I juss can't . . . can't . . ."

"For goodness' sake, Charley!" cried his wife, Janice, padding in breathlessly, zipping up the side of her pink skirt. "What have you been doing—trying to fly again?"

"Yeah," he mumbled, winking at me through his tears ("Ros is the only one," he used to say while reproaching himself, with that comical hangdog look in his eyes, for his clumsy haste and artlessness in lovemaking—"The nicest thing about Charley," Janice liked to say, "is that there's none of that wham-bam-thank-you-ma'am stuff with him—it's always quicker than that!"—"who's ever *thanked* me after . . ."), "I awmoss had it there f'ra minute!"

"Hey, everybody!" Janny cried, bouncing up and down. "Let's hear it for Choo-Choo Trainer!" She hiked her skirt and dropped into her cheerleader's squat, one arm out stiffly in front of her, the other cocked behind, and slowly, as Patrick and Jim took a grip on Charley's fat knees, got the old school locomotive going again. "*CHOO-oo-oo!*" Pause. "*CHOO-oo-oo!*" Yes, I thought as I watched Jim and Patrick,

grunting, press Charley's knees back against his chest, the crowd in the hall all joining Janny now as she started to get up steam—"Come on, everybody! *Choo-oo! Choo-oo!* That's it! *Choo-oo! Choo-oo!*"—time may or may not be passing, who's to say, but, damn it, *something* is. "*Choo! Choo! Choo! Choo!*" Above us, Woody and Cynthia were kissing now, Woody holding her hips firmly yet somehow chastely in his square hairy hands, her hands resting on his shoulders as though knighting him with all her rings and bangles, and though there was an undeniable tenderness in their embrace and even a certain touching vulnerability in the plainness of their underwear, the neatness of their carefully combed hair, the very narrowness of the step on which they stood, there above the chugging Choo-Choo Trainer locomotive—"*CHOO-choo! CHOO-choo! CHOO-choo! CHOO-choo!*"—Charley himself now out of sight behind his upraised rump, Dolph helping out, lending his weight—"*CHOO-choo-CHOO-choo! CHOO-choo-CHOO-choo!*"—there was also something disturbing, almost shocking, about their imperturbable composure as they kissed so discreetly, so properly, that seemed suddenly to make Ros's death (*Oh! Oh! oh!* I was thinking to the cheer's beat, *what have we lost—?!*) all the more poignant and immediate, and I might well have started to get, joining red-nosed Charley, truly maudlin, had I not spied Naomi's cock sock on Alison's middle finger, beckoning me from the dining room doorway. "*CHOO-choo-CHOO-choo CHOO-CHOO-CHOO-CHOO!*" the crowd roared, Janny's arm working like a flying piston. "Oh god, it hurts!" Charley cried, farting explosively ("Naughty boy!" exclaimed Patrick to everyone's delight)—and then in the sudden momentary silence that followed there was a hollow *KRR-POP!*, a burst of cheers and laughter, and from Charley as they lowered his mass to the floor and covered him up with the robe, a grateful "Oh, yeah . . . !" "*WHEE-EE-EE-ee-oo-OO-OO!*" the crowd shrilled in imitation of a train whistle, as Janny spun around then dropped into a still fairly passable split: "*CHOO-CHOO TRAINER!*"

While the crowd around Charley whistled and clapped, I slipped away toward the back, nearly bumping into Steve the plumber coming up from the basement with a big monkey wrench in his hand. "Hold on, hold on!" Inspector Pardew demanded behind me. "Is that someone having a game of darts down there?"

"A couple of women, sir," said Steve, "if you can call it a game."

"Hey, there," breathed Alison ("One of them's probably her, all

right," Bob was saying in back of me, while at our feet, Anatole, squatting down, asked: "You all right, Uncle Howard?"), "I've been looking for you, Superlover!"

"Ah, that must be my son you want."

"I assumed it ran in the family." The crowd around Charley was breaking up, many of them headed past us into the dining room ("No, no, no, no, *no!*" Howard blurted out petulantly, as though waking suddenly from a bad dream, or perhaps just talking in his sleep—Iris Draper was there, trying to feed him some soup), where Jim's wife Mavis was holding court, seemingly her old self once more. I could see people slipping in and out of the TV room with big grins on their faces and pausing, as they passed, to hear what Mavis had to say. Soapie was filling a brown bag with food from the table.

"Hey, Prissy Loo! I thought you took the veil!"

"No, some guy held me in escrow a while, that's all. Where'd you find the bug broth?"

"Yup," said Bob. "We're all set up for her."

"In here, there's buckets of it . . ."

Alison drilled my chest with her stiffened peckersweatered finger, parodying recruitment posters: "I want *you*, Gerald!" she declared throatily, clutching my belt with her free hand and knocking her pubes on mine. Which seemed to set off the phone: Regina answered it, Pardew saying: "Very well, you'd best get on with it then." "It's *show* time, Mister Bones! When do we open?"

"As soon as we can get off centerstage." I lifted the pointing finger to my mouth to tongue the base of it, under the sweater. I realized it had the same pattern as one of my ski caps. She spread her fingers and her breasts rose and fell in their silk pockets, as her eyes, sparkling, searched mine. "Hey, what's goin' down here, Vagina?" cried someone, banging in through the front door behind us, his voice small and squeaky. "Show me the card!" "In the living room, Vachel! It's Ros!" "Ros—?" "Only one problem," I murmured through her fingers, "I have to use the bathroom so badly my teeth are chiming!"

"Me, too," she admitted, letting go my belt to give her crotch a demonstrative little squeeze, "but they've turned this one into a darkroom, and upstairs . . ."

"Hey, that's cute," said Soapie, taking the sock off Alison's finger and peeking inside, then handing it back. "I could use one of those to keep my pencils warm." He was cradling a greasy paper sack full of

food and an unopened bottle of scotch. Alison had curled round under my far arm, and now ran her hand up my back under my shirt ("*We can go out back,*" I whispered: "*Yes, let's!*" she urged), as Soapie poked his nose down the basement steps and asked: "What's going on down below, d'you suppose?"

But we were already away, slipping through the kitchen door, Alison snatching up some paper cocktail napkins en route ("I always like something to read," she smiled), Woody saying something as we passed about "a lesson." "Yeah? Don't you believe it!" growled Vic, as the door whumped to behind us.

The kitchen seemed closed down for the night: things put away, counters clean, lights off and the room in shadows except for the night-light on the oven and the fluorescent over the butcherblock table, pots and pans hung up, appliances set back under the cabinets. "Your wife's such a great housekeeper," Alison said, still whispering. "I really envy her!" "Well, this is a bit unusual," I allowed. The general tidiness of the place was marred somewhat by the muddy tracks in and out of the back door: we were not the first, it seemed, to think of using the backyard. Also, now that I looked more closely, I could see that there was a pot simmering on a burner in the shadows, something cooking in the oven, some boiled eggs cooling on the counter near the sink, knives and tools laid out on the butcherblock, an apron—oilcloth, imprinted with foreign baggage stickers—draped over the breakfast bench. "It's strange," Alison murmured, turning to me as I paused, touched by some distant memory (but not of my wife, no—waiting for Ros in the wings during a performance of that toyland play, the toybox spotlit centerstage into which the other toys were all vanishing, Ros left on the floor outside, arms akimbo, as though forgotten . . .), "but I feel as though I were standing at some crossroads—or, rather, that I *am* a crossroads in some odd way, through which the world is passing. Does that sound silly?" She put her arms around my neck. "No." I took her small silken waist in my hands. Blinking, she tongued her lips, which seemed to have swollen. There was a soft blush on her skin, a warm fragrance, and her breath came in quick little gasps. "In fact, it's funny, but I was just thinking . . ." I let my hands slide down over her hips—then took them away again as her husband came in through the door behind her.

"Ah!" I said and cleared my throat. "We were just, eh . . ."

"You've found your earring," he said tersely, ignoring me.

"Yes, that nice man in the white pants discovered it for me," she replied, turning dreamily toward him. "On the living room floor—wasn't that lucky?" She smiled, touching the earring as though to show it to him, her free hand slipping into my back pocket to scratch subtly at my buttock, as though to sign her name there. "We're just going out for some fresh air."

"Yes, of course," he said with an abrupt pinched smile, glancing at me, then away again. He seemed to want to look back over his shoulder, but restrained himself, pushing his hands into his jacket pockets, biting briefly at his beard. "Watch where you step," he added as he marched past us.

Alison took my hand and pulled me out into the darkness of the back porch. "*Hurry—!*" She tore my wrap-tie shirt open, flung her arms around my bare back. "*Kiss me!*" she begged, pulling herself upward to meet my mouth with hers. Her mouth was open, her tongue pushing between my teeth as though to mate there, her perfumed breath mingling with the nostalgic country odors of the backyard and the sweet scents seeping up from within her dress. I clutched her body tight to mine—it was the right thing to do, I knew, the timing perfect!—and kissed her eyes, her cheeks, her mouth, her throat, my hands burrowing up under the whispering charmeuse skirt, childhood memories of camping trips, midnight hikes, forest dew, Inspiration Points filling my mind (it was a damp night, chilly, dense), and, her sash loosening, down into her tights. "*Oh Gerald!*" she gasped (her flesh down there was cool, sleek, so smooth it felt powdered, maybe it was, the fluff between her wriggling cheeks as soft as swansdown), jamming her hands inside my waistband, trying to, finally in frustration scrabbling frantically over the outside of my trousers ("No more rehearsals, Superlover," I seemed to hear her say, "I want climax, *I want the weenie!*"—but her mouth was pressed on mine), digging, fumbling for openings. I slid one hand around the curve of her hip onto her soft belly, and down into the damp velvety thatch between her thighs which heaved up to meet it, her legs spreading as in my mind's eye (and thus in truth! in truth!) they'd been spreading since the night we met. Yet even bare skin is a kind of mask, I thought wistfully, pushing deeper, my fingertips meeting, fore and aft, in the syrupy depths of her amazing furrow, maybe in fact it was something she had said that night during intermission: that desperate but futile

effort (but I was trying, I was trying) to touch what can never be touched. I had suggested that night that theater, like all art, was a kind of hallucination at the service of reality, and that full apprecia-tion of it required total abject surrender—like religion. "Yes," she'd said, setting her coffee cup down. "Or love . . ." "*Oh fuck!*" she whimpered now, tearing wildly at my trousers, clawing my back, tug-ging at my testicles, while thrusting violently (it was, yes, this incredi-ble impression of wholeness, this impression of radiance, of universal truth, the seeming apprehension of it, that surrender made possible, I thought, almost unable to think at all, unable to breathe—what had I just said?) into the little orifice I'd created with my two fingers and the bent knuckle of my thumb—"*You're the most beautiful man I've ever met!*" "Alison—!" I groaned, pushing deeper from behind. "(*Gasp!*) A *little* . . . *more*—!"

Someone squeezed my hand and I jerked it away. It was Dickie, his white suit glowing spectrally in the dim light. "Wondered what she was growing back there," he said, lifting Alison's skirt to peer closer, playing the heckler, the hick in the gallery. "Anyhow, I'm glad to see that, as an artist, Ger, you've got a good grasp of your subject." He slapped her behind as though blessing it. I started to squeak out some-thing, something stupid probably, but he had already turned away. "Hey, Hot Pot!" he laughed, stepping down off the porch. "Whad-daya say we go get some grass stains back behind the bushes!"

"It's filthy back there," Sally Ann retorted. "Like you, you creep!"

"Gerald," Alison gasped hoarsely—she lay collapsed against my chest now, breathing deeply, my arms around her shoulders, hers around my hips, "where can we go?"

"I'll have to think. They've taken over my study and—"

"How about the green room upstairs?"

"Green room?" I was still struggling to find my voice. I felt weirdly suspended, not quite outside time but not in it either.

"Where you kissed me . . ."

"Yes, the sewing room, okay . . ." Sally Ann stood nearby, star-ing—or probably staring, it was hard to tell—seemingly taken aback at finding us here, and I worried that if we didn't move, she wouldn't. "But first . . ." I unlocked my arms (a titter of laughter floated out and I noticed again the chill in the air) and led Alison down off the porch—we were both a bit unsteady, our bodies still making moves of their own, our legs more or less elsewhere.

· 153 ·

"Woops!"

"Steady now!"

It was a little brighter in the yard, lit up from inside, and I saw that her dress hem was caught in her tights: I pulled it out, smoothed it down, reveling (I don't like silk) in the feel of silk, and she cuddled closer. "Can I hold it for you, Gerald?" "Sure." Anyway, she already was, leaning on it like a cane. A swaggerstick. If she'd let go, she'd probably have fallen down. There were others out here, whispering, chatting quietly back in the bushes, grunting, and I felt once more— though not so intensely as a moment ago with my hands between Alison's legs—that nostalgic flush of country memories: campouts, bike hikes, an all-night picnic back in college (the girl who'd held it for me that night had stupidly pinched it, trying, she'd claimed, to dot an *i*), sweet harvest evenings along the Rhine and the Douro, our Alpine honeymoon, star-gazing with my father at my grandmother's place ("Look, Gerry! there by the Fishes: the Chained Lady!"): there even seemed to be a fragrance of apples in the air.

I led Alison over toward a shadowy corner near the toolshed (there were muddy tracks everywhere, puddles, wadded-up cocktail napkins, cigarette butts), and she knelt to undo my fly. "God! it's *gorgeous!*" she exclaimed softly as she opened up my shorts and let it fall out, pale as a stone pillar, into the night. She stroked it gently. I felt nothing: it was all puffed up, numb with excitement and anticipation. Inside, somebody squealed, and I could hear what sounded like the clacking of spoons, someone blowing on a sweet potato. A tall man stood, shadowed, in one gaping window, looking out as though to mirror me. "Where shall we point it?"

"Well, away from the flowerbeds—" But she was gone. "Alison—?"

"Hate to tinkle all over your wife's garden," rumbled Lloyd Draper, standing beside me, "but I'm an old man and I just can't hold it in anymore." I thought I heard her whispering behind me—I couldn't be sure, it might have been anyone: "Is there room . . . ?" "Sure, honey, sit down, sit down . . ." I looked around, but it was too dark to see anything but a few bushes, squatting like luminous trigrams, black at the roots. "What's the matter, son? For a young lad, you seem to be having trouble making water there," Lloyd remarked, squinting down through his bifocals. "Oh, I see." He spurted briefly, stopped, spurted again. "Well, that takes me back a bit . . ."

"I just hope there isn't any poison ivy back here . . ."

"You avvertisin' that ugly tally-whacker, Big G, or juss givin' direck-shuns?" asked Charley, leaning boozily over my shoulder, my wife's dustmop under his arm as a crutch, Jim helping at the other elbow.

"Yup, vanished days and all that . . ."

"Don't laugh, Charley. It hurts."

"Seen a lot of 'em like that in my day," sighed Lloyd, still squirting from time to time. "They weren't workin' too well either, of course . . ."

"Who's laughin'? I'll trayja even'n throw in m'new alligator golf-shoes b'sides!"

"Whoo-*EEEE!* Jes' call me Pipi 'cuz Ah'm all *your'n!*" hooted Earl Elstob, joining us ("Thieves' hangouts, we called 'em in the trade . . ."), shooting a stream out over the flowerbeds and—*thrummm!*—against the toolshed wall. Jim and Charley were already firing away at shorter range and I was able at last to join in as well. Our radiant streams gleamed in the pallid glow from the windows (the man who had been standing there had disappeared) like a row of footlights. Tania had once spent six months on a painting she'd called "The Garden," trying to capture this glow, this strange yearning (she'd related it to what she'd called "the sleeping dragon, the hidden force of nature"), and what she'd ended up with, she'd said, was a fair facsimile of an illustration from a children's book she'd had as a little girl.

"Hey, Earl," laughed Charley, "didja hear the one about the guy who takes his wife to the theater, 'n atta—ha ha!—innermission—"

"The thee-ater?"

"Move over, ladies," said Fats, joining us, "I gotta re-hearse the scenery here!"

"Yeah, n'atta innermission he's gotta take a leak, so he hurries off to the can. But he goes through a wrong door somehow 'n ends up inna goddamn garden!"

"Oh yeah? Huh huh," snorted Elstob from under his overbite, still managing to hit the wall but no longer threatening to drill a hole through it, and Fats, crossing Earl's stream with one of his own, said: "Too-chay!"

"Well, the garden's very fancy, y'know—inna *French* style, as y'might say—"

"Yuh huh hee," Earl sniggered, jiggling around. Lloyd had left us, but his place was taken almost immediately by a guy in corduroys and

a tweed jacket with suede elbows: "This the place?" he asked, smiling apologetically around his bent briar pipe, and someone in the bushes behind us, grunting, said: "Well—*ungh!*—there goes a little bit of eternity . . ."

"And in a fancy garden like 'at, Earl, he don' wanna weewee onna lotuses nor leave no nasty puddles around, right? So, real careful-like, he lifts a plant out of a flowerpot 'n unloads in 'at, 'n'en putsa plant back 'n—hoff!—tippytoes back to his seat—"

"Sounds like the one about the audience catharsis at the tragical farces," remarked Jim, winding down.

"Yes," I said, meaning something else. Alison had made some remark about intermissions that night at the theater, giving them an importance that haunted me now. "Exactly . . ."

"Onlya goddamn play's awready started up again when he gess back to his seat, see—"

"My name's Gottfried," the man beside me offered, extending his free hand. I changed hands and took it.

"Oh yes—you came with Fiona."

" 'N he leans over to his ole lady," Charley rumbled, leaning over toward Earl, " 'n he says to her, he says ("Fiona—?"): 'Hey, sugar-puss, whuzz happen so far iniss act?' " What Alison had said that night we met, smiling up at me over her fresh cup of coffee, was that perhaps without intermissions there could *be* no catharsis in modern theater—and only much later did it occur to me ("I feel like all my energy's just leaking away," someone murmured behind us, "and it gives me a very mystical feeling, like I'm in tune with the universe or something . . .") that what she'd really said was "intromissions" . . .

" 'You oughta know, you dumb shit,' his wife says," Charley was saying, "all scrunched down 'n mad as a bear with a bee up its ass: '*you were in it!*' "

Earl staggered backward, yaw-hawing uncontrollably, making us all duck, just as Leonard skipped out from behind the toolshed in front of us and started popping photos: "Help! I'm blind!" wailed Fats, shooting straight up in the air.

"Come on, Leonard, what're you doing?"

"This goin' in the sports pages or the church announcements?"

"God, all I see are spots!"

"The hard thing sometimes," sighed Gottfried beside me sucking on his drooping pipe, "is just letting go . . ."

"Obishuaries, mos' like . . ."

"Jesus, I thought those two yoyos left when they took Yvonne away!"

"*Yvonne—?*" cried Fats (". . . And then, other times, there's nothing to it . . ."). "*Who* did?"

"Hurry!" Alison whispered urgently behind me, rushing past. "I'm almost done!" I gasped, trying to blink away my momentary blindness, but she was already gone, vanished like an apparition. "Wait!" Then Leonard's flashgun went off again and I saw her, running barefoot toward the back porch (how small she looked!), clutching her tights like a spare wrap, her green sash loose and fluttering behind, pursued by Dickie and that guy in the chalkstriped suit—"*Hey!*" I shouted, just as Dickie caught a toe in a croquet wicket and slapped into the mud. Leonard missed it, shooting instead at a confused and bedraggled Howard being helped down the porch steps by Daffie and Anatole ("Ugh! just don't look back," someone muttered behind me), Noble following them out, holding his crotch, his glass eye lighting up with the pop of the flash. "Oh Christ," Dickie swore, brushing futilely at the dark stains on his bright white trousers, as Alison, with a desperate backward glance, crashed into Noble, "not *shit—!*" "Yvonne?" Fats was blubbering. "I can't *believe* it!" Leonard's flashgun went off again (Howard stuck his tongue out at it, Anatole threw his hand up): Alison, Noble, and the guy in the chalkstripes had disappeared.

"Well, folks—*shlup!*—Godspeed!" announced Earl Elstob with a toothy self-congratulating grin, doing himself up and wandering off. He headed toward the porch, but seemed to lose his way, circling back into the bushes behind us instead.

"No need for you guys to rush away on our account," Daffie announced, her tongue slurred with gin, as she and Anatole dragged Howard over and propped him up beside us (Fats had just gone charging off, crying: "*Bren!* My *god*, Bren! It's Yvonne! They've *took* our *Yvonne* . . . !" and Jim was zipping up). "Nothing going on in there but a goddamn funeral."

"'Ass pretty much whuzz goin' on out here," remarked Charley, shaking his member out. "Well, anyway I won' be hard to find inna dark . . ."

"Funeral?"

". . . Juss feel around, it won' be hard . . ."

"Yeah, for Ros. Fucking ghost festival, they're calling it, talking to spirits—they're outa their conks." She opened up Howard's pants, fished around inside. She was having trouble keeping her footing. Someone shrieked back in the bushes, Elstob sniggered giddily, there was a thump, and Earl reappeared, doubled over, making his way once more toward the back porch. "Jesus, Howard, where *is* the damned thing—?"

"Can I help?" offered Jim.

"I c'n do't *myself!*" Howard cried out, but it was all bravado, he was helpless. Distantly there were squeals and laughter coming from the upstairs bedroom, largely drowned out by the squeals and laughter behind us as Leonard's flash went off in the bushes.

"By the way, Ger, that guy with the French tickler on his chin said he had something he wanted to tell you. He—no, stop, Howard! *Wait'll I get it out!*"

"Cyril?"

"He probably wanted to tell you about the body in the basement," Jim said. "You about ready, Charley?"

"Body? What body—?!"

"Goddamn it, Howard . . . now see what you've done . . ."

"Down in the rec room, you mean," said Dolph, joining us as Gottfried strolled away ("Whuzzat guy got a tape recorder for?" Charley asked), and lifting his stream into a wheel barrow back beside the toolshed. "I wondered about that. I saw the feet sticking out behind the ping-pong table, but I didn't look closer—thought I might be interrupting something."

"Just as well you didn't," Jim said. "It wasn't a pleasant sight."

"I think he's a sociologist . . ."

"But what are you saying—*the rec room—*?"

"That's right. The dart pierced the back of the head and penetrated the medulla, and that always makes for a rather pathetic disorganized death, I'm afraid. Probably just an accident but—"

"But—my wife was—!"

"Your wife's all right," Dolph assured me. "She's in there in the kitchen. The cops are, uh, with her . . ."

"Assholes!" Anatole muttered under his breath, as I hurried away (she'd been trying to tell me something about an interview, I remembered this now, I hadn't been listening), and Howard whined: "My panz're all wet!"

"Of course they are, Howard—what do you expect?"

At the steps I caught a glimpse of something glittering in the grass, a little ring of light: Ah, she's dropped it again, I thought as I reached down to pick it up, this time just for me perhaps. I smiled. Or had Noble—? Someone cried out—I thought it might have been Alison, or else my wife, and I rushed forward (that bastard! I was thinking, meaning no one in particular), but at the kitchen door a man was blocking my way. "Excuse me—!"

"My wife," the man said stonily. It was Alison's husband. He stood rigidly in the open doorway, silhouetted against the kitchen lights (yes, my wife was in there, I saw her, the two policemen as well, both looking flushed and sweaty, their clothes disheveled, Fred still in his bulky neckbrace, Bob's tie undone), one hand in his jacket pocket, the other gripping the carved bowl of his meerschaum. "Where is she?"

"I don't know," I gasped. "Inside someplace, I think, I was just—"

"No."

I couldn't see his face at all, and it made his voice, cold, uncompromising, seem alarmingly disembodied. It was important that I reach my wife ("We better get some blood, too, Fred," the tall cop was muttering, and Fred, struggling with some pulleys above the butcherblock table, nodded stiffly), but I knew better than to try to push past him.

"You came out here together."

"Yes, we, uh, sort of ran into each other—but then of course we separated—"

"You touched her breasts—"

"No—"

"And other parts." It was like a recitation, an arraignment, distant, mechanical, menacing. And utterly (I thought, chilled by it) insane.

"Listen, you've got it all wrong," I explained, tried to, "it's only a party—"

"Yes, I know about parties." I could hear Charley clambering heavily up the steps behind me, assisted by Dolph and Jim. "You brought her out here—now what have you done with her?"

"I told you—"

"Have you raped her?"

"No—!"

"Raped who?" wheezed Charley at my shoulder.

"Whom," Dolph corrected.

"I can smell her on you," said Alison's husband.

"We *all* can," said Dolph. "Worse than a damn barnyard. No accounting for some people's tastes!"

"Say," Charley yuff-huffed amiably, "speakin' a that, didja heara one 'bout the two actors out inna sticks playin' the front 'n back end of a cow—?"

"Are you in love with her?"

"What?"

"They get chased offa goddamn stage, see, 'n—haw haw!—they get separated—"

"I asked you—"

"C'mon, Charley," said Dolph, leading him away. "I think Ger's about to get the punchline without our help."

"Awright, awright," sighed Charley, limping. "Foo! I'm feelin' awful! Whereza booze? I think I got too much blood'n my alcohol stream!"

"Very funny," Jim said, keeping Charley from tipping over onto Alison's husband, "but the truth is, you've had enough." I started to follow them, but the space through which they moved seemed to close up behind them. "You ought to take it easy. It's slow poison, you know."

" 'Ass okay, Jim, I'm in no hurry . . ."

"I asked you if you were in love with her."

His silhouette, which had dissolved momentarily into the larger mass of the others, now came into sharp focus once more as the light filled in behind him. As though he were honing it, I thought. "Don't you think you're, well, letting your imagination—?"

"Believe me, I know what it is to be a victim of love." Through all of this he hadn't moved. Not even when Charley and the others had jostled past him (they were in there talking to my wife and the short cop now, Charley shaking his big head and saying something about growing older, or colder, Jim examining a small tool Bob was using)— he could have been a cardboard cutout posted at the kitchen door with a recorded message. He sighed. "It's a kind of madness . . ."

"Yes, well—I don't know what you saw, or thought you saw, but in reality—"

"I know, it's the chemistry of it that most disturbs me. How it warps everything so you can't trust your senses. It's like some kind of powerful hallucinogen, transforming our conventional reality into

something stark and dangerous—I always feel as though a hole is being opened up in the universe and I'm being pitched into it. Is that what you feel?"

"Well, ah, something like that . . ." I didn't like conversations like this, and felt unfairly singled out. "But, honestly, as far as Alison—your wife—is concerned—"

"Inhumane. Utterly amoral. Atavistic. Yet transcendent. I sometimes wonder if it's what atoms feel as they're drawn together in molecules—or stars as they burst and implode . . ."

I could hear Wilma chatting with someone on the steps behind me, complaining about the discomfort of wet garter belts. Woody and Cynthia came out, still in their underwear, and Woody, sizing things up quickly, nodded back over his shoulder and said: "Your wife needs you, Gerry, you'd better get in there." "I know . . ." Fred was attaching something to her ankle; Bob stood by with a pot of Dijonais mustard in his hands.

"Certainly it has nothing to do with marriage, I know that, you can't tame it, you can't institutionalize it—the raw force of it just smashes through all that." For the first time he moved: he put his pipe—a pale hovering presence between us—in his mouth, drew on it, took it out again. I didn't know whether to be encouraged by this or not.

"Look, I know what you're trying to say, and your wife's very attractive of course, but—"

"I thought at first that marriage might be a way to isolate it, contain it, to give it a time and place, so that at least I could get ahold of the rest of my life—but I was wrong . . ."

Behind me, Wilma was expressing her condolences to Woody: "She was so *brave!*" "Yes, I know." I had faced situations like this before, of course. All too often perhaps. Always there were misunderstandings. . . . "I would have just fallen to pieces!" "We all have to make adjustments. Eh, where's the best place?" "Well, *not* where I went!" The important thing was to keep them talking. "You might try back by the swing set."

"I've known all along, I suppose, but it finally came home to me just tonight, watching you and Alison . . ."

"Hi, Gerry, getting a bit of fresh air?"

"Actually, Wilma, I was just—"

"Say, that's a smashing shirt! Maybe I could get one of those for

Talbot—not that it'd look as good on him as it does on you! By the way, do you know Peg's sister Teresa?"

"No," it was the woman in the yellow dress, "but—"

"Pleased, I'm sure!"

"There was a kind of awe, a kind of electricity in the way you looked at each other—especially when you were stroking her inside her tights . . ."

"Who did?" Wilma asked.

"No one," I said. Maybe if I linked arms with these two, sandwiched myself between them . . . "It's a . . . story. . . ."

"Oh, I *like* stories," gushed Teresa. "And I like *parties!*"

"And then, later, when she knelt down to put your member in her mouth—"

"That's not what—"

"It was like a revelation . . ."

"Some people have all the fun," Wilma sighed, patting her hair. "If I knelt down, I'd just pop all my stays."

". . . Like the end of something, innocence for example—and at first I didn't know what to do with it . . ."

"And is that your wife in there on the butcherblock?"

"Yes, in fact I was about to—"

"Come on, Teresa," said Wilma. "I'll introduce you."

"I thought of a lot of things I might do—violent things mostly . . ." They were gone, I was alone with him again, the chance lost—almost as though I'd never had it. I heard soft mutterings behind me, near the porch, something about being afraid of the dark. Or the dart. I'd caught the word "violent"—it had seemed to key a new tension in his voice, a slightly higher pitch. "The worst part, I realized, was not the way you played with each other's genitals—a mere appetite, after all, we all go through that—but rather the peculiar rapport between you, that strange intense *sympathy* you seem to share. I sensed this already that night we met at the theater. It was as though, when you spoke to each other, the very geography of the world had shifted, moving her to a place I could not reach."

He was completely mad, that was obvious. It was dangerous, I knew, to ignore him—impossible in fact ("Come along, Teresa," Wilma was saying in the kitchen, "it's best not to interfere . . .")— but you couldn't reason with him either. "All right," I said ("Well, what I'm saying," Teresa argued—all I could see of my wife were her

feet above Teresa's head—as Bob frowned and slid a knife back and forth through our electric sharpener, "is that it seems a silly way to go about it!"), "what do you want me to do?"

"I hate these destructive feelings. They're completely contrary to my life's work. I want you to help me free myself from them." I wasn't sure what he meant, but I didn't like the sound of it. In the kitchen Peg's sister Teresa leaned down to my wife and said: "Anyway, I'm delighted to meet you! It's a wonderful party!" I couldn't hear my wife's reply, if there was one, but I was thinking, maybe Vic was right, maybe these parties were a mistake. Perhaps we should travel more instead, or take up some hobby. . . . "I want you to give Alison what she wants," her husband said. "Or thinks she wants . . ."

"But I—"

"On one condition." I settled back on my heels. He'd startled me at first, but I knew where I was now. There was always a condition . . . "I want you to teach me about theater," he said.

"I see . . ." I had been right of course, but not in the way I'd imagined. "The theater, you say." Ros, I recalled, had once, while sucking me off, paused for a moment, looked up, and asked me to teach her ("There must be an easier way to make a living," Fred was complaining in the kitchen, as he wiped his flushed brow with a dishtowel) about marriage, and I had felt as inadequate then as I did now. "It's . . . it's a complicated subject."

"I want to find my way back to her," he said simply. "And I feel somehow it's the key to it all." He had pivoted slightly and light from the kitchen now fell on half his face. I could see the worry and fatigue in his eyes as he studied me. "From what I've heard about you," he added, stepping aside to allow me to enter, "I'm sure you will help."

It seemed to me, as I stepped over the threshold, that an age had passed since I'd crossed it going the other way, and for some reason I thought of that phrase that Tania had been so fond of and had concealed in several of her paintings—in "Orthodoxy," for example, and in (or on) "Gulliver's Peter": "*What was without's within, within, without.*" "Awright, ma'am, try to be a little more helpful if you can," Fred was saying, more or less echoing Alison's husband (I felt him close behind me like an arbiter, a referee), and I thought: Tania was right, everything—even going out for a pee in the garden—was full

of mystery. "We'd hate to have to bring in the old exploding sausage . . ."

"Just a moment," I protested. "This really isn't necessary. My wife had nothing to do with—"

"It's all right, Gerald," she said weakly, craning her head around under the bright fluorescent lamp. "It's only a routine—"

"That's right, so just move along now, fella—"

"But I tell you, you're wasting your time! She doesn't know anything!"

"She knows more than you think, sir," Bob said, pulling on rubber gloves from the sink, and my wife whispered: "Your fly's undone, Gerald."

"Ah! Sorry . . ."

"What's that . . . in your hand?"

"What—? Oh yes, nothing. . . ." I'd almost forgotten it was there. I realized I must have been rubbing it like a talisman throughout my encounter with Alison's husband, who now leaned closer to see what it was. "Just something I, uh, found outside—"

"Looks like one of my buttons," said Fred. We all looked: indeed it was. He searched his jacket, which gaped still around his bloodstained belly. "Yeah, there it is. Musta come off when I was trying to button up out there in the dark . . ."

"Outside . . . ?" my wife asked faintly, her face puffy. Bob was holding a damp tab of litmus paper up to the light. "Are my . . . flowers all right?"

"Well . . ."

"I guess I owe you one," Fred acknowledged, pocketing the button. Alison's husband had pulled back, but I could smell his pipe still (I was thinking about hidden fortunes, something a woman had once said to me down in some catacombs: "All these bones—like buried pearls, dried semen . . ."—whatever happened to that woman?), its aroma hovering like a subtle doubt. "The Old Man woulda raised hell with me if I'd lost it!"

"You could start," I suggested, "by letting her down."

Fred hesitated, glancing at his partner. Bob shrugged, nodded: Fred loosened the ropes and eased her down, though he kept her legs still in their shackles, a foot or so off the table. My wife looked greatly relieved and exchanged a tender glance with me. How tired she looked! "Some more people have arrived," she said with a pained sigh.

"Yes." I could hear them wailing in the next room. "Ros's friends mostly." The blood, which had before rushed to her head, now drained away, and the old pallor returned, making the bruises there seem darker. Or maybe it was just the cold light of the fluorescent lamp. "Listen, love, when this is all over, let's take a few days off, have an old-fashioned holiday—we can go away somewhere, somewhere where there's sun—even Mrs. Draper said . . ." She smiled faintly.

"Sounds good to me," said Fred, rigging up a lamp with an odd-shaped bulb ("Ultraviolet," he added when he saw me staring: "certain, um, substances usually always fluoresce . . ."), while his partner fiddled with a little rubber tube of some sort.

Eileen came in for some ice: "For Vic," she said. The bruises on her face made her seem wistful and sullen at the same time. "He's just been down to the rec room, he *needs* a drink."

"That sonuvabitch," Fred muttered, touching his neckbrace, and Bob grunted: "Don't worry, pardner. We'll get him."

"Have you been up . . . to see Tania?" my wife asked, as though to change the subject.

It was strange. As I started to speak, I felt everything that had happened during the evening roll up behind me to feed my reply—and then, even before I got the words out, it faded . . . "Not . . . not—"

"It's like . . . she was trying to . . . to put the fire out," she added. I felt as though something were unfinished, like an interrupted sneeze. As though ("*Ouch!*" she cried, wincing, and I felt my own eyes screw up in sympathy) I'd been preparing all night to do something—and then forgot what it was. My wife closed her eyes for a moment while Bob put his mouth to one end of the tube. "It must have been happening—*ngh!*—all night. I don't know why I . . . didn't notice . . ."

"Well, we all see only what we want to see . . ."

"Maybe she just got tired of waiting," said Eileen wearily.

"I . . . I let the water . . . out of the tub . . ." Her knuckles, clenched tight, were white as burnished salt. Eileen had left. "If you do go up, Gerald . . . ," she added, then gasped and held her breath a moment, "could you—*oh!* . . . check on Mark? He . . . can't seem to settle down."

"Of course . . ." Iris Draper pushed through the dining room door now with Michelle, the chants from the other side augmenting momentarily. They seemed to be parading around the table in there. "It

was the same day," Michelle was saying, "that Roger had that dream about the old hunchback with her drawers full of gold." "Was that a dream?"

"He dropped a bag of water on Louise's head. It . . . ." She gulped for air. I stared down at the bald spot on the top of Bob's head and thought about the Inspector's view of time and what he called—how did he put it?—the specious present . . .

"Yes, and apparently what happened, you see, is that Ros just opened the door and stepped out."

"It . . . made her cry . . ."

"Really!" Iris exclaimed, as they stepped outside. "She might have been killed!"

. . . The mysterious spread toward futurity . . .

"Well, she was on acid or something . . ."

"Perhaps, in the end, all self-gratification leads to tragedy," Alison's husband murmured behind my shoulder. Fred was looking for a wall plug. "We'll have to use an extension cord," he muttered, and Bob, peering closely at a little bottle, wiped his mouth and grunted. "But then, what doesn't . . . ?"

"It was so sad. In the old days, I'm sure . . . she would have laughed." She opened her eyes again. There were tears in them. "Do you remember that big jolly laugh Louise used to have . . . ?"

"That was a long time ago."

"I don't think you want to watch this," Fred said, uncoiling cord. "We'll let you know—"

"No, I'm not leaving," I insisted, but just then Alison came through from the back, barefoot and unbuttoned, hair loose, eyes dilated from the darkness. She shot me a glance full of—love? betrayal? desire? fear? ("And Dolph was so funny," my wife was saying, "we always had . . . such good times then . . .")—then padded hastily on into the dining room, Noble and the man in the chalkstriped suit banging in behind her, their shirttails out: "Where'd she go?" they laughed.

"You must hurry!" whispered Alison's husband, clearly shaken (we shared this), and my wife reached out to touch my hand. "Yes, Gerald," she sighed, "it's all right . . . you might be needed . . ."

"I'll—I'll go find the Inspector!" I declared (Noble, lumbering through the dining room door, had glanced back to smirk one-eyed at me, a streak of red down one cheek, Alison's green tights tied round his thick neck like a superhero's cape). "He'll put a stop to this!"

"Now, now," admonished Fred, peering round at me past his neck-brace (I was already at the door), "none of that . . . !"

"Wait, Gerald!" my wife called out faintly. "I nearly forgot . . . !" Maybe, I was thinking, I should say something to the Inspector about Noble, the hairbrush and all that—he's capable of anything. "I've made some nachos. They're . . . they're on a cookie tray in the oven . . . Could you . . . ?"

"Nachos! But—?!"

"These what you're looking for?" Steve the plumber asked, bumping in behind me with an assortment of small red-handled pliers in his callused hands, and Bob, setting down a can of hairspray, said: "That's them."

"Please, Gerald . . . they've been in there . . . too long already!"

"I changed the washers on the downstairs taps and reset the drum on your dryer," Steve said, moving over to the foot of the table, "but I haven't been able to do anything yet about the stool upstairs."

"Please . . ."

From this angle I couldn't see my wife's face—my view was blocked by Fred and Steve between her legs—but I knew she must be near to tears. I hurried over to the stove, stuffed my hands impatiently into oven mitts (Alison's husband was chewing on his beard again), and opened the oven door. "Good god!" I exclaimed as I pulled the tray of nachos out. "There's a *turkey* in here!"

"Yes . . . it's from the freezer," she gasped. Steve looked up and said: "I've rung my partner. He'll bring the tools we need for the biffy." "It could use another . . . twenty minutes or so . . ."

"But—!"

"Don't worry, we'll watch the timer," Fred assured me, and went over to open the dining room door for me, seemingly eager to get me out of there. I heard the chants still, but more distantly, interspersed with waves of silence: they'd moved off to some other part of the house. "And don't you be bothering the Inspector," he added, snatching up a couple of hot nachos and juggling them in his hands (Steve was watching closely as the tall cop plugged in his vacuum cleaner and limped toward my wife with the suction hose), then popping one in his mouth. "He's got a lot on his mind right now."

His warning seemed almost a challenge, a dare, and as I carried the tray of nachos into the dining room (Dolph was there at the table,

scraping at the remains of a bowl of moussaka, Dickie using a candle to light up a joint), I thought: It's clear, I've got to meet Pardew head-on right now. In fact, hadn't I already made this decision before coming back in from outside? "Dolph, could you move that bowl so I can use the hot plate?"

"Hey, nachos! Your wife finally remembered us beer drinkers!"

Across the room, Mavis, surrounded by those stragglers not interested in Quagg's funeral parade in the next room, stretched her arms up, palms out flat, as though pressing them against some unseen wall: I sympathized with this. "And that's coriander she's traipsing through, if I'm not mistaken, and there's sweet calamus," Iris Draper was saying nearby, identifying the plants in Tania's painting for Eileen, who stood leaning against a wall, staring puffily into space. "And those look like jujube trees, which the ancients got mixed up with something else, and this is probably sandalwood . . ." Between them, Vic, looking battered and unsteady but still strong, poured himself another drink. "Looks like you stepped pretty deep in the dew, Gerry," Dolph remarked around a mouthful of half-chewed nacho. "It's halfway up your pantleg there . . ."

"A fucking mess," Dickie agreed, taking a swift drag on his joint and handing it to me: I pulled off the oven mitts and joined him ("I wonder if all that adds up to something . . . ?" Iris mused, and Vic grunted: "The question to ask is, what's she selling?"), sucking the sweet smoke deep into my lungs as though, I felt, to mark some turning, the completion of something, or the beginning, something perhaps not quite present yet nearby . . . "All the style's gone out of your parties, Ger ("That's not a very generous view of art," Iris remarked, peering over her spectacles), there's too much shit and blood."

"Maybe you're just growing up," Vic growled, wheeling around slowly. "Unlikely as that seems." I caught a glimpse of Ros, her extremities concealed in translucent bags, being carried around on a kind of litter made of one of our living room drapes tied at the corners to three croquet mallets and a golfclub (it looked like a five-iron), held high, Hoo-Sin in her kimono wheeling around below, eyes closed, keening rhythmically. "Ritualized lives need ritualized forms of release. Parties were invented by priests, after all—just another power gimmick in the end."

"Not for me, old man," said Dickie with a cold smile, taking the

joint back. "For me, they're like solving a puzzle—I keep thinking each time I'll find just the little piece I'm looking for." Vic's jaw tightened—Dickie turned toward me and winked, then glanced back over his shoulder toward the living room, seeing what I saw: Alison among the mourners, looking frightened, hemmed in by Noble and that guy in the chalkstriped suit and some of Zack Quagg's crowd—Vachel the dwarf, that actor who played the wooden soldier, Hilario the Panamanian tapdancer—"Speaking of which," Dickie murmured ("Please, Vic," Eileen whispered), moving away, hand fluttering at his bald spot once more. "Like so many open but unenterable doors," I thought I heard Mavis say, just as Dolph, scratching now with both hands, said: "The top cop's there in the TV room, Gerry, if that's who you're looking for."

"Yes . . ." I'd lost sight of her. Fats was doing a kind of dance in the front room around Hoo-Sin, who was down on her knees now, twisting her torso round and round, moaning ecstatically, some guy with a camera circling around her, getting it all on videotape. They'd lowered Ros to the floor and Hoo-Sin swept the corpse with her long shiny hair, back and forth, wailing something repetitive through her nose, while the others chanted and clapped or slapped the walls and furniture. Hilario banged a tambourine, Vachel clacked spoons, Fats danced, eyes closed, smiling toothily, his big body bobbing around the room above the others as though afloat on the rhythms.

While Quagg—directing the camera crew, shifting the lights, calling the angles—pulled the others into a circle around Ros, Regina swooped into the center, eyes and hands raised as though in supplication. She called out Ros's name in a hollow stage whisper, and the others picked it up as a kind of chant. Alison (I saw her now) made a move in my direction, but Quagg stopped her, led her back into the circle, in a gap between Dickie and that wooden soldier actor. I tried to catch her eye, but she was peering anxiously back over her shoulder, where Noble and Talbot, digging at his crotch as though looking for the switch, were squeezing up behind her.

Malcolm Mee appeared then, as if from nowhere, in his ragged jeans and striped sailor shirt: he knelt solemnly beside Ros's body, bent stiffly forward, and pressed his head against her breast. When he straightened up there was fresh blood dripping down his forehead between his eyes. Regina let out a shriek and fell to the floor, her eyes

rolled back (I'd seen her do this as "Tendresse" in *The Lover's Lexicon*), Fats paused, the music stopped. "Ros!" Fats whispered, and the others picked it up once more, chanting airily as though taking deep breaths together.

"What's all this supposed to mean?" asked Alison's husband, who'd stepped up unnoticed beside me, but Quagg shushed him angrily, pointing at the camera.

All eyes were on Mee, who knelt beside Ros still, back arched, staring up the ceiling as though in a trance. His pants seemed to have opened up by themselves, and now his penis crept out like a worm, looking one way, then the other, finally rearing up in the lights like a flower opening to the sun. There were gasps mingled with the whispered chants of "*Ros! Ros! Ros!*" Mee's eyes closed and his lips drew back as though in pain. The head of his penis began to move in and out of its foreskin like a piston, plunging faster and faster—or perhaps it was the foreskin that was moving. "Look!" someone rasped. "It's getting wet!" This was true: it was glistening now as though with sweat. Or saliva. Mee's hips were jerking uncontrollably, his head thrown back, bloodstreaked face contorted, the scar on his cheek livid, his penis pumping. The others, still chanting, pressed round—I too found myself squeezing closer to watch. Suddenly Malcolm bucked forward, went rigid: the swollen head of his member, now wet and empurpled, thrust up out of its fleshy sleeve at full stretch, seemed to pucker up, and then let fly—but even as his sperm spewed forth (we all shrank back) it seemed to disappear into thin air. There were gasps of amazement and people fell to the floor. Regina, emerging from her own trance, searched her dress: it was dry. The carpet too. It had been like an explosion of yoghurt and now we couldn't see a trace of it. Mee lay there, gasping, quivering, his eyes squeezed shut, the blood dripping down between them. Regina, with gestures grand and devotional, tucked his penis away and zipped his jeans up. "All right!" exclaimed Zack Quagg, beaming, and he slapped the cameraman on the shoulder. "All *right!*"

"I may be thick or insensitive or something," sighed Alison's husband, "but I just don't get it. I mean, is that what theater's supposed to be about, communication with the dead?"

She was gone. Mee had distracted me. And Noble as well, Talbot, that guy in the lilac shirt and gray chalkstripes, they'd all vanished. Dickie was still there: he'd spied Sally Ann nearby, staring at me, one

hand in her blue jeans as though playing with herself. Holding my gaze, she withdrew her hand, held her fingertips in front of her lips, and blew—Dickie reached out as though to intercept her dispatch, closing his hand around it and drawing it, grinning, toward his nose. She made a face, pushed around him, and came toward me. "Whoa there, Greased Crease!" he laughed, and caught her by a back pocket. "At heart, theater doesn't entertain *or* instruct, goddamn it—it's an atavistic folk rite," Quagg was explaining, somewhat irritably. "Oh, I see," said Alison's husband, adding in a whisper to me: "She went out through that door to the dining room . . ." "Ah . . ." It was over on the other side of the room. How had I wandered so far away from it? It was as though the room itself had circled around me. "Jesus, Cyril and Peg shoulda seen that one!" "Weren't they just here?" Regina was mopping the blood from Malcolm's forehead and nose with a white scarf. "*That*, bison gulls, is what you call ad-*lipping* it!" Vachel squeaked, drawing tense laughter ("Off the *elbow*, man!" "No, haven't you heard?"), and Fats, his bald dome shiny with sweat, stopped me in the doorway: "Doggone! What happened, Ger? I had my eyes closed!"

But she wasn't in the dining room either. There were some people in there eating and drinking, and Mavis was carrying on still in her hollow and melancholic way, but neither Alison nor the guys chasing her around were to be seen. "Death came to me there as a woman," Mavis was saying—some of her audience had drifted to the doorway to catch Malcolm's act, but were now drifting back—while behind me, Wilma sighed and said: "Dear me, what a waste!"

"Ah well, spunk's cheap," someone answered her, and Mavis said: "Her hair seemed to float around her head as though caught in a wind. She had a large fleshy mouth, and when she opened it the inside glowed with a strange fluorescent light." I turned back, but Alison's husband was standing in the doorway, also looking puzzled. "Her breath smelled of wormwood and gentian root and her eyes were shriveled like dried mushrooms. Bruised fruit. She looked . . . like my mother . . ."

"*What—?!*" bellowed Vic, whirling around and staring fiercely past my shoulder, just as the man in the chalkstriped suit came, grinning, out of the TV room.

"She was blind and clumsy and the labyrinth of ice was impenetrable even for one who could see—it was easy to lose her—"

"That goddamn sonuvabitch—!"

"You got buried treasure down there, Dolph?"

"Look at him go! Moves like a man half his age!"

"He's ripe for a coronary . . ."

"I think I musta caught something . . ."

"But then, after I'd escaped from her, I grew lonely and longed, even in my awful fright, to see her again . . ."

Nor in the TV room, where Jim sat facing the Inspector across the games table ("It's a problem of dynamics, a subject-object relation," Pardew was saying, "for in a sense it is the victim who shapes and molds the criminal . . ."), Patrick just behind him, old Lloyd Draper over in the easy chair, sleepily watching the TV screen, Knud snoring on the sofa. There was a technician working behind the set, rigging up some kind of switcher between the cassette recorder on top, a lot of gear strewn around on the floor, and the tube itself, where now Mavis appeared in extreme close-up as though being interviewed, saying: "I went searching for her but I couldn't find her . . ." The technician flicked a switch and the image of Mavis gave way to a static wide-angle shot of a man in highheeled boots, a leather vest, and a thick black beard, coming through the front door with a tripod over his shoulder: it was the technician himself, I realized, as humorless on the screen as he was at his work. "Did the victim suffer perhaps from extreme sensibility?" the Inspector asked.

Jim smiled, glanced up at me—"Hardly," he said with a wink—and the Inspector peered around. "Ah," he exclaimed, waving at me with what looked like a knitting needle, "perhaps you can help!"

"Well, I was just looking for—"

"The good doctor here seems reluctant to provide us with the full medical history of the victim on the rather unprofessional grounds that it is not relevant," he went on snappishly. Some of Mark's toy soldiers had been set up on the table in front of him, apparently to illustrate some theory or other, and it occurred to me suddenly what those "marbles" were I'd found in my pocket. There was also another of Mark's drawings there—the one Mark said was of Santa Claus killing the Indians—as well as Peedie, his stuffed bunny. "And I am trying to persuade him that there is a definite mutuality here, that the criminal and his prey are working on each other constantly, long before the moment of disaster, before they've even met each other, and that, in the war against crime, to know the one," here he pointed with the knitting

needle at one of the little soldiers, "we must know the other!" He pointed at another soldier, then gave a sharp little thrust and tipped it over. "By the way, why are all the heads gone off these things?"

"I don't know . . ."

"All that may be very well with wolves and tigers," Jim said, "but it has nothing whatsoever to do with human beings."

"I can see that you have a higher—and a lower—estimation of humanity than I have," replied the Inspector, setting the needle down and lighting his pipe. Without the scarf, the back of his neck looked raw and naked. I caught a glimpse now of Janny Trainer behind the open closet door, her pink skirt hiked above her waist, some guy's hand in her heart-shaped bikini panties. On the TV screen there was a wide-angle shot of my study with Roger's lifeless body upside down in the far corner. Nothing moved. Yet the relentless intensity of the unblinking shot was almost unbearable. Pardew turned around to look at me, holding up the needle. "Does your boy *knit*, by the way?"

"No—!"

"There he is," Wilma said, leading Peg's sister Teresa into the room and over to the sofa.

"We found it in his room."

"Oh my! I'd like to be in *his* dreams!"

"Kitty says you probably *wouldn't* like it."

"It's probably his grandmother's, my wife's—"

"Who was the *victim's* mother?"

"Look, Wilma!" exclaimed Teresa, pointing. "There's Talbot on the TV!"

"Ros? She was an orphan—"

"Aha!" He banged the table with the needle, sending the little soldiers flying. Jim looked pained and shook his head at me (my wife, I recalled, had been trying to tell me something about Mark), and Wilma said: "I wish at least the ninny'd stop scratching his pants!" "An orphan! Now it's all coming *clear!*"

Charley entered, groaning lugubriously with each slow step, and the guy with Janny—it was Steve the plumber—hurried over to help the bearded technician behind the TV, fumbling abashedly with his overall buttons. What was Teresa saying? Something about a "little boy" or "little boys." " 'Sno good, Janny! I'm all—I'm all washed up . . . !"

"Oh, Charley, stop blubbering! Why don't you just push a cocktail stirrer in it or something?"

The camera, which had followed Talbot and Dolph and the others (Talbot, in response to an interviewer's question, had been describing his appetite for reflected sex) to the door of our master bedroom, now panned back down the hallway to the bathroom, and I saw as it slid past my son's door that it was ajar: the room was apparently empty, toys and bedclothes flung violently about—and was that a foot stretched out behind the closet door? "Now about the hole in this stuffed rabbit," Pardew was saying and the TV camera had entered the bathroom, where the shower curtain was being pulled aside, but I was already on my way out of the room: I remembered now, there'd been a bloody handprint on Mark's door when I'd passed it before—how had I failed to register it at the time?!—*there was not a moment to lose!*

I bumped up against Hilario in the doorway—"Oops!" "Perdón!" he exclaimed. "I am all left *foots!*"—and over his shoulder ruffles I spied Alison in the group around Mavis: Noble was there, too, Earl Elstob, Dolph . . . "I saw her at last," Mavis was saying, "but she was trapped behind a high wall of shimmering ice—she was hideous, yet pathetic, and I felt a terrible closeness and a terrible distance at the same time." Alison mouthed something with a questioning look on her face—it looked like "the green room?"—and pointed down at her crotch. "(*Just be a minute!*)" I mouthed in return, and Dolph, cupping a hand to his ear (the other hand was out of sight), mouthed back: "(*What?*)" "And then, *suddenly,*" Mavis intoned as Alison, wincing, lurched slightly and cast me a panicked glance—but what could I do? there was the bloody handprint, my son's torn-up room ("*What—?!* Down in the *rec room?*" cried Brenda. "Oh *no!*")—"*everything began to melt . . . !*"

"Wasn't Malcolm's number something else?" someone at the table remarked as I pushed past it—Quagg's crowd were all in here pressing around the food now—and Hoo-Sin replied ("Fats! *Fats!*"): "It was like the meeting of clouds and rain, tall mountains piercing the soft mist of the valley!"

"I tell you she was *there,* man!" It was the guy who'd played the wooden soldier, standing near the telephone: "Didn't you catch her *smell?* That could *only* be Ros!"

"You'll never *believe* it, Fats . . . !"

"I didn't smell anything, but I could *feel* her," sighed Michelle be-

low me as I took the steps three at a time. "It was like she was blowing through my clothes!"

"But I thought Mee's cock was tattooed like a serpent . . . ?"

Just as I hit the top, Ginger came wobbling out of the bathroom, looking unwell. She glanced up, met wide-eyed my startled gaze, and, as though in shock, all the stiff little pigtails ringing her face went limp. She snatched a kerchief away from one breast, clutched it to her mouth, covering her breast with her other hand, and went clattering down the stairs.

When I reached my son's room, I found there was no blood on the door after all, maybe I'd been mistaken—but inside, the room was, as I'd seen it on the TV, all torn up. And the bed was empty, there were stains—! "*Mark—?!*"

"Stick 'em up, Daddy! It's the Red Pimple!" he cried, jumping out from behind the closet door.

"Hey—!"

"Did I scare you, Daddy?" he giggled, as my mother-in-law came in with a glass of milk. His face was painted bright red and he had a towel tied around his neck for a cape. My heart was pounding.

"Boy, you sure *did!*"

"The police were in here," his grandmother said without looking at me. The room was a mess, things strewn about everywhere, books, toys, bedding, unwound balls of yarn.

"I'm sorry . . ."

"They took Peedie away!"

"They'll bring him back, son." What had I been afraid of? I didn't want to think about it.

"They better! That's *my* Peedie!"

"Now they are in the kitchen." She seemed to be talking to the closet. She handed Mark his milk.

"I know. I've just come from—"

"That towel is filthy, Mark. And what have you done to your face?"

"Yuck! This stuff tastes like soap!" He now had a white moustache on his crimson face.

His grandmother gathered up the sheets and blankets, spread them on the bed, her movements slow and forced, as if causing her physical pain. "I'll get a washcloth," she said, taking the towel with her as she went.

"Why did the policemen throw all my things on the floor?"

"They were probably looking for something. It's part of their job."

"Are they the ones who broke my soldiers?"

"I don't think so. Crawl in here now, it's late and Grandma's getting upset."

"Not without Peedie! I can't sleep without Peedie!"

I knew this. He curled round it and put his finger in a hole he'd dug. We had to take the rabbit everywhere we went. "Maybe if I told you a story . . ."

"Gramma already told me one. About a bad man who cut ladies' heads off. Daddy, what's 'happy the other laughter'?"

"Happily ever after? Nothing, just a way to end a story."

"Why don't they just say 'the end'?"

"Sometimes they do."

"Or 'hugs and kisses,' like on a letter?"

I smiled. His grandmother began working on his paint job with the washcloth, and he screwed his face up in disgust: "Oww!" My grandmother used to sign her letters: "Please don't forget me." My father: "Be brave." My mother never wrote. "What's a French letter, Daddy?"

"I suppose, uh, that's a letter from France."

"No, it isn't, it's a balloon. That girl told me."

"Well, all right, a balloon." I gazed down at him as he sucked his thumb there on the pillow (his grandmother had retired to her rocking chair and was staring furiously at the blank screen of the drawn window shade), recalling a young girl I'd known in Schleswig-Holstein, an afternoon in a wildlife preserve, lying naked in the tall grass out of sight, more or less out of sight (what did it matter, we were young and one with the wildness around us, flesh then was *truth*, this was a long time ago), teaching each other all the sex words of our respective languages. That day, I'd lost my condom inside her, and she'd exclaimed irritably, fishing for it: "Ach, die miserable Franch Post! Fot can you hexpect?" "Well, anyway the delivery's been made," I'd muttered lamely, feeling guilty (the truth of flesh is complex and disturbing and never quite enough, that beautiful oneness with nature ultimately a bed with stones and ants that bit: perhaps, there in the sun, I was beginning to think about this), and she'd shot back: "Ja, gut, only zo zere ist no postage due!"

"But it isn't, is it, Daddy? Ever . . ."

"What's that, son?" As he sucked, he pulled his nose down with his index finger.

"The end."

I hesitated. There was such a sadness in his little eyes, his stretched-down nose. I wanted to relieve it with a little joke, but I couldn't demean his question, even though it meant, I knew, a kind of betrayal. His eyes seemed to widen, then they went dull. "Ask Mommy to come up and kiss me good night," he said around his thumb.

"Well, she's . . . busy, but she'll—"

"Now," said my mother-in-law coldly from her chair.

"Yes, right *now*, Daddy," Mark repeated.

"Of course." I could understand her feelings—I hated the police, after all, even more than she hated my guests—but it seemed to me that her expectations of me were not all that different from Mark's: I'd become in her eyes, as I was naturally in his, a kind of generalized cause.

"And get my Peedie!"

The sewing room as I passed it was darkened, the door half-closed. *"Hold on to it!"* someone gasped from behind the door—or *"to her"*—and there was a muffled sound as though someone were struggling. I stopped short. But then I caught a glimpse of my mother-in-law out of her chair and watching me sternly from Mark's doorway. "I'll be right back!" I said to her—and to anyone else who might be listening—and as though in reply, someone whispered from in there: *"Do you know what you're doing?"*

In front of the mirror at the foot of the stairs (on the landing, Wilma, showing Teresa Tania's painting, said: "Well, as you can see, she never really tried to flatter herself—but I *do* think she always looked better with her clothes on . . ."), Jim was treating Eileen's left eye, which, puffy and red, now matched the right. "Not again!" I exclaimed, stepping down, and Jim shrugged. "She told Vic he was nothing but a utopian sentimentalist, something like that, and he proved it by belting her one."

"My father's out of control," Sally Ann said, then smiled up at me, her throat coloring.

"It's going to get worse," Eileen muttered. Nearby, Ginger was diapering herself in Pardew's silk scarf, pinning it front and back to a kind of serape she'd fashioned out of what remained of her ker-

chiefs. "I tried to tell him, to get him to go before it's too late, but he won't listen."

"Mmm. By the way, I tried in the kitchen," Jim remarked, glancing up at me, "but they won't listen either."

"I know. I've had enough. I'm going to do something about it right now."

"If you need any help . . ."

"Thanks, Jim. I'll let you know."

Ginger, Pardew's fedora perched on her wiry pigtails, her fingertips at the brim to keep it from falling off, went tottering into the front room on her high red heels, watched leeringly by Vachel the dwarf. Vachel was chewing a fat black cigar nearly as big as he was. "*Gudjus!*" he piped.

"God! it's awful!" Brenda was saying. She was nearly crying. She and Fats had apparently just come up from the basement. They were leaning on each other and Fats was blinking still in the bright light of the hallway. "Just *look*, Gerry!" She showed me a photograph: it was Ros on her hands and knees, looking over her shoulder at her raised bum—or rather, not a bum at all, but a rich banker, a snowman capitalist with greedy black-button eyes on each pale cheek, a carrot-nose stuck in her anus, top hat perched on top, and a wet bearded mouth about to ingest a shining gold rod. The photograph was full of holes. "They've been throwing *darts* at it, Gerry! Who'd ever *do* such a thing?"

"It's somethin' else down there, man!" said Fats, wiping his face with a big bandanna.

Daffie, wandering in from the back with a somewhat dazed Anatole, guiding him toward the stairs, took the photo away and said: "That popsicle looks familiar—I think I've seen one somewhere just like it." She winked at me drunkenly and immediately, as though cued, the telephone rang. I turned to answer it and nearly bumped into Louise, moving heavily toward the back of the house with a fresh bathtowel. Her glance was withering. "Have you been out on the mall communing with nature, sweetie?" Brenda asked, making Anatole blush, and the actor who played the wooden soldier in the toyland melo picked up the phone and said: "Hullo? No, Horner's the name."

"If it's a man, it's for me," called Peg's sister Teresa, leaning over the railing.

"No, there's nobody here named Gerald, fuckface—you must have

the wrong number." "Wait—!" But he'd already hung up. "I could tell right away that shit-for-brains didn't have your class, baby!" he said, grinning up at Teresa, who, as though in reflex, pushed one knee through the railings ("I-I've already been," Anatole was stammering as Brenda hooked her arm in his: "Well, you can help *me*, honey . . ."), and in the dining room there was a burst of applause.

But then I saw her, free at last, in by the table with Janny Trainer and Hoo-Sin—

"Hey!" I exclaimed softly, hugging her from behind.

"Why, Gerry, what a nice surprise!" It was Knud's wife Kitty, her mouth packed with bread and salami.

"Oh, I'm sorry—I thought it was my wife . . . !"

"What's to be sorry?" she laughed, spewing food. "Oops! See how excited you got me?" She wiped her chin with a cocktail napkin, examined her front. Though my wife had a dress something like that and they were both about the same size, I was nevertheless amazed that I could have confused the two of them. Alison was gone, as I'd known she would be—Mavis, seated now in a captain's chair, was surrounded mostly by women. Only Talbot was there among them, his ear bandage dirty and unraveling now like some kind of primitive headdress. "I borrowed some of your wife's clothes, I hope she won't mind, mine were all . . ." Kitty's chirpy manner faded. She swallowed. "Once, at a party, when he was, you know, in one of his moods," she said, staring off at Mavis (Janny sighed, Hoo-Sin nodded, Brenda came through from the front, popping gum, a reluctant Anatole in tow), "I tried to cheer him up by saying, 'Relax, Roger, it's all just a game, what the hell.' Without taking his eyes off me, Gerry, he bit right through the glass he was drinking from and started chewing up the pieces—God! I nearly fainted!"

"When the lotus blooms in the midst of a fire, it is never destroyed," Hoo-Sin said solemnly.

"Oh no!" cried Janny. Brenda and Anatole, trying to push out through the kitchen door, had got stopped by someone trying to push in ("But I'm in a bigger *hurry* than you are!" Brenda laughed, shouting through the door). "Don't *tell* me there's going to be a *fire!*"

"Only in my heart," crooned Fats, putting his arms around them both: Hoo-Sin elbowed him sharply in the gut and he backed off goggle-eyed and wheezing, bumping into Hilario, just emerging from the

TV room, who exclaimed: "Eh! Fats! You muss learn to not fock your-self aroun' weeth the moveeng force off nature!"

As Brenda got her way and, laughing, dragged Anatole on through to the kitchen ("I think Uncle Howard needs me!" he was pleading, trying to hang back), I felt suddenly overtaken by a terrible sadness—I don't know what it was that brought it on, that image of Roger chewing glass maybe, or Hoo-Sin knocking the wind out of Fats, or perhaps it was just an accumulation of everything that had happened all night, Ros and Roger, Eileen, Tania kneeling at the tub with pink soap scum up to her elbows, the police and all their gear and Ros's rolled-down stockings, my wife boiling eggs, all these people, my torn-up study, the food mashed in the carpet, the mess in the rec room, the look on Yvonne's face as she vanished through the front door or on my son's face just now when I left him or on Daffie's right this minute—whatever it was, it stopped me cold for a moment, such that when Woody came in from the kitchen with Cynthia ("Tech-nically maybe," she was saying, fingering her medallion at the cross-strap of her bra, "but, I don't know, somehow it just doesn't seem—"), a sudden look of concern crossed his face and he interrupted her to ask: "Is everything all right, Gerry?"

"You know it's not," I said, my voice catching. "You know what they're doing." The door behind him was moving still, chafing subtly the doorjamb. "Can you help?"

He observed me closely, one hand gripping a strap of his ribbed undershirt. His counselor's deadpan calm returned. "Sure, Gerry. I can at least try. Don't worry, there are laws, precedents—things will work out. Why don't you get Cynthia a drink meanwhile?"

"Yes, you've been neglecting me," she said, gazing at me with that same worried look she'd been giving Yvonne earlier. She took my arm and led me like an invalid toward the sideboard. "What was that spe-cial drink you fixed for me earlier tonight?"

"An old-fashioned, I think."

"No, it had gin in it. It was a funny color." Fats, with a pained grin on his face, was moving in on Hoo-Sin once more, Hilario cau-tioning him from the sidelines: "Theenk two times wut you do, my frien'."

"A blue moon?"

"That's it."

People seemed to be drifting about without focus. We pushed

through them. It was like happy hour back at the ski lodge. Maybe the last play in the world would be like this: an endless intermission. Above us, Susanna stepped out into nothing. No, I was mistaken: there were no gold loops in her ears.

"All we got is love, baby, in this crazy mazy world," Fats rumbled at Hoo-Sin's back, doing a hopeful little shuffle, and Kitty, joining the crowd gathering now around Mavis (Michelle glanced back over her shoulder at me: the resemblance was still there but she and Susanna had grown apart, the one toward mystery, or the fear of it, the other toward sorrow), said: "Tell us again, Mavis, about how you first met Ros . . ." We ducked as Fats arched slowly, almost gracefully, into the air over Hoo-Sin and crashed to the floor behind us, and I thought ("Are those back in fashion?" Iris Draper inquired, bending down and adjusting her spectacles. "I wonder if I threw all mine away . . . ?"), Vic was right, who was I to mix drinks and answer doorbells? I wished I could just go home.

"I know," Cynthia said, patting my arm with a ring-laden hand. Had I been talking out loud? "We all feel that way sometimes."

"It all began one day when Jim was called to an orphanage to deal with a peculiar medical emergency," Mavis said in a hollow portentous tone, and Iris, turning away, whispered: "Ah! I don't want to miss this!" I dug out the crème yvette, checked the ice bucket: three cubes, a puddle of discolored water, some soggy cigarette butts . . . and the wooden-handled pick. "He was often called in, of course, for circumcisions, hot douches, infibulations, and the like, when the girls reached puberty, but in this case the child was only ten years old— yet so precocious that they had already lost, through scandal, three tutors, a handyman, and two members of the board of trustees. As for the other girls . . ."

"Here," I said, straining the drink into a cocktail glass and handing it to her. My hand was shaking. I glanced past her shoulder, creased by its heavy strap, into the TV room, where Charley had Steve the plumber in a huddle, apparently trying to sell him something. The Inspector stood just behind them, watching the television, his back to the door. Well, I thought, if things seemed out of focus, I could do something about it. I reached into the ice bucket for the pick. The handle felt worn and comfortable in my grip. "Now if you don't mind, my son asked me . . ."

"I'll go in with you." She didn't seem to want to let go of me.

Charley passed us in the doorway, giving the thumbs-up sign. "I may get group outa this," he growled happily, "if I c'n juss fine—hah, *there* she is!"

As though this were an announcement, Pardew turned around and said: "Good, our engineer! Perhaps she can help!"

Steve was squatting behind the TV set once again, assisting the bearded technician. Images were flickering intermittently on the screen, and sometimes in montage, as though the switching cables had somehow fused. "Such commotions had a way of flarin' up at public executions in olden times—and recent ones, too, y'know," Lloyd Draper remarked, peering down his nose at the set (I caught fleeting glimpses there of the back of Jim's head, Noble doing an obscene handkerchief trick, Fats on the floor, the stopped-up toilet, Elstob yipping and snorting, Mee testing a razorblade across the palm of his hand, a patch on Sally Ann's fly that said "OPEN CAREFULLY AND IN-SERT TAB HERE," Horner with her, getting a message in his ear, some-one's fist in a bowl of peanuts, bright lights, out of focus), and Pardew said: "I know. Contagious hysteroid reactions of this sort are typical wherever masses are assembled—it's an imitative ritualization of the bizarre and hallucinatory tendencies of the odd few, and al-ways, I've noted, with a tinge of the burlesque. Frankly, it's the sort of thing I see too much of." Patrick, not far from the Inspector's el-bow, gave a sympathic little sigh.

"I think we've got it now," Cynthia said, detaching some cables, plugging in others. The image had stabilized on Mavis ("—determined that it was best for all concerned to bring the child home to live with my husband and me for a while," she was saying into the camera, her gaze intent yet misty, "in order to keep her under daily observation, and perhaps to assist her—through close personal guidance and a more precise education—to transcend her singular and somewhat—") and they switched it now to Quagg, being interviewed, or perhaps inter-viewing himself.

"Okay," said the technician, crawling out from behind the set, ad-justing slightly the color. "I'll go pick up the camera."

"That's right," Quagg was saying, "Ros had just got the lead in our new feature spasm, *Socialist Head*. It's a radical and theatrically mind-blowing miracle play that examines the modes and variations of oral sex in a revolutionary society—dynamite stuff really, and of course Ros

was like handmade for the part. Howzat? Something special? You betcher ass, baby! We'd really hoped to hit the nut on this one, get our tokus outa the tub, but now . . . with poor Ros on ice . . ." His voice broke. "Aw shit . . ."

As the camera, hand-held, began to move away from Zack past Vic and Daffie, Eileen, Scarborough in a gloomy hangdog slump, Alison's husband, the crowd around Mavis ("—but little did we imagine—" I heard her say), and on out into the hall, where Horner and the man in the chalkstriped suit could be seen racing each other for the basement stairs, Teresa peeking into the downstairs toilet (the camera seemed to be headed either out or up: now the front door came into view), the Inspector, clutching my son's stuffed rabbit in his arms, his finger in its hole, continued his angry harangue about what he called "this compulsive attraction for the new, for sensations, thrills, overloaded circuits, the human imagination unchecked by the proper and necessary intervention of sober critical faculties, and so laid open to all manner of excess and delirium." Patrick punctuated this monologue with his infatuated yea-saying ("Oh yes! Absolutely! Dreadful! Utterly insane!"—his split lip had made his lisp worse), all the while trying to touch the bunny in Pardew's arms. Staring at the glass eyes of the stuffed bunny, I seemed to see my mother-in-law's stern demanding gaze. Right *now*, she'd said. I cleared my throat. "Excuse me, Inspector, I—"

"*Sshh!*" Pardew hissed, squinting at the set, and Patrick snapped: "Yes, Gerald, don't interrupt!"

"But you *must*—the police—your two officers—in the kitchen, *my—!*"

"Not now, damn you!"

"*But—!*" My throat was all knotted up, I could hardly speak. "My son *needs* her! It's not *fair!*" I might as well have been shouting into the wind. I held up the ice pick in my trembling fist: "*Look!*" Cynthia glanced up in alarm. "*Here's* what you've been—!*"

"*There! You see?!*" Pardew was pointing excitedly at the TV, where Ginger, seemingly in a state of shock, her pigtails collapsed, wavered at the top of the stairs. "Who was that man with her just then?" "I didn't see, we'll get it on playback . . ." Clutching a kerchief to her mouth and a hand to her bared breast, she wobbled forward, but as if unaware of the stairs in front of her: she hovered there a moment with one foot out in space like a divining rod, then came down hard, striking the edge of the first step with her thin stiletto heel, her ankle warp-

ing, knee buckling, and down she pitched, looping arse over elbow, kerchiefs flying, limbs outflung in all directions, all of it slowed down and thus mockingly balletic in its effects, like someone tumbling on the moon. "A *redhead! Of course . . . !*" Somehow she hit the landing on her feet, sinking softly into a kind of frog squat, her back to the camera, which was slowly zooming in—but not for long: her narrow bottom bounced in slow motion off the floor like the head of a twin-peened hammer and she began to rise again, floating up into space once more, arcing head-first and heels high toward the camera. "It should have been obvious to me!"

"In Greek theater, you know," Patrick confided at his elbow, "they put these lovely red wigs—"

"*What's happened—?!*" Pardew cried, so startling Patrick that he fell backward onto Knud, who grunted irritably and rolled over. The screen had gone blank just as Ginger in full tilt was revolving feet-first toward the in-zooming camera, and now the Inspector beat on it with his fists: "*Come on, damn you!*"

"I don't think it's the CRT," Cynthia said. She worked the switches, picked up Mavis (" '—is what it's *for*, Aunty May,' the sweet child explained, touching me. I . . . I didn't even know I *had* one . . . !"), then Daffie tapping her gleaming teeth with a spoon, Noble with a straw up his nose, but only a blank screen where Ginger should be. I lowered my arm, which ached now with its dull news.

"*It's a plot!*" Pardew raged, kicking the set and swatting it with Peedie so hard one of the ears flew off.

"Uh . . . I'll go check the camera," Steve the plumber mumbled, slipping away.

"*Where are my officers—?!*"

"*That's what I've been trying to tell you!*" I cried, pointing past his shoulder with the weapon in my hand. But I was pointing in the wrong direction. The two of them were in the doorway behind me.

"Uh, Chief, we got a bit of trouble . . ."

"*Trouble? You don't know the half of it!*" the Inspector roared. They glanced at me uneasily. Or maybe respectfully, I couldn't tell. "*If I don't get this picture back—!*"

Fred turned to Bob, who shrugged, and they came forward into the room.

"*It's not the set, you imbeciles!*" the Inspector cried, shaking the stuffed rabbit at them. "*It's the camera! Out in the hall! MOVE, damn you! We're missing everything!*"

"Yes, sir," Fred said and they lumbered out, Bob muttering something sullenly under his breath. On the television, Regina clutched her shoulders and stared. Then Mavis, filling the screen, said something about Jim's tongue. Vic belched, Prissy Loo lifted her toga to show Dolph her military longjohns. "I think you were looking for this," I insisted, offering Pardew the pick.

"We've got it now!" cried Cynthia.

"Aha . . . !"

The fall was over. The camera seemed to be in the living room now. Ginger, wearing the Inspector's white scarf as a kind of diaper or loincloth beneath what kerchiefs remained, was standing, knees out, in the doorway, trying on his crushed fedora.

"*Now* what?!"

"I'll take that," Cynthia said, coming over.

"It really doesn't matter," I sighed. "I don't know where it came from anyway."

"I know. We'll let Woody handle it."

"They got the camera going again," Fred said in the doorway.

"You think I'm blind?" the Inspector growled, chewing his lip and digging irritably in Peedie's hole. "*Damn* her!"

The fedora lay springily on top of Ginger's revived pigtails, bobbing above her head as she walked. When she stopped, the hat leaned forward over her eyes, then rocked back. When she stepped forward, it seemed to hesitate a moment before following her.

"Most places I've been," Lloyd Draper put in, "red hair's pretty unlucky. Folks have a way of choppin' it off, don't y'know, head and all . . ."

"*What's happened to my overcoat—?!*" the Inspector bellowed. Ginger was pulling it on now, her thin arms lost in its long floppy sleeves. It was wrinkled, misshapen, and had huge dark blotches all over it. It seemed to weigh her down, and her knees bowed out another couple of inches.

"You ask any Hindoo, he'll tell you that red, heh heh, is just bad news. Once when we were up in India, Iris and me, we got tickets to a—"

"They been using it," Bob said (Ginger was now staggering about in the coat's bulk, the fedora bouncing on her head, peering at everything through an oversized magnifying glass that stuck out of one sleeve like an artificial claw), "to catch the drip from the upstairs crapper."

"What—?!"

"I said, when Iris and me were in India—"

"Enough!" barked Pardew, twisting Peedie's other ear off. He pointed with it toward the front of the house, and the two officers, unsheathing their clubs, disappeared.

Ginger had now discovered Ros's body (the wake seemed to have started up around her again) and was down on her bony knees with her head under the skirt. She emerged with a look of triumph on her face and the fedora squashed down around her ears. She pushed a thick sleeve back, reached in and fished about, her eyes rolling, then began to pull on something: she tugged, strained, her eyes crossed— it gave way and she tumbled backward. She held it up: it was the Inspector's briar pipe. "Damn!" he muttered, slapping his pockets. Ginger gazed at it curiously, sniffed it, then prepared to fit it into the pucker of her mouth—but something over her shoulder alarmed her: she staggered to her feet and went stumbling and tripping through the mourners off-camera, dragging the tail of her thick checkered coat behind her. Bob and Fred appeared on the screen. They looked around in confusion—then, swinging their nightsticks, charged off in pursuit. My heart leaped to my throat. The camera, following the cops' exit, had come to rest on Alison. Slowly it zoomed in, Alison staring straight at it with that same look of terror and supplication I'd last seen in the dining room. Noble, Dickie, Horner, the man in the chalkstripes, all crowded around her—and beneath her charmeuse skirt there were not two legs but four—Vachel! "Now what was it," the Inspector asked, turning toward me, "that you wanted to—?"

But I was already out the door, pushing through the pack-up in the dining room ("—watching the child's astonishing performance through the two-way mirror, as if art and life were somehow separate," Mavis was saying, breathing heavily now and stroking her pale white thighs below her rucked-up skirt, "but then, suddenly, overtaken by excitement and desire . . ."), fighting my way as though through a briary nightmare toward the living room—but to no purpose. Except for Vic, slumped in an armchair near Ros, and Malcolm Mee in the sunroom, his head bent solemnly over a handmirror ("I've never done anything like this before," some guy was crooning hollowly on the hi-fi), the room was empty. That must have been a tape replay on the TV. In fact, now that I thought about it for a moment, I'd just seen the cops

in the dining room, setting out silverware and stacks of plates on the table, and the camera, of course, was on Mavis.

There were too many lights on in here. The wreckage, the debris, was all too visible. It was like a theater after the play is over, deserted and garish, its illusions exposed. I gathered up some crumpled napkins, fallen ashtrays, half a bun smeared with catsup, a shattered cigar butt, a couple of glasses and a roach holder—but then I didn't know what to do with them, so I set them down again. This time on the coffee table. There, by one foot, lay Alison's green silk sash. I picked it up, held it to my lips.

"Mustn't take it too hard," Vic said, but I wasn't sure whether he was talking to me or to himself. He was staring down at Ros, unrecognizable now except for the tatters of her silvery frock. "It's fucking sad, but what the hell, there's nothing tragic about it."

"No . . ."

"Life's too horrible to be tragic. We all know that. That's for adolescents who still haven't adjusted to the shit." He shook the ice around in his drink, watching it. "Nonetheless . . ." He was struggling still with his sense of loss. I understood this. I'd said the same things many times, half believing them. When I'd found my father, for example. In a room much like this one, his last hotel suite. The consoling overview: catastrophe as the mechanism that makes life possible, sorrow a morbid inflammation of the ego. A line, like any other . . . "You know, I've been thinking about that play Ros was in, the pillar of salt thing . . ."

"You went to that?"

"Yeah. I wasn't about to make a fool of myself down there on stage, if that's what you're wondering, crazy as I was about her, but I watched the others who did. And it gave me time to think about that story. God saved Lot, you'll remember, so Lot afterward could fuck his daughters, but he froze the wife for looking back. On the surface, that doesn't make a lot of sense. But the radical message of that legend is that incest, sodomy, betrayal and all that are not crimes—only turning back is: rigidified memory, attachment to the past. That play was one attempt to subvert the legend, unfreeze the memory, reconnect to the here and now." He scowled into his glass. I was thinking of Ros, salted blue, warming to rose under all those tongues. Ros, who never looked back, not even for a soft place to fall. "And maybe . . . maybe her murder was another . . ."

"How's that?"

"Or maybe . . ." He grunted, sighed, drank deeply. "Who knows?" He shuddered slightly. "Why can't I shake this off, Gerry?"

"Well, perhaps," I suggested, recalling the feel, on the back porch, of Alison's sash giving way, thinking then of love as a kind of affectionate surrender, an alternative to both resignation and confrontation (Mee floated past us on his way to the dining room, wearing my soggy ascot now as a headband), "you should stop fighting it."

"Hmpf, you're as bad as that dead battery I'm with tonight," he grumped. "Know what she called me? A fucking sentimental humanist! Hah! A goddamn affront to the universe, she said!" The faint trace of a wry smile flickered across his craggy features. "That's not bad, I have to admit . . . but goddamn it, Gerry, I *hate* sentimentality! I *hate* fantasy, mooning around—*I hate confused emotions!*"

"Too bad," said Jim, coming in from the hallway, his jacket on once more, a drink in his hand, "that's probably the only kind there are." My own now were mixed with guilt: that terrified appeal on her face on the TV screen just moments ago, and then before that in the dining room—or was it in here?—and in the kitchen . . . "How's your wife, Gerry?"

"What? Oh, I don't know, Jim. The police . . ."

"The police what?" Vic wanted to know, looking up.

"You know, their inquiries, a while ago they were—"

"What—your wife? Those goddamn fucking—what have you *done* about it?"

"Well, I spoke to Woody—"

"Ah. Good . . ." He seemed lost again in his own thoughts, his elbows on his knees, staring into his glass. Jim watched him with concern. I was thinking of something my father said; it was the last time I saw him alive, about six months before he'd, as he liked to put it, reached for the inevitable. "Why don't you let me check your blood pressure, Vic?"

"What—with that gizmo they were blowing up around Ros's neck a while ago? No, thanks!"

"They were just getting a fingerpint. Trying to. They had to use it to clamp the X-ray film cassette to the skin, that's all." He smiled. "What's the problem? Figure it might be catching?"

"It's not that . . ."

"Yneh!" groaned Regina, sweeping into the room in her wispy

gown, her hands upraised as though in protest. "That lady in there is too much!"

"Lady—?"

"That—that child molester! That geed-up dip with her fat hands in her pants! I can't *believe* it!" Time is hard and full of calamities, my father had said, but man is soft and malleable. If he chooses to endure, then he also chooses metamorphosis, perhaps of an unexpected and even unimaginable nature, such that choice itself may no longer be part of his condition. A signal, of course, which I hadn't heeded. I draped the sash around my neck, thinking about my own metamorphoses, my diffluent condition. "She's giving a blow-by-blow description—and I choose my *mots* carefully!—of a frantic three-way grope, featuring her, her old man, and Ros when she wasn't ten years old yet and hadn't even got her *hair!* Oh my God! *Poor Ros!*"

"It didn't seem to do her any harm," Jim said quietly. Lloyd Draper came in with a screen and slide projector and started setting up in the sunroom. "Oh yes, many children," he was saying. "One feller strung ten of 'em up at a time, called it a warnin' to men and a—heh heh— spectacle for the angels! I got pictures here, you'll see!" "We're probably too emotional about pedophilia. In a lot of societies, children have sex with their parents, grandparents, brothers and sisters, aunts and uncles, all the time, and as far as we can tell they don't seem adversely affected."

"I believe it," said Vic, his temples throbbing, hand squeezing his glass as though to crush it like one of Dolph's beer cans, "but I don't believe it."

"In fact, sex with their grandparents is probably *good* for them."

"Blah! Mine would've given me the clap!" Regina retorted, crossing her hands over her breast. "I gotta admit, though, that little kid in there is sure eating it up!" The telephone rang. "I'll get it, it may be Beni!"

"What little kid?" I called after her.

"I think she means Mark," Jim said, sipping at his drink. "He came down looking for his rabbit, he said."

"What—?!"

At the door (how many times had I been through here? I felt like I was chasing after lost luggage in an airport or something) I bumped into Alison's husband, who turned pale when he saw the silk sash around my neck. "Is it . . . over?"

"Not yet," I said and sneezed. "I haven't even—"

"*Sshh!*" someone scolded.

He frowned and looked about, pipe clamped in his teeth, craning his head. She wasn't in here but Mark was: right up front in his SUPER-LOVER sweatshirt, sitting on the prie-dieu next to Vachel the dwarf. I had the impression Vachel might have his hands on him, but my view was blocked by all the others pressing around, I couldn't be sure. Mavis, her skirts dragged up past her marbled thighs now, both hands digging frantically inside her shiny balloonlike drawers, was apparently describing Ros's childish body ("—like cherries, and—*unf!*—her little cheeks were—*ooh!*—suffused with the—*ah!*—tint of roses . . . !") as she squatted over Mavis's face while manipulating her with one hand and stroking Jim with the other, sucking one of them—I couldn't tell which, maybe both, it didn't matter—I just wanted to get Mark out of there.

"Hey, come on! Stop pushing!"

"We were here first!"

"*Psst! Mark!*"

"Ouch!"

"—With her velvety tongue and with her—*gasp!*—fingers in me like the feet of—*oh!*—little birds, I felt my mind just explode and spread through my—*whoof!*—whole body, surrendering, ah—abjectly—an incredible—*grunt!*—radiance and—and *truth—!*"

Vachel leered at me over his shoulder as I pulled on Mark. Mavis was now hauling at her vulva as though scrubbing clothes at a washboard, her hips slapping the chair, head lolling, eyes glazed over, mouth bubbly with drool. "I don't *wanna—!*" Mark whined, and some of Quagg's crowd hissed and booed me playfully, grinning the while in open-faced admiration of Mavis's mounting orgasm. "*Go! Go!*" some of them chanted. "No, Daddy! I wanna hear the *story!*"

"It's all over," I insisted, dragging him away as though out of a dense thicket. All but anyway: nothing now but yelps, groans, squeals, a few blurted phrases (something about "miracles" and "sweet vapors" and "groves of wild angels" or "dangers"—Ros, apparently, had changed positions), and the rhythmical whoppety-whop of her huge soft buttocks against the seat of her chair. "Hang on to your pajamas!"

Too late, he'd lost them. He dropped to his hands and knees and went scuttling back in after them, but I pulled him out again—and in

the nick of time, for Mavis suddenly shrieked rapturously and fell out of her chair, sending all the people around her staggering backward and all over each other—"You might have been stepped on, son!" I scolded as the others choked and giggled, muttered apologies ("But my *jamapants*, Daddy—!" "You've got others . . .") , or caught their breath. "W*ow*—!"

"And then . . . !" Mavis gasped from the floor, and the crowd fell silent again. Her breathing was labored, her voice raw and as though miles away. "And then . . . Jim . . . Jim *kissed* me!"

Her audience, some of them still picking themselves up, whooped and whistled, giving her a big hand. "God, that was one helluva moving story!" someone exclaimed. "Wild—but *real!*"

"Why doesn't Gramma read me stories like that?" Mark wanted to know.

"Style, man—some people got it, some don't."

"Where is Grandma anyway?"

"She's with some man."

"She on the spike, you think?"

"Grandma—?"

"Didn't you notice when her skirt was up?"

"These yours, Mark?" Kitty asked, emerging from the crowd now milling about. She held them up in front of her like an apron. "One thing for sure, you can tell they're not mine!"

Mark laughed, and Kitty knelt to help him put them on, a bit flushed still from Mavis's tale and none too steady. "Been in to see your old man, Kitty?" Talbot asked, tilting his head toward his good ear.

"What's there to see?" The bearded technician in cowboy boots now crouched behind her shoulder, his camera focused on Mark and Kitty's fumbling hands—I stepped forward to block his view, but just then the two police officers came staggering in from the kitchen, supporting a huge turkey between them, shouting at me: "Hey, *you!* Move that empty tray, will ya? *Hurry!*" "Just appearances, Talbot—believe me, dreams are never as good as the real thing! Isn't that right, Mark?"

"What real thing?"

"Hey! Lookit the little birdie!"

"Easy!" grunted Fred as they lowered the turkey gingerly onto the hot plate, the others in the room beginning to press around the table.

"Here, gimme that rag!" he cried, snatching the sash from around my neck.

"Wait!"

"Back off now!"

"Jesus, whoever lives here really opens up his pockets!"

"You shoulda been here earlier, Gudrun—there was a curried shrimp dip you wouldn't believe!"

"Say," Zack Quagg whispered in my ear, nodding toward Alison's husband in the doorway ("But I heard him *say* he was going to do it," Janny Trainer was insisting with tears in her eyes, "right in her chest like that!"), "that bearded dude got any green?"

"And mushroom turnovers!"

"He does all right, I think."

"He's so cute!"

"Thanks, man—that's what I wanted to hear."

"I'll get a bowl for the stuffing," Bob said, taking his oven gloves off, and Janice Trainer, beside me, gasped in disbelief, clutching her bosom: "Oh no! You mean he sits right on their faces and—?!" "And that blade you just honed!" Fred called after him.

"That's right, you little dope," said Daffie sourly, blowing smoke. "And now you've driven him away with your nasty little rumors."

"Well, *I* didn't know!"

"What? Has Dickie gone?"

"He's just leaving," said Dolph, wandering in ("Is it . . . is it fun?"), a boozy smile on his face. He winked at Talbot, nodded back over his shoulder toward the hallway. "H'lo, Mark. Say, you're on a real toot tonight, aren't you?"

"It can be felt," Hoo-Sin explained at Janny's shoulder, "but it cannot be grasped."

"Yeah? Try telling Dolph that!" groaned Kitty, slapping his hand away, as I took Mark's. "Uncle Dolph's got ants in his pants, Daddy."

"Hey, what's Mavis doing down there on the floor?"

"Whatever it is," Regina declared, fluttering in from the living room, you can bet it's something *dirty!*"

"It has no surface . . ."

"Trouble with Dolph is, he starts at the bottom but never works his way up!"

"Don't put the act down, Vadge, the big lady's got talent," admonished Zack Quagg, working his way away from the table with a thick

slab of breast, just as Fats came waddling up behind Regina, crooning: "Ruh-gina! Won't you be my Valentine-a!" She grimaced and shrank away.

". . . No inside . . ."

"Man, this turkey's a fuckin' flyer!" Quagg had apparently dunked it in the mustard; it was running down his chin and dripping on his unitard. Regina pushed Fats' hands away, glowering toward Hoo-Sin ("Gee, it sounds *nice*," Janny was saying, and Hoo-Sin, smiling enigmatically, left her). "Did you get ahold of Benedetto?"

"He's coming as soon as his show's over," said Regina. Hoo-Sin now had Fats in a half nelson. "Wait—! Have a heart!" he gasped. "To have mercy on wolves is to be tyrannical toward sheep," Hoo-Sin replied, as though intoning Scripture. "He'll be bringing some of the cast." Fats was in the air again.

"Terrific! Hey, we got the goods—let's frame a show here! Malcolm—?"

I realized too late we should have gone the other way. We'd made it as far as the hall door, but were blocked there by incoming traffic. "Malcolm may be down in the dungeon, Zack—something's on the boards down there . . ." Mark pulled back so I took him up in my arms. "Is that little man a dorf, Daddy?" "Yes." "A real one?" It was like having to go the wrong way in a train station at rush hour. "Lemme at that roast canary, boys! I gotta round out my saggin' career!" But there was no turning back either, people were pushing toward the table and away from it at the same time. Fred had backed off, gingerly holding his neckbrace: they were tearing the bird apart in there with their bare hands, it was as though we hadn't put anything out to eat all night.

"Are real dorfs naughty?"

It was the tall cop, Bob, limping through with the butcher knife, who finally opened up a gap we could slip through. He scowled angrily at us as he squeezed past, and, glancing up, I saw that Mark was sticking his tongue out at him. "Hey, Mark! That's not nice!"

"I don't like him, Daddy. He *pinched* me."

"The policeman pinched you—?"

"Whaddaya say, Mark?" grinned Charley on his way in. "How's yer ole rusty dusty?"

"How's your ole boo-boo, Unca Charley!" Mark replied, giggling.

Charley rolled his eyes and did a sad little flat-footed dance around us. "My ole boo-boo's gone blooey!" he declared mournfully. There were people piling up and down the basement stairs ("Whoo! game, set and *snatch!*" "Ha ha! you goin' down again?" "Yeah, man, one more time . . ."), but it was less crowded out here. "It's bye-bye, boo-boo, Mark ole buddy!" Charley called. Mark laughed and jumped up and down in my arms as I carried him toward the stairs. My study door had been pulled to, but the toilet door was open, the darkroom light still on. It glowed from the inside like hell in a melodrama. "Boo-hoo-hoo-hoo!" Quagg had used just such a scene in *The Naughty Dollies' Nightmare*, when the wooden soldier sold his soul to the golliwog. "How's your ole *poo-poo*, Unca Charley!" Mark squealed.

"That's enough, Mark. You're getting overexcited—"

"Wait, Daddy!"

"No, Uncle Charley's gone now, it's time—"

"But *Peedie!*" he wailed. "*I want my Peedie!*"

"Ah." This was a different matter. In fact, if I wanted any peace, I had no choice. But the TV room was impossibly distant, I didn't know if I had the strength to go all the way back through there again. I felt as though I'd crossed one border too many: I just wanted to book in somewhere. Sit back and use room service. What made me think we wanted to go traveling again? "Do you think you really need it, Mark? Maybe we should try to go to sleep once with—all right, all right, stop crying." He was heavy, or seemed so suddenly. I set him down. The front room looked empty but there was music playing. A dance tune, "Learning About Love"—it sounded tinny and hollow. "Wait here, I'll go get it."

But when I turned around, there was Cynthia holding the rabbit up, waving it like a flag. Mark ran to her, arms outstretched, and I followed. It even had its ears on again. "Thanks, you saved my life," I said.

"His ears are all funny!" Mark exclaimed. She'd pinned them on backward.

"Oh, I'm sorry—I guess I don't know much about rabbits!"

"He's wearing them that way for the party," I suggested. "You know Peedie—anything for a laugh." I winked wearily and Cynthia smiled. There was a faint blush on her skin from the darkroom light. "We'll fix them back tomorrow."

"Naughty Peedie!" Mark scolded, giving the thing a thump. Then

he hugged it close, pushing a finger up its hole, a thumb in his mouth.

"You're so good with children," Cynthia said.

"Did you get into the TV room?" Woody asked her, coming up from the cellar stairs as I was leading Mark away.

"Yes. It was a disappointment." Someone behind us laughed at that: "It always is!" Woody, I'd noticed, was still in his underwear, but his shorts were on backward now. His hair was mussed, his eyes dilated from the cellar dark. "They're in there now watching slow-motion replays of the doctor's wife."

"Mavis . . . ?"

". . . A story . . ."

My grandmother used to tell me a story about a man who had to climb a staircase with a thousand steps to get to heaven. She'd start at the bottom and take them one by one, and I'd always fall asleep, of course, before the man reached the top. I remembered—would always remember—the terrible ordeal of that climb, as I struggled desperately to keep my eyes open to the end, and I still had dreams about it: poised halfway up an infinite staircase, my legs gone to lead. For a while I even supposed a thousand might *be* an infinite number, but I tried counting it in the daytime and found it only took me ten or fifteen minutes. In fact, as I learned on mountain holidays with my father, it's not even that high a climb. Of course my grandmother always counted slower than I did, but that still didn't explain why I always fell asleep halfway up and usually sooner. I thought it might be the sleepy rhythm of the counting itself, so to counteract it I tried to distract myself with puzzles and memories and silent stories of my own. This was even less successful than concentrating on the counting, and what was worse, I seemed to lose the stories and memories I used that way. It was as if they were getting sucked up into the counting and there erased. Not that I wouldn't have sacrificed them willingly to reach the top, to be able to see what the man saw, but clearly they were not the route. It seemed that nothing was, and I even began to worry that there might be something wrong with me, something having to do with words I'd been learning about like "souls" and "corruption" and "predestination." I remembered startling my parents one day on a drive to my grandmother's house by asking them what was original sin. "Not being able to read a roadmap," my mother said drily, and my father laughed and said: "Being born." Then one day I suddenly discovered my grandmother's secret. It was simple. There was al-

ways a preamble to the climb, a story about who the man was or how he'd died—often she claimed it was a relative or someone who'd lived there in town—and then a more or less elaborate account of his travels through the next world before he finally reached the stairs. And of course my grandmother was tailoring the length of this prologue to my own apparent sleepiness and the lateness of the hour. So I laid a trap for her, curling up in a corner early as though exhausted, pretending to fall asleep on her shoulder as she put my pajamas on, yawning and dozing through her preliminary tale until she got the man to the bottom step, letting him climb the first dozen or so, so there'd be no turning back. During these first ponderous footfalls, as I lay there with my eyes closed, I felt a momentary rush of guilt for having done this to my grandmother, and I nearly chose to carry the deception right on into feigned sleep—or real sleep, it might have got mixed up. But curiosity got the best of me, I'd waited too long for this: before I even knew it, I was sitting bolt upright in bed, hugging my knees, my eyes wide open, watching her intently. She gave no sign that anything was different, proceeding resolutely, step by step, toward the top, as though this was the way she'd always told it—and how could I be sure she hadn't? The first four hundred steps or so were excruciatingly difficult—I was partly right about the incantatory powers of the slow ascent, and in spite of all my preparations, they nearly did me in. I perked up a bit after that, animated by the challenge of getting at least halfway, but then faded again around seven hundred, even losing a number of steps altogether—or perhaps my grandmother, seeing my eyes cross and my head dip, skipped a few. As the man started up the last hundred steps, I felt a surge of excitement—suddenly it was the best story I'd ever heard and I was wide awake. At last! But, typically, I'd peaked too early. Fifty steps later I was sinking again, overwhelmed by a thick numbing stupor. I couldn't believe it. What was the matter, I asked myself fiercely, didn't I want to see it? Didn't I want to know what it was like? I pinched myself, shook my head, bugged my eyes, tried to bob up and down in the bed, but I couldn't shake it off. Each step the man took fell like lead in my brain. It was as though my whole body had turned against me, refusing me at the last moment all I'd struggled for. I couldn't see my grandmother, just the steps, looming high above me. The numbers tolled hollowly in the back of my head like heavy bells. It was my first true test of will, if there is such a thing, and as the man climbed the last steps up through the clouds, I must

have looked a bit like him—largely lifeless, staring rigidly, teeth bared, grimly hanging in. Amazingly, we both made it. When he pulled himself up that final step, I was paralyzed with fatigue and anxiety, but I was at least able to see my grandmother again. "And what do you think he found?" she asked. Her expression was the same as when she'd begun. "What?" I responded hoarsely, almost afraid. "You tell me," she said. I thought it might be a riddle, a final test, or her way of helping me wake up enough to hear the end. "Angels," I said. The back of my neck ached from trying to hold my head up. "And lots of toys and candy and things." This didn't seem serious enough. I was trying to remember things I'd read or been told. "God—and his own father and mother. And grandmother." "Yes . . ." She seemed to want something more. I sank back on the pillow, trying to think. "Streets made of gold. Flowers that taste good, and . . . and happiness . . ." "That's right." I hesitated. My tongue was sore where I'd been biting. And my eyes, which hurt from holding them open, wouldn't close now. "Is that . . . is that all?" She tucked me in and gave me a kiss. "He found everything he wanted," she said and left me. It was a terrible disappointment. I stayed awake for hours thinking about it and it made my head ache for days after. I couldn't quite think what it was, but I felt I'd lost something valuable—the story for one thing, of course: that special bond, while it remained unfinished, between my grandmother and me, now gone forever. And especially those preambles about the different climbers and how they'd died and then their travels in the afterlife—I found I'd enjoyed them more than I'd realized at the time, obsessed then by the need for denouement, and I wanted them back, but they'd lost their footing, as it were. No stairs at the end now, just an abyss. I kept wondering for a long time afterward if I'd missed something, if I'd maybe dozed off at the wrong moment after all or failed to understand a vital clue. Only years later, about the time my grandmother died and began her own climb—or rather, vice versa—did I finally understand that there was nothing more to search for, that I had indeed got the point. It was, as my grandmother had intended from the first step on, her principal legacy to me . . .

Mark was right, there *was* someone in there with her. I could hear them talking. My mother-in-law was saying something in that flat moralistic tone of hers about "sucking the mother's finger." A euphemism, I supposed, leaning toward the door: I hadn't heard her speak

like that before. "So he was married, then," the man said, his voice muffled, "and raped a woman who was as well as dead."

"Yes. And then he left her and forgot her, as you might expect. Though later, he went back and prolonged his illicit amours, it being his dissolute nature."

"I see. So it's not true about the mother-in-law, the accusations, I mean, that she murdered—or at least tried—"

"How could it be? It's impossible when you think about it. No, it was his wife, who, with good reason, put in execution those so-called horrible desires . . ."

"That's a very serious accusation, m'um. Yet my own experience tells me it must be so. Funny how, with repetition, it gets all turned around."

"What are we waiting *outside* for, Daddy?"

"Sshh! Don't bother Grandma!" I whispered and eased the door on open.

I was sure they'd heard us, but if so, they gave no indication. She was in her rocking chair and the man was on the floor at her feet, his head in her lap. "You've been so much help to me," he said. It was Inspector Pardew. She seemed to be stroking his temples. "I'd always thought of that story as a parable on time—the hundred years compressed to a dream, the bastard birth of chronology, then our irrational fear of losing it. The destruction of dawn and all our days, our sun, our moon, seemed so horrible that only something beyond our imagination, like a demon or an ogre, could be responsible. But, of course, all it takes is a jealous wife . . ."

"Yes, but one mustn't forget the prior crime, the one that set the rest in motion—"

"Daddy? There's something *hard* inside Peedie."

"Yes, all right . . ."

"Why are we whispering?"

The Inspector looked up. "Come in, come in," he said irritably, and put his head back down in her lap. He was wearing his scarf again, clasping the ends with one hand. I pushed the door shut behind us. "You were saying, m'um, the original—?"

"You know, the party, the disgruntled guest, the curse. The stabbing . . ."

"Ah yes—but was it really a crime? Or only a sort of prior condition?"

"Get it *out*, Daddy!"

"All right, all right." I laid him in his bed and drew a loose sheet up over him (he kicked it off), took up the stuffed bunny. I knew, even before I'd pushed my finger in the hole and touched it, what it was. "It makes him stronger, Mark, like a backbone—you sure you don't want to leave it in there—?"

"I want it *out!* It *hurts* him!" The Inspector sighed impatiently and closed his eyes. Mark was tired and on edge from all the excitement— the least thing and he could break into one of his tantrums. I reached in with two fingers, clamping the handle, pushing down on the point from the outside.

"Perhaps, like you say, I've been struggling with this problem too long," Pardew brooded. "I feel as I circle around it, groping, scrutinizing, probing, that something *is* trying to be born here—but that, unfortunately, it might already be dead." My mother-in-law flinched at this. "I'm sorry, did I—?"

"No . . . a memory . . ."

The end of the handle was protruding now: I drew it out, remembering something my wife had said, shortly after she came home from the hospital: "It's not the loss, Gerald, there are others waiting to be born, but rather . . ."

"Daddy, I'm afraid of the dark."

I stooped to kiss him and tuck him in. "Rather," my wife had said, "it's the way it *hated* me at the end, I knew everything it was thinking, the terrible bitterness and rage it felt, it would have *killed* me if it could—and what was worse, I agreed with it . . ." "Well, it's not dark now."

"When I go to sleep, it *gets* dark."

"I only meant that truth, when it is no longer pertinent, is not in the same sense truth any longer, do you follow, m'um? I may solve the crime, you see, only to discover that its very definition has moved on to another plane." The Inspector seemed not to want to be interrupted, so I set the ice pick on the emptied shelves near him, where he could find it later. My mother-in-law frowned at it, glanced sharply up at me. I shrugged. "It's as if that prince of yours were to hack his way through his thicket of briars and brambles, only to arouse a creature suffering from a fatal disease, as it were, or one who's lost her wits."

"Or perhaps to find a host of competing Beauties," she suggested, turning back to the Inspector, her face dark with consternation, "each

seemingly fairer than the rest, and then what's he to do? Awaken only one and condemn the rest to death in life? No, yet if he should kiss them all, their multitudinous awakenings would reduce his own life to chaos and madness . . ."

"Yes! Strange! I-I was just thinking the same . . . !"

"I know," she sighed and stroked his head.

"It all goes round and round," the Inspector said, his voice quavering slightly. "Sometimes I . . . I don't know where I am!"

"Yes, yes . . . it's all right . . ."

I turned to leave, but I heard a lot of people outside the door—Wilma, Patrick, Vachel, Kitty, Cyril perhaps ("Fiona—?" someone asked), Teresa, others—and I didn't feel up to facing them. Anyway, Mark was settling down at last, his eyelids fluttering, it seemed best not to let anything or anyone disturb that.

"May I . . . may I tell you a story, m'um? It's been bothering me and I—"

"Certainly." My mother-in-law had stacked some dirty plates and glasses on the chest of drawers near the door—I found half a warm old-fashioned and something else with ice and mixed them.

"Well, many years ago, you see, when I was just getting started in the force, I was called in to assist on a strange case that had utterly baffled the shrewdest and most experienced minds in our division. A famous historian—his field was actually prehistory, I believe: would that have made him a prehistorian? no, it doesn't sound right—at any rate, this historian was found in his library one morning, bound hand and foot, and strangled to death with a garrote believed to have been of ancient Iberian origin. At first it had seemed a case of simple robbery—several gold and silver artifacts were reported missing, the window had been jimmied, there were footprints in the garden—but in fact it had seemed *too* simple, too *self-referential*, if you take my meaning. A careful examination of the impression made in the window frame by the jimmy revealed it to have been an exotic Iron Age relic, and that plus the murder weapon itself pointed to someone familiar with the victim's scholarly field. This suspicion was soon confirmed by a laboratory analysis of certain fibers the dead man was clutching in one closed fist and a lone fingerprint on the garrote itself, which turned out in both cases to belong to the historian's young assistant, a man known for his adventurism and unbridled ambition. But before the arrest could be made, the suspect died suddenly of a

rare subtropical disease. Poetic justice, one might say. Some of the missing artifacts were found in the young man's quarters and—even more damning—the exotic jimmy. The case seemed closed—until a meticulous autopsy revealed, about three inches inside the young man's rectum, the remains of a suppository containing traces of a deadly bacterial toxin. Intimacy with his assailant was assumed, needless to say, leading the Inspector on the case to suspect the historian's daughter, who, according to the family butler, had once been ravished by the young man and had subsequently become, though engaged to another man, his slave and paramour—I quote the butler, of course, m'um, who, as a native of the Andes, spoke with a certain quaint frankness. It is true, other suppositories of a more innocent nature were found in the man's medicine cabinet, such that theoretically the murder weapon could have been, as it were, self-administered, but there were other reasons that the daughter fell under the strong shadow of suspicion, not only for his murder, but for her father's as well. With the young assistant out of the way, she was now the sole heiress to her father's works, published and unpublished, together with all the research materials gathered by both of them. Her public rivalry with the young man was well known, as well as her violent amatory relationship, which no doubt exacerbated what hostile feelings she might have harbored, and it was also no secret that she bore no natural affection for her father, a man so hermetically enclosed in his work, he had paid her, throughout her life, scant attention. I hardly need point out to you, m'um, the dismal consequences that so often attend the negligence of one's paternal duties. Moreover, it was she who had found her father's body, in all crimes a suspicious circumstance, and it was now remembered that she had been wearing white gloves at the time, the sort worn by museum personnel when moving valuable displays, or by technicians handling film. It was altogether possible that the butler had surprised her at the conclusion of her murderous act such that she had had to, quote, discover the body sooner than she had intended, if you follow my drift. When, finally, one of her personal hairs was found embedded in the, admittedly, minuscule remains of the suppository inside the young man's lower anatomy, the evidence against her, as you can imagine, was irresistible. Of course, it was possible the young man might somehow have swallowed the hair, but the means of doing so, in those days anyway and in such august circles, seemed quite beyond the imagination—as perhaps it

is beyond your imagination now, m'um, in spite of the depraved times in which we live. At any rate, the Inspector gathered all the suspects together in the father's library, scene of the prior and, as it were, primal murder, and—with the appropriate dramaturgical preliminaries—announced his suspicions. The young woman looked shocked, pained—but it was real pain as it happened, for in fact she was dying, poisoned it would seem by someone in that very room, her glass of cascarilla, as we soon discovered, having been laced with deadly aconite. It was at this point that I was brought into the case, a young lieutenant with a specialization at that time in forensic anthropology. I needn't go into the details. The butler, who had been near the scene of the crime on all three occasions and who, by virtue of his service, had left traces of himself everywhere, including, as it turned out, his telltale footprints in the garden, seemed clearly to have been the ingenious perpetrator of this baffling triple murder, motivated evidently by a desire to revenge the ruthless pillaging of his nation's treasures by these foreign intellectuals and perhaps to create thereby the legend of a curse upon these artifacts in order to encourage their eventual return to his people—but no sooner did we seem to have the goods on him than he too was suddenly done away with, in this instance by particularly brutal means: he was savaged, m'um, by the family's pet lynx, believed to have been crazed by a fagot of rare tropical herbs tossed into its pen. And so it went, from one suspect to another—the historian's semi-invalid wife, the young creole maid, a former student of the historian suspected of ties with an unfriendly foreign government, an elder colleague at the historical society—each in his turn found, a suspected murderer, murdered." The Inspector paused in his story. Mark, snuggled up around Peedie, was asleep at last and the traffic outside the door had subsided. It was a good moment to slip away, but I really didn't know where to go—like Mark, I was feeling lulled by all this genteel violence and hesitated to make any move that might break the spell. "It was my first challenge, m'um, and I was failing. I'd . . . I'd even begun to wonder if our efforts were, in some bizarre way . . . well . . . I mean, it was almost as if we were selecting the victims . . ." His voice broke slightly.

"It was like a trial," she said. "You were being tested."

"That's true . . . those were dark days, m'um . . ."

"But you won through in the end . . ."

"Well, I did. But not as I might have foreseen. As a young criminal-

istician, I was committed to the classical empirical tradition, to pure scientific analysis and the deductive enterprise. But, in the end, the solution came to me, I must tell you . . . in a dream . . ." He heaved a tremulous sigh that shook his chest. "A . . . a young woman . . ."

"I see . . ."

"She was so . . . so . . ." He clutched his face in his hands, his shoulders quaking.

"There, there," my mother-in-law said, patting his pate.

There was a pause. His trembling subsided. When he took up his story again, he had regained his composure, but there was a quaver yet in his voice, the cords tensed. "She . . . she came to me across a vast expanse of what in the dream seemed more like time than space. A barren wasteland—like truth itself, I thought when I awoke."

"Yes . . ."

"There was something before this about a city, or more than one perhaps—I'd been traveling, I think, through ancient iniquitous realms, dream representations no doubt of those deplorable consequences of man's incorrigible nature which it had become my lot to study, to live among—but now we were alone together in this infinite desolation. She wore a pure white tunic, a girdle at her waist, her head and shoulders bare, her feet too perhaps, I don't remember. A common stereotype, you will say, a storybook cliché—and it is true, as I watched her glide toward me across the flats with a grace that was itself archetypal, I felt reduced to a certain helpless innocence, simplified, stripped of all my pretensions, my professional habits, my learning—literally stripped perhaps, for I felt a certain unwonted vulnerability, not unlike nakedness, though of a spiritual sort, I'm sure you'll appreciate . . ."

"I know . . ."

"But she was not as she seemed. Oh no! It was as though she had dressed herself up as a commonplace, the more to set off her very uniqueness, her extraordinary, her special—what can I say?—her profound *selfness*. Instinctively, I understood: she was the *truth*. The rest of my life seemed like those ruined cities I had just visited, teeming with congested activity and feverish aspirations, but inwardly empty and aimless. And utterly condemned. So you can imagine how I felt, standing transfixed there in that boundless space—or time—feeling naked and unworthy, yet flushed with a kind of bewildered awe that I should have been singled out, chosen among all men, to receive her. Nothing like this had ever happened to me, in or out of dreams. I was

struck dumb with wonder. As she drew near, the very barrenness around me seemed to glow, to pulsate with an inner frenzy. And then she stopped. Not near enough to touch, but I wouldn't have touched her had I been able, m'um, I couldn't even move. She smiled—or rather, the serene smile she bore by nature deepened—and she spoke. What she said was: "The victim is the killer." He paused as though redigesting this news. The hand clutching the scarf at his throat trembled slightly. "Even now I can hear her voice . . ."

"A riddle . . ."

"So I thought, though later I was to learn otherwise. Now, in fear and trembling, I asked her to repeat herself, but she would not, she only smiled. I begged for another word, some understanding, had I heard her right? But she only continued to smile. Or rather, the smile seemed locked onto her face, for she no longer seemed quite real, an image rather, a kind of statue, but slowly fading—my heart leaped to my throat! I was about to lose her, lose everything! I reached out at last toward that silvery presence—but into nothing, she was turning into thin air! In fact, she *was* thin air—I was sitting up in my bed, groping in the dawn light, and staring at a pale frozen figure across the room: myself in the floor-length mirror on the far wall." So he stared now, his face drawn, his moustaches hanging heavy as anchors, seeming to drag the flesh down after them.

My mother-in-law drew his head into her lap once more, caressed his temples. "It was not a riddle?"

"No." His voice was muffled now, shaken, but, when he resumed, resigned. "I wrestled with it as though it were, alone of course, reluctant to mention it to my dour and earnest colleagues—they would have thought me mad, as I thought myself at times. But then another suspect died—a former lover of the historian, a teacher of Hellenic romances who fell, or was pushed, down a pothole in the Pindus Mountains whereto she'd evidently fled—and suddenly the whole sinister pattern of this bizarre case became clear to me. Without explaining myself but hinting at my suspicions, I asked that the historian's private diaries be unlocked. My colleagues scoffed—"Audacity don't win no medals around here, son," the Inspector on the case said, being as he was from the old school, you see—but I warned them that if we didn't act quickly other victims would almost certainly be caught up in this deadly chain. Reluctantly, they let me have my way—and sure enough, hidden away in the more recent entries, encoded to appear

nothing more than notations on an ancient Mayan calendric stela, lay the historian's ingenious plan to set into motion, with his own suicide, an infinite and ineluctable series of murders. Some he had merely foreseen, others he had himself committed—the poisoning of his daughter, for example: with his profound knowledge of historical—and prehistorical—theatrics, he had foreseen our gathering there in his library that night, known of his daughter's singular weakness for cascarilla, and so on, obtaining in advance the unsuspecting butler's fingerprints on the decanter. The lover in the pothole had been found clutching what looked like an old-fashioned treasure map drawn with vegetable inks, and these too were found in the historian's safe. The elder colleague at the historical society had sat on a poisoned tack in the very room in which the police interviewed him, a room kept locked except for occasions, as the prehistorian was well aware, when extreme privacy was required. On the other hand, it was fairly likely the former student *had* shot the creole maid, a necessary link in the chain, but hardly less inevitable than the others."

"It's quite extraordinary!"

"Yes, m'um, the fatal series might have run on forever had we not, upon deciphering the encoded plot, stopped the historian's brother-in-law from taking the late daughter's fiancé out hunting. And in the nick of time. It was a celebrated case, the turning point of my career. With it I won advancement, fame, the respect of my colleagues." He sighed. "But . . ."

"It's not why you've told me the story."

"No . . ." The Inspector withdrew one of Ginger's kerchiefs and blew his nose in it. "Are you sure you want to hear all this?"

"Of course . . ."

"I . . . I'm not married, you see . . ."

"The young woman in the dream . . ."

"Yes. I thought you'd . . . you'd understand. I've needed to tell someone about it for a very long time. I've kept it . . . kept it bottled up all these years. It was a very strange period in my life . . ." He lay his head back again. "An intermingling of life and dream that was very much like madness . . ."

"Was that the only time—?"

"No, over the next few years, she reappeared every now and then in my dreams, often to assist me in a case, sometimes to bring me consolation or courage, once to provide, if you'll pardon my opening my

heart to you in this way, m'um, a kind of pleasure—the only pleasure of, well, that sort I've ever known or wish to know, unless it should come from her lips, her hands . . . and so forth."

"It's very rare. To fall in love in a dream, I mean . . ."

"I know. And you can take my word for it, it's a very dangerous sort of love. A kind of possession, really. Like all lovers everywhere, I was given to violent extremes of passion and desire, but they had no living object. Though my beloved was less even than a phantom, I loved her more than life itself, which without her was unbearable, and more phantasmal than my dreams. My appetite declined, I was easily distracted, easily enraged. Never more so than when awakened from sleep. It was, at that time, all I longed for: the chance—the *only* chance—to be with her again. I spent more and more of my life in bed, forcing sleep, searching for her through half-real, half-nightmarish landscapes, begging her to reappear. She did so only rarely but often with a certain timeliness: without her insights I probably would have failed utterly at my neglected work and lost my position on the force. She rescued me from that. But not from my mad passion, as boundless and ultimately as barren as that vast plain where first we met. I once asked her whence she came. 'From far away, in another place,' she replied, and again I was sure she meant 'time.' I never dared to try to touch her after what had happened that first time, though once she . . ." Again a racking sigh broke from the Inspector's chest, and his face seemed momentarily flushed and swollen, his eyes feverish.

"I understand . . ."

"Finally, fearing for my sanity, I consulted a specialist, a psychiatrist who had often assisted us in cases requiring the interpretation of dreams. He convinced me that my original insight had been the correct one: she was indeed the truth. Only not an abstract external truth, mysteriously turning up from nowhere, but the more complex and profound truths I carried within. I had to admit that everything she had said I had probably intuited myself, in some form or another, but, through timidity or professional caution, or even fear or shame perhaps, I had hidden these thoughts away in some deep recess of my inner self: she was the figurative representation of the beauty, the serenity, that attends their release from what he in his profession called repression. Once I had been able to accept that, though I loved her still and would never love another, she at least and at last disappeared from my dreams, allowing me to return to the waking world, and I

never . . . saw her . . . again." He was beginning to choke up. He pressed his trembling fingers to his brows, as though trying to stop his head from splitting open there, took a deep rasping breath. "Until . . . until tonight . . . !"

"Oh dear!"

"That girl . . . down there!" She reached for him as he began to sob. "In the—*gasp!*—the *silvery frock!*"

"Now, now . . ."

"It was *her!* I *know* it was!" he wept. "*I've missed her so! Boo hoo! And now . . . !*"

"That's right, let the tears come, you'll feel better."

"*Oh m'um—!*" His chest heaved and he pitched forward into her lap, burying his face there, just as someone or something hit the door with tremendous force, making us all jump.

My mother-in-law swung round to glower at me—then they hit it again. The whole room shook, a string of pennants fell, a crack appeared above the door. "*Stand back!*" someone shouted—it sounded like the tall cop, Bob.

"*It's not locked!*" I yelled, lurching for the knob—but too late, the door gave way with a splintering crash, and Bob and Fred tumbled head over heels into the room. They leaped up and sprang at the bed, pitching the mattress over, Mark and all. "*Hey, wait—!!*"

"*We can't wait, we got a hot tip!*" hollered Fred, scrabbling through the bedclothes and under the bed. I rushed over to help my mother-in-law pull Mark out from under the mattress—his eyes were wide open but so far he hadn't let out a peep. He didn't even seem to know where he was. Or who I was as I picked him up. "*There it is!*" cried Bob.

They ripped Peedie out of his arms and tore it apart, flinging the stuffing into the air like snow. Now Mark did open up: he began to scream at the top of his lungs. The Inspector was on his feet, his back to us, cleaning out his nose with Ginger's kerchief; he turned to scowl over his shoulder at Mark with reddened eyes. My mother-in-law took him, still howling, from my arms: "*Now* see what you've done!" she fumed.

"It ain't in there," said Fred; not on the bookshelf now either, I noticed. All that was left of the rabbit was a limp rag. Fred looked up at the people crowding into the room behind me ("What's happening?" a woman called from out in the hall—"They're beating up the kid!"),

then shrugged: "Ah well, win a few, lose a few. Here, boy." He handed the empty pelt back to Mark, who shrank away ("Yeah? Let *me* see!"), shrieking in terror.

There was no turning him off now, he was completely out of control. My mother-in-law, in an ice-cold rage, snatched the rag out of the cop's hands and started gathering up the stuffing, Mark ("I *love* it!" someone exclaimed) still kicking and squalling madly in her arms. "Before you go, you can put that mattress back!" she ordered, and with a murmur of sullen "Yes'm's," the two officers dutifully heaved it back on its box springs again.

"What's the matter with that damned child?" Inspector Pardew complained, brushing irritably at his gray suit.

"I'll go get his mother," I offered, not knowing what else to do. Mark, I knew, could scream like that for hours. Fred looked up at me with raised brows, glanced at Bob, who looked away. "*And* the bedding!" my mother-in-law commanded. "We ain't housemaids," Bob grumbled, but they did as they were told.

"That young man needs a little discipline," remarked Pardew gruffly, nodding at his cops.

I pushed out through the jam-up in the splintered doorway (Patrick was out there, pacing nervously: "Do you think I can go in now?" he asked Woody), thinking that what *I* needed right now was a long cold drink. It was what my mother always said whenever my father began to wax philosophical. He was never very happy on such occasions; that always made him feel a lot worse. She tried it on me once when I started to tell her what I wanted to be when I grew up; I could imagine how he felt. Of course, an excess of philosophy was not exactly my problem right now ("Oops! excuse me, Gerry," said Wilma, catching me in the ribs with her elbow, "is Talbot in there?"), but something of the rotten moods that always attended my father's disquisitions was working its way deep inside me—sometimes on long family drives it got almost unbearable, and (Mark was still shrieking, Pardew was shouting, his assistants shouting back, I was surrounded by drunk and irascible guests, sour boozy breaths, total strangers, the guy with the TV camera shoved past me like he owned the place, my house was coming down around my ears) it was almost unbearable now, such that when Kitty touched my forearm at the head of the stairs, I nearly threw her down them. "There's someone," she whispered. "*What*—?!" I bellowed angrily. "In there," she said, shying

from my outburst and ("Oh, get off your high horse," my mother would say, my father having just remarked that "Beauty is like the rescue of an enchained maiden from some monster from the deeps—but Truth is that poor damned beast," "and fix me a cold drink!") nodding toward the sewing room. "Waiting for you." "Ah . . . ! Sorry. . . ."

I could hardly move. I'd all but given up and now, suddenly. . . . No, no, it's often like that, I reminded myself, my heart pounding: Don't be afraid. But I was afraid. I'd waited too long: now ("And Goodness is the reckless stupidity of the maiden," he'd add, turning to me with the cocktail shaker in his hands, "the beast's wistful surrender . . .") it seemed unreal. And just an arm's reach away. I stepped toward the door, ordering my legs to move. The air was heavy near the bathroom, it was almost like swimming. "Alison—?" I whispered. The door was a couple of inches ajar: the lights were out, it was dark inside. I saw the peckersweater on her finger then and, after a quick glance down at the landing (it was empty), followed it in.

"Hey, keep the door closed," someone muttered from across the room. "Alison!" She pulled me inside and threw her arms around me with a whimper almost of pain. I felt it too: a constriction in my chest (the peckersweater was what she was dressed in!) that took my breath away. "At last!" I cried, clasping her flesh in my arms, flooding over with the joy of it, the familiarity, the suppleness—"I can't believe it! I thought you'd—!" "Sshh!" she hissed, and pressed her mouth against mine, running her hands up inside my shirt, loosening the tie, fumbling with the belt, her excitement making her almost childish in her clumsiness: I was clumsy, too, my hands trembling, my breath coming in short gulps—this was it then! it was happening! "Hurry!" she whispered, dragging me toward the sewing area (the studio couch in the corner was taken, I could hear rustlings and mumblings: "Well, it's different," someone acknowledged) where pillows had been tossed down and heaped with clean laundry. I was shackled by my trousers: I managed to kick one canvas shoe off and free a leg. I felt rushed, as though something important (distantly Mark was screaming, I didn't hear him) had been passed over, but I understood it—it was like what Tania used to say about painting: you plan and you plan, but when it happens, it's a total shock, sudden and overwhelming, and you have to take it as it comes, trust your craft and surrender to the unexpected. She held my penis with her bare hand (I surrendered it, not at all

wistfully, the unexpected encasing me like a condom), stroking my testicles with the furry cock sock, her mouth at my throat. I buried my face in her hair which was almost crackly with excitement, its sweet smell mingling with the deeper aroma now wafting up between her legs, she was spending freely, if that was the word, it sounded too commercial, my hands wallowed there, reaching as it were for that magic moment on the back porch, though everything was harder now, more real, no, for all the familiarity of it, this had *not* happened before, this was new—and *now*: the comings and goings were over, *it was on!* "Oh yes! *good* boy!" gasped some woman in the corner. "That's not him, it's me," another woman said, her voice muffled. I knelt, sliding my mouth (*Craft! Craft!* I was shouting at my exploding mind) down her taut trembling body toward that sweet flow below, but she pulled away, sinking back onto the pile of pillows and laundry and dragging me with her. Yes, true, it was not to be wasted—she was coming, her whole body was shaking as I rolled between her legs, and my own excitement was surging toward hers—we were rushing pell-mell toward that denouement we'd share, the cracker, as Quagg would say, the blow-off, the final spasm. Which in the end is achieved, as I might have said that night at the theater, and perhaps did, neither by art nor by nature, but by a perfect synthesis (I could still remember such words: synthesis) of both. There was such an abundance of secretions between her legs that I slipped right past the entry, squeezing down the greasy aisle between the cheeks of her behind: she reached under (she was clutching my neck tightly with her other hand, her mouth at my ear, the fragrant laundry billowing around us like some kind of magical cloud) and guided me in: she was amazingly tight as though resisting her own mounting excitement, holding back, waiting for me. I thrust fiercely at her (the people on the studio couch were climaxing, too, I could hear them gasping and grunting—"God, I'm hot!" one of them wheezed), just as she pitched upward to meet me, driving her thighs up under my arms, whimpering: "Oh, I *love* you, Gerry! I *love* you!" in my ear.

"*Sally Ann—!!*" I bellowed, with such a shout that, startled, her whole body constricted in a violent spasm, locking me into her, my penis gripped just under the crown by the knifelike edge of her half-ruptured hymen. "*For god's sake, let go!*" I cried.

"*I can't!*" she wailed. "*Owww!*"

"*Damn* you, Sally Ann! You're *hurting* me!"

"What's going on?" asked one of the women on the studio couch.

"Are you all the way in, Gerry?" Sally Ann choked, her voice squeaky with shock and pain.

"No—*ow!*—I'm not in *or* out, it's much *worse* than that!"

"That's all right, I'm all done anyway," a man said. "I'll go splash 'em." I could hear him padding across the room toward the door.

"*Please*, Gerry! Don't stop now! I don't care *how* it hurts!"

The lights came on, blinding us for a moment. Sally Ann, in anguish, continued to pump away, hugging me tight, trying to lodge me deeper, but I'd long since gone limp with pain.

"Well, well, what have we here?" It was Horner, that wooden soldier, at the light switch, one hand holding his pants up. Teresa was frantically pulling on her yellow knit dress, Daffie stretched out naked on the studio couch beside her, legs wearily aspraddle. "You could have waited a minute!" Teresa called out from inside the dress, jerking the hem down past the swell of her midriff.

I had torn Sally Ann's hands away and was trying to extricate myself, but the door, as they say, had swung shut on that domain. "I didn't know it would *be* like this, Gerry! I'm *sorry!*" she groaned, her eye paint-smudged, making her look like some theatrical parody of the living dead. I drew my knees up under her thrashing rear and leaned back on my haunches—not very comfortable, but I could hold her down that way, keep her from scissoring the thing off.

The door opened and Zack Quagg poked his nose in from the hall— "Hey, Horn, I been looking for you, what's going on?"—followed by Woody and Cynthia (Horner, winking, licked his thumb as though to turn a page), holding hands: "Oh no," Woody said, his eyes crinkling up with compassion when he saw me. "I'll go get Jim."

"Yes, please!" I gasped. "*Hurry!*" I could hear Mark again—his wailing was now sleepy and rhythmical, dirgelike. "Stay still, Sally Ann!"

"I *want* to—but it's all moving by *itself!*"

"For goodness' sake! What have you been *doing?!*" asked Wilma, arriving short of breath as though after a run. "Lloyd Draper's giving a slide show downstairs, Teresa, and we've been *waiting* for you!" Cynthia knelt beside us, holding back my pubic hairs to have a closer look. "Can you relax a bit?" she asked, and Sally Ann wailed: "I *am* relaxing!" Quagg was pulling Horner ("This place looks too busy," said Janny Trainer, peeping in, our plumber Steve in tow), still blowing kisses back over his shoulder, out the door: "Come on, we got

something on the boil, man—something *great!*" "Yeah, okay, Zack, but first lemme get something to eat . . ."

"He *said* he was casting me for a part," explained Teresa, smoothing down her skirt, looking around on the floor for something more, and Wilma said: "Well, just try telling that to Peg!" "What? Is my sister still here?" Cynthia was wiggling my member back and forth as though trying to free a key from a broken lock: "Ow, don't!" I cried. "That's not helping!"

"You're bleeding, Sally Ann," Cynthia observed, looking at her fingers. "Am I?" Sally Ann lifted herself up on her elbows to see for herself. "Yeah!" she gasped, and lay back smiling, her face wet with sweat. "God! I'm bleeding!"

"It may be *me!*" I whimpered.

"And this is our sewing room," my wife said. "Soyng?" She stood in the doorway with Iris Draper, Alison's husband, Hilario the Panamanian tapdancer ("Ah! Zo-eeng! Weeth the leetle, how you say, pointed theeng!"), that guy with the elbow patches I'd met out in the backyard, and two people I'd never seen before. "It hasn't been redecorated for a few years, I'm afraid."

"It's very nice," said Iris, and my wife sighed and said: "It serves its purpose, I guess." Alison's husband frowned when he saw me; what's-his-name (Geoffrey?) from outside smiled and waved. "Do you need any help, Gerald?"

"Jim's coming," I gasped, gritting my teeth, and Wilma, buttoning Teresa up the back, said: "You should have seen Cyril just now on television! You really missed it! He's a natural!" "He's a pig." "How can you say that?" "Haven't you heard?" Gottfried, that was his name ("Fiona? Really—?"), I could hardly think. My head seemed to be full of little sparks. "But you're . . . all right—?"

"All right?"

"The—*gasp!*—interview . . ."

"Oh yes, Woody was very helpful. Some of the things they were doing were apparently illegal." She was wearing that plasticky apron with the old soap ad on it, and it made her look stiff and mechanical somehow. "He made them take the candle out, for example." Iris came by, evidently studying the paintwork, or maybe all the childish decals on everything. "Goodness, I suppose it was a mistake to do all that laundry . . ."

The bearded guy with the video camera on his shoulder pushed in

behind the others, viewfinder to his eye, one hand working the zoom. I tried to turn my back to him, but it hurt too much to move. Iris spied the fallen peckersweater and picked it up: "Interesting!" she said, adjusting her spectacles. Sally Ann reached up and covered herself as the cameraman closed in. "If you haven't really done it, Gerry, don't let him see."

"Wait for me!" called Teresa (Wilma was in the doorway, introducing herself to the two strangers, a stout man in a brown three-piece suit and a white-haired lady in lime slacks, a pink-and-lemon shirt, Iris saying something about having to go through her catalogues when she got home, see if she could find one, Lloyd was always getting a chill). "My other shoe . . ."

"I think I'm lying on it," Daffie grumbled, and Hilario, turning to go, asked: "Ees peenk woe-man, no?"

"Any color you can get, lover."

"The only trouble," Iris decided, after a stroll through the room ("What's she trying to hide?" the cameraman wanted to know, and Cynthia tugged Sally Ann's hands away: "Don't worry, dear, it's all right . . ."), "is that there's not enough light."

"I know, it's on the north side."

"No, I meant the wallpaper."

"Well, now, let's see what we have here," Jim said, announcing himself, and the cameraman moved on ("It's called 'Paintbox Green,'" my wife was saying) to pick up Daffie. "What do you think about the breakdown of law and order in our society?" he asked as he zoomed in. "She seized up on him," Cynthia explained quietly, lifting the root of my penis. "Just here at the neck." Jim set his bag down and knelt beside us. "Hmmm," he said, probing Sally Ann's thighs and the muscles around her anus. "All this handcream she has packed in here might've helped if she'd put it in the right place . . ."

"That's the sort of sewing machine I've been telling you about, honey," the lady in the lime slacks said.

"Ah, yes . . ."

"These are our new neighbors from down the street, Gerald. Mr. and Mrs. Waddilow."

I craned around to look at them. "We heard the music and just stopped in to say hello," Mr. Waddilow smiled. "Hope you don't mind." Alison's husband had disappeared, Hilario as well, but Howard was in the room now, over in the far corner near the ironingboard

closet, wearing Tania's half-lens reading glasses on the fat part of his nose, watching the cameraman as he panned the horizon of Daffie's body. "You've got a nice place here," said Mr. Waddilow.

"Why don't you stuff that ray gun up your ass, cowboy?" Daffie suggested.

"It's lightweight and almost entirely automatic, with a special attachment for lace edging," Mrs. Waddilow called from across the room.

"What?" her husband toddled over to look at it, his pantcuffs riding an inch or two above his white socks and two-toned shoes, crossing paths with Howard, who floated out now without saying a word, hands clapped decorously over his brassiere cups. "Oh yes, I see. Very good."

"Mr. Waddilow is an airline pilot, Gerald." "Does this hurt?" asked Jim. "Yes!" cried Sally Ann, and I yelped as well. "I don't think we've ever had a real pilot in our neighborhood before, have we?"

"No . . . but—ow!—if you don't mind . . ."

"Retired, actually," Mr. Waddilow said, hooking his thumbs in the pockets of his brown vest. "I'm in travel now."

"This old sewing basket is nice, too," Mrs. Waddilow added.

"You should check on Mark," I gasped, "they broke the door down—"

"I know, I was just in there. Mother's fixing Peedie." That's right, I noticed now, I couldn't hear him anymore. "Someone put the ears on backward."

"I'm afraid that was my fault," smiled Cynthia, looking up over her shoulder. "I don't know much about rabbits."

"Wah—!"

"Sorry . . ."

"If I can be of any help," Mr. Waddilow said. "I used to raise rabbits."

"You can feel here the adductor muscles," Jim was explaining (Woody had returned and now squatted by Cynthia, pursing his lips thoughtfully), "the so-called 'pillars of virginity,' how tense they are, right up into the vagina." "Oh yes . . ." He searched through his bag, watched closely by the cameraman, who, kneeling beside us, focused now on Jim's hands. "What are you going to do?" Sally Ann asked apprehensively, propping herself up on her elbows.

"Take your tonsils out," Jim smiled. "Now just settle back . . ."

"I haven't seen one of these things in years," Woody murmured. His shorts, still on backward, bagged up oddly above his thighs.

"Come, I'll show you our guest room," said my wife.

"When you think about it," Cynthia whispered, gently separating with ringed fingers Sally Ann's spongy outer lips, "it's really a kind of packaging problem."

"Though actually right now it's being used by my mother."

"Catch you later," Mr. Waddilow called, following my wife out, and Gottfried tucked his long bent pipe in his mouth and waved again. "Oh, do you have your mother staying with you?" someone said out in the hall. "You're very fortunate!"

"I'm going to make a very tiny incision," Jim explained, and I felt her flinch again. "And then you can do the rest with your fingers."

"Won't it hurt . . . ?"

"Only a little." He pulled a stick of gum out of his pocket and handed it to her. "Here, this will take your mind off it."

Sally Ann lay back and unwrapped the gum, her eyes dark with worry and smeared makeup. "Is she no longer a virgin then?" the cameraman asked, zooming in as Jim leaned forward.

"Who can say? Technically, she's neither one thing nor the other, but—"

"*Yow!!*" I cried.

"Sorry, Gerry."

Woody cleared his throat. "Well, legally—"

"Something *stabbed* me!"

"I know. Here, hold this up for me, will you?" he said to Cynthia, pincering the shaft gently between thumb and forefinger. "Don't let it sag . . ." Sally Ann's jaws snapped at the gum as though trying to speed up time, and for a brief moment I felt a certain empathy with the child, roughly but intimately linked with her as I was, as though I'd been giving birth to her and the navel string had knotted up and needed cutting. Not (I shuddered, and Cynthia patted my member gently: "Won't be long now . . .") that the image was a comforting one.

"A little more . . ."

Sally Ann groaned. Her jaws were clamped now, her teeth bared, a little bubble of gum sticking up between them like a fleshy growth: she gasped as Jim broke through and the gum disappeared. "Oh my gosh," she choked, "I think I *swallowed* it!"

"You're doing fine," Jim said, guiding her hands down. "Now just take hold here and slowly stretch yourself apart . . ."

"I thought this was supposed to be fun," she whimpered. Over on the couch, Daffie laughed and said: "You been going to the wrong church, kiddo."

Our midwife Cynthia, jiggling the key again, gave a quick tug and I was free, sliding out through Sally Ann's clenched knuckles as though on rails. I fell back, struggling to unbend my legs. One of them was still tangled in my trousers: Cynthia pulled my shoe off and stripped the rest away. I stretched out, ignoring the cameraman who hovered above me, thinking: So this is what it comes to, all the artful preparations, all the garnering of experience and sensual fine-tuning, and you're just another curiosity, a kind of decorous monster who pees on his wife's flowers and hurts children.

Sally Ann was crying, curled up on her side with her hands between her thighs, the cameraman moving in over her blood-streaked buttocks onto her tear-streaked face, then switching off. He unbelted the camera, took the weight off his shoulder: "Good show," he grunted, and put a lens cap on. "I don't really think that's necessary, Woody," Jim was saying, and Woody, holding hands with Cynthia above me, said: "Perhaps not, but he's a client. I have an ethical responsibility to let him know."

Jim shook his head as they left, then stooped to put his gear back in the bag. "Here, put this between your legs," he said, handing Sally Ann one of our kitchen curtains. "If you'll come to see me, I'll teach you how to pass graduated heated pneumatic dilators up to half a foot or so, then you won't have any more problems." Sally Ann only moaned, doubled up there in her nest of laundry and clutching the curtain to her fork like a child its security blanket, but the cameraman said: "I wonder if you'd look at this cut on my face, Doc."

"Hmm. I hadn't noticed it there, under the beard. It's quite deep—"

"Yeah, stiletto heels. Very sharp."

"I think there's some antibacterial cream in the bathroom."

"Too bad she didn't get him in the eye," Daffie grumbled, as Jim led the cameraman out. "If it hadn't been for him, Dickie and the others'd still be here." I was searching around for my clothes, but all I could find were my shirt and socks. "Your pants are over here, Ger."

I struggled to my feet and crossed the room, but my knees were so weak I could hardly walk. "Do you mind?"

"Sit down, sit down . . ."

My trousers were all knotted up and inside out. It was as if someone had tried to make a cat's cradle out of them. Just getting the underwear separated from the pants was like a Chinese puzzle. "Dickie's gone then, it's true," I said.

"Yeah. Between the cops, the mess his pretty clothes were in, and little young bung's maniacal old man . . ." She took a pull on her cheroot and then sighed, expelling dark smoke past my hip. Sally Ann was also beginning to stir, pushing up on one elbow to examine the curtains between her legs, the three of us alone now in the room.

"Why didn't you go along?"

"He had a full load." So that was it then. No point asking who he'd taken in her place. I sighed, surrendering to the inevitable as though learning a new habit. "Why all these *preparations?*" Ros had once asked me. "What are we *waiting* for?" I should have been listening. Sally Ann, waddling about now in her bikini underpants with extra padding in the crotch, had discovered a mirror (the frame was a cartoonish clown's face, the mirror his laughing—or gaping—mouth: little Gerald, I thought, was with us still) and was wiping the eye paint out of her eyes with a pillowcase. "You wanna know the truth, Ger?" Daffie said, her voice constricted. "I hate this fucking piece of meat. It makes me a lot of money, but I hate it." She stubbed her glowing cigar out on her pubis.

"Daffie—! *Hey!*" I pushed her hand away. There was a fresh pink wound just above her mound, and in the air the faint aroma of burnt hair and flesh. There were a lot of scars there, I saw. "I . . . I wondered why you never did full frontal poses," I said, touching them. They were glossy and unyielding, nubbly, rippling across her abdomen like faults, as though the flesh had been strip-mined. Her navel was blurred with overlaid scar tissue like the scratched-out face in Tania's painting.

"I wanna believe that the mind is something unique, Ger, that there's something called spirit or soul in me that's all my own and different from the body, and that someday it can somehow get out of it: it's my main desire. And it's all just a fucking fairy tale, isn't it? Her old man is right. And poor dumb Roger. Body is what we got. A bag of worms . . ."

Her act had sent a chill through me. It was as though she were trying to turn her flesh to stone. Tania liked to say that the idea of empti-

ness consoled her. Which I took as an ultimate form of madness: the mind rising to its nadir. I squeezed Daffie's hand. "Maybe," I said, the tears starting. "But yours is more beautiful than most. For our sake, you should keep it that way."

Sally Ann, standing beside us, also had a glitter in her eyes, though maybe it was just from scrubbing the paint away. She had a patch on the thigh of her jeans now that said "OPEN FOR BUSINESS"—probably she'd been saving it. "Thank you, Gerry," she said tenderly, knotting her shirttails. "It was beautiful. It was the most beautiful moment of my life." She stared charitably down at my limp organ. "And don't try to explain. I understand. Honest, Gerry, I wasn't at all disappointed, it was more than—"

"It was a cheap trick, Sally Ann. I ought to tan your britches!"

"Oh groan," she said, unwrapping another stick of gum, "all you dirty old men are just alike! Well, go ahead then!" She folded the gum into her mouth, switched around and arched her fanny up in front of my face: I couldn't resist. I reared back and cracked it with all my might. She yelped in surprise, then started gagging. "Oh *pee*, Gerry!" she wailed. "*You made me swallow my gum again!*" She took a wild swing at me, which I parried, then she went running, bawling, out of the room. "Boy, that felt good!" I said.

Daffie laughed, then raised herself up on one elbow and picked up my penis to have a look. "Anyway, it hasn't been husked." She slid the foreskin back with a deft finger.

"Ouch!"

"Oh yeah, I see. It's all raw there under the nub as if somebody'd tried to bite the nozzle off. Well, it's pretty, Ger, you know that, but it's just not callused enough." She dropped it and pushed herself up off the couch, stood there weaving, her feet planted wide apart. I'd got one pantleg free from the shorts, but the other was bound up in some kind of hitch knot. I untied it and turned the pantlegs rightside out. "You got anything here I can wear? My rig's all assed up."

"Whatever you find, help yourself." I pulled the shorts on, watching her stagger through the clutter (she dipped to one knee briefly, but got back up again), remembering the time we first fixed this room up as a nursery: everything in its place then like stage props. So long ago. And so much had happened. But then, I thought, recalling my wife in the doorway just now (she'd seemed her old self, hardly affected by all I'd seen her having to go through in the kitchen—that was coming back to me now, as I drew my trousers on, as though from some cir-

cuitous journey: the dark bruises on the backs of her thighs, for example, her tummy fanfolding, the faint trickle of blood radiating across
her pale nether cheeks—like cracked porcelain, I'd thought at the
time, overwhelmed just then by an inexpressible compassion . . . or
at least it had seemed inexpressible, and probably it was), not so
much. What had Pardew said? Change is an illusion of the human
condition, something like that. The passing images our senses delivered to us on our obligatory exploration of the space-time continuum,
pieced together like film frames to create the fiction of movement
and change, thereby inventing motive. Like this frame in front of me
now of Daffie's internationally famous derrière, glittering with perspiration, as she bent drunkenly from the waist to muddle about in the
scattered laundry: a way-station on the trajectory like any other. Just
the same, I was glad not to have missed it.

She held up a pair of my pale blue stretch denims that my wife had
up here for mending. "These okay?"

"Sure."

She got one foot in all right, but had trouble managing the other,
stumbling and loping through the pillows and laundry until she hit a
wall that propped her up. "Tell me something, Ger," she panted,
"that *was* your joystick in the photos with Ros, wasn't it?" I nodded,
feeling a prickling in my eyes again. "I thought I recognized it when
you were outside hosing down the roses. Who took the shots?"

"Some guy. We spent all afternoon at it." Daffie had the jeans up
past her thighs but was having difficulty, in spite of the give in the
material, squeezing the rest in. "A funny thing, there was a matinee
on that afternoon, and Ros was supposed to make a final brief appear-
ance as one of a group of resistance fighters, which she forgot about
until she heard them shouting for her. She went drifting dreamily
away from us and, through the wrong entrance, out onto the set,
wearing luminous green paint, some feathers on her tail, and a golden
crown, which of course brought the house down. Then, apropos of
nothing happening on stage, she delivered her one line: '*Follow me,
brothers, we have lost the battle, but we have not lost the war!*'"
Daffie laughed, but she was crying too. I wiped at my own eyes with
my shirtsleeve. "Probably her finest hour . . ."

Daffie took my arm. The jeans were stretched so tightly around her
hips they seemed almost to glow, but the waistband gaped above like
an open barrel. "Come on, Ger, stop your snuffling, let's go get
juiced."

"Do you want a shirt?"

"Nah, it's too hot . . ."

Earl Elstob came dragging a dazed Michelle into the room as we left it. "Huh!" he slobbered, weaving a bit, his eyes crossing. "Yuh know how tuh—shlup!—make a gal's eyes light up?"

"Listen, Michelle," Daffie said, reaching for her free hand, "let's go suck a turkey leg."

"It's all right," Michelle murmured, "I don't mind."

"Yeah, but come *on*, honey, *this* birdseed?"

"*Yuh plug her in!*" Elstob hollered, falling back against the door-jamb. Steve the plumber and some older guy, I saw, were trying to repair the door into my son's room, watched grimly by my mother-in-law; Janny stood by, looking bored, chatting with Hoo-Sin.

"I know how he feels," Michelle said gently. "I had a dream once that I had teeth like that in my vagina." Hoo-Sin was sweeping her hands about as though describing a vast space: "In the West you think of it as a river, but in the East it is a placid silent pool," she said. Mark seemed to have settled down at last. "Everybody laughed at me and pushed awful things up me to watch me chew. My Daddy took me to an orthodontist, but when he pointed to the problem, I ate my Daddy's finger off." She sighed. "Yuh huh huh!" Earl snorted, slapping his knee, and Janny said: "I guess I mostly think of it as a leaky faucet." "After that, the teeth weren't there anymore, it was a different dream . . ."

"Hey—*huh!*—yuh know what a bedspring is?"

"Spare me!" begged Daffie, pulling me toward the stairs, where we nearly crashed into our new neighbor, Mrs. Waddilow, stumbling pale-faced out of the bathroom, her eyes popping from their sockets: "For the love of God, why didn't somebody *tell* me—?!" she croaked, and went clambering weak-kneed down the stairs ahead of us. "I know what a buzz you get outa your wonky guest lists, Ger, but where'd you ever dig up *that* squirrelly suck-egg?"

"Charley brought him . . ."

The porch door flew open at the foot of the stairs and in strode Benedetto and four or five friends, all dressed up still in their Renaissance theater costumes. Discovering me on the landing, Beni flung his arms wide and cried: "Sir! What sort of affair *is* this? There's a *body* out there in the bushes!"

"What—?!"

Daffie seemed to stumble and she clutched my arm. "Was he . . . dressed in white?"

"Madame, I am not even certain it was a *he!* Which is not, I hasten to add, a *present* dilemma . . . !" He twirled the tip of his false moustache, ogling her bosom grandly, then swept off his plumed hat and bowed.

"I'll give him a call," I said, pulling away. Hilario, standing at the foot with two drinks in his hands—a highball and what looked like dregs from the bottom of a mop bucket—said: "Beni, you haff see anytheeng yet, I theenk!"

I remembered a play I'd seen, Ros wasn't in it, in which the actors, once on stage—it was ostensibly some sort of conventional drawing-room comedy—couldn't seem to get off again. The old pros in the cast had tried to carry on, but the stage had soon got jammed up with bit actors—messengers, butlers, maids and the like—who, trapped and without lines, had become increasingly panic-stricken. In the commotion, the principal actors had got pushed upstage and out of sight, only a few scattered lines coming through as testimony to their professionalism. Some had tried to save the show, some each other, most just themselves. It was intended to produce a kind of gathering terror, but though I hadn't felt it then (a stage is finally just a stage), I was suddenly feeling it now.

I dialed the number, turned back to Daffie, who'd been stopped by Hilario: "I cannot find peenk, so I meex violent and green—hokay?"

"Hello?"

"Benedetto!" cried Quagg, brushing past me, his cape flying.

"Zachariah! My friend!"

"Hello? Is that you, Dickie?" Daffie, without looking at the drink, tossed half of it back—then, wheezing, held it out at arm's length, bugging her eyes at it. Zack was carrying on noisily about the act he was getting up ("We got this wild frame, man, about a jealous old hag who spooked Roger and cast a spell on Ros—a kind of fairy godmother, ancient sex queen, and death-demon all in one, see . . ."), Beni approving exclamatorily and booming out introductions, while behind me people were clambering up and down the cellar stairs, or coming in from the backyard, there was music pouring out of the living room—I couldn't hear a thing. "Dickie—?"

"Who is this? Ger?"

"Benedetto!" cried Regina, sweeping past.

"Dickie! Are you all right?" I shouted. Daffie, her damp breasts drooping with relief, slumped back against the stairway and, wrinkling her nose up ("Regina! My little dumpling!"), carried on with her drinking.

"Hell, I dunno, I think I drank too much. Listen, Ger, call me in the morning when I'm feeling better, okay?"

"Ach! Regina!"

"Olga!"

"I'm sorry, Dickie, there's a . . . a body outside—and we thought—"

"Yeah, I saw it. Hey, what did you *do* to my little Nay, Ger?"

"What do you mean?" I glanced at the traffic on the basement stairs. Noble came up holding his crotch, his good eye dilated from the dark, the mock one apparently having fallen out. "Christ," he groaned happily, "I think my goddamn balls are turning blue!" He was wearing my new herringbone shirt—I hadn't even taken the pins out yet; it was stretched out of shape and already sweaty in the armpits. I turned away.

"Well, she's over the moon, Ger, you're all she talks about."

"She's there with you?" Vic had appeared in the living room doorway, looking rumpled and tired, ready to go home probably. The song on the hi-fi was a melancholic old showtune, "It's All Happened Before," a song from one of Ros's plays, *The Lover's Lexicon.*

"Yeah, well, I admit I'm only second best. You've got the touch, Ger—she's taken a real *shine* to you, as you might say." It was a relief to know she was all right. What had I been thinking? "I don't know if it's over," the vocalist was singing, "or if it's just begun . . ." Quagg had found Alison's husband somewhere and now dragged him over to meet the newcomers. One of the women kissed him. Benedetto gave him a big hug and planted his floppy wide-brimmed hat on his head. He flushed and, pulling on his beard, grinned sheepishly underneath it. Vic watched benignly, seeming to hover at some empyrean remove. I felt his detachment like a kind of balm and began, myself (". . . but tonight," came the song, "you're the only one . . ."), to disengage. After all, I thought, what else was there to do? "She says you're the kindest sweetest man she's ever known."

"All I did was oil her behind, Dickie."

"Well, you know what they say in showbiz, Ger, it's not the egg—"

"I know . . ." It's how you lay it. Or crack it. But sometimes, as

my wife would say ("It's how you scramble it," Dickie was saying distantly, not to me but, off-mike as it were, to someone there in the room with him), it *is* the egg. Woody had joined Vic in the living room doorway, watching me over Vic's shoulder. I smiled and nodded, but he didn't return it. Vic was toying wistfully with a fork in his hand, looking as resigned and serene as I'd seen him all night. I remembered something he'd told me about so-called "waves of silence" in the brain—perceived by some apparently as a kind of local conspiracy at the cellular level to shut down briefly and rest up—which he'd denounced as an example of "ideological biology," but which I saw, having more faith in chemistry than in will, as fundamentally applicable to all behavior, human and otherwise. I felt momentarily suspended in such a wave right now, in fact, as though this quiescent mood were not in me but in the hall itself, maybe the whole house, a conspiratorial nourishing, as it were, of the appetite for tranquillity.

"Hold on a sec, Ger! I got another beautiful lady here who wants to say hello!" I could hear her shushing him. I'd supposed he'd have to rub it in. Her husband, Benedetto's plumed hat down around his ears and a look of flushed infatuation on his face, was now preening for Quagg, who was peering at him through a circle of thumb and index finger as though giving him a screen test. I saw this as though peering through a lens myself, as though watching it on an editing table or in some darkened theater. "So, for the skeet, we use the faht lady, no?" "She's been holding out on us, Ger."

"The Arctic explorer? Nah, she's in there purring like a cat, Hilly, but we can work in her crazy story—a kind of initiation bit, the sacred cave—"

"She's terrific . . ."

"I'm sure," I said and swallowed. "Sacred cave?" her husband asked from under the brim of Beni's hat. He didn't seem to know. Or if he did, he accepted it. Maybe I wasn't the only one he'd struck a deal with. My head was starting to ache. "Yeah, it's a symbol for the unconscious," Quagg was explaining to him. He looked pained. "You know, where all the action takes place." I closed my eyes. "Give her . . . my love," I whispered, remembering something she'd said that night we met: beauty in the theater is not a question of language *or* action, she'd insisted (I'd tried to argue it was a balance of both), but of the *hidden* voice and the mysterious illusion of *crossed des-*

tinies. Yes (I opened my eyes), I could see that . . . Vic, his gray head tilted toward Woody (he was still peering at me, past Vic's hunched shoulder), seemed to be boiling up again: perhaps the wave was passing. I turned to look into the dining room ("You won't believe what she's got tattooed on her handsome little ass, Ger!"), but caught a glimpse of (*"What?!"* Vic roared—*"With Sally Ann—?!"*) Horner, mouth agape, eyes startled: *"Duck!"* he yelped.

"You! You goddamn traitorous sonuvabitch—YOU were the one!"

I whirled around just in time to see Vic lunging toward me, a terrible look on his ravaged face I'd never seen before, not frontally like this, his bloodshot eyes ablaze, lips drawn back, fist clenched around the fork, raised to strike—*"Vic! Wait—!"*

Two shots rang out, something hit me in the shoulder, there was a shriek and a tumble, people falling all around me—Vic slumped to one knee, a look of awe and wonder erasing his rage, then pitched forward and fell into my arms. The tall cop, Bob, crouched in the living room doorway (Woody had vanished), the smoking barrel of his revolver staring me in the face. "Oh my god! *Vic—!"*

I felt something warm and wet on my hands. Vic groaned, his shaggy head heavy on my chest. The cop limped toward us, keeping his gun on him. "What have you *done—?"* I cried.

"He was going for you, so I shot him."

"But—he was my best *friend!"* The cop grabbed Vic by the collar, threw him backward to the floor. There was a big hole in his chest. "All he had was a damned *fork!"* I was nearly screaming.

"I missed him once—this time I made fucking sure." He kicked Vic but got no response. Vic was breathing in short gasps, his eyelids fluttering.

The others started picking themselves up. "What happened?" asked Teresa, coming in from the dining room with a dessert plate heaped with turkey stuffing, cheese balls, and pickles. I stared at my bloody hands, my eyes watering, then knelt by Vic. It had all happened so fast . . . "Hey, old man . . . ?" There was no reply: his head lolled, his mouth gaped. "So that's it," Eileen said stonily, standing framed in the living room doorway. "I knew it'd end like this." Perhaps she had known. I recalled her oracle on the toilet and even before that I remembered thinking, when she was lying on the couch in the living room, Vic having just struck her, that she had glimpsed something that none of the rest of us were aware of yet. Maybe Vic had seen it,

too, and had merely been swinging blindly at a truth that enraged him. "I tried to warn him, and the sonuvabitch beat me up."

Cynthia eased past her, squatted by Vic ("You can come on back now, tiger," Daffie was saying, having picked up the fallen phone receiver, "they just shot that little girl's old man . . ."), touched his throat. This seemed to help for some reason: he closed his mouth, blinked, tried to focus. When he saw me, a pained look crossed his face, then faded. "Get Sally Ann . . ." he whispered.

"Sure, Vic, but—"

"And a drink."

"Listen, I'm sorry, but—"

"*Fuck* sorry! Get me a goddamn *drink!*" he croaked.

"Vic—?"

"He won't listen to you," Eileen said dully. The others watched us now at a distance, keeping a wary eye at the same time on the cop, who was reloading his revolver. "He's a smart guy. He knows it all."

"I'll get him something," Teresa offered, sucking a pickle. "What's his—?"

"Bourbon."

"The kid? Nah, last I saw, that chirpy fatassed welfare worker was taking him out on the back patch to get his stake tolled," said Daffie glumly on the phone. "I've had nothing but the goddamn losers, Dickie, I don't like it here."

"Where the hell *am* I?" Vic wheezed. He groped weakly for his chest as though looking for something in his pocket there.

"You're at my house, Vic. A party—"

"Jesus Christ! I'm *bleeding!* Oh, shit, Gerry! What have you done . . . ?"

"Hey, maybe we can work this in," mused Quagg, squinting down at Vic, as he slumped there against Cynthia ("Well, who knows . . . maybe it's the—*gasp!*—the way I wanted it . . ."), clutching his wound. "I *like* the fast action!" Malcolm Mee, who'd joined him, nodded, then mimed the draw. "*Right!* Blue *lightning*, man!" laughed Quagg.

"Yeah, well, when you're done, you can kiss mine," Daffie mumbled tearfully, and banged the receiver in its cradle.

"Only maybe the guy who gets his lights blown out is the one playing Roger on the stage, and it's Roger himself, out in the audience, who does the shooting!"

"Roger's dead, Zack."

"Listen, I know, you think I'm crazy? I'm talking about the *play*, man!"

"Roger—?"

"It's been a long night, Prissy Loo."

Teresa returned with a tumbler of iced bourbon. "Here," she said and, bending over, spilled her plate of food in Vic's lap. "Oops! Darn, that's all the stuffing there was left!"

Cynthia took the glass and held it to his lips—he slurped at it greedily, choking and spluttering, then knocked it to the floor; it rolled across the hall, the ice cubes scattering like thrown dice.

"Hey," warned Bob, waggling his revolver.

"Do you mind?" asked Teresa, picking the food off his lap with her fingers and eating it. "It's a shame to waste it."

"The way I see it, we got Ros playing herself—we use the corpse, I mean—but the rest of the cast interacts with it like she's alive, you dig? The trick being to make the audience get the sense she really *is* alive!"

Vic peered up at us under his shaggy gray brows, his eyes crossing. "*Another one!*" he demanded, and broke into a fit of coughing.

"I don't like it," Regina objected. "It's like abusing the dead or something."

"I think he's going . . ."

"We're not abusing Ros, baby, we're abusing death itself *through* Ros—really, it's an affirmation!"

"I dunno, Zack, somehow it's like that time you pulled that on-stage autopsy—"

"He needs help," said Cynthia. "Is that doctor—?"

Bob twirled the revolver on his index finger ("But that was *beautiful*, Vadge!"), slapped it into the holster. "I think I seen him in the kitchen."

"Yeah, if you could stop from throwing up."

"I'll get him," I said.

Before I could reach the kitchen door, though ("Say, where's that sewer hog?" Quagg turned to ask as I passed him. "We could use him as an extra grip to help the Scar." "There's two of 'em here now, Zack," said Horner, "him and his partner . . ."), Talbot, Dolph, and the guy in the chalkstriped suit came whooping and hallooing through it, bearing Anatole on their shoulders. "Ta-*DAHH!*" they cried. Ana-

tole, half-dressed and grinning sheepishly, begged to be put down, but his porters only hooted the louder, parading him around the room, getting everyone to clap and join in on a chorus of "Pop! Goes the Weasel!" The door whumped open behind them and Brenda came streaking through, holding her red pants in front of her face—"*Hip hip HIP!*" they shouted—and I slipped through behind her.

Jim was at the kitchen stove, sterilizing a needle in what looked like a sardine can. "Jim!" I cried. The room had dimmed, things had been put away, a kind of calm had descended here. Or been imposed. But I did not feel calm. I made it to the butcherblock and leaned against it. Fred, the short cop, sat in his shirtsleeves and neckbrace at the breakfast bench, eating sausage with chilled vodka from the fridge, my wife on a chair nearby sewing the brass button on his coat. There was something incongruously domestic, almost emblematic, about the three of them—cooking, sewing, eating there in the stillness, the subdued light; behind me the others reveled as though at some other party. "It's Vic! *He's been shot!*"

"All right," he said wearily. "Won't be a minute."

"It's *urgent*, Jim!" I held up my bloody hands.

He glanced over at me. "Yes, I know, it's always—say, what's the matter with your shoulder?"

My wife looked up in alarm. "It's nothing, a scratch—"

"Come here, let me take a look at it."

The other policeman stuck his head in the door behind me. "Got him, Fred."

"Yeah, thanks, I just heard."

"Looks like you've been grazed by a bullet. Were you near Vic when—?"

"Yes, I was on the phone, but—!"

"Mmm. That explains it." He turned the fire off under the needle, knelt to search through the black bag at his feet. "Do you need help, Jim?" my wife asked.

"No . . ."

"I do wish people wouldn't use guns in the house." There was a tremor in her voice.

"Vic's been hit bad, Jim. I think you ought to—"

"First things first, Gerry. That's not a serious wound, but it should be cleaned up right away." He came up with a bottle of iodine, a

swab, and some bandages, and set them on the stove, then went to the sink and rinsed a gray dishrag out under hot water.

"If I had my way, I'd outlaw the things, ma'am," said Fred around a mouthful of garlic sausage, "but you might as well outlaw eating and sh—uh, shaving." Louise stepped out from a dark corner—I hadn't noticed her there before—and, as though pursued, rushed on out of the room, watched sorrowfully by my wife. Fred washed the sausage down with vodka. "I hope I didn't say nothing—"

"No . . ."

"Now let's see what we've got here," said Jim, ripping my shirt away from the wound. "This may sting a bit . . ."

"Yes—OW!"

"He's such a baby," my wife smiled. This was true. I dreaded the iodine to come more than being shot again—just the gritty dishrag was bringing tears to my eyes.

"A millimeter more," Jim said, the gray lock flopping over his brow, "and you might have lost some bone."

"You gave me a button like this once, Gerald. Do you remember?"

"No . . ." Instead I remembered, for some reason, Naomi bent over the toilet, Dickie looking frazzled, Tania saying something (and there was this strange sensation of having just completed some kind of antiphonal figure, like a round of passed bids: echoes as it were of those shots still ringing in my ears) about cowardice and hysteria. Maybe it was the musty-smelling rag in Jim's hand. . . .

"You know, you should stop worrying about others so much, Gerry," he counseled now, "and start thinking a little about yourself for a change."

"My wages, you said." She turned to Fred. "He said if I gave him a good time I'd get a second one." She sighed. "But I never did."

Fred chuckled, winking at me. Jim dipped the swab in the iodine. "He got it in the chest, Jim. At least twice. I really think you ought to—YOW!"

"My goodness, Gerald—you're worse than Mark when he's having a sliver out!"

"Don't let him fool you, he's braver than you think, ma'am," said Fred with another wink.

"Come *on*, Jim, *that's enough!*"

"Easy! A little more . . ."

"Did you see the look on Cyril's face when Peg told him she was leaving him?" my wife asked as though to distract me.

"I don't know if I've seen them all night," I gasped, and Jim said: "You're kidding! Not Cyril and Peg—?!"

"Yes, I don't understand it at all, do you, Gerald?"

"What? No! Yes! *Ow!* I'm not sure!"

"What *are* you trying to say, Gerald?"

"I think Tania told me," I explained, pushing the words out through gritted teeth. Was this true? It seemed unlikely, even as the words came to me. Cyril and Peg? "Or was about to. *Oh! Ah!* It has something to do with Ros, the lines from some play and wanting to ad-lib or something, I don't know—*OUCH!*"

"Well, that certainly makes it all clear as pie," my wife remarked wryly, raising her eyebrows at Fred, who laughed and forked another hunk of sausage in his mouth.

"I really find it hard to believe," said Jim. He had stopped molesting the wound with his swab and was now unrolling a bandage. He pressed a fold of gauze to my shoulder. "Hold that, Gerry."

"Anyway, I guess that's one party we'll miss out on," said my wife. She bit the thread off, pinned the needle in her calico apron, held the coat up. "That must make you and Mavis the real veterans here tonight, Jim."

"I think probably Charley and Janny . . ."

"Well, they may not be doing so well either," she said, folding the coat gently and laying it on the bench across from the policeman. "From what I've heard . . ."

"Thanks, ma'am."

Jim was taping the bandage to my shoulder, muttering, "It's strange, they were almost a legend . . ." I was staring out at the backyard, where a dark heavy hush had settled, pressing up against the back door as though to embrace us. Ah well . . . I recalled the soft furry V of her pubes as they thrust against my fingers out there, the nubbly caress of her tongue as it coiled between my teeth, her hands scrabbling over me like hungry little crabs—but it was not an erotic memory, no, it was more like a solemn meditation on memory itself: the warm slippery stuff of time, the dry but somehow radiant impressions that remained. Like the muddy tracks (the voices were stilled now, the traipsing in and out) on the kitchen floor.

"I cleaned it all up," my wife said, following my gaze, "but then Anatole and Brenda and all that crowd came through."

"I know, I saw him on exhibit in there . . ."

"Yes, that was nice. I think he'd been feeling a bit lonely, especially

since . . . since his aunt . . ." She stared at her hands, her eyes watering. Jim capped the iodine and fit it back in the bag, rolled up the bandage, snapped the protective metal ring around the tape. "We should invite more young people next time."

"Maybe it'll milk some of the piss and vinegar outa the little jerk," grumped Fred, "pardon the French, ma'am. He's been giving the Chief a lotta stick, and we're pretty darn tired of it."

"He's still very young," my wife reminded him.

"Yeah, but he don't appreciate the difficulties—it ain't an easy job."

"I think the Inspector makes his own difficulties," I said.

Fred bristled momentarily, but then, thinking it over, cut himself another hunk of sausage. "Well, the Old Man's got his weaknesses, I admit. We all do. He spent all that time in there with them watches, for example, just to figure out the murder took place exactly thirty minutes after we *got* here. Huh huh!" Jim fit one of the sterilized needles in a syringe, put the others in a plastic box, emptied the little pan in the sink, then tossed it in the garbage. "Bob and me bailed him outa that one by taking a temperature fix with that stabhole in the liver, but it ain't always so simple like that—he's a pretty ingenious fella, like you seen, and sometimes we don't have a clue how to clean things up after. Sometimes we don't even know what the hell he's talking about. But, listen, loopy as he may seem, old Nigel's solved a lotta crimes. He's got a special knack." He poured himself a shot of vodka and tossed it down, smacked his lips, poured another. "He does it by somehow sinking into the heart of the crime itself, making a kinda transmitter outa hisself, don't ask me how. As far as he's concerned, see, there ain't no such thing as a isolated crime, it's always part of something bigger, and he figures the only way to get at this bigger thing is to use, not just the brain, but the whole waterworks— it's what he calls 'seeing through' a crime. He's a artist at it, best I ever seen!"

Jim had left us meanwhile with his syringe needle-up like a pointing finger. My wife was rinsing out the bloody dishrag. "So it's true what they've been saying about Mavis—that she's . . ."

"Yes, she's an epileptic, Gerald. I thought you knew."

"Old Nigel once told me something pretty weird," Fred continued, sipping thoughtfully at his vodka. Epileptic? "He said if a fella could become fond of the *evil* in the world, he'd find hisself *embracing delight*. Them were the Chief's exact words: *embracing delight*. Of

course, evil, that takes in death, disease, cruelty, crime, the whole toot and scramble—so not much chance, hunh?" He got up, brushed the crumbs from his lap, went over to the sink to wash his hands. "In the end, though, it's gotta be said, for all his fancy talk, old Nigel still seems to suspect foreigners, perverts, freaks and bums, just like the rest of us."

"That's not very charitable," my wife remarked, wiping off the breakfast table with the damp rag Jim had used on my shoulder.

"By the way," I said (I realized I'd been staring for some time at a little heart-shaped stain on the butcherblock next to the can of body spray: something someone had said . . . ?), "it turns out that valentine Naomi had was one I once gave you—"

"Yes, I know. Dickie asked me to go through her bag before they left and it was in there. She had your electric razor as well, and somebody's scout knife, Mother's hairnet, a yellow ball painted with an eye, even Mark's old potty and a bunch of inky thumbprints." Fred glanced up and winked at me over his neckbrace, shaking the water from his hands. "But Cyril said she couldn't help it."

"Cyril?"

"Yes, he was there to see Peg off, of course." She put the vodka and leftover sausage back in the fridge, then stood staring into it as though watching a movie there. "Now I wonder what I could—"

"Peg . . . !" It was slowly, very slowly, dawning on me. . . .

"Yes, when she left with Dickie—why! what's the matter with you, Gerald? We were just talking about—"

"Right . . . !" I turned to gaze out once more on the back porch where the dense tide of night seemed suddenly to be falling back: of course, it was Peg who had gone with him, her tattooed bottom, Dickie had mentioned—it hit me now like a revelation: *Alison was still here then!*

"Maybe I could make some brandied stuffed eggs . . ."

"Exactly!" But where? "What?"

"You were right about that sleazy bastard, by the way," said Fred. "Whisked his redheaded baggage right outa here just as we was bringing charges. Accessory after the—*wurr-RRP!*" He belched loudly, patting his stomach. "Whoo, that's better!" He belched again, a kind of brief little afterclap (yes, I thought, hugging myself, even for artless fools there are second chances!), then asked: "You ain't never thought of taking up police work, have you?"

"Not right now. . . ." My mind was elsewhere, searching, as it were, the premises.

"Too bad. We could use a fella like you. You got the gourd for it. And a good eye."

"What? Ah, well . . . but no stomach." Those others were giving her a bad time; maybe she went outside to hide. I seemed to see someone on the back porch. But, no, all those guys had just come in from there. . . .

"You get used to it. You got the right attitude and that's what counts. Of course, as a career, it ain't what it once was, I admit that, not since they legalized fornication, as we used to call it." He pulled on his coat, exercising his shoulders against the seams, then buttoned up. My wife put some water on to boil (where had I last seen her? the living room? I couldn't remember, it seemed so long ago . . .), got some tomatoes and green beans out of the fridge, some cottage cheese and butter, a carton of brown eggs. "I hope we still have some capers," she said. "Them were the days—crime everywhere and even them not guilty of fornication was all the more likely to be guilty of something else: fantasy or murder or virulent possession—an excess of sentiment, as the old statutes put it. The force was the place to be in them days, I'll never forget it, it had something special." Maybe the first thing, I thought, is to see if there's any vermouth left, pick up somehow where we . . . "Of course I was young then—but we had a lotta professional pride and enthusiasm, it was a kinda golden age for the old P.D., all the best brains was in it—that's when old Nigel joined up, for example—but now, well, most of them boys are gone. The new breed's got a whole different slant on things. It's all statistics now, stemming the tide like they like to say—in fact, fornication's a kinda police weapon these days to keep the citizens confused—these young fellas've got no time for dickprints or cuff debris or sussing out a hidden motive. And there's all this do-gooder crime now, bomb-throwing and food riots in the camps and computer-bashing and the like, most of it happening way over my head—though that don't mean I won't lose an arm or a leg from it. Just defending a poker game down at city hall these days can get you napooed." He tucked his cap under his arm, adjusted the knot of his tie under the neckbrace, checked his weapons. Quiet deliberation, that's the important thing, I thought. No more impulsive leaps in the dark. Harmony and balance—I was very excited . . . ! "No, the fun's mostly gone outa crime these days,

what you might call the personal touch—I mean, it's a real kick for us to get a old-fashioned murder like this one, it sets us up for a week after, even if it *is* something of a luxury—you shoulda seen old Nigel on the way over, he was tickled pink."

"That reminds me, Gerald," said my wife, prying the lid off a flour tin, "what *is* the way you find out if a girl is ticklish?"

"What's that?" The green room, we'd said. Right! But then . . . ?

"Mmm, looks good," said Fred, staring into the boiling water.

"That man with the buckteeth," she replied vaguely, fishing around now among the dishes in the sink. "He was saying . . ."

"Earl's joke, you mean? You give her a couple of test tickles."

"Well, that's what *he* said, but what does that prove?"

"Test-tickles. Testicles." I pointed. They were stirring again. I smiled.

"Oh, I see." She sighed and peered dismally into the empty pot of Dijonais mustard. "What did you want to talk to Alison about?"

"Who—?" She had an amazing way of juxtaposing things (the smile had become a wince: I touched my shoulder gingerly). Maybe it was the secret of her cooking.

"That woman we met at the theater. Louise overheard Sally Ann telling her you were waiting for her down in the rec room."

For a moment I couldn't think. "What?" What did she say? I was suddenly locked in somewhere, deep inside. And then something broke open, it felt like the police smashing in through Mark's bedroom door, a splintering crash, and I staggered back. Or perhaps I was already staggering. The rec room! I should have known: all those wisecracks, the traffic up and down the stairs (had somebody mentioned bondage?), Alison's husband staring fearfully down them as I was carrying Mark up to bed, Noble's sweaty armpits and insolent complaint—it all came together now, I saw things plainly, all too plainly, and it took my knees right out from under me. I slumped weakly against the butcherblock. Going down.

"Gerald? What's the matter—?!"

"It's his wound, ma'am. He's probably in a bit of shock."

What was worse, she'd suppose I'd set her up for it—she'd never been to one of our parties before, how could she know it wasn't a game we played with all our first-timers? I felt like crying. I *was* crying. Goddamn Sally Ann! The lights in the kitchen seemed to dim and a wave of nausea rippled through me.

"Maybe he should lie down."

"It's usually better to try to walk it off."

"Hey, Ger, what's wrong? You look terrible!"

"He's been wounded, sir, nothing serious."

I realized we were in the dining room. I seemed to be making progress through it without any effort of my own, held up by Fred and my wife. I still felt lightheaded and queasy. All I could think of for the moment was Tania staring despairingly into the bathtub full of pink suds, overcome—this was clear to me now, it was the only thing that was clear to me—by a paroxysm of self-hatred.

"Here, try this."

They were holding something alcoholic to my lips. It dribbled down my chin. Somehow I'd forgotten how to swallow.

Jim turned up then and said, no, I should be lying down, my feet higher than my head.

"That's what *I* thought," said my wife.

"I've had 'em die on me like that," Fred disagreed. "We like to keep 'em moving around."

They made some room for me in front of the sideboard, dragging Mavis out of the way, and stretched me out. Something was pounding in my ears. It might have been my heart. But it sounded more like feet thumping up and down the stairs. Someone brought our camel-saddle in from the TV room and propped it under my ankles. Fred made it clear that if I popped off, he wasn't to be blamed, and Wilma, standing nearby, said I reminded her of the last time she'd seen her third husband Archie. "He had that same blue look in the face."

"Open his shirt there, give him some air!"

"Loosen his belt!"

Heads dipped over me and bobbed away again like those little drinking birds sold in novelty shops. The ceiling, too, seemed to be throbbing, at times pressing down, at others vanishing into some vast distance, like the empty horizon of Pardew's dream. Shadows flickered across it like faint images on a cinema screen or a drawn windowshade. I remembered Alison saying: "There *is* no audience, Gerald, that's what makes it so sad." Or perhaps my wife had said that. In any case . . .

"Oh dear, look at that bruise under his navel," she said now.

"He looks pretty tender all over."

"Is there anything else we can do?"

"You might wet a washcloth with cold water," Jim said.

"Has he been crying?"

"Well, Vic was his best friend, after all."

"Listen," said Fred, leaning close, "I gotta go now, and I just wondered if you got any more hot tips for us?" His breath reeked of garlic and vodka. I turned my head away. I found myself looking up somebody's skirt and closed my eyes. "You'd be doing us a real favor . . ."

"No . . . ," I whispered faintly, or meant to—what I found myself saying was: "No . . . ble . . ."

"I think he said something."

"That's a good sign."

"That ham wizard with the glass lamp, you mean?" murmured Fred in my ear. I shuddered. "Hmm, pretty tricky—he's got that lawyer buddy, family of some sort. Still . . ."

"He seems to be getting some of his color back, too."

"Gosh, it was *great*, Uncle Howard!" Anatole was saying somewhere just past my vision. "I never realized doing it was so *easy*!"

". . . I'll see what I can do."

"No, that's probably just fever."

"And now I'm going to be a playwright!"

"Gerry? Can you hear me?"

"Mr. Quagg said I'm to be the brains for the show!"

"Wait—!" I whispered, turning back ("Don't be silly, he was with me," I seemed to hear my wife say), but the policeman was gone. What I saw instead was Fats floating high above me, as though suspended in midair: he hung up there, startled, looking like he was about to sail off into distant space—then he came crashing down, making the whole room shake.

"What?"

"The more things change, the more they are the same," said Hoo-Sin.

"It's gettin' rough in here, Scar—wanta go up and try on the county fair?"

"No, thanks, she's fulla fleas and I got this preem to mount. Anyhow I just been fannin' the rubber in the dungeon, man, I got no more snap."

"What am I doin' wrong?" Fats groaned from the floor ("That opus still pullin' 'em in?"), and someone said: "I love what you've done with the space in here, this delicate balance of old and new."

"Yeah, but not for much longer—if you wanta catch her act, you better get on down there."

"Hey, you come on like a ice wagon, Fats, you gonna get wrecked!"

"Material goin' a bit stale?"

"You're kidding—!"

"It's just terrible about Tania, Howard. Such a tragedy!"

"Pregnant?"

"Well, the tread's a bit worn—but what's really closin' the show down is this dyke out there at the head of the stairs, doin' a soapbox number on anybody with an honest bone-on . . ."

"I know how you must feel."

"Do you indeed."

". . . I mean, man, she sorta takes the starch out . . ."

"I only meant . . ."

I closed my eyes again and found myself recalling ("So that's why Cyril . . ."), or trying to recall, something that woman in Istanbul had said to me. We were crossing an arched bridge, I remembered ("Eileen?" someone asked, this was very far away), there were over-laden carts pulled by mules, a leaden sky, a certain spiciness in the air. "This will soon be over," she'd said. Yes. Tin cooking ware was clink-ing on the back of one of the carts, and there was a dull rumbling continuo underfoot. "In a sense, it was over before it began. We have been living with the last moment ever since the first. That's been the magic of it all: experiencing the future with the sensual immediacy of the present and all the nostalgia of the past . . ."

But then . . .

"Papanash," someone said. What? I heard ice tinkling in glasses, smelled hot food, or perhaps I *felt* these things: a chill, a flush . . . "I've never felt *anything*," Janny Trainer was saying, and someone asked: "Vomedy?" Someone had placed a wet dishtowel on my fore-head. "Yum!" "Quagg's casting!" "Oh yeah?" "I always did it because I thought I was *supposed* to, but suddenly I don't feel as *dumb* as I used to!" "Oh, I see—I thought it was a vomit remedy!" This was Jim. I opened my eyes. There was a lot of excited activity around me. People preening, straightening stockings, tucking their shirttails in. Fats was on his feet again. "Hey, man, can you use a good piana player?" "Right now," said Quagg, "I need a coupla grips to help Scarborough skate the flats!" Maybe I'd dozed off. My head was thick and there was a metallic taste on my tongue. "It's like letting men

shove their thing in me all the time was making my brain all sticky and stupid . . ." "Feeling better?" Jim was bending over me. "Hot as a junked-up canary, man!" "Hey, where you guys been?" "Vot? Chunk?" "Noble," I murmured. "I have to tell him . . ." "He's all right. The police are talking to him. Do you want to try sitting up?" "Down the well, Zack, you know—so what's on the menu, somethin' special?" What's on the menu. The line stuck in my head for a moment. As Quagg read it off ("Ach, yah, zeks!"), I seemed to see real menus, one-page books, tantalizing, yet unreadable, opening out before my eyes. Choices could be made, they said. They are always the same choices. "Gerry . . . ?"

"Let one who knows your nature," breathed Hoo-Sin soothingly, "feel your pulse."

"Well, it hasn't got a name, though the kid's working on that. But it's about time and memory and lost illusions . . ."

"Oh yeah! Is that the one where the director comes running in and says: 'No, no, Ros! you're supposed to pick up the clock and—'?"

"Or how 'bout a little soft-shoe," wheedled Fats. "And play the piana!"

"No, this is all new, man!"

"The way I heard it, she was—ha ha—supposed to pick up the jewels and run . . ."

"Both at the same time, Zack, both at the same time!"

Menus, my mother used to say, were fun's bait, misery's disguise. She could be epigrammatic like that. She'd sit over hot coffee, smoking nervously, thinking up these depressing little aphorisms. Happiness, she'd say, is a missed connection. . . .

"Come on, Gerry . . ." Jim was slapping my cheeks gently. I felt very remote. The menus had become cue cards, curtains, candles, calendars, the white wakes of ocean liners (Regina said something about the "last act" or maybe "elastic," and there was distant laughter like the sound of waterclocks), wet laundry . . .

"To experience perfect interfusion, let all the knots be dissolved."

"Well, I suppose it's all right . . . ," said Janny.

"Here, we don't need every fucking 'i' dotted, son—just give us the nub and a zinger or two and we can pong along on the rest."

". . . Though I'm a little bit ticklish there!"

"What's Scarborough doing in there?"

"Uh, what'd he say, Uncle Howard?"

"Has to do with some saint, he said."

"Yeah? Well, it's *wild*, man!"

"I believe he wants you to prepare an outline."

"You ever *seen* me bang the dogs, Zack?"

"Gerry . . . ?"

I opened my eyes again (this took effort) and found myself staring across the floor at Mavis, staring pitiably back. Her own eyes were glazed over ("Hoo! hah! Just—*puff!*—clamp your lamps on *this* move, man!") and she was grinning, but she didn't seem to be dead. Just listening. The pale rolls of flesh on her arms and legs lay spread out on the carpet as though deflated. Or deboned. I tried to flex my own arms, but couldn't.

"Jesus, he looks like he's fucking had it!" muttered Dolph.

"No, I'm all right," I whispered. But he wasn't talking about me, he was looking at someone across the room.

"Whoo, all bets off on that one!"

I twisted my head around. Steve the plumber and an older guy were hauling Vic in feet first through the crowd, Hilario and Daffie clearing the way. The older guy had his name stitched over his overalls pocket like Steve, but I couldn't read it. He seemed to resent having to drag Vic in and bumped him along irritably, knocking his lolling head against the doorjamb and table leg, elbowing people (Fats was huffing out a nasal tune and bobbing about recklessly, making little Vachel duck and scowl, and Hoo-Sin, kneading Janny's kidneys— "Ooh, that feels good, I was just itching there!"—backheeled him deftly in the crotch just as Dolph popped a beer can open) out of the way. With every step, blood bubbled out of Vic's chest wound, staining darkly his pale blue workshirt. "What . . . what are you *do- ing—?!*" I gasped.

"In *drag?*" whimpered Fats, hobbling around, doubled over. "*Hunh*, Zack? Whaddaya say? And *falsies?*"

"We breeng the chackass to the reever," Hilario smiled, helping the two workmen prop Vic up in the corner of sideboard and wall. He was still clutching the fork, but more like a standard than a weapon.

"He was asking for a fresh drink every five minutes," Daffie panted, wiping the sweat off her breasts ("With *high heels?* Eh? And striped *longjohns?* How 'bout it, Zack?"). "He was getting to be a goddamn nuisance."

Vic groaned and blood dribbled down his chin. "Looks like his

valves are shot, Goldy," sighed Steve, digging at the blackened crotch of his overalls. "Yeah, well, for that I *ain't* got the right tools."

"Who the hell did that?" Dolph wanted to know.

"I dunno. Gerry ("Olga—?") was there. . . ."

"Vic—?" I tried to sit up but ("Oh yah, anudder, bitte!") I was too lightheaded.

"Aw, Zack, c'mon—y'mean that lollypop who useta moon around Ros's door?" Vachel was whining. "You gotta be kidding!"

"I'm sorry, Gerry," Jim said. "The second bullet apparently ("Dot's enuff!") ricocheted off a rib and lodged in his heart, there's nothing I can do."

"Whaddaya mean? It's your kinda role, Vaych! Look at him, he's a real downstage sorta guy! And you can interpret it any way you—"

"In fact, probably lucky for you it did."

"Tank you."

"Wha—? That bushwah tinpot? That fashion-mag foof?"

"That's the guy there, Goldy, the one with the blue belly hanging out. It's his spread."

"Cheez, Zack! Have a *heart!*"

"All right, all right, I hear ya talking . . ."

"Hey, mister, is there anything else?" I opened my eyes again: it was the older plumber, standing over me, squat and jowly, wiping his hands on a greasy rag. He had a wad of something in one cheek, which now he shifted.

"I tell ya what, man, we'll make it the main speaking part, whaddaya say?"

"Come on, pal, I ain't got all fucking night, you know."

"Okay, okay," squeaked Vachel, "just so you don't stick me in a robot suit like last time," and Steve said: "I think his wife said something about the dishwasher making a funny noise, Goldy."

"Yeah? Where is it then? Let's get it over with, goddamn it—you took me out of a good movie on the box."

My head was a sieve, everything just came rattling in. It was like a frequency scan. White noise. My shoulder was beginning to hurt again, though, which was probably a good sign.

"A *drink!*" burbled Vic.

"What do you think, Jim?"

"Sure, what harm can it do?"

"Poor Veek! He ees, how you say, crosseeng out, no?"

"Yeah. Does his daughter know?"

"What's that? Vic goin' out?" asked Fats, lumbering over. "Don't step on Gerry," someone said. "Hey, can he bring back some fresh coronas?"

"I think Woody's breaking it to her."

"No, no, Fats, I mean, he ees feenesh, all gone over, goode-uh-bahee!"

"Okay, now the actual murder scene, we're gonna do in the nude, so we need somebody who strips well."

"Finished?" Fats, tottering above me, rocked back on his heels. "Who, Vic—?!"

"Great idea! What about the Vagina?"

"Oh no," at least two people said at once, and Daffie, pouring out a tumbler of bourbon, murmured: "That Woody's a busy little boy." "She's tripping over her bags these days and her goddamn cheeks(*"Bren! It's Vic! Oh my god, Bren! He's been shot!"*)'re hanging down behind her *knees!*"

"*Beautiful!*" rumbled Charley Trainer, hobbling up to the sideboard, as Fats staggered away. I seemed to hear people cheering in another room. "Hullo, Dollfish, Howard—hey, I *like* the bra, Howard!" And booing. "'Ass cute!" I rose up on my elbows (there was another burst of cheering) and stared down at my exposed navel, trying to get my bearings. There *was* a bruise there—had Sally Ann kicked me? No, that's right, Roger . . . I fell back again. "Whatcha call keepin' abreast a the times, hunh?"

And more boos: seemed to be coming from the TV room. It was like a kind of voting. Jim propped the camel-saddle under my head.

"Say, getcher paw outa Olga's muu-muu for jussa sec, Dolph ole pal, 'n pour yer ole dad one, wudja?"

"I got it, Zack! How about that ripe chunk in the yellow knittie?"

"So *dot's* vot it vass! I *tot* I haff *vorms* back dere!"

"Chunk?"

"*Sock it to him, gimpy!*" someone shouted from the other room. "*Put him on ice!*"

"You mean that suburban hausfrau of yours? C'mon, get serious!"

"'Ass ole Dolfer, m'love—haw haw!—awways takin' a backseat!"

"*Yay!*"

"We're not doing farce here, Horn, we don't want any goddamn travesty!"

"Fartz?"

"No, wait, Zack, think about it. Anybody here would be a travesty of Ros, am I right? So all right, you *accept* that and you push on *through* into something *else!* You dig?"

"Make it a short one, Dolph," Jim cautioned. "Charley's had too much already."

"*Send him up the country!*"

"*Boo!*"

"I mean, you're not just tryin' to give these people some cheap fantasy, are you?"

"What are they yelling about in there?"

"Okay, Horner, maybe you got something. Why not? See if she'll do it."

"Hey! Wha' happena ressa my *drink*, Dolf-ball? 'Ass oney *half* of it!"

"They're watching old videotapes. Weird stuff. Full of sex and violence."

"Sorry, Charley, Jim said—"

"What's weird about that?"

"What? W*hat?!*"

"It's so fucking *cold* . . . my legs . . ."

"I take 'iss drink as a *insult*, ole buddy!"

"Easy, Vic."

"Did you catch the slow-mo sequence with the croquet mallets?"

"Yeah, hairy, man! All that squoosh and splat—really shook me up!"

"Forshunately, bein' a easy-goin' fella, I can *swallow* a insult!"

"I still can't understand what caused them to break up," Jim was saying ("But beautifully filmed!"), zipping up my fly. "After all this time . . ."

"I don't know," said Daffie. "Maybe they thought people weren't paying enough attention to them."

"*Daddy—?!*"

"Woops, watch it, here she comes!"

"Oh, *Daddy!*" Sally Ann cried, her voice breaking. She stumbled over me, falling heavily into Vic's arms. "What have you *done?*"

"Sally Ann? Is that . . . you?"

"Yes, Daddy. Don't try to talk . . . !"

"I've had it . . . this time, kid! It's the—*whoof! hack!*—the end!" He gasped for breath. ("He's not got much longer," someone said,

and Olga asked: "Much longer don whoose?") "I never really thought I'd . . . have to . . . have to die . . ."

"Is that all you can do, Olga, talk funny?"

"I-I've always known what life," Vic spluttered, ". . . what life was about . . ."

"Yah, vell, it's *sum*-ting."

"Mmm—goodness, what *is* this?"

"And I never kidded myself about—oh damn! it *hurts*, baby . . . ! —about death . . ."

"It's a sort of pilaf. With yoghurt sauce."

"But I could never imagine . . . that moment . . ."

"Gee, I don't know," Teresa was saying ("Well, it's *delicious!* I don't know how you do it!"), "in front of everybody?"

". . . In between . . ."

"Don't, Daddy. You scare me when you talk like that."

"Come on, sweetheart! This is your *big chance!*"

"The truth's . . ."

"The break you been waiting for!"

"Just leftovers, I'm afraid."

". . . Always scary, girl . . ."

"Well, if it's art, I guess it's all right."

"And in any case it's about all I've got left . . ."

"Atta girl!"

". . . To give you," Vic was mumbling ("So get *in* there and tear it *down*, baby!"). He seemed to be fading again. "And what's inside these fan-*tas*-tic *eggs?*" "I'll give you the recipe," my wife said, and Quagg shouted out: "Okay, all you lot, into the parlor! It's time for the apotheosis of Ros!"

"Tell Mom . . . I'm sorry, and . . ."

"Oh oh," somebody cried out ("I already called her, Dad, and she said she didn't know who I was talking about . . ."), "here comes that lady guerrilla again!" I felt someone's hands in my armpits. "You'd better get out of her way, Gerry," Jim was saying somewhere behind my ear ("And do me a favor, baby . . .") as I rose, lifted, from the floor: "Could you—*ngh!*—give us a hand, please?" It was Eileen: she was wearing a trenchcoat with the collar turned up, her hands stuffed in the pockets, a scarf around her head.

"He's weak . . . and frivolous . . . confused . . ."

"Don't worry, Daddy, I won't . . ."

"Well, we meet again," said Mr. Waddilow. He was one of those

holding me up. The other one (". . . Anyway he's too old . . .") was the older plumber, Goldy; Jim, letting go, was getting dragged away by Quagg's set-builder Scarborough, who was explaining: "We're using her as part of the scenery, you dig, and we need you to get her ready . . ."

"I don't know . . ."

"And hang on to the—*kaff! huff! hoo* . . . !—present, baby! It's all you've—"

"Oh, Daddy, stop it! You're spitting blood all over!"

"No, listen—!"

Eileen stepped up and kicked the glass out of his hands. "What are you carrying that fork around for, greedyguts? Nobody's going to insist on good manners when you're eating cold mud." Vic, grinning, wheezed appreciatively, his hand searching for the lost glass. I realized ("I've never *seen* Eileen like this before!") my whole right side had turned to stone. "You liked that? Try this one!" She kicked him in the mouth: his head bounced off the wall, teeth flew.

"Jesus, that hurt!" Vic whimpered, laughing.

"Don't talk to her, Daddy."

"Way to go, sister!" Goldy grinned, spitting thickly into a plastic cup he was holding in his free hand, and Charley, pushing out his thick soft mitt past my petrified elbow ("When Jim told her Vic had a bullet in his heart, you know what she said? She said, 'Then why don't you just reach inside his asshole and pull it out!'"), said: "Don' believe I've hadda pleasure. Trainer here, Mushual Life."

"This is Mr. Waddilow, Charley," I gasped, trying to stand alone. "New neighbors . . ."

"The next one in the goolies, tough guy!"

"Oh ha ha! *Spare* me!" Vic groaned.

"Neighbors, hunh?"

"I left your bill on the dishwasher, mister," the plumber said around his chaw, squinting up at me. "Easy, Eileen, he's dying," Daffie cautioned, touching her forearm. Eileen shook her off. "So? Who isn't? Some just have more fun at it than others, that's all." "Thank you," I said, gripping the sideboard. "You're welcome to stay . . . have a drink or something . . ." "No, thanks." He spat another oyster. "I got no time for this shit."

"In fact he looks good drooling blood like that—it's like the mask's finally off the bastard."

"Steve's a young kid, it's all new to him, he can hang around if he

wants to. Me, I seen it all. I got a job to do, that's it." He turned to go. "Can I give you a ride somewhere, sister?"

"No, thanks. I'll walk."

"Hey," Kitty asked, "where *is* everybody?"

"Don't be stupid, girlie, it's dangerous out there."

I looked around. Kitty was right ("Anatole has written a play," Howard was explaining to her—he'd cleaned up some, wore Tania's glasses on a chain around his neck now, his red tie and the bra, but no shirt, and my white boating cap, "you just missed the casting . . ."): the dining room had emptied out, there were only the few of us clustered around the drinks now like refugees, Mrs. Waddilow alone over at the table, Mavis grinning up at us from the floor, Cynthia and Woody in the next room watching television.

"And relax, sister, I'm off fucking for life. I mean it, I'm into beer, old movies, and model trains. When I'm not unplugging rich guys' toilets." His partner Steve came in with Scarborough and Horner and they commenced to move the dining table out from under Mrs. Waddilow. " 'Scuse us, ma'am." "So whuzz your poison, Waterloo?" Charley asked, slumping heavily against the sideboard. "You like model trains?"

"Just a bit of tonic, thank you. Not a drinking man myself."

"I don't know," Eileen said, staring down at Goldy, hands stuffed in her pockets, her face swollen and blue with bruises. "I don't think so."

"Gerry?" It was Sally Ann, her voice anxious. "I think Dad's getting worse!"

"You oughta come and see my layout, I got everything, uses up half my basement, whole fucking county in miniature."

So he was: his head, eyes rolled back, had fallen to one side, blood dribbled down his chin still ("Just like real life. Only without the horseshit . . ."), his breath was coming in hoarse erratic gasps. There was a tooth lying loose on his chin like a beached castaway. "Vic?" His lips were moving ("You're as bad as this guy," Eileen was saying, "just another closet idealist!" and Goldy said: "Hey, you like horseshit? I'll put in horseshit!"), but only the odd word or two were getting out: ". . . nihilistic bastard . . . what? . . . and hope, shit . . . what I *hate*—kaff! foo! . . . so goddamn wet—" "I'll go get Jim," I said.

"Hurry . . . !"

It wasn't easy to hurry. I seemed to be carrying a hundred pounds of dead weight on my right side, and my knees were like jelly. I heaved myself to the doorway and leaned dizzily against it, staring into Scarborough's transformation of our living room. Nothing was in its place, except perhaps my wife, who was vacuuming the rug. It was like some kind of spectacular fusing of the familiar, the whole room tented in sheets, towels, bloody drapes and curtains, all meant to suggest some sort of cave, I supposed ("I won't be a moment, Zack," my wife shouted from inside it as Quagg flung his cape about in mimed protest, "I just want to get up this plaster dust before it gets tracked into the carpet!"), lit from behind—or rather from atop: Scarborough had drilled holes through the ceiling and mounted table and floor lamps up there above the sheeting. At the cavemouth, Teresa stood naked and frightened ("I feel so stupid," she was complaining, trying to cover, not her breasts—which Gudrun was rouging—or her genitals, but the whitened rolls of fat on her tummy), while nearby Jim leaned over Ros's cadaver, laid out amid pilaf, cheese balls, and sliced salami on our dining room table, a butcher knife in his hand. He seemed shorter than usual. "No, no, I want the video camera *inside* the cave, looking *out* at the *audience!*" Quagg shouted over the sweeper's roar, and Scarborough cried: "Goddamn it, Fats, get outa here! You're knockin' everything over!" "I'm just trying to help, Scar!" "Well, go help Gudrun!" Oddly, this was all reminiscent of something I'd seen before, as though—I was thinking about Inspector Pardew's whimsical speculations about "the geography of time"—I'd somehow got switched onto some kind of reverse loop (had I just heard Goldy say something about this to Eileen? now certainly she said: "Sounds like the story of my life," but perhaps he'd been describing his shunting operations), such that though the space had changed and the approach was from an opposite angle, this was a point on time's map I'd passed through before. I squeezed my eyes shut, shook my head.

"They said the dining room table was too high and wanted to saw the legs down," my wife said suddenly beside me, "but I talked them out of it."

"*What*—?!" I lurched back, banging my head on the doorframe.

"I didn't mean to startle you, Gerald. It's all right." What was happening? It was as though we'd jumped over something! One moment she'd been vacuuming the carpet and Quagg, prancing about in

his white unitard, had been shouting over the noise, the next she was in front of me discussing the dining room table, Louise was carting the sweeper off, Fats was on his knees, smearing Teresa's legs with clown white, and Quagg, wrapped up like a sleeping bat in his purple cape, was quietly explaining to Alison's husband ("In theater, dialogue *is* action, man!") what the play was all about. What had happened to that moment *in between?* "I made up something off the top of my head about the proper height of altars, and luckily they accepted it." Behind her there was a reek of pot and incense. "No, no, *no*, Fats!" Gudrun was exclaiming. "I said *not* in her bush—now go away, *I'll* do it!" "In fact, I overdid it, I'm afraid, and then the table turned out to be too low, so they had to raise it up on some of your records."

"Ah. Good." I really didn't know what I was saying. Regina came sweeping in, drew up short when she spied Teresa, cried out: "How come *she* got the part?!" and went storming out again in a stylized pique I was sure I'd seen before. I was totally confused. I didn't know whether the night was running forward or backward. I was afraid the doorbell would ring and it would be Ros at the door. Backing out, her cloak wrapping her, her welcoming hug dissolving into a wishful fancy—and then the doorbell *did* ring! "Oh no!" I cried.

"Not *more* people!" my wife groaned, and took my arm. But it was: little Bunky Baird, the actress who'd played "Honeyed Glances" in *The Lover's Lexicon*, one of Lot's daughters, and Jesus's nymphomaniac sister in *The Beatitudes*, escorted by some older guy in his fifties and a young gigolo who might have been partnering either or both. Quagg had just been explaining to Alison's husband that, "So what we're going for here is the transmutation of stuff from deep down in the inner life, see, into something out front that we can watch, something made outa language and movement, you dig, to show forth the—" when Bunky let out a terrible shriek from the doorway: "*Stop him! he's going to kill her!*"

Teresa squealed as though Gudrun, now rouging her bottom, might have jabbed her with something, Olga yelped and dropped her drink, Jim looked up: "Don't be silly," he sighed ("We need a butterfly on that float at the mouth," shouted Scarborough), shaking his loose shock of gray hair, "I'm only trying to chip this damned plaster off."

"It's all right, Bunky," Quagg explained, his arm around her. "She's

already dead. It's Ros." "Okay, hit it—that's it, now make it hot!" "She had a big heart, I wanta use it in this production."

"It's getting so confusing," my wife murmured, her hand on my leaden elbow ("Yeah, I heard a rumor you had something going on the boards, Zack—looks fab!" Bunky was saying, calming down as deftly as she'd aroused herself, and Vachel, flipping irritably through Anatole's script, complained: "Wah, don't I getta do any *fucking?*"), "I don't even know a lot of these people."

"That's good, kill it!"

"Hey, what took you guys so long?" Quagg asked, as Steve the plumber and Horner came in, lugging the ping-pong table.

"Catchin' the reruns in the pit, Zack."

"Isn't that your athletic supporter Vachel is wearing on his head?"

"Looks like it." Also my golf shoes and Bermuda shorts, my ski goggles on his bulbous rump, and Mark's blue SUPERLOVER sweatshirt.

"This where you want it?"

"Yeah." They set the table down, still collapsed, at the entrance to the cave: apparently it was meant to serve as a kind of stage. "See what you think, Hillie," Quagg said, then, shifting his penis from the left to the right side of his unitard crotch, turned to Bunky: "What're you doing these days, kid?"

"I'm, uh, between shows, Zack."

"I-I don't know what to say," I said, and my wife said ("C'mon," Quagg smiled, "we'll spot you in"): "I'll go put the coffee on."

"Thanks, Zack," said Bunky softly, touching him under the cape. She already had her coat off, her two men bumping past me into the dining room with it, on their way to the sideboard. Back there, I could still hear Vic babbling on helplessly: "Turned to salt . . . *what—?* . . . exactly the problem . . . ice all gone . . . who—*whoof! harff!—* wanted that . . . ? No, goddamn it!" Yes, I thought, feeling a little better, coffee would help.

"Now lemme see that script, kid."

I moved out of the traffic toward Jim (he seemed suddenly very weary, his hair in his eyes and square jaw adroop, as he dug away at the plaster on Ros's breast), Hilario rapping out a vigorous staccato on the ping-pong table as I passed that sounded like machine-gun fire. Behind his fierce rat-a-tat-tat, I could hear Anatole explaining excitedly that his play was really a kind of metaphysical fairy tale, a

poetic meditation on the death of beauty and on the beast of violence lurking in all love, Vachel grousing in his squeaky voice: "Yeah, but at *least* I oughta get to squeeze some goddamn *tit*, hunh, Zack?" "Christ, so much—*gasp!*—waste . . . over and over . . ." You could hear him all the way in here, growling and spluttering. "Got a side for me, honey?" Bunky asked. "Am I right . . . ? *story*—kaff! snort!—what? *kills!*" "Vic's in bad shape, Jim," I said. It was a relief to be around a familiar face. "I think he needs you."

Jim sighed, staring down at Ros. "Some damn party *I'm* having," he said. One of Ros's bagged-up hands was in the pilaf. There was a loose scatter of paper napkins, turkey bones ("Damn it, you gotta dumb it down, kid," Quagg was remonstrating, Alison's husband hovering over his shoulder, trying to read the script, "you're outa school now, so cut the fancy shit—this is *theater!*"), Alison's silk sash, chorizo chunks, somebody's vibrator, used silverware. Like Time's dropped breadcrumbs, I thought: no, we were not going around in circles, Ros wasn't anyway. And the sash: it was greasier than ever. There are no reverse loops, it seemed to say. The borders are absolute. Things end. Replay, instant or delayed (the TV cameraman had just moved off Jim's hands to focus on Teresa, clown white from head to toe, except for her bright red breasts and bottom, now being urged up onto the ping-pong table to dance with Hilario, Scarborough meanwhile nailing my skis to the front corners of the table, apparently creating some kind of proscenium arch, the raps of his hammer syncopating contrapuntally with Hilario's chattering tapdance and Zack Quagg's barking lecture to a deflated Anatole: "You might as well learn right now, son: keep it simple! The mystery just gets chewed up in all this razzamatazz. If you got something to say, come straight out with it!"), was a manipulation not of time but of matter. Benedetto came in, pulling on Roger's bloodsoaked business suit (this was new): "It's still *sopping!*" he complained (he hadn't said this before), trying to stretch it around his operatic belly. "Gudrun, old sock, could you let this out a bit?" "How's the shoulder, Gerry?" "Stiff . . ."

"Just remember, kid, the most mysterious sentence in the world has only three letters in it. Everything else is nothing but a fucking footnote to it, variations on a—hey, why so glum?"

"There's only about an inch or so back here," Gudrun said, examining the seam in the seat of Roger's pants, Benedetto peering

down at her over his shoulder. "Why don't we just make you a cod-piece?"

"I'm sorry, Mr. Quagg. It's my fault. I guess I really don't know much about this—"

"Whaddaya mean, you're doing great!"

"I am?"

"Hey, Scar, look what I found!" exclaimed Horner, coming in with Mark's pedalcar. Scarborough was up on a stepladder, his mouth full of pins, hanging our drapes over the ski uprights like theater curtains, so folding them as to make the splotches of blood resemble large crude hearts. "Terriff," he called down lugubriously, taking a tuck, "see if he'll fit," and Vachel squeaked: "No, man, I'm *not* getting *in* that thing!" Gudrun was meanwhile measuring Beni for his codpiece and it reminded me, as I settled back against the table, accepting it all now, Ros, Roger, Tania, the police, the wounds and bruises, every-thing, or almost everything ("Sure, kid! You got *bucketsa* talent!" Quagg was booming), of the time Ros, holding the head of my ex-hausted member up in the air, said: "I don't care how big it is, Gerry. I don't even care how hard it is. I just care how *here* it is . . ." Yes, I thought—I was watching Teresa's crimson cheeks bob like ripe ap-ples as Hilario, looking pained, clapped her along—this is the one sweet thing we have: the eternal present. Our only freedom. It seemed to flatten out beneath me, all resistance crumbling at last.

"Gerry . . . ?"

"I mean, I *love* the fairy tale bit, kid, that old granny in the ice castle, little orphan Ros at the door—like, we'll put her in a basket maybe, shaking a rattle or sucking a dildo or something—flash all that in the hello frame to key some motifs, ring a few bells, then punch in this torture number to set up the death dance and Last Supper routine: shit, man, it's a fucking *classic!*"

"It is?"

"No, no, no, Teresita! You are the, how you say? the goddess off *loave*, no?"

"And this line about bats in daylight—I mean, *wow!*"

Clock time might take things—Ros, for example—further and fur-ther away, or seem to, but human time ("So awright, kid, get *on* with it!")—what had the Inspector said?

"Now, anybody here get off on a git-box?"

"Gerry, you're, uh . . ."

"You muss *leeft!* and *leeft!* So!"

Pulsations, yes. Perhaps. (He said.) But flow, no.

"Whew, I don't *believe* this!"

"How 'bout *me*, Zack? Gimme a kit, I'm magic, man!"

"Vic's daughter plays, I think."

"Gerry . . . ? Hey . . . !"

"What?" I realized Jim had been trying to get my attention for some time. I leaned back toward him ("She's in the dining room, Zack. Her old man's got a problem . . ."), cradling my numb arm in my live one and recalling that game Ros and I used to play with our toes and noses—toeses and noses, we called it—and the delicious pucker of concentration on her lips, the tip of her tongue slithering out between them like an animal's erection . . .

"Okay, sign her on. Now—hey, sweetheart, whaddaya *doing*—?!"

". . . Sitting on her hand," Jim said.

"Oh—!" I lurched away from the table, and her arm swung loose. "*No . . . !*" I'd almost forgotten she was there. Jim put her hand back. The fingers, knuckled, looked more like a bag of marbles inside their plastic wrap.

"This is not a singalong, baby! We're not watching the bouncing ball! This is a dance of *death!* Doesn't that *mean* anything to you?"

"It's just . . . I-I've never *done* anything like this before," Teresa whimpered, her hands trembling, white on white, on her tummy.

"That story about Roger and Ros and the old lady, you know, is a complete fabrication," Jim added. "And Zack knows it."

I nodded, feeling too weak to stand alone, yet too appalled to lean back against the table again (I still felt her brittle fingers, knuckled into my rump like some kind of summons), or even to look at it, keeping my eyes fixed instead on stubby Teresa, now trying, coached by Hilario and Quagg, to "fly like a beard" (as Hilario said)—"No, no, guapa! like a *doave*, not a *tour-key!*"

"Is this what you'd call a metaphor?" asked Alison's husband from under his floppy hat. Olga, it seemed to me, had her hand in his pocket.

"Ros came to see me that day. Somebody had apparently given her a hallucinogen of some kind without her knowing what it was, and she was frightened. Not by the visions, but by the feeling it gave her, she said, of being alone."

"Mate a—*vot?*"

"Curious . . ."

"Wait a minute! *Wait* a minute! Let's get *serious!* This is *death* we're talking about, baby, *death!*—you know, the last fucking call, the deep end, so long forever: now, come *on,* what does it make you *think* of?"

"Why don't you stick a feather up her butt, Zack, and let her try it on all fours?"

"Ros hated to be alone. She even wanted someone in the bathroom with her when she was brushing her teeth or . . ."

"I know . . ."

"I-I once imitated a person flushing herself down a toilet," Teresa offered timidly. "Of course it was a long time ago . . ."

"His blind daughter?" Bunky asked, studying Anatole's script. Lloyd Draper had entered the room in his hat and coat, photo albums under his arm, Iris beside him. "Yeh heh heh!" he exclaimed, discovering me, and they came strolling over.

"At . . . at church camp . . ."

"Beautiful!" enthused Benedetto, admiring the silky patch Gudrun was holding up to his gaping fly. "Whose *were* those?"

"Awright," Zack barked, losing patience ("Take your pants off," Gudrun said around the needle in her mouth, "and I'll sew it on . . ."), "let's *see* it!"

"Everything was just delicious!" Iris exclaimed, and Lloyd agreed: "Yes indeedy! I'll second that!" He grabbed my right arm and gave it a painful shake. Someone behind me was tuning up a guitar. "God, she's terrible!" Zack groaned, hand clapped to his eyes, peeking out between his fingers at Teresa trying to flush herself. "We sure been travelin' first class tonight, haven't we, Mother?"

"I didn't even know he *had* a daughter!"

"Yeah," laughed Horner. "It's wonderful!"

"Thank you so much for asking us!" She was wearing the pecker-sweater, I saw, pinned to her dress like a corsage or a political button. "We looked for your wife . . ."

"How is he, Sally Ann?" Jim asked behind me.

"She's probably in the kitchen . . ."

"Well, please tell her . . ."

"Still about the same." She plunked at a guitar, picking out a chord. "He doesn't seem to be bleeding as bad, but his mind's getting worse."

"Can I stop flushing now?"

"Say, Mother, doesn't that remind you of those dancers we saw in the East—you remember . . ."

"No, guapa, ees byootifool!"

"Poor Dad. I don't think he's got much longer."

"Oh yes. The red paint, you mean. It was quite lovely, as I recall, dear, and very skillful—but I didn't like the heads on the stakes after."

"*Now* theenk like you are toilet *all stop opp!*"

"What—?"

"And flow! Effrywhere! *Ffflo-oo-ow!*"

Lloyd and Iris Draper, saying their goodbyes along the way, had stopped to talk with Alison's husband. He pivoted toward them, causing Olga to stumble and fall to her knees. "Well, I love my father very much," Sally Ann was saying (someone had just asked her why she'd left him alone in his condition, in fact I had), "but, after all, Gerry, I do have my own career to think about." "Don't worry, I'll check on him," Jim assured her, as Alison's husband shrugged and glanced over at me. "I don't know," he said, or probably said. Olga and the Drapers, following his glance, also peered back over their shoulders.

I turned away, just as Eileen came strolling in in her khaki raincoat, collar up, hands in pockets, staring right at—or through—me. "You look ridiculous!" she said. "I know," I slumped a bit, and there was an echo just behind me: she'd been speaking, I realized, not to me but to Teresa. "Can—can you please find Wilma?" Teresa whimpered, and Eileen ("This bearded fruitcake's driving me nuts, Priss!" Zack was hissing) said: "She and Talbot've already gone, Teresa. And we're going, too." She bumped past me, pulling off her raincoat. "Put this on."

"Why don't you and Olga take the sonuvabitch up and get him laid?"

"Who, this boiled hat, Zack?"

"I don't know if I *can*—"

"Sure you can, Teresa. All it takes is two feet. Come on, I'm fed up with all this cheap sensationalism. Let's get the hell out of here."

"Yeah, he's loaded, Priss, I'm cultivating him—*hey*, hold up there! That's our *star!* Leave her alone, goddamn it!"

"You see?" Teresa shrank into the raincoat that Eileen wrapped around her, as Horner, Scarborough, and Quagg started crowding

menacingly around. Goldy, at my elbow, spat into a cup and said: "You know, if I was them guys, I wouldn't fuck with that broad . . ."

"That's far enough, you cold-ass bitch!" Horner snarled, blocking their exit. Eileen coolly snapped her knee up and Horner crumpled, howling pathetically, the others backing off a step. "Like I said," laughed Goldy, and—*poytt!*—shot another gob into the cup.

"All right," said Eileen impassively, "who's next?"

In reply, there was a sudden gasp from the onlookers crowded up near the hallway door, and they all fell back: standing there was a weird naked figure wrapped like a mummy in plastic cleaning bags, with a condom pulled over his head. It was Malcolm Mee. He looked like something from outer space—or inner space, rather: a kind of aborted fetus. He took two bounding steps into the room (Prissy Loo screamed, Fats fell over a coffee table, pulling down part of the cave wall), paused, crouching; in his raised hand: *the ice pick!* "Oh no . . . !"

"Hey, man, we're not ready for this!" Scarborough protested, and Mee mutely flashed the pick at him as though to strike. He was breathing heavily, erratically, through a tiny puncture in the condom, the rubber snapping in and popping out with each breath. I wasn't sure, but he seemed to be smiling. The TV cameraman was squatting, shooting up at the flapping rubber under his nostrils. Beni said: "What is this?! I haven't even got my codpiece yet!"—but he went quickly silent when Mee turned on him, swishing the pick through the air, making it whistle.

"Christ, I think he's serious . . . !"

"Malcolm—?"

"You've got to *stop* him, Zack!" a woman cried out.

"Shut up!" Quagg snapped, drawing his purple cape across his body like a shield, and Prissy Loo seemed to faint. Or maybe she just tripped over her heavy galoshes. Horner, clutching his scrotum and grunting painfully, dragged himself off across the carpet, out of the way, watching Mee warily. "Shit fire . . . !"

"Is this some sort of protest—?"

Mee leapt lithely out of the shadows onto the spotlit stage and posed there rigidly, pick upraised. Everyone crept back except Teresa and Eileen, who were seemingly unable to move. "Please . . . !" Teresa whimpered, the raincoat falling away from her painted breasts, bright now in the overhead lights. Eileen, clutching the coat to Te-

resa's shoulders, watched Mee intently; Quagg knelt; Fats stared goggle-eyed, wrapped in collapsed cave wall.

"Come on, Mee," I said, finding my voice, or some of it anyway. "Enough's enough, damn it!"

He appeared not to hear me, took a lurching step toward Teresa as though losing control, seemingly transfixed (his dilated eyes were clearly visible through the stretched rubber sheath, the flesh around them mashed back like shiny scar tissue) by her heaving red spots, the pick quivering in his poised fist.

Beni, in Roger's ill-fitting jacket and his own theatrical longjohns, threw his arms open and stepped forward: "Malcolm, my old friend!"

"Don't, Beni! He knows what he's doing!" shouted Quagg.

"But she's not one of us," Beni argued, "she wouldn't understand!" Mee's free hand shot forward and grabbed one of Teresa's crimson breasts—she squeaked in terror, slumping backward into Eileen's arms as he drew the breast toward him. Beni tore off his false moustache. "Malcolm, my friend, it's your old comrade Benedetto, remember?"

"Isn't this getting a bit dangerous?" Alison's husband murmured, his face pale now under the drooping brim of Beni's hat, his lips pulled back in a frightened grimace. If Beni distracts him, I thought, maybe I can somehow disarm him. Malcolm was stronger than I was, though, I'd need help. I glanced around for the police: amazingly, they were watching me, not Mee!

"This is theater, man!" Quagg was saying, his voice a fierce whisper. "Theater is hard. It's real. Did you think we were just fucking around?"

"But I thought—"

"Do me a favor, would you, dear friend," Beni insisted, interposing himself boldly between Mee and Teresa, "and loan me that—" Mee struck. Beni gasped, disbelievingly, staggered back a step, clutching the handle of the pick that now seemed to grow out of his chest like a thick warty finger, pointing back at Mee. "*Oh no . . . !*" he wheezed, and sat back in amazement—*splat!*—as though someone might have pulled a chair out from under him. Blood began to spread outward from the wound.

"My god—!"

"*Now* see what you've done!" I cried. I didn't know who I was shouting at—Mee maybe, Quagg, the police, or perhaps the whole damned crowd—but I was suddenly angry, a ferocious rage was boil-

ing up in me: "*You've gone too goddamned far!*" Someone seemed to be crying. I shoved Mee aside brusquely, knelt at Beni's side: he was bleeding badly now, and when he tried to mutter something about "a surprise ending," blood bubbled out the corner of his mouth and down his plump chin. "*Jim—!*" I screamed—I couldn't seem to *stop* screaming. "*Someone get Jim! Hurry, for god's sake!*" But no one moved: they seemed frozen with shock or fear. I leaped to my feet: "*Jim! Come in here! Quickly!*" I yelled, then turned on the two cops: "Why didn't you *do* something, goddamn it? What did you just *stand* there for?" They looked utterly bewildered, as though they didn't even understand the question. The room was silent except for the suppressed whimpering, Beni's rasping groans, my own labored breathing. I swung on Mee and beat him on the chest with my good arm: "*You vicious creep!*" He took my blows without response, as though stunned by his own action. "Never seem to make it . . . ," Beni gasped hoarsely, "to the final curtain . . . !" "*You're a maniac, Mee!*" I screamed, shoving him off the stage. "*You ought to be locked up!*"

"It's time . . . to put a silk on it, friends . . . lower the asbestos," Beni moaned. I turned to him. He was sprawled against one of my wife's potted plants (had someone moved it there?), his eyes rolled back, blood dribbling profusely from his mouth and stabwound. "They're . . . yanking the show on . . . old Benedetto, boys . . . it's the last stanza . . . !" Oh no . . . I leaned closer, a new fury intruding on the old: "Beni . . . ?" He rolled his eyes back down, focusing on me, winked, pushed a half-chewed blood capsule between his teeth like a peashooter. "*Damn* you!" I snatched the pick out of his hands: a stage weapon with a contracting point! The sniggering (I hadn't been hearing whimpering at all) changed to laughter and a loud burst of applause. I looked up and found myself staring into the lens of the video camera. Mee was peeling off his facemask, smirking toothily. Even Eileen had a grin on her face as she wrapped Teresa up again, and Fats asked: "How'd I do, Zack?" "You were fantastic!" Quagg laughed. "Ah, screw you guys!" I said, hurling the pick across the room, and pushed out, drawing another burst of cheers and applause.

In the dining room doorway, Kitty and that white-haired neighbor lady in the lime pants and pink-and-lemon shirt were laughing at a photo: "Look at that cute little thing!" "Is that Gerry?" I snatched it

away from them and ripped it in half: I was tired of this abuse. They stared at me in some astonishment. On looking closer, I saw it was not one of the photographs I'd made with Ros, as I'd supposed, but a picture of Mark being held in my arms. Behind me, Quagg was saying: "Okay, now for the second number, whaddaya say we exhume that old gag from Ros's widow play, the one where she mistakes a pick for a prick and reaches in a guy's pants—"

"Isn't that a bit slapstick for the occasion, Zack?"

"Excuse me," I mumbled, and shouldered on past the two women, feeling like some kind of maimed and brutish fool.

"We'll play it straight—you know, reenactment of a sacred legend, take it apart and slow it down, like we did in *Bluebeard's Secret* . . ."

"Anyway, I thought it was a pecker for a pucker . . ."

I pulled up short just inside the dining room. Entering, I'd brushed silk. She was standing in the shadows by the doorway. Perhaps she'd been waiting for me. I took no hope from this: I'd betrayed her, after all, in her eyes anyway—and in my own as well (hadn't I said at the theater that night we met that the last word was, artistically, the inevitable consequence of the first, that truth was an aesthetic principle, beauty moral?), it was a goddamn mess. I couldn't even look at her. Over by the sideboard, Vic groaned. There were several people around him, but they were talking only to each other—even Jim had turned away to fix himself a drink. Above him, Tania's "Susanna" stepped out into oblivion. "She's making one mistake," Vic once said of her. "She's looking backward, back at the establishment, the elders. She's turned the pool, the stream of life, into a bottomless pit. What she ought to do is step back, turn around, and kick the shit out of them once and for all. Then she can take her fucking bath in peace." But what if the real cause of her terror, I thought, trembling, is that there's no one back there? That it's only she who's watching herself, or rather—*what*? She was crying! I turned at last and, tears springing to my own eyes, took her in my arms—or arm: my right one was still pretty useless. "I-I'm sorry!" I blurted out. I felt certain, somehow, she'd forgive me.

"Me too!" she sobbed. "Poor Vic!" Vic? It was Brenda: I let go her pudgy body, naked and lumpy under the silk. "Such a super guy, Gerry!"

"Where'd you get that dress?"

"Fats found it somewhere. Is it your wife's? I couldn't get back into that damned pants suit."

"Gerald would never let me buy a dress like that," my wife said, passing by with a sponge cake. "He doesn't like silk."

"Enough? What's ever enough?" Vic moaned. I could tell him. In the living room, someone was singing about "the old man," Sally Ann maybe, and I could hear Kitty and Mrs. Waddilow oohing and ahing over the sponge cake. "There are strawberries to go with it," my wife said, and Vic broke into a new fit of coughing. "You think it's all some kinda—*wheeze!* choke!—*joke?*"

"He's such a brave guy," snuffled Brenda, blowing her nose in the hem of the dress. I felt utterly wasted. Emptied out. Like Brenda's nose. Steve the plumber and the character with the pipe and the leather elbow patches came in behind her, talking about Mee's act ("You know, he looked a bit like that dead girl, all bagged up like that!" "Well, that was probably his intention . . ."), laughing when they saw me, and I felt the humiliation of it all over again. Where had all the beauty gone? "You probably ate it," Vic might have said. That "aesthetics of truth" line I'd used at the theater was his too actually, I'd borrowed it for the occasion. She hadn't quarreled with it ("It felt like a lifetime," Sally Ann, or whoever, was singing, "our little husband-and-wife time . . ."), but she'd had a reply of course. To wit: that from another perspective (mine had been of her soft lips pursed above a cup of steaming coffee that matched her eyes and velvet suit, and to tell the truth, thoughts of ethics didn't even enter into it) it was the *first* word that was the consequence of the *last*. "And he's still got presence," Brenda added, taking a chewed wad of gum from behind her ear and stuffing it in her jaws. She wiped her eyes on a slashed sleeve and took my arm. "I know he's not making a lot of—*crack! pop!*—sense, but he makes you *feel* like he is."

"God *damn* you!" he shouted now as we drew near (there was applause in the living room), and Mr. Waddilow, hooking his thumbs in his vest, said: "Isn't that a bit sacrilegious?" Mavis was sitting up now, propped against a chair, though her eyes were still glazed over and her jaw sagged loosely. Her husband, Jim, some distance away, held his drink up to the light, just under Tania's "Susanna," taking her fateful step, and it was almost as though she were stepping into his glass. Steve, smiling, said something to Bunky's two friends, who stared back dully, and Charley, who'd seemed locked in some kind of

elbowbender's freeze (he often went rigid before falling over at the end of a night), suddenly reared up and seized Mr. Waddilow's lapels. "*Damned right!*" be bellowed. Mr. Waddilow rocked back on his heels in alarm.

"By the way, Gerry, who's that cute guy in the tweed jacket?"

"His name's Gottfried, that's all I—"

"Oh, is *that* the famous Gottfried . . ."

"Where are the lights? Turn on the . . . goddamn lights!" Vic begged.

"*Hey, Big Ger!*" Charley boomed out, wheeling around heavily. "Where ya *been?*" Jim lowered his glass as though pulling the ground out from under Susanna, though of course she didn't fall. No, that abyss awaited her forever. It wouldn't even be there without her. This thought somehow picked me up a bit, like something I'd forgotten but finally remembered. "It's been *awful* here since you been gone!"

Howard in his bra, red tie, half-lens reading glasses, and sailing cap sniffed petulantly as Steve, shrugging, reached in past Bunky's friends for the gin bottle. I remembered the older guy now: he was the angel who had put up the money for that mock sci-fi film Ros and Bunky had starred in, *The Invasion of the Panty Snarfers.* The younger one, the gigolo type, had directed it. A terrible film. Or so it had seemed at the time. Now I wished for nothing more than to be able to go sit down somewhere and watch it. Or maybe I only wanted to (I seemed to hear someone telling me to do this: sit down) sit down.

"We *miss* ya, ole buddy! Nothin' *happens* when ya go away! Eh, Waterloo?"

"I beg your pardon?" Steve asked, his hand hesitating over the gin bottle, and Gottfried, putting pipe to mouth, said: "No, she was with some older gentleman, I believe—the one with the goatee."

I poured myself a brandy and stared up at the "Susanna," thinking: My father was right, we're the products of calamity, metamorphosed by our very will to endure, meshed alive into the unraveling fabric of the universe—that's where all creation happens. "Before I forget it, Howard," I said, gazing at Susanna's small foot poised tenderly over the void, "I want to buy Tania's 'Bluebeard' painting."

"Cyril? You must be mistaken," Brenda was saying to Gottfried, smiling up at him, her jaws working strenuously, as Steve staggered back, shoved by the younger guy. The tall cop limped up with his

toolbox, muttering something about a missing dynamometer, and Howard said: "I'm afraid you can't really afford it, Gerald."

"What do you mean? It's not even finished, Howard—"

"There's some forceps gone, too," Bob grumbled, and Brenda, looking puzzled (Steve also looked puzzled: "Who you calling a shit-face?" he asked), said: "They've *what* . . . ?"

"All the more reason," replied Howard huffily ("I think I saw those on the turkey dish," Jim said). "It's priceless probably. You're lucky to have the pieces you own now."

"Oh yes?" Mr. Waddilow asked, reaching in his breast pocket for a pair of spectacles. "Is this one of them?"

"*Oh no!*" Brenda cried. "*Not Cyril and Peg!*" Steve, eyes asquint, reached for the gin bottle again, but the gigolo blocked his way. "Is that an advertisement, sweetheart?" the older man asked with a sneer, pointing to the name stitched over Steve's pocket. "I can't *believe* it! *Fats—?*" I felt I understood now what Tania had meant when she said that truth ("That's not art, it's a piece of trash," Bob was objecting, "she don't even know how to draw!"), dispersed into the clashing incongruities of the world, returns as beauty: which, with memory, is all we have of substance. "You're not *listening!*" Vic yelled, and Brenda, running off ("Hey, mister, you wanting trouble?" Steve asked): "*Fats? Oh my god, Fats—!*"

"*Fuck* your shadows! Man is—*glurgle! splut!*—something *hard!*"

What? Was Vic talking to me? Kitty came over from the doorway with Mrs. Waddilow and said: "Hey, you guys in here are missing it all!" "Oh yeah?" yuffhuffed Charley confusedly, and Vic, breathing with great difficulty ("How much you sell your ass for, working man?" the gigolo taunted, blowing smoke), gasped out something about "the disappearing eye" or "I." No, not to me or to anyone else: Vic had fallen through that hole in the world Tania spoke of, he was far away, in another place. I felt a sudden pang of loss, of disconnection from something valuable. Something like the truth. "Ah well, what the fuck, it's all just a—*farff! foo!*—fiction anyway," he babbled now. I turned, sipping brandy, to watch Steve take a halfhearted swing which the gigolo parried. No ("Yeah," Kitty was laughing, "they've got Vachel rigged out like a kind of walking joystick, smeared all over with petroleum jelly and blowing off about murder and paradox as time's French ticklers—it's a *scream!*"), not the truth so much, but commitment, engagement, the force of life itself: this is what

Vic had meant to me. The *idea* of *vocation*. The young plumber, wary now, drew himself erect, flexing his strong shoulders. The older guy ("Look at this interesting painting, dear," Mr. Waddilow said) knocked his cap off. "Yes, it's very nice. Did you see the icon in the front room?" "We've *got* to have revolutions," Vic used to argue, banging his fists on the table, or bar, or lectern, wherever he was, "hope'd *die* if we didn't!" It was beautiful (Kitty, speaking of little Bunky Baird's new makeup job, had just said more or less the same thing): "Watch out for art," he'd exclaim, "it's a parlor trick for making the world disappear!" Or: "You know what I hate, Gerry? The idea of original sin—in *any* disguise! Do it new! Don't be afraid! Change yourself, goddamn it, and you inhabit a renovated world!" I didn't believe any of it, of course. But I loved the fervor.

"No, Bunky's playing 'the Lady in Red,' and she's really in great form! Regina tried to upstage her by swooping in wrapped in nothing but herself, but unfortunately her birthday suit's about fifteen years outa fashion!"

"Yeah, I just saw that on the box!" laughed the man in the gray chalkstriped suit, joining us from the TV room, an empty glass in his hand. "The poor toad!" Steve, lurching blindly to his feet—reaching down for his cap just a moment before, he'd taken a chop in the neck, a kick in the ribs, a drink thrown in his face—crashed into him. "*Whoa!*" the man whooped as his glass went flying, and Kitty, ducking (Bob, watching her, reached for his revolver), said: "Are they showing it on TV?"

"Yeah, the best bits anyway, along with—hey! talk of your show stoppers!" he hooted, picking up his glass and pointing at me. "You really tumbled for that old chestnut!"

"Whuzzat?" Charley grinned, swiveling his big head back and forth between us: it was the only part of him that still worked, the rest seemed totally immobilized. Bob had relaxed again, was showing Howard some of his own drawings of the crime scene.

"A stage sticker!" the guy in the chalkstripes laughed. "The old collapsible pick trick—ha ha! he really cut a gut!"

Charley's face sagged. "Whuzz funny 'bout that?" he wanted to know. " 'Assa fuckin' *trazhedy!*"

"Well, certainly they show skill, sensibility, a consciousness of form and architecture," Howard was expounding, peering down at arm's length through Tania's narrow spectacles at Bob's drawings. "But

they lack, what can I say, a certain density, mythic complexity, inno-
vation . . ."

"Argh . . . ," groaned Vic as though, were he at all rational, in
mockery, "say it . . . *kaff!* ain't so!"

"How about, uh, percipience?" Bob asked hopefully. The kitchen
door swung open and Woody and Cynthia came in, holding hands.
"If by percipience you mean a discerning eye for detail, yes," acknowledged Howard, "but true intuitive apperception: not yet." Bob looked
a bit downcast, but Gottfried, removing his pipe from his mouth
(over his shoulder, the gigolo had Steve in a hammerlock, and the
other guy was kicking him in the stomach), leaned intently toward
Howard and said: "Ah! you're interested in myth, then . . . ?"

"Gerry, thanks for the party," Woody smiled, as Bunky's older
friend took the monkey wrench out of Steve's back pocket and shoved
it in his mouth, "but we've got to be going."

"So soon?"

"You've been very kind," Cynthia said, and gave my hand a squeeze,
her own hand knobbled with rings. There was a soft flush in her
cheeks and just above her cross-strapped bra, partly hidden by the
vulgar fur she wore around her shoulders. "We both appreciate it."

"Hey, you're not goin', are ya, Woodpecker?" Charley protested.
Beside him, Howard was talking to Gottfried about orchestral ren-
derings of symbol and prophecy, and the dark roots of creation, Vic
wheezing and blowing agonizingly below. "Night's still young, goddamn it! Like you'n me!"

"I'm afraid so, Charley. I've got a big case tomorrow, and now all
of Roger's damned work besides. Sorry." Cynthia let my hand go.

"An immersion into mystery, don't you see, into pain . . ."

"So what's . . . next, Howard?" Vic gasped. "The old—*hah!
harff!*—'language of the fucking wound'—?" He was getting testy
again. His face was haggard, bleached out, his mouth gaped, blood
stained his blue workshirt darkly and his pants were wet with urine.
"The artist-as-visionary shuh—*whooff!*—shit?" Howard's eyes were watering up in anger. I too felt unaccountably annoyed (he was still
clutching that silly fork) and turned away to watch Bunky's friends
haul Steve, kicking, still eating his monkey wrench, out of the room
toward the front door. All that hard-won wisdom, that shrewd and
stubborn intellect, turned to pudding in the end: a lesson I really didn't
need tonight. "You're a fuh—*fooff! shit!*—fucking whore, Howard!"

"Have you seen Noble, by the way?" Woody asked, raising his voice to be heard. Bob, staring deadpan at me, winked. As did Earl Elstob, wandering in, when Charley asked him: "What? Back awready, Earl?"

"Ah, I think he—"

"Yup, well, huh! as one rabbit—shlup!—said t'other: 'This won't take long, yuh huck! *did* it?' "

"Last I saw," said the guy in the chalkstripes, "your coz was in high gear—even his gold eye was lit up and blinkin' like a turn signal!"

"I see. Well, Noble deserves a little fun. If you see him, tell him I'll call him in the morning."

"What I—*huff! whoo!*—hate," Vic rattled on fiercely, "is fucking contrivance! Triviality, obfus . . . obfuscation . . ."

"Poor old Jack the Forker," said Scarborough morosely, coming in from the living room with Gudrun. "Still at it, is he?" He held a bottle up to the light. "Tenor's farewell," remarked Gudrun. She was smeared randomly with greasepaint, though her hands were principally scarlet: as she rubbed her nose (". . . All that—*wheeze!*—'all-is-vanity' horseshit!"), she moustachioed herself. "Bah!" Scarborough pitched the empty bottle over his shoulder impatiently. It hit the doorframe, clattered into the TV room.

"There's more underneath—"

"I want . . . *lucidity* . . . Authen—*gasp!*—"

"Uh, huh! you seen sister?"

"What do you suppose this one could do?" Gudrun mused, looking Bob over.

"Ole Glad's relaxin', Earl! Don' worry, you juss zip up there'n'n *joy* yourself."

"Well, he sure as hell can't dance," muttered Scarborough, squatting.

"Yuh, I thought I'd just leave it open so's I don't hafta—huh!—lose time!"

"Could you repeat that?" Gottfried asked, bending toward Vic. It was true, I saw it now: he did have a tape recorder.

"What I want . . . in art . . . is a knowing . . ."

"*Everything's . . . changed . . . ,*" Mavis intoned gravely. She was on her feet now, leaning against the wall, legs spread wide, eyes staring zombielike into some remote distance. Bunky's young friend, back and breathing heavily, took a swig from the brandy bottle, handed it to the older man. "*I seem to remember . . . a statue . . .*"

"Say, yuh know what's—yuh huh!—worse'n pecker tracks on your zipper?"

". . . A *knowing moral center!*"

". . . *Of ice . . . with mirrors for eyes . . .*"

"Well, who doesn't?" snapped Howard, glancing contemptuously down at Vic (". . . *And a little man where the heart should be . . .*"), Gottfried sidling in between the two men with his mike. "But that's simply too narrow a view of art. Every act of creation, no matter how frivolous it might seem, is, in its essence, *an act of magic!*"

"Ah, that's very good," said Gottfried, stopping up one ear against Mavis behind him. Gudrun clapped her scarlet hands, as Scarborough, rummaging around in the shelves below, came out with a bottle of Tennessee sourmash. "But by 'magic' do you mean—?"

". . . *Showing his behind . . .*"

"No, goddamn it, that's . . . too narrow a view . . . of action!" Vic cut in, snorting and sputtering. "It takes a long . . . a long— shit! can't seem to . . ." As he sucked in air, it made an awesome bubbly sound, rattling through him as though ripping everything apart in there. His eyelids fluttered open, but his eyes were rolled back, unseeing, halfscreened by his unruly gray hair. ". . . A long time to find out . . . that the only *magic* in the world . . . is *action!*"

". . . *With a wart on it . . .*" Mavis pushed herself away from the wall and stood there, her feet planted far apart, rocking unsteadily.

"God, that poor devastated sonuvabitch has had it," murmured Bunky's gigolo friend, taking the brandy bottle back. It was true. Vic looked feverish now, an unnatural flush in his craggy cheeks, his breath coming in abrupt little gasps. The gigolo, taking a deep swig and pushing the bottle away ("Is there anything left to eat?" Gudrun asked, accepting a tumbler of whiskey. "If I toss this down the void, it'll take me with it!"), belched and said: "He's gonna get put beddybye tonight with a fucking shovel, that one!"

"Don't count on it," laughed the older man, picking up the bottle again. Vic tongued his swollen lips—Howard was carrying on grandly about art as "man's transcendence of the specious present, his romance with eternity, with timelessness" ("But then what about Malcolm's tattooed prick?" Kitty interrupted)—and his eyelids fluttered again. "Doesn't *exist!*" he bellowed. "I beg your pardon?" said Gottfried. "Yes, it does," Kitty insisted. "I've seen it." "I think some strawberry shortcake passed me, going into the living room." "*Eter-*

nity!" "Doesn't sound like the right thing to go with bourbon." "What're they up to in there now?" the man in the chalkstriped suit asked Scarborough. "Another . . . fucking *illusion!*" Vic yelled. It was pathetic to watch him. "I once knew a guy," this was Bunky's older friend, putting the bottle down after a long guzzle ("And the present is . . .") and carrying on, "got shot like that and took *days* to die."

". . . Is *not* specious . . . goddamn it!"

"Some kid's grisly visit-to-the-underworld spasm," Scarborough replied ("That guy's death rattle *alone* lasted eight hours!"), "called 'Rec Room Resurrection,' or some such shit," and Gudrun reminded him: "He's still just a boy, such things are important to him right now. He'll grow out of it."

"Did I . . . only imagine it?" Mavis asked herself, rocking gently.

"What you're trying to say, as I understand it," Gottfried interposed, leaning toward Vic with his mike, "is that action is a sort of rude language, emanating from the reflex centers of the—"

"*I'M NOT FINISHED YET!*" roared Vic, startling us all. "Sorry," whispered Gottfried, having reared back into Howard, and Mavis, still mumbling hollowly to herself, added: "And am I . . . imagining it now . . . ?" Earl Elstob was wheeling about, doubled over, yuck-yucking noisily: someone told him to shut up. "Huh—?" We waited. This was it. Or might be. Vic sucked in air, let it rattle out again. There was a trickle of blood at his lips: he licked at it. "What was I . . . ?" His eyelids fluttered open, his eyes rolled down out of their contemplation of the top of his skull, searching for me. "Is . . . is that you, Gerry . . . ?"

I squatted in front of him and his eyes closed again. "Yes. Take it easy, old man. It's all right . . ."

"Don't . . . shit me it's all right, goddamn it . . . I know better. Listen . . . is one of those—*oof!* damn . . . !—one of those cops around?"

"Yes, but—"

"This is *important*, goddamn it!" Mavis had lumbered slump-shouldered away, rocking heavily from one foot to the other, still half-dazed, but the rest of us were crowding around, watching Vic. He wheezed and snorted laboriously. "Ignore him, he's a stupid and intolerant monomaniac," Howard declared petulantly, but in fact it was Howard who was being ignored. "Can he . . . hear me?"

"Sure." I glanced up: Bob watched Vic without emotion, leaning against the sideboard.

"All right. Tell him . . . tell him I did it . . . I killed them!"

"What? Killed who, Vic?"

"*All* of them, goddamn it!" He struggled to sit up, but his coordination was gone, and the effort seemed to be tearing him apart. "Ros, Roger . . ."

"Vic, listen, you don't know what—"

"Who else?" he groaned. "Who *else*, goddamn it—I can't *think*—!"

"You mean Tania?"

"Yeah, that's right . . . Tania, stabbed her . . . too!"

"She wasn't stabbed, Vic."

"Strangled, I mean!"

"She was drowned."

"Drowned, that's what I . . . what I—*choke!*—said!"

"Hey, listen, nice try, Vic, but—"

"No! I held her under, I—just look at my hands . . . ! They're the hands . . . of a murderer, they—*what*—?!" His chin shot up, one leg straightened, a shoulder twitched. "Where *are* they? My *hands*, Gerry! *Where are my goddamn . . . hands*—?!"

"Here, Vic, easy . . . !"

"You see?" sniffed Howard.

"Jesus," somebody muttered softly, "someone oughta put the poor bastard outa his misery!"

"Oh shit," Vic was weeping, "I can't . . . I can't *feel* them . . . I can't feel *anything!*"

I glanced up at Jim, who shook his head sadly. Howard looked disgusted. "You'd be doing him a favor," the police officer said.

"What?"

"It's true, Gerry," said Jim quietly. Indeed, it was very quiet all around, broken only by Vic's rasping breath, the ice tinkling brassily in someone's glass, Earl's chronic sucking noise. The cop took his revolver out of his holster, checked the chambers. "It'll only get worse for him."

"A *drink!*" he yelled, making us jump. "*For chrissake, Gerry*—!"

Jim handed me his own glass. I sniffed it. "Is it—?" "He won't know the difference."

"Where *is* everybody—?!"

"Right here, Vic." I held the glass to his lips. He sucked and slob-

bered, most of it ending up as a kind of bloody foam that dribbled down his chin and shirtfront like baby drool. "Easy now . . ."

"*More!*" he demanded, jerking his head about, batting the glass with his nose, thumping his head on the wall. Once, when I was very small (I was thinking of this now, watching Vic try to keep his head up, his eyes open), we found a dead tomcat in my grandmother's backyard. A few nights later, she incorporated him into her bedtime story about the climb to heaven. The cat was not well-suited for this climb and I probably fell asleep very near the bottom, but I did hear the preamble and remembered it still. Interested in a lady cat next door, the tom had come out to serenade her and had got shot by an irate neighbor who didn't want his sleep interrupted. At the entrance to the stairway, there was a kind of ticket-taker, like the ones outside carnival rides and circus tents, and the cat complained to him about the injustice of being shot for singing: "Is that what you get for bringing a little beauty into the world?" he protested. "It's not fair!" "What do you mean, you were lucky!" the ticket-taker replied. "There's no big deal in a long life—what counts is the *quality* of the *departure*. Yours was beautiful! You died quickly, more or less painlessly, and at the moment of your greatest happiness!" "No, you don't understand," the cat objected, "the singing was only the *preparations*." "Exactly!" smiled the ticket-taker. Indeed, now that I thought about it, I'd said something very much like this to someone earlier tonight, only . . .

"Ah, *listen!*" Vic barked.

"*What—?!*"

"I said, listen, damn it! I'm talking . . . about what's happening . . . here tonight . . ."

"Ah . . ." My heart was pounding. Bob, I realized, was holding his gun out to me, butt first. Jim took the empty glass. "But . . . do you really think—?"

"You *know* . . . what kind . . . what kind of a world . . . we live in . . . !"

"You can see for yourself," said Jim. "The size of the wound, the blood lost, kidney and bowel dysfunction, numbness in the extremities—"

"So why . . . are they letting you . . . ?"

"And that rattle means his lungs are filling up: he's slowly choking to death, Gerry. Then, as he loses oxygen, the brain—well, just listen to him . . ."

". . . Letting you even . . . *have* parties like this?"

"The poor guy," said Gudrun. Howard snorted scornfully. "Yeah? Whuzzamatter?" asked Charley blearily.

"I-I've never . . ."

"Here," said Bob, showing me the safety catch. "It's easy." There was a soft whirring noise behind me and the lights brightened: the guy with the video camera again. "Angle's bad," he said. "Hang on, I'll get a chair."

"Damn it, Gerry! I . . . asked you—!" Vic burbled.

"What? I don't know, Vic. Maybe they don't know any better." The weight of the thing surprised me: I nearly dropped it. It seemed nose-heavy or something. "Oh, I *love* the *cowboy boots!*" Patrick was gushing behind me in his swollen lisp. "They're so well *tooled!*" My sudden shadow, which had been clouding Vic's chest, now fell off him below my knees. Certainly he was a mess, I couldn't deny that. "Grip it a little higher up the handle," the cop said, and Gudrun asked: "How are the skin tones?"

"Don't . . . underestimate them . . . !"

"Not bad—could use a touch at the back maybe," said a voice high above me. "Under the hairline."

"Whoa! Whoozat tall sumbitch?" Charley asked.

"He's not tall, Charley, he's on a—"

"No? Jesus, then maybe's *me!* Maybe I'm *shrinkin'!*"

My shoulder ached with this sudden awkward weight. Vic looked ghastly in the hot glare: it hurt to see him like this. "I've got a lot of things to do. I don't think I like this . . ."

"You're okay, just hold it steady."

"Grrr-rrr-*rr-rr!*" said Patrick, drawing a nervous laugh or two.

"That's it. Now all you have to do is squeeze."

"I just want to *eat* them!"

"You get any goddamn spit on my boots, you old tart, and you'll get one of 'em down your fucking throat—now get that mike outa the way!"

Gottfried ducked down beside me, squatting into my shadow. "Oh, what a *brute!*" exclaimed Patrick giddily. "Isn't he simply fe-*ro*-cious!"

"Don't pull on it or jerk it, just close your fist, easy-like," said Bob.

"In some way or other," Vic gasped, his shaggy head lolling under the bright lights ("Hey, where you off to—is it getting too much for you?" somebody asked), "you're . . . *useful* to them . . ."

"No, I wanta catch it live on the tube." Someone was stroking the back of my neck ("It's live here . . ."), taking the pain away. "I-I don't think they know I exist, Vic," I sighed ("Yeah, but I miss the zooms!"), and Bob said: "Listen, maybe you oughta use both hands."

"And pivot about thirty degrees, so I can see your cannon!" the guy on the chair called down. "Wow! Funkybuns! C'mere! Lemme see ya!" "Whaddaya mean . . . ?" Vic growled, just as little Bunky Baird, stark naked and painted a gleaming scarlet from head to toe (stark, that is, because even her hair was shaved away, her skull a gleaming red dome, her pubis sleek as a creased plum), pranced into the light between us. "*Hey—!*" "Isn't it just *smashing?*" she exclaimed breathlessly, one hand on hip, the other behind her ear ("They're *here,* Gerry," came the gravelly voice between her legs, "it's a matter of record . . . !"), switching through a sequence of fluid poses to make the paint sparkle. "Gudrun here did it! It's a *masterpiece!*" I stepped back out of her way, gave my arm a rest. She was bound loosely with a fine metallic thread that made her flesh bulge in peculiar places, and decorated with little silver ribbons, randomly attached to the thread. She looked like someone who'd got tangled up in the tail of a kite. "It's for Zack's *terrific* new *show!* It's called *Party Time,* and I've got this *great* part—it's so *exciting!*" She glanced up at the lights as though discovering them for the first time, flashed a bright innocent smile ("Watch out you don't shoot your foot," Bob muttered irritably in my ear): "Oh, hello! Am I interrupting something?"

"Yeah, stop catching flies, sweetie, and move your fat act! We got something heavy going down here!"

"What—?" She turned to gaze down at Vic, gasped audibly, her hands before her face. She held this pose rigidly a moment, then let her fingertips slide slowly down her seamed body ("Even pleasure . . . ," he was muttering on the other side, "has its fucking consequences . . ."), coming to rest just at the crease between thighs and shiny buttocks, her shoulders bowed but back straight, bare feet straddling his body. When she turned around, two tears glistened in the corners of her uplifted eyes.

"Oh yeah!" applauded her younger friend ("Gesture, stylized gesture," I'd remarked that night at the theater—perhaps it was her uplifted eyes that had reminded me of this, or else the heavy weapon in my hand—"is really a disguise for uncertainty: which is why we're so attracted to it"—but perhaps I'd been wrong about this), and the

older one said: "Ha ha, come over here, baby, and see what your old man's got for you!"

Because it might just as well be said (I wish I'd thought of this at the time) that what fascinates us is not the ritualized gestures themselves—for, in a sense, no gesture is original, or can be—but rather that strange secondary phenomenon which repetition, the overt stylization of gesture, creates: namely, those mysterious spaces *in between.* "What . . . what are you going . . . to do, Gerry . . . ?"

"Pardon?" His eyes were open. One of them anyway: it was fixed on the revolver in my hand. "Ah. I'm sorry, Vic," I said, waggling it about ambiguously ("God, it's *gorgeous!*" Bunky was raving behind me, and Howard, staring grimly at my hand, said: "Would you watch where you're *pointing* that thing, Gerald?"), "I'm only, you know . . ." I lowered it. His open eye ("Is it a sapphire?") rolled up to meet mine briefly, then closed. "Ah well, it . . . it beats . . . senility, I guess," he wheezed, and effected a jerky little movement with one shoulder that was perhaps meant as a shrug. "Yeah, a little something to celebrate your new success, baby—slip it on your pinkie, there!" "Anyway, it's—it's almost over, Vic, and I thought—"

"*No*, goddamn it, it's *not!*" he blustered, spewing blood. "The sooner you get it over with, the better it's gonna be for everyone," Bob growled in my ear. "It's so *big!*" "More's . . . more's gonna happen, but I won't . . . be here . . . to see it . . . and that . . . that scares me . . ." I shared his dread: that door closed forever. Not being. Eternal absence. "Well, you're a big *star*, sweetheart!" It made me shudder just to think about it. This consciousness was what I had and, like him, I didn't want it to— "I *don't* . . . want it . . . *to end!*"

"I know," I said through the catch in my throat. "In fact, oddly, I was just—"

"If I had a wish," he spluttered ("Hey, don't get that red stuff all over me!" laughed the gigolo behind me, as Bunky passed out thanksgiving hugs and kisses), "I'd wish always to have . . . one . . . more . . . *minute* . . . !" Of course, death itself caused no suffering, only this gnawing terror of it—it was, more or less, what I was saving him from. "Is . . . is my daughter . . . ?"

"She's in the next room, Vic. She's got a part in Zack's play. Shall I—?"

"No . . . just tell her for me . . . tell her to watch out for words like . . . like mind and . . . and soul, spirit . . ."

"You better point it a little higher," Bob murmured, "or you'll just cause him more useless damage."

Jim knelt and tipped Vic's head to one side. "The best place, Gerry, is here behind the ear . . ."

"All that junk . . . just . . . just a metaphor, tell her . . . old animistic habit . . ."

"That way, you'll penetrate the medulla at the top of the spine, which is the center for regulating all the internal functions . . ."

" 'Assa pretty bad *sun*burn, li'l lady," Charley was rumbling behind me.

". . . There's nothing in there, goddamn it . . . no me, no I . . ."

"Breathing, for example."

". . . The brain . . . just makes all that up . . . the first person . . ."

"Or speaking."

"Iss even got *scabs!*"

". . . Is a hoax, an arrogant sham . . . the first person . . ."

"That little place does it all?"

"Yes, the smallest damage to it causes death in a few minutes."

". . . Is no person . . . at all! Tell her . . ."

"So what's all this baloney about thinking with the whole body, old man?" I muttered hoarsely to myself as I took off the safety.

"Did I say that?" He looked up at me, cocking one yellowish eye (this startled me), and a wet sardonic grin formed at one corner of his mouth. He seemed disconcertingly alert all of a sudden. "Well, just watch me . . . *twitch* after . . . !" he grunted.

"Vic?" But he was delirious again, rumbling on about "militant time" and "the living organic arena . . ." ("That often happens," Jim was explaining softly, "a kind of involuntary hypoglossal reflex . . .") ". . . of choice and freedom . . ." I heard someone behind me say something about "the host," then ask for a drink. Or perhaps offer one. "Yeah, he's a sweet guy . . ." Vic was fondling his knee with his free hand (he clutched the fork in the other still like some kind of credo) and I supposed he was thinking about Ros again. Well, why not? For all his dogma about the oppression of the past: who was I, locked even now in reverie (that quiet talk we'd had earlier in my bedroom, now so poignant: it was ancient history!), to hold him to it? This unexpected weakness had in fact endeared him to me even more. "One in a million," someone murmured, and my wife

called out from somewhere back there: "Gerald, can you help with the coffee, please?"

"Yes, in a minute." My shoulder throbbed, and something was blurring my vision. Tears maybe. I couldn't see his face at all, it was like that face in Tania's painting.

"Why don't you . . . wise up, old buddy?" he gasped. I found the place. I hoped Jim was right. "There's not . . . much time . . . !"

"To tell the truth, Vic," I sighed, "I wouldn't know where to start."

"Famous last words," he grunted, and I squeezed the trigger.

There was less kick than I'd expected, less noise. I'd been braced for worse. And Vic was mistaken. I waited patiently (no, that's not true, it wasn't patience: I was rooted to the spot, frozen, a waxworks figure, legs spread, body and neck rigid, arm outstretched, lips pulled back over my clenched teeth—I wasn't any good at this), watching him, but nothing twitched. Except my shoulder, after the cop pried the gun out of my hand. "That wasn't so bad, was it?" he said. Jim, kneeling by Vic with his stethoscope, looked up at me and nodded solemnly. He reached for Vic's eyes, now wide open as though startled by something he'd just seen (or remembered?), and closed them. "Okay!" someone said, a chair scraped, the lights dimmed—then brightened again and wheeled around: "*Daddy—?*" My arm dropped and my fossilized spine unlocked and sagged as the light spun away. "*Oh no! Daddy—!*"

As Jim rose, concern pinching his tired face, to gaze over my shoulder toward the living room door, I turned the other way, weary of concern itself. "How do you feel about nihilism, then, as a viable art form?" Gottfried was asking, the mike thrust in front of my face, but I pushed away, out past Scarborough and Patrick and the guy on the chair, across the room ("Gerry, your wife—" "I know, I know . . ."), and on through the swinging door into the kitchen.

"Ah, just in time, Gerald," she said, switching off the oven timer. "The coffee's ready. Could you take that tray of cups in, please? We'll get the chocolates and the whipped cream—"

"*In a minute!*" I snapped. I'd made it as far as the butcherblock table in the middle of the room, and stood there now, leaning against it. The stains were gone, it had been scrubbed clean.

"You look exhausted, Gerald." At least she was able to see that much. I could feel her ego, callous and swollen, billowing out of her,

packing the kitchen, crushing me. Or perhaps that was my own ego, her own infuriating in its evanescence. Or maybe Vic was right, maybe it had nothing to do with egos. "Is Vic . . . ?"

"He's dead," I shot back.

"Well," she sighed, "it's probably for the best." She brought the bowl of whipped cream over and set it on the butcherblock. I clutched my head in my hands. "Oh, I'm sorry, Gerald, I forgot about your shoulder—don't worry about the cups. Instead, why don't you—"

"My god!" I cried. "What's the *matter* with you? He's *dead*, I tell you, his life is *ended*, it's *all over—!*"

"I know, you just—"

"But how can it be for the *best?* That's *crazy!*"

"Yes, I'm probably mistaken, Gerald, please don't shout at me." She glanced back over her shoulder. "Maybe what you could do is bring in the brandy. And anything else people might like with their—"

"*You* get the damned brandy! I'll—I'll—" I felt like picking up the bowl in front of me and heaving it across the room. I had to struggle to get control of myself. "*I'll bring the whipped cream!*" I yelled.

"Well, if you wish, but Alison had offered—"

"What?" All along I'd been seeing Louise over at the breakfast bench, as usual. But it was Alison. She sat there, watching sullenly, huddled up in a heavy checkered overcoat. "Ah . . ." I wiped my eyes with my sleeve. Her hair was snarled, her makeup gone, her eye shadow smudged. As she got up, I saw she was barefooted as well, and there were welts on her ankles. "I'm sorry, it's all right, I'll, uh, take this in, then—"

"No, I'm the novelty act here tonight, allow me," she cut in acidly and snatched up the bowl of whipped cream. She glanced briefly at me as she padded by, her brown eyes hard and dull like hammers.

"Does she always walk that way," my wife wondered as the door whumped shut behind her, "or is it just the funny coat . . . ?"

"Does the Inspector know she—?"

"Oh, is that whose it is? She came in hungry and cold, so I fixed her something to eat, while Woody went to find her a wrap. She seems to have misplaced all her own things." She put on mitts, opened the oven door, and took out a pie, set it on the counter, reached in for another. "I must say, Gerald, I've never known anyone to have such an uncharitable view of you."

"Well . . . I probably deserve it."

"Oh no. She feels slighted, but I'm sure you've done everything you could, Gerald. It's all these extra guests." She sliced the pies, ran her fingers along the knife blade and licked them, wiped them on her apron (it was that handwoven red-green-rye-and-gold one that we'd bought at a mountainside roadstand on our way back from Delphi), sprinkled some powdered sugar on. "Just because she didn't get enough attention, that's no reason to blame you for everything that's happened! Even poor Roger, and Cyril and Peg—really, she got quite nasty about it, said it was all your fault, you were no better than a petty thief!"

"Yes . . ." She'd mentioned thievery that night at the play. Or I had. The theatrical transaction . . .

"She might have been talking about her watch, I don't remember, but it got Louise so upset she went storming out of the kitchen!" She filled a large basket with fresh fruit from the refrigerator, brought in some boxes of chocolates from the pantry, got down a stack of dessert plates from the cabinets, stood on a chair to reach a pair of silver bowls on the top shelf. "Honestly, I'd just fixed her a nice hot soup and some fresh spinach crêpes; you'd think no matter what had happened to make her so grouchy, she might have been a *little* more gracious." She topped up the sugar canister, filled the cream pitcher— "But some people are just never satisfied!"—then touched the coffee-pot gingerly. "Good, still hot. If you can bring in the coffee and the fruit, I can carry the rest."

"Sure. Is that all?" I felt much subdued now.

"I think so. For now. Except . . . well . . ." She smiled up at me, wrinkling her nose slightly as though looking into the sun. "I know Alison's acting rather unpleasant, Gerald, but she *is* our guest. I think you should try to make it up to her somehow."

"I don't know really . . . what I could do . . ." I tried to recall that happier time, now so long ago, when her eyes had another look in them, but all I could think of was her husband on the back porch, blocking my way into the house. What had he said? "It was as if the very geography of the world had shifted." Yes, "something anarchical and dangerous"—it was coming back to me now. "You were stroking her thighs," he'd said, "she bent down to put your—" "But I'll try," I said.

"And please forgive me for what I said before. I'm truly sorry about Vic."

"Vic?" I looked down at her. She was smiling still, but there were tears in the corners of her eyes. "Oh, right . . ."

"Hey, you two lovebugs!" Fats sang out, thumping grandly in through the dining room door, the Inspector's gray fedora, its crown punched out, perched on top of his big head like a party hat, Scarborough, Gudrun, Michelle, Benedetto, Earl Elstob, and others in his wake. "You get outa here now and go enjoy yourselves! Ole Fats is takin' over!"

"Oh dear. Fats, I've just cleaned up in here—!"

"No backtalkin', little lady! We got some citizens with a desp'rate belly-wrinkles crisis, but you has done did your duty!" He warbled out a striptease tune while untying my wife's apron, jigging around her as he peeled it off. "La-la-la-*la*-la-la-la!" sang Beni, practicing his scales and strutting around in his silken codpiece. "We is gettin' up a *do!*" He tied on the apron on his way to the refrigerator, tipped the fedora down over his nose as he peered inside. "Whaddawe got? Cottage cheese? Good! Cocktail onions, grape jelly, ketchup—what's in these little tin cans?" "Why are we here?" Michelle asked vaguely, looking around, and Beni, a halftone higher than before, responded: "La-la-la-LA-la-la-la!"

My wife glanced at me, shrugged helplessly, picked up the tray of cups. "What's that you're tracking in, Mr. Elstob?"

"Huh? Aw—yuh!—whuppin' cream!"

"I'm afraid it's all over your hallway floor," Dolph said, lifting a foot to show us. "I think they're trying to ski in it or something."

"Oh dear . . . I think that was the last of the cream . . ."

"Here, Gerry, I'll help with that, if you'll rescue Zack," said Gudrun, picking up the bowl of pink pears and melon balls in her scarlet hands and bumping out backward through the door ahead of me. "Come on, there's some old bawd in here queering the pitch, and Zack's going bonkers."

"Ho-boy! Get ready to sink your pegs into the real bony fido, friends! Ole Fats is homin' in on the range!"

"La-la-la-LA-la-la-la!"

Out in the hall, people were laughing and cheering: "Go get her, gangbusters!" they shouted up the stairs. "Hair *wut?*" I glanced hopefully into the dining room where the brandy bottles were ("*Can*busters, more like! Ha ha!"), but she wasn't there: only Sally Ann,

wearing Tania's heavy peasant dress now and wistfully cradling her dead father in her arms in front of the cameraman's bright lamps and video lens; Patrick was helping with the lights, and Gottfried seemed to be interviewing Brenda, or vice versa—they were drifting, heads bent over the mike, past the abandoned sideboard toward the TV room—but all the rest were gone, and it seemed peculiarly barren and lonely in there. Some awful absence . . . "Okay!" the cameraman barked. "Now tip his head the other way!"

"It's nice to have those guys around, they add a little *color!*" Horner laughed, turning away from the foot of the stairs, and Mr. Waddilow, standing on the landing, blushed perceptibly. Or perhaps he was trying to lift something up. Beneath him, Daffie stepped out of the toilet, holding her forearm pressed against one bare breast. "Hey," she said with a vague glittering smile. Malcolm Mee was still in there behind her, under the red darkroom bulb, back to the open door. "Eet wass like night off fool moon, no?" grinned Hilario, picking up the fallen overcoat, just as Zack Quagg came fuming out of the living room, sliding through the floor's flocking of whipped cream, his dark cape flying: "Where the hell's Hoo-Sin? *Hillie—?* Jesus! What am I *working* with here, a buncha *amateurs?* We got a fucking *show* on the boards in there, goddamn it! Where's that extra grip? *Horner—?*"

"Easy, Zack," Horner said, "that mudlark's been pulped."

"*What—?!* Holy shit, Jacko! We've lost our goddamn band, half the deck crew, our new end-man's off banging tail, that bearded dude's pulled his lens outa the show—*we're gonna die standing up in there, if we don't move our ass!*" He kicked the fallen cream bowl across the hallway in pale-faced anger.

"Awright, screw your tits on, Zack, we're doin' what we—"

"*Aha!*" Quagg cried, grabbing my arm. "I been *looking* for you!" He dragged me toward the living room. "There's some old scud in here *murdering* our production! She's up the fucking *flue,* man, and taking me *with* her! You gotta *do* something!"

My mother-in-law stood calmly on the collapsed ping-pong table, her arms folded. That's what it was now: a collapsed ping-pong table. Her presence had quite effortlessly disenchanted our living room. The sacred cave had become a bunch of dirty laundry, the altar a table with a dead body on it (this latter, most of the skirt now cut away, was being removed by Vachel and Gudrun to make some room, my

wife, bracing one edge of the tray of cups and plates against the table, instructing), the proscenium arch merely my skis with nailholes in them. I half-expected the lamps to drop off the ceiling in sheer embarrassment. "It's time to go home," my mother-in-law said flatly.

"Put it down! Put it down!" Vachel screamed, his head slick still with petroleum jelly. *"Yeu-uck!"*

"You see what I *mean?*" moaned Zack, waving his arms around wildly. My mother-in-law only set her jaws the tighter. "Thank you, Vachel," my wife was saying. "I know it's not pleasant, but it can't be helped. Now could you move that bowl of fruit nearer the center, Louise?" "You *gotta* get this dry hole *outa* here, man!"

I glanced questioningly at my wife, now spreading the cups and dessert plates out on the table: she smiled toward her mother and shook her head, sent Louise off to the kitchen for the pies, slapped at Vachel's fingers as he dipped them in the chocolate sauce. "I'm afraid there's not much I can do, Zack," I said. "She's not going to budge."

"You can't be *serious!*" He clutched at his hair ("God! I'm starved!" said Gudrun, peeling a banana) as though to tear it out. "We've just hit the nub, man, the weenie, the *payoff!* This is everything we've been *working* for tonight! What are we going to *do—?!*"

"Well, Zack," my wife put in, taking the coffeepot from Michelle, who stood dazedly by, "I suppose you'll just have to exercise your imagination. Could you please move the strawberries, Gerald, so I can set the coffee down?"

"Maybe we oughta fold it up, Zack," mumbled Gudrun around her mouthful of half-chewed banana.

"No, wait," he said, gazing thoughtfully at my mother-in-law ("That's funny," said my wife, lifting up the sponge cake: "where did the plate go?"), "if the old bat wants to become part of the set, then, goddamn it, we'll just build the show *around* her!"

"Actually, there's an old lady *in* the next scene," Anatole pointed out. "It's the dream sequence in which—"

"Hey, you're right! Lemme see that script a minute!" My mother-in-law looked disconcerted, but stubbornly held her ground. "Meanwhile, kid, go in there and get our guitarist back—even if you have to pick her ass up and *haul* it in here—!"

"Yes sir, Mr. Quagg!"

"I once had a dream about an old woman," Michelle remarked lan-

guidly. "She was standing on a mountain, or some high place. She said she'd been there for a very long time."

"Do you suppose someone took it?" my wife asked. I gazed down at the cake, sitting there on the bare table as though after a pratfall, trying to think what it was that was bothering me.

"Her clothes were all worn away and her skin was covered with sores and scabs and a thick dust almost like sand . . ." Michelle touched her breast, her privates—

"Oh no . . . !"

"What is it, Gerald? What's the matter?"

"This woman in the dream, I mean . . ."

I turned toward the dining room: yes, it had been nagging at me since I left the kitchen—that peculiar sensation of barrenness, of erasure . . .

" 'But the worst thing about getting old,' she said," Michelle was saying, " 'is what happens to your navel . . .' "

"Right! The Ice Palace, the wet dream stuff, free will versus necessity, the Old Lady—this script is terrific! The kid's got talent!"

"The 'Susanna' . . . !" I whispered.

"What? What are you talking about, Gerald?"

" 'It keeps getting deeper and deeper . . .' "

"Hey, Jack! Go find the Scar! Tell him we want the panes out of all the windows in the house and as many mirrors as he can lay his hands on! We still got a *show* here!"

"It's gone."

"Gone?"

"Yum!" enthused Bunky, stepping over Ros's body and plucking a melon ball.

"Tania's painting," I explained, my throat constricted.

"I saw it now. The navel. In the middle of the old woman's tummy. Like a nailhole."

"I just realized—"

"Only much bigger . . ."

"It isn't there anymore."

"What—?!"

". . . Like a kind of tunnel, going nowhere . . ."

"And Gudrun! Listen, go strip all this red shit off Bunky!"

" 'You can go in and look around if you want to,' she said, but I was afraid."

My wife rushed over to the doorway. Those thoughts of oblivion I'd had when entering from the kitchen, glancing toward Vic (I'd been looking for something): almost as though she had somehow, after all, completed that terrible step . . .

"I want her midnight blue now, top to bot! With a scatter of sequins if you can find some—and a silver skullcap!"

"Right, Zack." Gudrun stuffed the end of one banana in her mouth, picked up another and pointed with it. "Wha' you wahme do wiwode wady?"

"What?"

"But I did see lots of things crawling in and out of her navel," Michelle said now, scratching idly, "and at the very back there was a little spot of light, like when you turn the TV off . . ."

Such an emptiness, that wall: it wasn't even a wall in my mind's eye, but infinite space, appallingly indifferent. I felt her disappearance as if it were, in part, my own, and great relief when my wife came back ("Ah, the old lady—leave her like she is, Gud! This is gonna be the weirdest goddamn peel you ever saw in showbiz!") and took my hand: "Do you suppose . . . it's been stolen?"

" 'That's where heaven is,' someone said—I think it was one of those things crawling in and out . . ."

"Hey, that was Prissy Loo's part!" Vachel was objecting (she released my hand as though I'd answered her—in fact, I had), and Zack said: "She's off doing a little business for me, Vaych, she'll never know—now listen, you said you wanted a sex scene, right?"

". . . But I didn't believe it."

"Someone must have overheard you," my wife suggested ("Yeah! Hey, can I have the guitarist? Hunh, Zack?"), "when you were negotiating with Howard."

"Yes . . ."

"No, she's the only orchestra we got, Vaych—I was figuring we'd use Bunky for the—"

"Bunky?"

"When I looked closer," Michelle went on, "I saw that these little things crawling in and out of her navel were tiny people . . ." I gazed at her there, clutching her thin arms, lost in her dream story ("Okay! Great! Luff-ly! Thanks, Zack! I get Bunky!" "Well, not exactly, Vaych . . ."), thinking: she seems younger suddenly, as though she were shrinking back into her vanished image . . . "And whenever they turned their heads and looked at me . . ."

"Actually, this is a kind of dream sequence . . ."

". . . They curled up like waterbugs and dropped off somewhere below . . ."

"No kidding!" grinned Anatole as he came through the door with Sally Ann ("At first it *seems* like Bunky, you see—or what she stands for," Zack was explaining, my mother-in-law looking on with increasing apprehension), her guitar slung round her neck: "You too? Tonight?"

"But when I tried to see where the little things fell to," Michelle murmured, "I discovered I was standing there all by myself . . ."

"Oh *no*—! Wait a minute, *wait a minute!*" squawked Vachel, backing off. "*Not* this moldy old *crowbait—!*"

"Yeah, well, almost," said Sally Ann, glancing darkly up at me as she passed, and my wife, breaking out of her worried silence, exclaimed: "*Oh, Louise!*" She stood there behind us, her round face red as a beet, holding two steaming hot pies in her bare hands. "Why don't you use the oven gloves, for goodness' sake?"

"What *is* this shit, Vachel? I thought you were a goddamn pro!"

"Well, sure, but—*cheez!*"

". . . The wind was blowing, it had gotten dark . . ."

"Well, look at the *power* in this scene, man! the *risks!* the levels of *meaning!*" He grabbed the hem of my mother-in-law's skirt and dragged it up past her garter belt: she turned pale, staggered back a step, her jaw dropping. "This ain't *beautiful* enough for you, god-damn it? Is *that* it?"

"The old lady was gone, I was all alone."

My wife cleared a space on the table and helped Louise set the pies down. Louise clapped her hands in her armpits ("Actually, my original idea," said Anatole, "was to take a couple of old archetypes and re—" "Right!" Quagg rolled on, slapping my mother-in-law's corseted behind. "It's original, it's ancient, it's archetypal—I mean, are you *good* enough for this or *not*, Vaych?"), her eyes damp and bulging, and Michelle said, as though from some distant place: "All my clothes had blown away somehow . . ." My wife glanced up at Michelle, a flicker of a smile curling her lips. ". . . And now *mine* was the navel with the hole in it . . ."

"I think this is where I came in," my wife said. "I'll go see if I can win the kitchen back from Fats."

"*No* one," said a commanding voice from the hallway door, "goes *anywhere!*" It was Inspector Pardew, clutching his lapels, white scarf

draped loosely around his neck, thick moustaches bristling. "Oh oh," someone said. "Where's the, uh, toilet?" "It's all right, m'um," Pardew added, nodding firmly, and my mother-in-law took a deep breath, smoothed her skirt down with trembling hands. "We have all we need now. Thank you for your assistance."

"Wait a minute—!" objected Zack Quagg. My mother-in-law straightened her back, drew her chin in, and, glaring at Quagg, stepped down off the ping-pong table. "*Hey*—! You can't do this! We're just *cli*-maxing this spasm!" Others had started drifting in, some shepherded by the two police officers, Bob and Fred. "I'll check upstairs," said Fred. My wife, taking my arm, whispered: "I'm afraid the coffee's going to get cold," and the Inspector glanced up sharply: "Did someone say something?" "Yeah, *I* did, you hick dick! This is *our* pitch, man, get outa here, this space is *booked*—!" Bob lashed out with his baton: "*Whuff-ff-FF-FOOO!*" Quagg wheezed, crumpling to the floor, curled up in his purple cape. "I hope," said the Inspector, withdrawing his briar pipe from a jacket pocket and tapping it in the palm of his hand as he gazed around at us all (Anatole interposed himself between Zack and the cop, Sally Ann kneeling to whisper: "You okay, Mr. Quagg?"), "there will be no further disturbances."

He filled the pipe from his leather pouch, cupping his hand around the bowl to form a funnel, then, tugging the drawstrings of the pouch closed with his teeth (Quagg groaned and stretched out: "Ow, something's . . . caught . . . !" he gasped), stepped aside as Fred came down the stairs behind him, herding a group of people toward us, Hilario leading the pack and showing off with a complicated set of hops and pirouettes down the steps, followed by Kitty, Dolph, Janny and Hoo-Sin in each other's clothes, Charley, Regina, the guy in the chalkstriped suit—or pants rather: down to an undershirt on top now and a towel around his neck. His jaw gleamed as though he might have been shaving. Regina, wrapped up in one of our sheets (Sally Ann, on her knees, was tugging speculatively at the seam of Zack's white crotch: "Here, you mean, Mr. Quagg?"), swept past Hilario into the room, eyes rolled up and the back of one wrist clapped to her pale forehead, crying: "Is *nothing* sacred?" "Caught her jerking off," Fred explained to the Inspector behind his hand, Dolph meanwhile slipping off behind him, unnoticed, toward the kitchen. "There's a few more upstairs'll be down in a minute, Chief. Meantime I'll go check out back." Pardew nodded, slapped his pockets for a light.

Bunky's gigolo friend took a wooden match from behind his ear, popped it ablaze with his thumb, and held it, shielded with his cupped hand, over Pardew's pipebowl. "Ah! Thank you," said the Inspector, Zack Quagg echoing him throatily from the floor (Sally Ann, stretching the crotch of his unitard down, was carefully easing his testicles to one side). "Now, I've gathered you all together here in this—"

"Hey, *big Ger!*" Charley boomed out, stumbling heavily into the room through a tangle of collapsed cave wall, his arms wrapped around Janny and Hoo-Sin. Janny looked radiant in her kimono, Hoo-Sin in the wrinkled pink outfit oddly weathered and innocent at the same time. "I've riz *up* in the *world* again, ole son! I'm standin' *firm!* Thanks to these two lovely ladies, I got a *bone* t'pick with *anyone!*"

"Easy, Charley," I cautioned, nodding toward Bob, who was just behind him, scowling darkly, club at the ready.

Charley reared up heedlessly, swung round, his big head swiveling. "Who, ole Bobbers here? Nah, he's one a my bess *clients,* Ger! Him'n his pardner both, I give 'em a fan*tas*tic deal! A—yaw haw!—*joint policy!*" He grinned expectantly, his head bobbing drunkenly. "C'mon, ole scout, 'sbeen a long night, give us a smile! A *joint* policy!"

Bob had turned toward the dining room door, through which Fred was now prodding another group of guests: "Whoa, man, you gonna make me char the hash!" Fats was protesting, the Inspector's gray fedora rocking back and forth on top of his head.

Pardew, pipe clamped in his jaws, was smoking vehemently. "Now, as I say, I have called you all here, here to the scene of the crime, in order to—"

"All I'm sayin' is you guys got no respect for the inner man!" Fats complained, then "*Rrnkh-HH!*" grunted as Fred suddenly jabbed him fiercely in his aproned belly with the end of his nightstick, doubling him over: the hat fell off, Fred caught it, handed it to the Inspector. "Ah . . . yes . . ."

" 'Swhut I love about you, ole buddy," Charley rumbled, wrapping a fat arm around me, "you laugh at my jokes. Goddamn it, ole son, you *lissen!*"

"What?"

"Where you want these, Zack?" called out Scarborough, carrying in, with Benedetto helping, a stack of windowpanes, and Earl Elstob asked: "Hey, huh! yuh hear about the gal who couldn't tell putty from Vaseline?" Charley winked at my wife, Regina flung herself on

the couch in seeming despair, Dolph popped the top on a can of beer, and Kitty, helping Fats straighten up, said: "Well, that's one way to kill an appetite!" Pardew, brushing irritably at his hat, looked up as though about to speak, but just then Charley hollered out: "*Whoa!* I smell *coffee*, girls!" and pushed away, startling Louise, who, backing off, stepped crunchingly on Fred's foot. "*Oww! SHIT!*" he yelled, and whirled on Louise, nightstick flashing—Dolph reached up, almost casually it seemed, and caught it on the upswing, stopping it dead. He handed his beer to Earl and slowly, Fred resisting, brought the club toward him, gripped the end of it with his other hand, and—*crok!*—snapped it in two. "Thanks, Dolph," Louise said softly, her face flushed. Fred, scratching the back of his head above the neckbrace, gaped in amazement at the shattered stub of nightstick in his hand, and Earl said: "Yuh, well, huh! all her windows fell out!"

"Ah, fuck everything," said Daffie vaguely, and left the room.

Pardew, biting down on his pipe, continued to fuss with his fedora, but, attempting to put the crease back in, chopped at it so fiercely in his rage that he knocked it out of his own hand. Angrily, he reached down for it, but somehow managed to step on it at the same time. "Damnation!" he mumbled around the pipe. "*Cream 'n sugar, girls?*" Charley called out. "*SSSHH!*" Patrick hissed. "Hunh?" Charley looked around blearily at the quiet that had descended. We were all watching the Inspector. He was trying to lift his foot off the hat, but it seemed stuck to his shoe. He studied the situation, one hand in a jacket pocket, the other holding the bowl of the pipe in his mouth. Bob approached him, but he waved him away, knelt, untied the shoe, took his foot out. Except for a light titter from some of the women at the holes in his sock, the room was hushed. Regina was sitting up now, watching; Zack, too, helped by Sally Ann and Horner. The Inspector lifted the shoe off the hat: no problem. He gazed quizzically at the sole of the shoe, shrugged, put it back on, tied it. Unfortunately, he was stepping on the hat as he did so, and when he lifted his foot, he found the hat was stuck again. He scratched at the back of his neck, under the scarf, thinking about this. He stepped on the hat with the other foot to hold it down, tried to lift the first foot off but without success. Then he discovered that the second one was stuck as well. He struggled with his problem for a moment, doing a kind of sticky shuffle, peevishly muttering something about the sense he'd had all night of having "intruded on some accursed place, some forbidden domain, which was

not what it seemed to be." Finally he looked up at the taller cop and nodded toward his holster: Bob handed him the gun. The Inspector checked the chamber, sucking thoughtfully on the pipe: "One thing about homicides I've learned to watch out for," he said around the stem, his pate gleaming under the overhead lights, "is the murderer's attempt to conceal the fact that what we've got is indeed a murder." He took a firm grip on the revolver with his right hand, took the pipe out of his mouth with his left. "There's been no limit to the ingenuity of murderers in masquerading their act—or even of removing all evidence of both victim *and* act. Bodies have been burned, blasted, buried, embedded in concrete, dissolved in acid, disassembled, and devoured." Sighting down the barrel, he let his arm fall in a slow arc until pointing between his feet. "You name it, it's been tried." There was a terrific explosion that startled us all, even though we'd been expecting it. "Of course, in this case, we've not only got a victim plain to see," the Inspector went on, handing the revolver back to the policeman, taking his feet off the hat, and reaching down to pick it up, "she's also got a hole in her"—he held it up and brushed at it lightly—"as big as your hat!" This got a burst of applause and laughter, led by Patrick (even Zack Quagg was joining in, if reluctantly), and the Inspector, handing the hat to Bob, nodded curtly.

"Damn! I missed it!" whispered the cameraman, staring at the equipment in his hand.

"Nothing, however," Pardew continued, beginning to move slowly about the room, gazing first at one of us, then another (Scarborough and Benedetto, grunting, set the windowpanes down against the table), "is ever so straightforward as it seems on the face of it. We have facts, yes, a body, a place and a time, and all this associative evidence we've so painstakingly collected—but facts in the end are little more than surface scramblings of a hidden truth whose vaporous configuration escapes us even as it draws us on, insisting upon itself, absorbing our attention, compelling revelation." He peered abruptly up at the guy in the chalkstriped pants and undershirt, who was wiping his face with the towel but now stopped. "Yes, *compelling!*" Pardew repeated, raising one bony index finger, and the man stepped back a step. "Deduction, I am convinced, is linked *au fond* in an intimate but mysterious relation to this quest for the invariant, the hidden but essential core truth, this compulsive search for the nut." Dolph, who had just picked one up from the bowl, put it back. "It is, at any rate, *my* main

desire," the Inspector went on, continuing his rounds, followed now by the TV cameraman, "and in pursuit of it, I had to ask myself"—and now, pausing for effect, taking a contemplative puff on his pipe, he glanced up at my wife (her hand tightened on my arm, I clasped it, he watched this)—"*why?* Eh? Whatever possessed—and I choose my words with care—whatever possessed our perpetrator, or perpetrators"—he squinted briefly up at me, then turned to the others—"to commit this foul deed, this useless insolent vanity? I ask you!" He had, moving on (my wife's hand had relaxed and dropped away: "Were those once mine, Beni?" she whispered over her shoulder), stopped in front of Regina, who, startled, shrank back, cronelike, in her bedsheet. "Was it fear? Jealousy? Moral outrage? Cupidity?" Regina made a little squeaky noise and shook her head. Beni was whispering something to my wife about the inexpressible gratitude of his pudenda. "Well, I hope they were clean," she said. Pardew cocked his head up toward the rest of us. "Of course, all crime—even fraud, perfidy, indecent exposure, excessive indulgence"—he was staring at each of us in turn, as the cameraman panned past the gaping faces—"all crime is at heart a form of life depreciation, a kind of psychic epilepsy, and so, in a real sense, there is always only one motive. Nevertheless . . ." He gazed off, drawing meditatively on his pipe, then pinched the back of his neck under the white scarf. He studied his fingers and, smiling faintly, pressed a thumbnail against the pad of his index finger. "I was reminded," he said around the pipestem, brushing his hands together ("They take an empty fist as containing something real," Hoo-Sin was murmuring to Janny, "and the pointing finger as the object pointed . . ." "*Really?!*"), "of a curious case I had some years ago in which the murderer, as it turned out, was an unborn fetus. The victim was its putative father, who in a drunken rage had struck the pregnant woman several times in the stomach. The fetus used the only weapon at its command: false labor. It was a wintry night, the man was heavily inebriated, there was a terrible accident on the way to the hospital. The woman, who survived for a time, spoke of maddening pains en route, and it seems likely she grabbed the steering wheel in her delirium or lashed out with her foot against the accelerator. Was the fetus attacking its assailant or its host? This was perhaps a subtlety which, in its circumstances, escaped it. Certainly it achieved its ends, and though it could be argued that it had acted in self-defense, it seemed obvious to me that the true

motive, as so often, was *revenge*." He paused to let that sink in, striking a fresh match to his pipebowl. "The strawberries are starting to go soft," my wife whispered. "In any event, we'll never know. Prosecution was impossible because the fetus—a harelip—was stillborn. But the point—"

"Wait a minute," Dolph interrupted. "You trying to suggest Ros was killed out of revenge?" Pardew watched Dolph without expression, holding the match over his pipebowl. "I dunno, I just can't see that, not Ros."

"Nor can I," said Pardew, looking around for some place to drop the match; he chose one of the potted plants Scarborough had lined up around the cavemouth. "No, revenge is a noble passion, an instinctive search for order, the effort to restore a certain balance in the universe. Our murder here tonight seems much more sinister than that: a search for disjunction, a corrupt desire to disturb, distort—a murder committed perhaps out of curiosity or impudence"—my wife, watched by a frowning Pardew, stifled a yawn ("Sorry," she murmured)—"or even love, which is well-known for its destructive powers. No, what reminded me of the Case of the Vengeful Fetus was the sense that the motive here was not merely irrational, it was *pre*rational, atavistic, shared by all, you might say, and thus criminal in the deepest sense of the word. Once I recognized this, my task was eased. It was simply a matter of recalling certain ancient codes, making the obvious associations, then following the discretionary principles of professional criminalistics. Whereupon our crime was, for all practical purposes, solved." He nodded toward his two assistants, and they fanned out, blocking the two doorways, cutting Fats off from one, Bunky's boyfriends from the other. "Yikes," someone said. The TV guy lowered his camera, looked around as though for an exit. Suddenly it wasn't amusing anymore. "Who . . . ?" Howard shrank back toward the far window, Michelle seemed to offer herself up. Earl Elstob was trying to close his lips around his buckteeth as though to draw a curtain. The Inspector, spotlit from above, watched all this, hands in pockets, pipe in mouth, as though, silently, weaving the final strands of his web—then, glancing toward Fred and turning his back, he jerked his thumb toward the rest of us. "*Now!*" "Ah, shit," Charley groaned, slumping a bit, and Fats whimpered: "Hey, wait a minute, anybody seen Bren?" Fred, hand on holster, pushed past him (he yipped reflexively), headed in my direction. Ours, rather: my wife tightened

her grip again. "It's all right," I muttered huskily (others were ducking, stumbling back)—and so it was: Fred broke past us in pursuit of Vachel, who, squeaking in alarm, went scrambling behind pots and props. "It's a *frame-up!* I been *skunked!*" he screamed, shoving the pedalcar in Fred's direction. Fred went crashing, but Bob had joined him in the chase and now tackled the dwarf cleanly (Charley in confusion cheered him, and Regina wheezed, falling back: "God! I thought it was going to be me!") near the back wall. Vachel, greasy with petroleum jelly, slipped a foot free, brained the cop with the fireplace poker, and took off running, but by now Fred was on his feet again and had him in a bearhug: Vachel's little legs churned in midair, going nowhere. Bob, enraged, holding his bloodied head, staggered toward them. "*Let me go, you shitheads!*" Vachel shrieked, feet and fists flying. "*You can't do this to me!*" "Pop him one on the gourd there, Bob!" Fred grunted, hanging on desperately, and Bob, leaning into it on his short leg ("Oh dear," my wife said, wincing), brought his stick down so hard that it did indeed sound like he'd crushed a pumpkin. "Shit," Quagg sighed from the floor, "there goes our show," and Fred, now holding the unconscious Vachel under one arm like a duffelbag and picking up his hat with the other, said: "Whew!"

"If that don't beat my grandmaw!" Fats gasped, and someone belched eloquently, Dolph probably. "Vachel! Who'da guessed it?"

"Guessed what?"

"Eet wass how you say a brow-eye leefter, no?" exclaimed Hilario, rolling his eyes.

"Fucking little degenerate!" growled Bob, still sore, blood streaming down past one eye, and he gave the dwarf another blow which oddly made his feet bob as well as his head.

"That'll do," said Pardew. "Come along now," and my wife, letting go my arm, said: "I'll see them to the door."

I sat back against the arm of the couch where Regina lay all akimbo in a crumpled white heap, the back of one wrist pressed melodramatically against her brow ("Goodness, Sally Ann—that dress is still wet!" my wife remarked in passing, there were people crossing now between us, I could only catch glimpses), taking great heaving bolts of air. I too felt short of breath, one half of me sinking leadenly, the other half dangerously afloat. "Do not try to grasp it," I could hear Hoo-Sin murmuring to Janny out there somewhere in that unfocused blur of movement before my eyes: the tension in the room had dissolved into

a kind of generalized backstage flutter, as people slipped out of folds in the cave wall or crept out from behind one another, exchanging laughter and snorts of relief, ducking off for drinks or helping themselves to the dessert and coffee. "Causal thought is for fools. It is the burying of oneself in emptiness."

"You said it, Hoo! Juss what I been doin' for—*ruff! haw!* ("Ffoof-*hrarf!* I swallowed one of those damned—*choke!*—cookies *whole!*" rasped the guy in the chalkstriped pants)—twenny years!" laughed Charley, drawing both of them into his arms. My grandmother had had a story about this, or something like this, I remembered, something about a dead cousin. "I *love* it!"

"*Now* what, Mr. Quagg?"

Or aunt. I pushed off a canvas shoe, and scratched my foot.

"*Hroaf! ch-wheeze!*"

Beside me, the cameraman was changing cartridges, Zack Quagg was doing deep kneebends, Gudrun was tying Janny's hair up in a tight coil, powdering her face white. "Don't worry, kids," Quagg panted. "We'll—*grunt!*—clean it up and recast it, mount the whole uproar again!" Janny sneezed, Scarborough swore, Regina groaned, and the guy in the chalkstripes—"*Pwwfff-FWWOOO!*"—spewed cookie as Kitty reached round from behind and squeezed his diaphragm. "We'll call it 'The Feast of Saint Valentine,' use Mee as the vampire, make it a revue maybe, a kinda funerary tribute to the bourgeois theater . . ." "That better?" "What happened?" asked Brenda, standing dim-eyed in the traffic of the dining room doorway, Gottfried peering sheepishly over her shoulder. The green charmeuse dress hung askew on her, one plump arm sticking out of the sleeve's slash instead of the cuff. She pulled a string of gum out of her mouth, let it droop ("Write some new tunes, give it some bounce!"), then lifted her chin and nibbled it back in again. "We were, um, watching TV." Regina sat up and studied her nails. "It's so unfair!" she said, and Fats, lapping up pie and chocolate sauce, spluttered: "You'll never believe it, Bren!" "You know, uh, I think I've lost my tape recorder," said Gottfried, reddening. "They've just took *Vachel!*" "Unfair?" "Poor old Vachel, I mean," said Regina. "Enh," Horner shrugged, rolling himself a cigarette, "he made a good exit . . ." "Yeah, but does he *know* that?" "Oh *no!* not—*snap!*—*Vachel!*" yawned Brenda (it was catching, my own jaws began to spread), and Michelle said: "I think I'll put a record on."

"That reminds me," said the Inspector, turning around at the door. "Our ice pick . . ."

"I got it," said Bob, holding it up, then he tucked it back in his rear pocket.

Fred must have seen my gape of surprise (I'd been caught midyawn) as I rose up off the couch arm, because he winked and came over (I pressed my jaws together), wagging Vachel under his arm. "One of the Old Man's favorite tricks," he grinned. "His probe, he calls it. Stick it in, see what surfaces. You know."

"I thought somehow I-I'd—!"

"But of course we couldn't fool you! Oh, and by the way . . ." He leaned closer, switching Vachel to his other arm. It was my bloated self I saw in Vachel's goggles, dwarfed twice over by the lenses' convexity. "I just wanted to tell you: you know that ultraviolet exam . . ." He nodded toward the hall door, where my wife stood, smiling wearily. She was waiting for the Inspector, who, stopped now by Patrick, was patting his pockets helplessly. "Well, sir, clean as a whistle!" He gave me a knowing nudge. "Just thought you'd like to know . . ." He sidled closer. Kitty, poking around at Vachel's head behind his back, scrunched up her nose and said: "Ouch!" "And listen, that wasn't blood on the knife the Chief found, it was tomata juice—we knew that, we knew it all the time." He slapped my butt with his free hand. "You got a great little lady, fella. Hang on to her!"

Vachel's dripping head bobbed at Fred's rear under the blue SUPER-LOVER sweatshirt as the officer walked away through what was left of the proscenium arch. One of my skis, cracked at the binding, tipped forward now at a crazy angle, making it seem as if the stage were reaching out to stop him, and Scarborough, trying to right it, snapped it in two. "Piss on it," he grumped and planted the broken end impatiently in a fern pot.

"Forget it, Scar, we're blowing this stand," said Zack.

"Hey, where's ole Earl?"

"We're moving the show up-country!"

"Yeah? Who's providin' the nut?"

"Cyril? Out back with Malcolm, I think, Charley."

"Probably getting stoned, the poor bastard."

"Don't worry, I got somebody. We're working on him now."

"Naw, I meant—"

"Is it true Peg left him because he liked to do it with mirrors?"

"No, that was someone else."

"I hear it was because she wanted to surprise him on their silver wedding anniversary, and it was the only thing she could think of."

"I *love* it!" Charley yuff-huffed. " 'Ass like the ole folks who went back t'their honeymoon hotel, an' . . ."

"You mean Peg and—?"

"You know, I don't think that guy's playin' with a full deck!"

"Lissen, this'll knock your pants off! They went back t'the goddamn hotel, see . . ."

"Well, according to Cyril . . ."

"Say, did you hear about that play Ros was in where she was supposed to pick up this deck of cards and cut it?"

" 'N—hee hoff!—the ole fella says . . ."

"That's not the way I heard it . . ."

"Ros?"

"Yeah, and—ha ha!—the director says—"

"Well then . . ."

"No . . ."

"He says . . ."

"*He* said . . ."

I was tired of stories and moved away. Perhaps my wife needed me. I remembered her hand on my arm a few moments ago, clutching at it as though for strength, and then the paleness of her face a little later as she smiled vacantly, sorrowfully, into the room past Pardew before she led him out. As I crossed to the door, little particolored Bunky Baird came bouncing through it, shouting: "Zack! Zack! they've done something to Vachel!" "Yeah, I know, they popped his blister, Bunko—and ours too. The show's blown, kid. So get outa your skin, we're pulling stakes!" A proscenium arch, I thought, passing under it, is like a huge mouth, but the sensation that it is the audience that is being fed through it is just another of theater's illusions. Theater is never a stripping down (Bunky was bright blue and pimpled with sequins from the waist up, scarlet still from the thighs down, but in between a damp fleshy smear, ugly and shockingly naked), but always a putting on: theater fattened on boxed time. To be a member of the audience, then (so many thoughts, one after another, I staggered on, feeling myself consumed by my own consciousness), was a form of martyrdom . . . .

Gudrun as I lumbered past gave me an understanding glance as

though in sympathy with my troubled thoughts ("Okay, before we go, everyone together for the flash!" Zack shouted) and rubbed her nose with a blue finger. "I think someone stole your wife's dressing table," she said.

"Come on! Curtain calls!"

"What—?"

"This is *exciting!* You know, Mr. Quagg, I *really love the theater life!*"

I leaned up against the doorframe. Even the dressing table . . . My wife was at the front door, saying good night to Inspector Pardew and Fred. They didn't seem to want to leave. Or maybe they didn't know how. She wanted me near, I knew—I caught it in her sorrowful gaze as she glanced up at me from Vachel's lifeless and begoggled buttocks—but between us the tall cop Bob had Patrick slap up against the wall, jabbing him with his stick, cursing him out for being a nuisance and a whore, and I lacked the will, or maybe even the courage, to push on past. "If you don't stop bugging the Inspector, you scummy little poufta, you're gonna get your goddamn place of business tweezed!" "*Well!* Is that a *promise?*" Patrick simpered brazenly, twitching his puffy lips up at the black-bearded TV cameraman now looming behind the cop's shoulder. "You goddamn prevert—!" "You got problems, little buddy?" asked the cameraman, taking a fierce grip on Bob's neck that made the cop whistle and drop his nightstick. In the living room (to be at a crossroads, I realized, was actually to be nowhere: there was unexpected comfort in this) applause erupted as the actors took their curtain calls, Mee joining them now, sliding spookily past me out of the toilet, as though sucked in by the slapping hands. Scarborough focused the lights, Regina doffed her bedsheet (there was a lot of good-natured booing), Zack dragged Fats on stage to take a bow. Fats, feigning shyness, shuffled up doing a little hunched-shoulders soft-shoe routine, hands in his pockets and rolling his eyes. "Spread it, sweetie!" laughed Brenda, clapping the loudest: "Let's hear it for him, folks! the one and lonely!" "Now if you'll just pick up my gear there, pardner, and haul it along with us," the cameraman said beside me, making Patrick gasp and flutter his lashes ("Oh my! yes!"), then he highstepped the cop to the front door, one hand gripping his skinny nape, the other the seat of his pants, Bob's gimpy leg brushing through the scum of whipped cream on the floor like a dan-

gling plummet. "Hot it up, Scar!" shouted Quagg. My wife opened the door and the cameraman heaved the cop through it, then turned to wait for Patrick. "Okay, strike it and take it away, crew, we're sloughing this dime museum!" People were starting to head out this way: I joined my wife.

"Such in the main are the degenerate dregs of humanity, whom we have never, I regret to admit, learned to curb or eliminate," Pardew was saying, as though into some kind of closing recitation, "characterized chiefly by their stupidity and depravity and their inability to play the game—"

"Oh yes?" said my wife vaguely.

Patrick, his hands full of camera gear, paused at the door to pucker his battered lips at me and wink, then pranced out after the cameraman, my wife still holding the door open. Her lips moved as though she might be counting. Behind us, the actors, laughing and shouting ("And their, eh, deformed personalities, you see . . ."), were flowing into the hallway. "Well, back to selling pencils!" "Christ, Vadge, get those things in a hammock before somebody steps on 'em!" "No, believe me, baby, we *got* a *backer!*" "I believe you, Zack. Call me at the beach." "Somebody gimme a chaser!" Fats called out, hauling on his down jacket. "A tailpiece for ole Fats—*lemme hear it from the heart!*" The Inspector had long since fallen silent. He peered down at my wife, nibbling his moustache. "Thank you so much for coming," she said.

Fats chasséd past us, waggling his hands beside his face and singing, "You're gonna miss me when I'm gone," my wife pushing the storm door open just in time to keep him from crashing through it. "Ta-DAAA-AA-*aa-aaa* . . ." The police marched out behind him. "Watch where you step," I could hear the Inspector mutter peevishly, his voice echoey in the night. "It's really too bad about Vachel," my wife said with a sigh.

"Yes, well . . . I never did like him very much, though."

"I know." The actors had applauded Fats' exit and Brenda was now giving them all a hug. "But he was always good with children."

"Next party at our house, everybody! Promise!"

Hilario leaned toward us and said: "Your keetchen, do you know, she ees smokeeng!"

"What—?!" Yes, I could see it, rolling in from the back like some kind of mephitic vapors.

"It's all right, Gerald," my wife said. "Fats just left some things on the burner. As usual."

"Ees what you call a bloody mass, no?"

"Shall I go see if—?"

"No." She took my arm. "I already turned it off." There was a peculiar gentle flush in her cheeks. "Dolph and Louise are back there, making up," she whispered.

"Ah . . ."

"*Bren!*" cried Fats, staggering wide-eyed back in through the front door, making us all jump. "My *god*, Bren! It's that plumber! *Whatsisface!*"

"What—? Oh *no!* Not—?!" She came rushing silkily past us, but paused to give us both a hug—"You're a super guy, Ger," she breathed in my ear, her gum snapping, "you've got a great heart . . . and *wonderful* hands!"—then clambered on out behind Fats: "*God!* I can't *believe* it, Fats!"

"Hey, poison curls!" Zack Quagg exclaimed. "Our angel descends!"

I looked up, we all did: it was Alison's husband, escorting Alison down the stairs in front of him, followed by Olga and Prissy Loo. Alison was dressed now in Brenda's red pants suit, a couple of sizes too big for her, stained at the knees, the cuffs flopping around her bare feet. The actors all applauded. Alison, her makeup smeared across her face, hair snarled, stumbled when she saw me. Her eyes searched mine. Was her lip quivering? She held the baggy-kneed red pants up with one hand. There was a patch sewn on the crotch now, probably one of Sally Ann's, which, even from here, I could see was in the shape of a road sign.

"And have *we* got a show for *you!*"

Alison's husband sniffed. "Theater," he said frostily, "is dead."

"What—?" Zack laughed, staggering back a step. "I told you, Zack."

"Is it time for my part?" asked Prissy Loo. She was wearing Beni's plumed hat and false moustache, my fingerless golfing gloves, and one of my mother-in-law's girdles, ornamented with what looked like rolled-up bloody socks. Olga was trying to stretch my wife's yellow nightie down below her high muscular croup. Zack spread wide his caped arms as though unfolding a curtain. "Hey, ha ha! you gotta be *kidding*, man!"

Alison's husband shook his head. "No, it's dead. All over. I see that now." He prodded Alison on down the stairs.

"Aw, goddamn it, Prissy, you overdid it!"

"Well, that was a short run."

"Don't blame me, Zack, it was Olga's idea."

"What idea?"

"Yah, goot! In a minute!"

"DANGER: BUSY CROSSROADS," the patch said. She stood there in front of me, echoed dismally in the hall mirror, clutching the baggy pants, looking lost. "Did you bring a coat?" my wife asked politely. "It's boring, it's repetitious, and it's dead-ended," said Alison's husband. "And it's a lie."

"Wait a minute, what do you know about theater, you dumb fuck?" Quagg exploded.

"Hell, he's nothing but a goddamn preacher, Zack."

"One goddamn night of pissing around, and you think you've seen it all? You weren't even in at the death, fer chrissake!"

"Don't tell me it's all over!" Prissy Loo wailed, her moustache listing. "Zack, you promised!"

"What do you know about blocking and backing, asshole? Glue guns and gobos?" Alison's husband only smiled faintly. "What about conventions, eh? Peripety, goddamn it? Teasers, timing—"

"Timing?" Alison's husband gazed round at us, stroking his beard. "Peripety?" He reached forward suddenly and yanked at the top half of the red pants suit as though to whip it off: Alison clutched at it and her pants fell down. He stepped on them and, as she bent over to grab them up, he shoved his hand in under his shirt and cracked a mock fart in his armpit. She blushed, tugging frantically at the trapped pants; he reached forward and grasped the nape of his wife's neck, pressing her head down. He poked his finger up her rectum, felt around, came out with one of Ginger's kerchiefs—in fact a whole string of them, knotted together: out they came, one after another, fluttering in the air as he tossed them high, more kerchiefs than you could imagine there'd be room for in there. And at the end, knotted to the last kerchief: the Inspector's white silk scarf! The door opened behind us: it was Fred. "Excuse me, the Chief seems to have left his—ah! thank you . . ." There was a burst of applause and whistles (Fred backed out with the scarf, hand to holster, looking nonplussed, or pretending to), even Zack had to join in. "You know, I think that sonuvabitch was just using me!" he laughed.

"You!" cried Prissy Loo.

"Yah?" said Olga.

My wife was giggling beside me; I think it was the first time I'd seen her laugh all night. I smiled: just as Alison straightened up, flushed and hurt, to stare at me. I tried to erase the smile, but it seemed frozen there, as though stretched forcibly over my teeth. "The bright moon is serenely reflected on the stream," Hoo-Sin said, gazing into the hall mirror behind Alison: "What is it for?" Well. I could only hope she understood. I tried to think of some way of explaining it all to her ("Gosh, I give up," Janny yawned, "can you give me a hint?"), or at least of deflecting some of her anger, something about theater perhaps, or time, but before I could come up with anything, she had stumbled out past me, red pants binding her ankles, had tripped at the threshold, and completed her exit on her hands and knees, chased by another round of laughter and applause.

"Whoo-*hoo!*"

"Look at them blue hereafters!"

"Just as well her parents missed that," my wife murmured.

"That was somethin' *special!*"

Alison's husband paused at the door, all eyes on him still, his on me. Out in the front yard, someone shouted: "Hey *hey!* What wuz-*zat* just creeped past?" "I dunno, Dugan, but it was wearin' the biggest *smile* I ever seen!" "I believe you still have our watches," he said.

"Oh yes, sorry! I'll get them!" But my wife stopped me: "I'm afraid someone . . . they're not there anymore, Gerald."

"The watches, too—?!"

"*This* way, squad! I think we found the *source!*"

Alison's husband snorted disdainfully and touched his beard. Outside there was drunken laughter, curses, stumbling on the steps: "Wah! Look out! This place is *alive!*"

"However, if they turn up later—" my wife began, reaching forward to take his hand, but he turned his back on her and strode stiffly out the door, a final ripple of appreciative applause trailing in his wake.

"*Whoa!*" exclaimed someone outside who, from the sound of it, had just tumbled down the porch stairs.

"*Down, boy!*"

"*Yowzer!*"

"Where was *that* dude goin'?"

"Hard to say, Doog, but he was either *awful sober*—or *awful drunk!*"

"I dunno when I've had so much fun!" Charley Trainer laughed,

throwing his arms around us both. Janny stood by with her hands pressed together below her chin, eyes closed, listening to Hoo-Sin, while around us, some people I'd never seen before were pounding and clattering through the door, singing, shouting greetings, brandishing bottles and bits of clothing. "Oh dear," my wife sighed, shrinking into Charley's arms. One guy was carrying a woman, wall-eyed with drink, on his shoulders: she failed to see the doorframe as he passed under it and smacked it with her face. "Somebody knock?" asked the guy confusedly, swinging around, still holding the woman's ankles and so wearing her collapsed body over his shoulders like a cape. "Ha ha! Who's there?" called another and Charley hugged us close: "You guys're the *cream!*"

"*Leda!*"

"Leda who, Moose?"

"I *mean* it, Big G! My heart is *full!*"

I could feel my wife's heart emptying out, but she smiled and said, her voice catching: "I-I'm so glad you could all come . . ." No one heard her but me—and Charley Trainer, who, pitching forward drunkenly, knocked his head on hers and growled: "Me too—but lemme tell ya, *I hadda work like hell!*"

"Hey hey hey! Izzat little Bunky Baird?"

"Leda horse to water?"

"Axel!"

"Do we know these people?" I whispered.

"Naw! Guess again!"

"And I'll tell you no lies?"

"I think we may have met some of them at Wilma's house a long time ago, when she was still married to Miles . . ."

"Miles?"

"*Benedetto!*"

"A Leda goes a long way?"

"*Gwendoline! My love!*"

"*Love* the silk pocket, Beni! Très charmant!"

The new arrivals were spreading recklessly through the house, as though the place itself were hemorrhaging. "Please," I said, but no one was listening, they were all ("Ha ha, we give up, Moose!") hooting and laughing. "My oh my, look what's *not* in that nightie!" "Hey, I'm looking for Serena!" "Is that rhubarb pie?" "She ain't here, Ralphie!" "Vot's hoo-bob?" asked Olga, grinning stupidly and push-

ing the nightie down past her navel: at the back, it climbed halfway
to her shoulders. ". . . Like so many particles of dust . . . ," Hoo-
Sin was murmuring in Janny's ear, and Charley ("Am I drunk, or are
those lamps up onna ceiling?"), dipping his heavy head, smirked
hopefully: "Hey, Ger, heard any good jokes lately?" At the back, they
were fanning the kitchen door (*"Leda me beside distilled waters—!"*)
to clear the smoke. I could hear the refrigerator door whumping, drawers being opened and closed like marching feet.

". . . Floating, rising . . ."

"You're drunk, Claudine—*and* the lamps are on the ceiling!"

". . . Disappearing like clouds . . ."

"*—Before da party's SOBER!*"

"Send your ole dad home with a li'l chuckle, whaddaya say?"

"Haw haw!"

"I'm fresh out, Charley. Nothing's funny."

". . . In the vast emptiness of unending space . . ."

"Moose, you're a scream!"

"Aw, c'mon, Big G, have a heart!" Charley pleaded, and Janny, her
head tipping to Hoo-Sin's shoulder, sighed: "You've got such a nice
voice, Hoo-Sin . . ."

"Do you think they'll want something to eat, Gerald?"

"No!"

". . . It nearly puts me to sleep . . ."

"Well, y'don' hafta be *sore* about it, buddy!"

"Sorry, Charley, I meant—"

"Whatever thoughts you have, they are not to dwell on anything,"
Hoo-Sin said softly as Janny's head snuggled in under her chin and
her hands dropped to her sides. "That's easy, Hoo-Sin . . ."

"Why don't you tell him the one about giving the testicles to the
girl, Gerald," my wife suggested, looking small and vulnerable under
Charley's arm.

"Testicles?" Charley grinned broadly.

"You already have," I said.

Hoo-Sin reached down under Janny's sagging knees to pick her up.
"We return to the origin," she whispered, as Janny wriggled closer,
"and remain where we have always been . . ."

"Flo! Where'd you find the fodder?"

"No, the one about how you find out if she's ticklish or not."

"In the back there, Rocco, but you gotta scrape it off the pans . . ."

"How you find out—oh, Jesus!" Charley doubled up, roaring with laughter.

"You find that funny?" I asked in some amazement. At the foot of the stairs, Prissy Loo shook her plumed hat ("Chet!") and stamped her foot. "But you said you'd *wait*, Zack!"

"I guess—*whoosh! hah!*—I guess it's all," Charley wheezed, falling back on the hall bench, holding his quaking sides ("Ha ha! Not Chet!"), "*in how you tell it!*"

"I knew he'd like it, Gerald," my wife said. "Now go ahead and tell it." Whereupon Charley, tears in his eyes ("You're a real heel, Zack!"), nearly fell off the bench.

"You kids off?"

"Careful, Charley, you'll hurt your back again."

"Oh shit!—hoo ha hah—!"

"Yes, thanks a lot, Mr. Quagg! As soon as we're in our new place—"

"—I awready did!"

"Better come quick, Zack! One of those drunken yobs gave Olga something heavy and she's freaking! She thinks she's a bird and keeps throwing herself at all the walls!"

"What am I, some kinda nursemaid?" Zack protested.

"Say, where'd you hide your sewing machine?" asked Prissy Loo, slapping over ("Well, keep in touch, kid—!") in her big galoshes. "I went in there to sew these sanitary napkins on my costume and—"

"You mean it isn't there?" my wife exclaimed.

"And let me see what you write!"

"It *probably* cost me my part!"

"That's right," someone said ("You bet!"), "your dressing table was gone, too," I said.

"Unh, Big G . . . ? I—*hoof!*—I can' get up . . . !"

"The dressing table! But that old thing is worthless!"

"Well, aw-*moss!*" yuffhuffed Charley, struggling clumsily, "but, Jesus, don' go *tellin'* everybody!"

Anatole gave me a hand pulling him to his feet, while Hoo-Sin stood patiently by, holding Janny, now breathing deeply, in her arms. Howard had joined us and, peering down through Tania's half-lens glasses, was trying to button his coat, while at the same time holding on to the sheaf of drawings the tall cop had made of the scene of the crime. "Here, let me help, Uncle Howard," Sally Ann said.

"What I don't understand, Gerald, is how they got all those things

out of here?" In the dining room we could hear Olga crashing around, yelling: "Tveet! Tveet!" "Tell her she's a fucking *flower!*" Zack was shouting. "Or a *stone!*"

"Cute," said Prissy Loo, fingering Sally Ann's dirndl.

"You gotta catch her first, Zack!"

" 'At wuzza bess laugh I had all night! *Hoo!*"

"Do you think they had a truck?"

Anatole cleared his throat. "Uh, do you want to tell them, Sally Ann . . . ?" he said, blushing.

"Well . . ." She took Anatole's arm, looked at each of us in turn. "Tveet—*squawk!*"

"Oh oh," said Prissy Loo, puckering up.

"We're . . . we're going to get married."

"I knew it!" wailed Prissy Loo and burst into tears. "I always cry at the clinches!" She planted a blubbery moustachioed kiss on Sally Ann's cheek and Anatole's ("That's wonderful," my wife was saying, "I'm so happy for you!"), then went clopping off into the living room in her plumed hat and decorated girdle. "Whuzzat? Whuzzat?" asked Charley blearily, careening around, and I said: "But how will you live?"

"Oh, Gerald!" my wife scolded, taking my arm. "Hush now!"

"That's all right," said Sally Ann gently. "I knew he'd be upset."

"I'm going to drop out of school and write for Mr. Quagg," Anatole explained. "And Dickie's getting Sally Ann a job in one of his massage parlors."

"You see, Gerald?"

"And we're going to live with Uncle Howard," Sally Ann added, taking the older man's arm. "He needs us, and we need him. Now that . . ." Her voice broke and Anatole's eyes began to water up.

"I assume you are aware, Gerald, that the 'Susanna' is missing," Howard said in his rigid pedantic way.

I nodded. "And not only that, Howard, they even took—"

"Such carelessness, Gerald, is utterly inexcusable."

"Come along now, Uncle Howard," Anatole said huskily.

"Whoa there, young fella!" exclaimed Charley, holding Anatole back. " 'Sa tough ole world out there, son—you can' go get married on nothin'!"

Anatole looked offended. "It's not nothing, Mr. Trainer. Mr. Quagg says I have a lot of talent and—"

"No, hell, I know that, but juss hole on, goddamn it!" He fumbled in his pockets. "Art, Gerald," Howard harrumphed, scowling at me over the spectacles, "is all we have. It is not a joke." Olga came bounding through on all fours, more like a lamb or a goat now than a bird, the yellow nightie up around her ears, pursued by Gudrun, Zack, and some of the newcomers. "*Maaa-aa-aa!*" she bleated, frisking along into the living room, her head stretched high. "Come here, Olga! Stop that!" "It is not a decoration, simple bric-a-brac. It is *not* a mere entertainment." "Maybe if she thought she was a dog, we could get a leash on her!" "*Maa-aa-aa!*" "Just so she don't start droppin' pellets!" panted Horner, limping along behind, and the guy with him stopped and pointed: "Hey! I know you jokers! Ha! I seen you in the photos!" "Art, Gerald—" "Photos?" my wife asked. "—*Is the precipitate of the human spirit* . . ." Charley dumped all his change into the pockets of Sally Ann's dress—or in that general direction: coins splattered the floor, rolled at our feet. "Yeah, some guy from the newspaper's floggin' 'em out in your front yard like souvenirs. " "There! 'Sall I got, kids," said Charley, emptying his wallet and thrusting the bills at Anatole, "but, well—I mean, god-*damn* it—!"

"I don't go much for the shots of stiffs or all the blood and shit . . ."

"Oh, Uncle Charley!" cried Sally Ann, throwing her arms around him.

". . . The repository of the only meaning we *have* in this world . . ."

". . . But there's one of some ole girl peein' off the teeter-totter out in the backyard that'll—Christ!—break your heart!"

"I know, Howard, but—"

"That must have been Wilma," my wife said.

"In the end, Gerald, and I say this with all seriousness, you are a dangerous person!"

Hoo-Sin, carrying Janny, bowed slightly and backed out the door, Howard ("I intend therefore to sue you for the remaining pieces in your possession," he declared, and my wife said: "Yes, you must come again soon!"), Anatole, and then Charley following. Some of the people chasing Olga had peeled off here in the hallway and it was filling up again. Not a familiar face among them. "Is that the only bottle you could find, Carmody?" one of them asked. I recognized it. Alas. Central to the art of love, I knew ("Yeah'n taze like piss, buh' this time nigh', who givshit?"), as to the art of theater, was the essential

fusion of process and product, an acknowledgment of the inherent doubleness—one's particularity, one's universality, one's self, one's persona—of the actor/lover. In fact ("I'm so glad you found each other," my wife was saying, "it's just about the nicest thing that happened all night!"), I'd said something like this to her earlier tonight, and she'd agreed, probably it was while she was fingering my nipple, we'd seemed in perfect harmony, perfect collusion, and yet . . . "Gerry?" I realized Sally Ann, hanging back from the others, had taken my hand. "Try not to be so sad, Gerry, it's for the best, believe me—but I promise I'll never forget you!" Her eyes were full of tears and they were tumbling down her cheeks. "I-I was blind until you opened my eyes to love . . . !" She tried to say something more, but it was choked off by a stifled sob. She kissed my mouth and went running out the door.

My wife, looking on, smiled and took my arm. There was a loud spewing sound behind us, someone gagging. "Young love . . . !" she sighed.

"Goddamn it, Carmody! This *is* piss!"

"We'll have to think of something for a wedding present . . ."

"Hey, you guys! Come in here! You don't wanna miss this!" I could hear toward the back what sounded like (" 'Fya don' like it, shifface, giv't back!") wild guttural laughter, utterly insane, and the crack of whips. Or belts.

"Madre de dios! ees getteeng roff!" Hilario gasped, staggering out of the dining room just as the others (something crashed) went pushing in. He wobbled toward us with his legs exaggeratedly bowed and his eyes bugged out. "Now Olga theenk he ees a horse and everybody ees rideeng heem! Hair."

"Where have they all come from, Hillie?" This never used to happen. Michelle's dream of the old lady's infested navel came to mind: it's what comes from growing old. "What am I going to *do?*"

"You wan' get reed?"

"Sure, but—?"

"Seemple like a tart, Cherry! Don' cry!"

My wife, rummaging through the hall closet, said: "My good fur wrap is missing, too."

"La serpiente—what you say the dance-sneak, no?" He reached forward as though gripping a waist and did a little rumba step. The guy they were calling Carmody, hugging his pale green bottle and mutter-

ing, "I *know* wha'm *doing*," wobbled past us (*"Yippee! Let 'er rip!"* shouted someone in the dining room) and disappeared through the front door.

"*Look out!*"

"Yow—!!" *Crash!*

"Eet *always* work!"

"That would be nice, Hillie, I'll put some music on," my wife offered, but just then Charley came banging back through the front door and grabbed us both: "Wait, you guys! I forgot!" "Pairmeet me!" Hilario smiled, bowing from the waist. He shuffled gracefully off toward the living room, hands still on the imaginary waist. "I sold my car!"

"Your car?"

"Yeah, the big station wagon. Your buddy—travel agent guy. Hey, whaddaya cryin' about, Ger? I got a fan-*tas*-tic deal!" He fished around in his jacket pockets, came up with a crumpled check. The crazy whinnying had stopped. I could hear the music now in the living room. Hilario was turning the volume up. "See? Awmoss *twice* what I paid for it!"

"Charley, isn't this check signed 'Waterloo'?"

"'Ass right—hah! ole Waterloo—you 'member! That dumb shit!"

I glanced up at my wife: she sighed and shook her head. "I showed them everything . . ."

"Whuzzamatter?" He stared in puzzlement at the check, held it up to the light.

"Listen, Charley, you take my car for now." I handed him the keys. The music was getting louder.

"Hunh? Oh yeah, thanks, ole buddy!" He wrapped his arms heavily around me. "Hey, I *love* ya, Ger! I *mean* it!" He hauled out his handkerchief and wiped my eyes and then his own. Over his shoulder I could see a line of people, hands on one another's hips and led by Hilario (he winked and raised his long fingers in a V), come hopping and kicking out of the living room, all singing along with the music, now turned up full volume: *"Don't LAUGH, it may be LOVE . . . !"* The woman who'd hit the door lintel with her face was still out cold, the guy who'd carried her in now dragging her along by one ankle. As they wound toward the back into the dining room ("Hey! wait for me!" people shouted, grabbing on to the tail), Dolph and Louise came squeezing out past them, holding hands, looking flustered and

confused. Beside me, my wife caught her breath, and Charley, pulling away (*"It's YOU I'm thinkin' OF!"*), said: "Great goddamn party, Big G! Bess I ever wen' to!"

"I guess we gotta second that," Dolph grinned.

"Is it true, then?" asked my wife, and Louise blushed and nodded. They fell into a big tearful embrace and then Dolph hugged my wife and Louise hugged me: she was trembling and I thought I heard her gasp something about "love you" or "because of you," it was hard to tell because things were getting pretty noisy. They both hugged Charley, who seemed to have no idea what it was all about, then hugged us again (they'd been standing in the smoke too long and smelled a bit charred), Louise now almost unable to breathe for excitement. While Dolph had his arms around me ("I *love* it!" Charley was saying. "God-*damn* it, Louise!"), I stage-whispered in his ear: *"If you grab my buttocks, Dolph, I'll bite your ear off!"* Dolph laughed, a squeaky but joyful laugh, unlike any we'd heard in over a year, and my wife, in tears, hugged them both again. "I'm so happy for you!" she cried, and Charley, punching Dolph in the ribs, said: " 'S*beaut*-iful! I *mean* it!"

Hilario's snake dance, meanwhile, had come winding out of the living room again, led now by Olga, who seemed to think she was a frog: she was down on her haunches, hopping along, her big cheeks bouncing rhythmically off the floor, and shouting *"Borp!"* every time she leaped into the air. The line coiled to the rear of the hall, Olga going *"Borp! Borp!"* in front of them, then swung round and hopped toward us again.

"Life is ONLY what you SEE . . . !"

Dolph said something about influence, but the noise in the hall was deafening. *"WHAT—?"*

"I SAID YOU GUYS—"

"Borp!"

"Here they come!"

"So come DANCE along with ME!"

"Look out—!"

My wife flung the door open and we pulled apart to let them by, but Olga, as though in panic, stopped dead at the threshold. Hilario prodded her effectively—"BORP!"—in the behind.

"You're a genius, Hillie!" I shouted.

He laughed, kicking. *"I promeese dem all w'en we outside we EAT*

de FROG!" And then he was gone, the long line hopping and whooping behind: *"Won't you TRY to under-STAND . . ."*

My wife seemed to be saying something. *"WHAT?"* I cried. Horner had his hand up the skirt of the woman in front of him: she bounced rigidly as though on coiled springs, her eyes glazed, mouth agape. *"I said, I get the feeling half my wardrobe walked out the door tonight!"* She pointed at Beni, who, one hand cupping his silk codpiece affectionately, winked and shouted out a *"Ciao!"* *"Or hopped!"*

"If you're the GLOVE, then I'm the HAND!"

A guy with a runny nose and what looked like dried vomit down his shirtfront staggered out of the line and threw his arms around us. *"G'nigh'!"* he shouted. *" 'Nkyou fr'inviding us!"* He seemed to be crying. *"C'mon, Boomer! you'll get left behind!"* *" 'S been so . . . shit! . . . so—"* *"Soup's on, Boomer!"* *"So goddamn . . . I don' know howta . . . God! yareally SWELL!"* he sobbed and grabbed up my wife's hand and kissed it. Or maybe he was only wiping his nose on it. Then he stumbled back into the line, disappearing through the door.

Slowly the sound wound away from us as the dancers snaked past. A guy with an eyepatch waved a bottle at me, Bunky blew a kiss—*"Noble said to say thanks, Gerry, thanks a lot!"*—Scarborough moved lugubriously out of step. *"If I'm the HAND, then you're the GLOVE . . . !"* they sang, kicking, the music still blasting away. The woman getting dragged along at the tail seemed to be coming around at last. "Phil . . . ?" she asked as her head bumped over the threshold. "Where am I, Phil . . . ?"

"So don't LAUGH . . ."

I shoved the door shut, leaned against it, turned the latch. *"Whew!"* I gasped.

"What happened to Dolph and Louise?" my wife asked, looking around in amazement. *"And Charley—?!"*

"I don't know!" I said. We were still shouting. *"They must have joined in!"* She shrugged, then said something I couldn't hear. About the kitchen maybe: she wandered off that way. *"I'll go turn the music down!"*

In the empty living room, Michelle danced alone, wan under the bright lights from the ceiling, drifting wraithlike through the wreckage, hands crossed at her breast, eyes closed. When I rejected the

tone-arm, the sudden silence was shocking, almost physical in its impact, and I heard her gasp faintly, frozen in her movement. "I guess it's that time, Michelle." The deadly silence was eery and I was almost tempted to put another record on. I thought: it used to be more subtle than this.

"Have you been crying?" she whispered.

"Yes, well," I said, and wiped my cheek, "I hate goodbyes."

"Once, when I was modeling for Tania . . ." She hesitated. ". . . This was a long time ago . . . I was young then . . ." Her head dipped slightly. ". . . Just a little bit of hair . . . 'like a boy's moustache,' she said . . ." She seemed lost in her own reverie. ". . . Trying to help me feel more . . . relaxed . . ."

"Michelle?"

"What? Yes . . ." She clasped her hands at the back of her neck, her elbows in front of her face. Her intricate lace blouse was unbuttoned, tails out over a wrinkled skirt. "That day, she was apologizing for keeping me in the same pose for so long . . . and it was true . . . my whole body ached . . . it was awful . . . I wanted to fly right out of myself . . ." She lifted her head, stretching her neck against her clasped hands, then let her hands separate to slide forward and support her chin. " 'But an unfinished painting frightens me,' she said . . ." Yes, "a bare patch of canvas," she'd once remarked to me, "is like some terrible ultimate nakedness . . ." ". . . I can still see her face as she said it . . . her eyes . . ." ". . . Reality exposing itself obscenely . . ." " 'I can't sleep,' she said, 'I can't eat, I can't even think properly until I've completed it . . . I become cruel to myself and cruel to others . . .' " I remembered how she'd turned away and seemed almost to shudder. ". . . 'And then . . . when it's suddenly done . . .' " Michelle dropped her hands limply at her sides, lowered her chin. ". . . 'There's this terrible emptiness . . .' "

I watched her drift away, stepping barefoot through the butts and crumpled napkins, spilled food, the debris from Scarborough's set (near the cavemouth, Malcolm Mee's cast-off plastic wrap lay like an insect's husk, glittering and dead), and, though I wanted her to leave, I felt abandoned at the same time, left behind in a room (why were the windows so bare, the lights so harsh?) full of grave disquiet. The bloodied drapes and linens had turned dark and dirty. Sticking out from under the collapsed ping-pong table: the chalk drawing of a pair of legs. Scarborough had rigged the cords of all the

lamps to a kind of switching system in a box dangling just behind the proscenium arch, but I was afraid to touch it. It had a rickety yet lethal look, as though it might go off. I needed a drink, but I didn't want to go in where Vic was, so I stepped into the makeshift cave, away from the flat lights and stripped windows, and sniffed at the half-filled glasses. I found one that smelled more or less like scotch, but just as I tipped it back, I noticed what looked like pubic hairs floating in it—I spat it out. But it was only someone's false eyelashes. I sank back into the gold couch in there, feeling suddenly very tired. We'd have to clean up tomorrow. Outside, in the hallway, I could hear my wife saying good night to Michelle, her voice thin in the hollow silence ("Goodness, Michelle, where did you—*yawn!*—get those nasty toothmarks . . . ?"), and it reminded me of the time when, spelunking in Greece, we'd come on this cavernous pit of human bones. What she'd said then—thinly, hollowly—was: "Did you notice? None of them have heads . . . !"

Of course . . . that wasn't my wife . . .

"Somehow," she said now, gazing around wearily (she was standing in front of me, easing her shoes off: I hadn't seen her come up), "parties don't seem as much fun as they used to." She sat down beside me, curling under my arm, the one I could still move, and tucked her feet up. "It's almost as though the parties have started giving us instead of us giving the parties . . ." She loosened my shirt, lay her head sleepily against my chest. "It gives me a . . . funny feeling . . ."

"Yes . . ."

"Still, I guess it's worth it . . ."

The woman in Greece had said something much like that about making love. She'd had an appetite for the unusual, the perverse even, and I too was pretty jaded in those days, frustrated by the commonplaces of sex, bored with all its trite conventions—the state of the art, so to speak—and so in need of ever greater novelty, ever greater risk-taking, in order to arouse myself to any kind of performance. What worked for her—and thus for us both—was to be unexpectedly violated in a more or less public place, the key to a successful orgasm being not so much the setting or the use of force, as the element of surprise. It was a kind of essential trigger for her—like having to scare someone out of her hiccups. Thus, I might walk her through public parks, churches, department stores, taunting her with exotic possibility while yet denying her, only to jump on her back in the busy hotel

lobby while asking for the key. Or I might arrange a night out at some mysterious destination, coax her into dressing up elaborately, then get her out of the hotel, hail a taxi—and suddenly violate her on the sidewalk just as she was stepping into the cab. I don't know why I thought that pitful of decayed atrocity victims would work. Perhaps because it seemed so unlikely. But nothing happened. In fact it was a disaster. We got filthy, she hurt her back on the bones, got her nose bloodied, I cracked my elbow, we were both choking with dust, and when it was over—or rather, when there was no point in going on—she told me just to leave her alone and go away. I never saw her again, my last vision of her being sprawled out there in the— "*Ouch!*"

"Sorry, Gerald, is something . . . ?" She had been stroking me through the trousers and had caught the place where Jim had nicked me. She opened my trousers carefully, eased my shorts down. "Oh, I see . . ." She licked it gently, then took the crown into her mouth, coating it with warm saliva. "Bat's a bad bwuise, too," she observed, touching my tummy, then let her mouth slide gradually down the shaft. I reached for the hem of her dress and she shifted her hips, turning her knees toward the back of the couch.

There was a sudden crash, the whole house shook—I lurched away, reared up—and then a scraping, another crash, a rumble, something rolling in the street. She closed her mouth around my penis again, curled her hands behind my hips, tugged at the back of my trousers.

"But . . . my god, what *was* that—?!"

"Pwobabwy Chawwey puwwing out ubba dwibe . . ."

"Ah . . ." She eased my trousers down below my hips—outside, there was another crunch, the distant squealing of tires—then pulled them away from between my thighs. She put my hand back on the hem of her dress. There was a tag there, I noticed, stamped by the city police department. "Wewacsh, Gewawd," she whispered. I liked the pushing of her tongue against the consonants and, surrendering to that, slid down toward her knees. "Tell me again . . ."

"Wewacsh, Gewawd . . . ?"

"Yes . . . good . . ." It all comes down to words, as I might have argued with Vic. Or parts of them. "Is this a new dress?"

"Yeumf," she said, working my trousers down to my ankles: I lifted one foot out and raised it to the couch. "Do woo wike it?"

"Right now, it's in my way . . ."

"You say the nicest things, Gerald," she sighed, taking her mouth

away. She located the fastener, unhooked it, pushed at the skirt: I pulled it away and, stretching forward, eased it past her feet. "What are you doing with pancake makeup on the back of your neck?" she asked.

"I don't remember."

I tugged at her panty girdle, stretching it down past her soft hips, and she took my penis in her mouth again, warming it all over, closing one hand tenderly around my testicles. She kneaded them softly, pulling them toward her as though gently pumping them, sliding her other hand around to stroke my buttocks, finger my anus. Only one arm worked for getting her clothes off her: I left the dead one between her legs for the time being and she squeezed her thighs around it. "Just . . . a minute . . ." The panties and stockings came off in a tangle. I ran my tongue slowly up her leg from her calf, past her knee, and up the inside of her thigh: she spread her legs and, as I nosed into her vulva, lifted the top one over my head. "Mmmmf!" She had her finger up my anus now and was sucking rhythmically, her mouth full of foamy saliva like a warm bubble bath. I had found the nub of her clitoris with the tip of my tongue and now worked against it as though trying to pry it open. I reached round from behind, dipped my fingers into her moist vagina, pushed one of them up her rectum—"*Ouch!*" she cried, letting my penis go.

"Sorry . . ." I pushed my nose deeper between her thighs to have a closer look: her anus was drawn up in a tight little pucker, inflamed and cracked, slightly discolored as though rubbed with ashes. "How did you—?"

"You know. The police." She paused, holding my penis by the root. Perhaps she was studying it. Or simply reflecting.

I pressed my chin against the hood of her clitoris, gazing thoughtfully at her crinkled anus, remembering now her position on the butcherblock (as though being changed, I'd thought as they lowered her), her thighs stretching back, belly wrinkling, tiny little red lines running down her cheeks. "What . . . what's an exploding sausage . . . ?" I asked uneasily.

"Oh, Gerald!" she laughed and wagged my penis playfully. "Don't you know a joke when you hear one?"

"Ah . . ." I stroked her buttocks gently as my penis returned to its soothing bath, rubbing my chin rhythmically against her pubic knoll. Like veined marble, they'd seemed to me at the time, as I remem-

bered, something like that, though now they sparkled with a kind of
fresh dewy innocence (it was the kind of feeling I had between my
own legs now) under the bright overhead light. She was beginning to
grind vigorously against my chin, thighs cuffing my ears, so I moved
my mouth back over her rosy lips, dipping my tongue into their warm
mushy depths—I was aswim in warm mushy depths, we were both—

"Say, uh . . . where the hell *is* everybody?" someone asked. I
peered up between my wife's convulsing thighs, my own hips bucking
against the cushions: it was Knud, standing bleary-eyed over us, rubbing the back of his neck. "Crikey!" he muttered, his voice phlegmy
with sleep. "You'll never believe the dream I just had!"

"Everybody's gone home, Knud," I gasped, my chin sliding now in
the dense juices beneath it.

"Hunh?" He frowned at his empty wrist. My wife had stopped
pumping her head up and down the shaft of my penis, but she was
still sucking at it rhythmically and stroking it with her tongue, marking time, as it were, her throbbing clitoris searching for my mouth.
"Even Kitty? Jeez, what time is it?"

"*Everybody's* gone, Knud. It's *late*."

"Holy cow, I must have slept through the whole goldarn party," he
rumbled, still staring at his wrist. He yawned, belched. "Boy! What a
dream, though!" My wife's hips had stopped pitching. She held my
testicles and one buttock firmly, but had let my penis slide past her
teeth into one cheek. "I was like in some kind of war zone, see, only
everyone was all mixed up and you didn't know who was on your
side—"

"Not now, Knud," my wife panted, letting me go and twisting
round to look up at him. Her buttocks spread a bit, giving me a clearer
view of Knud: he was puffy-eyed and rumpled, tie undone, shirttail
out, pants damp and sticky, and he looked like he needed a shave.

"No, listen, it was a lot longer. And really weird. Since you couldn't
be sure who anybody was, see, just to be safe you naturally had to kill
everyone—right? Ha ha! you wouldn't *believe* the blood and gore!
And all in 3-D and full color, too, I kid you not! I kept running into
people and asking them: 'Where *am* I?' They'd say: 'What a *loony*,'
or something like that—and then I'd chop their heads off, right?"

"Please, Knud—?"

He glanced down at my penis withering in my wife's hand, at
her buttocks flattening out in front of my face. "Oh, right . . .
sorry . . ." He gazed around at the living room, running his hand

through his snarled hair. "Say, do you remember, was I wearing a watch when I came here tonight?"

"Well . . ." my wife began tentatively, raising herself up on one elbow, and I cut in: "I can't remember, Knud."

He seemed to accept that. He squinted up at the lights on the ceiling for a moment, yawning. "Kitty been gone long?"

"No, you can probably catch her." I was beginning to feel my wife's weight: I gave a little push and she lifted herself off my face.

"Don't get up," Knud insisted. "I can find my own way out." He stumbled away, stuffing his shirttail in. My wife, sitting up, let her hand fall idly on my hip. We could hear Knud peeing noisily in the toilet bowl. It was a lonely sound, but not so lonely as the silence all around it. "At least it's working," my wife said. She picked up her stockings and panty girdle, toweled between her legs with them. "Hey, thanks," said Knud from the doorway. "See you at the next one."

"Flush it, please, Knud!" my wife called, but he was already out the door. "Oh well." I curled around her from behind, hugging her close, and she patted my hip with sleepy affection. My penis nuzzled between her cheeks. It felt good there. It was something to think about. "Do you notice a kind of chill in here?" she murmured sleepily.

"Well, all the windowpanes are out," I said. I ran my hand along her thigh where it met the couch. "We could try the TV room now that Knud's vacated it . . ."

She smiled, a bit wearily, then took my good hand and pulled me to my feet. I kicked off the trousers, still tangled around one foot, and, holding hands, we stepped out from under the tented drapes and linens into the glare and wreckage of what was once our living room. She drew close to me suddenly, pressing her naked hip against mine. I was feeling it, too. As though the house had not been emptying out so much as filling up. The windows, stripped bare and paneless, seemed to crowd in on us, letting the dark night at their edges leak in like some kind of deadly miasma. Hugging each other's waists, we picked our way barefoot through the shards of broken pots and glassware, the food squashed into the carpet, the chalk outlines and bent cocktail skewers. The wall next to the dining room doorway was splattered and streaked with a mince pie someone must have thrown, and even that, innocent as it was, seemed to add to our feelings of apprehension and melancholy.

The wall above the dining room sideboard was eloquently vacant,

the picture hooks sitting on it like a pair of pinned insects. Bottles lay tipped like fallen soldiers, liquor still, amazingly enough, gurgling from one of the open mouths. "What exactly happened to Vic?" my wife whispered.

"He . . . got shot . . ."

"He makes you think of Tania's painting, doesn't he? The one with the eyes . . ."

"Well . . ."

I tugged her on into the TV room. We seemed safer in here somehow. Maybe because the lights were softer ("Our antique lamps are missing," she remarked quietly as though in explanation) or because the drapes were still on the windows and the furniture more or less where it ought to be. Or just the soothing blueness of the walls. I could feel my wife's hip soften and I too seemed to walk less stiffly, my knees unlocking, my scrotum sliding back into place. Snow played on the TV screen, making a scratchy noise like a needle caught on the outer lip of a record, but I didn't want to turn it off. It was company of sorts. "I'll put a cassette on," I said, letting go her waist, and she sat down on the sofa to wait. "Don't be long, Gerald," she yawned.

I couldn't seem to find any of our old tapes, but there were plenty of new ones scattered about to choose from. "How about 'The Ancient Arse?'" I proposed, reading the labels. "Or 'Cold Show at the Ice Palace'—or here's one: 'The Garden Peers.'"

"I think that's *pee*-ers. I've seen that one. I don't want to see it again." Ah. I understood now. "Below the Stairs," "Butcherblock Blues," "Party Time," "Life's Mysterious Currents," "The Host's Hang-up," they all fell dismally into place. "Candid Coppers." "Some Dish." "Special Favors." I felt defeated even before I'd begun. There were tears in my eyes and a strange airy tingling on my exposed behind, like a ghostly remembrance of cold knuckles. I shuddered. "Put on 'Hidden Treasure,'" my wife suggested, unbuttoning her blouse and jacket.

I searched through the pile of cassettes, intent on doing my best, getting through it somehow, but my appetite had faded. "It . . . it will never be the same again," I muttered, my throat tight.

"Tsk. You said that last time, Gerald. After Archie and Emma and . . ."

"Yes, well . . ." It was true, I'd all but forgotten. "But Ros, Vic, Tania . . ."

"Roger, Noble . . ."

"Yes, that's right, Roger . . ."

"Fiona . . ."

"Fiona—?" I took off the cassette labeled "The Wayward Finger," and inserted "Hidden Treasure," rewound it to the beginning, punched the "Play" button, wishing it were all so easy as that.

"Yes, that was why Cyril was so upset." She was completely naked now, stretched out on the sofa, hands behind her head, eyes half-closed, scratching the bottom of her foot with one toe. "How do you think Peg found out?"

"Found out what?" I took off my shirt, folded it neatly over the back of the sofa, stalling for time. On the TV, my mother-in-law was getting Mark into his pajama bottoms. "That's better," she was saying. Mark was holding Peedie, which now had one of Sally Ann's patches sewn on its underside. "HOT TWOT," it said.

"Well, she was pregnant."

"Peg was?"

"No, Fiona." I sat down beside her and stroked her thighs, pushing into the warm place between her legs, but my heart wasn't in it. Mark, on the television screen, was asking: "What's a 'twot,' Gramma?" Behind him, his bedroom door was all smashed in. "That's the whole point, Gerald. Didn't you notice? It was very obvious."

"It's a . . . a faraway place," my mother-in-law was explaining. "A kind of secret garden . . ."

"I'm not sure I saw her all night," I said. Maybe it was the scar, cold and bluish in the light from the flickering TV image, that was bothering me. I looked around, spied one of her aprons hanging over the edge of the games table.

"Is it always hot, Gramma?"

"But you heard Peg carrying on when she left—she was telling everybody!"

"No, it's warm. Like a bed. Now you crawl up into yours there, young man."

"I guess I missed that." I brought the apron over: "Listen, do you mind—?"

"But then that's why everyone was feeling so sorry for Cyril after." She raised her hips so I could tie the apron on. "Will I ever go there someday?" Mark was asking. "You know, to lose them both in one night . . ."

"Both—?"

"It seems inevitable, child . . ."

"Yes—my goodness, Gerald, where *were* you?" I slid my hand up under the apron: yes, this was better. There was a faint stirring at last between my legs, which my mother-in-law appeared to be overseeing from the TV screen, her face marked by a kind of compassionate sorrow mixed with amusement. "Tell me a story about it, Gramma," Mark was pleading sleepily, as she led him to the bed. "You missed just about everything!"

"About what?" she asked.

"You know, the Twot," said Mark, as my hand reached my wife's pubis. I let my fingers scratch gently in the hair there, while my thumb slid between her thighs and curled into her vagina. "Well, once upon a time," she began, lifting Mark onto the bed, and I too lifted slightly, then let her down again. "You know . . . sometimes, Gerald . . . ," she sighed, closing her hands gently over mine, ". . . it's almost as if . . ." "There was a young prince . . ."

". . . You were at a different party . . ."

"Was his name Mark?"

I edged closer to my wife's hips, my thumb working rhythmically against the ball of my index finger ("Oh yes . . . good . . ."), and she took my wilted organ in her hand. On the television screen, my mother-in-law was tucking Mark in. "All right then, a young prince named Mark—but get down under the covers, or I won't tell it."

I pushed my thumb as deep as it would go, while at the same time stretching my fingers up her belly, her pubis thrusting at me under the apron, closing around my thumb, her own hand (my mother-in-law had already launched Prince Mark out on his "unique adventure," but Mark wanted to know: "Where's his mommy and daddy? Is he a orphan?") stroking me with a gentle but insistent cadence, slowly helping me forget what I'd seen sticking out from under the games table a moment ago when I'd reached for her apron: a foot, wrapped in a plastic bag, one toe poking out. Its nail painted. Cherry red. "No, he was the little boy of Beauty and the—her husband . . . ," my mother-in-law was saying, as the prospect of orgasm swelled in my mind like a numbing intuition. I gazed down at my wife, her hair unrolled now and loose about her pale shoulders, her thin lips parted, nostrils flared, and thought I could hear Ros whispering: *Oh yes, let's!*

Oh no . . .

". . . But he was a big boy now and it was time to leave home and seek his own fortune . . ."

I was frightened and wanted to stop ("We are in it, Gerry, we cannot get out of it," I seemed to hear Vic mumble right outside the door—had he moved somehow?!), but my wife was blindly pulling me toward her, spreading her legs, the apron wrinkling up between us, and my genitals, it seemed, were quite willing to carry on without the rest of me. "We can only stand up to it or chicken out . . ."

What? Vic—?

"Was the Beast nice now?"

"Oh yes, yes . . . !" my wife was gasping.

"Most of the time . . ."

I'd let go my thumbhold on her pubic handle and, twisting my hand around, my mouth sucking at a breast now (ah, what was it I *really* wanted? I didn't want to think about it . . .), had slid my handful of fingers down there instead, my bodily parts separating out like a houseful of drunken and unruly guests, everybody on his own. She tugged still at that most prodigious member, the host, as it were ("He paused at the edge of the Enchanted Forest: it was dreary and dangerous and . . ."), pumping it harder and harder, her other hand grasping my testicles like a doorknob: she gave them a turn, opened, and, going up on my knees as though to offer my behind to the invading emptiness ("And . . . dark?" asked Mark fearfully, hugging his Peedie under the blankets), mouth still at her breast, I crossed over between her legs.

"Yes . . . !"

"Hurry, Gerald!"

"I'm afraid, Gramma!"

There was a congestion now of fingers and organs, a kind of rubbery crowding up around the portal ("But he was not alone," my mother-in-law was explaining in an encouraging voice), but then she slipped her hands out to snatch at my buttocks, yanking them fiercely toward her as though to keep them from floating away like hot-air balloons— perhaps I'd been worrying about this, I felt like I was coming apart and falling together at the same time—and as her legs jerked upward ("Little Prince Mark was protected by his faithful companion Peedie the Brave Rabbit . . ."), I dropped in through the ooze as though casting anchor. *This*, I was thinking with some excitement, and with some bewilderment as well—what *is* this "we" when the I's are gone?—

is my *wife!* Under my tongue, her nipple (". . . and by his Magical Blue Shirt . . . ," her mother was saying) had sprung erect like a little mushroom stem (". . . for forfending demons . . ."), and I moved now—I say I, certainly *something* moved—across her flushed and heaving chest to suck intrepidly at the other one.

". . . And his good Fairy Godmother, who watched over him wherever he went . . ."

"Oh, Gerald! You're so . . . so . . . !"

I gripped her buttocks now, one taut flexing cheek in each hand ("Did she look like you, Gramma?"), feeling the first distant tremors deep in the black hole of my bowels ("A bit . . .") and remembering one night at the theater when, the stage littered with fornicating couples meant to represent the Forms of Rhetoric (the sketch was called "A Meeting of Minds"), she'd leaned toward me and whispered: "I know they want us to feel time differently here, Gerald, more like an eternal present than the usual past, present, and future, but the only moment that ever works for me is at the end when the lights go down ("No, Peedie doesn't die," her mother was saying, "not yet . . .") and the curtains close. And I'm"—her feet kicked up over my back, crowding her own hands away, so she reached up to clutch my neck and hair—"not sure I like it." "*Great!*" she moaned now, her head tipping back off the edge of the sofa, her back arching, her hips convulsing, and mine too were hammering away, completely ("Don't worry . . .") out of control—it was a kind of pelvic hilarity, a muscular hiccup (had Pardew compared this to murder?), our pubes crashing together like remote underwater collisions, as ineluctible as punchlines.

"That's what fairy godmothers are for . . ."

Only not too soon, I begged (as did my wife: "Wait, Gerald! "Not . . . *ooh! ah* . . . ! yet . . . !"), wanting to hold on to this moment, like so many before, but her vagina seemed to have filled up like a fist and to be clinging to my penis for dear life, pumping and pumping in tight muscular spasms, and even as I was looking forward to its arrival, it was already ("*Yes—!!*" my wife cried out, her head out of sight) gone.

I lay sprawled across her breasts, my head jammed into the linty corner between the armrest and back of the sofa, trying to conceive of the idea of eternity as a single violent spasm. I couldn't even imagine it. For that matter I couldn't imagine much of anything. It was as

though I carried my semen in my head and orgasm had sucked it hollow. Distantly, I could hear my mother-in-law describing for Mark the "mysterious Walled Garden" in the middle of the Enchanted Forest, "where fairies play and rubies hang from bushes like berries and you never get old or lose your way," which might have been quite soothing had she not sounded like she was scolding. We were still linked in a soft aromatic congestion. I wanted to say, "I love you," but instead found myself saying: "You focus . . . my attention . . ." "Oh, Gerald," she sighed from below, reaching up to pat my hip, "your sweet nothings are not always sweet . . . but at least . . ."

We slipped apart, my wife's pelvis sliding away to the floor to join the rest of her. Mark's grandmother was telling him about a hidden treasure in the Walled Garden, "guarded by a wicked and spiteful Tattooed Dragon that breathed both ice and fire." As I fell back, I seemed to catch her televised eye: a kind of warning . . . "And what the Prince had to do to reach the treasure," she went on as my wife sat up and reached for the off button ("Sorry, mother . . ."), "was chop—"

Click.

There was a sudden dreadful silence. "Goodness," my wife murmured, looked around, "I almost don't know where I am . . ." Somewhere, I seemed to hear some sort of knocking sound. Like darts hitting a dartboard. "Do you think we should . . . ?"

"No, leave it all till morning." I was thinking about the ice pick, that improbable object. When the officer carried it away, I was glad to see it go—I thought at the time: Free at last! But now I was not so sure. I seemed to feel its presence again, as though it had got back in the house somehow.

She struggled to her feet, then turned to gaze down at me with a compassionate smile. She was still wearing the apron. It was the one with the candystripes. From Amsterdam. "I love you, Gerald."

"I know . . ." Or Monaco.

"You might as well stay where you are." Her eyes were damp, I saw, the pupils dilated, and her lips were flushed and puffy. "I'll sleep on the studio couch in the sewing room." Perhaps I frowned at that, or looked puzzled, because she added: "Our bed's filled up, I'm afraid. Mr. and Mrs. Elstob are evidently staying the night." There seemed something wrong with that, but I couldn't remember what. "It will be a while before we want to use *that* bed again." She leaned over, her

breasts brushing my arm, and kissed me. "It's all right, Gerald," she whispered, resting one hand on my tummy. I seemed to hear Vic snort at that ("Don't shit me it's all right!"), and I trembled, so she took her hand away. "Is anything—?"

"No . . . well . . . it's like there's an echo in here. Or . . ."

"That's probably the people out in the backyard," she said, rising.

"The backyard? But what are they doing out there?"

"Nothing. Just telling stories, as far as I could tell. You know, the usual stragglers. But don't worry, I've locked up. Tomorrow . . ." Her voice seemed to be receding. "No, wait—!" I called, but she was already gone. Only the faintest fragrance remained and that, too, was fading. I lay there on my back, alone and frightened, remembering all too well why it was we held these parties. And would, as though compelled, hold another. At least she had turned the TV back on. Perhaps I had asked her to do this. Prince Mark was now riding through the Enchanted Forest. Or maybe this was the Walled Garden, maybe the Tattooed Dragon was dead already, quite likely. "'Ass usin' yer ole gourd, Mark," Peedie was saying, with a loose drunken chortle. "I think we're awmoss there, ole son—juss keep it up'n—yuff! huff!—*don' look back!*" "Look! There she is! I can see her now! She's *beautiful!*" Yes, this *was* the Garden, I could see her, too: she was running bouncily toward me through the lotus blossoms, radiant with joy and anticipation, her blond hair flowing behind her, eyes sparkling, arms outstretched, her soft white dress wrapping her limbs like the frailest of gauze. I felt myself awash in glowing sunshine. "Gerry!" she cried, leaping across some impossible abyss, and threw her arms around me. Oh, what a hug! Oh! It felt great! I could hardly get my breath! Tears came to my eyes and I hugged her back with all my strength. But then suddenly she grabbed my testicles and seemed to want to rip them out by their roots! I screamed with pain and terror, fell writhing to the ground. "No, no, Ros!" I heard someone shout. I couldn't see who it was. I couldn't even open my eyes. "That's 'Grab up the *bells* and ring them,' goddamn it—!" Oh my god! Get up! I told myself. (But I couldn't even move.) Turn it off. "Gee, I'm sorry . . ." (But I *had* to!) "Now c'mon, let's try that again! From the beginning!" No! *Now—!*

ABOUT THE AUTHOR

Robert Coover was born in Iowa in 1932. His first novel, *The Origin of the Brunists,* was the winner of the 1966 William Faulkner Award. His other works include *The Universal Baseball Association, J. Henry Waugh, Prop., Pricksongs & Descants, A Theological Position, The Public Burning, A Political Fable,* and *Spanking the Maid.* Coover lives with his wife in Providence, Rhode Island, where he teaches at Brown University.

168546

5505   02 771840   01 4   (IC=0)
COOVER, ROBERT   02/21/86
GERALD'S PARTY
(1) 1985 F

DATE DUE